LITERARY CIRCLES IN BYZANTINE ICONOCLASM

Iconoclasm was the name given to the stance of that portion of Eastern Christianity that rejected worshipping God through images (*eikones*) representing Christ, the Virgin or the saints and was the official doctrine of the Byzantine Empire for most of the period between 726 and 843. It was a period marked by violent passions on either side. This is the first comprehensive account of the extant contemporary texts relating to this phenomenon and their impact on society, politics and identity. By examining the literary circles emerging both during the time of persecution and immediately after the restoration of icons in 843, the volume casts new light on the striking (re)construction of Byzantine society, whose iconophile identity was biasedly redefined by the political parties led by Theodoros Stoudites, Gregorios Dekapolites and Empress Theodora or the patriarchs Methodios, Ignatios and Photios. It thereby offers an innovative paradigm for approaching Byzantine literature.

óscar prieto domínguez is a Lecturer in Greek Language and Literature at the University of Salamanca, Spain. He works on literary, historical and philological aspects of Greek literary production of Late Antiquity and the Middle Byzantine Ages and is the author of *Casia de Constantinopla: Poemas* (2019) and *Literature Squared: Self-Reflexivity in Late Antique Literature* (2020).

LITERARY CIRCLES IN BYZANTINE ICONOCLASM

Patrons, Politics and Saints

ÓSCAR PRIETO DOMÍNGUEZ
Universidad de Salamanca, Spain

CAMBRIDGE
UNIVERSITY PRESS

University Printing House, Cambridge CB2 8BS, United Kingdom

One Liberty Plaza, 20th Floor, New York, NY 10006, USA

477 Williamstown Road, Port Melbourne, VIC 3207, Australia

314–321, 3rd Floor, Plot 3, Splendor Forum, Jasola District Centre, New Delhi – 110025, India

79 Anson Road, #06–04/06, Singapore 079906

Cambridge University Press is part of the University of Cambridge.

It furthers the University's mission by disseminating knowledge in the pursuit of education, learning, and research at the highest international levels of excellence.

www.cambridge.org
Information on this title: www.cambridge.org/9781108491303
DOI: 10.1017/9781108868129

© Óscar Prieto Domínguez 2020

This publication is in copyright. Subject to statutory exception and to the provisions of relevant collective licensing agreements, no reproduction of any part may take place without the written permission of Cambridge University Press.

First published 2020

A catalogue record for this publication is available from the British Library.

Library of Congress Cataloging-in-Publication Data
NAMES: Prieto Domínguez, Óscar, 1981– author.
TITLE: Literary circles in Byzantine iconoclasm : patrons, politics, and saints / Óscar Prieto Domínguez.
DESCRIPTION: Cambridge, United Kingdom ; New York, N, USA : Cambridge University Press, 2021. | Includes bibliographical references and index.
IDENTIFIERS: LCCN 2020037687 (print) | LCCN 2020037688 (ebook) | ISBN 9781108491303 (hardback) | ISBN 9781108811828 (paperback) | ISBN 9781108868129 (epub)
SUBJECTS: LCSH: Byzantine literature–History and criticism. | Iconoclasm in literature. | Literature and society–Byzantine Empire. | Byzantine Empire–Politics and government.
CLASSIFICATION: LCC PA5130.I26 P75 2021 (print) | LCC PA5130.I26 (ebook) | DDC 880.9/3826157–dc23
LC record available at https://lccn.loc.gov/2020037687
LC ebook record available at https://lccn.loc.gov/2020037688

ISBN 978-1-108-49130-3 Hardback

Cambridge University Press has no responsibility for the persistence or accuracy of URLs for external or third-party internet websites referred to in this publication and does not guarantee that any content on such websites is, or will remain, accurate or appropriate.

Contents

List of Figures and Maps	*page* vii
Acknowledgements	viii
Note to the Reader	ix
List of Abbreviations	x

	Introduction	1
1	The Stoudite Milieu: The Foundations of the Literature of Iconoclasm	41
2	The Methodian Milieu: Literature Conceived in the Patriarchate after the Iconoclastic Crisis	99
3	The Dekapolitan Milieu: The Integration of the Third Way after the Restoration of Icons	168
4	The Secular Milieux and Their Rewriting of the Second Iconoclasm: The Aristocracy, the Army, the Court and the Imperial Family	225
5	The Ignatian Milieu: The Management of Inherited Iconodule Literature	273
6	The Photian Milieu: Rewriting and Updating Iconodule Literature	330
7	Mobility between Milieux: The Hagiographer Sabas, from the Bithynian Olympos to the Constantinopolitan Milieux	391
8	Final Remarks	428

Appendix A Chronology of the Patriarchs, Emperors, Popes and Hegoumenoi of Stoudios from 787 to 896	441
Appendix B Network Chart of Writers and Their Literary Relations under Iconoclasm and in Its Aftermath	446
Bibliography	448
General Index	525
Index of Manuscripts	541

Figures and Maps

Figures

3.1 Family tree of the Dekapolitan network (*birth, †death)   *page* 208

Maps

1 Constantinople: Principal monasteries in Middle Byzantium   441
2 Bithynia: Principal monasteries in Middle Byzantium   442

Acknowledgements

In 2011, the Spanish Ministry of Science, Innovation and Universities awarded me a two-year research contract to carry out a project focusing on Byzantine literature at the École des hautes études en sciences sociales (EHESS) in Paris, France. That postdoctoral project was the beginning of this book and of a personal change of perspective about what Byzantine literature really was and how it should be approached. I am sincerely grateful to Prof. Paolo Odorico, Filippo Ronconi and Charis Messis for their enlightening comments and advice and to the Bibliothèque byzantine for granting me access to its rich collection. I could continue working on this time-consuming monograph during the following years thanks to the generosity of the Spanish Ministry, the Junta de Castilla y León (Project SA014G19) and the University of Salamanca. Their research funding opportunities let me spend some time at institutions such as the University of Oxford, King's College London, the Vatican Library in Rome and the Historical Library of the Orthodox Patriarchate in Jerusalem. Many thought-provoking conversations were held here and there with many colleagues who deserve my deepest gratitude. I am afraid they are too many to be listed here but hope they all will recognise their influence on this work. Further thanks are due to the three outstanding readers for Cambridge University Press, who provided learned suggestions for improvement. The commissioning editor, Michael Sharp, has always supported this project and diligently supervised this book's production. Finally, Prof. D. Olson polished my English. I am also deeply indebted to J. Hernández Lobato, who – among many other things – painted the cover image.

Writing and finishing this book has been exhausting and often even disheartening. I am sure that it would never exist without my family and friends, my main source of encouragement and support. For his love, joy and patience, this book is fondly dedicated to my husband.

Note to the Reader

I must confess that I am not fully convinced by the blanket designation of iconoclasts as heretics, and the reader may perhaps agree with me. This affirmation reflects the viewpoint of the literary discourse with which this book is concerned; I have maintained it merely for the sake of clarity.

I have chosen not to anglicise the personal names of Middle Byzantine individuals and have therefore preferred Ioannes Grammatikos to John the Grammarian, with a transliteration that reflects spelling, rather than phonology. On the other hand, city names have been given their English form, in order to provide a more readable text.

Unless otherwise indicated, translations from the Greek are my own.

Salamanca,
December 2019

Abbreviations

AASS	*Acta Sanctorum.* Antwerp-Brussels. 1643–1925
ABSA	*Annual of the British School at Athens*
ACO	*Acta Conciliorum Oecumenicorum*, eds. E. Schwartz et al. Berlin. 1927–
AHG	*Analecta Hymnica Graeca e codicibus eruta Italiae inferioris*, eds. A. Kominis and G. Schirò. Rome: Istituto di Studi Bizantini e Neoellenici. 1960–1983
AIHS	*Archives Internationales d'Historie des Sciences*
AnBoll	*Analecta Bollandiana*
ASEER	*The American Slavic and East European Review*
BBGG	*Bollettino della Badia Greca di Grottaferrata*
BollClass	*Bollettino dei Classici*
BF	*Byzantinische Forschungen*
BHG	*Bibliotheca Hagiographica Graeca. Novum Auctarium* I–III, ed. F. Halkin. Brussels. 1957; 1984 (3rd ed.)
BIC	Bulletin d'Information et de coordination
BK	*Bedi Kartlisa. Revue de Kartvélologie*
BMGS	*Byzantine and Modern Greek Studies*
BNJ	*Byzantinisch-neugriechische Jahrbücher*
BSl	*Byzantinoslavica*
Byz	*Byzantion*
ByzSt	*Byzantine Studies/Etudes Byzantines*
BZ	*Byzantinische Zeitschrift*
CahArch	*Cahiers Archéologiques*
CCSG	*Corpus Christianorum, Series Graeca*
CFHB	*Corpus Fontium Historiae Byzantinae*
CHRC	*Church History and Religious Culture*

List of Abbreviations

CIG	*Corpus Inscriptionum Graecarum*. I–IV. Berlin. 1828–1877
CPG	*Clavis Patrum Graecorum*, ed. M. Geerard. Vols. I–v. Supplementum. Turnhout. 1974–1998
CSCO	*Corpus Scriptorum Christianorum Orientalium*
CSHB	*Corpus Scriptorum Historiae Byzantinae*
DA	*Deutsches Archiv für Erforschung des Mittelalters*
DChAE	Δελτίον τῆς Χριστιανικῆς Ἀρχαιολογικῆς Ἑταιρείας
Dölger, *Regesten*	*Regesten der Kaiserurkunden des Oströmischen Reiches von 565–1453. I. Teil: Regesten von 565–1015*, ed. F. Dölger, Munich-Berlin. 1924 (repr. Hildesheim. 1976)
Dölger-Müller, *Regesten*	*Regesten der Kaiserurkunden des Oströmischen Reiches von 565–1453. 2. Halbband: Regesten 867–1025*, eds. F. Dölger and A. E. Müller, Munich. 2003
DOP	*Dumbarton Oaks Papers*
DOS	*Dumbarton Oaks Studies*
DOT	*Dumbarton Oaks Texts*
DS	*Dictionnaire de Spiritualité*. 17 vols. Paris. 1937–1995
EEBS	Ἐπετηρὶς Ἑταιρείας Βυζαντινῶν Σπουδῶν
ΕΕΦΣΠΑ	Ἐπιστημονικὴ Ἐπετηρὶς Φιλοσοφικῆς Σχολῆς Πανεπηστιμίου Ἀθηνῶν
EHR	*English Historical Review*
EkTh	Ἐκκλησία καὶ Θεολογία
EO	*Échos d'Orient*
ΕΦΣ	Ὁ ἐν Κωνσταντινουπόλει Ἑλληνικὸς Φιλολογικὸς Σύλλογος
FM	*Fontes Minores*
GBBNPh	*Göttinger Beiträge zur Byzantinischen und Neugriechischen Philologie*
GOTR	*Greek Orthodox Theological Review*
GRBS	*Greek, Roman and Byzantine Studies*
Hell	Ἑλληνικά
HUS	*Harvard Ukrainian Studies*
IRAIK	*Izvestija Russkago Archeologičeskago Instituta v Konstantinopol'e*
JAOS	*Journal of the American Oriental Society*
JEH	*Journal of Ecclesiastical History*

JIAN	*Journal International d'Archéologie Numismatique*
JLARC	*Journal for Late Antique Religion and Culture*
JÖB	*Jahrbuch der Österreichischen Byzantinistik* (1969–)
JThSt	*Journal of Theological Studies*
LBG	*Lexikon zur byzantinischen Gräzität*, eds. E. Trapp et al. Vienna. 2001
LSJ	H. G. Liddell, R. Scott, H. Stuart Jones and R. McKenzie, *A Greek-English Lexicon*. Oxford. 9th ed. 1925–1940. Revised Supplement, ed. P. G. W. Glare with the assistance of A. A. Thompson. Oxford. 1996
Mansi	*Sacrorum conciliorum nova et amplissima collectio*, ed. G. D. Mansi. Florence-Venice. 1759–1798 (repr. Graz. 1960)
MBM	*Miscellanea Byzantina Monacensia*
MEFREM	*Mélanges de l'École française de Rome. Moyen age*
Megas Synaxaristes	Μέγας συναξαριστής, ed. K. X. Doukakis. xii vols. Athens. 1891–1896
Menaion	Μηναῖα τοῦ ὅλου ἐνιαυτοῦ (*Liturgical Books of the Months*). vi vols. Rome. 1888–1901
Menaion of Bartholomaios	Μηναῖα διορθωθέντα ὑπὸ Βαρθολομαίου Κουτλουμουσιανοῦ τοῦ Ἰμβρίου. xii vols. Venice. 1843
Menaion of Makariem	*Velikija Minei ceti: sobrannyja vserossijskim mitropolitom Makariem*. xxv vols. Saint Petersburg. 1868–1917
MEG	*Medioevo Greco*
MGH	*Monumenta Germaniae Historica*
OC	*Orientalia Christiana*
OCA	*Orientalia Christiana Analecta*
OCP	*Orientalia Christiana Periódica*
ODB	*The Oxford Dictionary of Byzantium*, eds. A. P. Kazhdan et al. Vols. i–iii. New York-Oxford. 1991
PBE I	*The Prosopography of the Byzantine Empire*. i: 641–867, ed. J. Martindale. Aldershot. 2001 (CD-ROM)
PBR	*Patristic and Byzantine Review*
PLRE	*The Prosopography of the Later Roman Empire, Volume III: A.D. 527–641*, eds. J. R. Martindale, A. H. M. Jones and J. Morris. Cambridge. 1992

Pitra, *Analecta*	*Analecta Sacra Spicilegio Solesmensi parata*, ed. J. B. Pitra. VIII vols. Paris. 1876–1888
Pitra, *Monumenta*	*Iuris ecclesiastici graecorum historia et monumenta*, ed. J. B. Pitra. II vols. Rome. 1864–1868 (repr. 1963)
Pitra, *Spic. Solesmense*	*Spicilegium Solesmense complectens sanctorum patrum scriptorumque . . .*, ed. J. B. Pitra. IV vols. Paris. 1852–1858 (repr. Graz. 1962)
PG	*Patrologiae cursus completus. Series graeca*, ed. J. P. Migne. 161 vols. Paris. 1857–1866
PL	*Patrologiae cursus completus. Series latina*, ed. J. P. Migne. 221 vols. Paris. 1844–1880
PmbZ	*Prosopographie der mittelbyzantinischen Zeit*, eds. R. J. Lilie et al. Berlin. 1999–
PO	*Patrologia Orientalis*, eds. R. Graffin and F. Nau. Paris. 1904–
PRK	*Das Register des Patriarchats von Konstantinopel*, hrsg. v. H. Hunger–O. Kresten et al., 1–. Vienna 1981–
RE	*Paulys Realencyclopädie der classischen Altertumswissenschaft. Neue Bearbeitung . . .*, eds. G. Wissowa et al. 66 Halbbde, 15 Suppl. Stuttgart-Munich. 1893–1978
Regestes	*Les regestes des actes du Patriarcat de Constantinople. Vol. I. Les Actes des Patriarches. Fasc. II et III: Les Regestes de 715 a 1206*, ed. V. Grumel. Paris. 1989, 2nd ed. (rev. J. Darrouzès)
REA	*Revue des Études Arméniennes*
REB	*Revue des Études Byzantines*
REG	*Revue des Études Grecques*
RES	*Revue des Études Slaves*
RESEE	*Revue des Études Sud-Est-Européennes*
RhM	*Rheinisches Museum für Philogie*
ROC	*Revue de l'Orient Chrétien*
RechSR	*Recherches de Science Religieuse*
RSBN	*Rivista di Studi Bizantini e Neoellenici*
SBN	*Studi Bizantini e Neoellenici*
SBS	*Studies in Byzantine Sigillography*
SC	*Sources Chrétiennes*

SJBMGS	*Scandanavian Journal of Byzantine and Modern Greek Studies*
StFB	*Studi di filologia bizantina*
StT	*Studi e Testi*
SynaxCP	*Synaxarium ecclesiae Constantinopolitanae*, ed. H. Delehaye. Brussels. 1902
Synaxarion Evergetis	*The Synaxarion of the Monastery of the Theotokos Evergetis*, ed. R. H. Jordan. Belfast. 2000–2005. Vol. I: September–February; Vol. II: March–August.
Tameion	Ταμεῖον ἀνεκδότων βυζαντινῶν ἀσματικῶν κανόνων. *Seu analecta hymnica Graeca e codicibus eruta orientis christiani*, ed. E. Papaeliopoulou-Photopoulou. Athens. 1996.
Tgl	*Thesaurus Graecae Linguae*
TLG	*Thesaurus Linguae Graecae*. CD-ROM. University of California. 1999
TM	*Travaux et Mémoires*
TU	*Texte und Untersuchungen*
VChr	*Vigiliae Christianae*
WBS	*Wiener Byzantinistische Studien*
WSt	*Wiener Studien*
ZRVI	*Zbornik Radova Vizantološkog Instituta*

Introduction

Iconoclasm – *eikonomachia* for the Byzantines[1] – was the name given to the stance of that portion of Eastern Christianity that rejected worshipping God through images (*eikones*) representing Christ, the Virgin or the saints. By imperial imposition, this was the official doctrine of the Byzantine Empire between 726 and 843, in two clearly differentiated stages separated by a period of iconoduly, or veneration of icons, between 787 and 815. It was declared a heretical dogma by several Councils and therefore one that should be persecuted, including by the Second Council of Nicaea (787). Defenders of icons vigorously opposed iconoclasm and its supporters in a process of identity construction that would irrevocably mark Byzantine society. Much of this opposition found support in literature, producing texts that told the story from the authors' own point of view.[2] The substantial impact on the mindset of the age meant that subsequent generations continued to speak and write about the iconoclast controversy, with the inevitable consequence of rewriting recent history, often in a premeditated fashion.

Some initial caveats should be noted. This is not a book about iconoclasm per se, or about its theological or dogmatic dimensions, but about its social, political and ecclesiastical repercussions. In short, its topic is literature, the texts referring to the crisis that were written during the years of the iconoclastic controversy and its defeat. In recent decades, there has been a great deal of productive research into the Middle Byzantine era and the iconoclast conflict.[3] But modern scholarship has downgraded the real impact of iconoclasm in shaping everyday experience and the economic landscape of eighth- and ninth-century Byzantium, by suggesting that the

---

[1] For the terminology currently used, cf. Bremmer 2008.
[2] Karlin-Hayter 1993; Criscuolo 1994b; Auzépy 2004a; Odorico 2014.
[3] Bryer and Herrin 1977; Brubaker and Haldon 2001; 2011; Auzépy 2007; Brubaker 2012; Kaplan 2017.

most significant role of the controversy regarding images was to trigger social and literary debate.[4] The relevance of such debates was in fact routinely overemphasised by extant Byzantine sources. Modern studies illustrate how, why and by what means the veneration of images was persecuted. But the study of the literary production of this age, which resulted in a set of intriguing texts composed during a time of instability and controversy, has advanced very little. Due to political prohibitions, some of those texts often circulated in a clandestine manner, but always with well-defined ideological and propaganda objectives.[5]

Nor is this book a history of Byzantine literature in the iconoclastic period in a traditional sense. A detailed survey of the texts produced during the period is offered, but the real aim of this study is to shed light on how such texts worked. To that end, each work is analysed in a way intended to explain its form and functions, dating, authorship, historical background, political and religious impact and the motivations of the author and the commissioner, as well as the manners of diffusion and (where necessary) the manuscript tradition. Particular attention is given to the interrelationships of a number of works involving common authors or a common patron (the patriarch of Constantinople, a monastic superior, or the like), which are collected together and critically examined in order to reconstruct the circle of writers within which they were penned.

Time has made its own selection of the texts. The Byzantines sieved their own literary production, and we tend to think that many iconoclastic works were forgotten by the iconodules. Sometimes they were condemned as heretical and burnt, but most often they were simply ignored, becoming alien and sliding into oblivion. The First Iconoclasm (726–787) is within the limits of the Dark Age, which means that its literary output was already very poor in terms of quantity, with extremely few excellent authors.[6] Some of the missing texts were also integrated into later works, as is true of the chronicles that used earlier historiographical narratives as sources. The case of *Theophanes Continuatus* is well known; he got his information about the Arab invasion of Sicily between 826 and 829 from the lost text of Theognostos.[7] Although positive evidence for this work exists, reconstructing the original composition, identifying the literary context in which

---

[4] Brubaker and Haldon 2011; Brubaker 2012.
[5] Garzya 1981; Magdalino 1993; Cameron 1994; Auzépy 2007; Cunningham 2011; Spanos 2014.
[6] Kazhdan 1999: 19–165; Auzépy 2004a: 155–66; Haldon 2014.
[7] Theoph. Cont. II, 27,17–20. On Theognostos, see *PmbZ* # 8012; *PBE* I: Theognostos 7; Treadgold 2013: 79–90.

it was produced, and sketching its early dissemination is almost impossible and, in any case, beyond the scope of this study.

Extant texts from the First Iconoclasm are scarce and correspond to the limited number of individual authors who met with great acclaim from their contemporaries. Even if there was some subsequent censorship or purge, we do not know of any important individual writer of this era who suffered a *damnatio memoriae* condemning his compositions to oblivion. After the cruel seventh century and its decline,[8] much of the eighth century was also almost barren from a literary point of view. Although Mullett has rightly characterised those years as a 'period of reduced literacy',[9] some innovative literary themes and styles developed.[10] Since the Dark Age, three genres had been privileged and continued to be cultivated with special emphasis: homiletics, hymnography and hagiography (the 'three H's'). Overproduction of them determines our study and explains why less attention is paid here to historiographical texts, which, although usually preferred by scholars, had been largely neglected since the seventh century and were not so widely produced in the ninth century.[11] Finally, men of letters of the First Iconoclasm seem to modern eyes like isolated islands, remote from one another. Their reduced number and greater autonomy prevent us from describing the hypothetical group that may have conditioned their literary production, since we cannot trawl for the reciprocal contacts of these alleged primitive literary circles. The foreign origin of such authors – Andreas of Crete, Ioannes Damaskenos and Kosmas the Melode were born in Damascus, Syria, and later settled in Palestine[12] – implies that they had no definite readers or established audience to respond to their compositions in literary form.

On the other hand, literary production increased exponentially during the iconodule interlude (787–815) and thereafter had closer links with Constantinople and its hinterland, making relevant data more accessible to the modern scholar.[13] This allows for interpretative commentary describing the interconnected network within which a specific work was written, the politics of literature underlying its production and how the texts that form part of this circle worked politically and socially to promote the self-interested veneration of various saints. During the First Iconoclasm, in fact, the intellectual level of Byzantine society and rates of literacy

---

[8] Haldon 1990. [9] Mullett 1990: 161. [10] Kazhdan 1999: 137–65.
[11] For this 'historiographical fatigue' see Kazhdan 1999: 19–35. Cf. Ševčenko 1992.
[12] For Andreas of Crete, see *PmbZ* # 362 and # 388; *PBE* I: Andreas 3; On Ioannes Damaskenos, see *PmbZ* # 2969; *PBE* I: Ioannes 11. For Kosmas the Melode, see *PmbZ* # 4089.
[13] Auzépy 2004a: 166–73.

increased significantly as a result of the theological controversy, multiplying the number of texts and specific details of their circulation that have reached us.[14] This is the main reason why the period examined in this monograph largely coincides with the century of the Byzantine revival, that is, from the Iconodule hiatus (787–815) up to the end of the reign of Basileios I (867–886), covering the Second Iconoclasm (815–843) and the years after the Triumph of Orthodoxy. The accession of Leon VI the Wise to the throne in 886 meant the deposition of the erudite patriarch Photios and the birth of a new literary scenario,[15] the greatest representative of which would be the learned Konstantinos VII Porphyrogennetos (913–959).[16]

Iconoclasm is in essence a religious phenomenon, and it is therefore not unrelated to the demographic explosion of Byzantine monasticism in the second half of the eighth century. The increase in population owing to better living conditions[17] meant a corresponding increase in the number of monks and priests unheard of until that time. This change in turn led more and more lay persons to choose the religious life, with a consequent exponential increase in the proportion of monks, priests and nuns to lay people. To this increase in the number of the professed must be added the different social extraction of the monks: more and more noble, wealthy individuals, well-educated and with good chances of prospering in society, chose to take vows.[18] As a consequence, monastic culture flourished in all its splendour starting in 787. Reforms implemented in the monasteries promoted the intellectual training of their members. Educated individuals took advantage of the independence and serenity of monastic retreat to create an abundance of new literature in which it was not only the formulations that were new, but also the approach to traditional genres. At the same time, the high level of education of many new monks and the social and family networks they had before joining their monastery made them key players in the political evolution of the Empire. Their involvement in worldly events became more and more intense, their opposition to imperial power firmer and firmer and, thanks to the new literature they

---

[14] Efthymiadis 2017 with previous bibliography.
[15] Mango 1960; Odorico 1983; Magdalino 1988b; Tougher 1994; Antonopoulou 1997; 2017; Tougher 1997: 110–32; Kazhdan 1999: 53–65; Riedel 2018.
[16] Toynbee 1973; Huxley 1980; Schminck 1989; Kazhdan 1999: 133–84; Koutava-Delivoria 2002; Magdalino 2017.
[17] Treadgold 1988: 36–41, 163–64, 360–67; Haldon 1998; Brubaker and Haldon 2011: 455–59.
[18] For the large number of figures who founded or entered monasteries at the same time as Theodoros Stoudites, see Ringrose 1979; Déroche 1993; Kountoura-Galaki 1996; Hatlie 2007a: 283–86. Regarding the new socio-cultural extraction of monks and their large increase, cf. ibid., 399–408.

were producing, more and more effective. We thus find a highly educated monastic generation that in the first half of the ninth century did not hesitate to take the reins of public life, dictating the paths to follow in the daily life of the provinces and in imperial policy to preserve Orthodoxy, that is, their interpretation of Christian dogma. Of all the conflicts that occurred, one stands out as a result of the constant reinterpretation and reappropriation of it by subsequent generations: the defeat of iconoclasm. As a heresy, iconoclasm not only demanded the destruction of images representing Christ, the Virgin Mary and the saints as being contrary to divine law, but also meant an interpretation of previous Councils and ultimately a revision of Christology, since by denying the possibility of representing Christ, the iconoclasts were held to be denying his human nature.

Beyond its theological and apologetic texts, anti-iconoclast writing is above all a literature about saints, whose lives were taken as pretexts for narrating history in order to create a group identity and thus influence society. Not only was iconoclasm a dogmatic dispute that turned into a civil confrontation after the emperor took an official position,[19] but it also created the situation of zealous men ready to sacrifice everything, even their own lives, in defence of their ideals. This attitude produced flight, gaol and torture, but also solidarity among the persecuted, and cohesion among those who found in their opposition to imperial power a form of religious life that could only be compared to that of the first Christians. Like the martyrs who gave their lives in the arenas before pagan emperors, the new heroes of Orthodoxy, often simply confessors (those who suffered for their faith), were an ideal subject for the writing of vivid narratives that testified to their exploits and their pious way of life. These stories were also perfect tools for bringing a monastic or social group together, for creating an identity and even for entering politics.

According to Theodoros Stoudites, devotion to saints required both texts and images to assist with a Christian understanding of their virtues.[20] The promotion of this devotion for those killed in the iconoclast persecution includes an initial ideological and political element that is then confirmed by the contents of the narratives created for that promotion. Much of the literature produced during iconoclasm was thus directed towards gathering proof of the holiness of the neo-martyrs and denouncing the outrages of the heretics in a liturgical context. Usually, the

---

[19] Treadgold 2012.
[20] Theod. Stoud., *epist.* 499; Gouillard 1961b; Sansterre 1994: 227, n. 131; Crostini 2013: 117–20.

commemoration of saints was first recorded at a local level (in a specific *menologion*) and then recognised by the rest of the Byzantine Church without an official canonisation process.[21] There were doubtless many oral traditions that were never put in writing and of which we know nothing.[22] Others, however, were written down to praise these heroes, preserving them for posterity and making them models of behaviour. They have come down to us in an immense variety of literary forms ranging from long *vitae*, hagiographies that offer details of the life, good deeds and miracles of the saint, to liturgical hymns (*kanones*, *kontakia*, etc.) and entries for the *synaxaria* (calendar of saint's days), to homiletic pieces such as panegyrics (*enkomia*) and accounts of the translation of relics (*anakomidai*).[23] Regardless of their form, these texts were much loved by the public and also very abundant, to the extent that they can be considered the bestsellers of the Byzantine Empire.[24] What is more, both writing/copying them and reading them were considered proof of holiness.[25] The patriarch Nikephoros and Tarasios, in fact, both dedicated the churches of their monasteries to the martyr saints, which is proof of the importance they attached to the confession (*homologia*) of the iconodules.[26]

During the two stages of Iconoclasm (726–787 and 815–843), the quality and quantity of the literature produced varied, giving the impression that literature first disappeared and then took refuge behind the walls of the monasteries, following in the footsteps of some of the most outstanding intellectuals. Kazhdan and Talbot, in their study of iconodule heroes, list some seventy-five testimonies among the *vitae* and notices from the *Synaxarion of Constantinople*,[27] drawing attention to the great disparity

---

[21] In the ninth century, there was no canonisation process in Constantinople; this was not to occur in the Byzantine Empire before the fourteenth century, see *ODB* 1, 372, s.v. 'Canonization'. For the ways in which holiness could be publicly recognised in our period, see Delehaye 1927; Ehrhard 1936–1939: vol. I, 28–33; Ševčenko 1977b: 97–98; Patlagean 1981; Kaplan 1990; 2000; 2002; Auzépy 1995; Efthymiadis 2006. As to the function of the hagiographic text in support of the sanctification process, see Pratsch 2005: 413–21; Efthymiadis 2011a: 1–14.

[22] Theod. Stoud., *epist*. 386,62–64: σχεδὸν πάντα τὰ μαρτυρογράφια ἀνεπίγραφά εἰσιν· ἀλλ' ὅμως βέβαιά εἰσιν, κἀκεῖθεν οἱ διδάσκαλοι ἀφορμίζονται ποιεῖν τὰ τῶν μαρτυρησάντων ἐγκώμια.

[23] Delehaye 1966; Kazhdan 1999: 140–42; Giannouli 2014; Hinterberger 2014a.

[24] Halkin 1967: 345.

[25] *Vita of Georgios of Amastris* 13–14. On the work of the copyists and their self-awareness, see Ronconi 2014.

[26] With regard to the church of the monastery of Nikephoros, cf. Ruggieri 1991: 203, n. 81; *Translation of the Patriarch Nikephoros* 5, p. 120; Janin 1975: 27. For the monastery founded by Tarasios, which furthermore was decorated with a complex iconographic cycle, see *Vita of the Patriarch Tarasios* 49–52; Wolska-Conus 1980; Brubaker 1989b: 19–23; Ruggieri 1991: 179 and 202.

[27] Kazhdan and Talbot 1991: 405–7 (appendix A).

between the saints commemorated in the two stages. In the first, which lasted almost twice as long (over sixty years), we know of few confessors who were persecuted, and curiously enough – or perhaps not so curiously – none of the hagiographical texts treating them was contemporary. Indeed, in the eighth century nothing seems to have been written in honour of any new heroes of Orthodoxy, in striking contrast to the comparatively abundant compositions in honour of the primitive martyrs and traditional saints.[28] Only five hagiographic texts were certainly written in the first half of that century, and they were mostly not about iconodules: the Roman *Miracles of Anastasios the Persian*; the anonymous *Vita of David of Thessalonike*; Andreas' *Vita of St Patapios* and *Vita of St Therapon* and Ioannes Damaskenos' *Enkomion of St Barbara*.[29] The case of hagiography is paradigmatic and exemplifies what was taking place in other genres.

In the ninth century, however, there was a noteworthy proliferation of texts written after the initial restoration of icons at the Second Council of Nicaea: in about the year 800, Konstantinos of Tios composed the *translatio* of the relics of Euphemia of Chalcedon (*BHG* 621), who was martyred in 303 and venerated in Constantinople from antiquity until the iconoclast Emperor Leon III (717–741) desecrated her remains and threw them into the sea.[30] The interlude of restoration initiated by Empress Eirene produced only ca. 809 a *vita* of an iconophile martyr, Stephanos the Younger (d. 764–765?), written by the deacon of Hagia Sophia (*BHG* 1666).[31] By contrast, the second iconoclastic period (815–843) and the years following the Triumph of Orthodoxy produced a true hotbed of religious fervour and literary inspiration, including an exponential upsurge in *vitae* about contemporary individuals persecuted for venerating images (but almost never as far as being executed, since mere harassment or exile was enough to earn a reputation as an iconodule confessor). At that time (the first quarter of the ninth century), the nerve centre of the genre was not yet exclusively Constantinople, as is shown by the texts written in

---

[28] As already said, in the eighth century literariness was limited with extremely little textual production. This is likely the main reason for the lack of testimonies, see Haldon 2014.
[29] Nonetheless, there are indications that the patriarch Tarasios wrote *enkomia* in honour of the martyrs of the end of the century, see *Vita of the Patriarch Tarasios* 49 and 55.
[30] Apparently, the body of Euphemia of Chalcedon remained uncorrupted but in pieces and her sepulchre ended up arriving on the island of Lemnos, a destination that the Empress Eirene had learned of through a vision. The official hagiographer of her repatriation was Konstantinos of Tios (*PmbZ* # 3878), who provides further details in his work *On the Relics of St Euphemia*.
[31] *Vita of Stephanos the Younger* 47,22–27; ch. 53 and pp. 5–9. For the different forms of ecclesiastical propaganda during these years, see Auzépy 1998: 95–99.

Palestine.[32] But texts composed about the capital and in it were gradually accumulating and referred to events that took place there or were addressed to an audience with strong ties to the court.

It was during the Second Iconoclasm (815–843) that there was a creative explosion that would set the foundations of the literature against iconoclasm and of a new Byzantine identity.[33] The texts written during these years of resistance were complemented by new narratives during the early decades of the post-iconoclast Church, which was led successively by Methodios, Ignatios and Photios. These men approached events during the iconoclast crisis as justifying situations that affected them directly, at the same time that they culled previous materials[34] and voluntarily or involuntarily rewrote historical fact. Our idea of what iconoclasm was and how it operated is due to these biased texts, but also to the lack of evidence from the opposing faction. We must therefore not fall into the trap of assuming that the absence of evidence is evidence of absence, and should envisage the possibility that iconodule hagiography was at least partly shaped by dialogue with a now lost iconoclast literary discourse. A case in point is the conclusion of Methodios' *Vita of Euthymios of Sardis*, which includes a theological controversy regarding the relationship between *eikon* and *logos* that can be seen as a refutation of Ioannes VII Grammatikos' thesis that *logos* is the only true form of representation. Most important, it has been clear since Ševčenko's seminal article that there was a tradition of iconoclast hagiography, the vestiges of which somehow survived the iconodule purge.[35]

The selective preservation of sources, many of which were destroyed by the victors, means that the extent of the written production of the iconoclasts can be estimated only with difficulty today. Many texts (for example, medical treatises) must have been copied, written and read by the iconoclasts,[36] but those related to the controversy were condemned to oblivion or drastically rewritten. The iconodules succeeded brilliantly in directing their project in such a way that their contemporaries and subsequent generations got the impression that literature during and after the

---

[32] Stephen the Sabaite's *Martyrion of the Twenty Sabaites*, see Kazhdan 1999: 169–81. On Leontios of Damascus' *Vita of Stephen the Sabaite*, see Kazhdan 1999: 171.
[33] Karlin-Hayter 1993; Criscuolo 1994b; Auzépy 2004a: 174–82; Odorico 2014.
[34] As shown by the case study analysed by Ronconi 2017, who focused on the letters of Theodoros of Stoudios and their initial sifting.
[35] Ševčenko 1977a; 1977b; Auzépy 1992. See Chapter 4.
[36] This was the case of the *Synopsis artis medicae*, a short medical encyclopaedia in seven volumes edited by Ermerins 1840: 79–221 and attributed to Leon the Mathematician by Ieraci Bio 1989: 217–18.

Second Iconoclasm was essentially an anti-iconoclast enterprise, an intellectual weapon of resistance to a persecuting regime distinguished by basically non-intellectual methods. Unfortunately, the lack of iconoclast texts is compounded by the problem that those we know of or that can be reconstructed are oases in the desert. The independent nature and the isolated and decontextualised transmission of the surviving texts (such as Leon's medical encyclopaedia and the *Vita of Pankratios of Taormina*) do not allow us to carry out a sociological study of their underlying relationships. The impression created, moreover, is that they played an unimportant part in the creation of a collective identity and were not determinant in the evolution of the major currents of Byzantine literature, in contrast to iconodule material. Such is the case with the texts written by the most prominent iconoclasts we can trace: the patriarch Ioannes VII Grammatikos completed an assignment from Emperor Leon V to compile a florilegium,[37] wrote two biblical *catenae*,[38] penned an apologetic work,[39] compiled the collection of *gnomai* in the *Florilegium Marcianum*[40] and even seems to have composed iconoclastic poems.[41]

Leon the Mathematician, a relative of the patriarch Ioannes Grammatikos who was the archbishop of Thessaloniki between 840 and 843, is also considered a great exponent of the iconoclast establishment.[42] Although the sources do not describe him as a bitter enemy of images, his literary production is generally taken to be iconoclast. His scientific interests set him apart from the more humanist trend or school 'of letters' followed by iconodule authors such as Methodios or Photios, to the extent that modern scholars have seen in this opposition a parallel to the image controversy: scientific contents (arithmetic, astronomy, geometry, etc.) were characteristic of the iconoclasts, in contrast to the humanistic knowledge cultivated by the iconodules.[43] A good example of this position is the

---

[37] *Vita of the Patriarch Nikephoros* 165,20–30; Alexander 1958a: 126–28. On Ioannes Grammatikos, see *PmbZ* # 3199 and # 3304; *PBE* I: Ioannes 5; Gero 1974/1975; Lilie 1999: 169–82; Katsiampoura 2010; Magdalino 2015a.
[38] Ceulemans and Van Deun 2017: 372–75.
[39] Gouillard 1966; Magdalino 1998: esp. 196–202 and 206–13.   [40] Odorico 1986: 17–25.
[41] Criscuolo 1994a; Lauxtermann 2003: 277–84.
[42] He was probably his cousin or perhaps his nephew, as the terms ἀνεψιός 'nephew' and ἐξαδέλφος 'cousin' used by Byzantine historians are interchangeable, cf. Nicol 1984: 84. On Leon, see *PmbZ* # 4440; 24312 and 24313; *PBE* I: Leon 19; *ODB*, s.v. Leo the Philosopher; Bury 1912: 436–42; Kolias 1939: 65ff.; Mango 1960; Lemerle 1971: 148–76. On Leon's literary production, see Laurent 1964; Lemerle 1971: 185–91; Westerink 1986; Lauxtermann 2019: 142–44 and 146–47.
[43] Signes Codoñer 2002, esp. 438–48. On the iconoclast command of scientific disciplines, see Tihon 1993; Magdalino 2006: 65–68.

complete contempt of the author of the *Vita of Ioannes Psichaites* for these disciplines – syllogisms, sophisms, Astronomy, Geometry and Arithmetic 'are non-existent things' – which he considers typical of iconoclasts.[44] The passing from one model to another and the friction between them can be seen in some short poems by Konstantinos Sikelos, who abandoned the teachings of Leon the Mathematician to continue his training in the circle of the patriarch Photios.[45] In a *psógos* against his first teacher, Konstantinos accused him of being a poor Christian because he was devoted to pagans such as Homer, Aratus, Euclid and Ptolemy. After Leon's death, Konstantinos dedicated an *Apology* to him in which he repeated his accusations and which was accompanied with other verses in which he affirmed that he had finally found the source of salvation, 'the Christian rhetoric of Photios that paves the way to heaven'.[46]

Leon's surviving work is not sufficiently representative and does not allow us to corroborate or refute the image transmitted by his iconodule contemporaries (monks) that scholars like him, who were linked to iconoclasm and patriarchal hierarchy, cultivated pagan disciplines during the Second Iconoclasm. The evidence indicates that this circle was very interested in Neoplatonism, erotic poetry, astronomy and divination.[47] Be that as it may, two texts that are more or less similar to those discussed in the following chapters allow us to qualify their approach. Leon's homily on the Annunciation of the Virgin has several intertexts with sermons by Gregorios of Nazianzus, but no attacks on icons or defence of iconoclasm by this 'disciple of Pythagoras'.[48] His long poem *Job, or, On Indifference to Grief and on Patience* (Ἰὼβ ἢ περὶ ἀλυπίας καὶ ὑπομονῆς) is along the same lines and in a sense can be considered hagiographical. It is a version in 638 dactylic hexameters of the biblical Book of Job, which stands out for mixing pagan characters and mythological figures with biblical protagonists and Christian martyrs.[49] As models for enduring family hardship, Leon accordingly proposes Thales, who decided to have no children so as not to suffer, and Xenophon, who lost his son in war and was able to overcome this misfortune (ll. 227–315), in the same way King David and Abraham were able to accept the deaths of theirs (ll. 339–56). In the consolation he produces, Leon goes so far as to compare the death of Socrates to the martyrdom of the saints who confronted the tyrants (ll. 395–99).

---

[44] *Vita of Ioannes Psichaites* 109; Dvornik 1933: 29–31.
[45] Spadaro 1971; Lauxtermann 2003: 98–99 and 106. On Konstantinos, see *PmbZ* # 23741.
[46] Spadaro 1971: 202.   [47] Lauxtermann 1999; Magdalino 2006: 55–69; Ronconi 2012b: 148–52.
[48] Laurent 1964: 286; Senina 2008a: 328–33.
[49] Westerink 1986: 201–22; Lauxtermann 2019: 146–47; Senina 2019.

This practice of fully incorporating pagan themes cannot be extrapolated to the other lost iconoclast texts, nor can we assume that it absolutely differentiates them from works produced by iconodule authors. But this does characterise the work of a non-iconodule author such as Leon, who clearly says as much in the stylistic reflections that precede his poem about Job. In these reflexions, Leon affirms that he will use a 'more pedestrian and more Homeric' style in order to achieve greater clarity and to give the reader more pleasure.[50] It is well established that literacy rates declined after the cultural collapse of the seventh century, and also that the political anarchy of the early eighth century and the military origin of the leaders of the First Iconoclasm led by Leon III the Isaurian discouraged a complex or involved style. Compared with the senior iconoclast leaders and their military background, many iconodules who took up the pen during the Second Iconoclasm held important posts in public office or in the administration of the patriarchate, both of which required substantial knowledge and erudition. We have no way of knowing whether most iconoclast authors sought a low, simple style devoid of flourishes of their own accord, but we do know that icon worshippers chose to use a pompous style. Whether this was to create a distance between popular texts and genres or to make reading their works difficult for the uneducated, the fact is that by the early ninth century verbal expression had reached a very high level and had become more obscure and recondite. Methodios' extraordinarily idiosyncratic and difficult style required the *metaphrasis* of two of his hagiographies by a subsequent generation to make them fully understandable, while Ignatios Diakonos, the learned author of the ponderous and verbose *Vita of the Patriarch Nikephoros*, was replaced with a minor writer to continue his narrative by offering an account of Nikephoros' relics.[51]

The sudden importance, courtesy of Theodoros Stoudites, of epistolography as a literary genre in its own right may have meant that traditionally lofty texts (e.g., *enkomia* of saints) had to be reshaped with an even more affected style. It is in any case reasonable to assume that iconodule writers cultivated their literary sophistication as a badge of ideological identity or even superiority. The 'epigram war' between Theodoros Stoudites and the four poets (Ioannes Grammatikos, Ignatios (Diakonos?), Sergios and Stephanos Kapetolites)[52] in the service of the

---

[50] Leon Mathem., *Protheoria* 6–8: ἰστέον δὲ ὅτι σαφηνείας ἕνεκα καὶ γλυκύτητος τὰς τραχυτέρας ὁ λόγος ἀποστρέφεται λέξεις, χρῆται δὲ πεζοτέραις καὶ μᾶλλον Ὁμηρικαῖς.
[51] See Chapter 2. On the inflated style of Methodios, see Hinterberger 2008.
[52] For the poet Sergios, see *PmbZ* # 6659. For Stephanos Kapetolites, see *PmbZ* # 7059 and 7074.

iconoclast Emperor Leon V who wrote verse inscriptions for the Chalke Gate of the imperial palace suggests a tendency to attribute a cultural dimension to theological controversy.[53] The latter group of authors were well aware of this and aroused a vehement literary debate by using acrostics: the iconodule inscription of 797–802 contains a simple acrostic, the iconoclast inscription of 815/816 conceals a more complicated one and the final iconodule inscription of 816/818 represents a real acrostic tour de force. While Theodoros showed off his expertise by placing the mesostich (the central acrostic) at the very beginning of the seventh syllable of the verse, the iconoclast poets were accused of a lack of poetic ability.[54] This accusation became a cliché that reappears in the *Vita of Michael the Synkellos* in an evaluation of the iambics of a certain Christodoulos that are to be tattooed on the foreheads of Theodoros and Theophanes Graptoi. The Emperor Theophilos and the rest of the court noticed the poor quality of the verses, and one of those present exclaimed: 'My lord, these persons do not deserve that the iambs be any better'.[55]

From this dialectic and formal duel, a style arose, which, for those who cultivated it, was clearly iconodule in nature and which they used as a propaganda tool, although they never theorised about it or defined it as different from a so-called iconoclast style. The best examples are certainly the lofty hagiographies written by Ignatios Diakonos, Methodios and Michael Synkellos, with their periodic structure, recondite vocabulary, *hapax legomena* pattern based on ancient words, classical quotations, obscurity, etc.[56] In one of his letters, Theodoros Stoudites praises the 'now developed discourse' (τὴν προκόπτουσαν διάλεξιν) of his disciple Naukratios and affirms that the orthodox must be skilful in their discourse to combat iconoclasts and thus defeat their arguments.[57] It was on the basis of this type of expression that Photios developed his theory of style, showing himself to be a scholar with an enviable command of Greek and building a new Christian literary theory that introduces ethical values.[58]

It is difficult to be sure to what extent the hypothetical 'iconoclast style' was separate from that of iconodules in terms of verbal expression, as the rhetoric taught continued to be that of the classics and was common to all

---

[53] Lauxterman 2003: 274–84; Pentcheva 2010: 77–88.
[54] Theod. Stoud., *Refutation of the Iconoclasts* 437; Theod. Stoud., *epist.* 356.
[55] *Vita of Michael the Synkellos* 84–86 and 160–61; Sode 2001: 86–89 and 127–31. See Chapter 6.
[56] Ševčenko 1981: 291 and 301–3; Ševčenko 1982; *Vita of Leon of Catania*, pp. 39–59. On the style of Ignatios Diakonos and his classical quotations, see Lampakis 2001.
[57] Theod. Stoud., *epist.* 49,4–14.
[58] Kustas 1962; Afinogenov 1995. For the wording in the Dark Century, see Kazhdan 1999: 161–65.

citizens of the Empire. Establishments of higher education proper did not appear until the mid-ninth century, when Theophilos founded one in the Magnaura Palace.[59] As a consequence, the writers of the iconoclast era had to educate themselves in a private system about which we do not know as much as we would like.[60] Literary conventions and the characteristics of the texts themselves, in which the author's humility and a lack of biographical references are the norm, prevent us from identifying where the writers were trained; they claim to have been educated simply by studying religious texts and to have asked God and the saints to grant them the ability to write, denying that their skill was the result of years of training.[61] Details of this sort might have indicated shared school experiences between ideological allies or even enemies. As we lack them, we must attempt to reconstruct the main aspects of the authors' biographies from the surviving texts they wrote. More information must accordingly be extracted via close reading of the latter, combined with detailed analysis of the reasons for their composition, the public they aimed at, the purpose of the texts and the manner in which they are crafted (often involving intertextuality and cast in the form of a dialogue with other authors and contemporary events). A similar contextualisation of these works allows us to identify the main milieux in which literature flourished during the iconoclast period.

1.1 The Literary Milieux under Iconoclasm

The large number and variety of extant texts produced throughout this period prove that their writing and initial reception took place within specific power groups, networks with a common interest in producing them or, more precisely put, milieux receptive to reading and disseminating them. The chapters of this book are accordingly organised by reference to these literary circles, identifying the main networks, the texts they supported and their setting, in order to contextualise how each work came into being and make sense of its literary, social and political dimensions. Studies carried out in recent decades in the framework of (social) network

---

[59] Speck 1974c; Treadgold 1979b:187. This higher school was later revitalised by Caesar Bardas.
[60] Lemerle 1971: 100–8; Moffatt 1977: 88–92; Demoen 1998; Hatlie 2007a: 419–22; Markopoulos 2015; Efthymiadis 2017; Markopoulos 2017 with previous bibliography.
[61] Odorico 2002; Papaioannou 2014; Pizzone 2014; Rapp 2015. On the status of the man of letters within middle Byzantine hagiography, see Efthymiadis and Kalogeras 2014; Hinterberger 2014b; Kaplan 2015.

analysis offer an excellent model for research.[62] In fact, Byzantine studies already incorporate this scientific approach to historical phenomena based on the concept of complex systems, and Mullett's pioneering monograph on the collected letters of Theophylaktos of Ohrid is no longer unique.[63] Such work was once founded on *network analysis*, which – as its name suggests – is interested in the relations and relationships that structure a society, since 'not only ties matter, but they are organised in a significant way so that this or that individual has an interesting position in terms of his or her ties'.[64] This concern for identifying and defining the connections between individuals in a group and examining their influence within the group, as well as their impact on the rest of society, is characteristic of network analysis. The systematic gathering of data allows further mathematical analysis, which can be presented via visualisation tools.

The following pages will inevitably deal with the dynamics of interaction between authors, patrons, religious and political leaders, and even protagonists of the texts (as shown in Appendix B: Network Chart of Writers and Their Literary Relations under Iconoclasm and in Its Aftermath). The literary and textual aim of the present study nonetheless requires that these matters be approached as a different reality and given a different name. I will therefore speak of 'milieux', and the chapters will be structured in accord with them. I will not concentrate so much on networks and their relationships, as on what lies behind them: the reasons they were forged, the way this was done and the texts they produced. The term 'milieu' is conceptually less strict and broader than 'network', since it refers to the cultural setting of the members of a network and to the setting for the composition of their written works. In addition, equal importance is given to phenomena such as the type of performance, publication/distribution, reading/listening, intertextuality, *imitatio* and *aemulatio*. This rubric also allows greater flexibility to reflect the fluidity of interpersonal relationships (e.g., between the patron and the writer, whose collaboration is accentuated by ideological proximity) and the influence exercised upon both of them by the socio-political context. In Byzantium, working groups were often created for a specific enterprise,

---

[62] Boissevain 1974; H.C. White 2008; Scott and Carrington 2011; Prell 2012.
[63] Mullett 1997; Ruffini 2008; Schor 2011; Mitsiou 2012; Steckel 2014; Preiser-Kapeller 2020. See also the Colloquium in Dumbarton Oaks: 'The Social Network in Byzantium and Its Neighbors' held in 2012.
[64] Lemercier 2012: 22, apud Preiser-Kapeller 2020: 433.

and their composition was not necessarily reproduced exactly when a similar new enterprise became necessary.[65]

As will become apparent in the case of Sabas, mobility between such circles was not unusual: not all members of a milieu had the same level of commitment to it, especially when its raison d'être (the defence of Orthodoxy) was always the same and what varied were the common or private interests that drew the group together at any particular moment. This interconnection between individuals from different milieux, and between the milieux themselves, implies partial overlapping, since they shared spatial and temporal coordinates. In the interests of clarity, and at the risk of offering an overly fragmented image of Byzantine society, each chapter concentrates on one of these groups, although references to others will be constant. This is not a case of isolated blocks or of monastic communities on the fringe of society and set apart from other individuals, but the opposite: people came together to have a greater possibility of success by mixing with others.

As a final methodological comment, the identification of the various milieux and the assignment of individuals to each corresponds not simply to historical research, but to the literary products that have come down to us. The written production of an individual author marks him as belonging to one or more groups; this assignment is confirmed or qualified by the historical situation and other surviving evidence.

After a survey of the main works written under iconoclasm and in its aftermath, this book analyses and interprets these works in light of their background. The goal is to be forensic, in the sense that the enquiry sets out to systematically expose the context, motivation and intertextual and interpersonal connections of every literary composition examined. These texts are grouped not by genre, stylistic level or even authorship, but by the 'milieu' of common interests shared by protagonists, authors, patrons and other intended readers, that is, according to production and reception circles. My aim is not only to highlight and make sense of their interrelationship but to gain insights into the dynamics of composition and rewriting. The result should be a major advance in the study of the construction of sainthood in Byzantium and the development of hagiographical *metaphrasis*.

---

[65] This is the case, for example, of the two versions of the *Imperial Menologion*, which were both written within a very short period during the reign of Michael IV (1034–1041) but for different recipients. A number of discrepancies between them regarding format, script and miniature style reveals that their scribes were different, even if the manuscripts were painted by the same brush, see D'Aiuto 2012; Patterson Ševčenko 2013.

The demographic explosion of Byzantine monasticism in the second half of the eighth century, which introduced new methods of organisation and 'networking' phenomena, be it by forming networks of monasteries or building the dynastic inheritances of the establishments, two key elements of milieux, has been mentioned. Apart from the famous Stoudite case, where at least another eight monasteries depended directly on the one at Stoudios and its hegoumenos (Sakkoudion, Symboloi, Kathara, Tripyliana, St Christophoros, St Georgios, St Tryphon and later Sabas, all governed by the same rule),[66] we know of similar structures (perhaps less rigid) in the first half of the ninth century. This was the situation, for example, of the monastery of Medikion, which owned a separate monastery founded by Niketas on the island of Prote, one of the Princes' Islands in the Sea of Marmara.[67] It is here, in this *metochion* of Medikion, that Empress Theodosia stayed after she was widowed by Leon V. A third monastery was founded by Niketas after his exile, when he purchased a new *metochion* north of Constantinople, although not far from the capital, where he established himself until his death in 824.[68]

Theophanes of Sigriane founded the monastery of Megas Agros, but also administered that of Polichniou, to which he retired, along with another monastery on the island of Kalonymos, as well as the monastery of Christophoros, which should probably be identified with Mikros Agros.[69] Makarios of Pelekete similarly led three establishments: one in Pelekete, another in Aphousia and a third in Chrysopolis.[70] Ioannikios likewise administered the monasteries of Eustathiou in Lydia, of the Theotokos, and of the Holy Apostles Peter and Paul.[71] Symeon Dekapolites controlled a number of monasteries of the Dekapolis in Isauria, as well as the one owned by his family in Thessaloniki and the

---

[66] Leroy 1958a; Rezác 1958: 117–25; Pratsch 1998: 129–31; 2007; Delouis 2005: 203–32; Hatlie 2007a: 323–26. For their rule, see Thomas et al. 2000: vol. 1, 67–115. See Chapter 1 and Maps 1 and 2.

[67] Rosenqvist 2002: 66–68; Auzépy et al. 2005.

[68] *Vita of Niketas of Medikion* 47; Alexakis 1994: 197. The influence of the Stoudite model is clear, as Niketas was very close to Theodoros Stoudites, cf. Delouis 2005: 315–16.

[69] Method., *Vita of Theophanes the Confessor* 21, 15,20–22 (exiled to Polichniou); 22, 15,32–16,6 (foundation in Kalonymos); 24, 16,23–30 (stay in Christophoros); 24, 17,1–13 (foundation of Megas Agros).

[70] Van de Vorst 1913b: 273.

[71] On the monastery of Eustathiou, see *Vita of Ioannikios by Petros* 22,396C; *Vita of Ioannikios by Sabas* 18,350A; On that of the Theotokos, see *Vita of Ioannikios by Petros* 23,397A; *Vita of Ioannikios by Sabas* 19–20,351C–D. On that of the Holy Apostles, see *Vita of Ioannikios by Sabas* 20,352A–B; *Vita of Ioannikios by Petros* 23,397A–B, who specifies the dedication of the monastery to Peter and Paul.

one that accommodated Gregorios Dekapolites.[72] In the same fashion, Petros of Atroa (773–837) appears at the head of the network formed by the Bithynian monasteries of St Zacharias, Hagios Porphyrios, Balaiou and Balentia, together with the chapels of Kalonoros and Hippos and a convent in Lydia.[73] The same can be said of the future patriarch Ignatios, who, before attaining the throne of Constantinople, founded and administered at least three monasteries on the Princes' Islands situated between the capital and Chalcedon, to be specific, on Terebinthos, Niandros and Plate.[74] To these must be added the monastery of Satyros (also known as that of Anatellon), which was built in 873–874 on the Bithynian coast facing Ignatios' previous monasteries, and whither he transferred the remains of his father Michael I Rhangabe.[75]

During his lifetime, the patriarch Nikephoros founded three monasteries at his own expense: Ta Agathou, Theodoros and another of uncertain name on the Asian coast of the Bosphorus.[76] To these must be added the monastery of his mother Eudokia.[77] The monastery of Agauroi for its part had at least six *metochia* of considerable dimensions administered by the same abbot: St Agapios, St Kosmas, St Elijah, Leukades, Bomoi and another whose name is unknown.[78] An additional well-known case is the indeterminate (although doubtless large) number of monastic centres successively founded by Symeon the Stylite of Lesbos, which were directed by a single spiritual father. In principle, this was Symeon itself. But his journey to Constantinople in 823 obliged him to delegate his duties to his brother Georgios, whom he ultimately made responsible for all his monasteries, whether in the *thema* of Thrakesioi or in Mytilene.[79] For twenty years, Georgios was in charge of all these foundations, until in 843 Symeon asked him to move to the capital to participate in the debates prior to the restoration of icons and the election of a new patriarch.

---

[72] *Vita of Gregorios Dekapolites* 5,12–13 (Symeon as *archimandrites* of the Dekapolis). For his monastery in Thessaloniki, see *Vita of Euthymios* 58–60. For that of Gregorios Dekapolites' community, see *Vita of Gregorios Dekapolites* 50.
[73] *Vita of Petros of Atroa*, intr. pp. 35–47; *Vita retractata of Petros of Atroa*, intr. pp. 44–45. Cf. Delouis 2005: 228–30.
[74] *Vita of Ignatios* 10–11; Janin 1975: 63, 65 and 67; Ruggieri 1991: 209. See also Pargoire 1901a.
[75] *Vita of Ignatios* 11; Janin 1975: 42–43; Ruggieri 1991: 201; Ricci 1998; 2012. The transfer of the body of Michael I is narrated by Theoph. Cont. I, 10,16–25.
[76] Agathou: *Vita of Nikephoros* 72,133a. Theodorou: *Vita of Nikephoros* 5, 120–21; 5,32–35; 72,133ab. Name not stated: *Vita of Nikephoros* 12, 53c–56a; 2,15–19; Alexander 1958a: 61–63.
[77] *Vita of Nikephoros* 7, 48d–49a; Theod. Stoud., *epist.* 286,15; Alexander 1958a: 56.
[78] Hergès 1898/1899; Janin 1975: 132–34. Many of its branches are quoted in *Vita of Ioannikios by Sabas* 356B: Agapios; 357B: Elijah; 361B: Kosmas; 368A: Leukades.
[79] *Acta of David, Symeon and Georgios* 18,20–25 and 25,3–6.

In all likelihood, the relationships between monasteries and their *metochia* and between monasteries that followed the same or similar monastic rules entailed an intertextual dependence between their *typika* (monastic foundation charters), as is proven by the extant texts.[80] Alongside the networks of cenobite foundations, there is evidence in the ninth century of monastic families based on blood ties, especially when choosing a successor to the spiritual father was involved.[81] This occurred in the monastery of Agauroi near Prousa, where Eustratios called together five of his uncles when he decided to take the monastic habit.[82] When his uncle Gregorios died, Eustratios succeeded him as hegoumenos of the monastery.[83] As is well known, the succession of the monastery of Stoudios passed from Platon of Sakkoudion to his nephew Theodoros Stoudites,[84] and the previous hegoumenos of Stoudios, Sabas, who is known for his vehement position at the Second Council of Nicaea, may well have been related to Theodoros through his mother and his uncle Platon.[85] In the case of the convent of Kloubiou, after the death of the abbess, her daughter took over its management, as Ioannikios had prophesied personally to them that she would.[86] Likewise, on the death of Niketas the Patrician, the monastery he had founded on land recently purchased in Katesia, to the north of the *thema* of the Optimatoi, was administered by his nephew, also named Niketas.[87] The *archimandrites* Symeon Dekapolites led his monasteries in Isauria while his nephew Gregorios was in charge of the new monastery in Thessaloniki, the name of which is unknown.[88]

Although studies of the subject are still lacking, this 'dynastic' model in the management of monasterial complexes must have been quite widespread, especially in the case of networks involving more than one centre. But we also find the practice in small, private monasteries: the

---

[80] Thomas et al. 2000.
[81] Flusin 1993: 48–49; Hatlie 2007a: 289–94. On the inheritance system of the Byzantine monasteries and their evolution following family links, see Patlagean 1981: 99–101; Kaplan 1993a; Krausmüller 2013c. Cf. Sot 1978.
[82] *Vita of Eustratios of Agauroi* 4, pp. 369–70.   [83] Ibid., ch. 7, p. 372. Cf. Menthon 1935: 51–59.
[84] *Vita B of Theodoros Stoud.* 248D–49B; *Vita C of Theodoros Stoud.* 16, p. 266.
[85] Pratsch 1998: 47; Theod. Stoud., *epist.*, p. 144*, n. 14; *PBE* I: Sabas 4; Afinogenov 1994: 54; Delouis 2005: 124–38.
[86] *Vita of Ioannikios by Sabas* 33–34, 361C–62B; *Vita of Ioannikios by Petros* 57–58, 421B–22C. On this convent, see Janin 1969: 282. Abbess Euphrosyne of Kloubiou is sent an epistle by Theodoros Stoudites (*epist.* 458), datable between 821 and 823. According to Topping 1986/1988: 386, Theodosia, the author of a *kanon* in honour of this ascetic saint, belonged to this community.
[87] *Vita of Niketas the Patrician* 31, p. 349. On Niketas, the saint's nephew, see *PmbZ* # 5473. On the monastery of Katesia, see Janin 1975: 95
[88] *Vita of Gregorios Dekapolites* 50,2–3.

management of the monastery of Psicha in Constantinople passed from Theodoros to his younger brother Ioannes when the former was appointed bishop.[89] The appointment by Petros of Atroa of his brother Paulos to run all the monasteries he had founded in Bithynia is well known.[90] When, seven years later, he was called to take charge of an episcopal see, the post passed to Iakobos, a nephew of both men.[91] There was a similar situation in the community led by St Anthousa of Mantineon,[92] the founder of a convent alongside a lake near Claudiopolis in Paphlagonia.[93] She chose her nephew to lead the monastery built in the vicinity that she supervised herself. Both were tortured by Konstantinos V (741–775), who sent the saint into exile.[94]

Earlier Byzantine monastic communities operated as families with a model for growing in ascetic maturity.[95] By the eighth century, however, the noble, wealthy background of the most important monks led to a new reality: monastic families. The dialectic between monastic life and family life was probably not based on real opposition, as the sources would have us believe; most monasteries were family affairs. The presence of these monastic families within the milieux must have contributed to the unity of their members, lending cohesion to the groups. At times, strong blood ties and spiritual kinship between individuals make it tempting to consider the group a 'clan'. But the milieu is a broader structure, since it includes external members who can be integrated only occasionally for a specific enterprise or for a short period.

Now that what is meant by 'milieu' has been made clear, it is appropriate to identify the main groups that form the core of the analysis that follows and the chapter divisions. The most well-known of these milieux was also the first to emerge: the Stoudite (Chapter 1), rooted in the famous monastery of St John of Stoudios in Constantinople, although it also included the members of the remaining monasteries of the federation (Sakkoudion, Kathara, etc.). We can identify a group of intellectuals gathered around the charismatic leader Theodoros (759–826), whose

---

[89] *Vita of Ioannes Psichaites* 5; For Costa-Louillet 1954/1955: 256–63 the see run by Theodoros was in Galatia, cf. *PmbZ* # 7613. For Ioannes Psichaites, see *PmbZ* # 3053.
[90] On Paulos of Atroa, see *PmbZ* # 5839; *PBE* I: Paulos 26. For Petros of Atroa, see *PmbZ* # 6022; *PBE* I: Petros 34.
[91] *PmbZ* # 2634; *PBE* I: Iakobos 4.
[92] *PmbZ* # 500; *PBE* I: Anthousa 2; *SynaxCP* 848,31–52,17 (27 July = *BHG* 2029h); Talbot 1998: 13–19.
[93] For the place where this convent was built, see Ruggieri 1991: 173–274 and 238–89; Belke 1996: 249–51.
[94] Peeters 1911; Mango 1982; Ruggieri 1985. [95] Krausmüller 2013c.

literary biography and political-religious ideology are cohesive enough to justify joint study in terms of what is usually considered a 'literary circle', that is, a social context built on a community of interests in which the literary component predominates or, put another way, a political group that uses literature to attain its goals.[96] We know that the interests of these men resulted in the ardent defence of their interpretation of Orthodoxy, which usually ended in direct opposition to the patriarch and the emperor. Their confrontations with iconoclast emperors and leaders are famous. But they also had conflicts with iconodules whose view of the Church did not coincide with theirs, as in the case of the defenders of the second marriage of Konstantinos VI, which gave rise to the Moechian conflict, or shortly afterwards in connection with the election of Nikephoros as Patriarch of Constantinople.[97] Far from comprising a homogeneous block, in fact, Orthodoxy included many currents, sometimes opposing each other, as can be seen in the confrontation between Stoudite monks and followers of the patriarch Methodios.[98]

An exhaustive analysis of the surviving literature testifies to the existence of other important milieux, which, like that of the Stoudites, formed around the spiritual leader of a monastic community: Nikephoros and Niketas of Medikion, the ascetic Ioannikios, Hilarion of Dalmatos, Euthymios of Sardis, Gregorios of Dekapolis, Makarios of Pelekete and Petros of Atroa. Although none of these men played as important a historical role as the monks of Stoudios, and their literary production is far less significant, the religious and literary dimension of these groups merits study. A group associated with the monastery of Medikion in Bithynia and its founders Nikephoros and Niketas, for example, extolled their memory and shared a specific view of ecclesiastical and even political life. The tentacles of this group, however, were not wide-ranging and therefore had little effect, and they proved incapable of involving other figures or writers in their cause. The testimonies that have been preserved thus do not permit in-depth study of them. Although these small circles (whose importance in the course of events cannot be ignored) were less effective at imposing their interests, it should not be assumed that power is always accompanied by great literature. Active and successful socio-

---

[96] Odorico 2006; 2014.
[97] Werner 1957; Fuentes Alonso 1984; Patlagean 1988; Karlin-Hayter 1994; Pratsch 1998; Cholij 2002; Delouis 2005.
[98] The confrontation between the Stoudites and the Methodians has already been studied, see Von Dobschütz 1909a; Grumel 1935; Doens and Hannick 1973; Löwe 1982; Darrouzès 1987; Lilie 1999: 248–60; Maksimovic 2000. See Chapters 1–2.

political circles in the Church did not always reinforce their activity through literature. Such is the case of Ioannikios, who was the point of reference of Bithynian iconodule monasticism and a major player in the restoration of icons and the defeat of heresy, but who never penned anything himself and does not seem to have encouraged his followers to write, despite the breadth of his network of contacts. The ramifications of this network extend over time and are clear even in the *vita* of Abbess Eirene of Chrysobalanton, written ca. 980, which claimed that the protagonist knew the saint of the Bithynian mountains personally.[99]

The opposite situation, of less powerful groups with a strong literary presence, also existed. A telling example is the disciples of Gregorios Dekapolites, who despite being uncommitted to the cause of the icons, were able to take advantage of the family ties of their spiritual father and the skilful instrumentalisation of their literary production to acquire a relevance to the new order that arose after the Triumph of Orthodoxy on 11 March 843 (Chapter 3). An intermediate situation can also be found, that is, that of groups with some literary production but a subtle cohesion that is difficult to trace, making it impossible to study them in an in-depth manner. This is the case of a hypothetical Palestinian milieu. In line with the importance of their compatriots during the Dark Age and the First Iconoclasm, some Palestinian monks and writers are quoted throughout the book creating the impression that a 'Palestinian lobby' influenced Byzantine society, which may be true to some extent. But literary evidence does not support that vision, for it does not reveal a true milieu, but rather Palestinian refugees individually integrated in some Constantinopolitan circles. It is worth mentioning their reception and activities at the Chora monastery, which was closely connected to the Patriarchate of Constantinople (see Chapters 2 and 6). But these men did not form an independent milieu, since they were not grouped around a charismatic leader and did not produce a significant amount of interconnected writings; their literary production was neither the result of a common ideological enterprise nor specifically Palestinian. In addition to the cold welcome afforded Syro-Palestinian hagiography in Constantinople,[100] recent research has shown that a process of liturgical Byzantinisation began in the ninth century in the Patriarchate of Jerusalem. This was to culminate in the thirteenth century and accompanies an overall process of cultural influence exerted on Palestine from the Byzantine capital.[101] Indeed, the oldest extant manuscript in minuscule script, the

---

[99] *Vita of Eirene Chrysobalanton* 3.   [100] Binggeli 2018.   [101] Galadza 2010; 2018.

Tetraeuangelium Uspenskij (St Petersburg RNB Gr. 219), was copied by Nikolaos Stoudites in the year 835 not in Constantinople but probably in Palestine, transferring this calligraphic innovation from the capital to the province.[102]

The unusual situation in provinces under Muslim domination, moreover, meant that the iconoclast conflict had a completely different dimension there and went unnoticed to a considerable extent. The iconodules' champion Theodore Abū Qurrah (ca. 750–ca. 820) was a native of Edessa in Syria who became a monk at the monastery of Mar Sabas in Palestine, where he followed the teachings of Ioannes Damaskenos. Abū Qurrah composed a long treatise in Arabic in defence of the veneration of icons at the end of the eighth century, when there was no communication with Constantinople.[103] The scenario in Jerusalem was quite different, and while the capital and its hinterland were concerned with iconoclasm and the theology of the images, within the Melkite Church, the predominant question continued to be Christology. Abū Qurrah's apologist text therefore addressed the religious challenges those Christians had to face when venerating icons amongst Jews and Muslims. He stood aloof from the debate over images that arose in Constantinople and its political implications, and said nothing about it, probably because he considered it irrelevant to the troubles of Melkite Christians living under Islamic rule.

The restoration of icons in 843 meant not only the defeat of heresy, but also the construction of a new discourse of identity in which it was necessary to be able to boast of iconodule credentials to facilitate or legitimate one's position in the new society. If the Second Iconoclasm favoured the strengthening of milieux with a noteworthy literary production regarding contemporary events, the new scenario that arose from the restoration of Orthodoxy required the adaptation of specific individuals and heterogeneous groups to the ecclesiastical policy pronounced by the newly elected patriarch Methodios.[104] These initiatives were henceforth to originate not exclusively in the most important monastic centres, but in major state institutions. This compounded the iconoclastic controversy and made it more important in Byzantine daily life. The various patriarchs promoted the creation of literature with a strong ideological content and with clear propaganda objectives by authors with common links. We can

---

[102] Kaplan 2017: 1059, following Ronconi's suggestion.
[103] Griffith 1982; 1985; 1993; 1997; Brubaker and Haldon 2011: 105–17 and 232–34; Signes Codoñer 2013a; Reynolds 2017.
[104] Pargoire 1903b; Afinogenov 1996a; 1996b; Karlin-Hayter 2006b. For the resurgence of monastic life after the Triumph of Orthodoxy, see Morris 1995: 9–30.

thus speak of a Methodian milieu (Chapter 2), an Ignatian milieu (Chapter 5) and a Photian milieu (Chapter 6) to match the writings produced under the auspices of Methodios (843–847), Ignatios (847–858 and 867–877) and Photios (858–867 and 877–886), who encouraged their disciples to promote the veneration of certain saints in order to strengthen their position as heads of the Byzantine Church. Even the imperial court and the secular elite (as will be explained in Chapter 4) began to forge a cultural policy that foreshadowed the great literary enterprises of the Macedonian regime, aimed at praising its members, redeeming the heretic iconoclast Emperor Theophilos, legitimizing the claim to the throne of the young heir Michael III and sanctifying his wife Theodora, the promoter of the restoration of icons, by recounting their participation in the Second Iconoclasm and the end of the crisis.

These circles or milieux were intended as strongly cohesive groups, due to their common interests and operated as social microstructures.[105] Reciprocal contact took place between their members to produce an interconnected network, and their links were often strengthened by oaths of loyalty.[106] Theodoros Stoudites demanded a serious commitment from his monks and did not hesitate to attack upstarts who defected in exchange for a post within the hierarchy, or even to punish deserters who betrayed him.[107] The seriousness of the iconoclastic conflict led the patriarch Tarasios to demand that declarations of loyalty be signed.[108] Both Ignatios and Photios maintained this custom[109] until *kanon* 8 of the anti-Photian Council of 869/870 prohibited the patriarch of Constantinople, whoever he might be, from having bishops or priests sign loyalty oaths. By order of Emperor Basileios I, moreover, if any documents of this kind were found in which the signatory had links with Photios, they were delivered to the papal legates to be cast into the flames.[110] The literary reflection suggested by membership in these groups makes it

---

[105] Kazhdan 1982; Déroche 1993: 243–45; Hatlie 2007a: 263–352.
[106] Svoronos 1951: 109 and 114; Auzépy 2007: 21–22; Delouis 2008b.
[107] As occurred with the upstart Leontios of Stoudios, see *PmbZ* # 4589; *PBE* I: Leontios 29; Hatlie 2007a: 273, n. 41. On the punishments imposed by the hegoumenos Theodoros, see Hatlie 2007a: 386, nn. 130 and 133 with references to Thedoros' epistles.
[108] *Vita of Ioannikios* by Sabas Monachos 372A; Karlin-Hayter 2006b: 57–58.
[109] *Vita of the Patriarch Ignatios* 17, pp. 26,29–31; 54, p. 80,5–7; 91, p. 124,26–28 and 92, p. 126,25–28. According to Anastasius the Librarian, Photios required all in his ranks (whether laymen or men of the Church) to sign a loyalty agreement, see Mansi XVI, 5D; Phot., *epist.* 276,21–23: λῆρος ἂν εἴη μακρὸς ἐπὶ χάρτῃ καὶ καλάμῳ καὶ μέλανι τὴν ἀληθινὴν ἡμῶν ἀγάπην ἐλπίζειν τῇ σῇ ποτε διαχαραχθῆναι ψυχῇ, 'it would be quite absurd to expect our true love on paper with pen and ink to be engraved on your soul one day'.
[110] Mansi XVI, 135E–36A; Delouis 2016.

possible to reconstruct the affiliation of the writers, if we analyse the objectives they pursued with their works and the extent to which they responded to the interests of their patrons.

Patronage was certainly a key element in these structures, both for the protection it gave some writers and for the commissioning of written works that have come down to us.[111] Although some patrons were laymen (high-ranking aristocrats linked to the court), most had professed a religious life, which meant that they chose ecclesiastical writers to draft the texts they commissioned. Throughout the whole iconoclast period (726–843) and even in succeeding decades, practically all the writers we know of are either monks or laymen who retreated to monasteries to write by taking advantage of the alleged peace of a monastic cell. The great service authors could render to their patrons' causes allowed them to achieve considerable social and geographical mobility. Although many are anonymous, they were determinant in the cultural life of the period, and it is therefore worth describing their status. To illustrate their freedom of movement and the rewards open to them for their literary work, the final chapter of this book includes by way of example a case study tracing the socio-ecclesiastic career of one such author, Sabas, an important hagiographer whose biography has not previously received systematic scholarly treatment (Chapter 7).

The social background of patrons and writers meant that the main subject of literature under iconoclasm was none other than the monks and patriarchs who had lived through the crisis as major figures, due to their influence on society and, in particular, on political life. This manner of narrating history through the persons involved not only allowed the presentation of a partial, biased view of events – often touched up or even distorted – but also permitted commissioners and writers to see themselves reflected in the texts' protagonists. The new 'martyrs' were mainly founders of monasteries born of rich and powerful families with excellent contacts in the corridors of power. Both during the persecution and after the Triumph of Orthodoxy in 843, most texts revolve around a saint, almost always a man, who is portrayed as a confessor, since hardly any of them actually lost their lives for defending their vision of faith. They not only had monastic support but were also socially accepted for having publicly defended icons, something that justified their political actions

---

[111] In common with other aspects, bibliography on Byzantine patronage is not non-existent but tends to concentrate on later periods, mainly the eleventh and twelfth centuries, see Mullett 1984; Morris 1995: 9–142; Lauxtermann 2003: 34–36; Jeffreys 2009; Bernard 2014: 291–333.

and their desire to influence society. A typical example of a saint of the Second Iconoclasm is the hegoumenos Theodoros of Stoudios, who confronted emperors and patriarchs as a champion of Orthodoxy and suffered for encouraging the veneration of images. Even when other protagonists did not fit this model of holiness particularly well, Theodoros became a point of reference, and accounts of him were imitated for other persons who needed a text to be celebrated liturgically and at the same time prove their holiness.

Most literature of the iconoclastic period is about iconoclasm and its heroic victims. This is due to the attitude with which writers addressed the blank page, since the narration of their sufferings is seen as an ascetic practice in itself, as well as a way to exercise authority and represent power at the same time that Christian identity was being defined (as naturally iconodule).[112] The process of writing these accounts was a form of re-creation of the incarnation of Christ: as Christ is the visible incarnation of the invisible Godhead, the iconodule saints incarnate and enact with their lives the abstract, immaterial theological principles that maintained the discourse of Orthodoxy.[113] This is the key to the choice of the literary genre of the lives of saints by iconophile writers. An author as committed to icons as the patriarch Methodios affirms that logographers (writers of words) resemble iconographers (writers of images) in their capacity to teach the incarnation of Christ (which justifies his visual representation in icons).[114] For iconoclasts, on the other hand, from the Synod of Hiereia (754) on, the virtues of the saints are the true sacred images, since they are εἰκόνες ἔμψυχοι (spiritual icons) that induce the faithful to imitate a prototype of holiness.[115]

Despite the great value of the new saints for describing events and helping create an ideology and identity capable of drawing different social groups together, they were more often political creations than objects of popular devotion by believers. This is why their veneration did not withstand the passage of time and they were quickly forgotten, despite

---

[112] Krueger 2004: 189–97.
[113] These dogmas were already defined by the Fathers of the Church such as Irenaeus of Lyons, who affirmed: 'for the Father is the invisible of the Son, but the Son the visible of the Father' (Invisibile etenim Filii Pater, visibile autem Patris Filius: Iren. 4.6.6, ed. Rousseau 1965, vol. II, p. 450). See Cameron 1992.
[114] ἔκθεσις περὶ τῶν ἁγίων εἰκόνων, in *Vaticanus Gr.* 1753, fol. 225r–30v, here fol. 228r, lines 15–21, see Bithos 2009: 76. As a matter of fact, the verb *graphein* is polysemic, meaning both 'to draw' and 'to write', see LSJ. On the iconophile theology of images, see Irmscher 1980; Sansterre 1994; Parry 1996; Featherstone 2015.
[115] Anastos 1954: esp. 153; Krueger 2004: 189–97; Magdalino 2015a.

the efforts made to promote them. Of the large number of figures sanctified during iconoclasm, only five attracted sufficient attention to be included in the *Metaphrastic Menologion*[116] compiled less than a century later: Andreas *en Krisei*, Ioannikios, Stephanos the Younger, Eudokimos and Theodoros Graptos, as well as the group of the forty-two martyrs of Amorion.[117] The ephemeral character of their liturgical celebration is striking and symptomatic of the fact that once their political function ended, continuing veneration of them made no sense. This may be why, despite the initial impact of this literature and its interest for its contemporaries, the works in question were not widely disseminated and tend to be preserved in no more than one or two manuscripts.

It goes without saying that much of the literature of this period has been poorly studied and that when it has attracted attention, it has been from the perspective of historians who see in it pro-monastic and pro-iconodule documents of opposition to imperial power.[118] This monograph, by contrast, attempts to understand these works in themselves as the literary production of a group of writers with common concerns. For this reason, I aim to contextualise each text in depth, taking into account the web of interests (political, monastic, ecclesiastical, iconodule or personal) active at each moment and place that produced its specific form and intentions.

The impossibility of successfully carrying out research into Byzantine literature within the methodological parameters established by Classical Philology, including the study of well-defined literary genres with powerful authorial rhetorical theorising, requires a reconsideration of approach and with it of the very concept of literature for medieval Greeks. As Bernard notes, 'Byzantine poetry is not poetry (it is a text in verse), and Byzantine poets are not poets (they are intellectuals who happen to write some verse).'[119] By the same token, Byzantine prose literature, although a special kind of communication, has its own artistic qualities and connotations, some imperceptible to the modern reader. Formalist theories should therefore be put aside in the recognition that scholarly methodologies that advocate 'literariness' as an immanent feature of the text are inappropriate for these writings. For the Byzantines, a literary text was considered such by convention and to the extent it complied with the functions that they expected from literature, regardless of style or narrative construction.[120]

---

[116] Høgel 2002; 2003; 2014.   [117] Høgel 2002: 110–26; Kazhdan 2006: 236–37.
[118] Halkin 1967; Patlagean 1968; Rydén 1986; Lifshitz 1994.   [119] Bernard 2014: 339–40.
[120] As has already been shown by literary theorists, see Even-Zohar 1978; 1990; 2005; Genette 1982; 1991.

The Literary Milieux under Iconoclasm 27

Attention must accordingly be focused on patrons, who commissioned texts with clear objectives, even if the passage of time appears to conceal them from our eyes. The relationship between writer and patron is vital for understanding how literature worked in the iconoclastic period. But this is equally true of the description of the objectives pursued by the writer in and through his work. The answers we can obtain from texts produced under iconoclasm are thus primarily to questions posed by the sociology of literature regarding the production of these texts and their impact on readers/listeners, literary affiliations and interconnexions among the authors: how texts shaped the ecclesiastical ideology of the period, how social identity was redefined through these texts, etc.[121]

In order to make sense of the circles of power that used literature to construct a biased image of the iconoclast controversy, this book presents the data by devoting a chapter to each of those milieux whose objectives and concerns are reflected in the texts. This is not really a study of the contents of the texts themselves, which means that matters such as the historicity or the reliability of the information they provide are not always treated in depth. Above all, what is offered is an analysis of the social, political and ecclesiastical (rather than theological or dogmatic) consequences of these texts, and thus of their literary nature and social dimension.

This study accordingly attempts to show how writers, anxious to provide their own version of events, but not always interested in how close it was to reality, worked. To do so, it relies on a substantial dose of innovation and interdisciplinarity, combining with more traditional methodologies the sociology of literature and textual studies, and analysing both liturgical veneration and the social and manuscript contexts of the works in question. In addition to the harmonious combination of words that make up a work, often exalted, the codices and manuscripts in which it is preserved are examined in an attempt to establish the true sense of its composition. This procedure yields more information than traditional philological studies of what the Byzantines understood by literature, how it operated and how it was received. In addition to an exhaustive study of contemporary texts on iconoclasm, this approach yields an analytical model that allows a definition and understanding of the real significance of Byzantine literature applied specifically to literary works produced under iconoclasm and in its aftermath, the textual consequence of a

---

[121] See, for example, previous articles on the receptive audience of these texts at that time: Rapp 1995: 42–44; Efthymiadis 1996; Efthymiadis and Kalogeras 2014; Papavarnavas 2016.

fascinating moment in history when literature, religion and power merged to produce a unique approach to the literary event.

I.2 The Texts and Their Manuscript Transmission: The Stoudite *Menologia*

Paratextual elements sometimes provide vital information about texts of any sort. This is very much the case for the works treated here, whose manuscript tradition informs us about the degree of success they enjoyed in their time and about whether they were disseminated together with other texts or in isolation. Manuscript transmission is often relevant, since the meaning of a text may change depending on the collection in which it is included or the nature of the texts surrounding it. This situation contrasts with the cultural phenomenon of *metaphraseis* ('translations'), which led to the rapid replacement of one work by a similar one expressed in a way more in keeping with contemporary norms. A good example is the *vitae* of Theodoros of Stoudios: the first we know of has been lost, and the second (*Vita* B) survives in some eleven manuscripts, but was replaced by *Vita* C, which is known only from two codices, Moskow RGB Gr. 128 and Athos Megistes Lauras Δ 78. The metaphrastic *Vita* A was written later and over two dozen copies survive because it found its place in the *Metaphrastic Menologion*.[122] The popularity of a text often has nothing to do with the devotion of its protagonist, as is the case with the *Vita of Makarios of Pelekete*, which survives only in the manuscript *Parisinus Gr.* 548, in contrast to the *Vita of Gregorios Dekapolites*, which has come down to us in over thirty manuscripts.

In any case, the codicological context within which these works were transmitted and disseminated is important. In the aforementioned *Parisinus Gr.* 548, Makarios of Pelekete is the only recent saint: his inclusion among a large number of Palaeo-Christian martyrs served to reaffirm his recently acquired sanctity and thus to strengthen his new cult. The situation of the *vita* of Theodoros of Chora in its two surviving manuscripts (Genoa Urbani 33 and Athos Pantokrator 13), always following the hagiography of Michael Synkellos, is further proof that the work was composed by the circle of Michael Synkellos. The presence of a text in a certain *menologion* not only indicates that the saint who is the protagonist was venerated on a certain date, but also identifies the monastic community that did so and shows that other saints received the same

[122] See the database of the *Institut de recherche et d'histoire des textes*: http://pinakes.irht.cnrs.fr.

treatment. The best-known case is that of the monastery of Stoudios, whose specific calendar of saints' days was already noted by Gedeon.[123] The Stoudite *synaxarion*, moreover, served as a model for subsequent *synaxaria* such as the *Evergetis*, so that study of them allows a partial reconstruction of what occurred in Stoudios throughout the ninth century.[124]

The contents of the manuscripts also provide information about connections and influences between different milieux, often thanks to the works of the copyists of the *menologia*. This is the case with the hagiographer Sabas, which is examined in depth in Chapter 7. Tracing Sabas' biography requires us to compile scattered information that may initially seem irrelevant and unconnected. The common connection is his literary production, which can be identified by certain peculiarities. These are hagiographical rewritings, which were not particularly common in the ninth century, and pragmatically, the author's motivations describe a clear policy of belonging to a number of monastic circles (which he sought to unite and promote), which end up becoming the Stoudite milieu. The best corroboration of the life story of this hagiographer, reconstructed for the first time here, is the textual transmission of his *vitae*. This is studied here paying detailed attention to the inclusion of these texts in specific codices and collections.

Hagiographical rewriting (*metaphrasis*), which was characteristic of the literary activities of Sabas, developed progressively throughout the ninth century and culminated with Symeon's great metaphrastic enterprise in the second half of the tenth century.[125] Although the Latin aspect of this phenomenon has been well studied,[126] no comprehensive analysis has been offered of its various stages. We know of revisions of *vitae* carried out in the seventh century[127] and of authors who revived this practice in the early ninth century;[128] curiously, this was also the period of the appearance of *menologia*, which are structured as we come to know them later and are a consequence of the patronage of both the patriarchate and monastic leaders. The minutes of the Second Council of Nicaea (787) show that the patriarchate already had such hagiographical collections.[129]

---

[123] Gedeon 1899.
[124] Taft 1994; Pentkovskij 2001: 142 and 425 (with an English summary); Delouis 2005: 493; Krausmüller 2013a: 297, n. 52, with bibliography.
[125] Høgel 2002; 2003; 2014.   [126] Goullet 2005.
[127] Ehrhard 1936–1939: vol. I, 152–53; Rapp 1995: 33–34. For a practical case, see Déroche 2011.
[128] Efthymiadis 1991b; Schiffer 1996; Krausmüller 2003; Resh 2015.
[129] Mansi XIII, 189. Cf. Ehrhard 1936–1939: vol. I, 20–21.

The patriarch Tarasios is praised for his *enkomia* (*Vita of Tarasios* 49 and 55), and Methodios personally copied a martyrology during his stay in Rome.[130] As far as the monastic circles are concerned, the situation at the monastery of Stoudios is well known, thanks to the testimony of Theodoros himself.[131]

Metaphrasis such as that carried out by Ioannes of Sardis, that is, the true transformation of an ancient text, which adapts its style and language to the expectations of a new readership and is at the same time more precise and historically accurate, like the work of Niketas David Paphlagon, is the precursor of what was done by Symeon Metaphrastes.[132] In the tenth century, the production of official *menologia* and *synaxaria* began to be promoted and administered by imperial power.[133] The rewritings of Sabas, however, are part of a practice characteristic of the monastery of Stoudios, which aimed to offer a partial, biased view of the events that occurred from the iconoclastic crisis.[134] A similar process, albeit on a smaller scale and probably possible only due to outside assistance, occurred at the Constantinopolitan convent of Krisis, where the non-iconodule saint traditionally linked to it (St Philaretos) was replaced by the legendary St Andreas *en Krisei*, who was fêted for his valour in having stood up to Konstantinos V until his death. The discovery of Andreas' alleged miraculous relics gave the community unbeatable iconodule credentials and made it a place of pilgrimage, due to which a second version of his life appeared in the years following the Triumph of Orthodoxy, producing the pre-metaphrastic *vita* that has survived (*BHG* 111). At the same time, a *kanon* was commissioned in Andreas' honour, written by Ioseph Hymnographos, who alludes to the convent of Krisis by means of a play on words comparing Andreas to a lily (Greek κρίνον).[135] The metaphrastic wording (*BHG* 112) dates from the second half of the century.

---

[130] Rapp 1995: 33.
[131] Theod. Stoud., *epist.* 2,67–70; *Vita* A *of Theodoros Stoud.* 152D–53A. See also Høgel 2002: 43–44; Van den Ven 1955–57.
[132] Paschalidis 1999; Flusin 2011. See also Ševčenko 1981; 1982.
[133] Ševčenko 1962; Odorico 2001; Høgel 2002: 127–34.
[134] See Afinogenov 2004c, which covers the versions of the hagiography of Nikolaos of Stoudios; Delouis 2011, regarding the reason for the various *vitae* of Theodoros Stoudites.
[135] *Menaion* I: 444–51. On the convent of Krisis, see Janin 1969: 28–31; Majeska 1984: 314–15 locates it on the western periphery of Constantinople. On Andreas *en Krisei* and his accounts, see Costa-Louillet 1954/1955: 214–16; Auzépy 1993; Kazhdan 1999: 203; Krausmüller 2007a. For the last-mentioned scholar, the figure of Andreas *en Krisei* has a historical origin based on the martyrdom of Andreas of Blachernai, beaten to death in 761–762 along with his companions Stephanos, Paulos and Petros. See Chapter 4.

This ambitious programme of rewriting was developed in Stoudios by means of the production of various *menologia*, which included hagiographical or homiletical texts on the saint to be commemorated each day, and whose successive ordination completed the liturgical year. It was generally a case of twelve volumes corresponding to each of the twelve months, beginning on 1 September, when the liturgical year began. The more detailed *menologia* covered only fifteen days, which meant that these collections consisted of twenty-four volumes.[136] The traditional saints (Apostles, early martyrs, Fathers of the Church, etc.) began to be joined by the new heroes of Orthodoxy, that is, those who had distinguished themselves in their opposition to iconoclastic heresy.[137] Theodoros Stoudites was absolutely committed to this project and did not hesitate to write pieces in honour of the usual saints juxtaposed with other, more recent ones (such as his uncle Platon of Sakkoudion) or figures with a less tangible holiness (such as his mother). Thanks to the new context into which they were inserted (a liturgical calendar followed in one of the monasteries of reference of Constantinople), the latter began to be venerated and to be considered models of virtue. The *Enkomion of Platon of Sakkoudion* can be found in the manuscript *Vaticanus Gr.* 1660, fol. 75v–108, among various *excerpta* from *vitae* of Palestine martyrs and the *vita* of the patriarch Eutychios of Constantinople (*BHG* 657). The *enkomion* in honour of Theoktiste, for its part, is inserted in the *menologion* of December included in *Parisinus Gr.* 1491, fol. 94–120v, followed by the *enkomion* to St Anastasia written by Ioannes Damaskenos.[138]

This practice is an identifying mark of the monastery of Stoudios, where a complete revision of the liturgical cycle was carried out to enhance the presence of saints from Late Antiquity related to the monastery and to introduce the new iconodule martyrs who had joined the battle on iconoclast heresy declared by Theodoros Stoudites. The ninth and tenth centuries therefore saw the publication of the *menologia* necessary for celebrating the feast days of the new calendar, for which new texts were written to replace old ones, existing *vitae* were touched up and hagiographies of more recent leaders related to the monastery (such as Blasios of Amorion or Nikolaos Stoudites) were produced. The *menologia* that resulted were highly successful and were rapidly disseminated within the Stoudite federation; they came to exercise considerable influence on the

---

[136] *ODB*, s.v. 'Menologion'; Delehaye 1897; Noret 1968; Velkovska 1996; 2003; Høgel 2002: 36–45.
[137] Rydén 1986; Auzépy 2004b.
[138] Ehrhard 1936–1939: vol. 1, 512–16; Høgel 2002: 49–50. On the vigorous promotion of the veneration of many of his allies by Theodoros Stoudites, see Chapter 1.

classification of the imperial *menologia* and outside Constantinople on Slav and Italian communities. According to Afinogenov, the oldest Slavonic manuscript containing the *menologion* of February derives from a Stoudite prototype written between 911 and 920,[139] while in the Italian case, Canart suggests that this was more the result of chance than of an aggressive policy of dissemination.[140] In his opinion, the new metaphrastic fashion led those in charge of the monastery of Stoudios to do away with the old *menologia* that were now obsolete.

Drawing up a specific *menologion* is not an activity exclusive to the Stoudites, since almost every important monastic centre had its own. The size and importance of this Constantinopolitan establishment, however, meant that its *menologion* had more influence and left an unmistakable mark. Thanks to the efforts of researchers such as Delouis,[141] we can reproduce the structure of the Stoudite *menologia* copied in the monastery itself in the early tenth century.[142] Ehrhard maintains that a twelve-volume collection of *menologia* coexisted at the monastery of Stoudios with another of twenty-four (two volumes per month).[143] Both collections followed the same Byzantine liturgical calendar, from which the following pre-metaphrastic *menologia* have come down to us:

– September (19th, 24th, 25th and 26th): *Vaticanus Gr.* 1853, tenth-century *scriptura inferior* of a palimpsest.[144]
– November (1st fortnight): *Vaticanus Gr.* 1669, copied by the same hand as *Vaticanus Gr.* 1660.[145]
– December (2nd fortnight): *Parisinus Gr.* 1491, the contents of which were doubtless compiled at the monastery of Stoudios.[146]

---

[139] It is the fifteenth-century manuscript Moskow RGB Fond. 173, nr. 92.I, see Afinogenov 2001; 2004c.
[140] Canart 1982. [141] Delouis 2005: 356–76.
[142] For the scribal work carried out in this important institution, see Volk 1955: 82–91; Eleopoulos 1967; Lemerle 1971: 121–28; Leroy 1973; 1977; Salucci 1973; Fonkitch 1980/1982: 83–92; Kavrus 1983; Corrigan 1992: 129–34; Perria 1993; Anderson 1998b; Brubaker and Haldon 2001: 41–44; Anderson 2006.
[143] Ehrhard 1936–1939: vol. I, 611.
[144] Garitte 1943: 44–8 believes that the same school of copyists also produced the manuscripts *Vaticanus Gr.* 415 (homilies by Basileios of Caesarea) and *Vaticanus Gr.* 2079, a collection of homilies including one by Theodoros Stoudites dedicated to the Dormition of the Virgin, see ibid., 47. On the codex *Vaticanus Gr.* 1853, see Ehrhard 1936–1939: vol. I, 440–42; Canart 1970: 341–47.
[145] Giannelli 1950: 416–19; Canart and Peri 1970: 628; Follieri 1977: 144; Canart 1982: 22, n. 6; Matantseva 1996b.
[146] It was however probably copied elsewhere since its characteristic bouletée style has never been found at Stoudios, but this research is still pending. On this manuscript, cf. Ehrhard 1936–1939: vol. I, 512–16; Halkin 1968: 182–3; Maltese 2014.

- February: *Parisinus Gr.* 1452.[147]
- April: *Vaticanus Gr.* 1660, copied on 21 March 916 by the monk Ioannes under the hegoumenos Anatolios of Stoudios.[148]
- June: *Vaticanus Gr.* 1667.[149]
- August: *Vaticanus Gr.* 1671, copied by the deacon Dorotheos under the hegoumenos Timotheos.[150]

This structure can be confirmed and completed thanks to two later lectionaries that gather Stoudite traditions and the special features of their calendar of feast days, *Parisinus Gr.* 382 from the late tenth century[151] and the Venezia, *Marcianus Gr.* II 115 from the eleventh-twelfth centuries.[152] In these manuscripts, the celebrations of clearly Stoudite saints accumulated: following each other such as that of Theodoros Stoudites (11 November with an unpublished *troparion*), Platon of Sakkoudion (4 April), the transfer of the relics of Theodoros and his brother Ioseph of Thessaloniki (26 January) and the consecration of the church of St John the Baptist of the monastery of Stoudios (23 June). Moreover, these celebrations are accompanied by other anniversaries not mentioned in non-Stoudite *synaxaria*, such as the memorial commemorations of the iconodule confessor Iakobos Stoudites (28 June), of the *patrikios* Stoudios, the founder of the monastery in the fifth century (20 July), and of the soldiers of the Emperor Nikephoros I murdered in Bulgaria (28 July). This was clearly a Stoudite feast day, since the famous abbot Theodoros took charge of promoting it.[153]

The contents of these codices reveal the true scope of the Stoudite project in drawing up a *menologion* of its own, since many of the saints are celebrated because of the interests of the community and its desire to establish itself as a monastic point of reference for the whole of Christendom in its fight against heresy and its defence of Orthodoxy against worldly powers. Homilies of Theodoros Stoudites or *vitae* of martyrs from the iconoclastic period were therefore carefully placed

---

[147] Halkin 1968: 161–62; Ehrhard 1936–1939: vol. I, 577–80.
[148] For the problem of whether this is the second hegoumenate of Anatolios or whether there were two hegoumenoi named Anatolios, Follieri 1969: 24–25; Canart 1982: 21, n. 5; *PmbZ* # 20347. On the copyist Ioannes, see *PmbZ* # 22913. For the manuscript, Giannelli 1950: 396–98.
[149] Giannelli 1950: 410–15; Canart 1982: 22, nn. 8 and 9.
[150] It is probably later than Anatolios and in any case from the early tenth century, *PmbZ* # 28351. On the copyist Dorotheos, see *PmbZ* # 21592; Follieri 1969: 25–26; Canart 1982: 22, n. 7. For the codex, see Giannelli 1950: 421–25.
[151] This was identified as an authentic Stoudite calendar by Halkin 1954a: 13, n. 4; Andreou 2005.
[152] Mioni 1967: 338–39; Andreou 2008.
[153] Follieri and Dujcev 1963; Tomadakes 1971b; Haldon 2017.

alongside texts of Fathers of the Church in an effort to make the modern authors of the Stoudite circle the equivalents of the Patristic theologians and to identify more recent victims of heresy with the martyrs cruelly murdered in early Christian times. This objective is particularly visible in the August *menologion*, in which *Vaticanus Gr.* 1671 gathers numerous texts in honour of the Theotokos (whose feast day was celebrated on 15 August) written by Theodoros Stoudites (*BHG* 1157), Ioannes Damaskenos (*BHG* 1114) and the patriarchs Germanos I (*BHG* 1086) and Euthymios (*BHG* 1138) together with the *vitae* of two outstanding leaders of early monasticism related to the federation, Isaac (*BHG* 956) and Dalmatos (*BHG* 482).

This perspective makes better sense of some of the texts collected in the other *menologia* and explains their relevance. *Vaticanus Gr.* 1669 contains the *Vita* B *of Theodoros Stoudites* written by Michael Monachos, two *enkomia* written by this same Stoudite monk[154] and the *vita* of Ioannikios by Sabas, who was honoured on 4 November. *Parisinus Gr.* 1491 presents the *vita* of Markellos Akoimetes (*BHG* 1027z), the precursor of the Stoudite hegoumenoi,[155] the *vita* of Blasios of Amorion (*BHG* 278) and the funeral oration produced by Theodoros Stoudites for his mother Theoktiste, whose memory was not celebrated outside the walls of the monastery of Stoudios.[156] For the month of February, *Parisinus Gr.* 1452 offers the *vitae* of Nikolaos Stoudites (*BHG* 1365), Alexandros Akoimetes (*BHG* 47), Georgios of Amastris (*BHG* 668) and the patriarch Tarasios (*BHG* 1698). The last two are by Ignatios Diakonos, being the copy of the *Vita Tarasii* the earliest testimony, and that of Georgios of Amastris the only surviving one. For its part, *Vaticanus Gr.* 1660 presents for April the eulogy dedicated to Platon of Sakkoudion by his nephew Theodoros Stoudites (*BHG* 1553) followed by the *vita* of the patriarch Eutychios of Constantinople (*BHG* 657). This *menologion* ends with the *vita* of Niketas of Medikion (*BHG* 1341). Finally, *Vaticanus Gr.* 1667 includes the *vitae* of the patriarch Nikephoros written by Ignatios Diakonos for 2 June, that of Ioannes of Gotthia (*BHG* 891) for the 26th, and for the 30th the *vita* of St Hypatios (*BHG* 760), in which the *akoimetai* monks (the first Stoudites) play a leading role due to their

---

[154] In honour of the archangels Michael and Gabriel and St Philip, Matantseva 1996a. On the authorship of the *Enkomion of the Apostle Philip* (*BHG* 1530a) written by Michael Monachos, see Matantseva 1996a: 123–24.
[155] Dagron 1968; Baguenard 1990; Kosinski 2016: 211–32. For the dating of the *vita* of Markellos Akoimetes between 482 and 518, see Déroche and Lesieur 2010.
[156] Theod. Stoud., *Laudatio of Theoktiste* (*BHG* 2422); Hermann 1919.

confrontation with the patriarch Nestorios. Finally, for 14 June it includes the *vita* of the patriarch Methodios (*BHG* 1278), which will be discussed at length in Chapter 7.

The picture of the liturgical calendar celebrated at the monastery of Stoudios in the early tenth century is thus a rich one. Even more details can be filled in if the *menologion* for May preserved in the codex München BSB *Gr.* 366 is added.[157] The content of this is clearly Stoudite and indicates that the texts were collected at this monastery, although further study is needed to determine exactly where it was copied. In any case, the handwriting is typical of the tenth century or perhaps the second half of the ninth century, according to Van den Ven.[158] The most recent work it contains must be the eulogy of the hieromartyr Mokios by Michael Synkellos (*BHG* 1298h) on fol. 236–43v, which puts us in the final third of the ninth century. The manuscript München BSB *Gr.* 366 stands out for including the *vitae* of a number of important iconodule saints of the early ninth century: the patriarch Germanos of Constantinople (*BHG* 697), Nikephoros of Medikion (*BHG* 2297) and Ioannes Psichaites (*BHG* 896). It likewise contains the *vita* of a fifth-century abbot confessor, Isaac (*BHG* 955), and two *enkomia* of Theodoros Stoudites intended to be read on 8 May, one in honour of St John the Evangelist (*BHG* 929), the other in honour of the anchorite St Arsenios (*BHG* 169).[159]

A final and somewhat bold contribution preserves information about the feast days celebrated in early March. A later manuscript, the fourteenth-century *Patmiacus Gr.* 736, reproduces on folios 1–116 the following pre-metaphrastic texts that appear to go back to the ninth century:[160] the *Vita Theodoti Cyrensis* (*BHG* 2436) for 2 March, *Martyrium Eutropii, Cleonici, Basilisci* (*BHG* 656a) for the 3rd, *Martyrium Theodoreti* (*BHG* 2425) for the 4th, *Martyrium Pauli et Iulianae* (*BHG* 964b) for the 5th, *Vita Cononis* (*BHG* 2079) also for the 5th, *Martyrium 42 mart. Amoriensium* (*BHG* 1214) for the 6th, *Martyrium Ephraim, Basilii, Eugenii et sociorum* (*BHG* 265) for the 7th, *Vita Theophylacti Nicomediae* (*BHG* 2452) for the 8th and *Martyrium XL mart. in Sebastea* (*BHG* 1202a and 1205) for the 9th. The maintenance of almost all these celebrations in the *Synaxarion Evergetis* supports the idea that they

---

[157] Hardt 1810: 76–87; Ehrhard 1936–1939: vol. I, 620–23. In the original sales catalogue description of 1544, this manuscript is described as '36 lives of saints and martyrs by Symeon Metaphrastes (nr. 42)', see Mondrian 1993: 232.
[158] Van den Ven 1902: 101.
[159] Van de Vorst and Delehaye 1913: 126, nr. 25; Ehrhard 1936–39: vol. I, 621, nr. 6 and n. 3.
[160] For the *Patmiacus Gr.* 736, see Ehrhard 1936–1939: vol. I, 587–88.

already took place at the Stoudite monasteries.[161] Several texts follow on the occasion of the Annunciation of the Virgin Mary celebrated on 25 March (*BHG* 1093g, 1116d, 1139n, 1128f, 1144h, 1085c).

Amidst this hagiographical catalogue, the anonymous *Vita* B *of Theophylaktos of Nicomedia* (*BHG* 2452) deserves closer consideration, since its composition includes some characteristic features of the hagiographical rewriting carried out at the monastery of Stoudios. This is an anonymous work based on a pre-existing *vita*, signed by the subject's namesake Theophylaktos (*BHG* 2451), which has been touched up and abbreviated to half its length to suit the liturgical needs of the *menologion*.[162] The Stoudites' interest in possessing this *vita* is the same as the one that led them to include the accounts of Georgios of Amastris (*BHG* 668), Ioannes of Gotthia (*BHG* 891), Niketas of Medikion (*BHG* 1341), Nikephoros of Medikion (*BHG* 2297) and Ioannes Psichaites (*BHG* 896), saints who seem to lack any link with this important monastery in the capital but who stood out in the fight against iconoclasm. Many of them, moreover, were the recipients of epistles of Theodoros Stoudites and shared his fate: torture, exile and so forth. In this sense, the case of Theophylaktos of Nicomedia is typical. A large portion of his religious life runs parallel to that of Michael of Synada. Both were tonsured by Tarasios in the monastery founded by this patriarch, who then had them called to Hagia Sophia. Once they were consecrated as bishops, they both confronted the iconoclastic Emperor Leon V and defended icons in the imperial palace.[163] Although they were tortured, imprisoned and exiled, from their places of exile they continued their pastoral work and received epistles from Theodoros Stoudites; Theophylaktos of Nicomedia was the recipient of two letters written in 817–818 (*epist.* 175 and 314), while Michael of Synada received a missive at the same time during his exile in Phrygia (*epist.* 364). Moreover, Theodoros mentions them repeatedly as examples of virtue[164] and even wrote a sermon narrating the life and works of Michael of Synada (*BHG* 2275).[165] It is also no coincidence that at the same time that Empress Theodora and the patriarch Methodios had the

---

[161] *Synaxarion Evergetis* II, 6–8 (days 3–9 March).
[162] Polemis 1989; Kazhdan 1999: 202–3. See also *SynaxCP* 519–22. See Chapter 1.
[163] *Vita of Niketas of Medikion* 34. On Theophylaktos, see *PmbZ* # 8295; *PBE* I: Theophylaktos 37. Concerning Michael of Synada, see *SynaxCP* 703–704; *PmbZ* # 5042; *PBE* I: Michael 6.
[164] Theod. Stoud., *Parvae catech.* 51 (p. 184 Auvray) quotes Theophylaktos. Theod. Stoud., *epist.* 533 and 542 alludes to the death of Michael of Synada.
[165] Theod. Stoud., *Parvae catech.* 21 (pp. 76–79 Auvray).

relics of Theophylaktos brought back,[166] those of Theodoros Stoudites and the patriarch Nikephoros were also moved.[167] One might well conjecture that this second *vita* of Theophylaktos of Nicomedia is the fruit of the literary skills of the hagiographer Sabas.

A final matter regarding the Stoudite *menologia* is particularly worth taking into account, both because it directly affects the hagiographical production of Sabas Monachos and because it increases our knowledge of the process of the shaping of the Stoudite *menologia*. For the month of June, not only *Vaticanus Gr.* 1667 has survived but also *Vaticanus Gr.* 984. The latter is a palimpsest rewritten in the year 1354 with works by Flavius Iosephus, whose *scriptura inferior* has been attributed to the ninth century[168] and which reveals a *menologion* similar to the one studied above, except that fol. 203v–206 include the *Vita of Hilarion of Dalmatos* written by our Sabas (*BHG* 2177), of which it is the *codex unicus*.[169] Although the manuscript contains only the texts intended to be read at the feast days from 1 to 17 June, comparison with the *menologion* of *Vaticanus Gr.* 1667 reveals more similarities than differences. Indeed, the feast days are the same, with the exception of the *vita* of Hilarion of Dalmatos found in *Vaticanus* 984 for 5 June, whereas *Vaticanus* 1667 includes the passion of the ten Egyptian martyrs (*BHG* 1194), the passion of Nikandros and Markianos (*BHG* 1330) and the passion of Kyrillos of Gortyn (*BHG* 467) for 3, 4 and 6 June respectively. A second exception involves 9 and 10 June, for which the *Vaticanus* 984 presents the *vita* of Kyrillos of Alexandria (*BHG* 2095) and the martyrdom of Timotheos of Prousa (*BHG* 2460), in contrast to *Vaticanus* 1667, which gives the passions of Theodotos (*BHG* 1782) and of Alexandros and Antonina (*BHG* 50). Finally, the life of St Hypatios (*BHG* 760), which is so important for Stoudite interests, is displaced to 17 June.

Given this situation, the presence of the *vita* of Hilarion of Dalmatos and the absence of the *vita* of the patriarch Methodios suggest that the *menologion* in *Vaticanus Gr.* 984 represents a liturgical moment prior to that evident in *Vaticanus Gr.* 1667. The inclusion of the *Vita Methodii* makes sense if we take into account the political and ecclesiastical interests

---

[166] *Vita A of Theophylaktos of Nicomedia* 18. For Vogt 1932: 68 this is the reason for the composition of said *vita*.
[167] For the contrast between both transfers, that of the remains of Theodoros Stoudites and that of the patriarch's relics, Afinogenov 1996a: 68–70. See Chapters 1–2.
[168] Franchi de' Cavalieri 1920: 107–10; Ehrhard 1936–1939: vol. I, 652 and 657; Turyn 1964: 149–50; Canart 2008b: 76.
[169] Matantseva 1993.

stirring in the monastic centre of Stoudios. The reason for the elimination of the *vita* of Hilarion of Dalmatos escapes us, although the process is well known from other cases. The relationship between the *menologion* of February preserved in *Parisinus Gr.* 1452 and the previous version, which can be reconstructed thanks to the Slavonic *menologion* of the Fond. 173, nr. 92.I of the Russian State Library of Moscow, has been well studied. The result is in one sense striking, since in the early tenth century the Stoudite *menologion* suppressed texts that were clearly useful for its promotion (the *vita* of Thaddaios Stoudites, the *vita* of Blasios of Amorion, a sermon of Theodoros Stoudites on the invention of the head of St John the Baptist [later transferred to the monastery of Stoudios itself]), replacing them with the two *vitae* of Ignatios Diakonos in honour of Georgios of Amastris and the patriarch Tarasios.[170]

Be that as it may, it is undeniable that the *vita* of Hilarion of Dalmatos touched up by Sabas was very successful in the Stoudite milieu, due to its great value in creating an official Stoudite ideology. A passage from this *vita* is quoted in an abbreviated version of the *Vita* A of Theodoros Stoudites (*BHG* 1755), pages 252–53 of which contain an inserted account of how St Hilarion predicted the death of Theodoros Stoudites.[171] This information was likely taken from the *vita* written by Sabas during the period when it was part of the pre-metaphrastic Stoudite *menologion*.[172] But the author of *Vita* A is wrong to date the prophecy of Hilarion during his gardener-monk period prior to the hegoumenate (before 806), which clearly contradicts historical chronology, since Theodoros Stoudites died in 826. In fact, this is a rather free interpretation of the text: the *vita* of Sabas places Hilarion in Constantinople between the years 822 to 828 on the land named *Marias* alongside the *Aethrion*, which had been transferred to him by a pious patrician lady. The author of the new version of the *vita* of Theodoros Stoudites (*Vita* A), aware that in those years Hilarion was not the hegoumenos of Dalmatos, took it for granted that during that period Hilarion resumed his duties in the garden as a simple monk.[173]

The two versions of the *vita* of Petros of Atroa, for their part, have come down to us in two tenth-century manuscripts included in two *menologia*

---

[170] Afinogenov 2001; 2004c; Delouis 2005: 367–71.
[171] On Hilarion of Dalmatos, see *PmbZ* # 2584; *PBE* I: Hilarion 1. See Chapter 3.
[172] See Chapter 7. Matantseva 1993: 29 proposed unnecessarily that it was a quote from the original *vita* of Hilarion that Sabas took as a basis for his adaptation, i.e., *VHil(Sab)**.
[173] This does not imply any chronological alteration that justifies resorting to a new source, as suggested by Matantseva 1996c: 151–52.

for the month of January: Venezia, *Marcianus Gr. Z* 583[174] and Glasgow BE 8.x.5, which the *vita retractata* offers for 2 January.[175] The substantial similarity in the collection of texts these codices present implies a connection between them, although the exact relationship is difficult to pinpoint. One might be tempted to restrict this liturgical selection to the Stoudite milieu, due to the presence of the *vita* of Petros of Atroa written by our Sabas (*BHG* 2364) together with the *vita* of Ioannes Kalybites (*BHG* 868), an *akoimetes* who was doubtless celebrated at the monastery of Stoudios like his companions Markellos and Alexandros. But no definitive arguments support this interpretation. Perhaps the large number of Palestinian and Egyptian saints,[176] indicating the strong influence of these Byzantine provinces, points to its real origin.[177] Of these two *menologia*, the Glasgow BE 8.x.5 is the most Constantinopolitan, since it adds the celebration on 8 January of Domnica, the renowned fifth-century hegoumene of Constantinople (*BHG* 562d).

Given that neither of the *menologia* for January can be attributed to the monastery of Stoudios, we can assume that Petros of Atroa was not commemorated there, despite the friendship and the common cause he shared with Theodoros Stoudites.[178] Indeed, the date when Petros' memory was honoured in the calendars of saints' days is highly significant. We know he died on 1 January, the feast day of the circumcision of the Lord and of Basileios of Caesarea, which meant that his celebration had to be moved. The following day, 2 January, was initially chosen, and for a long time this veneration only occurred in monastic communities (mainly Bithynian ones) that included the *vita* of Petros of Atroa in their *menologia* on that date. Upon their move to Constantinople, where the Forefeast of Lights or Basileios of Caesarea was celebrated on 2 January, it was decided to transfer the commemoration of Petros to a new date. This was 13 September, which was consecrated in the 'official' liturgical calendar,

---

[174] For the *Marcianus Gr. Z* 583, see Ehrhard 1929/1930; Ehrhard 1936–1939: vol. 1, 534–37; Mioni 1985: 501–3. The subscription signed by a copyist named Basileios indicates that the manuscript dates from the year 947, 958, 969, or 980, *Vita of Petros of Atroa*, p. 3.
[175] Concerning the Glasgow BE 8.x.5, see Halkin 1957; Cunningham 1982: nr. 64.
[176] Palestinian saints: the *vita* of Theodosios Archimandrites by Theodoros of Petra (*BHG* 1776), the Passion of the martyred monks of Sinai (*BHG* 1300); the *vita* of abbot Euthymios by Kyrillos of Scythopolis (*BHG* 647–48). Egyptian saints: the *vita* of Antonios the abbot of Thebes by Athanasios (*BHG* 140), the *vitae* of Athanasios of Alexandria (*BHG* 185), Paulos of Thebes (*BHG* 1466), Makarios of Egypt (*BHG* 999v) and *enkomia* of the Alexandrian martyrs Kyros and Ioannes (*BHG* 476–77).
[177] According to Halkin, the inclusion of three texts on the celebration of Anastasios of Perge means that the *menologion* was written in a monastery with such a dedication, see Halkin 1957: 70.
[178] *Vita* A *of Theodoros Stoud.* 226B–C: Πέτρος ὁ περιβόητος, ὁ τὴν ἀρετὴν ἀπαράμιλλος ἐκεῖνος.

according to tenth-century *synaxaria*.[179] Although the *Synaxarion of Constantinople* introduces a long notice on that date, it also records the original festival of 2 January.[180]

In essence, the selection of the *vitae* included in the Stoudite *menologia* constitutes a true declaration of principles and reveals a determination to appropriate the iconoclastic crisis (as can be seen from the unusual accumulation of recent saints and martyrs connected with the episode) and to have the monastery of Stoudios administer their memory and recall the events. Better put, what is recalled is a specific version of these events, in which any disputes with the patriarchate or the imperial throne are omitted, and its leader Theodoros Stoudites is remembered as an equal of the iconodule patriarchs Tarasios and Nikephoros. In order to do so, it was necessary to touch up or even rewrite some existing *vitae* in a process that actively involved the hegoumenoi of Stoudios, hagiographers such as Sabas and the monastic community as a whole. This case study of the manuscript evidence is complemented by that in Chapter 7 of Sabas as a writer. Codices as vehicles of transmission and authors as creators of texts shaping specific contexts are clearly the basis for the literature of the iconoclast period and the generation immediately following it. On these two pillars, a huge ideological edifice was constructed to redefine the identity of the Byzantine individual and reshape the society in which he or she lived.

---

[179] *SynaxCP* 42,4–19 (13 September); *Typikon of the Great Church* I, 27 (13 September) and 35 (15 September).
[180] *SynaxCP* 366,30–33. On his cult, see *Vita of Petros of Atroa*, pp. 51–56; *Vita retractata of Petros of Atroa*, pp. 49–54.

CHAPTER I

The Stoudite Milieu
The Foundations of the Literature of Iconoclasm

The surviving material suggests that the first socio-political group in Middle Byzantine times to make use of literary composition with clearly defined utilitarian purposes was the Constantinopolitan monastery of St John of Stoudios[1] and its charismatic abbot Theodoros (from 798 to his death in 826). Despite its long history – it was founded in 462 – the monastery flourished in the ninth and tenth centuries, increasing its influence exponentially thanks to the growing number of monks who entered it. It has been calculated that before the second stage of Iconoclasm began in 815, the Stoudite federation had over 1,000 members[2] – and numerous monasteries that followed its rules[3] throughout Byzantium, which, apart from the monastery of Stoudios, included those of Sakkoudion, Symboloi, Kathara, Tripyliana, St Christophoros, St Georgios, St Tryphon and in later times, Sabas.[4] In this process of acquiring power, great importance was attached to training boys and young men[5] and to promoting the *scriptorium* of the monastery, a renowned, innovative centre of manuscript production.[6] For the writers drawn together by the teachings of Theodoros Stoudites, the experiences

---

[1] The bibliography on this extremely famous monastery is extensive; see Van Millingen 1912: 35–61; Delehaye 1934; Janin 1969: 430–40; Mathews 1971: 19–27; Mango 1978a; Majeska 1984: 283–88, nr. 26; Kazhdan et al. 1991; Ruggieri 1991: 105–96; Delouis 2005.

[2] For this figure, cf. Hatlie 2007a: 322, n. 39. On the intense proselytising activity of Theodoros Stoudites and his search for new candidates willing to join his community, see Pratsch 1998: 123–34; Hatlie 2007a: 275–76.

[3] Leroy 1958a; Rezáč 1958: 117–25; Leroy 1969; Papachryssanthou 1973; Frazee 1981; Ruggieri 1991: 107–11; Pratsch 1998: 129–31; Delouis 2005: 203–32; Hatlie 2007b; Pratsch 2007. For the rule of the Stoudite confederation, see Thomas et al. 2000: vol. I, 67–80. For the testament of Theodoros Stoudites, see Thomas et al. 2000: vol. I, 84–119.

[4] Janin 1969; 1975; Hatlie 2007a: 312–51, esp. pp. 323–26, n. 42 with bibliography.

[5] On Stoudite education, cf. Lemerle 1971: 102–4; Moffatt 1977: 88–92; Hatlie 2007a: 346, n. 118 and pp. 419–422; Métivier and Papaconstantinou 2007.

[6] On the *scriptorium*, see Eleopoulos 1967; Leroy 1969: 71–76; Mango 1975a: 43–44; Kavrus 1983; Perria 1993; Brubaker 2000; Fonkitch 2000; Hatlie 2007a: 412–19; Fonkitch 2010; Ronconi 2017: 1312–13.

41

of those who confronted heresy during the second stage of Iconoclasm (815–843) were a primary literary motivation, to the extent that they became the first writers to document the facts and inevitably to modify them in their narratives.

The roots of this well-defined faction, however, are found in earlier times, when Theodoros was the hegoumenos (794–798) of the Bithynian monastery of Sakkoudion, which had been founded by his uncle Platon on Mount Olympos. Theodoros' resolute action during the Moechian conflict (795–798) and the Ioseph affair (806–811) was an essential part of the establishment of the alliances and friendships that allowed the subsequent organisation of resistance against iconoclast emperors and patriarchs.[7] Both disputes were of a religious, political and legal nature and were triggered by the second marriage of Emperor Konstantinos VI (771–ca. 797), who decided to divorce his wife Maria (who had already borne him two daughters) to marry his lover Theodote, a relative of Theodoros and Platon, who at that time served as Maria's *koubikoularea* (lady companion). Initially, the patriarch Tarasios opposed the new marriage, since the situation was unprecedented in the history of the Empire. Konstantinos, however, alleged that his wife had attempted to poison him and threatened Tarasios with a return to iconoclasm.[8]

The wedding was conducted in September 795 by Ioseph of Kathara, the *oikonomos* (steward) of Hagia Sophia,[9] and led to many ecclesiastics breaking relations with Tarasios. The emperor at first tried to calm the most impassioned among them, such as Platon of Sakkoudion and Theodoros Stoudites, but in 797 had them whipped and exiled. The intervention in the same year of the dowager Empress Eirene to dethrone her son allowed the monks to return and be reconciled with Tarasios, who then deposed Ioseph of Kathara.[10] The controversy appeared to have been resolved, until it was revived in 806 by the Ioseph affair, when the patriarch Nikephoros reinstated Ioseph of Kathara.[11] This was not a religious measure but a political decision by the new Emperor Nikephoros I (802–811), who was anxious to reward Ioseph for his service as mediator during the uprising of Bardanes Tourkos in 803. Reactions were not long in coming, and in 808, the archbishop of Thessaloniki,

---

[7] Hatlie 1993; Ševčenko 1995; Hatlie 1996b; Hatlie 2007a: 263–311, 338–51, 365–70 for his political agenda.
[8] *Narratio de sanctis patriarchis Tarasio et Nicephoro* 1852D. Although this threat is generally considered to be a slightly later fiction (mid-ninth century), cf. Speck 1978: 280–81.
[9] *PmbZ* # 3447; *PBE* I: Ioseph 2; Niavis 1990.
[10] Fuentes Alonso 1984; Hollingsworth 1991; Gemmiti 1993. [11] Afinogenov 1994.

Ioseph, the brother of Theodoros Stoudites, refused to accept the position of either the emperor or the patriarch. A synod in 809 confirmed the rehabilitation of Ioseph of Kathara, dismissed Ioseph of Thessaloniki as archbishop and anathematised all those who refused to apply *oikonomía* (moral concessions) in this dispute.[12] The Stoudite monks rejected the synod as 'adulterous', owing to which they were persecuted until, after the death of Emperor Nikephoros, his successor on the throne, Michael I Rhangabe (811–813), reinstated the Stoudites and deposed Ioseph of Kathara in 811.

Personalities such as the hermit Ioannikios,[13] whom Theodoros Stoudites initially considered his spiritual father (*pneumatikos pater*),[14] and the hegoumenoi Theophilos,[15] Euthymios[16] and Antonios of Hagios Petros,[17] among many others,[18] supported Theodoros Stoudites during the Ioseph affair and strengthened the ties that bound them in the face of the threat of the restoration of iconoclasm. Although its effect was more limited, the opposition of Theodoros and the Stoudites to the marriage of Emperor Michael II to the former nun Euphrosyne in 823–824 was inspired by the same principles of protesting against imperial power to defend the doctrine of the Church and its independence.[19] But it was during the second stage of this heresy when his circle of collaborators was the strongest,[20] to such an extent that the literature this group produced at that time regarding contemporary events had a clearly utilitarian purpose:

---

[12] Devreese 1950; Alexander 1958a: 80–101; Henry 1969; Hatlie 1995.

[13] On Ioannikios, see *PmbZ* # 3389; *PBE* I: Ioannikios 2. This important iconodule leader is referred to by one of the names in code given by Theodoros to his followers to prevent his correspondence being understood by the enemy, see Theod. Stoud., *epist*. 41, line 9, although the latter editor changes the traditional reading Ἰωαννικίου to Ἰωάννου, see Sirmond in *PG* 99/1, 1060AB, nr. 41.

[14] Theod. Stoud., *epist*. 490,80–81. Despite their subsequent differences, Theodoros sent him at least one letter: *epist*. 461.

[15] On Theophilos, cf. *PmbZ* # 8207; *PBE* I: Theophilos 52. Theod. Stoud., *epist*. 39, on his common position during the second stage of the Moechian controversy; Theod. Stoud., *epist*. 432, on the defence of images. We cannot be sure which monastery this Theophilos ran, but it was most likely that of Theotokos Photnai or Photeine, cf. Janin 1975: 437, the abbot of which took part in the Second Council of Nicaea in 787, cf. Mansi XIII, 153D; *PmbZ* # 8192.

[16] On Euthymios, cf. *PmbZ* # 1847; *PBE* I: Euthymios 16. Theod. Stoud., *epist*. 48 and 51. Although we do not know which monastery Euthymios led, it is recorded that it was in Thessaloniki.

[17] On Antonios, see *PmbZ* # 548; *PBE* I: Antonios 39. Theod. Stoud., *epist*. 56. The monastery of Hagios Petros may have been built in Poimanina south of Kyzikos, Theod. Stoud., *epist*. p. 200*, n. 196; Janin 1975: 207.

[18] See the list given by Theodoros himself in *epist*. 48,40–61: the hegoumenoi Theosostos, Stephanos, Antonios, Aimilianos, Leon Balelades, in addition to Stoudite monks, such as Naukratios, Arsenios, Basileios, Gregorios, Litoios, etc.

[19] Theod. Stoud., *epist*. 514,10–32; Theod. Stoud., *Parvae catech*. 74,12–23; Theoph. Cont. II, 24; Dobroklonskij 1913: vol. I, 914–18; Treadgold 1988: 246–47; Herrin 2001: 155–58.

[20] On Stoudite resistance to iconoclasm, see Ševčenko 1995: 91–105; Hatlie 2007a: 383–38.

to praise friends and allies who favoured images as saints worthy of veneration. The occasions for celebrating their memory in connection with the liturgy increased considerably, since the post-iconoclast reform of monasticism included an obligation to hold the Eucharist daily.[21] The Stoudite milieu includes many of the bishops appointed by Tarasios in his attempt to purge the iconoclast clergy after the Second Council of Nicaea. Their numbers include Theophylaktos of Nicomedia, Michael of Synada and the hegoumenoi of Medikion and Pelekete, whose pro-icon position, together with the personal links that can be traced, made them full members of the first network of the Second Iconoclasm.

1.1 The Literary Production of Theodoros Stoudites

Theodoros Stoudites is well known for both his theological works and his reform of Byzantine monasticism.[22] Born in 759 in Constantinople to a family of high-ranking iconodule officials, he died on 11 November 826 in exile due to his rebellious stance in defence of images.[23] He is famous for his confrontations with emperors and iconoclast leaders but also with iconodules whose vision of the Church did not coincide with his own, as for example, those who defended the second marriage of Konstantinos VI, which sparked the Moechian conflict, or shortly afterwards, as a result of the choice of Nikephoros as patriarch of Constantinople.[24] At the age of twenty, Theodoros entered the family monastery of Sakkoudion in Bithynia, which was run by his uncle Platon, and was subsequently ordained a priest by the patriarch Tarasios.[25] Having trained as a *notarios* under Platon, who had been a *zygostates* (a state functionary of the imperial treasury), fourteen years later, in 794, he became the hegoumenos of that community.

Known for opposing Konstantinos VI by refusing to approve his second marriage, Theodoros was always a point of reference for the ecclesiastical anti-establishment movement against the imperial court and compliance with the emperor's will. Nor did he hesitate to confront the orthodox patriarch Nikephoros I for his relaxed attitude to imperial pressure or

---

[21] Pott 2000: 120–33; Taft 2004.
[22] Dobroklonskij 1913; Leroy 1958a: 181–214; Leroy 1969; Frazee 1981; Morris 1995: 13–19; Leroy 2002. For his liturgical reform, see Hatlie 2007a: 436–39.
[23] For his biographical coordinates, see *PmbZ* # 7574; *PBE* I: Theodoros 15.
[24] Gardner 1905; Werner 1957; Patlagean 1988; Karlin-Hayter 1994; Pratsch 1998; Cholij 2002; Delouis 2005: 83–124.
[25] Theod. Stoud., *epist.* 38,74–79. Pratsch 1998: 76–81.

refuse to attend the Council of 815, at which iconoclasm was finally restored. His greatest achievement was doubtless the creation of an independent, united monastic system capable of resisting imperial coercion, in which all monasteries were governed by the same rules, inspired by those of Basileios the Great and based on discipline and community life as reflected in his two *Catecheseis* and in his collected letters. Although a large number of his epistles survive, approximately half of them have been lost due to the propagandising deselection carried out by his Stoudite successors.[26] Thus, for example, this operation, which aimed to normalise Theodoros' image (and that of the whole Stoudite federation), removed letters concerning monks who embraced iconoclasm, as is shown by the anthology ψ.[27] In the theological field, Theodoros produced a refutation of iconoclastic ideas, developing the theory of images of Ioannes Damaskenos.[28] But it is his hagiographical production (liturgical hymns, homilies and panegyrics) that has received less attention to date, which will concern us here. This established the basis of a new political process of literary production that was followed by Theodoros' disciples and would be imitated by other religious groups when they composed texts in honour of the many new iconodule saints.

1.1.1 *The* Laudatio of Theoktiste *(BHG 2422)*

According to the thinking of Theodoros Stoudites, the sanctification of his contemporaries who had suffered for defending Orthodoxy was a logical consequence of the emulation of the early martyrs he encouraged so actively among his followers.[29] In one of his earliest works, Theodoros used this method to promote the liturgical commemoration of someone very close to him: his mother Theoktiste. She was born ca. 743/744 to a Constantinopolitan family of imperial rank, and her relationship with the royal household was strengthened by the marriage of her niece Theodote to Konstantinos VI.[30] Due to the premature death of her parents from the plague when she was young, Theoktiste was only able to develop intellectually after her marriage to Photeinos. To this end, she devoted herself to

---

[26] Ronconi 2017: 1319–23.
[27] Theod. Stoud., *epist.* (ed. Fatouros), p. 105; Ronconi 2017: 1323, n. 143.
[28] Gendle 1981; Roth 1981; Brubaker 1989a; Parry 1989; 1996; Demoen 1998; Pelikan 2011; Pizzone 2012; Calisi 2013; Tollefsen 2018. For the written production of Theodoros, see *DS* XV, 401–14, s.v. 'Théodore Stoudite'; Cholij 2002: 65–77; Demoen 2019.
[29] Hatlie 1996b: 266–72 and 275–80.
[30] *PmbZ* # 8023; *PBE* I: Theoktiste 3; Hermann 1919; Pratsch 1998: 26–41.

the study of the Psalms whenever time permitted.[31] After giving birth to three boys and a girl, Theodoros' parents embraced chastity and a life of continence for five years. In 781 (when she was thirty-six or thirty-seven years old), Theoktiste entered a convent together with her family, after selling the family properties on the advice of her brother Platon of Sakkoudion.[32] The convent she entered with her daughter was presumably also in Bithynia, not far from Sakkoudion, where her son Theodoros lived with her brother. Death came to Theoktiste on 20 December although the year is unknown (perhaps 798 or 799).

Shortly afterwards, her son Theodoros wrote her epitaph in a hagiographical vein, as is emphasised by its inclusion from the outset in a collection of *vitae* and *passiones* from the early tenth century,[33] in the form of a catechesis. Apparently, no existing literary genre filled Theodoros' need to praise his mother as a saint while at the same time proposing her as a model of behaviour for his male monks.[34] According to Efthymiadis and Featherstone, the editors of the text, this funeral oration dates to the sole reign of Eirene, from 797 to 802. Depending on the date on which the funeral oration was delivered, the monastic community would have been gathered either in Sakkoudion (Bithynia) or, if it was after 799, in Stoudios (Constantinople), since by that time Theodoros was the hegoumenos of the monastery in the capital. This is neither a historical text nor one with historical pretensions that narrates the biography of the holy protagonist. Instead, it aims to reproduce an image of Theoktiste by means of rhetoric and to emphasise her spiritual feats.[35] Its objective was to promote a monastic ideal that would serve as a reference point for the monks who made up its readership, including Theodoros' uncle Platon, the brother of his dead mother. In order to do so, far from following standard

---

[31] Theod. Stoud., *Laudatio of Theoktiste* 3,1–4: τοῦ θείου πόθου αὔξοντος αὐτῆς ἐν τῇ καρδίᾳ, ἐπειδὴ ἦν ἀγράμματος ἐξ ὀρφανίας ἀγομένη, γραμματίζει ἑαυτὴν ἡ σοφὴ καὶ συνετίζει καὶ τὸ ψαλτήριον ἀποστηθίζει κάλλιστά τε καὶ συντομώτατα, 'when divine longing had increased in her heart, because she was illiterate in her orphan state, this wise one instructed and taught herself and she learnt the Psalter by heart in best and quickest fashion'.

[32] Theod. Stoud., *Laudatio of Platon* 824B–C; *Vita* A *of Theodoros Stoud.* 121D; *Vita* B *of Theodoros Stoud.* 241B.

[33] It is the manuscript *Parisinus Gr.* 1491, a *menologion* for the month of December, in which the *laudatio Theoctistae* corresponds to the fourteenth day of the month, appears on folios 96–103, and is preceded by the *passio* of Ignatios of Antioch (*BHG* 814), see Ehrhard 1936–1939: vol. I, 514–15 Halkin 1955: 55; 1968: 182–83.

[34] On genre problems and Theodoros' innovation, see Pignani 2007: 21–28; Pignani 2009; Maltese 2014.

[35] This epitaph has been studied by Diehl 1906; Kazhdan 1999: 244–47; Efthymiadis and Featherstone 2007.

hagiographical clichés, Theodoros depicts a firm, resolute woman capable of decisive action to guide her family towards salvation. He stresses her retreat from the world and her taking of the veil but also points to a clear continuity between her lifestyle as an always virtuous married laywoman and as an abbess. Theoktiste is by no means the only example of female asceticism within marriage.[36]

This is the first *enkomion* of a female saint in Middle Byzantine times.[37] At this stage of the renovation of hagiographical production, the values of female holiness were inspired by those of the new social elite and the strongly emerging monastic culture. Despite everything, Theodoros Stoudites established numerous close relations with women in a manner different from any other Byzantine author. In his abundant epistolary corpus of 560 missives, no less than 76 are addressed to women.[38] These include one letter sent to his mother Theoktiste (*epist.* 6), composed shortly before her death, in answer to a letter of hers saying that she was seriously ill. Theodoros comforts and encourages her and at the same time consoles her for the early death of her son Euthymios and an unnamed daughter.[39] In this letter, we can see that for Theodoros Stoudites his dead brother and sister were already saints (*epist.* 6, 9–11) and that although his mother was still alive, he did not hesitate to consider her too a saint (*epist.* 6, 54 and 69), since she had rejected worldly glory for the kingdom of heaven and had endured a bloodless martyrdom out of love for God. Despite the absence of an actual canonisation process during this period, Theodoros' sanctifying project was soon successful: this concept of family holiness that extends to the mother and the sister of a saint also appears in one of the first iconodule hagiographies, the *vita* of Stephanos the Younger (*BHG* 1666), which was written barely a decade after his funeral oration in ca. 809.[40]

Although the question of images does not arise in the funeral oration, there can be no question of Theoktiste's orthodoxy. This is due to the fact that Theodoros wrote this speech during the iconodule interlude, which extends from the restoration of images decreed at the Second Council of Nicaea in 787 to the restoration of iconoclasm in 815. Moreover, in the

---

[36] Abrahamse 1985: 53–54; Constantinou 2005.
[37] Patlagean 1976. On the hagiographies of this period praising female saints, see Chapter 4.
[38] Gouillard 1982; Hatlie 1996a.
[39] Sarris 2005: 401–2. Although we do not know her name, Theodoros must have had a close relationship with his sister as he dedicated one of his iambic poems to her, *Epigram* 105f, edited by Speck 1968.
[40] *Vita of Stephanos the Younger* 47,22–27 and ch. 53.

year it was written, the author had to attend to another highly topical matter: the Moechian controversy. Theoktiste suffered for her faith during the persecution ordered by Konstantinos VI, allowing her to be considered a confessor. But her sufferings are abstract: anguish, threats, tears, grief for the persecuted, etc. Theodoros' first period of exile involved deportation to Thessaloniki from Sakkoudion. During the journey, the exiles were briefly harboured by Theoktiste; the encounter appears to have taken place in Paula in Bithynia on 20 February 797.[41] Perhaps in reprisal, Theoktiste and the rest of her family were imprisoned for thirty days,[42] which meant that when Platon and Theodoros were recalled from exile by Empress Eirene, Theoktiste exemplified the resistance of Orthodoxy for both her family and the monastic community. Theodoros Stoudites was able to take advantage of this situation, since his mother's sanctification gave his monks a saint of their own capable of drawing the group closer together and reflecting the ideals of the Stoudite project. Theodoros completed this programme with an *enkomion* of his uncle Platon, but before this he wished to honour his mother's memory with an occasionally autobiographical hagiographical speech.[43] Her unconditional support of her son and defence of the same principles[44] meant that Theoktiste's sufferings always followed and to a large extent were triggered by her son's sufferings to defend his faith.

1.1.2 *The* Laudatio of Platon of Sakkoudion *(BHG 1553)*

Some fifteen years later, Theodoros Stoudites repeated the process. His uncle Platon, the abbot of Sakkoudion, died 4 April 814, and Theodoros wished to pay him tribute with a funeral oration in which he continued along the lines of the *laudatio* in honour of his mother to promote a family cult that the monks of the Stoudite federation adopted as their own. This epitaph (*Laudatio of Platon of Sakkoudion*) takes the form of a *vita* and was

---

[41] Theod. Stoud., *Laudatio of Theoktiste* 9; Cheynet and Flusin 1990. Cf. Theod. Stoud., *epist.* 3,75–76.
[42] Theod. Stoud., *Laudatio of Theoktiste* 10; Von Dobschütz 1909a: 60.
[43] On the autobiographical nature of this catechesis, see Efthymiadis 1996: 70; Hinterberger 1999: 152–53; Efthymiadis and Featherstone 2007: 23. In Byzantium, the autobiographical genre arises in monastic contexts, see Angold 1998.
[44] Theodoros did not receive this support unanimously from his whole family. His uncle, the hegoumenos Nikephoros (*PmbZ* # 5282), took the side of Theodote and the Moechians, Theod. Stoud., *epist.* 4. We also know of another relative who opposed his fanaticism: the *patrikios* and *logothetes tou genikou* Niketas (*PmbZ* # 5466), who held the position of *antiprosopos* of Emperor Nikephoros and did not hesitate to recommend moderation in the Ioseph affair, see Theod. Stoud., *epist.* 27.

written shortly after Platon's death at the monastery of Stoudios. Platon was born ca. 735 to a family of state officials and initially expected to follow in their footsteps as a notary. (In fact, he succeeded his father in charge of the *zygostasia*, a profitable position in the imperial treasury.) In 759, he entered the Bithynian monastery of Symboloi (or Symbola) on Mount Olympos.[45] His piety made him so popular with the monks of that monastery, that after the death of the abbot, Platon was chosen to replace him.[46] One of his disciples during this period would later be Theodoros' informant regarding the life of his uncle before their joint career.[47] Theodoros declares that Platon worked as a copyist reproducing works and *florilegia* of Church Fathers that were available in several monasteries.[48] No works or manuscripts written by him have however survived, and we have no evidence that he composed texts of his own.[49]

After rejecting the opportunity to become the hegoumenos of a Constantinopolitan monastery or the metropolitan of Nicomedia,[50] in 783, Platon decided to found the monastery of Sakkoudion with his nephew Theodoros on family land near the aforementioned holy mountain[51] and become its hegoumenos. A staunch defender of images, he took part in the Second Council of Nicaea in 787 in response to a personal request from the patriarch Tarasios[52] and did not hesitate to oppose the second marriage of Konstantinos VI, which led to his arrest between 795 and 797. During these years, the Sakkoudion community was dispersed and its monks exiled.[53] After the fall of Emperor Konstantinos, the monks returned to their monasteries in 798, but the threat of an enemy attack[54] meant that they then became concentrated in Constantinople.

---

[45] *PmbZ* # 6285; *PBE* I: Platon 1; Pargoire 1899; Costa-Louillet 1954/1955: 230–40; *ODB* III, 1684; Hatlie 2007a: 280–83.
[46] Theod. Stoud., *Laudatio of Platon* 817B.
[47] The monk Antonios is the informant in question, see *PmbZ* # 532–33; *PBE* I: Antonios 35; cf. Theod. Stoud., *Laudatio of Platon* 817Bff.
[48] Theod. Stoud., *Laudatio of Platon* 820A.
[49] The only exception is the odd epistle; indeed, Theod. Stoud., *epist.* 35 is by both of them. Likewise, a fragment of a letter from Platon is included in *epist.* 21,22, see Pratsch 1998: 97ff.; 2001.
[50] Theod. Stoud., *Laudatio of Platon* 821B–C.
[51] Janin 1975: 177–83; Ruggieri 1991: 225–26; Pratsch 1998: 71–76; Auzépy et al. 2005: 183–94.
[52] In addition to the hagiographical sources, the minutes of the Council certify his attendance at the second session (26 Sept.) and the fourth session (1 Oct.); in them he defended the traditional veneration of images, see Mansi XII, 1111 and Mansi XIII, 152.
[53] Theod. Stoud., *Laudatio of Platon* 829A–D.
[54] The reason traditionally given is an Arab raid, Theod. Stoud., *Laudatio of Platon* 833D; *Vita* A *of Theodoros Stoud.* 144D–45A; *Vita* B *of Theodoros Stoud.* 257D–60A; *Vita* C *of Theodoros Stoud.* 270,32–71,4. Although this view is still widely accepted (Pratsch 1998: 119–20; Cholij 2002: 43), it was questioned a long time ago, see Leroy 1958a: 201ff.

Platon took advantage of this situation to abandon the leadership of the federation in favour of Theodoros and was thus able to return to the hermit life he craved.[55] But the death of the patriarch Tarasios on 25 February 806 again lent Platon public importance, since he was one of those consulted by the emperor as to who should succeed the deceased patriarch. The angry response of Nikephoros I has led some researchers to suppose that Platon's candidate was Theodoros Stoudites himself, which would explain why Theodoros failed to mention the name given by his uncle.[56] The final decision of Emperor Nikephoros to appoint a layman (also named Nikephoros) as patriarch was widely opposed, since it was contrary to ecclesiastical canons. The Stoudite federation again fiercely defended religious regulations and its independence from the imperial throne.

When the Moechian conflict was revived, Platon again suffered for defending Orthodoxy: despite being advanced in years, he was imprisoned to prevent him from opposing the synod in January 809 being prepared by Emperor Nikephoros I. He was subsequently exiled together with his nephew Ioseph of Thessaloniki to the nearby island of St Mamas, where he fell ill.[57] The accession of Michael I Rhangabe meant that Platon was freed, but he did not recover and died at the monastery of Stoudios at the age of seventy-seven after a three-year illness.[58] Although he died on 4 April 814, a tribute to him was held on 18 April.

Theodoros himself ensured that this commemoration was held in a suitable manner, as is shown by his *Catecheseis*,[59] one of which was pronounced on the day after the tribute to Platon.[60] To promote this tribute and its liturgical celebration, Theodoros took special care over the composition of his speech in honour of his uncle. Anxious for the public to adopt the message he wished to transmit, Theodoros abandoned the literary technique of describing the good deeds of the holy protagonist by means of narrative scenes (as he does, for example, in his *enkomion* of St Arsenios the hermit) and instead stressed the virtues of the founder of Sakkoudion.[61] Platon's education, his ascetic life, his respect for the ecclesiastical hierarchy and his strict observance of the *kanones* and the

---

[55] Theod. Stoud., *Laudatio of Platon* 833D–36C.
[56] Costa-Louillet 1954/1955: 239; Theod. Stoud., *Laudatio of Platon* 833D–36C and 837B; Theod. Stoud., *epist.* 16,29–36; Dobroklonskij 1913: vol. 1, 598–604; Alexander 1958a: 66–67; Henry 1969: 505–6; Pratsch 1998: 135–42.
[57] Theod. Stoud., *Laudatio of Platon* 837C–40C.
[58] Theod. Stoud., *Laudatio of Platon* 844C–48B; Pargoire 1900/1901.
[59] Theod. Stoud., *Parvae catecheseis* 69 (ed. Auvray, pp. 240–41), lines 25–33.
[60] Theod. Stoud., *Parvae catecheseis* 33 (ed. Auvray, pp. 121–23).
[61] This epitaph has been studied by Sideras 1994: 97–100; Kazhdan 1999: 241–44.

new rules he drafted following that of St Basileios the Great and incarnated[62] are described time and time again. The result was a highly innovative text, due to its catechetical nature and communal reading of it within the Stoudite federation. No miracles are recounted, but there is mention of Platon's exemplary behaviour in defence of the faith and in compliance with his obligations as a monk, justifying his sanctification. The composition of an epigram on the subject of Platon's cell is another excuse used by Theodoros to emphasise his uncle's monastic virtues.[63] One can imagine that this poem – like many other epigrams of the Stoudites inscribed in the church of St John of Stoudios or in other parts of the monastery – was engraved or painted on the wall of Platon's old monastic cell. In this way, Theodoros encouraged the cult of his uncle and indicated a place of 'pilgrimage' strongly linked to the daily life of the community.

In common with the epitaph for his mother Theoktiste, the *vita* of Platon has a marked auto-hagiographical component that affects the holiness of Theodoros Stoudites himself. Both Platon and his nephew, for example, were responsible for the reform and organisation of monasticism.[64] The sufferings of Platon for condemning the Moechian affair were shared by Theodoros, who accompanied him in captivity and in exile and was also declared schismatic by the synod of 809.[65] Both men protested the accommodating attitude of the patriarch Tarasios towards Emperor Konstantinos VI and the choice of the layman Nikephoros as patriarch imposed by the new Emperor Nikephoros I. The literary resources and intertextual underpinning employed by Theodoros in his *Laudatio* effectively identify Platon with Basileios the Great, whose *Funeral Oration* Theodoros uses extensively.[66] As a consequence, Theodoros himself appears as the new Gregorios of Nazianzus (the author of Basileios' *Oration*), enabling his monks to appropriate the authority of the Cappadocian Fathers invoked by the iconoclasts at the Councils of Hiereia (754) and Hagia Sophia (815).[67] Moreover, the appointment of Theodoros as the leader of the Stoudite federation is described in detail with a quote from the Bible,[68] which in the mouth of Theodoros

---

[62] On the Stoudite model incarnated in Platon, see Van de Vorst 1914; Leroy 1958b.
[63] *Epigram* 2 (ed. Speck, pp. 111–13).
[64] Theod. Stoud., *Laudatio of Platon* 825C: συναγωνιστήν τε καί συλλήπτορα.
[65] Pratsch 1998: 153–78.   [66] MacDougall 2017.
[67] Alexander 1953; Gero 1977: 53–110; Krannich, Schubert and Sode 2002; Brubaker-Haldon 2011: 189–97 and 372–74.
[68] Jer 15: 10: Οἴμμοι ἐγώ, μῆτερ, ὡς τίνα με ἔτεκες· ἄνδρα δικαζόμενον καὶ διακρινόμενον πάσῃ τῇ γῇ· οὔτε ὠφέλησα, οὔτε ὠφέλησέν με οὐδείς· ἡ ἰσχύς μου ἐξέλιπεν ἐν τοῖς καταρωμένοις με, 'Woe is me, my mother, that thou hast borne me a man of strife and a man of contention to the whole earth!

represents a declaration of his intention to stand firm in his convictions and fight against anything that does not represent God's will.[69] Indeed, this *vita* mentions not so much the fight to defend images – no doubt because Platon died before iconoclasm was restored – but the opposition of the monastic party (represented by the Stoudites) to the patriarchal party, indulgent to the imperial power and given to transgressing the *kanones* to please the emperor's will. This is in fact another way of fighting to defend Orthodoxy that is no less important than protecting icons from heretics, and equally risky.

The holiness of the members of Theodoros' family was a result of their extreme practising Christian virtues and their apologetic defence of Orthodoxy, which led them to withstand persecution and physical punishment. Already before he vehemently praised his mother Theoktiste and his uncle Platon, Theodoros had encouraged his full brothers to suffer to defend his vision of the faith. When he writes Platon from exile in March or April 797, for example, Theodoros does not forget to encourage his younger brother Euthymios.[70] Along with the rest of the family, Euthymios had left everything to take vows as a monk, and, at that time, it was necessary for him to confirm his opposition to the second marriage of Emperor Konstantinos VI, as punishment for which he had already been dealt a number of blows. The prize would be the enjoyment of eternal life.[71]

The same can be said of Theodoros' elder brother Ioseph, who would end up as archbishop of Thessaloniki from 807 to 809.[72] Ioseph survived Theodoros, which means that the sanctification of Ioseph was not promoted by his brother. But this process was prepared for by the image projected of him by Theodoros and by the way the latter addresses him in his collected letters. Indeed, although Ioseph was still alive, Theodoros had no qualms about giving him reverential treatment like that afforded a saint. In *epistle* 43, he addresses him as 'your holiness', 'who in truth shines in our generation as a bishop in a similar way to the Church Fathers', and as

---

I have neither lent on usury, nor men have lent to me on usury; yet every one of them doth curse me'.

[69] Theod. Stoud., *Laudatio of Platon* 836A–C.   [70] *PmbZ* # 1844; *PBE* I: Euthymios 14.
[71] Theod. Stoud., *epist.* 1,63–74. We do not know the exact period, but Euthymios did not live much longer, see Theod. Stoud., *epist.* 6,24–25; *Parvae catecheseis* 95 (p. 327). According to his brother's testimony, Euthymios died in an accident at sea while travelling from Sakkoudion to Stoudios, Leroy 2008: 100, n. 42.
[72] For the biography of this individual, born in ca. 762 and died on 15 July 832 in exile in Thessaly, see *PmbZ* # 3448; *PBE* I: Ioseph 3; Pargoire 1906a; 1907; Van de Vorst 1913a.

'most holy'.[73] In Section 1.3.1, we will take a closer look at the origin of the cult of Ioseph of Thessaloniki, the seed of which was planted by his brother Theodoros in his collected letters. In the same way, the key factors that would make the liturgical celebration of Theodoros Stoudites possible are scattered throughout his letters, in which auto-hagiographical elements are common.[74] Indeed, the correspondence of Theodoros Stoudites contains all the material needed to write a *vita* in his honour, often presented in a hagiographical manner, making his missives an essential source for the composition of any text involving him.[75]

1.1.3 *The* Enkomion of Theophanes of Sigriane *(BHG 1792b)*

The next landmark in the literary production of Theodoros Stoudites was a panegyric in honour of Theophanes of Sigriane,[76] better known as Theophanes the Confessor and as the author of a famous chronicle.[77] Born in 760 to a wealthy, aristocratic Constantinopolitan family of officials loyal to the Isaurians,[78] after a period of secular life during which he married Megalo,

---

[73] Theod. Stoud., *epist.* 43,2–3: τῆς ἀδελφικῆς καὶ πατρικῆς σου ἁγιοσύνης. *epist.* 43,7–8: ἀληθείᾳ ἐκλάμψαι σε ἐν τῇ καθ' ἡμᾶς γενεᾷ ἐν τῷ τῆς ἀρχιερωσύνης ἀξιώματι καθ' ὁμοίωσιν τῶν ἁγίων πατέρων εἴρηκα. *epist.* 43,90: ὁσιώτατε. He also calls him ἁγιοσύνη in Theod. Stoud., *epist.* 37,35; *epist.* 43,73; *epist.* 72,2; *epist.* 73,2; *epist.* 111,31; *epist.* 195,2; *epist.* 222,2; *epist.* 333,10. Cf. also *epist.* 222,34 (ὅσιε); *epist.* 355,23 (ὁσιώτατε).

[74] Hatlie 1996b: 284–85. This autobiographical turn to Theodoros' literary production with the aim of supplying raw material to his future hagiographers can also be found in his collection of iamboi: *Epigram* 97 is dedicated to himself, while poems 98–101 deal with the jail in Chalkitos where he was a prisoner, Speck 1968: 257–66.

[75] Theod. Stoud., *epist.* 3,54ff. (*Vita* B, ch. 16, 253B); Theod. Stoud., *epist.* 25,70–73 (*Vita* B, ch. 25, 265B–68B [growing apart from the patriarch Nikephoros]); Theod. Stoud., *epist.* 28,45–48 and *epist.* 30,30–36 (*Vita* B, ch. 18, 256D = *Vita* A, ch. 43, 156A [synodic vote deposing and excommunicating Ioseph of Kathara]); Theod. Stoud., *epist.* 31,94–104 (*Vita* B, ch. 14, 252D = *Vita* A, ch. 19, 137B); Theod. Stoud., *epist.* 33,78–81 (*Vita* B, ch. 27, 269B = *Vita* A, ch. 48, 160BC); Theod. Stoud., *epist.* 24,17–27 (*Vita* B, ch. 25, 268A = *Vita* A, ch. 45, 157A [on the *Oikonomía* to Ioseph of Kathara]); Theod. Stoud., *epist.* 38,74–79 (*Vita* B, ch. 10, 248A); Theod. Stoud., *epist.* 48,78–117 (*Vita* B, ch. 27, 269B–D = *Vita* A, chs. 49–51, 160C–61D); Theod. Stoud., *epist.* 71,3–9 (*Vita* B, ch. 36, 285CD); Theod. Stoud., *epist.* 106 (*Vita* B, ch. 38, 288Dff. = *Vita* A, ch. 87, 194Cff. [interrogation in Boneta]); Theod. Stoud., *epist.* 112,37–45 (*Vita* A, ch. 87, 193C); Theod. Stoud., *epist.* 297,17–21 (*Vita* B, ch. 40, 293A [θυρίς]); Theod. Stoud., *epist.* 376,18–28 (*Vita* B, ch. 40, 292D–93A = *Vita* A, ch. 90, 196D–97A [harsh conditions of imprisonment]); Theod. Stoud., *epist.* 382,11–18 (*Vita* B, ch. 42, 296AB = *Vita* A, ch. 93, 200A); Theod. Stoud., *epist.* 443,21–24 (*Vita* B, ch. 14, 252C = *Vita* A, ch. 18, 136D [Moechian controversy]); Theod. Stoud., *epist.* 475,2–5 (*Vita* B, ch. 61, 320AB = *Vita* A, ch. 119, 221CD); Theod. Stoud., *epist.* 560 (*Vita* B, ch. 59, 317A = *Vita* A, ch. 117, 220D [letter in defence of Petros of Atroa]).

[76] *PmbZ* # 8107; *PBE* I: Theophanes 18; Yannopoulos 2013.

[77] The bibliography on this work is enormous, see for instance, Rochow 1991; Speck 1994; Kazhdan 1999: 205–34; Jankowiak and Montinaro 2015. See the end of this section (Section 1.1.3).

[78] Yannopoulos 2010.

Theophanes decided to take the monastic habit in 780–781 in the monastery of Mount Sigriane on the southern coast of the Sea of Marmara.[79] After the Council of Nicaea, construction of the monastery of Megas Agros[80] began on that spot with money Theophanes had borrowed.[81]

Although during the Moechian controversy and the Ioseph affair Theophanes decided to support the conciliatory position of the patriarchs Tarasios and Nikephoros, in contrast to the fierce opposition of Theodoros Stoudites, the persecution they suffered together under Leon V (813–820) ultimately united them.[82] Theophanes was imprisoned for two years in Constantinople (815–817) and then exiled to the island of Samothrace, where he died on 12 March 818.[83] Moved by the loss of one of the great intellectuals of iconoduly, Theodoros Stoudites lost no time in praising Theophanes, his ascetic struggle and his suffering in defence of Orthodoxy. Shortly after the news arrived, therefore, he wrote letters to the hegoumenos of Medikion, Niketas,[84] and his brother Ioseph of Thessaloniki, describing the martyrdom Theophanes had suffered: he had been seized, imprisoned and exiled.[85] He also took the opportunity to mention Theophanes' main feats in a missive he sent the nuns Megalo and Maria in the spring of the same year.[86] Megalo (the widow of Theophanes)[87] had written to inform him of the chronicler's death. Theodoros answered with an *enkomion* of Theophanes similar to those found in the entries in *synaxaria* (liturgical calendars of fixed feast days), in that it recalled the main events of his life, described his pious character and stressed his charisma as a confessor of Christ, a second Job, a great monk, etc. Theodoros also mentions Theophanes' tortures: two years' imprisonment in Constantinople, exile on an island, serious illness and death in exile. For all this, his reward is eternal life together with the martyrs who preceded him. Theodoros confirms the sanctification of Theophanes, which merits a liturgical celebration,[88] and finally asks him to intercede on his own behalf and on that of the whole Church before the Lord.[89]

---

[79] Thomson 2007.
[80] Mango and Ševčenko 1973: 259–67; Janin 1975: 195–97; Ruggieri 1991: 219–20.
[81] Alexakis 1995b; 1996b.
[82] Pargoire 1902. Theodoros sent two epistles to Theophanes, Theod. Stoud., *epist.* 214 and 291.
[83] Van de Vorst 1912b; Theod. Stoud., *Vita of Theophanes the Confessor* 263ff.
[84] Theod. Stoud., *epist.* 319,8–15.
[85] Theod. Stoud., *epist.* 333,25–35, where he affirms that he has also informed Petros of Nicaea of this.
[86] Theod. Stoud., *epist.* 323. Cf. Yannopoulos 2007a.
[87] *PmbZ* # 4930; *PBE* I: Megalo 1; Yannopoulos 2014.
[88] Theod. Stoud., *epist.* 323,30–32: ὦ, ὦ, πάτερ, πάτερ, ὡς καλός σου ὁ δρόμος, ὡς ὅσιον τὸ μνημόσυνόν σου, ὡς μακάριον τὸ ὑπόμνημά σου· ὅλος σὺ φαιδρός, ὅλος χαρίεις.
[89] Theod. Stoud., *epist.* 323,34–38: μέμνησο ὡς τῆς ποίμνης σου κἀμοῦ τοῦ σοῦ υἱοῦ, κἂν ἐλαχίστου καὶ ἐρριμμένου. οἶδας τὸν πόθον σου τὸν ἐν ἐμοὶ ὡς κἀγὼ τὸν ἐν σοὶ ἐμοί. βόησον ὑπὲρ πάσης τῆς

A few years later, during the reign of Michael II (820–829), who was much less aggressive against iconodules, the opportunity was taken to transfer the relics of Theophanes from Samothrace to the monastery of Megas Agros, where they were deposited in two stages in 821 and 822. On the occasion of this transfer, on Easter Sunday of the year 822, Theodoros Stoudites pronounced a panegyric (*BHG* 1792b) in which he extolled the holiness of Theophanes and legitimised his veneration.[90] This was a highly rhetorical *enkomion*, known as the *Vita of Theophanes the Confessor*, in a lofty style intended for a sophisticated audience that appreciated literary resources as much as the saint being honoured.[91] From the outset, it was triumphalist in tone, as was fitting in a celebration of the arrival of the body of a true saint who defended the Orthodox faith, a confessor in keeping with the monastic principles established by Theodoros Stoudites. In the introduction, Theodoros explains why pronouncing this tribute fell to him (ch. 2): for want of natural sons, he became Theophanes' son when during his vows Theophanes acted as his monastic godfather (ἀνάδοχος) and spiritual father.[92]

The tribute goes on to stress the nobility and wealth of the saint and his wife and their desire for chastity[93] and withdrawal from the world. Theophanes' tonsure is carefully and precisely narrated, along with the foundation of a new establishment (φροντιστήριον) at the foot of the mountain of Sigriane (ch. 6). After a review of Theophanes' ascetic practices (ch. 7) and good Christian qualities (ch. 8), Theodoros also mentions his attitude during the Moechian conflict. He began by calling Konstantinos VI 'a second Herod'[94] for having disowned his legitimate wife Maria of Amnia to marry one of her ladies-in-waiting, Theodote. Many iconodules (among others the new hegoumenos of Megas Agros)

ἐκκλησίας πρὸς Κύριον, δεήθητι καὶ περὶ ἐμοῦ τοῦ οἰκτροῦ τάχει ἐλθεῖν πρὸς σέ, ἐν ᾧ τρόπῳ τετελείωσαι.

[90] Van de Vorst 1912a; Efthymiadis 1993b, whose dating I accept. According to Senina 2015: 312–13, this panegyric should be dated one year before, i.e., at the end of March 821, during the first stop of the funeral procession at Hiereia.

[91] Other hagiographical accounts of Theophanes have also survived: a *vita* signed by the patriarch Methodios (see Section 2.1.1) and an *enkomion* written by Theodoros Daphnopates (*BHG* 1791) in the mid-tenth century that emphasises the blood ties between the iconodule chronicler and Emperor Konstantinos VII Porphyrogennetos, see Yannopoulos 2005; 2009.

[92] Theod. Stoud., *epist.* 214 and 323; Yannopoulos 2013: 30–4 and 119–20. Moreover, Theophanes had entrusted Theodoros to look after his sister, Theod. Stoud., *Vita of Theophanes the Confessor* 9,4–9; Yannopoulos 2013: 68–70.

[93] For other immediate parallels of the eighth and ninth centuries, see Krausmüller 2013b.

[94] Theod. Stoud., *Vita of Theophanes the Confessor* 10. He also used the same expression in the *Laudatio of Platon* 829B and 832AB and in his collected epistles, see Theod. Stoud., *epist.* 22,57 and 67; *epist.* 28,67; *epist.* 31,66–67; *epist.* 443,11–12.

were surprised that Theodoros attacked an Orthodox emperor this way, as can be seen from the answer Theodoros was forced to send the *hypatos* Demetrios to justify his choice of language.[95]

The Stoudites, led by Theodoros, fiercely opposed Konstantinos VI's marriage, also attacking the patriarch Nikephoros for his tolerant attitude towards it, as well as those such as Theophanes who supported him. In his panegyric, Theodoros recognised this difference of opinions and, thanks to a letter to his brother Ioseph of Thessaloniki, we know that Theodoros excused the abbot of Megas Agros for having accepted the emperor's second marriage, since he regarded the decision as strongly influenced by the fact that Theodote was Theodoros' niece.[96] The Stoudites considered this behavior cancelled out by the sufferings of Theophanes in defence of his faith shortly afterwards. Indeed, Theodoros lingers over the proclamation of heresy by Leon V (ch. 11) and the immediate resistance of Theophanes, who was unable to travel due to his delicate health. In spite of this, Theophanes used epistles to mobilise a significant number of hegoumenoi from different regions, including Bithynia, over which he had considerable *auctoritas* owing to his great virtue (ch. 12). A large number of iconodules were imprisoned while attending the liturgy, and Theophanes himself had to confront the patriarch Ioannes VII Grammatikos,[97] who tried to win him over to heresy (ch. 14). After his confession, Theophanes was imprisoned for two years, during which he remained faithful to Orthodoxy; this firmness led Theodoros to consider him 'a martyr of persecution' (ch. 15). When the decree of exile was issued, Theophanes is said to have received it with joy even though his route across the Propontis (Sea of Marmara) advanced like a funeral procession, which means that his death in exile was compared to that of Apostles who were far from home due to their faith (ch. 16).

A brief enumeration of Theophanes' major posthumous miracles (ch. 17: the expulsion of demons, healing a *haemorrhoissa*, a paralytic and a deaf-mute, among many others, together with the curing of animals)[98] precedes a highly rhetorical ending in two parts: first, Theodoros

---

[95] Theod. Stoud., *epist.* 443; Yannopoulos 2013: 33.
[96] Theod. Stoud., *epist.* 333,29–32: οὐ παρεῖδεν οὖν αὐτοῦ Κύριος τοὺς ὑποτακτικοὺς κόπους, ὁπόσους οἶσθα, κἂν ἑάλω κατὰ **τὰς ἁμαρτίας μου** ἐν τοῖς μοιχειανοῖς φειδοῖ τοῦ σώματος, οὐ συναιρούμενος τῷ φρονήματι, ὡς τὰ πράγματα ἐδείκνυ.
[97] On the patriarch Ioannes Grammatikos, see *PmbZ* # 3199 and # 3304; *PBE* I: Ioannes 5; Gero 1974/1975; Lilie 1999: 169–82; Katsiampoura 2010; Magdalino 2015a.
[98] These miracles always occur due to the mediation of relics or of oils from the tomb, but curiously no icon is involved, Brubaker 2003: 258–59.

reflects on Theophanes' courage and his defence of images (ch. 18); second, the tribute concentrates on an impassioned peroration that concludes with a request to the saint to aid and bless Theodoros as the author of the panegyric, as well as the new hegoumenos of Megas Agros, Theophanes' former disciple (ch. 19).[99] It is precisely the mention of the hegoumenos at the end of the *enkomion* that suggests that he must have commissioned this work from Theodoros Stoudites. The man's name was Stephanos, and Theodoros sent him one of his letters during this period (*epist.* 487) in which he mentions the qualities of his now deceased spiritual father (μακάριος) and encourages Stephanos to follow in the latter's footsteps. Theodoros ends by advising Stephanos about how to treat repentant iconoclasts. That the hegoumenos Stephanos ran the monastery of Megas Agros is confirmed by the fact that this was the name of the person who called on Methodios to draw up a *vita* to honour Theophanes.[100] The two abbots thus joined forces to encourage veneration of their spiritual father, while also indulging in politics, since the transfer of the relics of Theophanes was a major iconodule event designed to counteract the iconoclastic persecution of Michael II. The initiative was immediately successful, and in about 825 we have evidence of tribute paid to the relics of Theophanes by none other than Ioannikios, an important leader of the resistance.[101]

Although Theophanes was recognised as a saint, the true reason for the great fame he achieved in life was the composition of a universal *Chronography* covering the years 285–813.[102] This important historiographical work is characterised by an iconodule perspective of Byzantine history very close to the official propaganda issued by the Constantinopolitan patriarchate led by Tarasios.[103] Its purpose is not only to show the rightness of the veneration of icons, but also to make clear the superiority of the Church over imperial power, which had recently embraced heresy. Theophanes is an erudite historian, whose work

---

[99] *PmbZ* # 7064; Theod. Stoud., *Vita of Theophanes the Confessor* 264–65. On the monastery of Megas Agros, cf. Janin 1975: 195f.; Ruggieri 1991: 104–6 and 219–20; Mango and Ševčenko 1973: 259–67.

[100] As suggested from the term στεφώνυμε Methodios uses to address the hagiography's recipient: Ἔμπρακτον κάλλος καὶ προαιρετικὴν εὐμορφίαν λόγῳ διαγράψαι πάλαι κελευσθεὶς παρὰ τῆς σῆς ἀγάπης, στεφώνυμε, τρισὶν ἐκωλύθην προφάσεσι τὸ ἀπάρξασθαι, Method., *Vita of Theophanes the Confessor* 1, 1–3. See Chapter 2.

[101] *Vita of Ioannikios by Sabas* 31, p. 360; *Vita of Ioannikios by Petros* 37.

[102] Treadgold 2013: 38–77; Jankowiak Montinaro 2015; Neville 2018: 61–71, with previous bibliography.

[103] Varona and Prieto 2014.

completes a joint project initiated some years earlier by Georgios Synkellos,[104] who had drawn up a *Chronography* (literally *Extract of Chronography*) that ran from the creation of the world to the coming to imperial power of Diocletian in 284.[105] As Theophanes himself declares, Georgios had been the synkellos of the patriarch Tarasios, whose ideological premises he shares in his historical work: Georgios' concern to define precisely the moment of the incarnation of Christ (the definitive justification of iconoduly) is accompanied by a desire to refute the theories of Eusebios of Caesarea, whom the iconoclasts had used as a principal authority at the Council of Hiereia in 754.[106] This objective was already evident when Georgios helped Tarasios prepare the Second Council of Nicaea (787), which they attended with an iconodule *florilegium* of quotations taken from Fathers of the Church, in the production of which both Georgios Synkellos and the future patriarch Nikephoros probably participated.[107]

Georgios spent the final years of his life (post 806–ca. 810) in the monastery of Megas Agros, where his hegoumenos Theophanes helped him draw up his *Chronography*. By the time of his death, he had successfully concluded their common project of writing a universal history, composing his own chronography from where Synkellos stopped, in the year 284. According to Theophanes in the preface to his work: 'Since, however, he was overtaken by the end of his life and was unable to bring his plan to completion ... he both bequeathed to me, who was his close friend, the book he had written and provided materials with a view to completing what was missing.'[108]

Once Theophanes the Confessor was dead, the two works began to circulate together.[109] The *Chronicle* of Theophanes quickly went through several editions, and it has traditionally been thought that they were produced at the monastery of Stoudios.[110] Palaeographic study of the earliest surviving manuscripts, however, indicates that they come from Bithynia, suggesting that they were copied at Megas Agros. These manuscripts are *Vaticanus Gr. 155*, Oxford *Christ Church Wake 5* (both dated to

---

[104] *PmbZ* # 2180; *PBE* I: Georgios 137; Mango 1978b; Čičurov 1981; Ševčenko 1992.
[105] Treadgold 2013: 51–63; Neville 2018: 56–60.   [106] Gwynn 2007; Varona 2018.
[107] Alexakis 1996a: 228–33; *Vita of Tarasios*, pp. 15–17; *Second Council of Nicaea* (ed. Lambertz), 3.1, pp. xxvii–xxx; and 3.2, pp. xv–xxiii.
[108] Theoph., *Chronography*, Pref. 3,23–24,2: ἐπεὶ δὲ τὸ τέλος τοῦ βίου τοῦτον κατέλαβε καὶ εἰς πέρας ἀγαγεῖν τὸν ἑαυτοῦ σκοπὸν οὐκ ἴσχυσεν ... ἡμῖν, ὡς γνησίοις φίλοις, τήν τε βίβλον ἣν συνέταξε καταλέλοιπε καὶ ἀφορμὰς παρέσχε τὰ ἐλλείποντα ἀναπληρῶσαι.
[109] Torgerson 2015.   [110] Afinogenov 2006: 132–33; Yannopoulos 2000; 2013: 284–96.

the final years of the ninth century or the beginning of the tenth) and *Parisinus Gr.* 1710 (copied in the 960s).[111] According to the *De Ceremoniis*, Megas Agros had an important library when in the tenth century Konstantinos VII Porphyrogenitos (913–959) resorted to it in search of bibliographic material to compose his treatises.[112] At the same time, the *Chronography* of Theophanes was widely known early on, since it is used notably by Georgios Monachos in his *Chronicle* and by the author of the *Vita of Theodoros of Chora*, both of whom were members of the Methodian milieu.[113] There is nothing strange in this: although Tarasios died years earlier, the links of Georgios Synkellos and Theophanes the Confessor with the patriarchate as an institution continued over time with the dissemination of their memory and their work.

1.1.4 Other Hagiographical Compositions of Theodoros Stoudites

(a) Honouring Members of the Stoudite Federation

Along with these major hagiographical texts, Theodoros Stoudites also produced another genre of works in honour of iconodule martyrs intended to encourage their veneration, to give the monks of the Stoudite federation moral and political references and to create a precise image of the role a monk should play in society.[114] His iambic poems dedicated to Early-Christian saints (*epigrams* 61–84) are well known, since by means of them, Theodoros revives the classical tradition while adapting it to new political and religious coordinates; these include numerous martyrs, and a section is even devoted to monks and founding abbots of Constantinopolitan monasticism in Late Antiquity (*epigrams* 76–84).[115] St Antonios, Hilarion, Euthymios, Sabas, Dalmatos, Pachomios, Arsenios, Theodosios and Dios exemplified the behaviour and virtues Theodoros Stoudites considered desirable for iconodule hegoumenoi in their fight against heresy. Precisely these same monks (Antonios, Hilarion, Euthymios and Sabas) appear in several of the liturgical poems (*kontakia*) written by

---

[111] Ronconi 2015a.
[112] Yannopoulos 2013: 295–96; Signes Codoñer 2015: 164–66, who comments on the passage.
[113] Theoph., *Chronography*, p. xcviii; Schmit 1906: 9–16; Mango 2009. See Chapter 2.
[114] Concerning the promotion of the daily saints' veneration by Theodoros, see Theod. Stoud., *epist.* 42,52–56: καὶ μετὰ ταῦτα ἐπικαλοῦ τὴν ἁγίαν Θεοτόκον ἐλεῆσαί σε, τοὺς ἁγίους ἀγγέλους καὶ ὃν ἔχεις τῆς ζωῆς σου φύλακα ἄγγελον ἵνα σε φρουρῇ καὶ σκέπῃ, τὸν Πρόδρομον, τοὺς ἀποστόλους, τοὺς ἁγίους πάντας καὶ οὓς ἔχεις ἐξαιρέτως συνήθως ἐπικαλεῖσθαι, καὶ τὸν κατὰ τὴν ἡμέραν μνημονευόμενον.
[115] This collection of poems has been edited by Speck 1968. Cf. Demoen 2001.

Theodoros Stoudites, always in the same metre, a characteristic rhythm he created and cultivated.[116] Moreover, these same fathers of primitive monasticism are listed in one of his catechetical sermons.[117]

Theodoros' epigrams also feature individuals from his own generation (*epigrams* 111–23), denigrating those who did not follow the principles of Orthodoxy, such as the Stoudite monk Pamphilos Trimalethon,[118] honouring the patrons of monastic foundations, who often ended up embracing monastic life and to whom he often dedicated epitaphs,[119] and of course praising monks who suffered in defence of their faith even to the extent of losing their lives. This is the case of the noble Stephanos, who died at the age of twenty-five 'without having known a woman', which probably means that he had taken monastic vows.[120] Stephanos may perhaps be identified with the nephew or cousin of Theodoros Stoudites by the same name to whom *epist.* 92 is addressed.[121] The final reference in the poem, to the effect that Christ has crowned him with his right hand, is an unequivocal sign that Stephanos had achieved the crown of holiness reserved for martyrs.[122]

The same is true of the monk Dionysios, whom we know well thanks to the collected letters of the hegoumenos of Stoudios. Dionysios was a member of the Stoudite federation,[123] for which he was a courier, since in the time of Leon V he was charged with carrying letters and news between Theodoros, Ioseph of Thessaloniki and the bishop of Miletus, Ignatios. There can be no doubt that Theodoros trusted him, since he sent him with missives to Rome and Jerusalem, from where he returned with news of Theodoros' correspondents.[124] The epitaph in verse that

---

[116] These *kontakia* have been edited by Pitra, *Analecta*, pp. 338–40 (Euthymios), 377–80 (Antonios), 576–78 (Sabas) and 615–17 (Hilarion). See also Lowe 1976.
[117] Theod. Stoud., *Magnae catecheseis* 69, (ed. Cozza-Luzi, 194,8–14).
[118] Theod. Stoud., *epigram* 122, cf. *PmbZ* # 5672; *PBE* I: Pamphilos 1. Concerning pro-iconodule and anti-iconoclast epigrams, see Martin 1930: 174–82.
[119] To the *patrikios* Leon *epigram*s 106, 107, 109, 114 and 120, cf. *PmbZ* # 4432; *PBE* I: Leon 258. To his wife Anna *epigram* 115, cf. *PmbZ* # 457; Speck 1968: 310–14. To the *protospatharios* Theophylaktos *epigram* 113, see *PmbZ* # 8340. To the *patrikia* Euphrosyne *epigram* 105g, cf. *PmbZ* # 1709. To Eudokia *epigram* 116, cf. *PmbZ* # 1628; *PBE* I: Eudokia 7. To the *patrikia* Eirene *epigrams* 117 and 118, cf. *PmbZ* # 1446; Speck 1997: 42f., n. 17.
[120] Theod. Stoud., *epigram* 111, cf. *PmbZ* # 7068; *PBE* I: Stephanos 138. The context that must be reconstructed for *epigram* 121, dedicated to the *diakonos* Theophilos, cf. *PmbZ* # 8215; *PBE* I: Theophilos 50, is likely very similar.
[121] *PmbZ* # 7058; *PBE* I: Stephanos 133; Pratsch 1998: 55 and 59.
[122] On the crown as a prize for the martyr in Theodoros Stoudites' thinking, Speck 1968: 102–3.
[123] *PmbZ* # 1346; *PBE* I: Dionysios 6. Death came to him at an advanced age during the reign of Michael II, between 821 and 826.
[124] Theod. Stoud., *epist.* 273 and 377 (journey to Rome in late 817); *epist.* 276 (journey to Jerusalem in 818).

Theodoros dedicated to Dionysios relates that he devoted his life to fighting and travelling to defend Orthodoxy and that when he died, he received a martyr's reward.[125] On a spiritual plane, this reward was eternal life in heaven. On a worldly plane, it consisted of sanctification and the liturgical commemoration of his memory by his followers and the members of his monastic community. For this veneration to be possible, a textual element was needed. The person responsible for providing it was Theodoros, who no sooner heard of Dionysios' death at the monastery of Myele, than he wrote to the monks there, telling them to venerate him. This is related in *epist.* 456, which briefly enumerates Dionysios' deeds: he was known from his youth for his obedience, was imprisoned twice, travelled to Rome, followed God's orders, and stood out for his cenobitic virtues. Because of all this, Theodoros ends by exhorting the monks of Myele to preserve Dionysios' relics as a treasure[126] and to celebrate his memory with that of the other saints.[127] We do not know where the Myele establishment was built, but it is reasonable to think that it was one of the many centres into which Theodoros Stoudites divided his monks to face iconoclastic persecution. It was at the monastery of Myele that a group led by Dionysios was established, according to another letter from Theodoros, in which he affirms that 'those who lived with brother Dionysios' encouraged him to write *epist.* 271 and 272 to the Pope in Rome.'[128]

In parallel with *epist.* 456, Theodoros sent another missive of a catechetical nature to his disciples as a whole to inform them of the deaths of Dionysios and Anthos, another Stoudite monk known for the services he rendered to Ioseph of Thessaloniki, whom he accompanied into exile.[129] The passing of both monks is narrated emphasising their holiness, since they shared the call of heaven with the saints.[130] Dionysios was outstanding for working both for and on behalf of God, while Anthos, as a Lamb of God, withstood with the stoicism of Job a terrible disease (no doubt leprosy) that ultimately cost him his life. Both men cultivated monastic

---

[125] Theod. Stoud., *epigram* 119.
[126] Theod. Stoud., *epist.* 456,18: τηλικοῦτον λείψανον ἅγιον παρ' ὑμῖν ᾠκονομήθη ἀποθησαυρισθῆναι.
[127] Theod. Stoud., *epist.* 456,20–22: μετὰ ἀληθινῆς καρδίας ὑπεδέξασθε τὸν ὅσιον Διονύσιον, οὗ τὸ μνημόσυνον μετὰ τῶν ὁμοταγῶν ἁγίων.
[128] Theod. Stoud., *epist.* 377,4–6: οἱ γὰρ περὶ τὸν ἀδελφὸν Διονύσιον εὐδοκίᾳ θεοῦ καὶ ἀπεσώθησαν ἕως τῶν ἐκεῖ καὶ χρηστὰς ἐλπίδας ἤνεγκαν· πρὸς οὓς καὶ πάλιν ἐπιστεῖλαι εὖ ἐνόμισα.
[129] *PmbZ* # 498; *PBE* I: Anthos 1.
[130] Theod. Stoud., *epist.* 457,3–6: οἱ ἀποβεβιωκότες ἀδελφοὶ ἡμῶν ἅγιοι κλήσεως ἐπουρανίου μέτοχοι, Ἄνθος ὁ φερωνύμως ἠνθηκὼς τὰς ἀρετάς, καὶ Διονύσιος, ὁ διαπρέψας διονυσιακῶς καθ' ὁσιότητα.

obedience to the extent of suffering imprisonment,[131] which meant that Theodoros considered them martyrs.[132] Rather than pursuing the establishment of a liturgical cult in the other establishments, the proclamation of the holiness of these brothers of the Stoudite federation instead sought to provide models of holiness that could be imitated on a daily basis by any of its monks.[133]

For Theodoros Stoudites, these models of holiness are worthy of official veneration within liturgy, since they did not fall into heresy. Apart from the other qualities expected of a Byzantine saint, the main requirement imposed by Theodoros is firmness in Orthodoxy, as he affirms in one of the replies he offers regarding pastoral matters.[134] Faithful to this spirit, Theodoros canonised and encouraged veneration on the part of many members of his congregation who opposed iconoclasm, both in his letters and in his homilies, which have been gathered into two collections: *Magnae catecheseis* and *Parvae catecheseis*.[135] In addition to the cases already mentioned, particular attention should be paid to that of Domitianos, a Stoudite monk who valiantly survived the persecution of Leon V[136] and whom the community remembered as a saint, according to the texts of the *Parvae catecheseis*.[137] Another example is the monk Theodoros, a correspondent of Theodoros Stoudites known for the harsh punishment he proposed for iconoclasts.[138] The memory of this martyr (who probably did not belong to a monastery of the Stoudite federation) was celebrated on the same day that Theodoros pronounced the *Parvae catecheseis* 14.[139]

Of all the confessors of the Second Iconoclasm, however, one Stoudite monk stands out as the true neo-martyr of Orthodoxy: St Thaddaios.[140] Born in Bulgaria of Slavic origins, he had been a slave in childhood. Once

---

[131] Theod. Stoud., *epist.* 457,16–19: Διονύσιος, ὁ μέχρι γήρους τὸν τῆς ὑποταγῆς ἆθλον ἀπὸ νεότητος τετελεκώς, καὶ Ἄνθος, ὁ ἐκ παιδὸς ὁσιωθεὶς μέχρι μεσηλικιότητος καθ᾽ ὑποταγήν.
[132] Theod. Stoud., *epist.* 457,15: ἴδε οἱ μακάριοι ὡς καὶ αὐτοὶ μάρτυρες.
[133] Theod. Stoud., *epist.* 457,31–33: διὸ σπεύσωμεν, ἀδελφοί μου, καὶ ἡμεῖς ὁσίως ἀποβιῶσαι, ὡς ἂν φύγοιμεν αἰωνίας κρίσεως καὶ ἀξιωθείημεν βασιλείας οὐρανῶν. Theod. Stoud., *epist.* 457,59–62: Διὰ τοῦτο, ἀδελφοί μου, ὑπομιμνήσκω, παραινῶ, παρακαλῶ ὡς ὀφειλέτης, ὡς δοῦλος ὑμῶν διὰ Κύριον, δικαίως καὶ ὁσίως πολιτευσώμεθα καὶ πρὸς τὸ ἑξῆς, ἵνα κληρονομήσωμεν ζωὴν αἰώνιον ἐν Χριστῷ Ἰησοῦ τῷ Κυρίῳ ἡμῶν, ᾧ ἡ δόξα εἰς τοὺς αἰῶνας. ἀμήν.
[134] Theod. Stoud., *epist.* 552,139–46.   [135] Cholij 2002: 65–73; Lucà 2016.
[136] *PmbZ* # 1355; *PBE* I: Domitianos 1. *Vita* B *of Theodoros Stoud.* 46, 301C-D; *Vita* A *of Theodoros Stoud.* 205C; *Vita* C *of Theodoros Stoud.* 57, p. 291. Theodoros Stoudites sent *epist.* 180 to him in late 816 or early 817. Perhaps this monk can be identified with the hegoumenos of the same name who ran Sakkoudion, see *PmbZ* # 1354; *PBE* I: Domitianos 3; Theod. Stoud., *Magnae catecheseis* II, 58.
[137] Theod. Stoud., *Parvae catecheseis* 2,55–67. Cf. also Theod. Stoud., *Parvae catecheseis* 38,35.
[138] *PmbZ* # 7668 and # 7669; *PBE* I: Theodoros 323. He received *epist.* 427, 446 and 477.
[139] Theod. Stoud., *Parvae catecheseis* 14,56–64.
[140] *PmbZ* # 7252; *PBE* I: Thaddaios 1; Pargoire 1906b; Van de Vorst 1912c; Dobroklonskij 1913: vol. II, 291–94; Afinogenov 2001; Hatlie 2007a: 265.

freed, he was tonsured as a youth and played an active role in monastic life, first in Sakkoudion and later in Stoudios after 799. He subsequently decided to live in an individual cell as a recluse, as Platon had done. Thaddaios was persecuted in 809–811 during the second stage of the Moechian controversy.[141] In spring of the year 815, Emperor Leon V sent Theodoros and other Stoudite monks into exile, while the recluses appear to have remained in their cells. But Thaddaios was imprisoned shortly afterwards, before the beginning of summer 816.[142] While in prison, he corresponded with his hegoumenos, Theodoros Stoudites, who strengthened his position as a defender of Orthodoxy in *epistles* 126 and 183, which were sent in 816. During an interrogation, Thaddaios had the opportunity to make a fiery speech in favour of Orthodoxy,[143] which earned him punishment from the emperor: according to the Church Slavonic *vita*, Thaddaios attacked the heretic communion, but according to the *Synaxarion of Constantinople* he attempted to defend the icons themselves. After receiving 130 lashes[144] at the hands of a relative of Leon V named Bardas, Thaddaios died on the second[145] or third day.[146] According to the Greek sources, it was 22 November or 29 December, but the Church Slavonic *Vita* puts Thaddaios' death on 27 February 817.[147] His funeral was officiated by the priest Theophylaktos,[148] and nothing is known of what happened to his relics.

Thaddaios is a good example of the social mobility enjoyed by monks in the late eighth and early ninth centuries: despite his humble origins and the fact that he was a foreigner with a strong accent, the diligence with which he performed his monastic obligations earned him the highest possible social recognition and sanctification, veneration and imitation. The major player in this canonisation process was Theodoros Stoudites, who saw in Thaddaios the monastic ideal required to face up to the iconoclast heresy. Both in his correspondence and in his catechesis, Theodoros often quoted Thaddaios as a case in point,[149] calling him a 'saint' (ἅγιος), a 'martyr' (μάρτυς), and a 'crowned one' (στεφανίτης).[150]

---

[141] Theod. Stoud., *Parvae catecheseis* 39,49–50. [142] Theod. Stoud., *epist.* 126.
[143] *Vita of Thaddaios of Stoudios* 19 (p. 335).
[144] Theod. Stoud., *epist.* 186,20. On the number of lashes he received, see Pratsch 1998: 252, n. 225.
[145] Theod. Stoud., *epist.* 190,21. [146] Theod. Stoud., *Parvae catecheseis* 39,53.
[147] Afinogenov 2001.
[148] Theod. Stoud., *epist.* 251,6–7. Cf. *PmbZ* # 8338; *PBE* I: Theophylaktos 111.
[149] Theod. Stoud., *epist.* 185, 186, 187, 188, 190, 191, 194, 195, 198, 199, 204, 301, 381. Theod. Stoud., *Parvae catecheseis* 29,46–53 (= *BHG* 2414); 43,51–52 (= *BHG* 2415); 133,44–45.
[150] Theod. Stoud., *epist.* 185,8–9: ὁ ἡμέτερος Θαδδαῖος καὶ τῶν ἁγίων σύσκηνος. Theod. Stoud., *epist.* 194,20–21: μάρτυς Χριστοῦ ἀδελφὸς Θαδδαῖος. Theod. Stoud., *epist.* 194,23: Θαδδαῖος στεφανίτης.

Theodoros considered him the archetypal saint of the Stoudite confederation and repeatedly encouraged his monks to follow in the footsteps of Thaddaios and not to hesitate to request his intercession.[151]

In all versions of the *vita* of Theodoros Stoudites, Thaddaios plays an important part by performing a miracle to benefit his iconoclast torturer.[152] According to the hagiographical accounts, Bardas was a *strategos* of Smyrna (i.e., the *strategos* of the Thrakesion) when Theodoros Stoudites was imprisoned there in 819 or 820.[153] Bardas fell seriously ill and sought help at the episcopal palace of Smyrna, where he was urged to ask Theodoros to pray for him. The hegoumenos refused to do so, rebuking Bardas for his involvement in the persecution of iconophiles and for taking an active part in the death of Thaddaios, whom he had beaten to death. Bardas repented and managed to persuade Theodoros to send him an icon of the Theotokos with indications as to how he might receive Thaddaios' pardon and have him pray for him. Bardas recovered his health, but fell into heresy again, meaning that he suffered a relapse and died shortly afterwards.

The healing miracle attributed to Thaddaios is mentioned in no other source and contains legendary elements similar to those included in the entry in the *Synaxarion* of Constantinople dedicated to this saint.[154] Why this is the case, we do not know. But there are insuperable discrepancies in the *Synaxarion* compared with the other surviving sources, with the former affirming that the martyrdom took place under Michael II and Theophilos and that Thaddaios was ordered to appear at the palace together with Theodoros Stoudites (although we know that the latter was in exile). The episode in which Thaddaios is ordered to destroy an icon of the Saviour also appears to be a pious addition typical of hagiography, rather than historical fact. Regardless of the reasons for these deviations, found in the tenth century, the cult of Thaddaios was initiated by Theodoros Stoudites himself, who may have been the author of the first *vita* in his honour, written between 821 and 826.[155] The Greek text of this *vita* has been lost, but a very early translation into Old Church Slavonic has survived to prove

---

[151] Theod. Stoud., *epist.* 186,26–27: Δέομαί σου, ἅγιε τοῦ θεοῦ Θαδδαῖε, πρέσβεθε ὑπὲρ ἐμοῦ τοῦ ἀναξίου δούλου σου· οὐ γὰρ τολμῶ σε καλέσαι τέκνον.

[152] *Vita* B *of Theodoros Stoud.* 46, 300C–301C; *Vita* A *of Theodoros Stoud.* 204B–5C; *Vita* C *of Theodoros Stoud.* 55–56, pp. 290–91. Ignatios Diakonos also alludes to this episode in his *vita* of the patriarch Nikephoros, although he does not mention Thaddaios, see *Vita of Nikephoros* 201; Talbot 1998: 119.

[153] *PmbZ* # 789; *PBE* I: Bardas 30.   [154] *SynaxCP* 353/354,51–355/356,54 (29 December).

[155] Afinogenov 2001: 321. For the writing of a collection of *vitae* by Theodoros Stoudites, see Section 1.1.4.c.

its existence, which is perfectly in keeping with the ideology of Theodoros Stoudites.

(b) Honouring Non-Stoudite Iconophile Monks

According to Theodoros' thinking, the veneration of the ancient saints was as necessary as the imitation of their deeds. But current saints and modern martyrs also had to be imitated, as Theodoros himself asserts when speaking about Domitianos,[156] hence his striving to canonise many of the monks of his confederation. This predilection for praising Stoudite confessors did not preclude praising bishops and abbots from other monasteries who shared Theodoros' ideals and sacrifices for Orthodoxy. Such is the case with Athanasios of Paulopetrion and Michael of Synada, who appear later in the *Synaxarion of Constantinople*.[157]

The life story of Athanasios[158] is similar to that of Theodoros, which helps explain their good relationship. Athanasios had also been born to a rich Constantinopolitan family and decided to take monastic vows at an early age. To do so, he established himself at the monastery of Paulopetrion on the Gulf of Nicomedia, 8 km north of Cape Akritas,[159] where he later became the hegoumenos. Due to his defence of icons, Leon V had him tortured and exiled in spring 816. The place of exile was the fortress of Plateia Petra in Lydia, where Athanasios was visited by another iconodule saint, Petros of Atroa.[160] No doubt he returned with the change of government in 821. During his exile, Athanasios received several letters from Theodoros Stoudites,[161] and after his death in 826, he was praised in the *Parvae catecheseis* 21. Together with other hegoumenoi, Athanasios signed the two letters Theodoros sent to Pope Paschal I in 817 to gain his support for iconophilia. Although the other signatories were the hegoumenoi Makarios of Pelekete, Ioannes of Kathara, Hilarion of Dalmatos, Theophanes of Megas Agros, Theodosios of Pikridion and Ioannes of

---

[156] Theod. Stoud., *Parvae catecheseis* 38,31–34. On the comparison of Palaeo-Christian martyrs with the iconodule confessors in the hagiography of this period, see Ševčenko 1977a: 129.

[157] Athanasios in *SynaxCP* 483,22–36 (22 February). Michael of Synada in *SynaxCP* 703, 2–704,14 (23 May) and 703/704,56 (24 May). There is an unpublished *kanon* in honour of Athanasios of Paulopetrion, see *Tameion*, 170, nr. 510.

[158] *PmbZ* # 678 and # 677; *PBE* I: Athanasios 17 and Athanasios 3; Pargoire 1901b: 355–56; Dobroklonskij 1913: vol. II, 279ff. and 319.

[159] Janin 1975: 53; Ruggieri 1991: 223.   [160] *Vita of Petros of Atroa* 23–26, pp. 119–25.

[161] Theod. Stoud., *epist.* 169, 231, 321 (all were written between 816 and 818). Moreover, he is mentioned in *epist.* 267, 271 and 542. This Athanasios probably was also the recipient of *epist.* 79 in which Theodoros expresses his pride in the suffering he had faced in defence of images.

Eukairia, the Pope did not honour their request.[162] Athanasios of Paulopetrion also displayed a combative attitude towards the iconoclasts, as is confirmed by the letter he sent to the abbot of the monastery of Photeinoudion, who had fallen into heresy.[163]

Theodoros often praises Athanasios along with Michael of Synada, who died shortly afterwards on 23 or 24 March 826. This is mentioned in *epistle* 542 and in *Parvae catecheseis* 21, which was written after Michael's death.[164] After falling ill with a high fever and much pain, Michael died on the third day. Theodoros Stoudites declared that this event needed to be celebrated in a *panêgyris*, since the metropolitan of Synada was a confessor who remained firm. As a result, Michael could now intercede before God in the current situation, in which it was necessary to suffer in defence of Orthodoxy.[165]

Michael of Synada belonged to the circle of the patriarch Tarasios, under whose orders he served first as an *asekretis* and subsequently as a monk, since in 784 he accompanied Theophylaktos of Nicomedia to the monastery founded by Tarasios at the entrance to the Pontus.[166] On their return to Constantinople, they were both installed in Hagia Sophia, where their diligence was such that Tarasios decided to name them bishops.[167] As bishop of Synada (in Phrygia Salutaris), Michael attended all the sessions of the Second Council of Nicaea in 787.[168] Emperor Nikephoros I entrusted him with several diplomatic missions (to Charlemagne in 803 and 811; to Harun al-Rashid in 806),[169] owing to which his confrontation with Emperor Leon V in the imperial palace was particularly significant.[170] As punishment, he was exiled to Eudokias (Phrygia), from where he maintained contact with Niketas of Medikion.[171] After being

---

[162] Theod. Stoud., *epist.* 271 and 272. For the signatories, see Theod. Stoud., *epist.* 267,30–31. On the relationship between Theodoros Stoudites and the Pope, see Van de Vorst 1913c; Lilie 1999: 197. For the previous contacts of Theodoros with Rome, see Dobroklonskij 1913: vol. I, 624–28 and 673–75; Bernardakis 1903: 252–54; Hatlie 1996b.

[163] Theod. Stoud., *epist.* 169,19–20. On this monastery, see Janin 1975: 189; Ruggieri 1991: 224.

[164] Theod. Stoud., *Parvae catecheseis* 21 (= *BHG* 2275): Κατήχησις ΚΑ΄. Περὶ μνήμης θανάτου ἐν ᾧ καὶ περὶ τῆς κοιμήσεως Μιχαὴλ τοῦ ἁγιωτάτου μητροπολίτου Συνάδων.

[165] Theod. Stoud., *Parvae catecheseis* 21,6–11. On the *panêgyris*, see Vryonis 1981.

[166] *PmbZ* # 5042; *PBE* I: Michael 6; Pargoire 1901b: 347–50. The erudition of these high-ranking officials led to the attribution to Michael of Synada of an account on the miracles of St Michael the Archangel (*BHG* 1285–88) in the codex *Vaticanus Gr.* 1259 (thirteenth century), when it is in fact the work of Pantoleon, see Beck 1959: 636 and 800. On the circle of the patriarch Tarasios see Section 1.3.

[167] *Vita A of Theophylaktos of Nicomedia* 5–8.

[168] Mansi XII, 994, 1091 and 1151; Mansi XIII, 137, 189 and 365.

[169] Dölger, *Regesten*, nrs. 361, 366, 385; Treadgold 1988: 145–46.

[170] *Vita of Niketas of Medikion* 34, p. XXV.   [171] *Vita of Niketas of Medikion* 44, p. XXVII (year 815).

transferred to the capital, Michael received a letter from Theodoros Stoudites that encouraged him in his faith and addressed him as most holy and as a champion of Christ.[172] The process of sanctification of the metropolitan of Synada initiated by Theodoros was based on the deeds of Michael as a confessor; this characteristic is precisely the one stressed by the *Synaxarion of Constantinople* and the *Synodikon of Orthodoxy*, which includes him among the metropolitans acclaimed for defending icons,[173] as well as by the *vita* in his honour (*BHG* 2274x) that has come down to us[174] and three unpublished *kanones*.[175]

(c) Verse Compositions

Along with these prose texts, Theodoros Stoudites composed liturgical poetry (hymns, *kanones*, *kontakia*, etc.)[176] to celebrate the annual commemorations of his brave monks or to initiate the process of their sanctification. A *kontakion* survives dedicated to the monks who died during acts of obedience[177] while complying satisfactorily with the obligations of Stoudite monasticism: charity, industriousness, meekness, parrhesia and of course the physical suffering of confessors.[178] Three hymns honouring the hegoumenoi martyr saints have also come down to us.[179] These poems celebrate the memory of abbots who died defending their faith after retreating from the world, living as ascetics, undergoing interrogation and accepting martyrdom. These *kontakia* end by imploring assistance or intercession before Christ; their general nature and lack of detail meant that they could be used in the veneration of both the early saints and the neo-martyrs.

The manuscript *Vaticanus Gr.* 1510, f. 70, includes the first of these compositions on the occasion of the feast day of the Sabaite abbots on 20 March.[180] The final and longest hymn has an epigraph indicating that it was sung on 14 January in honour of the Palestinian fathers of the Sinai and the Rhaithou, who were annihilated in the fifth century by a Saracen raid.[181] On the other hand, a contemporary reading is possible in which

---

[172] Theod. Stoud., *epist.* 364 (c. 817/818). He is also mentioned in *epist.* 533 and 542.
[173] *Synodikon of Orthodoxy* 53,123; cf. Horos of the Synod of 843, p. 297,113; Lauritzen 2017.
[174] Ehrhard 1936–1939: vol. I, 638, n. 7; vol. III, 974, n. 3; Beck 1959: 512; Politis 1968: 363, nr. 93.
[175] *Tameion*, 203–4, nrs. 617–19.   [176] Wellesz 1961; Wolfram 2003; Demoen 2019.
[177] Κοντάκιον εἰς κοιμηθέντας μοναχοὺς ἐν ὑποταγῇ, edited by Pitra, *Analecta*, pp. 373–77.
[178] The sixth verse summarises perfectly the spirit of the composition: Θεσπεσίους ἀγῶνας ἐτέλεσας, ὑπηκόων ἀνύσας τὸ στάδιον, ὑποδὺς γὰρ θερμῶς ἐν τοῖς σκάμμασιν, ἐναθλῶν κατωθεὶς ἐπιθυμίαν, ἐν ᾗ κατῄσχυνας τὸν δράκοντα, τὸν αὐχένα ὑπέκλινας τῷ σαυτοῦ ποιμένι, μέχρι τέλους αὐτῷ συνεχόμενος.
[179] Pitra, *Analecta*, pp. 605–8.   [180] *SynaxCP* 549, 56–57. Cf. *SynaxCP* 548, 19–37 (19 March).
[181] *SynaxCP* 389, 16–391,17.

these *enkomia* are taken to refer to hegoumenoi who like Theodoros valiantly confronted the iconoclast heretics and whose veneration as saints he frequently encourages in his letters. Nothing in the text forbids this, but we have lost the original context. Fortunately, however, an interesting parallel allows us to reproduce the scenario and the reasons for these works. The *Messanensis Gr.* 153 codex includes in folios 127v–33 a *kanon* written by Theodoros to honour a dead monk.[182] From his verses, we know that this man renounced the world, lived as an ascetic and cultivated obedience. After exercising parrhesia during the conflicts, he received the martyrs' crown and now enjoyed the Kingdom of Heaven. No element in the poem identifies the hero with an iconodule saint or places his life within the context of the Second Iconoclasm. But Theodoros' declaration that he would attempt, God willing, to compose a *kanon* in honour of the Stoudite Iakobos who had recently died (so that it could be read by all the brothers of the federation) reveals the true intentions of the hegoumenos of Stoudios.[183]

Since childhood, Iakobos had aspired to the ascetic life of monasticism,[184] to which end he trained as a disciple of Theodoros himself.[185] During the persecution by Leon V, he was one of the monks led by Thaddaios,[186] which meant he suffered torture for defending the images to the point of being left for dead. As a result of these beatings, he was permanently disabled until he died in ca. 824, after having predicted his own passing.[187] The hegoumenos of Stoudios encouraged veneration of Iakobos by dedicating one of his sermons to him[188] and describing his martyrdom in detail in *epist.* 441. In this letter, Theodoros begins by lamenting the loss of Iakobos and goes on to offer a true panegyric: ever since his youth, Iakobos was inclined towards the spiritual life. He remained a virgin and led an ascetic lifestyle extreme enough to surprise those who saw him or heard his words. He did not hesitate to fight heresy as a soldier of Christ with no fear or doubts (ll. 21–22). The account of the

---

[182] Magrí 1971; 1978/1979.
[183] Theod. Stoud., *epist.* 441,50–53: περὶ τοῦ τιμίου αὐτοῦ λειψάνου, ὡς γέγραφα περὶ κανόνος, εἰ εὐδοκεῖ Κύριος, ποιήσω. ἀσπάσασθε ἀλλήλους ἐν φιλήματι ἁγίῳ· καὶ γὰρ πᾶσι τοῖς ἀδελφοῖς ἀναγνωστέον. The identification of this *kanon* for Iakobos with that he wrote for an anonymous monk was pointed out by Faturos, see Theod. Stoud., *epist.*, p. 38*, nr. 31.
[184] *PmbZ* # 2632; *PBE* I: Iakobos 14; Dobroklonskij 1913: vol. II, 295ff.
[185] He received, in fact, two missives from Theodoros: Theod. Stoud., *epist.* 189 and 328. He is also mentioned in *epist.* 186, 190, 195, 199 and 441.
[186] Theod. Stoud., *epist.* 186.   [187] Theod. Stoud., *epist.* 441,39–40.
[188] Theod. Stoud., *Parvae catecheseis* 115: Κατήχησις ΡΙΕ'. Περὶ μνήμης θανάτου καὶ τῆς κοιμήσεως ἀδελφοῦ Ἰακώβου καὶ περὶ μετανοίας. Cf. also Theod. Stoud., *Parvae catecheseis* 133,45.

confession Theodoros offers is rich in nuance; although it offers no bloody details, it does testify to his martyrdom in defence of icons (ll. 22–39). Theodoros Stoudites describes the massive funeral of the saint and goes on to affirm that Iakobos is now in heaven with the other martyrs, as a consequence of which he encourages his brothers to pray for him and implore his assistance (ll. 41–50).

Theodoros' success in promoting the cult of Iakobos can be seen in the various versions of the biography about the hegoumenos of Stoudios, since Iakobos' sacrifice meant that he was remembered as one of the most loyal followers of Theodoros to suffer together with their leader under Leon V.[189] Now that he had become a point of reference of the Stoudite confederation, its monks celebrated his feast day on 28 June each year with an entry in their lectionaries to remember his veneration of icons, his confession and his martyrdom, in addition to his Slavic origin and his affiliation to the monastery of Stoudios. This is shown by the *menologion* included in the two lectionaries that reflect the Stoudite tradition with the peculiarities of its feast day calendar: *Parisinus Gr.* 382, of the late tenth century, and the Venezia, *Marcianus Gr.* II 115, of the eleventh-twelfth centuries.[190] The high regard Theodoros had for Iakobos led him to affirm that he was a confessor of Christ, a martyr and a saint,[191] and Iakobos Stoudites is in fact the only contemporary saint of the Second Iconoclasm for whom a liturgical *kanon* signed by Theodoros Stoudites survives.[192] The dedication of this *kanon* to Iakobos is particularly significant if we also take into account that the other neo-martyr saint to whom Theodoros dedicates a hymn is none other than Stephanos the Younger, the iconodule martyr of the First Iconoclasm par excellence. This hymn is a liturgical *idiomelon* (i.e., of original and unique music)[193] preserved as part of the

---

[189] *Vita B of Theodoros Stoud.* 46, 301D: ὁ καρτερικώτατος Ἰάκωβος; *Vita A of Theodoros Stoud.* 205C; *Vita C of Theodoros Stoud.* 56, p. 291.

[190] Τῇ αὐτῇ ἡμέρᾳ (i.e., 28 June) τοῦ ὁσίου καὶ ὁμολογητοῦ Ἰακώβου μοναχοῦ τῶν Στουδίου τῷ γένει σκλάβος τυπτόμενος διὰ τὴν προσκύνησιν τῶν τιμίων εἰκόνων ἐκοιμήθη. Ζήτει τῇ ἀκολουθίᾳ εἰς ὁσίους (*Parisinus Gr.* 382, fol. 253v; *Marcianus Gr.* II 115, fol. 265v). On these *menologia*, see Andreou 2005: esp. 14–15 and 2008: esp. 37–38.

[191] Theod. Stoud., *epist.* 441,3: Ἰακώβου τοῦ ὁμολογητοῦ Χριστοῦ. Theod. Stoud., *epist.* 441,9–10: τί γὰρ οἴει τὸν ἄνδρα; ἀλλ' οὐχ ὁμολογητήν; ἀλλ' οὐχὶ μάρτυρα; ἀλλ' οὐχ ὅσιον;

[192] The remaining calendars of saints' days only commemorate a confessor named Iakobos, but they add that he came to be a bishop. We are not concerned, therefore, with the same person but with his namesake the bishop of Anchialos in Thrace, see *SynaxCP* 558, 2–9 (24 March) and 551/552, 42–54 (21 March); *Menologion Basilii* 361D–63A. He is equally remembered in the *Synaxarion Evergetis* II, 28. On this other confessor, see *PmbZ* # 2637; *PBE* I: Iakobos 16; Efthymiadis 1995: 146–48; Prieto Domínguez 2016b.

[193] Sixteen *idiomela* hymns written by Theodoros have come down to us, see Theod. Stoud., *epist.*, pp. 33*–34*.

November *menaion*,[194] the liturgical book that contains the variable parts of the daily liturgy. The martyrdom of Stephanos the Younger, whom Theodoros Stoudites considered his 'holy father', is remembered on 28 November[195] and probably represented a Stoudite response to the decision taken by the patriarchate to commission the *vita* of Stephanos the Younger (*BHG* 1666) in ca. 809 by Stephanos Diakonos in order to bring together different monastic factions against Stoudios.[196]

In addition to these two verse compositions devoted to contemporary saints, a third with an important political background survives: the hymn dedicated to other recent martyrs, the soldiers of Emperor Nikephoros I murdered in Bulgaria.[197] This unhappy event was later remembered in liturgical books, and we have a record of its commemoration in Stoudite monasteries.[198] In addition, we know that Theodoros composed many similar pieces, along with more extensive works in the form of *vitae*. The abbot of Stoudios himself clearly affirms this in letters addressed to Naukratios, his future successor. One of these is *epist*. 405, which was accompanied by hagiographical texts, which he urges his correspondent to disseminate and keep hidden in a safe place, to prevent them from being destroyed or used against him by the iconoclast authorities.[199]

Although these 'speeches and lives of our brothers written in rhythmical verse' (λόγοι καὶ βίοι τῶν ἀδελφῶν ἐμμέτροις στίχοις) might be identified with the iambic epigrams already mentioned, their editor, Speck, emphatically rejects this idea and considers this an epic *enkomion* in honour of a Stoudite monk put to the test by persecution.[200] According to the words of Theodoros, 'the small book and the fourteen quires' (Βιβλιδάκιον καὶ

---

[194] *Menaion of Bartholomaios*, p. 206; Theod. Stoud., *epist*., p. 34*, nr. XII.
[195] *SynaxCP* 261,24–63,19.
[196] Auzépy 1997: 41. For the intertextual dialogue between the *vita* of Stephanos the Younger and the writings of Theodoros Stoudites, see Hatlie 1998.
[197] Follieri and Dujcev 1963: 71–75; Tomadakes 1971a; Haldon 2017.
[198] As can be seen in the lectionaries including the mss. *Parisinus Gr*. 382, fol. 259r, and *Marcianus Gr*. II 115, fol. 271r, see Andreou 2008: 38–39.
[199] Theod. Stoud., *epist*. 405,28–34: Ἀπέσταλκά σοι βιβλιδάκιον καὶ τετράδας δεκατέσσαρας, ἐφ' οἷς εἰσι λόγοι καὶ βίοι τῶν ἀδελφῶν ἐμμέτροις στίχοις· ἅπερ ἀναγνοὺς αὐτός τε καί τινες τῶν πιστῶν ἀδελφῶν ἀσφαλῶς κατάκρυψον. οὐδὲν οὖν ποιῶ, ἀδελφέ, ἄξιον λόγου· ἀλλ' ἐπειδὴ εὐκαιρῶ καὶ ἐπειδὴ νύσσομαι ὡς ὑπὸ τοῦ ἁγίου μου πατρός, ἀκούων τε πάλιν τοῦ θείου Παύλου λέγοντος τῷ ἁγίῳ Τιμοθέῳ, μὴ ἀμέλει τοῦ ἐν σοὶ χαρίσματος, ὡς ἀνάξιος μετὰ φόβου καὶ τρόμου ποιῶ ἃ ποιῶ. 'I have sent you a small book and fourteen quires, containing discourses and lives of our brothers in verse. Once they have been read by yourself and some of the trustworthy brothers, hide them safely. Nothing of my work, brother, is worth mentioning. But since I have the opportunity and so was spured by my holy father, and listening once more to the divine Paul who says to the holy Timothy "do not neglect the gift in you" (1 Tim 4: 14), as an unworthy man, with fear and trembling, I do what I do.'
[200] Speck 1964: 31–32. Cf. Theod. Stoud., *epist*., p. 37*, nr. 28; Speck 1987b: 570.

τετράδες δεκατέσσαρες) contained discourses (perhaps in prose) and verses on the lives of iconodule monks. This was perhaps one of his original writings, which tend to ignore literary conventions and established genres, combining prose and poetry in the same work, as in his *Refutatio* of the iconoclast poems of Ioannes Grammatikos, Ignatios (Diakonos?), Sergios and Stephanos Kapetolites, in which Theodoros Stoudites mixes theological criticism in prose with ten short poems.[201] Or perhaps this was a manuscript in which liturgical poems such as those preserved were juxtaposed with hagiographies in the strict sense. If so, one of these *vitae* is no doubt the one dedicated to Thaddaios, the first version of which goes back to this period. It is also reasonable to consider them as brief biographical sketches, such as those found later in the *synaxaria*. This may be the origin of several entries of close collaborators of Theodoros later included in the *Synaxarion*, such as Athanasios of Paulopetrion,[202] Ioannes of Kathara,[203] Ioannes of Chalcedon,[204] and Petros of Nicaea.[205]

Be all that as it may, the function of these texts is clearly the same as that of hagiographical accounts. Indeed, the references to these writings by Theodoros in his own correspondence show that these texts circulated regularly, since their author wished to share them with his circle and did not hesitate to ask its members to disseminate and copy them for their preservation. In *epist.* 152, therefore, he mentions a 'quire' (τετράδιον) containing a work Theodoros had written in shorthand, but which had already been transcribed so that it could be read.[206] In the following letter, *epist.* 153, Theodoros asks Naukratios to transcribe the text he is sending him to allow it to escape iconoclast persecution.[207] In effect, the dissemination of these literary works among the members of a persecuted community, dispersed to the remotest parts of the empire and beyond

---

[201] Theod. Stoud., *epist.* 356; Grossu 1907: 192ff.; Speck 1987b: 570 and 576, n. 73. See Introduction.
[202] *SynaxCP* 483,22–36 (22 February).
[203] *SynaxCP* 444,38–40 (4 February); 631,41–34,46 (27 April = *BHG* 2184n). The death of this important hegoumenos of the Stoudite federation was on 27 April. The repetition of his feast day on 4 February, accordingly, seems to be due to the great celebration of Nikolaos Stoudites on that day (*SynaxCP* 443, 32–44,37). On Ioannes of Kathara, see *PmbZ* # 3139; *PBE* I: Ioannes 460; Costa-Louillet 1954–1955: 241–44; Stiernon 1970; Cheynet and Flusin 1990: 205–7. Theod. Stoud., *epist.* 267, 271, 272, 365. Moreover, Ioannes of Kathara signed the two missives sent to Pope Paschal in favour of iconophilia (Theod. Stoud., *epist.* 271 and 272).
[204] *SynaxCP* 830,39–40 (19 July); 853,54 (29 July). Theodoros dedicated numerous *enkomia* to him in his *Parvae catequeseis* 22 (*BHG* 2185). Concerning Ioannes of Chalcedon, see *PmbZ* # 3205; *PBE* I: Ioannes 439.
[205] *SynaxCP* 33,35 (10 September); 36,16–18 (11 September); 37,60 (13 September). On Petros of Nicaea, see *PmbZ* # 6067; *PBE* I: Petros 49.
[206] Theod. Stoud., *epist.* 152,47–56.   [207] Theod. Stoud., *epist.* 153,29–32.

72   The Stoudite Milieu

(Palestine, Rome, etc.) and in need of an ideological discourse to unite them as a group and strengthen them spiritually, was as necessary as the act of writing them. Given this scenario, these hagiographical texts in all their forms complied perfectly with the objectives of each of the parties and became mainstays of the politico-religious enterprise of the hegoumenos of Stoudios.

1.2   Promoting Veneration of Theodoros Stoudites: The *Vitae*

1.2.1   First Texts in Honour of Theodoros Stoudites

After the death of Theodoros on 11 November 826, his disciple and successor at the head of the Stoudite congregation, Naukratios,[208] sent an encyclical letter to its brothers dispersed throughout the empire due to the iconoclastic persecution (*BHG* 1756). What needed to be only a brief statement notifying them of the death of their leader became a true *enkomion* of a hagiographical nature.[209] The text relates in great detail the saint's final days and his death and funeral, making this *Encyclica de obitu* one source of Theodoros' future *vita*.[210] Due to a disease of the stomach aggravated by his periods in exile and his imprisonments,[211] Theodoros was hardly eating anything, which gave him a cadaverous appearance and forced him to stay in bed from 1–3 November owing to a sudden worsening of his condition. Theodoros tried to continue with his daily activities but, being incapable of teaching his famous catecheseis, he was forced to dictate the last of them.[212] On the night of 6 November, his pain was such that he woke up the monk sleeping near his cell. On the following day, he called the monks together in the morning to pronounce his final words in public[213] and to grant a general pardon to all those present. The news that the death of the hegoumenos was imminent spread like wildfire, and a crowd began to congregate around him on Prinkipos, the largest of the nine so-called Princes' Islands in the Sea of Marmara. Theodoros received each of them, until on the following Sunday (11 November), the day of St Menas, he felt weak and expired. Naukratios tells us the exact time of his death, using a timing indicator

---

[208] *PmbZ* # 5230; *PBE* I: Naukratios 1; Doens and Hannick 1973; Maksimovic 2000.
[209] Delouis 2008a.   [210] Vita B *of Theodoros Stoud.* 66,324D–25A.
[211] On the disease of Theodoros, see Cholij 2002: 63, n. 375.
[212] Naukratios includes it in his *Encyclica de obitu* 1837–41. It was subsequently featured in the collection of *Parvae catecheseis* under number 31.
[213] Naukratios, *Encyclica de obitu* 1844A–B.

that could easily be identified by his brothers in the monastic federation: at the sixth hour after lighting the candles, Psalm 119 (118) was read. At verse 93, Theodoros delivered his soul to the angels.[214] This precision is unusual in hagiography of any period. In a sense, it contravenes the literary principles of both epistolography and hagiography, and brings the text closer to documentary biography.

What occurred, according to Naukratios, at the moment of Theodoros' death, is particularly relevant in a literary context: a *Psalm*, that is, a poem praising God, was sung. This was not just any *Psalm*, but Psalm 118, the longest in the psalter, the reading of which is generally reserved for the Μεσονυκτικόν (Midnight Liturgy), Παννυχίδες (vigils) or κηδείες (funerals). The atmosphere was thus already mournful, and preparations for the death of the abbot were afoot. The precise moment of death, hard to determine scientifically in 826, probably corresponds to the point at which the passing was confirmed. One of the monks could have confirmed the event shortly beforehand, but the Psalm continued. We cannot pinpoint the motive for the detail given by Naukratios, but there must have been one. The verse he claims marked the passing to eternal life of Theodoros Stoudites reads as follows: εἰς τὸν αἰῶνα οὐ μὴ ἐπιλάθωμαι τῶν δικαιωμάτων σου, ὅτι ἐν αὐτοῖς ἔζησάς με, 'I will never forget thy precepts: for with them thou hast quickened me.' It is curious that Naukratios did not choose the following verse, which has a clear salvational and eschatological nature appropriate for imploring the salvation of a dead man's soul,[215] but the former, which has a more worldly interpretation and looks to the living who remain in this world. From them comes the obligation to observe the divine precepts.

Naukratios' choice perfectly illustrates the purpose of his encyclical to the Stoudite community and why he took the initiative in the process of the sanctification of Theodoros: his motivations were internal. His wish to strengthen his position at the head of the confederation as the successor to the deceased hegoumenos led him to demand from his brothers absolute obedience to the will of Theodoros, which according to his account confirmed him as the Stoudios leader after a vote by the monks that served to undermine the appointment of Kalogeros, which had caused controversy in the past.[216] Evidently, the rules dictated by the now sanctified

---

[214] Naukratios, *Encyclica de obitu* 1845.
[215] σός εἰμι ἐγώ, σῶσόν με, ὅτι τὰ δικαιώματά σου ἐξεζήτησα, 'I am thine, save me: for I have sought thy precepts'.
[216] Delouis 2008a: 184–86. On the monk Kalogeros, see *PmbZ* # 3612; *PBE* I: Kalogeros 1.

Theodoros had become divine. But the hegoumenos had not put this down in writing, and Naukratios was aware that this was one of the main demands of the other monks.[217] To achieve this, he did not hesitate to contribute towards the (re)creation of the texts and their dissemination as authentic. The *Testament of Theodoros Stoudites* (*BHG* 1759), which postdates the encyclical epistle of Naukratios, thus arose from the combination of fragments of texts written by the hegoumenos, which were preserved in a literal sense, but in a new context adapted to the change of government after his death.[218] For their part, the Stoudite regulations (*hypotyposis* or rule)[219] twice mention Theodoros as having passed, showing that they must post-date his death, even when their guidelines are faithfully reproduced, as is confirmed by the *Catecheseis*.[220]

The spiritual (and perhaps even material) authorship of these texts is unquestionably to be attributed to Naukratios, who likewise undertook between 826 and 842 to supervise the establishment of the corpus of Theodoros Stoudites' most important work for the confederation: the *Parvae catecheseis*.[221] This took place in any case before his death in the year 868. In this way, Naukratios made his encyclical and the *Testament* of Theodoros a kind of paratext of the *Parvae catecheseis*, intended to strengthen the monastic message of his predecessor and bring together his brothers with a document that made him the legitimate hegoumenos of the Stoudite confederation. The encyclical of Naukratios contributed to

---

[217] Naukratios, *Encyclica de obitu* 1836: τίς τε ἡ διαθήκη, καὶ διάταξις.
[218] English translation of the *Testament* in Thomas et al. 2000: vol. 1, 67–83. For Naukratios' authorship, see Delouis 2008a: 190.
[219] Two ancient versions have survived, both translated into English in Thomas et al. 2000: vol. 1, 84–119.
[220] Theod. Stoud., *Rule* 1704B: Θεοῦ δηλαδὴ παρέχοντος ἡμῖν ταῖς τοῦ ποιμένος ὑπὲρ ἡμῶν προσευχαῖς τὴν κατάλληλον ἁρμογὴν τῆς τοῦ λόγου συνθέσεως, εἰς τὸ ἐκθέσθαι ὑγιῶς τὰ ὀνησιφόρα τε καὶ σωτήρια τοῦ θεοφόρου Πατρὸς ἡμῶν ἐντάλματα, 'For, clearly, through our shepherd's prayers on our behalf, God provides us the appropriate style in composing this treatise in order to present in a sound fashion the helpful and salutary precepts of our inspired father.' Theod. Stoud., *Rule* 1709C: Χρὴ γινώσκειν ὅτι δ΄ καὶ Παρασκευῇ καὶ Κυριακῇ, τῶν ἀδελφῶν ἱσταμένων μετὰ πάσης εὐλαβείας, μετὰ τὴν ἀπόλυσιν τοῦ ὄρθρου ἀναγινώσκεται ἡ κατήχησις τοῦ θεοφόρου Πατρὸς ἡμῶν Θεοδώρου. Εἶτα λέγει καὶ τὰ παρ᾽ ἑαυτοῦ ὁ ἡγούμενος νουθετῶν τοὺς ἀδελφούς. Καὶ μετὰ τὴν συμπλήρωσιν τῆς κατηχήσεως, δοξάζουσιν, καὶ λέγεται τὸ Πάτερ ἡμῶν, καὶ εὐλογεῖτε, ἅγιοι, εὐλόγησον, Πάτερ, καὶ ἀπολύει. Οὕτως καθόλου τοῦ ἐνιαυτοῦ, 'It should be known that on Fridays and Sundays, the Catechesis of our God-bearing father Theodoros is read after the dismissal of matins, while the brothers stand with all reverence. Thereupon, the superior imparts his own [thoughts] to instruct the brothers. After this Catechesis is completed, they say the doxology together with the "Our Father" and the "Bless, O holy ones, bless O father." Then they are dismissed. This is the order throughout the whole year.'
[221] According to Leroy 1958b: 342.

the sanctification of Theodoros Stoudites, and the clarifications it contained regarding his life and the circumstances of his death were used to draw up brief hagiographical reports designed to perpetuate his memory. This is the case of the *Epigram in Honour of the Confessor Theodoros, Hegoumenos of Stoudios* (*BHG* 1758). Shortly afterwards came the entries celebrating his feast day in the various *synaxaria*[222] and liturgical poetry, as is proven by the extant *kanon* in honour of Theodoros, in which he is glorified together with the Palaeo-Christian martyrs Menas, Victor, Vicentius and Stephanides.[223]

When, after the Triumph of Orthodoxy on 26 January 844, his relics were transferred to Constantinople, a new occasion arose to celebrate the hegoumenos. The anonymous description of this event (*BHG* 1756t) not only relates how the remains of Theodoros and his brother Ioseph of Thessaloniki were transferred to the monastery of Stoudios, but also constitutes a further stage in the sanctification process of both men.[224] According to the hagiographical account, the transfer was possible thanks to the involvement of Naukratios and his pleas to Theodora and Michael III.[225] After the death of the iconoclast Theophilos, Naukratios returned from exile to take charge of the monastery of Stoudios,[226] and it is only logical that one of his first measures was to bring the remains of his master and predecessor back to the capital. In this enterprise, he had the assistance of the hegoumenos of Sakkoudion, Athanasios,[227] together with whom he would lead the Stoudites in important confrontations with the patriarchate, as well as of other leaders in the fight against iconoclasm, such as St Ioannikios.[228] Before these disagreements broke out, the transfer of Theodoros' relics was approved by the imperial and ecclesiastic governors. Indeed, the patriarch Methodios himself played a leading role, for not only did he pay homage to the saint in his new location, but he also wished to

---

[222] *SynaxCP* 213/214,37–215/216,34; 214,6–216,8 (11 November); 209/210,28 (10 November); 444,3f.; 819/820,36; *Menologion Basilii* 156A–C (11 November); *Typikon of the Great Church* I, 98, 15f. (11 November); *Synaxarion Evergetis* I, 186–88 (11 November).

[223] *AHG*, vol. III, 318–30 (11 November), and 600–602; *Vita B of Theodoros Stoud.* 233B. There are also two unpublished *kanones* dedicated only to Theodoros Stoudites, *Tameion*, 90–91, nrs. 220–21; Tsigkos 2001.

[224] *Translation of Theodoros of Stoudios and Ioseph of Thessaloniki* 27–62. See also *Vita B of Theodoros Stoud.* 328A; *Vita C of Theodoros Stoud.* 81; *Vita of Nikolaos Stoud.* 904B.

[225] *Translation of Theodoros Stoud. and Ioseph* 8.   [226] *Vita of Nikolaos Stoud.* 901C–D.

[227] *PmbZ* # 675; *PBE* I: Athanasios 8.

[228] On the confrontation with Methodios, see Von Dobschütz 1909a; Grumel 1935; Doens and Hannick 1973; Löwe 1982; Darrouzès 1987; Lilie 1999: 248–60; Maksimovic 2000. For the dissensions with Ioannikios, see *Vita of Ioannikios by Petros* 57 and 69–70.

cover his perfectly preserved body with priestly vestments.[229] Theodoros' inclusion in the *Synodikon of Orthodoxy* (*BHG* 1392) must be understood in this atmosphere of iconodule fervour and the vindication of the Stoudite leader.[230]

The date was certainly not chosen at random. On the next day, the Church was celebrating the translation to Constantinople of the remains of St John Chrysostom, the fourth-century archbishop, who was thus made to resemble Theodoros. With the aim of rendering this event as significant as possible, Naukratios and Athanasios made the arrival in Constantinople of Theodoros' relics coincide with that of the remains of his brother Ioseph of Thessaloniki,[231] which at their request had been discovered in Thessaly. According to the text, only a few bones and some dust were found,[232] since the body had been abandoned in a humid wooded area rather than being decently buried. The remains of Theodoros and Ioseph were deposited in the same sarcophagus as their uncle Platon, in a prominent place in the narthex of the church of St John the Forerunner of the monastery of Stoudios. The first part of the text (chs. 2–6) takes the form of an *enkomion* that reviews the biography of Theodoros to provide the necessary material for his veneration, insisting on his Orthodoxy and his holiness, together with his many sufferings in reforming monasticism and defending the veneration of images; there is even a mention of the miracles he performed after returning from exile.[233] The text also includes an example of the homage paid Theodoros by his devotees in the form of the hymns of praise they sang in his honour during the sea voyage when they accompanied the body to Constantinople.[234]

The account of this transfer was written shortly afterwards, on the occasion of an anniversary, which we assume was celebrated officially every year by the Stoudite confederation. The treatment given Naukratios, who is referred to as a θεῖος (saint) on several occasions,[235] yields a *post quem* date: 8 April 848, the day of his death. The account may have been written the following year, in 849. In any case, this occurred not long after the event, since the author is a Stoudite monk who clearly witnessed the

---

[229] *Translation of Theodoros Stoud. and Ioseph* 12.
[230] *Synodikon of Orthodoxy* 53, line 127: Θεοδώρου τοῦ πανοσίου ἡγουμένου τῶν Στουδίου αἰωνία ἡ μνήμη.
[231] *Translation of Theodoros Stoud. and Ioseph* 13–14.
[232] Ἀθανάσιος καὶ Ναυκράτιος οἱ μνημονευθέντες λάθρᾳ πως καὶ ἀσυμφανῶς ἐν ὀλίγοις ὀστέοις καὶ κόνει βραχείᾳ τὸν τούτου συλλέξαι νεκρόν. On the process of his sanctification, see Section 1.3.
[233] *Translation of Theodoros Stoud. and Ioseph* 6: ὃς καὶ ἀνὰ τὴν ὁδὸν διϊὼν πολλὰς μὲν εἰργάζετο τὰς θεοσημείας, πολλὰ δ' ἔπραττεν ἄλλα πρὸς ὠφέλειαν τῶν συνόντων.
[234] *Translation of Theodoros Stoud. and Ioseph* 11.   [235] *Translation of Theodoros Stoud. and Ioseph* 8.

transfer of the relics of Theodoros and lived for some time under the authority of Naukratios.[236] This narration also aims to consolidate the sanctification of Naukratios himself as soon as he was dead: not without reason, he too was buried in the church of the monastery of Stoudios, is referred to as a θεῖος and was celebrated in the same way he celebrated his master. An anonymous author praised his work in three elegiac distichs that have survived under the name of *Stichelegeia* 'στιχελεγεῖα' (*BHG* 1756a).

Moreover, the positive picture offered of Methodios, who died a few months before Naukratios, indicates that the conflict of the monastery of Stoudios with the patriarchate was coming to an end and that a compromise was being sought with its leader (probably at the beginning of the mandate of the new patriarch, Ignatios). Indeed, after the confrontations with Methodios, a new text appeared, the *Narratio de sanctis patriarchis Tarasio et Nicephoro* (= *De schismate Studitarum*, *BHG* 1757), which describes the position of Theodoros Stoudites during the Moechian controversy. The hegoumenos is praised as a saint and a committed defender of Orthodoxy against the whims of the emperor and the accommodating solutions of the patriarchs Tarasios and Nikephoros. The final words of Methodios to the Stoudites portray the restoring patriarch as a dictator and serve to justify the loss of influence of the confederation in the public life of Constantinople: Σὺ μοναχὸς εἶ, καὶ οὐκ ἔξεστί σοι ἐξετάζειν τὰ τῶν ἱερῶν, ἀλλ' ὑποτάσσεσθαί σε χρὴ, καὶ οὐχ ὑποτάσσειν οὐδὲ ἐξετάζειν αὐτούς. 'Thou art a monk and it is not thy place to interfere in the matters of priests; thou must obey and not undermine or question others.' Despite this, the monastery of Stoudios clearly attempted to play a part in the official account of post-iconoclast society, as the composition of a *kanon* to celebration the restoration of images (Κανὼν εἰς τὴν ἀναστήλωσιν τῶν ἁγίων εἰκόνων) shows. The manuscripts attribute this work to Theodoros Stoudites, but it is obviously by one of his disciples who survived to see the Triumph of Orthodoxy.[237] It is a narrative poem that attacks iconoclast heretics and denounces their errors, while at the same time iconodule confessors are praised for having withstood cruel tortures in defence of images.

---

[236] *Translation of Theodoros Stoud. and Ioseph* 8: Ναυκρατίῳ, τῷ ἡμετέρῳ φημὶ ποιμένι καὶ τοῦ πατρὸς διαδόχῳ.
[237] Kazhdan 1999: 262. For Gouillard 1961a: 380 the author of this *kanon* is none other than the patriarch Methodios, but the presence of a version of this text in the manuscript *Parisinus Gr.* 1104, eleventh century, which contains the *Catecheseis* of Theodoros Stoudites, suggests a Stoudite author, Halkin 1968: 112.

1.2.2 The Vitae of Theodoros Stoudites

The memory of Theodoros Stoudites was also celebrated by at least five different *vitae*. Certain traditional hagiographical motifs (such as miracles) are played down in these in favour of more desirable characteristics of Theodoros, such as his political side and his reform of monasticism. The first *vita* of which we have a record was written before 847 by none other than the patriarch Methodios in the final years of his life.[238] This hagiography has not survived, but we know that it served as a model for *Vita* B of Theodoros Stoudites (*BHG* 1754), which was composed by the Stoudite monk Michael, as the preface makes clear. Michael Monachos[239] was a prolific author who wrote mainly about iconoclasm and confessor heroes (see Section 5.2.2), displaying a hierarchical reverence for Theodoros as a consequence of his years as a monk in one of the monasteries of the Stoudite federation.[240] In this case, he followed his model faithfully, taking inspiration from the funeral speeches (especially that of Platon of Sakkoudion)[241] and carrying out a *metaphrasis* that insisted above all on matters of style rather than content, with the intention of making the text accessible to a less educated audience. The previous text by Methodios must have been unintelligible to most of the monks who took vows at Stoudios due to its pompous style, theological digressions, rhetoric and recherché vocabulary.[242]

We know that Michael wrote his *vita* after the death of Nikolaos Stoudites, the hegoumenos of Stoudios, in the year 868.[243] The exact date, however, is still subject to debate.[244] In any case, he wrote at the request of the Stoudite community, in order to adapt the hagiography to new social requirements and the new literary genres popular at the time.[245]

---

[238] Krausmüller 2006; Krausmüller 2013a. Methodios also dedicated a liturgical hymn to him, Pentkovskij 2001: 293–94. For the meaning of this *vita* in Methodian production, see Section 2.1.4.
[239] *PmbZ* # 5121 and 25099; *PBE* I: Michael 128.
[240] *Vita* B *of Theodoros Stoud.* 233A: ὁ τοῦ καθ' ἡμᾶς συλλόγου πεφηνὼς ποιμενάρχης.
[241] Pratsch 1998: 8.   [242] Krausmüller 2006; Hinterberger 2008: esp. 132.
[243] Nikolaos Stoudites is mentioned as μακαρίτης or 'blessed': *Vita* B *of Theodoros Stoud.* 42,296C; Kazhdan 1999: 235–36. See also the allusion to the journey to Sardinia made by the disciples of Gregorios of Syracuse, who died after 861, after mocking Theodoros Stoudites' hymns, *Vita* B *of Theodoros Stoud.* 56,312D.
[244] For Matantseva 1996a: 123–24 this occurred in the late ninth century. For Krausmüller 2013a: 287 it was the early tenth century.
[245] *Vita* B *of Theodoros Stoud.* 236A–B: ἀλλ' ἐπεὶ **τὸ κοινὸν τῆς ἀδελφότητος** καὶ ἡ τῶν πολλῶν διάνοια μικρὰ βλέπουσα, ὡς τὰ πολλά, τὸ πεζόν καὶ ἁπλοϊκώτερον τῆς φράσεως προτιμᾶν ἐπίσταται, ὡς ἀνύστακτον συντηροῦν τὸν ἐπόπτην τῶν λεγομένων νοῦν, καὶ ὄνησιν ἐμποιοῦν

It can readily be supposed that Michael also added some material not included by Methodios, such as the accounts of the miracles performed by Theodoros that were remembered at the monastery of Stoudios. These included in particular those he performed during his lifetime and which were echoed by the hegoumenos Sophronios, who was chosen by Nikolaos Stoudites to succeed him in 851 during his ascetic retreat.[246]

The *Vita* B was written during the hegoumenate of Anatolios (the abbot of Stoudios from 886 to 916)[247] along with other outstanding works of Stoudite hagiography such as the *vitae* of Blasios of Amorion (*BHG* 278)[248] and Nikolaos Stoudites (*BHG* 1365),[249] in addition to the *menologion Vaticanus Gr.* 1660. All of these clearly aim to create an identity and vindicate the values of Stoudite monasticism; they insist both on praising their spiritual father Theodoros and on proclaiming that his legacy is alive and well. Only in this light can we understand the poem Dionysios[250] wrote between 886 and 916 to honour Theodoros Stoudites (*BHG* 1758d).[251] The work consists of thirty-one dactylic hexameters and praises two hegoumenoi of the monastery of Stoudios, Theodoros (vv. 1–18) and Anatolios (vv. 19–31), who is compared to the famous abbot. In contrast to the iambic trimeters characteristic of the poetry of Theodoros Stoudites, Dionysios chose dactyls, a metre used more often after the restoration of icons by authors such as Ignatios Diakonos, Anastasios Traulos, Arethas, Theophanes and Kometas.[252]

A new hagiography of Theodoros Stoudites appeared shortly afterwards, the anonymous *Vita* C (*BHG* 1755d), which has been attributed to another monk of the monastery of Stoudios.[253] *Vita* A (*BHG* 1755) also

---

ταῖς σφῶν αὐτῶν ὑπὲρ τὸ σκληρὸν καὶ βαθύγλωσσον τῶν νοημάτων ψυχαῖς, φέρε **ταῖς ὑμετέραις πειθαρχήσαντες ἐντολαῖς, πατέρων αἰδεσιμώτατοι**, τοὺς περὶ τοῦ θείου τούτου προπάτορος ἡμῶν καὶ πανσόφου διδασκάλου τῆς οἰκουμένης λόγους καὶ ἡμεῖς οἱ ταπεινοὶ καὶ οὐδενὸς λόγου ἄξιοι, ὡς οἷόν τε καταθώμεθα· πολὺ μὲν κατόπιν τοῦ πρὸς ἀξίαν ἰόντας, ὡς ἐνὸν δὲ τῇ ἀσθενείᾳ ἡμῶν πρὸς τὸ εὐλη πτόν τε καὶ καταφανὲς μεταποιούμενος.

[246] *PmbZ* # 6848; *PBE* I: Sophronios 1. For Sophronios as an oral source of Michael Monachos, see *Vita* B *of Theodoros Stoud.* 308D, 309C, 312A.
[247] *PmbZ* # 20347; *Vita of Euthymios* 159–61.
[248] Grégoire 1929; Efthymiadis 1998: 45–46; Angelidi 2004; Delouis 2005: 340–56; Kazhdan 2006: 222–25. Anatolios is mentioned in *Vita of Blasios* 19, 666BC.
[249] Anatolios is also mentioned in it, see *Vita of Nikolaos Stoud.* 893A. On this *vita*, see Chapter 5.
[250] *PmbZ* # 21545. According to the acrostic of the poem, Dionysios came from Lydia like Anatolios. On Dionysios' literary production, see Lauxterman 2003: 70–72, 78, 143–44.
[251] *Epigram* 124, (ed. Speck 1968, 307–9). See Mercati 1953; Speck 1963: 49–51; Komines 1966: 122.
[252] See, for instance, their poems included in the *Anthologia Graeca* (*Anth. Gr.* xv, 28–40).
[253] Latysev 1914: 304, 13–20.

dates from the mid-tenth century and is attributed to the *magistros* Theodoros Daphnopates, the author of an *enkomion* of Theophanes the Confessor (*BHG* 1792).[254] If Daphnopates really wrote *Vita* A, he must have done so with the close collaboration of the Stoudites themselves.[255] Be that as it may, *Vita* C took *Vita* B as a model, while *Vita* A was mainly inspired by *Vita* C. In contrast to the hagiography of Michael Monachos, which was aimed at the members of the Stoudite federation, the latter two were intended for a wider public, their purpose being to propagandise about Theodoros and his important religious work. *Vita* C was aimed at readers who saw the monastery of Stoudios from the outside and contemplated the daily life of its monks, inspired by God.[256] The audience is invited to visit the monastery to see for itself its compliance with the doctrine of Theodoros, as a result of which the monks' behaviour is exemplary. *Vita* A contains all these elements, but in a more concise style and with less detailed description of the Stoudite community, stressing the role of Theodoros as a role model for any monk.[257] In this exercise of spiritual advertising, it appears that *Vita* C was unsuccessful, due to which another hagiographer of acknowledged talent and appreciated by readers was commissioned to write a new *vita*. This is doubtless why only two manuscripts of *Vita* C have survived (Moskow RGB Gr. 128 and Athos Megistes Lauras Δ 78), while *Vita* A appears in an important number of manuscripts included in the *Metaphrastic Menologion*, such as codex London *British Library Add.* 36636 (eleventh century).[258]

Finally, a *vita* of Theodoros in iambic verse (*BHG* 1755m) written by Stephanos Meles in the twelfth century survives,[259] together with a fragment of what must have been *Vita* D (*BHG* 1755f), of uncertain date and curiously contrary to Stoudite interests, in that it does not offer a positive image of the leader, but accuses him of breaking away from the Church.[260]

1.3 Sanctification of Other Members of the Stoudite Milieu: The Hegoumenoi of Tarasios

The promotion of the cult of Theodoros was, unsurprisingly, one of the main concerns of the Stoudite community, but these also included the

---

[254] *PmbZ* # 27694. On Daphnopates' hagiographical production, see Darrouzès and Westerink 1978: 2–4.
[255] Darrouzès and Westerink 1978: 5–6; Krausmüller 2013a: 291.
[256] *Vita* C *of Theodoros Stoud.* 258,15–59,7; Delouis 2011: 106–8; Krausmüller 2013a: 293–97.
[257] *Vita* A *of Theodoros Stoud.* 113A–16A. [258] Van de Vorst and Delehaye 1913: 276.
[259] Delouis 2014. [260] Matantseva 1996a.

strict observance of the rules he had issued. The regulations included the liturgical commemoration of monks who had been noted for holiness: 'It should be known that until Pentecost, even though we neither sing the hours nor bend our knees, we do sing the *kanones* for the dead on Saturdays, and we sing them on any other day if there happens to be a commemoration of a brother.'[261] This was not merely a case of an annual celebration of the memory of the saints already mentioned by their beloved hegoumenos, such as Theophanes of Sigriane, whose cult they continued to honour every 12 March[262] and whom (following their master's example) they praised with new hagiographies. Although later *vitae* in honour of Theophanes tend to draw on that of Methodios and add little to the patriarch's words, Nikolaos Stoudites may have been the author of a brief anonymous *vita* in honour of Theophanes,[263] while a certain Sabas, who was also probably linked to the monastery of Stoudios, signed another *vita* that survives only in an Old Church Slavonic translation.[264] But the Stoudites also imitated the model of Theodoros himself in promoting the veneration of his brothers and other hegoumenoi whose common interests led them into the Stoudite orbit.[265]

1.3.1 Ioseph of Thessaloniki

Almost necessarily, the first Stoudite monk sanctified after the death of Theodoros Stoudites was his full brother Ioseph of Thessaloniki.[266] The sources allow us to reconstruct Ioseph's biography in some detail. Born ca. 762, Ioseph, along with the rest of the family, accompanied Theodoros when he entered monastic life in Sakkoudion ca. 787. He also followed his brother in becoming archbishop of Thessaloniki, a position he held in the

---

[261] Theod. Stoud., *Rule* 1708A: ζ'. Ἰστέον δὲ ὅτι ἕως τῆς ν', εἰ καὶ ὥρας οὐ ψάλλομεν, οὐδὲ γόνυ κλίνομεν, ἀλλ' οὖν κανόνας νεκρωσίμους ἐν τοῖς Σάββασι ψάλλομεν· καὶ ἐν ἄλλῃ δὲ ἡμέρᾳ, εἰ τύχοι μνημόσυνον ἀδελφοῦ, ψάλλομεν.
[262] Gedeon 1899: 221.   [263] According to Latysev, see Kazhdan 1999: 215.
[264] Kazhdan 1999: 340. Likewise, the monks of Stoudios undertook to preserve and disseminate Theophanes' legacy, as is shown by the existence of a Stoudite edition of his famous chronicle, Yannopoulos 2013: 288–94. For a thorough reconsideration of this matter, see Ronconi 2015a.
[265] A detailed list of the saints celebrated at the monastery of Stoudios can be found in Gedeon 1899. The saints honoured by the Stoudites can be traced by the mark they left in subsequent *synaxaria* such as the *Synaxarion Evergetis*, see Taft 1994. For the elements of the Stoudite *synaxarion* reflected in the *Synaxarion Evergetis*, see Pentkovskij 2001: 142 and 425 (with an English summary); Delouis 2005: 493; Krausmüller 2013a: 297, n. 52, with bibliography. See Introduction.
[266] *PmbZ* # 3448; *PBE* I: Ioseph 3; Pargoire 1906a; *Translation of Theodoros Stoud. and Ioseph* 36–47.

years 807–809 and 811–815.[267] Along with the other Stoudite monks, he refused to agree with the patriarch Nikephoros about the 'Ioseph affair', which led to his exile and imprisonment.[268] In 814 and 815, we find him reinstated as archbishop of Thessaloniki, interceding with Emperor Leon V in an attempt to prevent the restoration of an iconoclast policy. After the failure of this enterprise, he was persecuted and exiled along with the other bishops who had addressed Leon V;[269] each of them was exiled to a different place, and Ioseph ended up in a fortress called Elpizon.[270] In 821, at the beginning of the reign of Michael II, he returned from exile,[271] and in April 824 he officiated (again as archbishop of Thessaloniki) at the funeral of Niketas of Medikion along with the archbishop of Ephesos, Theophilos, who also corresponded with the Stoudites.[272]

After his death on 15 July 832, in exile in Thessaly,[273] Ioseph came to be recognised as a saint within the Stoudite confederation. Now that he was dead, the words of praise his brother Theodoros had addressed to him[274] encouraged making his sufferings during the Moechian controversy and iconoclastic persecution a basis for proclaiming his holiness. Ioseph's written production in defence of images and his orthodox defenders, of course, also encouraged this process. His literary work included verses attacking iconoclast heretics and a slanderous pamphlet predicting the death of the iconoclast Emperor Theophilos, along with sermons and panegyrics.[275] He is known above all else, however, as a hymnographer.[276] The transfer of his relics to Constantinople after the Triumph of Orthodoxy, coinciding with the arrival there of the relics of his brother and their final placement in the sarcophagus of Platon of Sakkoudion, helped make a periodic liturgical commemoration possible.[277] Ioseph of

---

[267] Theoph. AM 6301 and AM 6304; *Vita B of Theodoros Stoud.* 244C–45A; *Vita C of Theodoros Stoud.* 12, p. 264; *Vita of Nikolaos Stoud.* 877A–B.

[268] *Vita B of Theodoros Stoud.* 269B; *Vita C of Theodoros Stoud.* 30, p. 275; *Vita A of Theodoros Stoud.* 160B.

[269] *Vita A of Theophylaktos of Nicomedia* 12–14.   [270] *Vita B of Theodoros Stoud.* 304D.

[271] This allowed a reunion with his brother Theodoros in Pteleai (now Balikesir in Turkey), *Vita B of Theodoros Stoud.* 304D; *Vita C of Theodoros Stoud.* 59, p. 292; *Vita A of Theodoros Stoud.* 208B.

[272] *Vita of Niketas of Medikion* 48. Theophilos of Ephesos was exiled by Leon V for defending images and during this period he corresponded with Athanasios as well as with Theodoros Stoudites, from whom he received three letters (*epist.* 385, 414 and 455), see *PmbZ* # 8209; *PBE* I: Theophilos 15.

[273] *Translation of Theodoros Stoud. and Ioseph* 47.

[274] Theod. Stoud., *epist.* 37, 43, 65, 72, 73, 111, 195, 222, 265, 333, 355; *Laudatio of Theoktiste* 889C, 892B; *Parvae catech.* 95.

[275] On the verses, see Theod. Stoud., *epist.* 222; Alexander 1977: 248–49. On the pamphlet, see *Vita of Euthymios of Sardis* 13, 270–72; 15, 300–304. For the sermons, see Beck 1959: 505–6.

[276] Pargoire 1907: 207–10; Eustratiadès 1941/1952; Follieri and Dujcev 1963; Stiernon 1973: 264–66; Kotzambassi 2007.

[277] *Translation of Theodoros Stoud. and Ioseph; Vita B of Theodoros Stoud.* 328A; *Vita C of Theodoros Stoud.* 81, p. 304; *Vita A of Theodoros Stoud.* 232B.

Thessaloniki appears among the metropolitans acclaimed in the *Synodikon of Orthodoxy*,[278] was included in the *synaxaria*[279] and was given special attention in the account of the transfer of his relics and those of his brother to Constantinople.[280] We also know at least two liturgical hymns (*kanones*) in his honour written by Stoudite monks, in which he is celebrated as a confessor of the faith.[281]

The celebration and dissemination of the cult of Ioseph of Thessaloniki within the Stoudite federation had ideological dimensions related to the reaffirmation of a group identity around the memory of one of its most outstanding members. But it also stems from ecclesiastical alliances initiated at the start of the century that aimed to defeat iconoclast heresy. A large number of these were forged at the instigation of the patriarch Tarasios (784–806), who was responsible for calling the Second Council of Nicaea in 787 and temporarily putting an end to iconoclasm.[282] In order to achieve the first restoration of images, Tarasios relied on the monks, many of whom had been promoted to important posts in order to clear the hierarchy of iconoclast heretics.[283] A number of these men ended up playing important roles in the fight against the Second Iconoclasm, which promoted their subsequent veneration. Among others, Tarasios ordained or consecrated Theodoros of Stoudios, Georgios of Amastris, Makarios of Pelekete, Ioannes Psichaites, Niketas of Medikion, Michael of Synada, Theophylaktos of Nicomedia, Ioannes of Sardis, Euthymios of Sardis, Petros of Atroa, Hilarion of Dalmatos and Ioseph of Thessaloniki.[284] The individuals present at the encounter of iconodules of December 814, which aimed to prevent the return of the heresy planned by Leon V, were drawn precisely from this group.[285] To them must be added figures such as Theophanes of Sigriane, an absolute bastion of support

---

[278] *Synodikon of Orthodoxy* 53,123 and 114,IX, line 5.
[279] *SynaxCP* 213/214,54; 519,18–20,1; 819/820,35–59; 822,19–21 (15 July); *Menologion Basilii* 541AB.
[280] *Translation of Theodoros Stoud. and Ioseph* 13–14.
[281] One of these has been fully edited by in *AHG*, vol. XI, 270–82. The other is still unpublished in ms. *Vallicell.* E 55, f. 49–51v, as only the *kathisma* following the third ode has been edited, Tomadakes 1971a: 83, n. 1.
[282] *PmbZ* # 7235; *PBE* I: Tarasios 1; Lilie 1999: 57–108.
[283] Auzépy 1988. From the earliest attempts to put an end to heresy, Platon of Sakkoudion and Theodoros Stoudites took the part of Tarasios, see ibid., pp. 18–20.
[284] Hatlie 2007a: 317–18, with reference to the sources.
[285] According to the *Vita of Niketas of Medikion*, those attending were: Aimilianos of Kyzikos, Michael of Synada, Theophylaktos of Nicomedia, Petros of Nicaea, Euthymios of Sardis and Theodoros Stoudites. According to the *Vita of Theophylaktos of Nicomedia*, they were: Euthymios of Sardis, Aimilianos of Kyzikos, Ioseph of Thessaloniki, Eudoxios of Amorion, Michael of Synada and Theophylaktos of Nicomedia, see Matantseva 1998.

for Tarasios, who was also seen as a symbol of the resistance to heresy. The sanctification of many members of this group depended on the work of the Stoudite confederation, as their inclusion in the *Synodikon of Orthodoxy* in its first phase of composition proves.[286] Due to the personal relationship these saints established with Theodoros and their common interests, they began to be venerated following the practice of the monastery of Stoudios. The initial readiness of Platon of Sakkoudion to appoint Tarasios as patriarch[287] and the fact that the differences with Theodoros Stoudites were restricted to matters of religious discipline and did not involve doctrinal matters, allowed the sincere veneration of many of their collaborators.

1.3.2 The Hegoumenoi of Medikion

A clear case is Michael of Synada, whose veneration was encouraged by Theodoros Stoudites himself, who was still alive when Michael died.[288] Michael maintained contact not only with Theodoros, but also with one of his other associates from outside the Stoudite federation, Niketas of Medikion, making this another clear example of the phenomenon in question. Niketas was born in Bithynia[289] in the town of Caesarea in ca. 760. According to his *vita*, after the death of his mother when he was a baby, he was raised by his grandmother. Once he had learnt his letters and the psalter, he entered the service of the Church as a *neokoros* (sacristan), although his desire to lead a truly religious life led him to approach the hermit Stephanos, who directed him towards monasticism (ch. 5). As a result, he entered the monastery of Medikion under the direction of its founder, the hegoumenos Nikephoros[290] (chs. 7–8). Some years later, he travelled to the capital to be ordained as a priest by the patriarch Tarasios.

Upon his return, the hegoumenos appointed Niketas as his successor, and his good management caused the number of brothers to increase considerably (ch. 10). In this work, he had the assistance of Athanasios, a young man who, after training in the *logothesion* (bureau) as a secretary,

---

[286] Lauritzen 2017.
[287] The fact that Platon was not one of the monks opposing Tarasios logically indicates that he decided to support him, Auzépy 1988: 18–19.
[288] See Section 1.1.4.b.
[289] *Vita of Niketas of Medikion* 44, p. xxvii (year 815). On Niketas, see *PmbZ* # 5443; *PBE* I: Niketas 43.
[290] *PmbZ* # 5280; *PBE* I: Nikephoros 21. For the monastery of Medikion, see Mango and Ševčenko 1973: 242–48; Janin 1975: 165–68; Ruggieri 1991: 221–22; Auzépy 2003a: 431–58; Auzépy et al. 2005: 183–94.

defied his father and entered the monastery of Symboloi.[291] Shortly afterwards, Niketas' reputation for piety and virtue (chs. 17–22) led to him being named hegoumenos when his predecessor died in 813 (ch. 24). This event in turn led to his confrontation with Emperor Leon V in 815, due to the latter's desire to reinstate iconoclasm, and then to persecution and exile. Despite his determination, in a moment of weakness he agreed to the iconoclasts' aspirations and took communion from the heretic patriarch Theodotos ca. 816, for which he was criticised by Theodoros Stoudites. After repenting and defending the images anew, he was again exiled, tortured and imprisoned by the iconoclasts on the island of Glykeria (ch. 43), until, with the accession to the throne of Michael II, he returned to the capital in 820. He purchased a house on the northern outskirts of Constantinople that he converted into a *metochion* of the monastery of Medikion, where he lived until his death on 3 April 824. His hagiography ends by affirming that his funeral was officiated at the same place by Ioseph of Thessaloniki and Theophilos of Ephesos (ch. 48).

The relationship between Niketas of Medikion and Theodoros Stoudites was good, to judge by the latter's letters.[292] The fact that Niketas acknowledged his error and returned to Orthodoxy was a source of joy for Theodoros; Niketas had approached him to admit his guilt and show repentance (*epist.* 280). Theodoros did not hesitate to write to him in March–April 818 to inform him of the death of Theophanes of Sigriane (*epist.* 319), and after returning from exile, Niketas made the effort to visit him at Cape Akritas (*epist.* 452). Moreover, their common interest in defending icons led to Niketas writing a work in defence of the veneration of images, which took the form of an anthology of passages from the Church Fathers and earlier authors in which he offered theological arguments for the Orthodoxy of iconoduly.[293] This iconophile florilegium is preserved in only one manuscript (*Vaticanus Gr.* 511), where it is followed by a short treatise on the prohibition of the orthodox having communion with heretics that concludes with a compilation of excerpts from the *Constitutiones Apostolicae*, Leontios of Neapolis and Ignatios of Antioch.[294] Niketas thus transmitted to Theodoros the confession of faith that had been confided to him by the ex-Empress Theodosia, who, after she became the widow of Leon V the Armenian, took refuge in the

---

[291] *PmbZ* # 673; *PBE* I: Athanasios 5. *Vita of Niketas of Medikion* 11–12.
[292] Who sent him many missives, Theod. Stoud., *epist.* 255, 280, 319, 422, 452. In many others, Theodoros mentions Niketas, cf. Theod. Stoud., *epist.* 136; 177, 197, 267, 281, 333, 432, 538. See also *epist.* 281 (on the repentance of Niketas).
[293] Thümmel 1993/1994; Alexakis 1994; 2011.   [294] Alexakis 2011: 48–50.

metochion directed by Niketas on the island of Prote, one of the Princes' Islands in the Sea of Marmara.[295] On learning that the dowager empress accepted the veneration of images, Theodoros congratulated her and her son on embracing Orthodoxy and comforted them in their forced monastic retreat (*epist.* 538). Theodoros Stoudites also had a close relationship with another monk from Medikion, Arsenios, a faithful collaborator of Niketas to whom Theodoros often sent greetings and on one occasion an epistle.[296]

The links between Medikion and the Stoudite federation were more wide-ranging than this, however, for Athanasios, the man appointed by Nikephoros to assist Niketas in running the monastery, came from the nearby monastery of Symboloi on Mount Olympos.[297] This was precisely where Platon of Sakkoudion had taken his vows in 759 and where he became hegoumenos after the death of abbot Theoktistos.[298] Once settled in Medikion, Athanasios was the loyal *oikonomos* to Niketas for many years.[299] It is likely that he was persecuted and tortured together with Niketas for making a confession of faith; he was therefore perhaps the recipient of an epistle from Theodoros Stoudites to a certain *oikonomos* that comforts him in his suffering and reminds him of his special link with the monastery of Symboloi, which the author calls 'my monastery'.[300] Another monk from the Stoudite federation was probably arrested together with Athanasios and Niketas; this was Timotheos of Symboloi, who was given 150 lashes ca. 817/818 for defending icons. Timotheos was a co-founder of the monastery of Sakkoudion and one of the monks loyal to Theodoros Stoudites, who sent him at least five epistles (nrs. 80, 198, 307, 315 and 360). The confession and the asceticism of Timotheos also meant that he was remembered in the *vitae* of the abbot of Stoudios.[301] Following

---

[295] Rosenqvist 2002: 66–68; Auzépy et al. 2005.
[296] *PmbZ* # 623; *PBE* I: Arsenios 5. It appears that this monk of Medikion also composed several liturgical hymns, Beck 1959: 602; Komines 1966: 123. For the important role of Arsenios in Niketas' repentance, see Senina 2015: 309–12.
[297] Mango and Ševčenko 1973: 242–48; Janin 1975: 181–83; Auzépy 2003a; Auzépy et al. 2005.
[298] Theod. Stoud., *Laudatio of Platon* 816C.
[299] *Vita of Niketas of Medikion* 23. They had an extremely close relationship, see ibid. 12: γίνονται οὖν ἀμφότεροι μία ψυχὴ καὶ γνώμη μία ἐν διαφόροις σώμασιν, ἐν καταστάσει γαληνιώδει τὸ πᾶν διέποντες.
[300] Theod. Stoud., *epist.* 306,6–8: προσθείην δ' ἂν ὅτιπερ καὶ τοῦ ἐμοῦ μοναστηρίου· τὸ γὰρ ἐκ Συμβόλων εἶναι, ἐν ᾧ ὁ μακάριός μου πατὴρ [i.e., Platon] καὶ ὑπετάγη τῷ ἱερῷ Θεοκτίστῳ καὶ ἠσκηκὼς ἐξέλαμψεν ἐν ἀρετῇ. See also Theod. Stoud., *epist.* 354: Τῷ οἰκονόμῳ τῆς Συμβόλου.
[301] *Vita B of Theodoros Stoud.* 245A, 301D; *Vita A of Theodoros Stoud.* 128B; *Vita C of Theodoros Stoud.* 12, p. 264; 57, p. 291; *Vita of Nikolaos Stoud.* 877B.

Sanctification of Other Members of the Stoudite Milieu

the dynamic already seen with other members of the Stoudite confederation, Timotheos was celebrated as a saint every 21 February.[302]

In addition, the man in charge of officiating at the funeral of Niketas of Medikion was the Stoudite Ioseph of Thessaloniki. And the author of a *kanon*[303] to commemorate Niketas liturgically each year, finally, was the hymnographer Klemes,[304] a Stoudite monk and the *hypographeus* (notary) of Theodoros, who ultimately became an abbot and entered the *synaxaria* as an iconodule confessor.[305] Klemes accompanied Theodoros on his visit to Ioannikios.[306] This Klemes is not to be identified with the hegoumenos of the same name who ran the monastery of Stoudios for a few months in 868 after the death of Nikolaos Stoudites.[307] Given all these elements, it is unsurprising that the *vita* of Niketas was ultimately preserved in a Stoudite manuscript.[308] This hagiography (*BHG* 1341)[309] was originally written shortly after the year 828 by Theosteriktos, a monk of Medikion and a disciple of the saint.[310] It can be dated due to indications given by its author. The patriarch Nikephoros was dead by then,[311] which means it post-dates 5 April 828. The date *ante quem* is 11 January 844, the day of the death of Michael I Rhangabe, who was still alive when Theosteriktos was writing.[312] The hagiographer was apparently unaware, however, of the persecution of the iconodules by Emperor Theophilos, since he makes no reference to it. Theosteriktos gave his work the title of a funeral *enkomion*

---

[302] In his honour a *troparion* has survived (*AHG*, vol. VI, 355–63). His memory is honoured in *synaxaria* of Stoudite tradition such as the *Synaxarion Evergetis* I, 554. On Timotheos, see *PmbZ* # 8499; # 8502; # 8503; *PBE* I: Timotheos 3; Timotheos 7.

[303] Edited in *AHG*, vol. VIII, 74–86. Kazhdan 1999: 261–69.

[304] *PmbZ* # 3653; Magrì 1979; Kazhdan 1992/1993; Efthymiadis 1995: 148–49. Klemes also dedicated a *kanon* to Eustathios of Kios, praising him as an iconodule confessor.

[305] *SynaxCP* 713,3–5 (27 May); 631/632,39f. (27 April); 633/634,50–52 (28 April); 641/642,57f. (30 April); *Typikon of the Great Church* I, 276,5f. (28 April). However, the *Synaxarion Evergetis* II, 84 commemorates it on 3 April. An *akoluthia* in his honour has been edited by Pétridès 1903. On his relationship with Theodoros Stoudites, Theod. Stoud., *epist*. 302, 326, 433 and 538.

[306] *Vita of Ioannikios by Sabas* 28, 357B; *Vita of Ioannikios by Petros* 36, 404C–405B; Pratsch 1998: 281–83. As abbot he is also mentioned in the *Vita of Petros of Atroa* 68, 5, p. 197, n. 4, cf. *PmbZ* # 3654; *PBE* I: Klemens 1.

[307] *PmbZ* # 23705; *PBE* I: Klemens 4.

[308] This is the *Vaticanus Gr.* 1660 (*olim Cryptensis* 20), a *menologion* of April signed by the Stoudite copyist Ioannes on 21 March 916 (fol. 408v), i.e., under the direction of the hegoumenos Anatolios, see Follieri 1969: 24, nr. 14; Ehrhard 1936–1939: vol. I, 608–11, see Section I.2.

[309] *AASS* Apr. I (3rd ed.): XVII–XVIII (at end of volume). A new edition was being prepared, see Kazhdan 1999: 198–99; Rosenqvist 2002.

[310] *PmbZ* # 8393; *PBE* I: Theosteriktos 1.

[311] *Vita of Niketas of Medikion* 24: ἔτυχεν δὲ ταύτης δι' ἐπιθέσεως τῶν χειρῶν τοῦ ἐν ἁγίοις Νικηφόρου, τοῦ τότε τὸν πατριαρχικὸν Κωνσταντινουπόλεως κατέχοντος θρόνον. Ibid. 36: καὶ ὑπομονὴ πολλὴ ἕως τῆς ἡμέρας τῆς πρὸς τὸν κύριον αὐτοῦ ἐκδημίας.

[312] *Vita of Niketas of Medikion* 31: εἶτα Μιχαήλ, ὁ νῦν ἔτι ἐν μοναδικῷ διαπρέπων ἀξιώματι.

(*epitaphios*), but actually ended up writing a *vita* (βίος καὶ πολιτεία), as Theodoros Stoudites himself had done previously to celebrate his uncle Platon of Sakkoudion.[313] His style is elegant, and his classicism very correct. The construction of the text is in keeping with the rules of ancient rhetoric, following the prescriptions of the *lógos basilikós* of Menander Rhetor. The result is a detailed and well-documented account of the revival of iconoclasm in 815 and of monastic attempts to resist it. Theosteriktos had witnessed many of the events in which Niketas took part: he accompanied him to Constantinople when the patriarch Nikephoros granted him the hegoumenate, and he was also present when his body was taken to Medikion. Indeed, he was one of those who, deeply moved, bore the relics on their shoulders while they sang hymns.[314]

The version in Greek that survives is from the pen of the copyist Ioannes Stoudites,[315] which has been seen as a sign of self-interested rewriting aimed at giving priority to Theodoros Stoudites, whose virtues are emphasised to the detriment of those of the saint being portrayed.[316] Theodoros is emphatically praised[317] and is the only person mentioned by name along with the patriarch Nikephoros, when Leon V orders his expulsion for disobeying his iconoclast will. (Remarkably, the Stoudites is mentioned first, to the detriment of the patriarch.)[318] But the copyist respects the desire of the hagiographer and does not alter the account of Niketas' behavior in any way. The softening of Niketas' lapse in failing the iconodule cause (ch. 41) is maintained without adapting it to the harsher version transmitted by Theodoros Stoudites himself.

We do not know why Ioannes copied the *vita* of Niketas in an unsuitable place in the *menologion* (at the very end, when the saint's feast

---

[313] Compare the title of the *Vita of Niketas of Medikion*: ἐπιτάφιος εἰς τὸν ὅσιον πατέρα ἡμῶν καὶ ὁμολογητήν, Νικήταν, συγγραφεὶς ὑπὸ Θεοστηρίκτου, μαθητοῦ αὐτοῦ μακαριωτάτου, with that of the epitaph of Platon: τοῦ ὁσίου πατρὸς ἡμῶν καὶ ὁμολογητοῦ Θεοδώρου ἡγουμένου τῶν Στουδιτῶν ἐπιτάφιος εἰς Πλάτωνα τὸν ἑαυτοῦ πνευματικὸν πατέρα (Theod. Stoud., *Laudatio of Platon* 804).

[314] *Vita of Niketas of Medikion* 48: ἦμεν δὲ ἡμεῖς ἐκδεχόμενοι εἰς τὸν αἰγιαλόν . . . καὶ ὡς ἔφθασεν πρὸς ἡμᾶς, ἐξενέγκαντες τοῦτον τοῦ πλοίου, προσεκυνήσαμεν σὺν δάκρυσι τὸ ἅγιον λείψανον· καὶ ἄραντες ἐπ' ὤμοις σὺν τῇ πρεπούσῃ ὑμνῳδίᾳ.

[315] *Vita of Niketas of Medikion* 50: τετέλεσται ἡ παροῦσα βίβλος μηνὶ μαρτίῳ κα', ἰνδικτιῶνι α', ἔτους κόσμου͵ϛυκδ', γραφεῖσα διὰ χειρὸς Ἰωάννου ταπεινοῦ καὶ ἐλαχίστου μοναχοῦ, ἐπὶ Ἀνατολίου τοῦ ὁσιωτάτου ἡγουμένου τῶν Στουδίου.

[316] Von Dobschütz 1909a: 81–83; Delouis 2011: 104–5.

[317] *Vita of Niketas of Medikion* 35: Θεόδωρος ὁ θερμὸς τῆς ἐκκλησίας διδάσκαλος, ὁ τῶν Στουδίου ἡγούμενος.

[318] *Vita of Niketas of Medikion* 36: ἀπεπέμψατο πάντας· τὸν δὲ ὅσιον Θεόδωρον ὑπερορίσας . . . ἐξορίζει δὲ τοὺς τῶν μεγάλων ἐκκλησιῶν προέδρους, οὓς μὲν ἐπὶ τὰ Ἀνατολικὰ κλίματα [λεγε· κλίματα], οὓς δὲ ἐπὶ τὰς τῆς Δύσεως νήσους, καὶ δηλοῖ τῷ ἁγιωτάτῳ Νικηφόρῳ τῷ πατριάρχῃ.

day is 3 April). Perhaps it was a later addition to the original manuscript. What we do know is that he was forced by a lack of space to abbreviate the original text he was copying. We know this thanks to the survival of a translation into Old Church Slavonic of the original text of Theosteriktos, which retains the full epilogue.[319] Long afterwards, a certain Ioannes Hagioelites produced a new version of the Greek *vita* of Niketas of Medikion, which has also come down to us (*BHG* 1342).[320]

The reasons that persuaded Theosteriktos to draw up a hagiography to honour his spiritual father (giving it the textual element needed by the incipient liturgical veneration in his honour by the monks of his monastery) take on their full significance if we recognise that they followed the model produced by the important Constantinopolitan monastery of Stoudios. The sanctification of monks persecuted by the iconoclast authorities was a growing tendency modelled on the treatment of a number of recent individuals. In the case of the community of Medikion, the promotion of the veneration of its hegoumenos Niketas was an essential objective, and was successful, to judge by the number of people who gathered around the saint to mourn his death, by the presence of all the monks of the monasteries of his community and by the numerous miraculous cures effected by his relics.[321] Given such a social movement, his entry into the *synaxarion* was inevitable.[322] But the identity of this monastic community had to face a minor inconvenience. Despite Niketas' historical significance in the fight against heresy, he was not the monastery's founder, and most of these practices (such as that of the Stoudites) revolved around the holy figure of the founder of the community. The need thus arose to draw up a new *vita* in honour of their own founder Nikephoros of Medikion (*BHG* 2297–98),[323] clearly sometime after Niketas' death (according to the hagiographer himself),[324] which however displays a patent lack of knowledge about the precise activities of the protagonist. This was a shrewd move by the monastery of Medikion,

---

[319] *Menaion of Makariem*, April, tetr. I, dni 1–8, cols. 42–102; Rosenqvist 2002: 64–72.
[320] Euangelides 1895: 286–313. A twelfth-century manuscript (the Athens EBE 2504, fol. 1–9v, 12–14) contains a third version: the *vita seu laudatio* (*BHG* 1342b), Ehrhard 1936–1939: vol. I, 409, n. 4.
[321] *Vita of Niketas of Medikion* 48.   [322] *SynaxCP* 581, 1–18 (3 April).
[323] Halkin 1960: 396–430.
[324] *Vita of Nikephoros of Medikion* 9,25–28: Οὗτινος Νικήτα τὴν ἐξαστράπτουσαν πολιτείαν οὐκ ἐν ἐπιτόμῳ διέξειμι λόγῳ· τετάσθω δέ, εἴπερ τῷ θεῷ φίλον, ἐν ἰδίᾳ χώρᾳ φιλευφήμοις. For its dating, see Sevcenko 1977a: 118 and n. 43. The failure of the hagiographer to summarise Niketas' brilliant career in no way presupposes that the *Vita Nicetae* had not yet been written or that the author was planning to write it, as is maintained by Halkin 1960: 413 n. 3, but rather the opposite.

which thus expanded the religious and liturgical scope of the cult of Niketas. This form of enhanced holiness was also emphasised by placing the bodies of both men in the same tomb in the monastery church, which was a place of pilgrimage due to the miracles and cures that occurred there.[325] The decision to place the body of Niketas in the tomb of his spiritual father and predecessor as the head of Medikion is in keeping with Naukratios' decision to place the relics of Theodoros Stoudites and Ioseph of Thessaloniki in the sarcophagus of their uncle Platon of Sakkoudion.

The *Vita of Nikephoros of Medikion* was written by a monk of Medikion at the same time as Theosteriktos drew up the *vita* of Niketas (i.e., shortly after 828, and certainly before 837).[326] This hagiography traces the career of Nikephoros, who was born in Constantinople in 755 to a well-established family (ch. 5). He took part in the Second Council of Nicaea in 787 led by Tarasios,[327] but was not affected by iconoclast reprisals. After the author tells of the foundation of the monastery of Medikion (ch. 10), he goes on to describe the rules Nikephoros gave to his monks (chs. 11–12), the principles of his governance and the way he provided spiritual direction (chs. 13–14). Nikephoros was obliged by illness to seek medical care in the capital and finally died on the island of Chalki on 4 May 813 at the age of fifty-eight (chs. 16–19). His role as monastic leader is stressed again when on his deathbed he issues his final recommendations to his community (ch. 17). Evidently, this model of holiness is the one expressed most clearly elsewhere in the figure of Theodoros Stoudites, whose example the author seems to have used to encourage the veneration of Nikephoros of Medikion. This hypothesis is confirmed by the nature of the miracles related at the end of the *vita*: not prodigious post-mortem healings, but three miracles performed while Nikephoros was still alive to benefit his monks. The first gave a dying monk three extra years of life, the second provided the monastery with wheat and the third supplied it with water (chs. 21–23).

The primary audience at which the *vita* of Nikephoros was aimed was the community of Medikion. But this hagiography was composed to be read at the annual commemoration held in his honour, where the general public was invited to take part in the liturgy.[328] The writer himself was aware of this and inserts hints and references in the text to believers near the monastery, for instance, when he encourages devotees with children to

---

[325] *Vita of Niketas of Medikion* 49.   [326] Halkin 1960: 398; Ševčenko 1977a: 118.
[327] Mansi XIII, 153A.
[328] *Vita of Nikephoros of Medikion* 24,9–12: ὄλβον ἐρικύδαιον διαμπὰξ τὸν ἐπέραστον θεϊκῆς θυμηδίας τοῖς τὴν ἐτήσιόν σου γεραίρουσι μνήμην, ἵν' ἤρεμον καὶ ἡσύχιον ἀστασιάστως ζοίημ' ἂν βίον.

educate them following Nikephoros' example.³²⁹ This is the seed of successful advertising for the monastery of Medikion and the guarantee of the dissemination of the cult of Nikephoros, which would allow his entry into the *synaxaria*.³³⁰ That Nikephoros suffered persecution, imprisonment and exile during the reign of Emperor Leon is affirmed here. This no doubt represents confusion with Nikephoros' disciple Niketas, who did in fact have to confront the iconoclast policy of Leon V.

The *vita* of Nikephoros is highly rhetorical and bombastic, full of artificial compound words and lengthy speeches, but offers little real information or precise details; it is preceded by a long prologue that is both pretentious and obscure, and which is full of *hapax legómena* and recherché syntactic devices, such as overuse of the dative. This is in contrast to the *vita* of Niketas of Medikion, which has a loftier and more correct style, although Theosteriktos may have been the author of both. Nothing proves this definitively, meaning that this must remain an anonymous work. In any case, it is important that the oldest testimony to the *vita* of Nikephoros of Medikion is again a manuscript with clearly Stoudite content. This is München BSB *Gr.* 366, fol. 228–35v, of the late ninth century, which also contains two hagiographical accounts by Theodoros Stoudites on fol. 57–75v: *Laudatio S. Iohannis Euangelistae* (*BHG* 929) and *Laudatio S. Arsenii Anachoretae* (*BHG* 169).³³¹ Another hagiography found in the same manuscript claims our full attention: that of Ioannes Psichaites.³³² Our knowledge of this iconodule saint, celebrated on 25 May, is restricted to the *vita* in his honour (*BHG* 896).³³³ We know that the patriarch Tarasios ordained him a *diakonos* and that after holding the position of *oikonomos* he became the hegoumenos of the monastery of Psicha in Constantinople.³³⁴ He suffered during the persecution of Leon V and was exiled to the Chersonesos, although he returned years later to die in his monastery. The *vita of Ioannes Psichaites* appears to have been written by one of his fellow monks for the greater glory of the monastery's most eminent abbot.³³⁵

---

[329] *Vita of Nikephoros of Medikion* 5,45–48: Παιδεύθητε ταῦτα, ὅσοι ἐν ὑμῖν παῖδας ἔχετε, καὶ μιμήσασθε ἀρίστην βίου μέθοδον καὶ κομψῶς ἀνάξατε τὰ ἔκγονα ὑμῶν, εἰ ἄρα γε κατ' ἐκείνην εἰσί τινες τεκνοφιλόστοργοι.

[330] *SynaxCP* 653,53 and 659,25–60,22 (4 May); Halkin 1970. See also *AHG*, vol. IX, 363–64.

[331] Van de Vorst and Delehaye 1913: 126, nr. 25; Ehrhard 1936–1939: vol. I, 621, nr. 6 and n. 3.

[332] *PmbZ* # 3053; Costa-Louillet 1954–1955: 256–63.

[333] Van den Ven 1902; Von Dobschütz 1909b. See also *AHG*, vol. IX, 424–26.

[334] Janin 1969: 242; Ruggieri 1991: 199; Senina 2008a: 321–24.

[335] Traditionally, this hagiography has been considered contemporary with its protagonist, i.e., of the ninth century, Beck 1959: 512. The editor does not exclude this possibility, but the handwriting is characteristic of the tenth century.

1.3.3 *Makarios of Pelekete*

Makarios of Pelekete, another model of iconodule confessors, who was declared a saint and venerated as such, is a similar case. The promotion of his liturgy involves precisely the dynamics used by Theodoros Stoudites, which were (as already noted) habitual in the Stoudios monastery of the capital. Makarios of Pelekete[336] was born before 752 in Constantinople to a noble family of imperial rank. According to his *vita*, he was orphaned as a small child and raised by his uncle, who educated him in religious piety. When he grew up, a full brother of Makarios attempted to oblige him to marry, but he felt the call of God and hastened to a cell adjacent to a chapel. He took refuge there and refused to speak to anyone except the local priest, to whom he said that he wished to initiate a monastic life (ch. 2). The priest described the place where the monastery of Pelekete had been established; Makarios was so impressed that he decided to be tonsured and resolved to surpass the other monks in virtue and holiness (ch. 3). Makarios' interest in the Scriptures and books in general, together with the considerable time he devoted to them, led the hegoumenos to entrust him with the copying of texts as his main obligation.[337] His skill at this led to his successive promotion through the stages of monk, diakonos, *kanonarches, oikonomos* and finally hegoumenos of the monastery. The hagiographer claims that, in his humility, the saint tended to be reluctant to accept these obligations (ch. 4). His fame spread to the extent that, when doctors could not cure the *komes* of the Opsikion, the *patrikios* Paulos,[338] the latter sent for Makarios. Shortly after the miraculous cure of this important general, his wife fell ill, and when doctors were unable to relieve her, Makarios was called upon again. The saint travelled to Constantinople, where, in addition to healing Paulos' wife, he also cured the wife of the *patrikios* Theognostos, who had contracted a serious disease (dropsy) (chs. 5–6). While in the capital, Makarios was received by the patriarch Tarasios, who confirmed him as hegoumenos and – once more against his wishes – ordained him a priest (ch. 7).

The facts collected by the hagiographer Sabas reveal that Makarios' promotion to the hegoumenate occurred at the time of the First Iconoclasm and thus was due to an iconoclast bishop. To rehabilitate

---

[336] *PmbZ* # 4672; *PBE* I: Makarios 9. For the Bithynian monastery of Pelekete, see Hergès 1898; Mango and Ševčenko 1973: 242–48; Janin 1975: 170–72; Ruggieri 1991: 224.
[337] *Vita of Makarios of Pelekete* 3, p. 145,23–31; Krausmüller 2013c: 348–9.
[338] *PmbZ* # 5830 and 5837; *PBE* I: Paulos 10.

Makarios and win him over to the cause of images, Tarasios interviewed him personally and confirmed him as an iconodule abbot, cancelling the previous consecration, which was considered heretical and hence 'of the devil'.[339] These events probably occurred prior to the Second Council of Nicaea in 787. The inclusion of miracles predating the anointment of Makarios by Tarasios shows the writer's attempt to legitimate his hero: even if the saint had agreed at one point with the heretics, his miracles proved his holiness. Another miraculous cure (the healing of a paralytic child, ch. 8) was added precisely to emphasise this, along with a great drought brought to an end by his intervention (ch. 9).

The iconoclast persecution of Leon V meant that Makarios was imprisoned and urged to renounce icons by the heretical patriarch Ioannes Grammatikos (chs. 10–11). As a consequence of his continued loyalty to Orthodoxy, he was exiled to the Propontis, where he spent time with the deposed patriarch Nikephoros and decided to found a new monastery (ch. 12). When Theophilos came to the throne in 829, Makarios was called to Constantinople, where he defended the veneration of images to the prefect of the city. He was unable to convince his opponents, however, as a result of which he was whipped and imprisoned (ch. 13). During this period in prison, he found himself among several Paulicians, and Makarios managed to convert one of them, who thus escaped a death sentence.[340] Despite being in gaol, Makarios continued to speak freely and was therefore exiled again, this time to the inaccessible island of Aphousia, where he put an end to a famine and began the construction of a new church (ch. 15). According to the *Synaxarion of Constantinople*, all these events occurred during the reign of Michael II. As he himself had predicted, he died of a sickness on 18 August (the year is unknown, but the event took place under Theophilos, i.e., between 829 and 842) and was buried there.[341] His tomb became a place of pilgrimage due to the miracles that occurred by it, mainly healings and the expulsion of demons (ch. 18).

Makarios' memory began to be celebrated on 19 August, but also on 1 April. Entries in the *Synaxarion of Constantinople* in his honour can be

---

[339] *Vita of Makarios of Pelekete* 7, p. 149,14–16: διὸ μεταστειλάμενος (sc. Ταράσιος) αὐτὸν τόν τε πόθον (sc. the desire to see Makarios) ἀφοσιοῦται καὶ τὴν ἡγεμονίαν ἐπικυροῖ, καὶ πρὸς ταύτῃ **τὴν τοῦ διαβόλου χειροτονίαν** ἐκβιάσας αὐτῷ ἐπιτίθησιν.
[340] *Vita of Makarios of Pelekete* 14; Ludwig 1998: 31.
[341] *Vita of Makarios of Pelekete* 16, p. 161,5–162, 15. Precisely on the island of Aphousia at this time the death occurred of another important iconodule hegoumenos closely connected to the monastery of Stoudios: Ioannes of Kathara (*PmbZ* # 3139; *PBE* I: Ioannes 460).

found on both dates.[342] Tradition required that the memory of the saint be celebrated annually on the date of his death. The striking change that occurs with the feast day of Makarios may have been determined by its proximity to that of the Dormition of the Virgin (15 August), which generally lasted several days. Perhaps the change to celebrating his memory on 1 April has to do with the creation of a cycle of iconodule saints; not for nothing Niketas of Medikion was celebrated on 3 April, Platon of Sakkoudion on the 4th and Georgios of Mytilene on the 7th. A liturgical *kanon* in honour of Makarios also survives[343] along with a contemporary *vita* (*BHG* 1003) that constitutes our main source of information on the saint and the monastery of Pelekete.[344] It was written by Sabas, a monk from this monastery, who years later replaced Makarios as hegoumenos of one of the monasteries he had founded (probably the one of Aphousia or that near Chrysopolis).[345] According to Senina, Makarios died after 835, which means that the author must have written the *vita* between 836 and 842. Sabas declares that he has seen the good works of the saint,[346] but his reliability as a witness appears to be no better than his literary abilities (which are mediocre).

There is no doubt, however, about the Stoudite connections of Makarios and the monastery of Pelekete,[347] as the correspondence he maintained with Theodoros Stoudites between 816 and 818 shows. Five epistles sent by the abbot of Stoudios survive, some of them replies to previous letters from the hegoumenos of Pelekete.[348] Along with the other pro-Stoudite leaders, moreover, Makarios was a signatory of the missive sent to Pope Paschal I.[349] We know that after Makarios was exiled by Leon V in 816, he never returned to the monastery of Pelekete, but Theodoros continued to maintain a close relationship with that community. He sent a missive there in which he laments the death of the abbot who had guided the monastery since Makarios was exiled.[350] It appears that the abbot had

---

[342] *SynaxCP* 577,26–80,34 (1 April); 909,34 and 45 (19 August).
[343] *AHG*, vol. XII, 217–31 (19 August). An unpublished *kanon* celebrates him along with the martyrs Phloros and Lauros, *Tameion*, 270, nr. 844.
[344] Van den Gheyn 1897. See Efthymiadis 1998: 42; Kazhdan 1999: 340–41.
[345] *PmbZ* # 6445; *PBE* I: Sabas 11; Senina 2014.
[346] *Vita of Makarios of Pelekete* 23, p. 163,17–19: Σάββας ὁ τῶν σῶν κατορθωμάτων αὐτόπτης διεξῆλθον, ἑτέρῳ μὲν χρησάμενος, αὐτὸς δὲ τὸν λόγον προστησάμενος.
[347] Van de Vorst 1913b.
[348] Theod. Stoud., *epist.* 159, 230, 294, 362, 371; Pratsch 1998: 238–41. Theodoros Stoudites also mentions him in two other letters: *epist.* 267 and 501.
[349] Along with Makarios of Pelekete the hegoumenoi of Pikridion, Paulopetrion, Megas Agros, Dalmatos and Kathara signed, Theod. Stoud., *epist.* 267,30–31; Van de Vorst 1913c. See Section 1.1.4.b.
[350] Theod. Stoud., *epist.* 501. On this anonymous abbot, see *PmbZ* # 11526.

sympathised with the iconoclasts, due to which Theodoros encourages the monks to observe Orthodoxy under the new leadership of Sergios,[351] who had Makarios' approval. Theodoros also sent an epistle to this Sergios in 823, when he was already an abbot, asking him to abandon his plan to visit, due to the uprising of Thomas the Slav and the Arab threat.[352] The desire of the new hegoumenos of Pelekete to visit Theodoros Stoudites implies the recognition of a superiority that may have been worldly as well as spiritual.

Finally, the circle of hegoumenoi ordained by the patriarch Tarasios and faithful to their commitment to Orthodoxy and the defence of images also included Theophylaktos of Nicomedia,[353] another correspondent of Theodoros Stoudites whose veneration was also established following the Stoudite pattern. To a large extent, Theophylaktos' religious life runs parallel to that of Michael of Synada: both men were tonsured by Tarasios in the monastery the patriarch had founded on the European shore of the Bosphorus (near St Mamas);[354] he subsequently called them to Hagia Sophia, where their behaviour was so outstanding that Tarasios decided to appoint them bishops.[355] Theophylaktos had been born in ca. 765 in the eastern part of the Empire, but by about 780 he was already in Constantinople working for the future patriarch Tarasios, who was still a *protasekretis*.[356] He was consecrated bishop of Nicomedia (before 806) together with Michael of Synada (who had already attended all the sessions of the Second Council of Nicaea as a bishop in 787)[357] and confronted the iconoclast Emperor Leon V; both men defended the icons in the imperial palace.[358] Although they were tortured, imprisoned and exiled, they continued their pastoral work in exile and received letters from Theodoros Stoudites.[359]

For the Stoudios leader, Theophylaktos was the example of an iconodule confessor who deserved a martyr's crown.[360] Theodoros also men-

---

[351] *PmbZ* # 6662; *PBE* I: Sergios 104.   [352] Theod. Stoud., *epist*. 512.
[353] *PmbZ* # 8295; *PBE* I: Theophylaktos 37.
[354] *Vita of Tarasios* 24, pp. 98–99; *Vita* A *of Theophylaktos of Nicomedia* 5 and p. 73, n. 1. On this monastery, see Janin 1969: 481–82; Thomas 1987: 123–24 and 136; Ruggieri 1991: 202–3.
[355] *Vita* A *of Theophylaktos of Nicomedia* 5–8.   [356] *Vita* A *of Theophylaktos of Nicomedia* 2.
[357] Mansi XII, 994, 1091 and 1151; Mansi XIII, 137, 189 and 365.
[358] *Vita of Niketas of Medikion* 34.
[359] Theophylaktos of Nicomedia was the recipient of two letters written in 817–818 while he was in Strobilos (probably in the *thema* of the Kibyrrhaiotai), Theod. Stoud., *epist*. 175 and 314. Michael of Synada received a missive at the same time during his exile in Phrygia, Theod. Stoud., *epist*. 364.
[360] Theod. Stoud., *epist*. 175,5–9.

tions him repeatedly as a model of virtue,[361] and as already noted, even wrote a sermon narrating the life and works of his companion Michael of Synada (*BHG* 2275).[362] Theophylaktos died of some illness in exile on 8 March, although we do not know the year.[363] If the relative dating Theodoros gives is precise, this must be 845, although the *vita* does not mention the reigns of either Michael II or Theophilos. For the editor of the hagiography, Theophylaktos' death occurred ca. 840.[364] Two *vitae* were composed in his honour, the first (*BHG* 2451) of which was written shortly after his death, and was then touched up and abbreviated to half its length in a second version (*BHG* 2452).[365] The author of the first *vita* was the subject's namesake Theophylaktos,[366] a writer located in Nicomedia, as is made clear when he narrates the construction work carried out by his protagonist 'in this town' (ch. 8: ἐν ταύτῃ τῇ πόλει), and by the fact that he knew which bishops succeeded the saint. He was probably a cleric linked to one of the institutions his hero had founded. The hagiographer does not indicate that he witnessed any of the events he narrates or that he knew the protagonist personally, which makes it difficult to discover what triggered the writing of this *vita*. Perhaps this was due to the transfer of Theophylaktos' relics to Nicomedia promoted by Empress Theodora and the patriarch Methodios.[367] This motivation coincides with the iconodule interest in including Theophylaktos among the metropolitans acclaimed in the *Synodikon of Orthodoxy*[368] and his promotion as a confessor by other hagiographers.[369] With such a dynamic cult, the memory of Theophylaktos of Nicomedia did not take long to enter the *synaxaria*[370] and to be celebrated with liturgical hymns.[371]

---

[361] Theod. Stoud., *Parvae catech.* 51 quotes Theophylaktos. Theod. Stoud., *epist.* 533 and 542 allude to the death of Michael of Synada.
[362] Theod. Stoud., *Parvae catech.* 21.
[363] *Vita A of Theophylaktos of Nicomedia* 17: καὶ φασὶν αὐτὸν τριάκοντα σχεδὸν ἔτη τῇ ὑπερορίᾳ διηνυκέναι.
[364] Vogt 1932: 69.
[365] The first *vita* was edited by Vogt 1932: 67–82. The second, which is anonymous, was edited by Halkin 1986: 170–84, cf. Polemis 1989; Kazhdan 1999: 202–3. In actual fact this second hagiography is a characteristic summary of the premetaphrastic *menologia* and *synaxaria*, see Detoraki 2011. See also Section I.2.
[366] PBE I: Theophylaktos 57; Vogt 1932: 68.
[367] *Vita A of Theophylaktos of Nicomedia* 18; Vogt 1932: 68. A tenth-century composition has also been suggested, see Sevcenko 1977a: 118 and n. 39; Kazhdan 1999: 203.
[368] *Synodikon of Orthodoxy* 53, 123; cf. Horos of the Synod of 843, p. 297,113; Lauritzen 2017.
[369] *Vita of Euthymios of Sardis* 70–71: σὺν τῷ Νικομηδέων προέδρῳ καὶ ὁμολογητῇ, Θεοφυλάκτῳ φημὶ τῷ τρισολβίῳ.
[370] *SynaxCP* 519–22 (8 March); *Typikon of the Great Church* I, 244, 14f. (8 March); *Georgian Calendar* 54 (7 March); *Synaxarion Evergetis* II, 8 (8 March).
[371] The codex *Sinaiticus Gr.* 609 contains an unpublished *kanon* for Theophylaktos, *Tameion*, 174, nr. 521.

1.4 Conclusions

Defining the Stoudite circle has allowed us to take a closer look at the literary construction of a religious and political lobby that had a profound effect on contemporary society and liturgy. The methods invented by Theodoros Stoudites – the way he sought successfully to canonise many of his collaborators, promoted their veneration and made space for them in the liturgical cycles – were used by his followers to extol his own memory and disseminate his holiness, relying on the *scriptorium* of Stoudios and its substantial textual production. The reconstruction, albeit partial, of the cult practices of this period is possible thanks to the textual testimony that survives. As we have seen, the writing of *vitae* was a vital element in the promotion of new cults, but the inclusion of these saints in psalters, *menologia* and *synaxaria* was also important. The use of psalters as propaganda against iconoclasm by the Stoudites is well known.[372] This was not an individual phenomenon, however, but a collective enterprise in which the other monasteries of the Stoudite federation took part, along with individuals who were independent of it but were attracted by the charismatic figure of Theodoros Stoudites and his monastic reform, and who thus entered its sphere of influence. The debt to the Stoudite cult and canonising model is visible even in the most marginal institutions of the system.

What Theodoros had accomplished with his uncle Platon of Sakkoudion, his mother Theoktiste, his monastic godfather Theophanes of Sigriane, his monks (Thaddaios, Iakobos, etc.) and associates (e.g., Athanasios of Paulopetrion, Michael of Synada, Ioannes of Kathara) was also done with other iconodule confessors, such as Ioseph of Thessaloniki, Niketas and Nikephoros of Medikion, Theophylaktos of Nicomedia, Ioannes Psichaites and Makarios of Pelekete, who began to be remembered and celebrated. And this method of proclaiming and promoting the holiness of influential hegoumenoi continued to be productive in the monasteries in which it was first implemented. A case in point is the Bithynian monastery of Pelekete, which also promoted the cult of Hilarion, another hegoumenos who favoured icons.[373] Hilarion is praised for defending the veneration of icons at some point between the mid-eighth century and the early ninth century, and after his death, miracles

---

[372] Cutler 1977: 102; Cormack 1977a: 40–41. On the Stoudite manuscripts of the first half of the ninth century, see Hatlie 2007a: 412–19.
[373] *PmbZ* # 2587; *PBE* I: Hilarion 9.

occurred one after another at his tomb. Although the historical sources for Hilarion are scanty (no *vita* in his honour survives) and nothing like those for his counterpart Makarios of Pelekete, he was venerated, entered the *synaxaria*[374] and was even the subject of two liturgical hymns composed by Ioseph Hymnographos and Georgios of Nicomedia.[375] This is yet more proof of the great force and extent of the Stoudite canonisation method, which made its hegoumenos Theodoros into the iconodule saint of reference for monasticism during the difficult years of the resistance and the first generations of the post-iconoclast Church.

---

[374] *SynaxCP* 564,5–6 (27 March); 565/566,37 (28 March); 573/574,33 (30 March); *Menologion Basilii* 376A (28 March); *Typikon Messinense* 144,30 (28 March).

[375] Follieri 1960–1966: vol. II, 159ff; Tomadakes 1971a: 152, nr. 219; *Tameion*, 181, nr. 546. See Chapters 3 and 6, respectively.

CHAPTER 2

The Methodian Milieu
Literature Conceived in the Patriarchate after the Iconoclastic Crisis

The patriarchal circle was not closed to literary production prior to the Triumph of Orthodoxy, although the texts written during the periods of iconoclast leadership were inevitably condemned. The erudite profile of Ioannes VII Grammatikos leads one to think of lofty compositions that defended positions resisting the veneration of images with theological arguments.[1] Regardless of the nature of these texts, the subsequent victory of the iconodules meant their prohibition, destruction or simple oblivion. Apart from *florilegia* (anthologies) intended to justify their vision of Christianity, it is reasonable to assume that hagiographical accounts that gave a different version of the dispute and praised figures unconnected with the cult of icons must have existed.[2] Not in vain, the Second Council of Nicaea in 787 had already used this type of literature to support its reasoning, validating the reading and use of saints' *vitae* not only as edifying in themselves, but as representing an argument in favour of iconodule practice over time.[3] This not only made texts treating saints important but encouraged the creation of new works, some of which, devoted to iconodule confessors who had recently suffered, have come down to us. The orthodox interlude between the First and Second Iconoclasms (i.e., from 787 to 815) meant a loss of urgency for the writing of such works, which were enthusiastically produced again after the return to heresy decreed by Leon V. Despite everything, the milieu of the patriarch Nikephoros encouraged and benefitted from the writing ca. 809 of the *vita* of the great martyr of the First Iconoclasm, Stephanos the Younger, by the deacon of Hagia Sophia.[4]

---

[1] Magdalino 2015a: 85–94.   [2] Auzépy 1992; 1999; 2003b. See Introduction and Chapter 4.
[3] Van den Ven 1955/1957; Cameron 1994.
[4] *Vita of Stephanos the Younger* 47,22–27; 53 and pp. 5–9. For the participation of its author in 787 at the Second Council of Nicaea, see Efthymiadis 1993a. On the various forms of ecclesiastical propaganda of this period, see Auzépy 1998: 95–99.

We do not know to what extent the iconoclast patriarchs implemented a cultural policy that used literature as a propaganda tool to counteract the version of events promoted by iconodule monastic authors, but something like this is highly probable[5]. By contrast, we do know that the ascension to the ecclesiastical throne of Methodios was a point of inflection due to his deliberate efforts to protect, encourage and even personally write all kinds of works describing the Triumph of Orthodoxy and spreading the victors' version of what had happened under heretical leaders. For the historiographical version, he entrusted Georgios Monachos[6] with the production of work similar to that created during the previous restoration of images by his predecessor Tarasios, who had been supported by his *synkellos* Georgios in this enterprise.[7] Methodios too relied on his *synkellos* to implement aggressive official propaganda, a vital part of which was texts praising monks fallen during the persecution. To write them, he used several hagiographers, such as Ignatios Diakonos and Theophanes, and also of course occupied himself with the task personally. Although his patriarchate was very brief (843–847), its literary production was extraordinary in abundance and quality.

2.1 The Literary Work of Methodios

The man destined to oversee the definitive defeat of iconoclastic heresy, after he was appointed patriarch in 843, had been born into a rich Syracuse family in the final years of the reign of Konstantinos V (741–775).[8] As we shall see, Methodios' literary production is essentially hagiographical, in that it consists of lives of saints, hymns and homilies.[9] While still very young, he moved to Constantinople, where he prospered in public office until an encounter with an anonymous ascetic led him to change

---

[5] Theodoros Stoudites shows how the iconoclasts composed new hymns and odes to replace iconodule ones in the liturgy, see Theod. Stoud., *epist.* 275,60–68 and *epist.* 276,74–77: παραστέλλονται ψαλμῳδίαι ἀρχαιοπαράδοτοι, ἐν αἷς περὶ εἰκόνων ᾄδεταί τι, ἀντᾴδεται τὰ νέα δόγματα, ἀσεβῆ εἰς προὔπτον κείμενα, ἀλλὰ τοῖς παισὶ πρὸς τῶν διδασκάλων παραδιδόμενα· καὶ μεταστοιχείωσις τῶν πάντων ἀθεωτάτη. Some iconoclastic poems attributed to the patriarch Ioannes Grammatikos also survive, see Beck 1959: 498ff; Criscuolo 1994a: 143–51; Lauxtermann 2003: 277–84. See Introduction.

[6] Afinogenov 1999b; 2004b; Conca 2010: 119–40; Detoraki 2015: 103–30.

[7] Treadgold 2013: 38–63. On Georgios Synkellos, cf. *PmbZ* # 2180; Mango 1978b; Čičurov 1981; Ševčenko 1992. See Chapter 1.

[8] For the life journey of Methodios, see *PmbZ* # 4977; *PBE* I: Methodios 1; Marino 1986; Lilie 1999: 183–260. On the youth of Methodios, see Pargoire 1903a. On the *vita* that survives in his honour, see Chapter 7.

[9] A survey of his work can be found in *DS* X, 1107–9; Bithos 2009: 169–244.

objectives. He then entered the Bithynian monastery of Chenolakkos, from where he witnessed the establishment of iconoclasm in 815 and the overthrow of the patriarch Nikephoros. In his flight from the new regime, he travelled to Rome, where he carried out important work as a copyist,[10] as well as writing a two-volume *menologion*,[11] a *passio* of St Dionysius the Areopagite (*BHG* 554d)[12] and *scholia* in honour of Sts Kosmas and Damian (*BHG* 377a)[13] and St Marina (*BHG* 1167m). Once Leon V had been assassinated, Methodios returned to Byzantium as a papal legate to ask Michael II to reinstate Nikephoros in the patriarchal chair.[14] Michael had him whipped, however, and imprisoned on St Andrew's Island, where he remained for nine years (821–829), since he refused to forswear images, until an imperial decree granted him his freedom. It is generally assumed that from this time until the new persecution began, as decreed by Theophilos in 833, Methodios remained on St Andrew's Island on Cape Akritas. When Euthymios of Sardis was exiled there in 831, to die from the torture he had suffered at his captors' hands, Methodios was present and did not hesitate to extol his bravery in a detailed hagiography (*BHG* 2145).[15] By this time, Methodios was over fifty years old and had written another important *vita* of one of the major bastions of the defence of the veneration of images, Theophanes the Confessor (*BHG* 1787z).[16]

2.1.1 Early Works: Non-Combative Writings

The monk Theophanes of Sigriane, alias Theophanes the Confessor, is well known for having written a chronicle of the years 285–813 and stands out for his opposition to the ecclesiastical policies of the Emperors Konstantinos VI (the Moechian controversy) and Leon V (the iconoclast

---

[10] On his stay in Rome (ca. 815–821) and his work there as a copyist, see Canart 1979; 2008a. In Rome he most likely copied a new codex putting together the model of the manuscripts *Parisinus Gr.* 1476 and 1470 (both of which were copied in 890 by the copyist Anastasios), see Prato 1986; 2000; Perria 1991.

[11] Ehrhard 1936–1939: vol. I, 22–24; Gounelle 2005: 63–65. The manuscript *Parisinus Gr.* 1470, which contains the *vita* of the Apostle Bartholomew by Theodoros Stouditos (*BHG* 230), is closely linked to this *menologion*, cf. Di Maria 2004.

[12] On its authorship, see Canart 1979: 348, n. 21.   [13] Deubner 1907: 41–42.

[14] *Vita of Methodios* 1248C: τόμους δογματικούς, ἤτοι ὅρους ὀρθοδοξίας, παρὰ τοῦ πάπα λαβών, ἀνέρχεται πρὸς τὸν διάδοχον Λέοντος, ἐλπίσας τοῦτον ἄξαι πρὸς τὴν ὀρθοδοξίαν, καὶ ἀποκαταστῆσαι τὸν ἐν ἁγίοις Νικηφόρον τῷ ἰδίῳ θρόνῳ, 'after collecting from the Pope some dogmatic volumes, in fact the definitions of Orthodoxy, Methodios approaches Leon's successor, waiting for him to move towards Orthodoxy and reinstate St Nikephoros on his own throne'.

[15] *Vita of Euthymios of Sardis* 16–21; Gouillard 1960; 1987.

[16] For a literary analysis of the work, see Hunger 1978: vol. I, 334–39; Kazhdan 1999: 372–74; Yannopoulos 2013: 34–9.

controversy).[17] In the *vita* Methodios dedicates to his memory, he praises Theophanes' role as a spiritual leader and as founder of the monastery of Megas Agros in Sigriane on the coast of the Sea of Marmara,[18] as well his decision to choose God to the detriment of his wife Megalo and his chaste marriage.[19] We do not know what relationship there was between the hagiographer and his hero; no surviving source reports that they knew each other or overlapped anywhere at any time. This text probably post-dates the *enkomion* written by Theodoros of Stoudios, which the future patriarch seems to have known and to have used in his work, along with oral sources and testimonies of the saint's disciples that he might have gathered during his detention on St Andrew's Island.[20] It was ultimately the *vita* of Methodios and not that of Theodoros Stoudites that served as a basis for subsequent biographies in honour of Theophanes and entries in the *synaxaria*.[21]

There can be no doubt that Methodios wrote the *vita* between 823 (the year of the second transfer of the relics of Theophanes, whose miracles after this event he relates) and 829, since he counted on the saint's help in getting released from prison.[22] The date of composition was certainly before 832 in any case, since the author included quotes from this hagiography in his other great *vita*, in honour of Euthymios of Sardis, of that year.[23] The relaxed imperial iconoclast policy and his personal situation – he was imprisoned far from Constantinople – explain the author's attitude to icons: only thus can the continuous omission of the active defence of images promoted by Theophanes be understood. It is curious that Methodios' position contrasts with that of other authors who praise Theophanes, as can be seen from the dithyramb in his honour, in which the historian is referred to as 'the martyr for the icon of Christ'.[24] The term 'icon' appears only here, in biblical reminiscences to the effect that God created man in his own image.[25] In this work, Methodios concerns himself above all else with the veneration of the relics of saints, and never with that of icons.[26] Even in the final *agon*, in which the saint confronts Emperor

---

[17] *PmbZ* # 8107; *PBE* I: Theophanes 18; Yannopoulos 2013: 27–212; Jankowiak and Montinaro 2015.
[18] Mango and Ševčenko 1973: 259–67; Janin 1975: 195–97; Ruggieri 1991: 104–6 and 219–20.
[19] Krausmüller 2013b.   [20] Yannopoulos 2008.   [21] Yannopoulos 2013: 39 and 63–191.
[22] *Vita of Theophanes the Confessor* 1,14–16: λάκκου ταλαιπωρίας καὶ φυλακῆς καὶ δεσμῶν. Yannopoulos 2007b.
[23] Efthymiadis 1993b: 260, n. 7.   [24] Krumbacher 1896: 617,7–8.
[25] *Vita of Theophanes the Confessor* 18,20; 23,31; 24,12. Cf. Gen 1:26; 5:1.
[26] *Vita of Theophanes the Confessor* 34,26–27; 30–31. On Methodios' defence of the cult of saints, see Krausmüller 2015; 2016.

Leon and the heretic patriarch Ioannes Grammatikos, who is characterised as an iconoclast and a magician, the theme of the veneration of images is absent.

Moreover, the restoration of icons implemented by Empress Eirene in 787 is mentioned only in an obscure reference to the 'end of the war of the Judaiophiles',[27] and the destruction of images by Leon V is also ignored. That this iconoclast emperor asked Theophanes to pray for him, in order that he might annihilate the barbarians, is nonetheless emphasised.[28] We lack definitive information about why Methodios took this stance, but there are indications that his imprisonment was not as onerous as subsequent hagiographers would have us believe. This delicate situation of political weakness and a desire not to change the attitude of Michael II concerning the images might be a good reason. An additional factor is the character of the man who commissioned the work, a certain Stephanos, who has not yet been identified.[29] Attempts to see in this Stephanos the hegoumenos of the monastery of Megas Agros have failed: the *vita* signed by Methodios is not conceived for a monastic milieu, particularly if one takes into account that this community already had a biographical sketch of its founder courtesy of the distinguished Theodoros Stoudites. By any reckoning, the author was a highly educated layman who could appreciate Methodios' abstruse, rhetorical style; he was probably a non-combative iconodule. He may have been the *asekretis* Stephanos,[30] the *magistros* and president of the senate of the same name[31] or someone else. In any case, he was a public person with a position at court who did not wish to attract attention or offend the emperor by honouring the memory of Theophanes.

Another of Methodios' literary patterns seem to be behind the low apologetic profile of the hagiographical texts he wrote in honour of Nicholas of Myra, in which he again does not concern himself with images. (There are no references at all to icons or even to iconoclasm.)[32] Theodoros, an important figure (*periphanestatos*) in Byzantine society, had asked Methodios to write an account of the life of this saint and the miracles performed by his relics; Methodios undertook production of a

---

[27] *Vita of Theophanes the Confessor* 14,2–3. The comparison of iconoclast heretics with the Jews, who also rejected representations of divinity, is a constant in iconodule reasoning, see below ch. 6.
[28] *Vita of Theophanes the Confessor* 29,14–15.   [29] PmbZ # 7064; Yannopoulos 2004.
[30] PmbZ # 7034 and 7069; Efthymiadis 1995: 149–51.
[31] PmbZ # 7063 and 7069; Efthymiadis 1995: 162.
[32] Ševčenko 1977a: 125–26. The two versions of the *vita* of Nicholas written by Methodios can be found in Anrich 1913: vol. I, 140–50 and vol. II, 546–56. See Kazhdan 1999: 378–79; Magdalino 2015b; Krausmüller 2016.

text (*BHG* 1352y) in a 'simple and straightforward' style. Nor can anything striking be found in the *enkomion* of Nicholas of Myra attributed to Methodios (*BHG* 1352z), which repeats the main landmarks of the saint's life, such as protecting sailors from a rough sea and saving three young sisters from prostitution. Other miracles are added to illustrate the intercession of St Nicholas, including three performed on monks. The future patriarch also wrote a *kanon* to honour Nicholas of Myra that likewise includes no allusion to the iconoclast crisis. Methodios' attitude towards icons suggests that these writings date after 829, when he had regained his freedom and was the object of much attention from the Emperor Theophilos.[33] The delicate situation at court when he wrote them likely deterred him from touching on controversial subjects; he was cautious after his years of imprisonment and lacked courage and determination after witnessing the martyrdom of Euthymios of Sardis.

Another liturgical poem, the *kanon* in honour of the Sicilian martyr St Lucia, may well be from this period.[34] The acrostic indicates that it was written by Methodios. The lack of controversial elements of the iconoclast conflict indicates that this *kanon* was composed before the Triumph of Orthodoxy. Both here and in the text in honour of St Nicholas, 'incarnation' (ἐνσάρκωσις) is a recurring element of Methodian thought. It is found in all periods of his life, since it is one of the main theological arguments used to support the veneration of images: since Christ is in God's image, it is legitimate to produce images of Christ and venerate them.[35] In the case of the *kanon* dedicated to St Lucia, the affirmation in the ninth verse that the saint inaugurated a new peace in the heart of the Church[36] is a solid argument for dating its composition to the iconoclastic period. Methodios' allusion in these verses to three youths shut up in an oven allows the composition of his *Canon in Danielem prophetam et tres pueros* to be assigned to this period. The lack of even veiled references to the controversy of the icons also places it at this time.[37] Similarly belonging to this period is the *enkomion* of St Agatha (*BHG* 38),[38] the other

---

[33] As is stated by Ševčenko 1977a: 126.
[34] *AHG*, vol. IV, 279–87. Ὁ κανὼν φέρων ἀκροστιχίδα· Ἄδω πολίτης, Λουκίη, σοὶ Μεθόδιος.
[35] Giakalis 1994; Parry 1996: 70–80.
[36] Λουκία, βρύεις καὶ μετ' ἀπόφασιν / εἰρηνικὴν κατάστασιν / τῇ ἐκκλησίᾳ προφητεύεις, ἁγνή.
[37] *AHG*, vol. IV, 343–50 and 829–31.
[38] However, Mioni 1950 believes that it was written after 832, probably during Methodios' patriarchate, because the *enkomion* says nothing of the iconoclast conflict but affirms that the truth, borne out by Agatha's martyrdom, is confirmed in justice and in peace (see p. 74). Crimi 2006: 156, n. 51 accepts this late dating. Cf. also Krausmüller 1999; 2009a; Angelidi 2012; Crimi 2017.

patron saint of Methodios' native Sicily, to whom he devoted a work in the form of a homily on 5 February. Nothing in the text allows us to identify the year, but the silence regarding icons speaks for itself, as does the specific reference to the subject of the incarnation of Christ,[39] a characteristic element of iconodule assumptions that could pass without arousing suspicion among even the most recalcitrant iconoclasts.

We know that after the death of Michael II in 829, the new Emperor Theophilos summoned Methodios to invite him to renounce icons; after a verbal confrontation, Methodios was again whipped and imprisoned.[40] In a fresh attempt (the third), Theophilos decided to fête Methodios to try to purchase his good will; he had him installed in his palace and made him a friend. Methodios took advantage of the situation to work for Orthodoxy and converted many of those close to the emperor, even persuading Theophilos to become less intransigent, according to his hagiographer.[41] It is not unreasonable to suppose that during this period our author kept a low profile, avoiding sensitive subjects and restricting himself to his protagonists' abilities to perform miracles. This may well have been one of the most fertile stages in Methodios' literary career.

2.1.2   The Vita *of Euthymios of Sardis (BHG 2145)*

Sometime later, at the beginning of the year 832, Methodios wrote the *vita* of the metropolitan of Sardis, Euthymios, exactly forty days after the death of the saint on 26 December.[42] This biography, which was commissioned by the *archimandrites* Symeon[43] to extol the saint's memory, includes the main landmarks of Euthymios' life journey and his ecclesiastical history.[44] Little is known of Euthymios' early life, but he appears to have taken part in the Second Council of Nicaea (787) in active defence of icons[45] after having been named metropolitan of Sardis by the patriarch Tarasios.[46] Empress Eirene sent him on a diplomatic mission to Baghdad, and he

---

[39] *Enkomion of St Agatha* 3, 10–11 and ch. 19.
[40] *Vita of Methodios* 1252B; Pargoire 1903b. On the author of the *vita* of the patriarch and the circumstances of its production, see Chapter 7.
[41] *Vita of Methodios* 1252C.
[42] *Vita of Euthymios of Sardis* 16–21; Gouillard 1960; 1987. For a literary analysis of this work, cf. Kazhdan 1999: 375–57; Kaplan 2015: 175–76.
[43] On this person, see Section 3.2.1 in the Dekapolitan Milieu.
[44] Concerning Euthymios' life (754–831), see *PmbZ* # 1838; *PBE* I: Euthymios 1; Pargoire 1901/1902.
[45] Mansi XII, 994, 1011, 1015, 1039, 1087, 1147; Mansi XIII, 37, 129–33, 136, 172, 365.
[46] According to his other hagiographer Metrophanes, *Enkomion of Euthymios of Sardis* 71–2, n. 11, see Section 5.2.1.

likely took the opportunity to visit the town of Edessa and venerate the *acheiropoietos* icon there (ch. 9). Emperor Nikephoros I accused him of treason and of having participated in the disturbance of the usurper Bardanes Tourkos, which led to his exile on the small island of Pantelleria (near Sicily) together with the bishops Theophylaktos of Nicomedia and Eudoxios of Amorion (chs. 5–6). According to Methodios, the true motive was not political, but the fact that Euthymios had consecrated as a nun a young girl whom the emperor wanted to take as his wife. In any case, Euthymios never again occupied his post in Sardis, although he continued to be the legitimate metropolitan until his death, since Tarasios did not yield to the pressure of Emperor Nikephoros, who wanted Euthymios deposed (ch. 7).

Methodios continues by relating that thanks to the efforts of his supporters, Euthymios returned in 806, but he was not reinstated in his high ecclesiastical post in Sardis. Like Theodoros Stoudites, he was the leader of the iconodule party under Leon V, and far from accepting the proposals of the iconoclasts that he agree with them in exchange for the patriarchate, he confronted the emperor in a fierce *agon*, in which he based his arguments on the Scriptures.[47] Because of all this, he was again exiled in 815 to Thasos, where he received two epistles of support from Theodoros Stoudites.[48] During the reign of Michael II, which was much more permissive with the iconodules, the emperor tried to calm both parties down by calling a meeting, at which Euthymios was so intransigent that the sovereign had him stripped naked and exiled once more (chs. 11–12). Despite everything, Michael II soon released him, and we know from *epistle* 545 of Theodoros Stoudites that at the end of the year 826 Euthymios was working as a teacher in Constantinople.

When a pamphlet was circulated in the early days of the reign of Theophilos predicting the emperor's death, an investigation of the conspiracy led to the arrest and interrogation of Euthymios. His refusal to cooperate earned him a third period of exile, on St Andrew's Island off Cape Akritas, where Methodios himself was already imprisoned.[49] In fact, similar pamphlets predicting the ends of the Emperors Leon V and Michael II had also been circulated, and Methodios appeared to be connected to their composition.[50] Euthymios' death in 831 as the result

---

[47] *Vita of Euthymios of Sardis* 8–10; *Vita of Niketas of Medikion* 35; *Vita* A *of Theophylaktos of Nicomedia* 12–14.
[48] Theod. Stoud., *epist.* 74 and 112. [49] *Vita of Euthymios of Sardis* 13–15.
[50] Treadgold 2004.

of a brutal whipping made him one of the few iconodule saints to be genuinely martyred.[51] The forty days that passed from his death to when Methodios began to write his *vita* lend the account pathos and allowed the inclusion of some miracles to ratify the hero's holiness (chs. 41–48). To the prediction of his own death are added the posthumous appearances of Euthymios and miraculous healings, which made it possible for him to be given an official liturgical tribute in the *Synaxarion of Constantinople* and in the main *synaxaria*.[52]

The testimony of Euthymios became a point of reference for Methodios in the fight against imperial power, the defence of Orthodoxy and the theological justification of the veneration of images. In contrast to his earlier works, here the subject of the icons constitutes the main storyline of the narration and of the personal vision of religion shared by protagonist and hagiographer. Throughout his account, Methodios emphasises the political dimension of his hero's confession in assuming the postulates of Theodoros Stoudites, with whom he had many points in common in regard to how holiness was to be represented, as for instance in the silences in the *vita* about Euthymios' origin, family and the like. Many hagiographical details unconnected with virtue had already been omitted by Theodoros Stoudites in his *Laudatio of Theoktiste*, in which he leaves out, for example, the place of birth, parents and childhood of his protagonist.[53] Indeed, Theodoros' brother, Ioseph Stoudites, the metropolitan of Thessaloniki, who is also praised by Methodios since he was arrested together with Euthymios in connection with the affair of the pamphlets, congratulated the saint for his valour and hoped for a similar opportunity to confront the iconoclasts (chs. 12–15). This ability of Euthymios to encourage others to follow his example, together with the deep impression that his last days must have made on Methodios, explains why, after the restoration of icons, the metropolitan of Sardis was celebrated in the *Synodikon of Orthodoxy*, where he is lauded for his iconoduly immediately after the patriarchs, as the first in the list of confessors and archbishops who suffered for defending images.[54]

---

[51] *Vita of Euthymios of Sardis* 16–21; *Acta of David, Symeon and Georgios* 229,10f. and 238,4–16. Both sources agree on the date (Tuesday, 26 December 831) but not the age: according to Methodios the saint was seventy-eight years old, and eighty according to the *Acta of David, Symeon and Georgios*, see Gouillard 1987: 10.

[52] *SynaxCP* 345,1–38; 345/346,49–55 (26 December); *Typikon of the Great Church* I, 160,61 (26 December); *Typikon Messinense* 85,241 (26 December); *Typika Dmitrievskij* I, 37, 358, 359 (26 December).

[53] Efthymiadis and Featherstone 2007: 17, n. 16.   [54] *Synodikon of Orthodoxy* 53,121.

The years of Theophilos' tenure are particularly obscure in the reconstruction of Methodios' biography. After the emperor's attempts to attract Methodios to iconoclasm and the severe punishment he got when he refused, Theophilos seems finally to have decided to install Methodios at the court in order to have him under close supervision and take advantage of his ability to foretell the future.[55] This reconstruction led Stiernon to believe the anonymous continuator of Theophanes (*Theophanes Continuatus*) and to postulate that Methodios accompanied Theophilos on the expedition to the Arab lands in 838 that was to end with the humiliating defeat at Amorion.[56] The point cannot be confirmed, but it is true that this measure would have nipped in the bud any possible iconodule rebellion in Constantinople led by Methodios that aimed to take advantage of the absence of the emperor and his troops.[57] There can nonetheless be no doubt that the position maintained by Methodios during the period was vital to his future appointment as patriarch by Theodora. His proactive efforts to defend icons meant that he was capable of restoring their veneration. Moreover, his inside knowledge of the situation at court and of the balance of forces there made him the right man to implement Theodora's will and at the same time to guarantee the rights of succession of little Michael III, the crown prince. The hagiographical work of Methodios' time as a patriarch is characterised not only by its apologetic nature in defence of icons, but also by its political orientation.

2.1.3 *His Writing As a Patriarch: The Fight against Heresy*

After his appointment as patriarch of Constantinople on 3 March 843, Methodios began a series of works that shaped the defeat of heresy in writing. This is the case of the *Speech about the Holy Icons* (Μεθοδίου λόγος περὶ τῶν ἁγίων εἰκόνων),[58] which may have been written on the occasion of the discussions of the synod in the capital that would finally take Methodios to the patriarchate.[59] Other controversial works by

---

[55] Ps-Symeon 645,3–7; Treadgold 2004.
[56] *DS* X, 1109; Theoph. Cont. III, 24,1–12; Genesios 35,73–76; Skylitzes 28,85–89.
[57] Lilie 1999: 208.
[58] Pitra, *Monumenta* II, 357–61; Bithos 2009: 67–73; *Regestes*, nr. 417, for whom it is a solemn profession of faith intended to be pronounced in March 843 by the new patriarch. Doubts about its authorship have arisen, since the style of the *Speech* differs from the convoluted style of other Methodian texts, see Hinterberger 2008: 119–50.
[59] In contrast, for Afinogenov 1996b: 83, n. 17 its date is earlier. On this particular synod, see Karlin-Hayter 2006b.

Methodios launching fierce attacks on iconoclasts and their theological arguments include the ἔκθεσις περὶ τῶν ἁγίων εἰκόνων[60] and three fragments of different homilies on the cross as an instrument of the Passion of Christ, in which Methodios attacks the iconoclast position and vindicates the suffering of Christ incarnate for our sake, to pronounce that Jesus' humanity is an integral part of Him.[61] All these compositions assume the constant reminder of the Triumph of Orthodoxy celebrated in a liturgical manner with a magnificent procession in which icons were again taken to the church of Hagia Sophia with the participation of all levels of Byzantine society. This ceremony took place on 11 March 843 and has been celebrated annually ever since on the first Sunday in Lent.[62]

The praise of the victorious heroes and the condemnation of the heretics were expressed in the *Synodicon Orthodoxiae* (*BHG* 1392), which was written by Methodios either on the inauguration of the feast day in 843 or on its first anniversary in 844.[63] The editor of the text, Gouillard, believes that the structure of this celebration goes back to its very origin, although contemporary sources (Georgios Monachos, *Synodicon vetus*, *Vita Theodorae*, *Vita Michaelis Syncelli*) do not mention it. Herrin is of the same opinion and believes that the restoration of icons and the annual celebration of this feast day coincide, since this first liturgy was largely maintained as it operated as an ecclesiastical council.[64] The testimony of some *vitae* (*Vita of Eirene*, *Vita of Nikolaos of Stoudios*) supports this interpretation. For Afinogenov, however, the ceremony is later and reflects the situation of the Macedonian period.[65] Basing his arguments on the anonymous *Narratio historica in festum restitutionis imaginum* (which he places in the ninth century), Afinogenov believes that the route of the original procession was similar to that of the emperor's triumphal marches, emphasising the penitence required to absolve Emperor Theophilos. In any case, the *Synodikon of Orthodoxy*, which describes the ecclesiastical ceremony of the restoration of image veneration,

---

[60] This text, which has survived in codex *Vaticanus Gr.* 1753, fol. 225r–30v, is strongly dependent on the aforementioned λόγος περὶ τῶν ἁγίων εἰκόνων, whose arguments it shares, see Alexakis 1996a: 110–16; Bithos 2009: 73–85.

[61] These three fragments of sermons were mistakenly edited by Migne among the works of Methodios of Olympos in *PG* 18, 397–404; Pitra, *Monumenta* II, 354.

[62] Theoph. Cont. III, 6,16–21; Genesios IV 3, p. 57,81ff.; Ps-Symeon 647,16–18; *Synodicon vetus* 156,6–8, p. 132; 156,24–25, p. 196; Skylitzes 81,3–84,83. Cf. *Regestes*, nr. 425; Lilie 1999: 228–30; Varona Codeso 2010: 80–82.

[63] For Gouillard 1961a: 380 Methodios is also alleged to have produced for this first anniversary a *Kanon on the Restoration of the Holy Icons*. However, manuscript tradition suggests that this work was from the Stoudite milieu, see Section 1.2.1.

[64] Herrin 2001: 209–10.   [65] Afinogenov 1999a.

was gradually enriched with later additions that expanded the list of orthodox patriarchs and emperors worthy of acclaim.[66] The *Typikon of the Great Church* also gradually increased the number of recent patriarchs to whom homage is paid by means of a procession: Nikephoros, Methodios, Photios, Stephanos and even Stephanos III (925–927).[67]

Practically all of Methodios' poetic work is related to the restoration of the veneration of images. The poem of twenty-seven iambic trimeters dedicated to the icon of Christ that watched over the main entrance to the palace, known as the Chalke Gate,[68] in which he declares the victory of iconoduly, summarises the basis in the incarnation of Christ for the theology of image worshippers (verses 3–10), denounces the errors of heretics and condemns Emperor Leon III (verses 11–20) but goes on to praise Empress Theodora for restoring Orthodoxy and the icons that had been destroyed (verses 17–27). Likewise, the poem of five iamboi *In crucem*[69] sings of the cross as the place where the Lord incarnate suffered. It is significant that the patron mentioned in the fourth line for having embellished this cross with gold is Michael. This reference to the young crown prince, together with the previous one to Empress Theodora (and implicitly again to the heir: σὺν τοῖς ἑαυτῆς χρυσοπορφύροις κλάδοις, v. 19), acts as a memorable diptych designed to guarantee his succession to the throne and to legitimise him as a faultless iconodule sovereign. This political bid of the patriarch to consolidate the dynastic rights of Michael III was due solely to his wish to certify the end of the iconoclast heresy and avoid new outbreaks of it.

Another clear example of this attitude of the patriarchate is the writing by Methodios himself of an *idiomelon* preserved in the liturgical *menaia* on the occasion of the feast day of the holy Emperor Konstantinos I and the holy dowager empress Helena, who were renowned for their support of Christianity and their discovery of the relics of the Passion of Christ.[70] These two imperial figures, to whom Methodios also dedicated a homily,[71] can be seen as the equivalents of Theodora the restorer and her son Michael III; this had been a frequent identification within iconodule rhetoric since 787, when Eirene, the regent of her son Konstantinos VI (780–797), undertook the first restoration of the veneration of icons.[72]

---

[66] Flusin 2010. [67] Connor 2016: 120–21
[68] *In imaginem sic dictae* τῆς Χαλκῆς *portae*, ed. Sternbach 1898: 150–51; Mango 1959: 126–32, who in actual fact reproduces the edition of Mercati 1920: 198–99.
[69] *In crucem*, ed. Sternbach 1898: 151; Mercati 1920: 199.
[70] Chris and Paranikas 1871: 99; *Menaion* V: 145.   [71] Chris and Paranikas 1871: 99.
[72] Lilie 1996; Herrin 2001: 51–129; Brubaker and Haldon 2011: 248–365.

After the final session of the Second Council of Nicaea, which was held in the Magnaura Palace in the presence of the emperor and empress, the bishops acclaimed them a new Konstantinos and Helena: 'Long live the emperors. Long live Konstantinos and his mother Eirene. Long live the Orthodox emperors. Long live the victorious emperors. Long live the peace-bringing emperors. New Konstantinos and New Helena eternal may be the memory. May God protect their Empire.'[73] The parallels between Eirene/Konstantinos VI and Theodora/Michael III returning to iconoduly were exploited by Methodios, to whom the synodal decree of March 843 ("Ορος τῆς συνόδου τῆς ὑπὸ Μιχαὴλ καὶ Θεοδώρας τῆς αὐτοῦ μητρός) is attributed.[74]

The Triumph of Orthodoxy not only meant the restoration of pious practices that had been abandoned for over a generation, such as the production of icons, prostrating oneself and bowing before them, kissing them as a sign of veneration and the like. But also and more important, it meant the restructuring of the ecclesiastical hierarchy, which had been led by the iconoclast Ioannes VII Grammatikos during the final years, and which mostly consisted of bishops and hegoumenoi who, after almost thirty years of iconoclasm, were heretics or had agreed with heretics. In order to prevent believers from continuing to labour under a religious error, Methodios had to contemplate a purge of these leaders, who had challenged the teachings of the patriarchs Tarasios and Nikephoros, replacing them with others of iconodule leanings who, as well as defending images and avoiding a return to heresy, would support his leadership.[75] During his patriarchate, Methodios thus adopted a series of measures that would have a direct impact on the literary production of the time, creating a breeding ground for hagiographical accounts vindicating the iconoduly of their protagonists. The decrees he passed against iconoclasts, who were anathematised, are reflected in the short work *Contra Iconomachos* (*Refutation of the Iconoclasts*) and in the letter he sent to the patriarch of Jerusalem, Sergios I, in which he fiercely attacks Ioannes Grammatikos and denounces his continuous attempts to defend and vindicate heresy even after the return of Orthodoxy.[76]

---

[73] Mansi XII, 416. On the continuous appropriation of this cult, see Brubaker 1994; Connor 2016: 115, nn. 83–84.
[74] *Synodikon of Orthodoxy* 293–98. For the doubts as to its authenticity, cf. *Regestes*, nr. 416 and p. 66.
[75] Pargoire 1903b; Afinogenov 1996a; 1996b; Karlin-Hayter 2006b.
[76] *Regestes*, nr. 434, who date this episode after 11 March 846; cf. Afinogenov 1996b: 84; Signes Codoñer 2013c: 102–6. For the patriarch of Jerusalem, Sergios I, see *PmbZ* # 6663. Some years previously, in March–April 843, Methodios had already written him a lost missive (nr. 419) on the

As a consequence, neither Ioannes nor any of his close collaborators were ever readmitted to the bosom of the Church. This was precisely one of Methodios' main concerns: how to reinstate those who had fallen into heresy or who had agreed with the iconoclasts. Children and elderly people, and those who had been tortured or coerced to accept iconoclasm, were reinstated if they atoned for their sins with prayer for a stipulated period.[77] Methodios was responsible for drawing up the canonical ordinances in the Church for those returning from apostasy,[78] together with the formulae for prayers of propitiation that were to be recited by the penitent. Adults who had voluntarily accepted heretical postulates would be readmitted after two years of penitence. In contrast, clerics and iconoclast leaders could only be admitted to communion on their deaths if they had spent the rest of their lives in repentance and receiving catechesis.

The Triumph of Orthodoxy not only defeated the iconoclasts but also prevailed over other forms of heresy. This is shown by the return to the Church of the sect of the followers of a certain Zelix, the Zelikians,[79] whose public conversion took place in a solemn procession in which the initiates were anointed and dressed in white.[80] By the same token, unanimity was lacking among the victors of the dispute (the iconodules), and the representatives of dissent ended up as monks of the monastery of Stoudios, although Methodios did not hesitate to excommunicate them en masse.[81] The decree he issued against the monastery's leaders, Naukratios and Athanasios, together with the surviving fragments of the correspondence he maintained with them, showed the tension that existed between the two parties. It was precisely the Stoudite faction that was ultimately behind the false accusation of fornication that a woman made against the patriarch.[82]

The traditional interpretation of these events imagines a polarised scenario with, on the one hand, radical iconodules (the heirs of the position of Theodoros Stoudites), who sought to defeat iconoclasm, avenging its persecuted leaders and preventing any new outbreak of heresy

---

same subject. Its writing is perhaps linked to the presence in his circle of collaborators such as Michael Synkellos, who was from Jerusalem, see Section 2.3.1.

[77] Grumel 1935; Darrouzès 1987: 16–18; Arranz 1990.   [78] *Regestes*, nr. 430; *PG* 100, 1300A-7.
[79] *PmbZ* # 8642; Gouillard 1961a: 373–75; Ahrweiler 1965: 361–63; Lemerle 1973: 42–43. See Section 7.2.2.
[80] Georgios Monachos 802,18–19 compares them to the Manicheans. Cf. Theoph. Cont. IV, 12; Genesios 60,84–88; Ps-Symeon 654,6–11.
[81] On the Stoudite schism, see Von Dobschütz 1909a; Grumel 1935; Doens and Hannick 1973; Löwe 1982; Darrouzès 1987; Lilie 1999: 248–60; Maksimovic 2000. See Chapter 1.
[82] *Vita of Ioannikios* by Petros 431B. See Section 2.2.1.

by force. On the other hand, there were the moderates, who wanted to establish an understanding with the now defeated iconoclasts in the interests of social and ecclesiastical peace. The moderate attitude of Methodios would have been determinant in having Theodora entrust him with restoring the cult of icons but avoiding revolts.[83] The extremist iconodules (the Zealots) regarded it as up to them to lead the post-iconoclastic Church and believed that their suffering, which had allowed Orthodoxy to be re-established, should not be in vain. The ordinations and appointments of Methodios, however, excluded them in favour of less capable candidates with fewer qualifications.[84] The support Methodios received from monastic leaders such as Ioannikios and the rejection of others such as the Stoudites, give us a sense of some of the tendencies that the literature promoted by the patriarchate developed during this period. Before we analyse the works of Methodios' collaborators, however, let us consider one of his most outstanding cultural policies: the processional and festive transfer of the relics of the main defenders of icons who had died in exile.

2.1.4 The Promotion of New Saints and Their Texts

Together with Empress Theodora, the patriarch Methodios promoted the transfer of the remains of Theophylaktos to Nicomedia from Strobilos, the place of exile where he had died, so that they could be buried in a church he himself had built.[85] Methodios had already praised this confessor in his *Vita Euthymii Sardensis*[86] and did not hesitate to include him among the metropolitans acclaimed in the *Synodikon of Orthodoxy*.[87] It is even possible that this transfer triggered the writing of one of the *vitae* in honour of Theophylaktos.[88] In a similar manner, the patriarchate of Methodios also saw the repatriation of the relics of Georgios, the bishop of Mytilene,[89] who had died in exile imposed by Leon V after the implementation of the

---

[83] Dvornik 1948: 13. In contrast, for other authors Methodios should be considered a radical due to his severity with the iconoclast leaders, cf. Grumel 1935: 390–91 and 393; Karlin-Hayter 1977: 141.
[84] *Vita of Methodios* 1257C; Dvornik 1948: 14; Morris 1995: 9–11; Karlin-Hayter 2006b; Hatlie 2007a: 392–93.
[85] *Vita A of Theophylaktos of Nicomedia* 18.
[86] *Vita of Euthymios of Sardis* 70–71: σὺν τῷ Νικομηδέων προέδρῳ καὶ ὁμολογητῇ, Θεοφυλάκτῳ φημὶ τῷ τρισολβίῳ.
[87] *Synodikon of Orthodoxy* 53,123; cf. the Horos of the Synod of 843, p. 297,113.
[88] *Vita A of Theophylaktos of Nicomedia* 68.
[89] *PmbZ* # 2160; *PBE* I: Georgios 134. See also *PmbZ* # 2110 and 2161; *PBE* I: Georgios 248. Halkin 1959; Talbot 1998: 165–6, n. 119.

Second Iconoclasm.[90] To judge from a *kanon* by Ignatios Diakonos, the relics of the patriarch Tarasios were also repatriated.[91] In Section 2.1.3, we saw how Methodios, with Theodora's approval, became personally involved in the repatriation of the relics of Theodoros Stoudites from the island of Prinkipos to Constantinople on 26 January 844.[92] That transfer compared Theodoros to St John Chrysostom, the fourth-century patriarch, whose translation was celebrated liturgically on the following day. Three years later, Methodios did the same with the relics of the patriarch Nikephoros, who had died in exile at his monastery of St Theodoros (near Chrysopolis on the Bosphorus).[93] In contrast to the previous transfer, which was of a more ecclesiastical nature, this one had strong political overtones: Nikephoros was honoured with what we today would term a state funeral.[94]

A hagiographical account (*BHG* 1336–37b) of this event survives, which is described in detail by the presbyteros Theophanes, a member of the literary circle of the patriarchate.[95] Methodios himself, as patriarch, addressed Empress Theodora, to request her assistance in the enterprise and thus dignify her tenure. Accompanied by a large delegation, Methodios travelled to the monastery to collect the relics of his predecessor in the patriarchate. As soon as he arrived, he prayed to St Nikephoros, comparing him to St John Chrysostom, who like him had been exiled for confronting the emperor in defence of the faith. Nikephoros' relics were transported in a *dromon* (a ship belonging to the imperial navy) that had been especially equipped for the purpose, and on their arrival in Constantinople were received by Emperor Michael III and the highest dignitaries of the court, who carried them on their shoulders to Hagia Sophia. Finally, on 13 March 846, to coincide with the anniversary of the exile of Nikephoros, his remains were solemnly paraded through the centre of Constantinople (expelling demons as they went) to the church of the Holy Apostles, where they were buried alongside emperors and other patriarchs such as John Chrysostom himself. The importance of this

---

[90] *Vita of Georgios of Mytilene* 4, 35,6–10. *SynaxCP* 589–90 (7 April) and 687.
[91] Papadopoulos-Kerameus 1902: 88–91; Wolska-Conus 1970: 334–35; Mango and Efthymiadis 1997: 16; Senina 2011/2012. For the attribution of this *kanon* to Ignatios, see *Synaxarion Evergetis* I, 566.
[92] *Translation of Theodoros of Stoudios and Ioseph* 58,10–16. See Section 1.2.1.
[93] Janin 1954: 96–98; 1975: 27; Ruggieri 1991: 203.
[94] For the contrast between the transfer of Theodoros Stoudites' remains and that of the patriarch Nikephoros' relics, see Afinogenov 1996a: 68–70. On the essential role played by the transfer of the saint's relics in the process of sanctification, see Talbot 2015.
[95] Concerning this Theophanes, see *PmbZ* # 8151; see Section 2.2.3.

transfer meant that the liturgical celebration of Nikephoros was a double one: both the day of his death (2 June) and that of his exile and subsequent transfer (13 March). The celebration was so lavish that it surpassed any previous event in honour of a patriarch or emperor. Methodios thus not only vindicated an iconodule confessor but celebrated the defeat of heresy and publicly fêted the triumph of the Church over the State.

The vindication of the defeat of iconoclasm and of the figure of the patriarch Nikephoros by Methodios also included his commissioning (and perhaps direct involvement in writing) three illuminated psalters that represented a milestone in Byzantine book production. The Khludov Psalter,[96] the Pantokrator Psalter[97] and the Paris Psalter (today incomplete)[98] made up a triad produced by a single team of professionals with a clear propaganda and apologetic purpose in defence of the theology of icons. In these manuscripts from the middle of the ninth century, the text of the Psalms is accompanied by illuminations in the margins showing an iconographic programme regarding the contemporary situation of the Church, in which the fight against iconoclast heresy is narrated. The patriarch Nikephoros appears in a very large number of representations in this cycle (absence from the heretical council of 815, *calcatio colli* or 'trampling the neck' of Ioannes Grammatikos, etc.), making iconography another weapon in the dispute. These miniatures probably reproduce an earlier model of the Second Iconoclasm, perhaps in monastic milieux.[99]

What is certain is that the three psalters include the liturgical uses of the church of Hagia Sophia, which meant that they were produced in the workshop of the patriarchate.[100] The vision they transmit must thus be the official version of triumphal Orthodoxy, whose origin lies in the patriarchate of Constantinople.[101] The fruits of this process are manuscripts that are

---

[96] Moskow GIM Khludov 129D; Full facsimile: *Salterio Chludov*, Madrid 2006; Corrigan 1992: 140–44 and 205–8; Pankova et al. 2007; Dobrynina 2010.

[97] Mount Athos, Pantokrator 61; Dufrenne 1965; Pelekanides et al. 1979: vol. III, 265–80 and figs. 180–237; Anderson 1994; 1998; Lechner 2002. Some leaves of it are preserved in the St Petersburg RNB Gr. 265 (Granstrem 80 and 346). See Anderson 1998a.

[98] *Parisinus Gr.* 20; Anderson 1998b.   [99] Auzépy 2003b; Evangelatou 2009.

[100] According to Grabar 1984: 284–86 these illustrated psalters were produced during the same period, in the same scriptorium, and perhaps partly by the same artist. Grabar however dates them later during Photios' patriarchate. It is not unreasonable to imagine competition in the book industry between the patriarchate and the scriptorium of the monastery of Stoudios, to judge by the intense copying of manuscripts that took place there in the mid-ninth century, see Hatlie 2007a: 412–49; Evangelatou 2009: 60–61.

[101] Walter 1970. The bibliography on this set of manuscripts is abundant, see Grabar 1965; Cormack 1977b: 160; Grabar 1984: 196–202 and 214–33; Kazhdan and Maguire 1991: 20; Auzépy 2003b; Fanar 2006; Crostini 2013: 112–13.

doubly illuminated, as the verse of the Psalms is accompanied by a New Testament illustration with a second parallel image with contemporary references. The general opinion today is that they were copied on the orders of the patriarch Methodios, that is, between 843 and 847,[102] and that the illustrations indicate the existence of a previous iconographic model perhaps coined by Methodios himself during his stay in Rome and subsequently brought to Constantinople.[103] The existence of this lost prototype seems confirmed by the inclusion in the Pantokrator Psalter of a poem of fourteen verses in Byzantine dodecasyllables celebrating the victory of the patriarch Nikephoros over his three enemies, Emperor Leon V and the iconoclast patriarchs Theodotos and Ioannes Grammatikos.[104]

The final years of Methodios' patriarchate were another particularly fertile time in his hagiographical production. The choice of his heroes clearly illustrates his intentions beyond paying tribute to and canonising confessors of iconodule Orthodoxy, establishing the pillars of the Church he had created after the purge of ecclesiastical heretics and strengthening the sectors most loyal to his legacy. To counteract the movements of Naukratios and other Stoudites, in what was both a skilful political move and no doubt the product of personal admiration,[105] Methodios wrote another important hagiography of one of the major defenders of icons, a confessor and the leader of Orthodoxy during the First and Second Iconoclasms. The man in question is Theodoros Stoudites. Although this final *vita* has not survived, we know that it served as a model for the *Vita B* of Theodoros Stoudites written faithfully by the Stoudite monk Michael, as he says in the preface.[106] Likewise the mention this hagiographer includes in another of his works (the *vita* of Nikolaos Stoudites) of the transfer of the relics of Theodoros to the Princes' Islands[107] makes it

---

[102] Walter 1987: 220; Corrigan 1992: 124–34; Brubaker and Haldon 2001: 43–47. It is possible that Michael Synkellos may have assisted him in the production of these illuminated books, see Hatlie 2007a: 412–13. In fact, the Khludov Psalter appears to be related to the *Vita* of Leon of Catania, see Section 2.3.1.c.
[103] Anderson 2006. See also Cutler 1977. [104] Ševčenko 1965; Kazhdan 1999: 279.
[105] As proven by the letter Theodoros Stoudites sent Methodios while he was in Rome, Theod. Stoud., *epist.* 274 (and perhaps also *epist.* 549). Cf. Prastch 1998: 254; Lilie 1999: 195–97.
[106] Krausmüller 2006: 144–50; 2013a. See Sections 1.2.2 and 5.2.2.
[107] *Vita of Nikolaos Stoud.* 900B: ἀλλὰ περὶ τούτου ἔνιοι τῶν τῆς ἐκκλησίας ἱερομυστῶν ἀνεγράψαντο δῶρον ὥσπερ τι φερωνύμως τὰς αὐτοῦ ἀριστείας κοινωφελὲς διαζωγραφήσαντες. Although this and other sources place Theodoros' death in the cape Akritas, the version given by the *Translation of Theodoros of Stoudios and Ioseph of Thessaloniki* (*BHG* 1756t) seems historically preferable. According to it, Theodoros died on Prinkipos and his relics were transferred to Stoudios in 844. For the inconsistencies of the narratives see Van de Vorst 1913a: 31–34.

clear that Methodios is being referred to. According to Michael's testimony, the *vita* was written in the characteristically intricate and affected style of the ecclesiastical leader, who was by this time quite old. It is not surprising that Methodios praised his former rival in this manner, since they had much in common, even if Theodoros' disciples had strayed from the Church and used their master's legacy against the patriarch. Indeed, the transfer of the relics of Theodoros Stoudites confirmed publicly the good relationship between Methodios and the hegoumenos to whom he paid a singular tribute, treating his remains with the greatest respect and praying before them. Perhaps his strong personal involvement in this celebration explains the production of the *vita*. This might also have triggered the composition of the hymn Methodios dedicated to Theodoros that was mentioned in the liturgical *Typikon* of the patriarch Alexios Stoudites (1025–1043), which includes a calendar of commemorations that reflects ninth-century Stoudite practice. This *kanon* produced by Methodios appears precisely during the saint's celebration on 11 November.[108]

This was in any case not the only canonisation process Methodios encouraged and took active part in before his death on 14 June 847. Despite his advanced age, he wrote another *idiomelon* to celebrate the forty-two martyrs of Amorion who died on 6 March 845.[109] As if the catastrophic defeat of Theophilos and the loss of the original homeland of the imperial dynasty in 838 had not been bad enough, the cruel martyrdom to which the caliph Al-Wathiq (842–847) subjected his prisoners was a great shock to the Byzantine mentality. A way of exorcising it and at the same time exonerating the current Byzantine rulers from any blame was the promotion of the cult of these heroes as champions of the new iconodule Orthodoxy who had been martyred by infidels. Proof of patriarchal promotion of the forty-two martyrs of Amorion is provided by the fact that two of the compositions on this event are by close collaborators of the patriarch. I refer to the hymn of Ignatios Diakonos and the hagiography of the forty-two martyrs of Amorion by Michael Synkellos (version Γ = *BHG* 1213).[110] At the end of Methodios' patriarchate, and perhaps sponsored by him, two other accounts of the martyrdom of the forty-two saints also appeared: the versions B (*BHG* 1212) and P (*BHG* 1214c), in which Theophilos and Theodora are highly praised in accord with the

---

[108] Pentkovskij 2001: 293–94. [109] *Menaion* IV: 29.
[110] For the relation between the two texts, cf. Tomadakes in *AHG* vol. VII, 86–98; Kotzambassi 1992: 123–24.

official propaganda imposed by the empress as a condition for the Triumph of Orthodoxy.[111]

In the same way, no sooner had Ioannikios died on 4 November 846 than Methodios decided to encourage his veneration by means of a religious *kanon* of his own making. The hymn presents the acrostic Ἰωαννικίῳ πατρὶ χριστοφόρῳ πατριάρχης ὁ Μεθόδιος.[112] In this composition, Methodios invokes the various levels of ascetic life (*praxis, theoria* and *gnosis*) incarnate in an exemplary fashion in his ally and good friend,[113] whom he compares to St John the Forerunner and without whose support he would not have become patriarch. What is more, the close friendship between Methodios and Ioannikios was strengthened by the fact that years before Methodios had founded his own monastery near where Ioannikios lived.[114] It is easy to see how the patriarch, whose strength was failing with age, was satisfied with writing a liturgical poem himself and entrusting someone else with the composition of a hagiography to encourage veneration of the saint who had recently died. This person would have been the monk Petros, one of Methodios' most loyal collaborators, along with Ignatios Diakonos, Theophanes Presbyteros, Georgios Monachos, the Graptoi brothers and Michael Synkellos.

2.2 The Men of Letters of the Methodian Milieu

The task of encouraging the veneration of iconodule confessors was too much for the patriarch of Constantinople with his multiple commitments, in particular, in the convulsed period in which Methodios was forced to govern, attempting to neutralise the threats of the heretics and temper internal disagreement among the orthodox. It is thus unsurprising that, despite his proven skills as a hagiographer, Methodios delegated to other authors the composition of the *vitae* needed to support the veneration of figures who had been a point of reference of his patriarchate: Ioannikios,

---

[111] Prieto Domínguez 2019b. See Chapter 4.
[112] *AHG*, vol. III, 134–45 and 569–72. As a counterpart to this composition by Methodios, the *melodos* Theodosia also wrote a *kanon* in honour of Ioannikios (the only one dedicated to a man by a Byzantine woman). By means of this text, the female author vindicates herself as the spiritual daughter of the ascetic, legitimates her situation as the head of the convent of Kloubiou and provides her establishment with undeniable iconodule credentials, cf. *AHG*, vol. III, 122–33; Szövérffy 1979: vol. II, 48; Topping 1986/1988; Kazhdan and Talbot 1991: 400–401.
[113] *Vita of Ioannikios by Sabas* 46–48, 372B–76A; 53, 381C–82C; *Vita of Ioannikios by Petros* 70–71, 432B–33A; Cunningham 1991: 102–5. See also Von Dobschütz 1909a: 93–100.
[114] The monastery stood within the limits of the bishopric of Kios (*Menologion Basilii* 500A) and was called Elegmoi/Eleobomon, see Janin 1975: 142–48; Ruggieri 1991: 217. See also *Vita of Michael the Synkellos* 26, 104,10–12; Lilie 1999: 190–91; Mango 1968a: 174ff. See Chapter 3.

the hegoumenos of Bithynia and his strong supporter in ecclesiastical policy, and the patriarchs Tarasios and Nikephoros, his orthodox predecessors who had distinguished themselves in the fight against iconoclasm, were for Methodios models to follow in his work as head of the Church. The monk Petros was chosen to extol the life of Ioannikios, while Ignatios Diakonos wrote the *vitae* of the two patriarchs and Theophanes Presbyteros the account of the transfer of the relics of Nikephoros. This group of writers working for Methodios was first identified by Afinogenov, based on quotes or allusions they make to the works of the patriarch Nikephoros (*Refutatio et eversio, Apologeticus maior, Antirrheticus III*).[115] These texts were in the possession of Methodios and then disappeared without trace until many years later, suggesting that Methodios' authors wrote during the period of his patriarchate and had access to volumes from his personal library. Under his leadership, these men put their command of literature at the service of an extensive ideological programme that went far beyond mere praise of the protagonists of their accounts. Their intellectual author was none other than the patriarch himself, and it is he who gives these works their full meaning and allows an understanding of the synergies and interrelations among them.

From a historiographical perspective, we also witness an attempt here to present the years of iconoclasm as part of the history of humankind from the point of view of the iconodules. In contrast to his predecessors in the patriarchate, who did write historiographical accounts,[116] Methodios preferred to delegate the composition to Georgios Monachos[117] of a chronicle whose central organising point was the fight to defend Orthodoxy. The absence of other indications does not allow us to fully reconstruct the relationship of patronage between the two men, but it is clear that this chronicle rested in and supported the patriarch's ideological programme. The resulting text takes the form of a universal history from Creation to 842, the final year of iconoclast heresy. Within it, Christian Orthodoxy based on historical fact explains the unfolding of events. Indeed, the main contribution of Georgios Monachos in his compilation of information from previous historians is the addition of digressions to explain or justify the events that occur, the guiding principle almost invariably being the

---

[115] Afinogenov 1999b: 445–47.
[116] Treadgold 2013: 17–26 (the work of Tarasios as a historian) and 26–31 (Nikephoros and his two historiographical works).
[117] Also called 'Hamartolos' (Sinner), see *PmbZ* # 2264; *PBE* I: Georgios 286. On Georgios Monachos' method of composition, see Ljubarskij 1994; Afinogenov 2004b; Kazhdan 2006: 43–52; Treadgold 2013: 114–19; Neville 2018: 87–92.

observance of Orthodoxy.[118] Due to the date when the text was written, after the restoration of images, the Orthodoxy in question is of course iconoduly, and this provides the basis for the author's historiographical discourse, which underlines the parallels between various other heresies and iconoclasm, creating an image of the ideal emperor in contrast to iconoclast sovereigns.[119] Despite the great interest in the work of Georgios Monachos and his edifying stories, the approach is far from original, since it recovers the principles of the chronicles of Georgios Synkellos and Theophanes the Confessor. The secondary treatment of information regarding the iconoclastic crisis (taken directly from various hagiographical sources, such as the *vita* of Niketas of Medikion),[120] moreover, means that analysis of other contemporary texts with greater immediate impact on the society of the time, such as that composed by Petros in honour of Ioannikios, is much more revealing.

2.2.1 *Petros Monachos and His* Vita of Ioannikios *(BHG 936)*

The death of Ioannikios must have been a serious blow to Methodios and his ecclesiastical party, since it deprived them of one of their main protectors, who to a large extent had acted as the representative of Bithynian hermit life when defining the new post-iconoclast Church. The *kanon* Methodios composed in Ioannikios' honour shows how quickly he was canonised. But in order to promote his veneration, a text was needed to relate the life, works and miracles of the hero.[121] This text (*BHG* 936) was pronounced in Methodios' lifetime, and it is not in vain that it declares itself a funeral epitaph for Ioannikios, who died in 846.[122] The man commissioned to write it was a monk named Petros, about whom we

---

[118] Conca 2010: 119–40; Detoraki 2015: 108 and 126–30.
[119] Afinogenov 1991 studies this phenomenon in the portrait of Theodosios I (347–395), while Afinogenov 2010 shows Georgios' condemnation of the humiliating end that the iconoclast Emperor Konstantinos V inflicted on the patriarch Konstantinos II (754–765).
[120] Afinogenov 2004b: 243.
[121] Sullivan 1994; Talbot 1998: 243–351; Kazhdan 1999: 327–40. Only a single manuscript of this hagiography has survived, *Parisinus Coislin Gr.* 303, fols. 304–53, tenth-eleventh centuries. In contrast, the *vita* written by Sabas survives in four manuscripts, Talbot 1998: 252, see Section 7.1.1.
[122] *Vita of Ioannikios by Petros* 72, 435C: ἀλλὰ μνήσθητί μου τοῦ ἀχρείου δούλου σου καὶ δέχοιο παρ' ἐμοῦ τουτὶ τὸ βραχύτατον **ἐπιτάφιον σύνταγμα**. The topos of the brevity of the epitaph is characteristic of hagiography, but it is still striking that Ignatios Diakonos should end his *vita of Nikephoros* in the same way: ταῦτα τῆς σῆς ἀλήπτου βιοτῆς ὡς ἐν ἐπιδρομῇ τὰ γνωρίσματα, p. 217. For the dating of the *vita* of Ioannikios during the first half of the year 847, see Mango 1983: 394, n. 5. According to Talbot 1998: 247, the first anniversary of the death of Ioannikios would be the best moment to place its production.

know very little.¹²³ Along with his four brothers, he lived in the monastery of Agauroi on the Mount Olympos of Bithynia.¹²⁴ One of these brothers, Antonios, must have had a great deal of authority, since he became the hegoumenos of the monastery during the iconoclastic persecution. This relationship of Antonios with the heretics, despite Ioannikios' insistence that he repent, seems to have been the cause of his illness and death.¹²⁵

In addition to these family links with religious leaders, the hagiographer Petros clearly hobnobbed with the cream of Bithynian monasticism, which after the Triumph of Orthodoxy saw itself as the guardian of iconoduly. We do not know to what extent this self-perception was correct, but Methodios certainly promoted many of his Bithynian colleagues to positions of power after 843: the bishop of Syllaion in Pamphilia, also called Petros, together with Ioannes, the bishop of Prousa, accompanied the author on a visit to Ioannikios before they had assumed these obligations.¹²⁶ Our hagiographer also prospered and ended up running a monastery, perhaps as acknowledgement for the services rendered in the composition of this *vita*.¹²⁷ Given that the monastery of Agauroi, where he had taken his vows and lived for so many years, continued to be run mainly by Eustratios, Petros was most likely the abbot of one of the *metochia* under Eustratios' influence. Could it have been the monastery of Bomoi after the death of Nikolaos?

The hagiography in question was not commissioned directly by the patriarch Methodios, but by an intermediary, the hegoumenos Eustratios,¹²⁸ a close collaborator of Ioannikios, together with whom he is mentioned on numerous occasions in the *vita*. Like Ioannikios,

---

¹²³ On Petros, cf. *PmbZ* # 6075; *PBE* I: Petros 126. No support has been found for the proposal that the author was Petros of Atroa, see Hergès 1898/1899: 234; *Vita of Eustratios of Agauroi* 370, n. 4. This hagiographer considers the writing of this *vita* an 'obligation' (ὑπόχρεων), *Vita of Ioannikios by Petros* 3, 385C: ἐπὶ τὴν προρρηθεῖσαν ὑπόχρεων πραγματείαν μέτειμι. *Vita of Ioannikios by Petros* 62, 425B: οὐκοῦν λοιπὸν ῥητέον κατὰ τὸ ἡμῖν θεμιτὸν καὶ τὰς λοιπάς, ὡς εἴρηται, **ὑποχρέους** σημειοφανίας τοῦ ἰσαγγέλου καὶ θεομιμήτου πατρός.
¹²⁴ Janin 1975: 132–34; Hergès 1898/1899: 230–38. His brothers were Gregorios (*PmbZ* # 2440), Basileios (*PmbZ* # 934), Agathon (*PmbZ* # 134) and Antonios (*PmbZ* # 561).
¹²⁵ *Vita of Ioannikios by Petros* 66, 427C–28A; *Vita of Ioannikios by Sabas* 36,365B–C; *Vita of Eustratios of Agauroi* 4, 370,4–12.
¹²⁶ *Vita of Ioannikios by Sabas* 43, 368C–69A; *Vita of Ioannikios by Petros* 68, 429B–C. This Petros was a hesychastic monk and belonged to the monastery of Herakleion, cf. *PmbZ* # 6076; *PBE* I: Petros 127. On the monastery of Herakleion, see Janin 1975: 152–53. On his bishopric in Syllaion, see Ruggieri and Nethercott 1986: 147; Fedalto 1988: 253. Ioannes of Prousa is known only from this reference, see *PmbZ* # 3238; *PBE* I: Ioannes 441.
¹²⁷ *Vita of Ioannikios by Sabas* 43, 368C: ὁ ἀββᾶς Πέτρος. See Section 7.1.1.
¹²⁸ Concerning Eustratios, cf. *PmbZ* # 1824; *PBE* I: Eustratios 19. An anonymous hagiographical text survives, the *Vita of Eustratios of Agauroi* (*BHG* 645), that to a large extent is a derivation of the life of Ioannikios written by Sabas.

Eustratios was a follower of Methodios and favoured implementing his policies against iconoclasts and Stoudites. Together with their intimate relations, this explains why he commissioned the writing of this work intended to strengthen the position of the patriarch and his view of Orthodoxy. The monastery of Agauroi had several *metochia* (St Agapios, St Kosmas, St Elijah, Leukades, Bomoi), some of which were very important, a fact that explains the political significance of the hegoumenos of Agauroi. In the mid-ninth century, the head of the monastery of Bomoi was precisely Nikolaos, Eustratios' brother.[129] It was there that Eustratios once miraculously healed a five-year-old deaf-mute boy[130] and where Eustratios decided to stay some years later, before he set out on his final journey to Constantinople. It was also there that his body was venerated for the first time after his death in the capital and where the first miracle occurred through the mediation of his relics: the healing of another boy who had been deaf-mute from birth.[131] Eustratios' body was subsequently taken to Agauroi by his brother Nikolaos and buried there.

The monastery of Bomoi must be the establishment mentioned by Petros and other sources under the name Elaiobomoi or Elegmoi.[132] This monastery stood within the boundaries of the bishopric of Kios and was founded by Methodios,[133] presumably after his formative period at Chenolakkos, before he travelled to Rome. Methodios was probably the first hegoumenos of this monastery, since in one of his letters Theodoros Stoudites gives him this title.[134] His successors at the head of Elaiobomoi were iconodules, as is shown by the fact that Antonios, the hegoumenos of the monastery, visited Ioannikios in the company of the *oikonomos* Basileios when he lived in Trichalix; they took a message from him to Inger, the metropolitan of Nicaea.[135] Shortly afterwards, however, the abbot was relieved of his duties[136] and replaced by a certain Ioannes, who sympathised with the patriarch's iconoclast line. A letter survives

---

[129] On Nikolaos, see *PmbZ* # 5586; *PBE* I: Nikolaos 71.   [130] *Vita of Eustratios of Agauroi* 23,383.
[131] *Vita of Eustratios of Agauroi* 51,396–97.
[132] Mango 1968a: 174ff.; Janin 1975: 142–48; Ruggieri 1991: 217.
[133] *Menologion Basilii* 500A: ἐν τῇ τοποθεσίᾳ τοῦ ὄρους τῆς ἐπισκοπῆς Χίου [corr. Κίου] μοναστήριον κτίσας ἐκεῖσε προσεκαθέζετο. Pargoire 1903b: 190; Lilie 1999: 190–91.
[134] Theod. Stoud., *epist.* 274. See also the *enkomion* of Nicholas of Myra by the hegoumenos Methodios, cf. Anrich 1913: vol. I, 140.
[135] *Vita of Ioannikios by Petros* 38,406; *Vita of Ioannikios by Sabas* 30,360. This reference confirms that the monastery of Bomoi was accountable to the metropolitan of Nicaea and not that of Nicomedia as is affirmed by Mango and Efthymiadis 1997: 175.
[136] Theod. Stoud., *epist.* 495,30–33. The confusion of Κωμῶν with Βωμῶν is common in the sources. However, this is always the same monastic centre, see *Vita of Ioannikios by Petros* 38,406: Ἐλαιοβωμῶν; *Vita of Ioannikios by Sabas* 30,360: Ἐλαιοκώμων.

addressed to this Ioannes from Ignatios Diakonos in his position as bishop of Nicaea, in which Ioannes is asked to give ecclesiastical asylum to a confessed murderer, who had repented, so that he could serve the sentence decreed by the patriarch under Ioannes' supervision.[137] The exceptional nature of the persecution suffered by Methodios during the reign of Michael II (due to his political attitudes rather than his religious stance) explains the harshness of the captivity and the fact that he was in the same prison as a man sentenced for attempted usurpation.[138] But it also helps us understand why his monastery was 'expropriated' by the highest iconoclast authorities.

Once heresy had been vanquished, Ioannikios was consulted as to who the future patriarch should be; after seven days of prayer, he mentioned Methodios, who was in exile in the monastery of Elaiobomoi.[139] In his story of the patriarch's visit to Ioannikios, however, Sabas specifies that Methodios stayed at his 'own monastery nearby',[140] clearly in the same geographic area. These references underline the strong link between the restorer patriarch and the monastery of Bomoi over time. Once icons had been restored, the decision to make Nikolaos, the brother of Eustratios of Agauroi,[141] the new hegoumenos, brought the monastery back into line with the iconodule policy established by Methodios. It is easy to understand the new patriarch's interest in this specific appointment, which saw his monastery return to Orthodoxy and at the same time gave him new allies within the Bithynian monastic milieu. The benefits were soon appreciated, and Eustratios received a substantial donation for his monastery at the foot of the Bithynian Mount Olympos from Empress Theodora (200 *nomismata* and whatever else the monastery might need).[142] In return, the iconodule party in the patriarchate had a *vita* written by Petros in honour of Ioannikios, which not only promoted the cult of one of his most unconditional supporters but also spread the patriarchal version of the Triumph of Orthodoxy and how it should be managed.

---

[137] Mango and Efthymiadis 1997: 54–57 (*epist.* 16).
[138] *Vita of Methodios* 1248C: ἐν ᾧ τάφῳ καὶ ἕτερος ἐπὶ τυραννίδι κατακέκλειστο, 'a tomb in which another had already been imprisoned for attempted usurpation.' See Pargoire 1903b; Dagron 1993: 144; Lilie 1999: 204; Brubaker and Haldon 2011: 389–90. The reign of Michael II was particularly permissive regarding icons and tolerated their veneration outside the city of Constantinople, see Section 7.2.2.
[139] *Vita of Michael the Synkellos* 26, 104,10–12: ἐν τῇ τῶν Ἐλεοβωμητῶν μονῇ.
[140] *Vita of Ioannikios by Sabas* 53, 382C: ὁ ἔνθεος ἀρχιεράρχης Μεθόδιος μετὰ ἀσπασμὸν τελευταῖον καὶ εὐχὴν αὐτοῦ θεοπαράθετον, κάτεισι ἐν τῷ **οἰκείῳ καὶ εὐλαβεῖ** σεμνείῳ.
[141] *PmbZ* # 5593.   [142] *Vita of Eustratios of Agauroi* 15, 378. See Kaplan 1993a: 214–15.

The ideological slant of the *vita* is clear, since the account stands out for its hostility to the Stoudite milieu, which Ioannikios did not hesitate to attack in order to favour Methodios, whose candidature for the patriarchate he had vehemently maintained.[143] The defence of the patriarchate as an institution had multiple facets with direct consequences: the hierarchical superiority of the patriarch over the monks was affirmed, and the patriarchs Tarasios and Nikephoros were vindicated, as their iconodule postulates were assumed by Methodios as his own. Ioannikios therefore gave a warm welcome to his visitor Ioseph of Kathara, the protagonist of the Moechian controversy, and predicted his pious death (ch. 36), which scandalised the Stoudites and simultaneously underlined patriarchal authority. The Emperors Konstantinos VI and Nikephoros I, who were attacked by the Stoudites for supporting Ioseph of Kathara, are specifically described as 'very pious' by Petros (chs. 5 and 14). Ioannikios is the leading figure, in fact, in an important military incident in which he saves the life of the 'adulterous' Konstantinos VI (probably a fictitious event created by Petros in imitation of the one described by Theophanes in his *Chronographia*).[144] The hagiography's attitude towards iconoclasts and Emperor Theophilos also seeks to ratify Methodios' decisions: the patriarch had agreed not to anathematise the iconoclast emperor for his heresy so that the restoration of Orthodoxy could succeed, a use of patriarchal *oikonomía* (dispensation) that was not easily accepted by all monastic sectors.[145] To play down the matter, Petros restricts his treatment of the iconoclast conflict to the reign of Leon V (ch. 18), scarcely alluding to icons and omitting any mention of Theophilos, the last iconoclast emperor.

But Petros' true hobby-horse is his attack on the Stoudite monks, against whom he produces something approaching a pamphlet in certain passages of the *vita*, calling them scandalmongers, for example, and accusing them of arrogance and of despising St Ioannikios.[146] On another occasion, Petros brands the Stoudite monks troublemakers and gossips who criticise saints with their vicious tongues.[147] Nor does he hesitate to accuse them of being party to the conspiracy against Methodios and of bribing a woman to commit perjury[148] or to put harsh words against them in the mouth of Ioannikios, as when he compares the Stoudites to the

---

[143] Von Dobschütz 1909a; Talbot 1998: 248–49.   [144] Sullivan 1994.
[145] See Chapter 4 on the rehabilitation of Theophilos.   [146] *Vita of Ioannikios* by Petros 36, 405B.
[147] *Vita of Ioannikios* by Petros 57, 422A.   [148] *Vita of Ioannikios* by Petros 69–70, 430C–32C.

iconoclasts and declares them 'most abominable'.[149] Likewise, Petros responds forcefully to Theodoros Stoudites' attacks on Ioannikios as the representative of provincial hermit life, in contrast to the Constantinopolitan monastery movement, when he presents his hero as a second Moses on three separate occasions.[150] This comparison is easily interpreted: the Bithynian Olympos is the new Sinai, and Constantinople represents the people of Israel, who have access to God thanks to the efforts of a charismatic leader (Moses-Ioannikios) who mediates with the Lord. The people of Israel were taken out of Egypt and thus brought out of darkness when they reached the Sinai, as happens with the Byzantines thanks to the efforts of Ioannikios. Because of all this, religious life in the capital is incomplete and cannot be considered superior to that of the hermit.

It is evident from the committed, belligerent position of Petros that he was not merely a monk who confined himself to recounting stories already circulating about his hero, but an author who used literature to influence politics and defend one of the main institutions of the Empire. It is impossible, however, to say to what extent Petros himself was responsible for this attitude. An important part may have been played by the abbot Eustratios, who participated actively in the writing of the *vita* and is repeatedly praised by the hagiographer. Petros demonstrates extensive knowledge of the life and works of his hero Ioannikios and relates their personal encounters.[151] But his main source of information was Eustratios, who had been a witness of these events for fifty years.[152] Petros seems to resort to this oral source on multiple occasions, although a passing reference makes it clear that the hegoumenos had also kept some written records to allow others to benefit from Ioannikios' example.[153] Be that as it may, Eustratios had known Ioannikios since his youth, and on the orders of his hegoumenos had twice built a cell for him to live in.[154] Eustratios was present when the saint predicted the death of Emperor Nikephoros to his relatives (ch. 14), was the messenger who conveyed the

---

[149] *Vita of Ioannikios by Petros* 70, 432B: λέγω ὑμῖν· ἀποσχίσθητε πάντες ἀπὸ τῶν δυσσεβῶν αἱρετικῶν, καὶ τῶν μυσαρωτάτων Στουδιτῶν.
[150] Talbot 1998: 250. [151] *Vita of Ioannikios by Petros* 1, 385A; 68, 428B–30A.
[152] *Vita of Ioannikios by Petros* 12, 390A–B; 40, 407C; 46, 410C; 54, 415B; and 62, 425B.
[153] *Vita of Ioannikios by Petros* 54, 410C: Εὐστρατίῳ, τῷ καὶ τὴν θαυμαστὴν ταύτην καὶ ὀνησιφόρον πραγματείαν θερμῶς καὶ μετὰ πίστεως ἀναταξαμένῳ καὶ τῇ μετέπειτα γενεᾷ μνημόσυνον αἰώνιον καταλείψαντι, 'Eustratios, who earnestly and with faith composed this wondrous and beneficial treatise and left to the next generation an eternal memorial'. For Mango 1983: 393 more than a work as such it was 'a memoir or set of notes'; cf. Talbot 1998: 246.
[154] *Vita of Ioannikios by Petros* 10 and 11.

question about the fate of Emperor Staurakios (ch. 15) and saw how Ioannikios prophesied to Bryennios the heretical persecution of his uncle Emperor Leon (ch. 17). The only man who knew where Ioannikios took refuge during the Second Iconoclasm was Eustratios, and it was to him that Ioannikios prophesied the imminent death of Emperor Leon (ch. 30). Eustratios was also present during the visits of Theodoros Stoudites and of the iconodule leaders (ch. 36), as well as during that of the hegoumene of the convent of Tou Kloubiou and her daughter (chs. 57–58). Eustratios followed Ioannikios when he retired to the monastery of Antidion (chs. 60–67) and was the recipient of his prophecy that after the death of Theophilos, Orthodoxy would be restored and Methodios would be appointed patriarch of Constantinople. And it was Eustratios who took to the new patriarch a letter of support from the saint that asked him to stand firm against the enemies of the Church (ch. 69). Despite the hagiographer's silence, it is reasonable to assume that Eustratios was also present at the funeral, at which the hegoumenos Ioseph officiated in his monastery of Antidion,[155] where Ioannikios was buried.

Due to his exceptional abilities, Ioannikios was often dubbed 'the Great'. A native of the town of Marykaton in Bithynia, he was born in 762, if we accept the chronology of the hagiographer Petros.[156] After working as a swineherd, he joined the militia as a soldier of the *exkoubitoi*, fighting against the Bulgarians in 792 at the Battle of Markellai, which was a resounding defeat for the Byzantines. Whether he was fleeing from the military disaster or owing to his religious vocation, Ioannikios took refuge on the Bithynian Mount Olympos and took vows as a monk. He spent the years of the Second Iconoclasm (815–842) wandering from place to place, keeping a low profile to avoid persecution. Indeed, although Ioannikios maintained contact with many iconodule leaders of the resistance, his attitude to the veneration of images was not always clear, and only after the Triumph of Orthodoxy did he strongly defend icons. This may be why Petros Monachos wished to create clear parallels between him and martyrs who had fallen at the hands of the iconoclasts, about whose attitudes there was no shadow of a doubt. In order to do so, he resorted to a powerful textual source: the *vita* of Niketas of Medikion written by Theosteriktos, the epilogue of which he copied with slight alterations.[157] Although the

---

[155] On this hegoumenos, see *PmbZ* # 3453; *PBE* I: Ioseph 19. On the Bithynian monastery of Antidion, see Janin 1975: 135–36.
[156] For the biography of Ioannikios, see *PmbZ* # 3389; *PBE* I: Ioannikios 2.
[157] Rosenqvist 2002: 69–71.

complete original Greek of the *vita* of Niketas has been lost, an early translation into Slavonic has survived and demonstrates the similarity of the two texts;[158] we thus have here something more like appropriation than inspiration. If Petros reused the epilogue of a hagiography well known to iconodules, he did so not from a lack of technical skill but as an intertextual measure, seeking to reaffirm his hero's commitment to Orthodoxy and to assimilate him to a fully established saint such as Niketas of Medikion.

2.2.2 Ignatios Diakonos

Along with Petros Monachos, another hagiographer, generally known as Ignatios Diakonos, worked in the interests of the patriarch Methodios. Ignatios is responsible for the two *vitae* praising the iconodule patriarchs Tarasios (*BHG* 1698) and Nikephoros (*BHG* 1335), the vindication of whom was for Methodios an essential point of post-iconoclast propaganda. But who was Ignatios Diakonos? He certainly had one of the most fascinating biographies of the men of letters of the period. During his lifetime, Ignatios held the positions of 'deacon, skeuophylax of the great Church of Constantinople, at one time metropolitan of Nicaea, a grammatikos'.[159] Depending on how these obligations were coordinated with the religious stages of Ignatios' life (iconodule, iconoclast, repentant iconodule), the meaning of his literary production changes.

The *communis opinio* takes Ignatios to have been born ca. 770;[160] in his youth, he was a member of the circle of the patriarch Tarasios (784–806), whom he served as a notary and under whose auspices he perfected his training in rhetoric.[161] After some contact with the patriarch Nikephoros, he accepted a commission to write iconoclast iamboi celebrating the replacement of the icon of Christ of the Chalke Gate with a representation of a plain cross courtesy of Emperor Leon V in 815–816.[162] He was the metropolitan of Nicaea during the Second Iconoclasm (probably between 815 and 830),[163] and during this period he not only wrote numerous epistles, but also produced two literary works, a lost panegyric of Michael II and his victory over the rebel Thomas the Slav (ca. 823)[164] and a *vita* in

---

[158] Afinogenov 2006: 127, n. 7; 2018: 338–39.
[159] According to the *Suidae Lexicon* I,84 (ed. Adler, vol. II, 607).
[160] Vasilevskij, *Trudy* 3 (1915) 93; Wolska-Conus 1970: 330.
[161] *PBE* I: Ignatios 9; Mango and Efthymiadis 1997: 3–24; *Vita of Tarasios*, pp. 38–46; Lauxtermann 1998: 397–401; Kazhdan 1999: 343–66; Efthymiadis 2002.
[162] Speck 1974a; Criscuolo 1994a; Lauxtermann 2003: 278–84.
[163] Kaplan 2001; 2006: 186–92.   [164] Lemerle 1965; Signes Codoñer 2014: 39–59 and 183–200.

honour of Georgios of Amastris (*BHG* 668).[165] The *terminus post quem* for the latter is the year 820, when the first Russian raid was recorded in the *vita*.[166] As Ignatios himself declares, this was his first hagiographical composition,[167] which means it saw the light before 830 as a result of a commission by a certain Ioannes.[168] It is not clear who this man was, but he may well have been the bishop of Amastris, about whom we know next to nothing,[169] or Ioannes Grammatikos, a correspondent of Theodoros Stoudites about whom we know a little more.[170]

The final period of iconoclasm is obscure, and we do not know precisely what Ignatios Diakonos did between 830 and 843. His collected letters suggest that he was for a time a monk on Mount Olympos, specifically at the monastery of Antidion.[171] But he then appears to have accepted the post as a teacher that was offered him by Emperor Theophilos himself and was awarded the title of 'ecumenical teacher' (οἰκουμενικὸς διδάσκαλος), which meant that he resumed contact with the iconoclast heretics. We know the names of some of his disciples, including Paulos and Konstantinos.[172] Compositions such as the poem of seven iambic verses on Lazarus and the rich man had an educational purpose,[173] but in a pedagogical vein he also produced a moralistic poem κατὰ ἀλφάβητον consisting of twenty-four verses that began with each letter of the alphabet and offered rhetorical and religious inspiration.[174] After the victory of Orthodoxy and the purge carried out by Methodios, Ignatios was shut up in the monastery of Pikridion[175] on the banks of the Golden Horn, although he was later readmitted among the members of the diaconate.

---

[165] Costa-Louillet 1954/1955: 479–92; Ševčenko 1977a: 120–26; 1977b: 150–73; Markopoulos 1979; Efthymiadis 1991a; Auzépy 1992; Kazhdan 1999: 356–66. The contents of the only manuscript that includes the *vita* of Georgios of Amastris, the tenth-century *Parisinus Gr.* 1452, also suggests that its author was Ignatios Diakonos, since it also contains his *Vita Tarasii* and several texts on Agatha, the Sicilian saint highly venerated by Methodios, cf. Halkin 1968: 161–62.
[166] Treadgold 1988/1990: 141–43. On this hagiography see Chapter 6.
[167] *Vita of Georgios of Amastris* 1, 1–2. [168] *Vita of Georgios of Amastris* 48, 73.
[169] Costa-Louillet 1954/1955: 479; *PmbZ* # 3252 and 2979.
[170] *PmbZ* # 3213; Theod. Stud., *epist.* 492, 528 and 546.
[171] The identification is due to Efthymiadis, *Vita of Tarasios*, p. 43, who bases himself on a reference in *epist.* 43,3 and on the fact that Ignatios Diakonos sent *epist.* 33 to the hegoumenos of the monastery of Antidion. This monastery had links with St Ioannikios, see Janin 1975: 135–36; Section 7.1.1.
[172] On the relationship of Ignatios with his students, *Anth. Gr.* XV, 29; Speck 1995; Ciccolella 2000: 33–55.
[173] Sternbach 1898: 154; Lauxtermann 2019: 237–41.
[174] Müller 1891; Wolska-Conus 1970: 333–34; Lauxtermann 2019: 212–15.
[175] The line of thought of the monastery of Pikridion was rather strict, as evidenced by the fact that its hegoumenos Theodosios signed along with Theodoros Stoudites two epistles addressed to Pope Paschal, see Theod. Stoud., *epist.* 271 and 272. On the periods that Ignatios spent there, see

It is under the patriarchate of Methodios that Ignatios' hagiographical writing flourished. After writing an initial *vita* in honour of Gregorios Dekapolites (*BHG* 711) commissioned by his disciples,[176] he soon began to concentrate on adapting to Methodios' ideas, perhaps seeking to improve his situation in the new post-iconoclast society or perhaps obliged to demonstrate that he had truly repented of his iconoclast past. Indeed, Ignatios' repentance becomes one of the main elements of the final years of his biography and is a prominent feature in the whole of his literary production, including his non-religious writings.[177] It was now, at any rate, that he wrote two works that constituted a true literary landmark: the *vitae* of the patriarchs Tarasios and Nikephoros,[178] supreme examples of elevated hagiography in which numerous allusions to classical culture help define a subgenre that became particularly prolific over the following decades: biographies of orthodox patriarchs. It is tempting to think that an appreciation of Ignatios' services allowed him not only to reinstate himself but to achieve the title of the patriarchal *skeuophylax* of Hagia Sophia by a grant from Methodios himself. It is assumed that Ignatios survived his final mentor, but he must have died shortly after him.

This interpretation of the biography of Ignatios most effectively relates well-known political and social events to the indirect data about him that have survived. It is also true, however, that some scholars have used the same information to propose a different reconstruction of certain stages of Ignatios Diakonos' life, moving his date of birth forward considerably.[179] In any case, the nickname his contemporaries gave him, *Kothornos* or 'timeserver',[180] is unanimously considered highly appropriate.[181] His ability (or need) to change sides explains why, after the defeat of heresy in 843, he did not hesitate to assume the ideological postulates of the new ecclesiastical leader, after subjecting himself necessarily to an inquisitorial process required for reinstatement.[182] We know that an important element of Methodios' iconodule propaganda was the vindication of his

---

Mango and Efthymiadis 1997: 195–97 (*epist.* 43–47). On this monastery, see Janin 1969: 403–4; Berger 1988a: 688; Ruggieri 1991: 195.

[176] See Chapter 3.
[177] For instance, in the self-referential elegy preserved in the *Anthologia Graeca* (*Anth. Gr.* XV, 29), which begins with a typical admission of sin: Ἰγνάτιος πολλῇσιν ἐν ἀμπλακίῃσι βιώσας, see Lauxtermann 2003: 111–13. See Section 2.2.2.c.
[178] Kaplan 2015: 176–78.
[179] *PmbZ* # 2665; Makris in *Vita of Gregorios Dekapolites*; Pratsch 2000.
[180] This is a classical allusion (from Aristophanes) and refers to a boot that could supposedly be worn on either foot, i.e., it referred to someone whose opinions changed with the political winds.
[181] Lauxtermann 1998: 397–401.   [182] Ignatios Diakonos, *epist.* 40,10–15.

predecessors, the patriarchs Tarasios and Nikephoros, in order to stress the coherence of the Church in its fight against iconoclasm and any other heresy. Methodios did not hesitate to encourage the veneration of these men as saints, converting the repatriation of the relics of Nikephoros into a state matter. The production of a *Vita Tarasii* ratified his model of ecclesiastical governance and matched his propaganda expectations. Indeed, Tarasios, who combined bureaucratic experience with monastic virtues, represented the episcopal ideal proposed for the post-iconoclast Church.[183] Moreover, his important role at the Second Council of Nicaea, the first defeat of heresy, the legislative work of the canons issued there and the rehabilitation of repentant heretics, together with his policy on ordinations and his uninhibited monastic patronage, made him a clear prefiguration of Methodios.

(a) The *Vita of the Patriarch Tarasios* (*BHG* 1698)

By means of his *Vita Tarasii*,[184] Ignatios Diakonos adopted Methodios' way of thinking as if it were his own and became a full member of Methodios' circle of collaborators. He produced the text after 843, during the patriarchate of Methodios,[185] when Ignatios was merely a monk (according to the title of the work) and was exhausted due to illness and old age (ch. 70: γήρᾳ καὶ νόσῳ καμπτόμενος). Like his earlier *Vita of Georgios of Amastris* and *Vita of Gregorios Dekapolites*, the hagiography was also a commission. Ignatios himself addressed his patron at its end with these words: 'It is right for us to divert the speech to you, servant of God, whoever you are; you who have urged us to take on this task against our will and have forced us to attempt something beyond our capacity. Accept our obedience.'[186] The openly political nature of the work led Von Dobschütz to conclude over a century ago that it was instigated by Methodios himself.[187] In his exemplary edition of the *vita*, Efthymiadis added that the infinitive μετοχετεῦσαι might well be a pun on the name of the patriarch.[188] On the other hand, the complete vocative used by Ignatios (θεοῦ θεράπον, ὅστις ποτὲ εἶ, 'servant of God, whoever you

---

[183] Kaplan 1999; 2006.
[184] Costa-Louillet 1954/1955: 217–29; Efthymiadis 1991a: 73–83; Kazhdan 1999: 343–66.
[185] For its dating, see Von Dobschütz 1909a: 54–59; Costa-Louillet 1954/1955: 217–18; *Vita of Tarasios*, pp. 48–49.
[186] *Vita of Tarasios* 70: ἡμᾶς δὲ λοιπὸν πρὸς σὲ τὸν λόγον **μετοχετεῦσαι** δίκαιον, θεοῦ θεράπον, ὅστις ποτὲ εἶ, ὁ πρὸς ἀγῶνα τοῦτον καὶ μὴ βουλομένους παρορμήσας καὶ τῶν ὑπὲρ δύναμιν ἐγχειρεῖν βιασάμενος· τῆς ὑπακοῆς ἀποδέχου. Efthymiadis' translation.
[187] Von Dobschütz 1909a: 59.   [188] *Vita of Tarasios*, p. 49.

are') affirms that he was unaware of the identity of his commissioner. This suggests that the *vita* was commissioned by an intermediary, who was probably a member of the clergy (θεοῦ θεράπον) and no doubt had a high position in the hierarchy, which meant that he requested that Ignatios' obedience be recognised (τῆς ὑπακοῆς ἀποδέχου). This obedience was clear both in the writing of the work and in Ignatios' alignment with the patriarchal party and its postulates. The *Vita Tarasii* therefore has a clear anti-Stoudite slant, defending the attitude of the patriarchate in the Moechian controversy and its moderate position towards the iconoclasts. This led Speck a number of years ago to argue that Ignatios had a personal aversion to Theodoros Stoudites, who is often criticised, in contrast to Tarasios, who is praised.[189]

But although Ignatios served Methodios' cause efficiently and the aim of this *vita* is clear, it is no less evident that his objective in writing it was more personal. His difficult situation after the Triumph of Orthodoxy, given that he had been a member of the iconoclast clergy, required all his efforts to achieve rehabilitation and acceptance in the emerging new society. Public demonstrations of repentance (see Section 8.1) were an initial step in this direction. It was thus necessary to show obedience to the new hierarchy, as Ignatios did by producing this hagiography. Aware of the literary possibilities the genre offered him, he decided to give special treatment to the events of 787 after the first defeat of iconoclasm, since they were by now (after 843) highly topical. Ignatios praised Tarasios for his moderation, in that all the bishops ordained by the iconoclasts were not suspended but continued in their posts after they renounced heresy in writing, as a way of guaranteeing peace within the Church.[190] Ignatios sought the kind of *oikonomía* rejected by Methodios, who preferred a harder line.[191] In this attempt, he praised Tarasios (the predecessor and up to a certain point the prefiguration of Methodios), emphasising his personal relationship with the saint by saying that he educated him in ancient prosody and heroic poetry and worked for him as a stenographer.[192] By means of harsh attacks on his former co-religionists the iconoclasts, and by praise of the moderate actions of Tarasios, Ignatios

---

[189] Von Dobschütz 1909a: 54–59; Speck 1987b: 568–71; 2003.
[190] *Vita of Tarasios* 31 and 63; Mansi XII, 1035C. The Stoudites, led by their hegoumenos Sabas, reacted in a hostile manner towards the half-heartedness of Tarasios, see Auzépy 1988: 13–21; Brubaker and Haldon 2011: 278. On Sabas of Stoudios, see *PmbZ* # 6442; *PBE* I: Sabas 4; Delouis 2005: 124–38.
[191] *Vita of Tarasios*, p. 50.   [192] *Vita of Tarasios* 69; Ronconi 2012a: 642.

vindicated the postulates of the Methodians and at the same time expressed his desire to belong to their milieu.

Tarasios, born ca. 730,[193] is described by Ignatios as above all else a defender of canonical Orthodoxy.[194] His character as a just man of independent judgement unaffected by the pressures of political power is anticipated by the work of his father, a prominent judge (chs. 4–5). Trained in public administration, he came to fill the post of *protasekretis* (imperial secretary), and despite the fact that he was a layman, Empress Eirene appointed him patriarch in 784. No sooner had Tarasios occupied the throne of Constantinople, than he imposed on the remainder of the clergy the observance of the ecclesiastical canons, requiring them to follow his example of temperance, modesty, humility and charity (chs. 18–24). If he stood out for one thing, however, it was for calling the Seventh Ecumenical Council, which was intended to put an end to heresy and restore the veneration of icons. It was at the Second Council of Nicaea in 787 that the status of religious images was theologically defined (chs. 25–32). Subsequently, Tarasios took action against simoniac clergy – men who had bought their posts – and soldiers who ignored ecclesiastical legislation.[195] The latter episode serves in Ignatios' account as a precedent for what would occur during the Moechian Affair, when the patriarch did not yield to the civil authorities, since it was his duty to preserve ecclesiastical order, which was divine in nature. Tarasios refused to bless the new union of Emperor Konstantinos VI (chs. 39–46), and although a compromise was finally found, Ignatios mentions the persecution he suffered (chs. 47–48).

Immediately afterwards, Ignatios switches his attention to the matter of images, so as to give the impression that Tarasios was persecuted for defending icons. First, he describes in detail the iconographical programme patronised by the patriarch,[196] after which he defends iconoduly theologically in a long excursus (chs. 53–55). Before narrating the death of Tarasios, which occurred on 18 February 806, Ignatios includes several chapters in which he praises him as a worthy successor to the Apostles and compares him to various Old Testament figures (chs. 56–61). It is particularly interesting to see Tarasios compared with Moses, a prophet the Methodians loved. (It should be remembered that the monk Petros also

---

[193] For a reconstruction of the biography of Tarasios, see *PmbZ* # 7235; *PBE* I: Tarasios 1; Lilie 1999: 57–108.
[194] *Vita of Tarasios*, pp. 33–38.   [195] *Vita of Tarasios* 33–37. Kaegi 1966: 62–63.
[196] *Vita of Tarasios* 49–52. Wolska-Conus 1980; Brubaker 1989b: 19–23.

uses this comparison with Ioannikios.) As Moses guided Israel to the true faith and gave it the tablets of the law, therefore, Tarasios, like a second Moses, eliminated the heresy of his people and delivered to them the dogmas of Orthodoxy issued at the Second Council of Nicaea (ch. 57). Not for nothing was the Second Council of Nicaea known as the Council of Tarasios (ἡ Ταρασίου σύνοδος).[197] The description of the general mourning into which Tarasios' death plunged the Church and the Empire precedes an account of his funeral in the All Saints' monastery, which he himself had founded on the Bosphorus, and several posthumous miracles.[198]

Veneration of Tarasios began immediately:[199] together with the acclamation of his holiness and expressions of affection by the public, the imperial throne recognised and encouraged his veneration. Emperor Nikephoros paid a heartfelt tribute to the patriarch before he was buried (ch. 62), as did Michael I and his wife Prokopia at the celebration of the liturgy on the anniversary of his burial in the year 813.[200] Since the devotion of Tarasios was concentrated on the monastery where his relics were preserved, it lost momentum during the Second Iconoclasm due to the slander of the heretics, who renamed him Taraxios (troublemaker).[201] The restoration and promotion of his cult by Methodios was a key element in post-iconoclast iconodule propaganda. Methodios did not hesitate to include him among the confessors of Orthodoxy acclaimed in the *Synodikon of Orthodoxy*.[202] Ignatios wished to contribute to that vindication with his hagiography, in an awareness that Tarasios had fallen into oblivion and, even worse, was the butt of envious and slanderous comments by the iconodules themselves, a clear reference to the Stoudite schism.[203] Moreover, Ignatios also wrote a liturgical hymn in honour of the patriarch.[204] On the other hand, the entry for Tarasios in the *Synaxarion of Constantinople* provides a physical description of him that

---

[197] Georgios Mon. Cont. 783.
[198] *Vita of Tarasios* 62–68. For the monastery of Tarasios, cf. Janin 1969: 481–82; Thomas 1987: 123–24 and 136; Berger 1988a: 706f.; Ruggieri 1991: 202–3.
[199] *Vita of Tarasios*, pp. 25–31.   [200] Theoph. 500,8–9, trans. Mango-Scott, p. 683.
[201] Theoph. Cont. I, 15,9–16; Genesios 11,29–30; Koutrakou 1994: 270 and n. 142.
[202] *Synodikon of Orthodoxy* 51,110; 53,114–15; 103,881.
[203] *Vita of Tarasios* 65: ὃν οὐ χρόνος μακρὸς καλύψαι δυνήσεται· χρόνου γὰρ παντός ἐστιν ὑψηλότερος. ἡ γὰρ τῆς ἀρετῆς φύσις οὐ λήθης ἀνέχεται, οὐ φθόνου τηκεδόσιν ἀμβλύνεται. 'Over him the long lapse of time will not cast a veil, for he stands above all Time. For by its nature, virtue is impervious to oblivion, nor is it blunted by the wasting effects of envy.' See also *Vita of Tarasios* 2.
[204] Papadopoulos-Kerameus 1902: 88–91; Wolska-Conus 1970: 334–35; Mango and Efthymiadis 1997: 16. The attribution of this *kanon* to Ignatios is confirmed by the *Synaxarion Evergetis* I, 566.

mentions his resemblance to Gregorios of Nazianzus and must be drawn from a parallel source.[205]

(b) The *Vita of the Patriarch Nikephoros* (*BHG* 1335)

The other great iconodule patriarch, Nikephoros, was also a vital element of post-iconoclast ideology used to justify the policies implemented by Methodios, who found one of his main motivations in the persecution of members of the clergy who betrayed Nikephoros in 815 by taking communion with the iconoclasts.[206] The pomp and splendour that characterised the repatriation of Nikephoros' relics is perhaps the strongest indication of the importance to Methodios of cultivating his memory. The sanctification of Nikephoros depended more on the will of the ruling elite, for whom it ultimately became a state matter, than on the popular fervour of believers. His overthrow in 815 and his death in exile years later doubtless contributed to his obscurity. Because of all this, a *vita* disseminated from the capital was necessary and also represented an efficient means of spreading iconodule values and above all the iconodule vision of recent events. This is the context of the writing of the *Vita Nicephorii patriarchae Constantinopolitani*, which was again produced by Ignatios Diakonos.[207]

For some time, this work has been considered a new commission from Methodios.[208] The *vita* contains forceful attacks on iconoclasm and Emperors Leon V (accused of treason) and Michael II (described as ignorant and as having inherited the coarseness of his ancestors).[209] But it also expresses the author's deep repentance for having fallen into heresy,[210] a sentiment that only makes sense after the restoration of Orthodoxy in 843. Given that the author does not mention the solemn *translatio* of the relics of his hero in 846, the work can be dated more or less precisely. This hagiography evidently belongs to the literary milieu of the patriarch Methodios. The only textual element that might refer to a commission, however, is an initial vocative (*my dear friend*),[211] which is actually a poetic usage to refer to the audience as a whole, since it is

---

[205] *SynaxCP* 487,24–88,34 (25 February); *Vita of Tarasios*, p. 30, n. 117.
[206] Afinogenov 1996b: 88–89.
[207] Alexander 1940; Costa-Louillet 1954/1955: 245–56; Efthymiadis 1991a; Mango and Efthymiadis 1997: 8–12; Kazhdan 1999: 352–56.
[208] Talbot 1998: 33, who bases herself on Von Dobschütz 1909a: 54; Ševčenko 1997: 123, 125 and n. 92; Efthymiadis 1991a: 83.
[209] *Vita of Nikephoros* 30, p. 163,6–8 (on Leon V); *Vita of Nikephoros* 82, p. 209,27–28 (on Michael II). See Makris 2013.
[210] *Vita of Nikephoros* 88, pp. 215–17.   [211] *Vita of Nikephoros* 1, p. 139: ὦ φιλότης.

preceded and followed by vocatives appealing in the plural to the author's listeners/readers.[212] Nor is there any reference to a commitment or to obedience due a patron. Was the work thus a private initiative by Ignatios'?

It is not unlikely that Ignatios was the author of this *vita* on his own initiative, with the aim of pandering to Methodios, who had been a disciple and close collaborator of Nikephoros, having been appointed an archdeacon by the latter.[213] Its aim will thus have been to strengthen Ignatios' position within the patriarch's circle and redeem himself for his iconoclast past. A pre-existing situation also simplified matters: Ignatios had already written some kind of hagiographical text in honour of the patriarch Nikephoros and therefore had the necessary materials and even a first draft. The vocatives mentioned above suggest that the text may have been a funeral *enkomion* delivered to the disciples of Nikephoros, who had gathered to pay him tribute and to whom Ignatios appeals. In the exordium, the hagiographer treats the death of his hero at the age of seventy as a recent event (ch. 1). The date given is 5 April 828,[214] although Nikephoros actually died on 2 June.[215] Ignatios appears in any case to be writing shortly after this, due to the references to the death of Michael II (2 October 829) in ch. 80, the continuing strength of iconoclasm at the time of writing,[216] the prophesied misfortune that befell Bardas, the nephew of Emperor Leon V, which was still a matter of general awareness,[217] and the repercussions 'to this day' of the disturbance of Thomas the Slav.[218] These elements have led some scholars to suggest an early date for the writing of the *vita*, ca. 830.[219] But the extensive apology in the epilogue, in which Ignatios bitterly regrets his iconoclast past, together with some traces of the recent defeat of heresy, suggest a reworking after the Triumph of Orthodoxy,[220] in which case, the text matches the ecclesiastical policy of the moment and the utilitarian use to which literature was being put then.

---

[212] *Vita of Nikephoros* 1, p. 139: ὦ ἄνδρες ... ὦ φιλότης ... ὦ τᾶν .... See also ch. 67, p. 197: ὦ τᾶν ....
[213] *Acta of David, Symeon and Georgios* 22, p. 237,6; Lilie 1999: 191–94.
[214] *Vita of Nikephoros* 86, p. 213,22–24.
[215] Halkin 1958: 231–32, who bases himself on the *menologia* and *SynaxCP* 725,16–17.
[216] *Vita of Nikephoros* 87, p. 214,26: ὅσην δὲ θυμηδίας καὶ παρρησίας ἀφορμὴν δεδωκὼς τοῖς κακόφροσιν.
[217] *Vita of Nikephoros* 70, p. 201,25–26; see Alexander 1958a: 148.
[218] *Vita of Nikephoros* 78, p. 207,20–22.
[219] Vasilevskij 1893: vol. 2, XCVII, n. 3; Alexander 1940: 204, n. 3; Wolska-Conus 1970: 339 and 348.
[220] Costa-Louillet 1954/1955: 245; Mango and Efthymiadis 1997: 8–12. See also Lemerle 1971: 131, who justifies this rewriting by the presence of interpolations such as that of *Vita of Nikephoros* 15–17, pp. 149–51.

The *Vita Nicephori* is the most extensive and the loftiest in style of those written by Ignatios. It skilfully combines biographical, theological and historical elements in a masterpiece of Byzantine hagiography. The patriarch Nikephoros is well known both for his defence of images[221] and for his literary works (*Short History; Refutatio et eversio, Against Eusebium,* etc.).[222] Born in Constantinople around 758 to a distinguished family and destined to follow in the footsteps of his father as an imperial notary,[223] Nikephoros received an excellent education despite the fact that he had to follow his father into exile. The latter was the head of the imperial chancery[224] but was denounced for venerating images, as a consequence of which Konstantinos V exiled him to Nicaea until his death (chs. 5–6). Nikephoros returned to the capital to work in the chancery under the supervision of the *protoasekretis* Tarasios, the future patriarch.[225] The iconodule credentials of Nikephoros and his working relationship with Tarasios led to his participation in organising the Second Council of Nicaea and to his being chosen to read the imperial proclamation in defence of icons.[226] Ten years later, in 797, he decided to withdraw from the world and found a monastery,[227] in which he shut himself away until he was appointed director of the main poorhouse of the capital ca. 802 at the request of the new Emperor Nikephoros I.[228] When Tarasios died, it was again the emperor's will that, although he was a layman, he should succeed to the patriarchal throne (chs. 21–22).

During his patriarchate, Nikephoros provided ample evidence of his concern for orthodox dogma (ch. 26) and for the morals of believers, for example, abolishing the double monasteries that housed both monks and nuns under a single authority with the same rule (ch. 27) and rejecting the adulterous marriage of the governor of Gotthia in Crimea.[229] Like his predecessor, however, he adopted a policy of compromise (*oikonomía*) regarding the rehabilitation of Ioseph of Kathara, a close collaborator of the emperor. The accession of Leon V in 813 gave rise to several clashes

---

[221] Travis 1984. [222] Blake 1939; Alexander 1958a: 156–88; Chryssostalis 2009.
[223] On the biography of the patriarch Nikephoros, cf. *PmbZ* # 5301; *PBE* I: Nikephoros 2; Alexander 1958a; Lilie 1999: 109–48.
[224] *PmbZ* # 7538; *PBE* I: Theodoros 176.
[225] *Vita of Nikephoros* 7, p. 144; Alexander 1958a: 57–59.
[226] *Vita of Nikephoros* 10, p. 146; *Vita of Tarasios* 28, p. 103,20.
[227] *Vita of Nikephoros* 12–13, pp. 147,18–49,42. Ignatios does not specify whether the monastery is that of Ta Agathou or that of St Theodoros. For the former, see Janin 1975: 23; Ruggieri 1991: 199–200. Concerning the monastery of Theodoros founded equally by Nikephoros, see Janin 1954: 96–98; Ruggieri 1991: 203.
[228] *Vita of Nikephoros* 10, p. 152,14–18; Constantelos 1968: 257–69.
[229] *Vita of Nikephoros* 28, p. 160,22–30. See *PmbZ* # 11315; Lilie 1999: 127–30.

with the patriarch concerning images in the form of long dialectic confrontations narrated in the *vita* in Platonic dialogue form, and these resulted in the return to iconoclasm and the overthrow and exile of Nikephoros (chs. 30–70). But his place of exile (his monastery of Ta Agathou in Chrysopolis) did not seem sufficiently distant to Leon V, who forced him to move further away from Constantinople. This was how Nikephoros came to the monastery of St Theodoros Teron, which he had also founded (ch. 70) and where he spent thirteen years until his death. Isolated from matters of government (except when the accession of Michael II led Nikephoros to send a declaration of Orthodoxy, the response to which was an offer for him to return as patriarch, provided he abandoned the subject of images: chs. 81–82), Nikephoros devoted his time to writing theological treatises in defence of icons (ch. 83).

The patriarch Nikephoros was thus not the typical martyr, who is tortured physically for his faith, and whose holiness is manifested through miracles visible to all. On the contrary, he was a distinguished exponent of Orthodoxy in his management and governance of the Church. His theological defence of icons makes him an intellectual point of reference giving dogmatic form to the resistance against imperial iconoclasm. Aware of this, Ignatios emphasises his moral integrity and great determination and presents him as an independent hero who knows what he must do for the good of Orthodoxy. By showing us Nikephoros as a solitary saint without support from a party or congregation, Ignatios highlights an important difference from Theodoros Stoudites, the patriarch's great rival. Theodoros used all the communities of the Stoudite congregation to launch a major campaign against Nikephoros, first because the latter was a layman before being appointed patriarch, and second because of his accommodating attitude during the Ioseph affair and his choice to combat iconoclasm in a discreet and quiet manner. Theodoros had chosen the vigorous public defence of images, an attitude he continued to maintain in exile, while Nikephoros preferred to shut himself away and delve into theology in order to defeat heresy by argument. Ignatios Diakonos decided to ignore even the presence of the Stoudites and other monastic groups so as to avoid having to mention the internal opposition his hero faced, while at the same time attributing the leading role in orthodox resistance exclusively to Nikephoros.[230]

---

[230] This silence even included the famous visit made by Theodoros Stoudites to the deposed Nikephoros in exile, cf. Theod. Stoud., *epist.* 475,11–13; *Vita* B *of Theodoros Stoud.* 316C; *Vita* C *of Theodoros Stoud.* 70–74, pp. 298–300; *Vita* A *of Theodoros Stoud.* 220AB; Alexander 1958a: 153–54.

The saint's charisma is exemplified by numerous comparisons with biblical figures. It is significant, for example, that he is compared to the patriarch Moses, the spiritual leader, governor and guide of the people of Israel, whom he led out of Egypt to the Promised Land after defeating the heresy into which they had fallen.[231] Nikephoros also spoke with God and served as an intermediary for his flock in an attempt to lead them out of the darkness (ch. 84). Nor did he hesitate to confront the heir to the Pharaoh (Leo V) and his magicians Iannes and Iambres (Ioannes VII Grammatikos and Antonios of Syllaion), the champions of the Antichrist.[232] On the other hand, a lack of miracles might have hindered the promotion of his veneration,[233] but the hagiographer solves this problem by introducing two scenes in which Nikephoros predicts future events: the imminent fall into heresy of Leon V (ch. 33) and the fall from grace of his envoy Bardas.[234] By this means, Ignatios gives to understand that the patriarch had the gift of prophecy inspired by God, creating a tradition to justify his holiness that would be fully accepted by later historians. When they describe Nikephoros' journey into exile, they therefore introduce a meeting between the deposed patriarch and Theophanes, after which Nikephoros prophesies that the chronicler will be persecuted and will die as a confessor of Orthodoxy.[235]

(c) Ignatios Diakonos' Liturgical Poetry

Ignatios Diakonos' commitment to the holy memory of Nikephoros subsequently led him to compose a liturgical hymn to complete his account of the vicissitudes of the life of his hero, celebrating the ceremonial transfer of patriarch's relics.[236] The composition begins with a heartfelt admission of guilt by Ignatios, who declares that he is trapped in the tomb of sin (Ἁμαρτιῶν τάφῳ δεινῷ συσχεθέντα με). His repentance for his iconoclastic past becomes a leitmotiv in the final texts he produced, as was also seen in the *kanon* dedicated to Tarasios. The latter – a repeated public penance – was likely the price imposed upon Ignatios for his rehabilitation and acceptance in the circle of the patriarch Methodios. In any event, the hymns he wrote during that period are a significant element of patriarchal

---

[231] Ex 13:17–18:27; Num 10:11–34; 13.
[232] *Vita of Nikephoros* 36, p. 166; Ševčenko 1965: 41–47; Abrahamse 1982; Gero 1995 on the magicians Iannes and Iambres as precursors of the iconoclasts; Senina 2016.
[233] Auzépy 1995; Kaplan 2000; Efthymiadis 2006.
[234] *Vita of Nikephoros* 70, p. 201,8–28; Timotin 2010: 154–55.
[235] Genesios I, 14; Theoph. Cont. I, 18; Zonaras XV, 19,36–39.
[236] *Menaion* IV: 80ff. The *Synaxarion Evergetis* II, 22 also attributes this *kanon* to Ignatios.

policy, of which the vindication of the forty-two martyrs of Amorion formed an essential part. Methodios himself had become personally involved in this, and Ignatios did not want to be left out. He therefore composed a hymn in honour of the Amorian martyrs that began with a renewed admission of his sin.[237] The other *kanones* he produced also show his close collaboration with the patriarch.[238] His involvement in the official ideology of the post-iconoclast Church was absolute, as is evident from the fact that he devoted several of them to the new saints promoted by Methodios: Georgios of Mytilene, whose relics Methodios had repatriated, is celebrated in a liturgical poem sung on 7 April.[239]

Other contemporary saints and confessors who were prominent in the fight against iconoclasm also seem to have been honoured by Ignatios. This is the case with Hilarion, the hegoumenos of the monastery of Dalmatos,[240] and with Bishop Iakobos,[241] who is known as Iakobos the Younger and held in high regard in *synaxaria* and *menologia* for his ascetic life.[242] The descriptions offered by these liturgical texts are vague, but they perfectly fit the former bishop of Anchialos in Thrace during the patriarchate of Tarasios.[243] After this period, Iakobos decided to live a hesychastic life in Bithynia, bringing him into contact with several saints. He appears in some hagiographies, first in the circle of Petros of Atroa,[244] and subsequently in that of Antonios the Younger, who chose him as his master of contemplative life and moved into a cell near him.[245] Iakobos died at the end of the reign of Theophilos, and his remains were buried in the monastery of the Eunuchs (i.e., that of Hagios Porphyrios),[246] where they remained, according to the wishes of his disciple Antonios the

---

[237] Significantly this *Kanon in Honour of the 42 Martyrs of Amorion* is part of the *akolouthia* that also includes the *idiomelon* that the patriarch Methodios produced in honour of the forty-two martyrs.

[238] For the hymns of Ignatios Diakonos, see Papadopoulos-Kerameus 1902: 88–91; Wolska-Conus 1970: 334–35; Mango and Efthymiadis 1997: 15–16; *Vita of Gregorios Dekapolites*, pp. 16–19.

[239] *Menaion* IV: 268–72: Αἴγλην εὐσπλαχνίας μοι; *Vita of Gregorios Dekapolites*, p. 18, n. 46; *Synaxarion Evergetis* II, 86.

[240] *Menaion* V: 235–39; Spanos 2010: 193–94 and 401–2. The attribution of this *kanon* (Ἐν φωτὶ αὔλῳ καὶ νοητῷ) to Ignatios seems clear in light of *Synaxarion Evergetis* II, 144. On Hilarion of Dalmatos see Section 7.2.2.

[241] *Menaion* IV: 124–28: Τὸν φωτισμὸν τοῦ σοῦ δεσπότου, Ἰάκωβε.

[242] *SynaxCP* 558,2–9 (24 March); 551/552,43–50. 52. 54 (21 March); *Menologion Basilii* 361D–63A (21 March); *Typika Dmitrievskij* III, 44 (21 March). *Synaxarion Evergetis* II, 28 supports the attribution of this *kanon* to Ignatios. On this Iakobos, see *PmbZ* # 2637.

[243] *PmbZ* # 2630; *PBE* 1: Iakobos 5. As was shown by Efthymiadis, he also received two letters from Theodoros Stoudites (*epist.* 462 and 466) ca. 823, cf. Efthymiadis 1995: 146–48; *PmbZ* # 2633.

[244] *Vita of Petros of Atroa* 65–70 and 75.

[245] *Vita of Antonios the Younger* 28–30, pp. 207,18–208,32; 35–39, pp. 212,22–14,10; *Vita of Antonios the Younger* (addit) 6, p. 213,19f.

[246] Janin 1975: 149 and 209; Ruggieri 1991: 225.

Younger, when the ex-Empress Prokopia tried to convey them to her own monastery in Constantinople.[247]

The memory of Iakobos was of course still very much alive in 843, when icons were restored and their defenders were acknowledged. Their liturgical praise was fully in accord with Methodian policy, as was the cult of St Eustolia of Constantinople, a strict nun who had become prominent for her monastic virtues.[248] The writing of a *kanon* by Ignatios to celebrate the model her life represented on 9 November should be taken as a sign of the satisfaction the new patriarchate aimed to give the monastic groups, the major bastions of iconodule resistance during the persecution. The catalogue of the liturgical poems of Ignatios Diakonos ends with a *kanon* in honour of Methodios himself, which is actually a very simple reworking of Ignatios' own work dedicated to Tarasios.[249] It is tempting to think that Ignatios also composed the hymn featuring Ioannikios, which was read on 4 November on the occasion of his celebration,[250] and he might in fact have known Ioannikios personally, since he mentions him in two of his epistles (*epist.* 31 and 33) and spent a great deal of time at the monastery of Antidion (much frequented by the saint and the place where he was buried).[251] But the acrostic in the theotokia indicates that it was written by Theodosia.[252]

All this intense literary production encouraging veneration of the new iconodule saints sponsored by Methodios is a good example of Ignatios' powerful position in the patriarch's circle and of the work he carried out in his service. The proximity of the man of letters to power made the circulation of the *vitae* he composed possible and encouraged copying them. Proof of the success of the ideological programme conducted by the patriarchate is provided by the large number of codices in which these works survive,[253] despite the difficulties the vast majority of the population

---

[247] *Vita of Antonios the Younger* 37, p. 213,9–26. On the monastery of Prokopia, cf. Janin 1969: 442–43; Ruggieri 1991: 195.
[248] *AHG*, vol. III, 260–68. The poem includes the traditional confession of sin: κἀμοῦ τὴν ἀχλὺν τοῦ πταίσματος λῦσον λάμψασά μοι φῶς (lines 100–101). See also Leontopoulos 1939.
[249] The *kanon* to Methodios is edited in *Menaion* V: 288–95; Senina 2011/2012. Another *kanon* in honour of the patriarch Methodios was collected in the *Menaion of Bartholomaios* X: 46–51; Spanos 2010: 237–39 and 409–10.
[250] *AHG*, vol. III, 122–33: Ἀχλύς με καὶ ζόφος ἁμαρτιῶν. For Makris, the authorship of Ignatios is clear from the similarities to several passages of the *vita* of Gregorios Dekapolites, see *Vita of Gregorios Dekapolites*, p. 16, n. 58.
[251] Ignatios Diakonos, *epist.* 43,3–4; Mango and Efthymiadis 1997: 118.
[252] *AHG*, vol. III, 569–71.
[253] No less than ten manuscripts contain the *Vita Tarasii*: the oldest two of these are the *Parisinus Gr.* 1452 and the Oxford *Bodleianus Barocci* 238, which go back to the tenth century. Two date from

would have faced in reading them. Ignatios Diakonos writes thinking of his ultimate reader, the erudite Methodios, and of gaining his approval and thus recovering his lost influence. The collected letters of Ignatios reflect the relations between the two men, since three letters addressed to Methodios survive in which Ignatios attempts to gain readmission into the Church by appealing to Methodios' piety and generosity.[254] Of these, *epistle* 54 is particularly worthy of attention, since in it Ignatios asks Methodios to intercede to persuade the bishop of Hierapolis to return a copy of the Gospel that was borrowed and not returned; after the death of his elder brother, Ignatios had inherited this book, which he lent to an *asekretis* named Stephanos, who passed it on to Michael of Synada.[255] When this saint died in 826, it came into the hands of the bishop of Hierapolis, who had not returned it. This resort to Methodios indicates the close collaboration between Ignatios and the patriarch and testifies to their rapprochement. Taking into account the fact that Michael of Synada belonged to the Stoudite milieu, it is reasonable to suppose that the bishop also supported the critics originating from the monastery of Stoudios; we can thus imagine that with this request Ignatios aimed to join the patriarch's circle and take advantage of his hostility to the Stoudite milieu in order to recover the aforementioned book.

If we understand literary production as a functional reality, the utilitarian aspect of the *vitae* of Ignatios confirms his progressive stabilisation within the post-iconoclast Church. In view of the *intitulationes* of his last two *vitae*, which were produced within the Methodian milieu, it is tempting to suggest the following chronology: the *Vita Tarasii* affirms that its author was Ignatios as a simple monk (Ἰγνατίου μοναχοῦ), while the *Vita Nicephori* maintains that Ignatios was a deacon and the *skeuophylax* of

---

the eleventh century: Istanbul Hagia Trias 95 and Vienna ÖNB Hist. Gr. 3. Two others belong to the twelfth century: *Sinaiticus Gr.* 515 and the London *British Library Add.* 36589. The four remaining manuscripts are from a later period: *Meteorensis Barlaam* 150, *Regius Monacensis Gr.* 32, *Vaticanus Ottobonianus Gr.* 92 and *Bollandianus Gr.* 192, see *Vita of Tarasios*, pp. 53–67. For its part, the *Vita Nicephori* has come down to us in eight different manuscripts from the Byzantine period, of which the oldest two date back to the ninth century: the *Vaticanus Gr.* 984 and the *Parisinus Gr.* 910. Three others correspond to the tenth: *Vaticanus Gr.* 1667, *Vaticanus Gr.* 1809 and *Vaticanus Gr.* 1882. The codex of Mount Athos, Philotheou 8, is from the eleventh century, while the other two are of later date.

[254] Ignatios Diakonos, *epist.* 52,8–9: μὴ δὴ βραδύνοι ἡ πρὸς πάντας ὑμῶν ταχεῖα ἐπισκοπή. Ignatios Diakonos, *epist.* 55,6–7: μὴ ζημιώσῃς τοὺς παῖδάς σου, κερδησείοντας ἐντεῦθεν ψυχικῆς ἀρετῆς μεγίστην ἐπίδοσιν. Mango and Efthymiadis 1997: 132 and 138.

[255] Mango and Efthymiadis 1997: 199–200. He also wrote *epist.* 53 to the deacon and *protonotarios* Theophilos, the director of the patriarchal offices, on the same subject; this shows the relations of Ignatios with the major institutions of Constantinople, see *PmbZ* # 8213.

Hagia Sophia (Ἰγνατίου διακόνου καὶ σκευοφύλακος τῆς ἁγιωτάτης μεγάλης ἐκκλησίας τῆς ἁγίας Σοφίας). We know that the former was commissioned by a man with good connections, to whom the hagiographer rendered obedience, which makes sense, since after 843 Ignatios was a simple monk. The latter work does not seem to have had a commissioner but was produced by the author's own volition. His change in social and ecclesiastical status between the two *vitae* is well known, and it is logical that it occurred in this order. The claim of Ignatios Diakonos in his *Vita Tarasii* that he had attained a great age (ch. 70: γήρᾳ καὶ νόσῳ καμπτόμενος) does not mean that this was his final work; he is simply resorting to *pathos* in a bid to improve his quality of life. Once that objective had been achieved, there was no sense in insisting on the point. In the same way, the intertextual relationship between chapters 57–58 of the *Vita Tarasii* and chapter 84 of the *Vita Nicephori*, in both of which the patriarchs are compared to Moses, does not indicate a relative chronology, although it has been maintained that the *Vita Tarasii* is Ignatios' final work.[256]

After the restoration of Orthodoxy, penitent iconoclasts were stripped of all their posts. Ignatios was shut away in the monastery of Pikridion and as a simple monk was put to the test, being commissioned with producing the *vita* of Tarasios. After completing his mission successfully and making clear his full support of iconoduly and his committed membership in the Methodian party (implying rejection of the Stoudites), he was readmitted as deacon and, in payment for services rendered to the patriarch, was also given the post of the *skeuophylax* of Hagia Sophia, on the condition that he continued to express his repentance in public, as he does in his liturgical hymns and especially in the final pages of the *Vita Nicephori*. It should not be forgotten that the obligations of the *skeuophylax* included looking after not only the liturgical vessels but also the icons,[257] hence the need for a declaration of permanent iconoduly. Moreover, the *skeuophylax* was appointed by the imperial power, which meant that Empress Theodora as regent accepted the appointment. As far as Ignatios Diakonos is concerned, the advantages of this promotion are obvious. But it was also highly beneficial to Methodios, even apart from the direct results of the literary work within his milieu. After the restoration of Orthodoxy, the

---

[256] Efthymiadis 1991a: 82, n. 60.
[257] On the *skeuophylax* and his duties, see Clugnet 1898: 147ff. and 262ff; Alexander 1958a: 133–34; Darrouzès 1970: 314–8; Papagianni and Troianos 1984: 87–97; *ODB*, s.v. 'skeuophylax', pp. 1909–10.

new patriarch had to show himself to be firm, as his attitude to Stoudites and iconoclasts proved he was. But he also had to be understanding, in order to defuse any possible rebellion by the defeated heretics. It was useful for the patriarchal ideology to have a public figure, someone relatively important and socially prominent, show repentance and provide a behavioural model for former heretics: Ignatios' public admission of sin in having embraced iconoclasm opened the door to the pardon of the iconodule Church and guaranteed social peace in the Empire.

2.2.3 *Theophanes and His* Translation of the Patriarch Nikephoros *(BHG 1336)*

When, on 13 March 846, the patriarch Methodios repatriated the relics of his predecessor Nikephoros, all the institutional machinery was set in motion to re-enact again the Triumph of Orthodoxy and the restoration of icons. The chosen date commemorated the overthrow and exile of the iconodule patriarch at the hands of Leon V on 13 March 815. One aim of providing the mistreated confessor with a burial befitting his position as patriarch in the church of the Holy Apostles of Constantinople was to make amends for how he had been abused. But another was to represent the subordination of imperial power to ecclesiastical power and the hierarchical superiority of the patriarch over all the iconodule groups the Church incorporated. Methodios, much aware of the propaganda resources of literature and hagiography in his own interests, could not fail to ensure that this event had an official narration. This materialised both in a *kanon* written by Ignatios Diakonos[258] and in the *Account of the exile of St Nikephoros patriarch of Constantinople and the transfer of his honourable remains* (*BHG* 1336–1337b).[259] Reading of the latter was added to the liturgical calendar, the effect being that the memory of Nikephoros was celebrated not only on 2 June (the anniversary of his death), but also on 13 March (the commemoration of his exile and subsequent transfer), as is attested by the *synaxaria* and *menologia*.[260] This account entered the

---

[258] *Menaion* IV: 80–4. *Vita of Gregorios Dekapolites*, p. 18, n. 44; Mango and Efthymiadis 1997: 16; *Synaxarion Evergetis* II, 22.

[259] It survives in the manuscript *Marcianus Gr. Z* 359, fol. 51v–59, of the early eleventh century. The *BHG* gives two references to this same work, separating the first part on exile (chs. 1–5) which would be *BHG* 1336 and the second about the transfer: chs. 6–13 = *BHG* 1337.

[260] *SynaxCP* 723,6–26,7 (2 June) and 533,11–34,18; 533/534,44–535/536,45 (13 March); Janin 1969: 46; *Typikon of the Great Church* I, 248,4–7 (13 March) and p. 302,10–17 (2 June); *Typikon Messinense* 129,3–4 (13 March) and 156,4 (2 June); *Typika Dmitrievskij* III, 42 (13 March) and 50 (2 June). See also Petit 1926: 207.

menologia in adapted and abbreviated form: in March only the portion of the text corresponding to the *translatio* of the relics was read,[261] while in June a much abbreviated *vita* of Nikephoros was read.[262]

The text begins with a reflection on the need to bear witness to the power of God, which manifests itself in amazing events such as those occurring at the time,[263] which have been revealed not privately or partially, but publicly to the entire clergy.[264] This elevated subject required writers who expressed themselves in a fine literary style, so that the lack of ornament did not diminish the importance of the events being narrated.[265] For this reason, our author, a certain Theophanes, renounced writing completely in the conviction that he could not express himself in an appropriate style or correctly.[266] But after his patron repeatedly insisted on commissioning the text, he obeyed, trusting that God would grant him the power of speech.[267]

The account looks back on the years of the reign of Emperor Nikephoros, when the dogmas of the Second Council of Nicaea were respected and icons were venerated. Nikephoros was succeeded by Michael, and Michael in turn by Leon, a cruel man from Armenia who confronted God and the emperor, making war even on icons with the aid of demons and false soothsayers (ch. 2). Leon V dismissed Nikephoros as patriarch, bringing much discredit upon himself, since he is compared to a wild boar, a wild beast and a viper (ch. 3). Nikephoros' attempts to confront the heretical tyrant were unsuccessful, and the emperor decided to exile him. Before leaving Constantinople, the patriarch addressed the members of the Church, attempting to strengthen them in Orthodoxy, since many of them were persecuted, tortured or exiled, while others

---

[261] BHG 1337b in *Menologion imperiale*, vol. I, 230–33. For its part, the thirteenth-century manuscript *Vaticanus Gr.* 1991, fol. 128–31v contains a version of the text in which the final prayers for the emperor have been removed (BHG 1337f), see Ehrhard 1936–1939: vol. III, 364(2) and 366, n. 1.

[262] BHG 1337e in *Menologion imperiale*, vol. II, 4–6.

[263] *Translation of Nikephoros* I, 115: τὰ νυνὶ τοῖς καθ' ἡμᾶς ἐπιδεδειγμένα χρόνοις.

[264] *Translation of Nikephoros* I, 115: οὐκ ἐν μέρει καὶ εἰδικῶς, οὔτε μὴν ἐν ἔθνει ἐλαχίστῳ καὶ τοῦ μηδενὸς ἀξίῳ αἱ τηλικαῦται τῶν ἀγαθῶν καταπεφοιτήκασι χάριτες, ἀλλὰ καθ' ὅλου καὶ γενικῶς καὶ τῷ Χριστῷ ἐπωνύμῳ καὶ ἐκλεκτῷ κλήρῳ.

[265] *Translation of Nikephoros* I, 116: αἱ τῶν μεγίστων λόγων ὑποθέσεις ἀρίστων καὶ τῶν ἐξηγητῶν δεδέηνται, ὡσὰν μὴ κατόπιν ἔλθοιεν ἑαυτῶν τῇ τῶν ἐγχειρούντων σμικρότητι ἐλασσούμεναι, μηδ' αὖ τῷ περιπεζίῳ τῆς λέξεως καὶ ἀκαλλεῖ πρὸς τὸ καταδεὲς ὑποτέμνοιτο τὸ ὑψηλὸν τῆς ἐκείνων μεγαληγορίας.

[266] *Translation of Nikephoros* I, 116: διὰ τοῦτο ἰλιγγιῶν ἀφασίᾳ πεπίεσμαι, καὶ τοῦ γράφειν ἀπείργομαι, λόγου εὐφραδοῦς εἰς ἅπαν ἡμοιρημένος.

[267] *Translation of Nikephoros* I, 116: Ὅμως, τῶν εἰς τοῦτο προτροπάδην κινούντων με, τῇ συνεχεῖ καὶ ἀπαραιτήτῳ σχολῇ παρωρμημένος, πρὸς τὴν ὑπακοὴν δεδιὼς ἐμαυτὸν καθυφῆκα, Θεὸν τοῦ λέγειν δοτῆρα καὶ ἀρωγὸν σχοίην πεπιστευκώς.

embraced iconoclasm out of fear or self-interest (ch. 4). Three heretical patriarchs then succeeded each other: Theodotos, Antonios and Ioannes, who attacked dogmas like hungry wolves for almost thirty years, fourteen of which Nikephoros spent in exile in the monastery of St Theodoros, where he led a pious and virtuous life until his death (ch. 5).

After an *enkomion* of the hero (ch. 6), the author jumps forward to the present: Theophilos has died, and his wife Theodora has inherited the Empire together with her son Michael. With iron will worthy of a man, the empress restored Orthodoxy, working to promote harmony (ch. 7). First, she called a synod at the palace to discuss the restoration of images, and a large number of monks and other members of the Church attended. Those who had embraced iconoclasm were anathematised, including the heretic leader Ioannes VII Grammatikos, who was deposed by a unanimous decision of the empress, the emperor and the ecclesiastical synod, and Methodios was appointed (ch. 8). The Second Council of Nicaea, held by Empress Eirene and the patriarch Tarasios to put an end to the First Iconoclasm, is described. Four years after the definitive restoration of images, Methodios asked Theodora for help repatriating the relics of Nikephoros, which were still in exile, to the shame of the iconodules. As when Joseph brought his father Isaac's bones from Egypt to Canaan, so too the remains of the patriarch were to return to Constantinople.[268] Theodora agreed with the objective of making up for the affront of the heretic emperors and committed herself to an active part in the celebration together with her son and daughters (ch. 10).

Accompanied by a large delegation, Methodios travelled to the monastery to collect the relics of his predecessor in the patriarchate. As soon as he arrived, he prayed to Nikephoros, comparing him to St John Chrysostom, who like him had been exiled for confronting the emperor in defence of the faith (ch. 11). Nikephoros' remains, which remained uncorrupted, were transported in a *dromon* that had been specially equipped for the occasion; on their arrival in Constantinople, they were received by Emperor Michael III and the most senior dignitaries of the court, who carried them on their shoulders to Hagia Sophia (ch. 12). Finally, they paraded the relics solemnly through the centre of Constantinople as far as the church of the Holy Apostles, where they were buried in a new sarcophagus on 13 March 846 to coincide with the anniversary of the exile of Nikephoros. The writer concludes with a series of prayers addressed to Nikephoros, asking him to intercede before God (ch. 13).

---

[268] *Translation of Nikephoros* 9, 124. See Genesios 50,5–13.

These prayers show that the hagiographer not only witnessed these events, but played an active part in them, approaching the saint in his definitive location to venerate him.[269] The author asked the saint to ensure that the Church remained at peace, and requested that his own faith remain unshaken.[270] To this end, he would follow the example Nikephoros gave his life for and defined in his writings. The prayer ends with the standard formula of iconodule authors to justify their theological position, commending themselves to God, the Holy Spirit and Christ, who was made flesh in order that he might be visible to our eyes.[271]

We know little of the author of this piece. According to the title of the manuscript, he is the presbyteros and hegoumenos Theophanes (Θεοφάνους πρεσβυτέρου καὶ ἡγουμένου). From the text, it can be deduced that he was a new writer who had had a good education and aspired to the inflated, verbose and overwritten Asiatic style. He had witnessed the solemn procession of the relics through Constantinople and perhaps even from the monastery of Theodoros, which means that he was a contemporary of the patriarch Methodios. Indeed, the production of the work immediately postdates the *translatio*, since its allusions prove that Methodios was still alive.[272] But who is this Theophanes?

He is hard to identify.[273] He cannot be Theophanes Graptos, the hegoumenos of the monastery of Chora discussed below, who died in 845. We have records of only one hegoumenos named Theophanes, the author of the *vita* of Ioseph Hymnographos and of a *kanon* dedicated to Ioannes, another disciple of Gregorios Dekapolites.[274] But this author was barely a youth when the relics were transferred, and he thus cannot have written this piece.[275] Few details have come down to us regarding ninth-century figures named Theophanes, and the prosopographies offer only

---

[269] *Translation of Nikephoros* 13, 127: ἡμεῖς δὲ, ὦ πατέρων ἀξιάγαστε πάτερ ... τῇ σῇ μετὰ πόθου προσίεμεν θήκῃ, καὶ ταύτην σεβασμίως περιπτυσσόμενοι, ταύτας ἀφίεμεν πρὸς σὲ τὰς φωνάς.

[270] *Translation of Nikephoros* 13, 128: τήν τε ἁγίαν Ἐκκλησίαν εἰρηναίως βραβεύεσθαι, καὶ τὴν πίστιν ἀκλονήτως περιφρουρεῖσθαι ἐσαεί.

[271] *Translation of Nikephoros* 13, 128: τοῦ δι' ἡμᾶς ἀνθρωπισθέντος, καὶ περιγραφῆς εἴδει κατὰ σάρκα ὀφθῆναι μὴ ἀπαξιώσαντος Χριστοῦ τοῦ Θεοῦ ἡμῶν.

[272] Methodios is thus described as a Θείῳ κινηθεὶς ὡς ἀληθῶς πνεύματι ὁ πανίερος Μεθόδιος (ch. 9, p. 124) and ὁ ἱερώτατος πατριάρχης at the beginning of ch. 12, p. 126. But he never uses expressions such as μακάριος or ὁ ἐν ἁγίοις to refer to him.

[273] *PmbZ* # 8151.

[274] *PmbZ* # 8143 and # 28075. He is probably also the author of two *kanones* in honour of Prokopios Dekapolites and his companion Basileios, see *PmbZ* # 8135; Eustratiadès 1936: 476, nrs. 62–63.

[275] As was suggested by Beck 1959: 561, who considers the text from the late ninth century instead of the mid-ninth century.

two additional candidates: the hymnographers Theophanes[276] and Theophanes Sikelos.[277] We know virtually nothing of their biographies, and their works have been confused with those of Theophanes Graptos, who has monopolised the authorship of virtually all the hymnographic production of the ninth century. The author of the *translatio* may be a third individual, but it is also possible that he is one of the men mentioned above, or we may be concerned with a single author whose different facets have been separated by tradition.

If so, the good relationship between Theophanes Sikelos and Methodios is logical: they were both from Sicily and took pleasure in praising local saints with the composition of liturgical poems. Moreover, their opposition to iconoclasm had been clear years previously. It is no coincidence that this Theophanes was the recipient of a letter from Theodoros Stoudites, in which he was encouraged to oppose a certain *chartoularios* who was encouraging iconoclasm in Sicily.[278] Theophanes also produced numerous *kanones* dedicated to Sicilian saints: Beryllos of Catania,[279] Theoktistos the hegoumenos of Cucumo,[280] Agatha of Palermo[281] and Markianos of Syracuse.[282] In addition, he likely wrote pieces in honour of Agrippina, the martyr buried in Sicily,[283] of Pankratios of Taormina (*BHG* 1412)[284] and of other iconodule saints, such as Aimilianos the Confessor of Kyzikos.[285] Unfortunately, the passage of time has confused the correct attribution of these compositions, many of which are traditionally assigned to the famous Theophanes Graptos, and it is no longer easy to know which texts belong to which author.[286]

We have no record of Theophanes Sikelos being the hegoumenos of any monastery, but it is logical to suppose that his iconodule credentials meant that Methodios saw in him an ideal candidate for running one of the many monasteries in the capital after the defeat of heresy and the consequent purge of ecclesiastical leaders. This would fit well with his membership in

---

[276] *PmbZ* # 8139; Follieri 1960–1966: vol. v,1, pp. 269–71.
[277] *PmbZ* # 8130; *PBE* I: Theophanes 51; Théarvič 1904; Giannelli 1963: 313–14; Kazhdan 1999: 272. The attribution to Theophanes Sikelos of the account on the transfer of Nikephoros' relics was already proposed by Théarvič 1904: 168.
[278] Theod. Stoud., *epist.* 524, written between 821 and 826.   [279] Papadopoulos-Kerameus 1900.
[280] *AHG*, vol. x, 350, n. 4.   [281] Papadopoulos-Kerameus 1901.   [282] Tarquini 1961.
[283] Follieri 1975.   [284] Rossi Taibbi 1965: vii–xvi.
[285] This is the *kanon* read on 8 August (*incipit*: Ταῖς ὑπερκοσμίαις συνοικῶν ταξιαρχίαις ...), see Eustratiadès 1937: 89, nr. 195. For Aimilianos, the metropolitan of Kyzikos, see *PmbZ* # 153; *PBE* I: Aimilianos 1.
[286] The situation is the same with that dedicated to Symeon Stylites for 1 September (*incipit*: Ὡς τῶν χρόνων ποιητής καὶ τῶν αἰώνων, Σωτήρ, κατάρχων ...): ed. *AHG*, vol. 1, 41–51 and 399–408. A detailed study of the works of Theophanes Sikelos has yet to be written.

the Methodian circle and his acceptance of the patriarchal postulates in his work: Theophanes is lavish in his praise of Methodios[287] and of the Empress Theodora, the patron of the restoration of icons as well as of the patriarch.[288] The vindication of Tarasios[289] is complemented by a belligerent attack on iconoclasm and its leading figures, especially in the first chapters. The comparison of Nikephoros to a Church Father such as St John Chrysostom, along with the biblical image of the repatriation from Egypt to Canaan of the relics of Joseph's father,[290] is part of the same conceptual universe as that used by Ignatios Diakonos in his *vita Nicephori*. The account of the *translatio* is a commission, either from a member of the patriarchal milieu or from Methodios himself, aimed primarily at a religious audience. The setting of the scene is excessive and unnecessary for the narration of the repatriation of the relics but is one of the essential objectives of the text. In its historicist approach, a desire to offer a partial (pro-iconodule) version of recent history is apparent. This patently ideological tendency of the patriarchate of Methodios is a key element of post-iconoclast propaganda, but on this occasion, it is more direct than usual.

This time Ignatios Diakonos was not chosen to transmit the message of the Triumph of Orthodoxy, the vindication of the iconodule patriarch and the superiority of the Church over the State by continuing the narration from the end of his *Vita Nicephori*. We do not know why. Perhaps his obligations in Hagia Sophia kept him too busy, or perhaps he was prevented from undertaking the commission by a new wave of inquisitorial fervour, as is indicated by the admission of sin with which Ignatios Diakonos initiates his *kanon* on the transfer of the relics of Nikephoros.[291] To judge from the texts that resulted, however, it is more likely that the institution was seeking a new form of communication to reach another audience. Compared to the expression of Theophanes Presbyteros, Ignatios' style was too learned: his language was an erudite Greek with a complex, archaic and even artificial grammar, with frequent allusions to classical antiquity and its mythology, history, literature and the like. Despite his almost Asiatic initial declaration of intentions,[292]

---

[287] *Translation of Nikephoros* 8, 123.   [288] *Translation of Nikephoros* 9, 124.
[289] *Translation of Nikephoros* 9, 124: Ταρασίου τοῦ μεγίστου καὶ παμμάκαρος πατριάρχου.
[290] Gen 50:1–13.
[291] *Menaion* IV: 80: Ἁμαρτίων τάφῳ δεινῷ συσχεθέντα με, / τῇ ἀθανάτῳ νεύσει σου / καὶ τῇ εὐσπλάγχνῳ σου ἀναστήσας παλάμῃ, / ζώωσον ὡς οἰκτίρμων καὶ πολυέλεος.
[292] Perhaps because lofty language is characteristic of ninth-century iconophile authors, in contrast to the lower and more direct style of the iconoclasts, as was suggested by Lemerle 1971: 120–68. See Introduction. For the style of Ignatios Diakonos, see Lampakis 2001.

Theophanes shuns the use of complex forms, obscure allusions and obsolete terms. But this search for more efficient, simple expression does not imply the rejection of the hagiography of Ignatios, with which Theophanes establishes a clear dialogue in the interests of the common good that goes beyond literature. Aware of Methodios' desire to promote and spread the holiness and the cult of his predecessor Nikephoros, Theophanes provides details to sustain this liturgical veneration that are not found in the *vita* of Ignatios, for example, the miraculous preservation of the uncorrupted body of the saint[293] and his capacity for performing miracles. Indeed, he takes pleasure in the scene of the mass healing of those possessed by the devil that takes place in Constantinople when the relics are solemnly paraded to the church of the Holy Apostles.[294]

2.3 The Milieu of Methodios in the Patriarchate: The *Synkelloi*

The difficulties the patriarch Methodios faced in accomplishing successfully the restoration of the cult of icons can be imagined. It was fortunate that, in addition to having the support of imperial power and the assistance of a significant ecclesiastical sector, he could rely on institutional figures whose main purpose was to aid him. These were the *synkelloi*, collective bodies generally made up of two members at the service of the patriarch but appointed by the emperor.[295] These men were so important, that they were frequently considered as successors of the current patriarch. During the iconodule interval of 787–815, the *synkelloi* had already shown their capacity to provide active cultural propaganda in the service of Orthodoxy through literature. Tarasios had been accompanied by the historian Georgios,[296] who produced an important world chronicle,[297] and by Ioannes,[298] the future bishop of Sardis, replacing Euthymios in 803/804, who wrote hagiographical texts.[299]

---

[293] *Translation of Nikephoros* 12, 126.   [294] *Translation of Nikephoros* 12, 127.
[295] Concerning the post of *synkellos* and its responsibilities, cf. Metr. Athenagoras 1927; Grumel 1945; *ODB*, s.v. *synkellos*; Oikonomides 1972: 308; Leontaritou 1996: 553–605; *Vita of Tarasios* 237.
[296] *PmbZ* # 2180; *PBE* I: Georgios 137; Laqueur, 'Synkellos,' in *RE* IV, 2 (1932) 1388–90; Auzépy 2012.
[297] According to his own testimony, Georgios began to write it in 807/808 (Georgios Mon. 2,32 and 6,12) and continued to do so two years later in 809/810, cf. Georgios Mon. 244,31.
[298] *PmbZ* # 3200; *PBE* I: Ioannes 461; Pargoire 1901/1902. The minutes of the Second Council of Nicaea (787) only mention Ioannes as the *synkellos* of Tarasios, see Mansi XIII, 134 and XIII, 380. On Georgios' absence, cf. Huxley 1981: 216.
[299] Efthymiadis 1991b. The overthrow of Euthymios was due to his alleged involvement in the riot of Bardanes Tourkos (802/803), see *Vita of Euthymios of Sardis*, 27,74–76; Niavis 1987: 120–21.

After the restoration of images in 843, Methodios also had the assistance of two *synkelloi*,[300] regarding whom the hagiographical sources offer various information. According to the *Acta* of the Lesbian brothers David, Symeon and Georgios, which coincide with the accession to the patriarchate of Methodios, Symeon the Stylite was appointed *synkellos* with the approval of Empress Theodora.[301] He can only have held the post briefly, however, since according to his hagiographer, he returned shortly afterwards with his brother to Lesbos, where he died in 844.[302] This decision seems surprising in a close collaborator of the patriarch, who necessarily had duties in the capital, and it has been suggested that Symeon was only assistant to the *synkellos*, a sufficiently important post to allow the flattering hagiographer to give him the higher position.[303] But the grant to Symeon of the Constantinopolitan monastery of Sts Sergios and Bakkhos, an establishment that had hitherto been run by the patriarch Ioannes Grammatikos, supports the idea that he was in fact appointed a patriarchal *synkellos*.[304] This seems even more likely if we consider that some years previously Emperor Theophilos made Ioannes Grammatikos a *synkellos* at the same time that he made him head of the same monastery.[305]

It is very likely, however, that it was not Symeon the Stylite of Lesbos who was chosen for the post of *synkellos*, but Symeon Dekapolites, an important *archimandrites* who years before had commissioned Methodios' *Vita Euthymii Sardensis*.[306] The homonymity of the two men led the hagiographer of the former to merge them into one person, so as to increase the importance of his hero. As a result of this confusion, the *synkellos* Symeon became a neo-martyr worthy of recognition, and the news of his appointment after the restoration of icons provided material for subsequent hagiographers, who praised him, told the Methodian version of

---

[300] It was the patriarch Sergios (610–638) who limited the number of patriarchal *synkelloi* to two, see Athenagoras 1927: 8; Konidaris 1982: 66 and 72. The custom of having two *synkelloi* must have been maintained over time, see *De ceremoniis* II, 531,7–8: εἰ δὲ τύχῃ εἶναι ἕτερον σύγκελλον.

[301] *PmbZ* # 7178; *PBE* I: Symeon 13. For his appointment as *synkellos*, see *Acta of David, Symeon and Georgios* 30, 250.

[302] *Acta of David, Symeon and Georgios* 33, 255. In any case, he is remembered in the *Synodikon of Orthodoxy* 53,132 for his defence of icons.

[303] Karlin-Hayter 2004: 348.

[304] *Acta of David, Symeon and Georgios* 30, 250: τὴν τε Σεργίου καὶ Βάκχου τῶν ἁγίων μονὴν πρὸς τὴν τῶν οἰκείων μαθητῶν καταγωγὴν καὶ ἀνάπαυσιν αὐτῷ προσδεδώκασι, τὴν τε τῶν ἱερῶν ἀναστήλωσιν ὁμοῦ καὶ προσκύνησιν εἰκόνων ἐξέθεντό τε καὶ ἐδογμάτισαν. On the monastery of Sts Sergios and Bakkhos, Janin 1969: 451–54; Mango 1975b; Bardill 2017.

[305] Theoph. Cont. IV, 7,7–9.

[306] *PmbZ* # 7199 and *PmbZ* # 7214. On Symeon Dekapolites, see Chapter 3. On the interpolation of his appointment as *synkellos* in the *Acta of David, Symeon and Georgios*, see Chapter 6.

the restoration of images and contributed to the creation of a post-iconoclast mentality in keeping with the principles decreed by the patriarchate. The *synkellos* Symeon thus came to be identified with Symeon of Lesbos, and information regarding his hegoumenate at the head of Sts Sergios and Bakkhos was added to the *vita* of the confessor, which was probably written after his death, but still during the mandate of Methodios. The *vita* was subsequently rewritten as *Acta*, however, as a consequence of which we will consider it later on.[307] The same thing happened with the other *synkellos* of Methodios, a certain Michael, who as well as featuring in a *vita* and being praised by the patriarchal circle[308] was also an active hagiographer.

2.3.1 Michael Synkellos

Michael was from Palestine, was born in Jerusalem in 761 and gave himself up to God at a very young age; he received an excellent education and entered the monastery of Mar Sabas.[309] According to the hagiographical sources,[310] the patriarch Thomas of Jerusalem named him his *synkellos* ca. 811, and when he needed a right-hand man to travel to Rome as an ambassador, chose him for the job. Michael went no further than Constantinople, however, where Leon V had just succeeded to the throne. Michael defended the Orthodoxy of icons and as a result suffered persecution and imprisonment, as is confirmed by the epistle sent to him by Theodoros Stoudites. As a consequence, he was imprisoned near Mount Olympos in Bithynia during the reign of Michael II.[311] Matters did not improve during the mandate of Theophilos, but Michael stood firm and sent several letters of encouragement to other persecuted iconodules, such as the *asekretis* Stephanos and the *spatharios* Kallonas.[312]

---

[307] See Chapter 6.
[308] An unpublished *kanon* celebrating Michael Synkellos has survived. The manuscripts affirm that its author was Ignatios (i.e., Diakonos), see *Sinaiticus Gr.* 583, fol. 133v–35v, or Theophanes, cf. *Sinaiticus Gr.* 581, fol. 20–24 (in this case it would be Theophanes Sikelos and not Graptos as the latter had died by then), see *Tameion*, 129, nr. 361.
[309] *PmbZ* # 5059; *PBE* I: Michael 51; Vailhé 1901; Hatlie 2007a: 267–69, 322 and 336.
[310] A premetaphrastic *vita* survives (*BHG* 1296), edited and translated into English by Cunningham 1991; see the review by Rosenqvist in *BSl* 53 (1992) 265–67; Loparev 1910: 212–24; Kazhdan 1999: 257–59; 2006: 204–5. To it can be added a much later fourteenth-century *vita* attributed to Nikephoros Gregoras (*BHG* 1297), see Schmit 1906; Guilland 1926: 175–77; Lukhovitskiy 2014. See the detailed discussion in Chapter 6.
[311] Theod. Stoud., *epist.* 547.
[312] *Vita of Michael the Synkellos* 17, 74,31–76,1; 76,14–17. For the *asekretis* Stephanos, see *PmbZ* # 7069. On the *spatharios* Kallonas, cf. *PmbZ* # 3611.

Once the last iconoclast emperor was dead, Methodios appointed him a patriarchal *synkellos* and the hegoumenos of the monastery of the Holy Saviour of Chora.[313] The monastery of Chora (the modern Karye Camii) had allegedly been founded in the sixth century by a relative of Empress Theodora I, and her husband Justinian had provided financial support for its construction.[314] As it was an imperial foundation,[315] it is unsurprising that it was delivered together with the appointment of the *synkellos*, especially if we take into account the important Palestinian connections of the monastery, which, according to the hagiographical accounts, went back to the time of its foundation, when St Sabas himself stayed there.[316] Although it is unclear that this visit ever took place, in the ninth century the monastery of Chora was continuously used as a refuge by Palestinian monks and clerics.[317] It is precisely to this spot in the capital that Michael Synkellos and his companions went for lodging when they arrived in the city, according to his *vita* (ch. 9). Regardless of what historical reasons brought Michael to the capital, after the restoration of icons he was thought to be an ideal candidate to participate in the creation of the post-iconoclastic Church, to the extent that he was allegedly offered the post of patriarch of Constantinople (ch. 25).

However, Michael rejected the offer and requested a consultation with Ioannikios, who indicated that Methodios should become the patriarch. Perhaps with the posts of *synkellos* and hegoumenos Methodios was purchasing Michael's loyalty and gaining a new ally to the cause of restoration. The monastery of Chora had remained faithful to icons during the First Iconoclasm. To illustrate this, the *vita* of the *synkellos* affirms that the patriarch Germanos I retired to Chora after being deposed by Leon III in 730 and that his remains lie in its church.[318] But the monastery finally embraced the iconoclast principles of Leon V, as Theodoros Stoudites noted.[319] Once Michael Synkellos took over the running of this important monastery, he not only put an end to its acceptance of heresy but also

---

[313] For the monastery of Chora, see Janin 1969: 531–38; Thomas 1987: 45; Berger 1988a: 660–67; Hatlie 2007a: 155–58, 165, 335–36.
[314] *Vita of Theodoros of Chora* 21–23.
[315] *Vita of Michael the Synkellos* 106,1; 116,22–23. Cf. Hatlie 2007a: 335–36.
[316] *Vita of Theodoros of Chora* 24–26.
[317] On the settling of Palestinian monks in Chora in the early ninth century, see Theoph. 499,15–31; Gouillard 1969; Kaplan 1992: 299–300; Auzépy 2012: 495. For the relations of Constantinople with this province throughout this period, see Mango 1991; Auzépy 1994; Griffith 1998; Auzépy 2001; Signes Codoñer 2013a.
[318] *PmbZ* # 2298; *PBE* I: Germanos 8; Lamza 1975; Lilie 1999: 5–21.
[319] Theod. Stoud., *epist.* 112,29.

converted it into a significant iconodule centre. The number of its monks grew to a hundred[320] and included confessors such as Theophanes Graptos, whose burial within its walls (like that of its new hegoumenos Michael after his death on 4 January 846) made it a place of pilgrimage and enhanced the spiritual reputation of the community.[321]

Proximity to the patriarch Methodios must soon have become close collaboration involving the imperial household. According to the testimony found in his *vita*, Michael was attended on his deathbed by the patriarch, who before he died took him to the empress and her son so that he could intercede for them.[322] Michael also supposedly shared the ideological programme of Methodios even before he met him, since on his journey to Constantinople he did not hesitate to confront some monks from Seleucia who rejected the Second Council of Nicaea and refused to 'mention the saints, confessors and great patriarchs Tarasios and Nikephoros in their holy diptychs'.[323] Their common interests were confirmed by the literary testimony of the work of Michael Synkellos itself.[324] This includes pieces with a clearly institutional function, which acquire their full meaning if they are understood as having been composed with patriarchal sponsorship. A good example is the Greek translation of the dogmatic epistle addressed to the Armenians, which had been written in Arabic in the name of Thomas the patriarch of Jerusalem by Theodore Abū Qurrah to defend the Chalcedonian faith.[325] Another is the profession of faith Michael wrote (*Libellus on the Orthodox Faith*), in which he affirms the principles of the iconodule Church of Constantinople, the subsequent success of which in the Slavic world is undeniable.

In keeping with the triumphalist feeling that pervaded the Church after the restoration of icons, moreover, and in imitation of the *kanon* to celebrate the Feast Day of Orthodoxy (*Kanon on the Restoration of the Holy Icons*), Michael also produced a long celebratory poem in Anacreontic verse.[326] The use of this verse-form implies an old-fashioned stance on the

---

[320] *Vita of Michael the Synkellos* 32. On this number, see Auzépy 1994: 209–17.
[321] *Vita of Michael the Synkellos* 29 and 37; *SynaxCP* 680,1–3; Auzépy 2001: 313, n. 86.
[322] *Vita of Michael the Synkellos* 36. For the literary representation of his death, see Agapitos 2004.
[323] *Vita of Michael the Synkellos* 8; Vailhé 1901: 325–32.
[324] For the written production of Michael Synkellos, see Vailhé 1901: 638–40; Beck 1959: 503–5; *DS* X, 1194–97; Cunningham 1991: 36–38; Kazhdan 1999: 257–59; 2006: 204–5; Sode 2001: 285–59. Some of the works attributed to him, such as the *Encomium Ignatii* (*BHG* 818), are in fact by Michael Monachos, see Chapter 5.
[325] Sode 2001: 286–87 and n. 13. For the original text in Arabic, Lamoreaux 1992; Griffith 1997: 9–10; Signes Codoñer 2013a: 161 and 164–65. On the ancient translations he became familiar with, see Thomson 1991.
[326] Crimi 1990a; D'Aiuto 1997.

part of this author, who was recovering classical forms that were in disuse but which inevitably referred back to the Anacreontics of Church Fathers such as Gregorios of Nazianzus and Synesios of Cyrene, who constituted the literary references of the piece.[327] Its ingenious language is characteristic of Methodios and the authors of his circle, and Ignatios Diakonos in particular had also used Anacreontic verse. Michael Synkellos and Ignatios Diakonos probably knew each other long before icons were restored. Not for nothing had Michael converted to iconoduly one of the companions of Ignatios commissioned to write iconoclastic *iamboi* to commemorate the replacement of the icon of Christ of the Chalke Gate with a representation of the bare cross carried out by Leon V in 815–816. This man was the *asekretis* Stephanos Kapetolites, and after the conversion, which occurred ca. 834, Michael was exiled by Theophilos, while Ignatios must have remained in Constantinople.[328] Be that as it may, the poem of Michael Synkellos is a work of iconodule propaganda whose controversial, combative verses not only extol icons and their veneration but also denigrate iconoclast heretics.[329] At the same time, they encourage the veneration of the hermit saints (icons of whom the author undertakes to paint) by means of a reference that inevitably recalls Ioannikios, one of the major protectors of Methodios in his race to the patriarchate and the man with whom Michael himself had requested a consultation in order to make a decision about the post.[330]

Finally, the *synkellos* joined other authors of the Methodian circle who encouraged the dissemination of the cult of the forty-two martyrs who fell at Amorion (but who were in fact martyred at Samarra, the capital of the Abbasid Caliphate). One surviving version of the *Passio of the 42 martyrs of Amorion* (version Γ = *BHG* 1213) is therefore unanimously attributed to him in the manuscripts. Although its authorship has been convincingly defended,[331] the attribution to Michael Synkellos remains problematic, since he died in January 846, scarcely a year after the martyrdom of

---

[327] As is apparent from verses 43–46; Crimi 1990a: 9–11; 1990b.
[328] *Vita of Michael the Synkellos* 17. For the *asekretis* Stephanos, a poet at Theophilos' court, see *PmbZ* # 7059 and # 7074; *PBE* I: Stephanos 162; Theoph. Cont. III, 43,39–47; Ps-Symeon 610,17–11,2; Speck 1974c: 74–5, n. 3; Mango and Efthymiadis 1997: 199; Lauxtermann 1998: 398; 2003: 278–84.
[329] Michael Synkellos, *In restaurationem imaginum* vv. 79–80: Εὐσεβέων ἄποθεν κύδεος ἔστω / λαβραγόρης ὁ ἔχων αἶσχος ἀπίστων. vv. 85–88: Ῥαφίσι στόμα φραγήτω / νοεραῖς νόον στεφούσαις, / ἀπὸ θαυμάτων ἰούσαις, / νεμεσῶν λεών θεοῖο. vv. 115–18: Ψιλὸς οὖν πέφηνε πᾶσι / πραπίδων, πλέος δὲ μᾶλλον / ὄφεως ἰοῦ φονῆος / ὁ θεουδέας κακίζων.
[330] Michael Synkellos, *In restaurationem imaginum* vv. 81–84: Πατέρων βίου μονήρους / ὀρέων ἄκροις ὀπαῖς τε / ἀγάπῃ θεοῦ τακέντων / ἰδέας γράφων σεβάζω.
[331] Lemerle 1973: 87, n. 9.

Amorion, and the text includes the official burial of the martyrs and the healing miracles that occurred on their tomb. It has been suggested that the author was Michael's young namesake Michael Monachos, who is often mentioned as Synkellos in the sources and is well known to us for having written the *vita* B of Theodoros of Stoudios and other *enkomia* in the second half of the ninth century.[332] There is no doubt that an early date of composition fits better with the remainder of the hagiographical dossier, of which an *idiomelon* of the patriarch Methodios and a *kanon* signed by Ignatios Diakonos survive. The difficulty may be overcome by seeing in the last news about the martyrs' burial a later interpolation.[333]

Michael Synkellos' written production is completed with a famous grammatical treatise entitled Μέθοδος περὶ τῆς τοῦ λόγου συντάξεως, which was widely distributed and reflects the author's erudite literary concerns,[334] and with an *enkomion* in honour of Dionysius the Areopagite (*BHG* 556), which stood out for the knowledge of classical culture apparent in it and for its historicist intentions.[335] This final composition may have been in imitation of Michael's leader, since Methodios too wrote a *passio* featuring St Dionysius (*BHG* 554d). Only four of Michael's liturgical poems have survived,[336] with the following central themes: the transfiguration of Christ, all the saints, a penitential *kanon* and one to be read in case of drought. The latter is particularly interesting and connects with the iconodule discourse that blamed the heresy of Theophilos for the constant droughts and other natural disasters that took place during his reign.[337] Although the icon conflict is not mention in any of these texts, the matter arises indirectly in the *vita* of Theodoros, the founder of the `monastery of Chora.

(a) **The *Vita* of Theodoros of Chora (*BHG* 1743)**

The *vita* of Theodoros of Chora was written shortly after the restoration of images in 843, that is, while Michael was the hegoumenos of the establishment.[338] This hagiography was not a commission but appears to have

---

[332] See Chapters 1 and 5. [333] Kotzambassi 1992.
[334] Donnet 1982; Robins 1993: 149–62. The work was written in the town of Edessa at the request of Deacon Lazaros, described as a 'philosopher and logothete', see Signes Codoñer 2013a: 164.
[335] Loenertz 1950; Podolak 2015; *Suidae lexicon* II, 108,33–109,20 corroborates the authorship of Michael Synkellos.
[336] *DS* X, 1197.
[337] The chronicler Georgios Monachos is the first to make these affirmations (Georgios Monachos 798), followed later by the *Vita Theodorae* 7,11–16 and Genesios III, 19.
[338] Loparev 1904; Schmidt 1906. For its dating as ca. 843, see Saradi 1995: 104–5; Auzépy 2001: 313; Hatlie 2007a: 14–15 and 155–64; Mango 2009: 188. This *vita* has only come down to us in two

been the fruit of the concern of its author (no doubt a monk of Chora) that there be an account of the alleged founder with which to celebrate his memory in future generations.[339] The protagonist is a fictitious saint, and the sixth century within which his life plays out no less so.[340] Indeed, no *synaxarion* or *typikon* includes any reference to this Theodoros.

Despite resorting to good historical sources and making extensive use of the Chronicle of Theophanes, which he copies verbatim at many points,[341] the hagiographer alters the facts. It is difficult to believe that these errors are due to inattention on the writer's part, especially since they are so numerous and since on important matters he does not follow the well-informed sources to which he had access. Identification of a clear purpose in this accumulation of anachronisms and alterations of history makes it possible to understand the reasons for producing the text. We are told that Theodoros was an uncle of Empress Theodora, the wife of Justinian I, who was an important army official until, after major military successes against Chosroes, he chose to take the monastic habit. Sometime later, when the emperor and empress located him, they decided to take him to Constantinople along with the bishops of Antioch, Palestine and Egypt to combat the Theopaschite heresy. At the same time, the Pope of Rome, Agapetus, arrived to take part in a synod in 536 that resulted in the overthrow of Anthimos as bishop of Constantinople and the appointment of Menas in his place. Three years later, the monastery of Chora was seriously damaged by a major earthquake that shook the Empire, but its restoration, financed by Justinian, was rapid enough for it to be finished by the time St Sabas came to stay there.[342]

The chronology of the *vita* is altered to create a logical parallel sequence to that of the time in which it was written. The *vita* thus narrates the same event twice: the defeat of heresy and the major role of the monastery of Chora in the administration of the resultant new Church. This also made the adulation of the imperial household more effective, and may even have

---

manuscripts, always placed after the hagiography of Michael Synkellos itself; these are codex Genoa Urbani 33, tenth century, and Athos Pantokrator 13), twelfth century, see Chapter 6.

[339] *Vita of Theodoros of Chora* 1: ἐπεὶ δὲ ... τὸν τοῦ ὁσίου πατρὸς ἡμῶν βίον Θεοδώρου ἀτέλεστον καταλελίπασι, μικράν τινα περὶ τούτου βραχυλογίαν ἐν τοῖς ἑαυτῶν πονήμασι γράψαντες καὶ ταύτην ὧδε κἀκεῖσε διὰ μνήμης ἐγκατασπείραντες, ἀφορμὰς παρασχόντες ταῖς μετέπειτα γενεαῖς τὰ ἐλλείποντα ἀναπληρῶσαι.

[340] In fact the personage of Theodoros is completely fictitious and seems to have been based on the *protopatrikios* named Priskos, the son-in-law of Emperor Phokas (602–610), cf. Kaegi, 'Priskos,' in *ODB*; *PLRE*, vol. III: 1052–57, s.v. 'Priscus 6'.

[341] Schmit 1906: 9–16; Mango 2009.

[342] The earthquake actually occurred in December 557 and the visit of Sabas was in 531, Mango 2009: 187.

extended it to the iconoclast Theophilos (829–842), whose memory Theodora wanted to safeguard at all costs. The famous defeat of the Persian Chosroes by the Byzantines at the Daras fortress in 530 is a reflection of the victory of Theophilos in 837 at Melitene in the same border area.[343] Both occurred six years before the restoration of Orthodoxy in Constantinople, in the first instance in place of the aforementioned Theopaschite heresy, and in the second, in place of iconoclasm. The characterisation of the wife of Justinian I similarly does not correspond to the other details we have about her, but is very appropriate for her namesake Theodora, the restorer of icons (ch. 3). The identification of Theodora with Empress Helena in this passage was also used by the patriarch Methodios to praise her.[344] As in the Methodian version of the defeat of iconoclasm, according to which Theodora decreed that a synod should be held in Kanikleion to put an end to heresy,[345] the *vita* of Theodoros of Chora affirms that the Theopaschite heresy was defeated on the initiative of the sovereigns who called the synod (ch. 15). After their beliefs were condemned as far removed from the Chalcedonian creed, the former patriarch and his followers were anathematised and excommunicated. Among them, Severos of Antioch (ch. 16), who was condemned not only as a heretic, but also for paganism and carrying out magical practices, was particularly important, as was Ioannes VII Grammatikos.[346] After the restoration of Orthodoxy, the account concentrates on the monastery of Chora, including several details with aetiological value. The alleged damage caused by the earthquake was repaid with imperial money, which set a precedent for Michael Synkellos to demand economic favours from the empress.[347] The alleged stay of St Sabas[348] justifies Chora's links with Palestinian monks, who were particularly important in the ninth century.

Finally, if we compare the absence of the tomb of the patriarch Germanos I from the *vita* of Theodoros with the extensive treatment it receives in the subsequent *vita* in honour of Michael the Synkellos himself, an interesting conclusion emerges. The *vita* of Theodoros uses a wealth of

---

[343] Signes Codoñer 2014: 263–78. [344] See Section 2.1.3.
[345] *Acta of David, Symeon and Georgios* 242–43 and 246; *Vita of Michael the Synkellos* 100,29; *Translation of Nikephoros* 8–9, 122–24; Genesios 57,76–86.
[346] Abrahamse 1982; Senina 2016.
[347] *Vita of Michael the Synkellos* 32. It is true that before asking Michael III and his mother to return the assets seized from the monastery during the iconoclast years, Michael Synkellos requested the patriarch's intermediation.
[348] *Vita of Theodoros of Chora* 24–26. In his visit to Constantinople, Sabas did not stay at any monastery but at the imperial palace itself, see *Vita of Sabas* (BHG 1608) 174. On this stay, see Festugière 1962: 22–23, III/1.

detail to describe the building work paid for by Justinian and lists each part of the monastery, the church, its chapels and their decoration, affirming that they could be seen by anyone, since they survived up 'until that time' (μέχρι τῆς δεῦρο).[349] The author then launches a harsh attack on the iconoclast emperors for having caused great damage here.[350] The failure to mention the tomb of the patriarch Germanos in the description of the chapel of the forty martyrs indicates that his remains were not yet there along with those of Theodoros and Theophanes Graptos. If the monastery had had such important relics, the author, as a fervent iconodule, would not have failed to mention them.

Two conclusions can be drawn. First, the *vita* of Theodoros of Chora was written between 843 and October 845, when Theophanes Graptos was buried.[351] Second, since the *vita* of Michael the Synkellos twice affirms that the body of Germanos lay alongside that of Theophanes Graptos in the chapel of the forty martyrs before Michael Synkellos died,[352] the relics of this iconodule patriarch must have been transferred during Michael's hegoumenate. Taking into account Methodios' propaganda policy with iconodule confessors who died in exile, it is reasonable to suppose that he welcomed the measure. Germanos had been overthrown by Leon III in 730 and imprisoned on paternal property known as 'Platanion'.[353] Although it cannot be ruled out that this was the monastery of Chora,[354] we have clear evidence that Germanos was initially buried at the monastery of *Ta Rhomaiou* in Petrion.[355] Sources dating immediately after this merely indicate that Germanos' relics were at Chora, not how they arrived there.[356] But the years immediately after the restoration of icons represent the best context for this transfer.

Although the *vita* of Theodoros of Chora is not a masterpiece of Middle Byzantine hagiography, as Mango notes,[357] it is worth taking into account as a good example of the motivation that led authors to write *vitae* of saints

---

[349] *Vita of Theodoros of Chora* 22.   [350] *Vita of Theodoros of Chora* 23.
[351] *Vita of Michael the Synkellos* 31.
[352] *Vita of Michael the Synkellos* 31, 114,11–15 and ch. 37, 124,31–26,4.
[353] Theoph. 409,9–10; Rochow 1991: 128. For Mango 2009: 191, n. 23 it is in the quarter of Blachernai.
[354] Auzépy 1999: 203–4. The identification seems clear for later Byzantine authors, including the anonymous writer of the *vita* of the famous abbot of Chora, see *Vita of Michael the Synkellos* 28, 108,13–18. However, the silence regarding the *vita of Theodoros of Chora*, which is earlier, would seem to indicate the opposite.
[355] See the preface to the Latin translation (early ninth century) of the *Acathist Hymn*, ed. Huglo 1951: 33: 'Qui sepultus in monasterio εἰς τὰ Ῥωμαίου vocablo in quo ... devotissime veneratur'. For this monastery see Janin 1969: 446–47.
[356] *SynaxCP* 677,55 and 680,3; and the *Typikon of Patmos*, see *Typika Dmitrievskij* I, 72,1–6. On the *vita* of the patriarch Germanos, see Section 5.2.3.a.
[357] Mango 2009. His final opinion of this work is a harsh one and rather unjust: 'the preposterous VTh'.

The Milieu of Methodios in the Patriarchate 159

after the restoration of icons. They sought to promote the cult of companions who had fallen during the persecution of the Second Iconoclasm, as did individuals in the Stoudite milieu. But they also aimed to construct a glorious past to legitimise the importance acquired by certain monasteries after the defeat of heresy, due in large part to their close connections with religious leaders or the patriarch himself and the imperial family. The assignment of this account to the Methodian milieu reflects the socio-political function it pursues and the contents it transmits in keeping with the official version of how the triumph of images was achieved. But the linguistic form itself shows that its author wished to make clear that the *vita* was a product of the patriarchal circle. This is evident from the use of a striking intertext[358] from the *vita* of Stephanos the Younger, the first iconodule hagiography written at the request of the patriarch to serve his ecclesiastical interests.

(b) The Graptoi Brothers

Byzantine tradition would have it that Michael Synkellos was accompanied by two disciples, the brothers Theophanes and Theodoros, who in addition to being celebrated as iconodule saints for their defence of Orthodoxy, also contributed actively to the creation of the cult of their companions who died during the iconoclast crisis. These brothers had been born in Moab in Palestine ca. 775, but their most important activities took place in Constantinople.[359] Together with their master Michael and another companion named Iob, after some time at the monastery of Chora, they were summoned to meet Emperor Leon V. Their defence of icons led to imprisonment in the palace at Phiale, and their perseverance in not sympathising with the iconoclasts meant that they were separated and exiled. The brothers were taken to the Island of Aphousia,[360] where they continued to work for Orthodoxy and to send letters defending the veneration of images.[361] Years later, in July 836, Theophilos had them brought into his presence and sentenced them to be marked on their faces with twelve iambic verses declaring that they had been expelled from Jerusalem as heretics and were now being expelled from Constantinople

---

[358] *Vita of Theodoros of Chora* 10: ὀρεόμονας καὶ σπηλοδιαίτους, cf. *Vita of Stephanos the Younger* 122,17.
[359] *PmbZ* # 7526; *PBE* I: Theodoros 68; *PmbZ* # 8093; *PBE* I: Theophanes 6; Vailhé 1901; Efthymiadis 1995: 141–44; Sode 2001. See Chapter 6.
[360] *Vita of Michael the Synkellos* 14; *Acta of David, Symeon and Georgios* 239, 2–18.
[361] *Vita of Michael the Synkellos* 14. For the brothers' activities between 815 and 836, see Cunningham 1991: 14–17.

as criminals. On 18 July, after they were whipped, the sentence was carried out at the prison of Praitorion in the presence of the author of the verses, Christodoulos.[362] Later Byzantine historians affirm that Theophilos himself composed the verses to refute the brothers' accusation that the emperor used false evidence in his defence of iconoclasm.[363] From then on, the brothers were known by the nickname *Graptoi* (the tattooed).

The *vita of Michael the Synkellos* affirms that the brothers were in contact in this period with Methodios, the future patriarch, who was also imprisoned in the Praitorion (ch. 24). The historiographical account differs from the hagiographical one as to the location, placing this relationship not in Constantinople, but in exile.[364] According to Pseudo-Symeon, Theophanes and Theodoros had been exiled to a place named Kartalimen on the Bithynian coast.[365] Tradition has it that Methodios (imprisoned in a hideout on the island of Antigonos) and the Graptoi brothers exchanged messages of support through a fisherman. Regardless of where they were imprisoned, Methodios had already written several missives to them when they were on Aphousia. The tone of these verses, which were sent first by the Graptoi, is very familiar and suggests the sincere friendship as well the intellectual affinity for poetry the three men shared.[366] Although the author of his *enkomion* and the historians of the Logothete group claim that Theodoros Graptos died in exile, most hagiographers and *Theophanes Continuatus* report that he survived to witness the Triumph of Orthodoxy and attended the celebrations in Constantinople presided over by Empress Theodora, at which he proudly showed off the marks inflicted on him by the heretics.[367] As for Theophanes, he was appointed the metropolitan bishop of Nicaea once Methodios was established as patriarch.[368] He was the leader of this see for four years, until his death on 11 October 845 at the age of sixty-seven. Death surprised him at the monastery of Chora, where he was buried by his master and friend Michael Synkellos.[369]

---

[362] *PmbZ* # 1080; *PBE* I: Christodoulos 3; *Vita of Michael the Synkellos* 23; Cunningham 1991: 86–87 and 157, n. 145; Barber 1999; Hatlie 2007a: 390–91; Senina 2008b.
[363] Cont. Theoph. III, 14. According to Ps-Symeon 641–43 the verses extended as far as their chests. For the exact date of these events, see Treadgold 1979b: 187–89.
[364] According to the *PmbZ* # 4977, Methodios was imprisoned in Constantinople and closely watched over by Theophilos. For the different versions, see Lilie 1999: 209 and 213–14.
[365] Ps-Symeon 642–43; Zon. XV 28.33–37.
[366] Pargoire 1903b; Cunningham 1991: 160–61; Bithos 2009: 237–38.
[367] Theoph. Cont. IV, 11; Ps-Symeon 653–54. Concerning the two different traditions on the death of Theodoros Graptos, see Chapter 6.
[368] *Vita of Michael the Synkellos* 29; *Vita of Nikolaos Stoud.* 900C–901A; Ps-Symeon 641–43 and 653.
[369] *Vita of Michael the Synkellos* 31.

The Milieu of Methodios in the Patriarchate

We see once again in the rapid process of sanctification and promotion of veneration of the Graptoi brothers the interests of the party installed in the patriarchate, which was anxious to find ways to exemplify the values of the new, post-iconoclast Church. The signs of the early cult are telling: no sooner had Theodoros died, than his brother Theophanes wrote a *kanon* to celebrate his memory liturgically,[370] in the same way he promoted the cult of his father Ionas.[371] The same can be said of the bishop of Nicaea, Theophanes, who is acclaimed in the *Synodikon of Orthodoxy*,[372] entered the first *synaxaria*[373] and was praised by a companion of the patriarch Photios (see Section 6.3.3). The collaboration of the Graptoi brothers with Methodios is well established, and events such as the appointment of Theophanes as leader of the see of Nicaea redounded to the benefit of the Orthodoxy they defended along with the iconodule leaders. Indeed, there is an unpublished *kanon* signed by a certain Methodios, probably the patriarch himself, to honour Theophanes Graptos every 11 October.[374]

The historical relationship of the Graptoi brothers with Michael Synkellos is obscure, and his contemporaries are sometimes thought to have tried to make it out to be closer and more intimate than it really was: some years ago, Auzépy suggested that they abandoned Palestine due to a confrontation with the patriarch of Jerusalem and not as part of a delegation he commissioned, whereas for Von Dobschütz and Sode they were pilgrims who accidentally ended up playing a part in the defence of images and who had scarcely any real contact with Michael Synkellos.[375] There can in any case be no doubt that the veneration of the Graptoi was based as much on their spectacular confession, which was harshly punished by

---

[370] *Menaion*, vol. II, Rome 1889, p. 698. His presence in the various *synaxaria* proves how widespread his celebration was: SynaxCP 352,4–54,3 (*BHG* 1746e) (28 December); 349,47ff. (27 December); 65,3 (21 September); 69/70,41 (22 September); 130,24–31,20 (11 October); *Menologion Basilii* 229B–C (28 December); *Typikon of the Great Church* I, 164 (27 December); 42 (22 September); Sode 2001: 249.

[371] The *kanon* in honour of his father has been edited in *AHG*, vol. I, 294–306. The canonising efforts of Theophanes were successful as the celebration of Ionas found a place in the SynaxCP 65,1–11 (21 September) and 69/70,40–49 (22 September); *Menologion Basilii* 68A–B (22 September); *Typikon of the Great Church* I, 42,9f. (22 September); *Synaxarion Evergetis* I, 83–85. For the father of the Graptoi brothers, see *PmbZ* # 3429.

[372] *Synodikon of Orthodoxy* 102, I and 268–69.

[373] SynaxCP 130,24–31,20 (11 October); *Typikon of the Great Church* I, 42 (22 September), 66 (11 October; Theophanes Sabaites), 164 (27 December); *Menologion Basilii* 229B (28 December)

[374] Codex *Sinaiticus Gr.* 562, fol. 54–56. The acrostic reads: Τὸν μυστολέκτην αἰνέσω Θεοφάνην. Ὁ Μεθόδιος, see *Tameion*, 58, nr. 105.

[375] Von Dobschütz 1909a: 84–92, esp. 91; Auzépy 1994: 209–13; Sode 2001; 2004: 187. See Chapter 6.

Theophilos, than on their literary production in the service of the Methodios cause.[376]

Theodoros Graptos appears to have written a book in which he quoted passages from the Bible and the Church Fathers to refute the iconoclast heresy. This apologetic work, known as *Kynolykos*,[377] is unfortunately lost, like all the *enkomia* Theodoros penned in honour of a number of saints.[378] These *enkomia* likely included one dedicated to iconodule heroes, as is true of the liturgical hymns by his brother Theophanes. We do have the epistle Theodoros sent to Ioannes, the bishop of Kyzikos, in which he relates the ordeal that he and his brother suffered in defense of icons.[379] The vast majority of his production, however, is hymnographic. The *vita* of Michael the Synkellos stresses the poetic abilities of both brothers,[380] and the large number of liturgical compositions bearing the name of Theophanes Graptos shows that this is not literary licence on the part of the hagiographer.[381] Many of these pieces were composed to be sung on the day when an iconodule saint was celebrated, and those that are a part of the ideological programme of the patriarch Methodios are of particular interest. This is the case with the *kanon* on the restoration of images that is sung during the *orthros* on the first Sunday in Lent and which amounts to a kind of diptych with the *kanon* on the same subject written by Methodios. Theophanes praises those who had defeated heresy in his eight odes addressed to Empress Theodora and her son Michael III.[382]

Likewise Theophanes Graptos promoted the veneration of the favourite saints of Methodios, such as Agatha or Emperor Konstantinos and Empress Helena,[383] while at the same time he dedicated hymns to the main

---

[376] For the written production of the Graptoi brothers, see Vailhé 1901: 640–42; Beck 1959: 516–17; Cunningham 1991: 38–39; Sode 2001: 292–98.

[377] *Vita of Michael the Synkellos* 30; *Enkomion of Theodoros Graptos* 125.

[378] *Enkomion of Theodoros Graptos* 112: οὗ τὴν ἐπιστήμην τοῦ λόγου καὶ τὸ κάλλος ἀποδείκνυσι μάλιστα τὰ εἰς ἄνδρας ἁγίους αὐτῷ πονηθέντα ἐγκώμια.

[379] Included in the *Vita of Theodoros Graptos* 672B–80A. See Sode 2001: 121–38, for whom this letter did not originally refer to the Graptoi brothers but to another pair of criminal brothers; Senina 2008b: 262–69; Høgel 2015. On its recipient Ioannes the bishop of Kyzikos, see *PmbZ* # 3216; *PBE* I: Ioannes 529.

[380] *Vita of Michael the Synkellos* 19: ἄριστα τούτοις ἤσκηται ἡ τῶν ποιητικῶν σκεμμάτων ἀκριβεία.

[381] A couple of *kanones*, dedicated to the Theotokos and the dead, have come down to us and are attributed to Theodoros Graptos. A large proportion of Byzantine *kanones* are signed by Theophanes. The latest study by Zervoudaki 2002 enumerates as authentic compositions of Theophanes Graptos 374 *kanones*, 5 triodia and diodia, 138 stichera (*prosomoia* and *idiomela*), 3 kontakia and 1 metrical prayer dedicated to the Virgin Theotokos. Cf. also Eustratiadès 1936; 1937; Follieri 1960–1966: vol. v,1, pp. 269–71.

[382] Gouillard 1961a: 381; *Synodikon of Orthodoxy* 121 and n. 12; *Synaxarion Evergetis* II, 385.

[383] *Synaxarion Evergetis* I, 519 (Saint Agatha); II, 133 (Konstantinos and Helena).

representatives of the iconodule party, Ioannikios, Theodoros Stoudites, Prokopios Dekapolites, Theophylaktos of Nicomedia, Theophanes of Sigriane, Niketas of Medikion, Georgios the metropolitan of Mytilene, the patriarch Germanos of Constantinople, Michael of Synada, Theodosia, Aimilianos of Kyzikos,[384] Petros of Nicaea, Hilarion of Pelekete and Ioannes Psichaites.[385]

The two *kanones* Theophanes Graptos wrote to celebrate the patriarch Nikephoros are an important example. The first is included in the *akolouthia* of the *Menaia*,[386] while the second consists of nine odes and survives only in the *Codex Lesbiacus Leimonos* 11.[387] Both praise the saint for having defended the doctrine of icons, and the second also highlights the exile he suffered (verses 61–63). Given that the repatriation of the remains of his predecessor was a matter of vital importance for Methodios, it is unsurprising that the members of his circle referred to it in their compositions. After Nikephoros' relics were deposited in the church of the Holy Apostles in Constantinople, a *sticheron* was added to celebrate his iconoduly and confirm that the celebration took place around his tomb, thus updating the *kanones* of Theophanes Graptos and allowing their use to continue over time.[388]

(c) **The *Vita* of Leon of Catania (*BHG* 981b)**

The *vita* of Leon of Catania represents the main evidence for this fictitious bishop from Sicily. No historical sources mention him, and all surviving information comes from hagiographical and liturgical texts (i.e., brief entries in the *synaxaria* and *menologia*).[389] Two hagiographies in Leon's honour survive: the longer (*BHG* 981b) was written in Constantinople in

---

[384] *Synaxarion Evergetis* I, 173 (Ioannikios), 189 (Theodoros Stoudites), 569 (Prokopios of Dekapolis); vol. II, 9 (Theophylaktos of Nicomedia), 23 (Theophanes the Confessor), 85 (Niketas of Medikion), 87 (Georgios of Mytilene), 125 (Germanos of Constantinople), 135 (Michael of Synada), 141 (Theodosia), 239 (Aimilianos of Kyzikos). On the *akolouthia* he dedicated to Theophanes the Confessor, see Yannopoulos 2013: 56–58 and 169–74.

[385] For the *kanon* dedicated to Hilarion of Pelekete (29 March), see Eustratiadès 1936: 531, nr. 90; that of Petros of Nicaea has been edited in *AHG*, vol. I, 219–26 and pp. 434ff. (12 September); that of Ioannes Psichaites in *AHG*, vol. IX, 270–79 and 424–26 (25 May).

[386] *Menaion* V: 215–19; Follieri 1960–1966: vol. IV, 220; cf. *Synaxarion Evergetis* II, 144.

[387] Spanos 2010: 27–31, 160–69 and 396–97.

[388] *Menaion* V: 219: λάρνακα κυκλοῦντες τὴν θείαν τοῦ θεοφόρου Νικηφόρου, δεῦτε χριστοφόροι προθύμως ὡς νικηφόρον τοῦτον ὑμνήσωμεν, καὶ τὴν αὐτοῦ πανήγυριν μετ' εὐφροσύνης ἑορτάσωμεν. Spanos 2010: 161,7–8: αὐτὸν δυσώπει, ὅσιε, τηρηθῆναι τοὺς παρεστῶτας τῇ τιμίᾳ σου, μάκαρ, καὶ θείᾳ λάρνακι.

[389] *SynaxCP* 477/478,17–27 (20 February); 479,22–80,12 (21 February); *Typikon of the Great Church* I, 236,8 (20 February); *Typikon Messinense* 122,29 (20 February); *Typika Dmitrievskij* I, 419 (21 February) and III,40 (20 February); *Menologion Basilii* 324A–B (20 February).

the mid-ninth century by an author from the circle of Michael Synkellos, while the shorter (*BHG* 981) was produced in Sicily some time later.[390] Both are anonymous and show the same lack of interest in the historical situation and biography of the protagonist, regarding whom the only clear information offered is that he was from Ravenna. The longer version sets the action during the reigns of Konstantinos IV and Justinian II (681–685), while various details in the shorter version correspond to the reign of 'Leo and Konstantinos', which has been interpreted as a reference to Leon IV and Konstantinos VI (775–780). The lack of precision is justified by the absence of a true hero, since all the action revolves around the antagonist, the magician Heliodoros. Heliodoros is the true object of attention, and his sorcery continuously threatens the city of Catania and Leon as its protector until the final confrontation, in which Heliodoros interrupts a liturgical celebration and Leon overpowers him physically and has him burnt alive before the amused gaze of the crowd. This account has traditionally been considered an iconoclast hagiography that managed to survive after suffering iconodule censorship.[391]

The true central figure of the plot of the *vita*, Heliodoros, has been much analysed in search of historical references. As Alexakis, the last editor of the long version, has shown, we are concerned here with a re-imagining of the last iconoclast patriarch, Ioannes VII Grammatikos, whose passion for magic and the occult is well known.[392] The rhetoric of identifying iconoclast heretics with sorcerers and pagans is not new, but it achieves its fullest expression in this text, albeit in a veiled manner: the archenemy is never mentioned by name. For Alexakis, it is clear that the entire work is an attack on the iconoclast authorities when they were still in power, obliging the author to be discreet and subtle. Despite everything, it is possible to glimpse the iconoclast Ioannes in the figure of Heliodoros, and the iconodule patriarch Nikephoros in his opponent Leon of Catania.[393] In all likelihood, the text was written somewhere around Constantinople during the years of the tenure of Theophilos (829–842), and perhaps more precisely during the patriarchate of Ioannes Grammatikos (838–843).[394]

Despite many attempts to identify the writer, he remains anonymous. It has been suggested that he might be the patriarch Methodios, who was

---

[390] Acconcia Longo 1989. On Leon of Catania, see *PmbZ* # 4277; *Vita of Leon of Catania*, pp. 79–85.
[391] Costa-Louillet 1959/1960: 89–95; Kazhdan 1988: 205–8; Acconcia Longo 1989; Turner 1990; Auzépy 1992.
[392] *PmbZ* #3199 and #3304; *PBE* I: Ioannes 5; *Vita of Nikephoros* 36, p. 166; Ševčenko 1965: 41–48; Abrahamse 1982; Gero 1995; Lilie 1999: 169–82; Senina 2016.
[393] *Vita of Leon of Catania*, pp. 79–85.   [394] *Vita of Leon of Catania*, p. 73.

from Sicily, or someone from his milieu. The range of possibilities can be narrowed by close examination of the text, since it is of high literary quality[395] and written in very correct Greek in the best rhetorical tradition of Antiquity. This points to Michael Synkellos as the most likely author, since he was well acquainted with classical syntax and grammar (although the style does not fully coincide with his) or perhaps a disciple from his circle.[396] In the same way that the *vita* of Leon of Catania mentions Ioannes VII Grammatikos in an indirect and allusive manner,[397] in fact, the *vita* of Michael the Synkellos resorts to a circumlocution to refer to him.[398] We have already seen, moreover, that the intellectuals linked to the monastery of Chora also resorted to a legendary saint, Theodoros of Chora, to describe the role of his monastery during the iconoclast crisis in an indirect manner. In addition, the *vita* of Leon of Catania has a close relationship with the cycle of miniatures present in the Khludov Psalter, which was copied on the orders of the patriarch Methodios shortly after 843.[399] According to Hatlie, Michael Synkellos himself might have assisted Methodios in producing these books and creating this new iconographic rhetoric.[400] What is significant here is that both the Khludov Psalter and the *Vita of Leon of Catania* paid tribute to the ideological programme of the patriarch Methodios, since they relied on the anti-iconoclast rhetoric he had created, for example, in the representation of Ioannes VII Grammatikos as a second Simon Magus, a comparison taken from the *kanon* of the restoration of images drawn up by Methodios.[401]

The service provided by the fictional figure of Leon of Catania to the iconodule patriarchate led to vigorous promotion of his veneration, initially in Constantinople, from where the cult spread to southern Italy. Ioseph Hymnographos devoted a *kanon* to him to be included in the Menaia on 20 February.[402]

2.4 Conclusions

The ideological agenda of the patriarchate under the management and sponsorship of Methodios of a common manner of ratifying the defeat of

---

[395] Kazhdan 1999: 296–302.   [396] *Vita of Leon of Catania*, p. 59.
[397] *Vita of Leon of Catania*, pp. 70–72.   [398] *Vita of Michael Synkellos* 13, p. 68.
[399] Walter 1987: 220; Corrigan 1992: 124–34; Brubaker and Haldon 2001: 43–47. See Section 2.1.4.
[400] Hatlie 2007a: 412–13.
[401] *Vita of Leon of Catania* 13,15–19 = Psalter Moskow GIM Khludov 129D, fol. 51v; *Vita of Leon of Catania* 28,9–10 = Khludov Psalter, fol. 53v. Cf. Corrigan 1992: 2 and 27–28; *Vita of Leon of Catania*, pp. 64–65 and 72–73.
[402] Tomadakes 1971a: 145, nr. 187.

heresy included the promotion of saints whose stories could be used to establish the influence of the patriarchate itself and achieve its objectives within the post-iconoclast Church. An effort was thus launched to retell recent history from the patriarchate's perspective as a Triumph of Orthodoxy over heresy, of ecclesiastical power over imperial power and even of the patriarchal hierarchy over monasticism.

At the same time that Methodios' milieu pursued the creation of new saints favourable to its interests (e.g., Ioannikios, Michael Synkellos, Theodoros Graptos, Georgios of Mytilene and the forty-two martyrs of Amorion), it also used fresh glorification to appropriate other saints who were already established but could serve the patriarchal cause (the patriarchs Tarasios and Nikephoros, or the neo-martyrs linked to them, such as Theophylaktos of Nicomedia, Michael of Synada and Niketas of Medikion).[403] Indeed, in the exhaustive catalogue of heroes of the Second Iconoclasm praised by Theophanes Graptos, it is obvious that the objective is to recover for the patriarchate, as the governing institution of the Church, saints promoted by specific monastic groups, appropriating them for the greater good, which is the management of the Triumph of Orthodoxy. Rather than providing the faithful with examples of virtue, the aim was to expropriate from a powerful monastic lobby (that of Stoudios) the exclusivity of their religious veneration and the literary description of their deeds, thus avoiding their politicisation in the confrontations with the patriarch Methodios.

The overpowering personality of Methodios not only made possible the restoration of icons but also allowed the creation of a compelling narrative focused on Orthodoxy and capable of retelling the history of the Second Iconoclasm, attaching less importance to monastic leaders than to patriarchs, and accommodating the demands of the imperial household for the rehabilitation of Emperor Theophilos (as will be shown in Chapter 4). This major propaganda project is still more remarkable if we take into account the successive rewritings that inevitably distorted it in attempts to impose other visions of events. This continuous purge was not only literary, but also physical, and affected the books of the patriarch himself. It is plausible that the personal library of Methodios ended up in the Constantinopolitan monastery of Stoudios, as has been suggested.[404] In Afinogenov's opinion, patriarch Ignatios, who had little interest in making use of Methodios' books, decided to send them to Stoudios, where a large

---

[403] It is worth noting that Medikion and Pelekete were patriarchal monasteries, see Ruggieri 1991: 116–17; Auzépy 2004b: 22.
[404] Afinogenov 2006.

part of the iconodule literature, and in particular the hagiography produced during the whole period, was sieved and disseminated. At the same time, as this hypothesis explains, the enormous volume of texts produced by the *scriptorium* of Stoudios also makes sense of significant bibliographical lacunae in the works handled by Ignatios' arch-enemy, the patriarch Photios. Despite his privileged access to the patriarchal library, Photios seems to have lacked access to works that were used by Methodios and the authors of his circle. The simplest explanation is that those volumes left the patriarchate for a place where Photios was unwelcome. If this is the case, Methodios' personal library was likely much larger than we imagine.

CHAPTER 3

The Dekapolitan Milieu
The Integration of the Third Way after the Restoration of Icons

The society that arose as a result of the defeat of the Second Iconoclasm is generally portrayed as emphasising iconodule fervour and enthusiasm for restoring images, which, according to the surviving sources, suffused the Empire. The new patriarch Methodios carried out a thorough purge in a public demonstration of his Orthodoxy, while monastic sectors called for harsher measures against heretics, and imperial institutions publicly professed their devotion for icons, following the example of Empress Theodora and her family. Despite this impassioned official version, a close reading of contemporary works allows the general euphoria of the writers describing these events to be qualified somewhat. Groups such as those formed around the monastery of Stoudios or the patriarchate confirm the existence of sectors that were very enthusiastic about the restoration, in which they saw not only the recognition of orthodox dogma but even a personal triumph. As seen in previous chapters, literature produced by authors immersed in these environments is apologetic and triumphalist and clearly aims to justify the contribution of each hero or monastery to the cause that had now prevailed. It can be assumed that there were other, opposing sectors, groups of committed iconoclasts or of people established in the prior political scene, that were against the change but were ultimately silenced, either by their contemporaries or by subsequent generations that failed to copy their writings.

A third major social element can also be identified, in that a large part of the population, although this might seem impossible, managed to live unaffected by this great dispute: some regions in the provinces and even many private individuals did not identify with the conflict. We can also think of hermits with a mystical spirituality, for instance, for whom the different traditions and forms of devotion were of secondary importance. Proof of the different traditions that coexisted with no apparent conflict is provided by the famous words of Michael II allowing his subjects 'to do whatever each one desires and considers appropriate' (ἕκαστος οὖν τὸ δοκοῦν αὐτῷ ποιείτω καὶ ἐφετόν).[1] It is impossible to quantify this third, doubtless large but silent group, which, in the view of some scholars, made up the vast majority of the individuals in the Byzantine Empire and who remained neutral or indifferent to the subject of icons.[2] But we do have a conspicuous example of this third way. Although he is considered an iconodule saint, Gregorios Dekapolites is not the typical combative confessor who defends the theology of icons, but quite the opposite. Fortunately for us, his disciples became full members of the social fabric that arose after the Triumph of Orthodoxy but also managed to retain the identity of their leader. Despite not having been particularly prolific in producing texts, this group has left valuable testimony to this segment of society, which (either owing to a lack of interest in images or to its specific personal circumstances) was not iconoclast but was also not clearly iconodule. Direct reflections of what Ševčenko in a seminal article called 'non-iconodule hagiography' are Georgios of Amastris, Leon of Catania, Philaretos and Eudokimos.[3] Gregorios Dekapolites, however, was the only one of the men of the third way who surrounded himself with a milieu of followers and writers.

3.1 Life and Works of Gregorios Dekapolites

We are familiar with the main events of the life of Gregorios Dekapolites from a hagiographical text (*BHG* 711) written by Ignatios Diakonos shortly after the subject's death.[4] These events were corroborated and expanded by the *vita* of Gregorios' disciple Ioseph Hymnographos (*BHG* 944–947D).[5] Studies to date have established the historicity of the information and clarified the chronology of the events described.[6] We know that Gregorios was born in Eirenopolis in the Isaurian Dekapolis in the year 795/796. On the eve of his wedding in 815, he fled to the hills to be able to give himself up to God. Once his parents accepted his decision,

---

[1] Theoph. Cont. II, 8; Genesios II, 35,68–77; *Vita B of Theodoros Stoud.* 317; *Acta of David, Symeon and Georgios* 230 and 237,1–8. On the mitigated iconoclasm of Michael II, see Pargoire 1903b; Bury 1912: 110–19; Martin 1930: 199–211; Treadgold 1988: 228–32; Pratsch 1998: 263–71; Lilie 1999: 204; Brubaker and Haldon 2011: 386–92.
[2] Speck 1978: 66–72. [3] Ševčenko 1977a: 127–29; Auzépy 1992.
[4] Dvornik 1926 was the first edition of the *Vita of Gregorios Dekapolites*. To this must be added that of Makris 1997. Unless otherwise specified, references correspond to this last edition.
[5] On these *vitae* see Section 3.2.2.a. On this follower of the Dekapolites, see Van de Vorst 1920; Colonna 1953; Costa-Louillet 1957: 812–23; Tomadakes 1971a; Stiernon 1973; *PmbZ* # 3454 and 23510; *PBE* I: Ioseph 12.
[6] For Gregorios, see *PmbZ* # 2486; *PBE* I: Gregorios 79; Mango 1985; Malamut 2004.

Gregorios entered the monastery in which his brother had taken vows. Due to disagreements with the hegoumenos, he was transferred to another monastery administered by his uncle Symeon, where he spent fourteen years. In about 830, he decided to live as a hermit until, after several visions, a voice from heaven urged him to travel. On his journeys, he passed through Ephesos, Prokonnesos (ca. 833), Ainos, Christoupolis, Thessaloniki, Corinth, Reggio, Naples, Rome, Syracuse and Otranto. On his return to Thessaloniki (ca. 834), he settled in this important city of the Empire and lived in a hermitage near the church of St Menas. His main miracles[7] and the creation of a fairly large circle of disciples correspond to this period. In about 836, he travelled to Constantinople and Bithynia, where he spent time in one of the monasteries of Mount Olympos.[8] He returned to Thessaloniki, where he performed more miracles before falling seriously ill, first of epilepsy and then of dropsy. When his uncle Symeon, who was imprisoned at the time for defending icons, heard of his nephew's illness, he asked to be allowed to see him for the last time. Gregorios then travelled to Constantinople to meet Symeon. Shortly after his uncle was released, Gregorios died. The date was probably 20 November 842, although it may have been a year earlier.[9]

The veneration of Gregorios began shortly after his death; for this to happen, a hagiography needed to be written recalling his good deeds and miracles, together with other evidence of his holiness.[10] The task fell to Ignatios Diakonos, a well-known writer who had already dealt with the genre of saints' lives twenty years earlier with the *Vita of Georgios of Amastris*. The date of the writing of the *Vita of Gregorios Dekapolites* is a matter of dispute,[11] but is in any case after January 842, the month of the death of Emperor Theophilos, who is mentioned as already deceased.[12] Before we analyse why the work was written and the objectives the saint's followers hoped to achieve with it, it is worth stressing one aspect of the

---

[7] Efthymiadis 2011b: 5–6. [8] *Vita of Gregorios Dekapolites* 53.
[9] The year 842 had been determined by Dvornik 1926: 26; Mango 1985: 643–44 proposed to bring forward the date to 841 or even 840.
[10] On the contribution of the hagiographical text to the sanctification process, see Kaplan 2000; Pratsch 2005: 413–21; Efthymiadis 2011a: 1–14.
[11] Mango 1985: 644 dates the *vita* between 843 and 850. Efthymiadis 1991a: 78 and 81, is of the same opinion. Malamut 2004: 1199 is more precise and locates it in the years 843–845. On the contrary, the last editor delays it until 855, when it would have been written on the occasion of the transfer of Gregorios' relics to the new monastery founded by Ioseph Hymnographos, see *Vita of Gregorios Dekapolites* 28–29. Kazhdan favours a later date, around 860–870, within the confrontation between the patriarchs Photios and Ignatios, see 'Gregory of Decapolis' (nr. 12), in *Dumbarton Oaks Hagiography Database*, Washington 1995.
[12] *Vita of Gregorios Dekapolites* 77,3: παρὰ τοῦ τηνικαῦτα κρατοῦντος.

contents of the text, for although Gregorios is a iconodule saint, he never suffered on account of icons. His hagiographer describes him as 'proclaimed a martyr without bruises' (μάρτυς ἀναδειχθεὶς ἄνευ μώλωπος)[13] precisely because, in contrast to the main saints of the Second Iconoclasm, he was not imprisoned, exiled or tortured for his faith. The only mention of physical punishment to be found refers to shortly after he was tonsured, when he publicly opposed the hegoumenos of his monastery,[14] which led to his receiving some blows. An attempt is made to justify the young Gregorios' lack of discipline via the iconoclastic contacts of the abbot, but at no point does the hagiographer claim this was a defence of images. The impression is also created that the argument with the abbot was invented to justify Gregorios' flight from the monastery, even though the ecclesiastical canons prescribed the *stabilitas loci* of all monks.[15]

Gregorios' numerous journeys appear to lack an objective; the text does not justify them either by God's will to put Gregorios to the test or by a human desire to establish contacts with important persons. (A well-meaning reader might be tempted to see in the journey to Rome in the year 834 an attempt to raise support for the iconodule faction against Emperor Theophilos,[16] although nothing in the text explicitly supports this inference.) On the way to Constantinople, in Prokonnesos, Gregorios received news of the imperial decree of 833 that made iconodules subject to persecution[17] and changed his route. The date of Theophilos' decree is uncertain, but is generally taken to be 833, since the measure is thought to have been imitated at the Abbasid court, when Al-Ma'mūn issued an edict on the creation of the Quran and the birth of the Miḥna (the Inquisition), which certainly dates to that year.[18] As a result, the main iconodule leaders were exiled to the island of Aphousia in the Propontis,[19] although Gregorios was able to continue on his way.

---

[13] *Vita of Gregorios Dekapolites* 73,25–26. [14] *PmbZ* # 11652.
[15] *Vita of Gregorios Dekapolites* 17,1–2.
[16] This possibility was already noted by Dvornik 1926: 26, for whom the purpose of his journeys was to turn to the Pope.
[17] Theoph. Cont. III, 10,23–26.
[18] Rosser 1983: 41–42; Jokisch 2007: 500–501. For his part, Treadgold 1988: 280–81 and 436, n. 386 thinks that this measure gave rise to a synod. Repercussions of this iconoclast decree are found in the hagiographies, as, for instance, in the *Vita of Petros of Atroa* 63,21–26, in the *Vita of Niketas the Patrician* 4, in the *Vita of Ignatios* 14, or in that of Hilarion of Dalmatos, see Matantseva 1993: 22.
[19] The exiled to Aphousia were Ioannes of Kathara (*SynaxCP* 633–34,35–38), Hilarion of Dalmatos (*SynaxCP* 733–34,48), Makarios of Pelekete (*Vita of Makarios of Pelekete* 159,26), Symeon of Lesbos (*Acta of David, Symeon and Georgios* 238–39) and the Graptoi brothers (*Vita of Michael the Synkellos* 14).

When he reached Thessaloniki, he happened to encounter a monk who was leaving for Rome, whom he accompanied as a servant as far as Corinth. Why did he not continue with him? Clearly this was because Gregorios had another aim. It appears that the impossibility of reaching Sicily, due to danger from pirates, took him to Reggio and thence to Rome, which was not his final destination; the hagiographer takes advantage of this fact to extol Gregorios' holiness, since he locates his first miracle, the curing of a man possessed by a demon, in the holy city.[20] When he finally reached Syracuse, Gregorios shut himself up in a tower adjacent to the port until, after having cured several individuals who were possessed, he travelled to Otranto. There a mob accused him of betraying Christians and attempted to execute him, but he was saved by the iconoclast bishop of the town.[21] The passage is problematic and difficult to interpret. It is clear that the crowd accuses Gregorios of betrayal and wants to punish him severely. Mango believes they took him for an Arab spy and wanted to put a turban on him, while G. Makris takes the item of clothing in question to be a shroud.[22] Ultimately, Gregorios returned to Thessaloniki, where he settled permanently.

The tale of Gregorios' travels seems neither to make sense nor to respond to any clear motivation. The travels in fact represent an odyssey, with the final destination being a return to the starting point. The *vita* does not tell us that the saint had to carry out a specific mission either divine or human; the stages of his journey seem to be the result of chance or external determinants, and his spiritual growth is not emphasised, making it difficult to see the itinerary as a reflection of an inner journey or a coming closer to God. As the hagiographer gives no literary or hagiographical justification for it, we must accordingly assume that his journey was necessary: although we do not know the reason for it, Gregorios' objective was clearly to reach Syracuse. The writer insists on this after Gregorios reaches Corinth[23] and when he abandons Rome.[24] In addition, the itinerary always aims at the island of Sicily: Thessaloniki, Corinth, Reggio, etc. Likewise, the detour to Rome via Naples does not allow

---

[20] *Vita of Gregorios Dekapolites* 25,3–5. For the significance of Rome in Middle-Byzantine hagiographies, see Delouis and Peters-Custot 2019.
[21] *Vita of Gregorios Dekapolites* 33,5–16.
[22] Mango 1985: 637; Makris in *Vita of Gregorios Dekapolites*, p. 97.
[23] *Vita of Gregorios Dekapolites* 22,9–10: Ἐκεῖθεν δὲ ἀναχθῆναι προσεποιεῖτο καὶ τῇ Σικελίᾳ προσβῆναι.
[24] *Vita of Gregorios Dekapolites* 26,1–2: Ὅθεν φυγῇ τὴν Ῥώμην ἀπολιπὼν ταῖς πρὸς τῇ Σικελίᾳ Συρακούσαις ἐπέβη.

Gregorios to change his goal, which he eventually attains. Finally, once Gregorios reached Syracuse, he set off for Thessaloniki again immediately.

The key to this puzzle may lie in another characteristic on which the hagiography insists and which has not previously been examined in detail: the social influence of the protagonist. Gregorios' skill at maintaining good relationships with iconoclast leaders is clear throughout the *vita*, although until he arrived in Rome, the well-meaning reader could assume that he moved only in iconodule circles, since after his arrival in Sicily, his connivance with prominent iconoclasts is evident.[25] The community of Syracuse was guided by Theodoros Krithinos, the former *oikonomos* of Hagia Sophia and a committed defender of iconoclasm, to whom Theophilos had granted the archbishopric after Theodoros completed two successful embassies in the West in 824 and 827.[26] In addition, the Caesar, *strategos* and Duke of Sicily was none other than Alexios Mouselé,[27] the son-in-law of Theophilos, who granted him the hand of his daughter Maria to make him a first-degree relative. The emperor also delivered to him the monastery of Philippikou in the Bosphorus (alternatively Chrysopolis),[28] where Stephanos the Younger had been imprisoned by the iconoclasts.[29] It is only logical to conclude that the state of siege to which the Arab fleet was subjecting the island meant that the iconoclastic imperial dogma was accepted in exchange for military support from the ruling classes of the island. Since 827, the Arabs had been threatening and besieging Sicily in an attempt to sack Syracuse. The epitaph of Athanasios of Methone proves that Catania was sacked around this time.[30] Moreover, in 831 the Arab campaigns were successful, and they took the city of Palermo,[31] encouraging the choice of iconoclasm as the lesser evil. The

---

[25] Malamut 2004: 1207–14. For the presence in Rome of iconodule monks from Constantinople, see Sansterre 1983: vol. 1, 32–48 and vol. 2, 87–105.

[26] *PmbZ* # 7675; *PBE* I: Theodoros 66; Gouillard 1961a; McCormick 1994: 148–53. During this stay, Krithinos probably commissioned the translation of the *vita* of Anastasia, cf. Gounelle 2005: 65–68. We know very little about the implementation of iconoclasm in the provinces. For its dissemination in Byzantine Italy, see Guillou et al. 1983: 207–11; Carile 1986; Von Falkenhausen 1989; Dell'Acqua and Gantner 2019.

[27] Ps-Symeon 630,15: στρατηγὸν καὶ δοῦκα Σικελίας πέμπει. Cf. *PmbZ* # 195; *PBE* I: Alexios 2; Guilland 1970: 596–97; Settipani 2006: 150–57.

[28] Theoph. Cont. III, 18,27–44; Ps-Symeon 631,21–32,2. From the imperial monastery of Philippikou, Alexios later founded the monastery of Anthemiou. On Philippikou, see Janin 1975: 24–25; Ruggieri 1991: 202.

[29] *Vita of Stephanos the Younger* 41, 141.11–26.

[30] Costa-Louillet 1961: 313–15; Crimi 1998. On Athanasios of Methone, see *PmbZ* # 683 and # 20663.

[31] Vasiliev 1935: 127–37 and 143–44; Falkenhausen 1978; Guillou et al. 1983: 267–70; Von Kreutz 1991: 9–35; Nef and Prigent 2013.

heretical character of the bishop of Otranto is explicitly referred to in our text,[32] which also mentions how he interceded for Gregorios with the mob; not only did he prevent it from continuing to strike him and from executing him on charges of betraying Christians, he even ordered that those who had assaulted him be whipped.

In Thessaloniki, these contacts are developed to the highest degree: the account stresses the prophetic ability of Gregorios, who warned the monk Anastasios of the dangers of a future journey he would make to Constantinople in the company of the *protokankelarios* Georgios, the representative of the *strategos* of Thessaloniki.[33] Following his advice that they go on foot and not by ship, Georgios and Anastasios were twice arrested: by the Caesar Alexios Mouselé in Christoupolis (now Kavala) and by the *magistros* Manuel in Boleron.[34] Their presence in the area is dated to 837. Although the *vita* does not specifically mention these two important personages of the court of Theophilos, there can be no doubt that reference is being made to them. As to the reasons for their presence at the head of the two fleets, Mango believes that this is due to the signing of an agreement with the Bulgarians.[35] Be that as it may, Anastasios had to beg both leaders to free Georgios, although on the second occasion he had the help of the Dekapolites.[36]

Although the hagiographer presents this as a simple plea to God, it seems likely that while his disciple was meeting with such important personages, Gregorios was meeting the *strategos* of Thessaloniki, who was responsible for the safety of the *protokankelarios* Georgios. The recent creation of the Thessaloniki *thema*, in about 836, implies that this high-ranking official settled in the city for the first time then,[37] nominated directly by the emperor[38] and necessarily an iconoclast. The lack of data

---

[32] *Vita of Gregorios Dekapolites* 33, 12–13: διὰ τὸ τῇ αἱρέσει αὐτὸν προσκεῖσθαι. See *PmbZ* # 11688.
[33] *PmbZ* # 2233. On the peculiarities of the city of Thessaloniki at that time, see Malamut 2005.
[34] On the *magistros* Manuel, to whom Theophilos perhaps gave his sister Helena as a wife, see *PmbZ* # 4707.
[35] Mango 1985: 639–40. This treaty probably contemplated the freeing of a group of hostages including the future Emperor Basileios I, see Adontz 1933; 1934: 50ff. A different interpretation is that of Yannopoulos 1993: 68–69.
[36] *Vita of Gregorios Dekapolites* 52,25–27: Ἱκέτης οὖν πάλιν τῷ μαγίστρῳ καταστάς, συνεπεργαζομένης τῆς τοῦ ὁσίου πρὸς τὸ κρεῖττον ἐντεύξεως τῆς μελλούσης κακώσεως ἐρρυσάμην Γεώργιον, 'I again appeared before the *magistros* as a supplicant and with the help of the intercession of the saint before the Almighty, I freed Georgios from imminent punishment.'
[37] On its creation, see *ODB* III, 2073.
[38] All surviving seals that belonged to a *strategos* of Thessaloniki also include an important title, normally that of *basilikós protospatharios*, although we also find a *strategos* who was a patrician and another who held the title of *basilikós spatharios*. All these show how close the emperor was to his aristocrats. The most frequent (*basilikós protospatharios*) was an honorary title (ἀξίαι διὰ βραβείου)

makes it impossible to identify this *strategos* of Thessaloniki, although prosopographical studies limit the list to just over a dozen candidates.[39] The end of the story is extremely telling: Georgios and Anastasios sail for Constantinople and arrive there, unscathed by pirates, to be granted an audience by Emperor Theophilos, who grants Georgios the title of *kandidatos*. The bestowal of the title was clearly in return for an order or service that benefitted the royal household or its cause. The fact that the two travellers were again arrested, despite the explanations Anastasios gave to the Caesar and the notice that Gregorios' intercession to the *strategos* was necessary, shows the importance of the mandate. Once the Thessaloniki *strategos* stepped in, therefore, their protection was guaranteed (by the Caesar's men or the *magistros*), so that they could reach Constantinople safe and sound.

The good relations Gregorios Dekapolites and his disciple Anastasios enjoyed with the iconoclast leaders are clear even without the hagiographer describing any theological dispute or confrontation owing to the images. Far from being temporary, this good relationship must be assumed to have been permanent, as is confirmed by the affirmation that closes ch. 49, when a journey that Gregorios had planned to a Slav settlement (σκλαβηνία) was allegedly cancelled by a vision of the saint that allowed him to predict a bloody uprising. Given the lack of precision, it has been assumed that this was a rebellion related to a Bulgarian expedition against the Smolyans.[40] But the Dekapolites' final words on the subject were that a lack of imperial permission prevented the journey.[41] In view of his two subsequent journeys to Constantinople during the period of Theophilos (the first followed by a visit to the Bithynian Mount Olympos, the second to see his uncle Symeon and to die in the capital), for which he had a safe-conduct from the emperor, it is reasonable to assume that he enjoyed the

---

that allowed participation in the Senate and at the court of honour that accompanied the emperor during certain ceremonies, see *De ceremoniis* 70, 72, 152, 174, 179, 542, 576, 604; Lemerle 1967; Oikonomidès 1972: 51,27; 53,24; 57,22; and 63,10.

[39] These are Arsaber (*PmbZ* # 604), Konstantinos (*PmbZ* # 3986), Marianos (*PmbZ* # 4766), Michael (*PmbZ* # 5107), Symeon (*PmbZ* # 7211), Theognios (*PmbZ* # 7998), Theognostos (*PmbZ* # 8009) and three anonymous *strategoi* (*PmbZ* # 11924, # 12121 and # 12122).

[40] Mango 1985: 639–40; Karayannopoulos 1986: 22; Besevliev 1992: 239; Yannopoulos 1993: 64–67; Curta 2011; Gkoutzioukostas 2017. For Dujcev 1966 the event must be linked to a passage of the *Vita retractata of Petros of Atroa* that mentions a Byzantine expedition in Bulgaria (ch. 111), which allows it to be dated in 837.

[41] *Vita of Gregorios Dekapolites* 49,13–15: Διεβεβαιοῦτο δὲ τῷ λόγῳ καὶ τοῦτο, ὡς "Ἄνευ σφραγίδος καὶ νεύσεως βασιλικῆς οὔ ποτέ μοι γέγονεν ἐκ τόπου εἰς τόπον μεταβιβάσαι τὸν πόδα", 'Moreover, he stated verbally: "without the seal and imperial approval I would not have been able to have moved from one place to another".'

same authorisation to reach Syracuse some years previously. This would explain how he managed to penetrate the Arab siege without danger both when entering and when leaving the town and also how he quickly obtained the support of the bishop of Otranto.

Gregorios' contacts extended to the ecclesiastical hierarchy, as is shown by the hagiographer's affirmation concerning his return to Thessaloniki, to the effect that the bishop (obviously an iconoclast) already knew him from his previous stay there.[42] On his way to Italy, in fact, Gregorios had been put up for a time by abbot Markos,[43] the director of an ascetic centre (καθηγούμενος ἀσκητικῆς μάνδρας), and they had had the opportunity to get to know each other. The incumbent of the Thessaloniki see had opposed images since 815, with the advent of the Second Iconoclasm, when Ioseph Stoudites, the brother of the famous Theodoros, was dismissed for his support of the iconophile cause. Although Ioseph did not die until July 832, first Ioannes and later Theodoros were appointed in his place at the head of the see.[44] Between 830 and 839, the Thessaloniki throne was occupied by another Ioannes,[45] who had been chosen by the patriarch Antonios I (an iconoclast, to the despair of the Stoudites), who was necessarily referred to in the *vita*. Although we do not know the nature of their relationship, Gregorios neither confronted him nor opposed the establishment of Leon the Mathematician as his substitute. Although Leon is not described in the sources as a bitter enemy of images, his direct kinship with the patriarch Ioannes VII Grammatikos[46] and his immediate purge in the spring of 843 by Methodios, who dismissed him, appointing in his place Antonios the bishop of Dyrrhachium,[47] show that he did not favour the veneration of icons.

---

[42] *Vita of Gregorios Dekapolites* 36: Τῇ δὲ Θεσσαλονίκῃ πάλιν προσπελάσας καὶ πρὸς τὸν ναὸν τοῦ ἁγίου μάρτυρος Μηνᾶ μονὴν ποιησάμενος ἐγνώσθη ὑπ' αὐτοῦ τοῦ τηνικαῦτα τὴν ἐκκλησίαν διέποντος.

[43] About this hegoumenos, see *PmbZ* # 4839; *PBE* I: Markos 4. The establishment he directed was the monastery of St Menas, whose church was founded by Zacharias near the port of the city, cf. Tafrali 1913: 175–77; Janin 1975: 397; Ruggieri 1991: 260; *Vita of Gregorios Dekapolites* 20. On its founder, the monk Zacharias, see *PmbZ* # 8627; *PBE* I: Zacharias 20.

[44] Petit 1900; 1916: 240–41 and 252; On Ioannes, see *PmbZ* # 3233. For Theodoros, see *PmbZ* # 7682. On Ioseph Stoudites, see *PmbZ* # 3448; *PBE* I: Ioseph 3; Pargoire 1906a. See Chapter 1.

[45] *PmbZ* # 3234; Fedalto 1988: 424.

[46] He was probably his cousin or perhaps his nephew, as the terms ἀνεψιός 'nephew' and ἐξαδέλφος 'cousin' used by Byzantine historians are interchangeable, see Nicol 1984: 84. On Leon, cf. *PmbZ* # 4440; *PBE* I: Leon 19; *ODB*, s.v. Leon the Philosopher; Bury 1912: 436–42; Kolias 1939: 65ff.; Mango 1960; Lemerle 1971: 148–76. On Leon's literary production, see Introduction.

[47] Zonaras 402, 3–5; Petit 1916: 240–41; *Regestes*, nr. 423. On Antonios of Dyrrhachium, see Paschalidis 1994a.

Apart from the personal relationships he may have had (onto which one can attempt to project a good deal of cynicism and survival instincts unbefitting an iconodule saint), in the end, the surviving literary production attributed to the Dekapolites[48] is iconoclastic. Although this amounts to only a single work, its contents are extremely telling. The text in question is a historical account (λόγος ἱστορικός or *Sermo historicus*) probably conceived to be read during one of the common meals characteristic of monastic life. It narrates the miraculous vision of the Eucharistic transubstantiation experienced by a Saracen nobleman (i.e., a Moslem) during the liturgy in a church dedicated to St Georgios, which triggered his conversion to Christianity.[49] To date, it has proven impossible to identify either the protagonist (a nephew of the Syrian Emir, who ruled during the Umayyad Caliphate of Damascus) or the informant (a *strategos* named Nikolaos Joulas) who transmitted an account of these events to Gregorios. But it seems clear that the scene of the events was Diospolis (modern Ramla) in the district of Jerusalem.[50] The existence of several versions of the same story with important variants[51] suggests that it is a development of an episode included in the *vita* of a famous convert of the time, Saint Antonios Ruwah, who was martyred on Christmas Day 799 by order of the Caliph Harun al-Rashid (786–809).[52] News of this may have reached Gregorios during his years as a novice in Dekapolis or perhaps through the contacts of the circle of Leon the Mathematician with the court of the Abbasid Caliph. The legend maintains that word of Leon's great wisdom reached Arab lands and that a disciple of his impressed the intellectuals of the court to the extent that the Caliph Al-Ma'mūn (813–833) invited the master to visit his dominions.[53] The details of the story seem incredible, and in any case they would have taken place in the time of Al-Mu'taṣim (833–842).[54]

Be all this as it may, this traditional account stands out for the all-embracing part played by the Eucharist: the miraculous vision of a child cut up on the paten and shared out by the priest among the faithful at

---

[48] The *intitulatio* included in the manuscript *Vaticanus Gr.* 1130 states categorically: Γρηγορίου τοῦ Δεκαπολίτου. The relatively recent date of the codex (sixteenth century) does not imply that this is an unfounded attribution, Franchi de' Cavalieri et al. 1899: 99.
[49] Kałżaniacki 1903; Festugière 1971: 294–307. English translation with a commentary in Sahas 1986.
[50] Hoyland 1997: 383–86, n. 142.
[51] Aufhauser 1913: 64–89 includes the narration along with another two of these versions.
[52] Dick 1961.   [53] Theoph. Cont. IV, 27–28.
[54] Treadgold 1979b; Speck 1987a; Magdalino 1998.

communion is the reason for conversion[55] but also the new believer's raison d'être for the rest of his life, since he aims only to experience again the vision granted to the chosen few. Despite the difficulty this entails – he is warned by the consecrating priest that even Fathers of the Church such as Basileios the Great, John Chrysostom and Gregorios of Nazianzus were unable to see this[56] – the sole objective of all his efforts is to achieve the vision again. To this end he does not hesitate to travel or to try to convert the emir,[57] which finally leads to his martyrdom.

In structural terms, it is the Eucharist that triggers the action rather than an icon of the Theotokos or of a saint, as tends to occur in iconodule texts. Moreover, the sacrament is imbued with mystic elements that indicate a specific type of spirituality. If we take into account that, according to the reasoning of Konstantinos V (741–775) in his *Peuseis*, iconoclast theology maintained that the sole icon of Christ that is valid for the Church was the Eucharist,[58] this narrative could hardly be less iconophile. Sahas' attempt to give it an iconodule reading is unconvincing.[59] According to him, the ability of the martyr to see with the grace of God the ontological reality that underlies the Eucharist is in fact an attack on iconoclastic theology, because it demonstrates that the sacrifice is real and not an image. But the same could be said of the icons: they do not represent reality, as is shown by the apparitions of the Virgin, the saints and the like. Finally, the audience at which the account is aimed – the monastic community as a whole – seems inappropriate for such theological subtleties.

3.1.1 The Testimony of the Vita Gregorii Decapolitae (BHG 711) of Ignatios Diakonos

To date, we have no commentary on or comprehensive study of this work despite its importance for understanding the society of the Second Iconoclasm. The mention of the Slavic peoples has attracted the attention of a few scholars,[60] but despite their skill in combining the anchoritic model (*Vita of Gregorios Dekapolites*, chs. 6–36) and the cenobitic model (chs. 37–78), we lack an overall reading of the text.[61] As far as content is

---

[55] In the case of Antonios Ruwah it was a lamb. For the variants of this miraculous vision, see Congourdeau 2009.
[56] Gregorios Dekapolites, *Sermo historicus* 1204D–5A.
[57] On his possible identity, see Sahas 1986: 66.   [58] Gero 1975; 1977: 37–52, 101–2 and 143–51.
[59] Sahas 1986: 65; cf. Papaconstantinou 2012: 331.
[60] Dvornik 1936; Dujcev 1957; Karayannopoulos 1989: 9–32; Georgiev 1993.
[61] Malamut 2004: 1201–2 and 1209–10; cf. Flusin 1993.

concerned, the *Vita* is noteworthy for its lack of attempts to defend the veneration of images and even of mention of icons. In regard to the theology of the image, the hagiographer includes a reflection in keeping with the dogma that emanated from the Second Council of Nicaea, but without this being motivated by its hero's confrontation with an iconoclast heretic.[62] This *excursus* is inserted between Gregorios' consecration as a priest and the point at which he falls seriously ill. This does not appear to be coincidence in the account. But how would the hagiographer like us to interpret it? As a reaffirmation of Gregorios in his iconodule faith? Or as a 'conversion' before death? Is this perhaps a simple literary device to arrest the action, prolong the emotion achieved after the consecration of the hero and thus play down his sickness and imminent death?

Outside this context, Ignatios Diakonos uses the term εἰκών only once, in the preface to the *vita*, where the saint is the subject of a comparison (*synkrisis*) with King David, who was 'the image of the heart of God'.[63] We know that iconoclast hagiography postulated that the image of God could be found in exemplary human behaviour and not 'in soulless pictorial representations' (ἀψύχοις εἰκόσι).[64] The studies by Ševčenko and Auzépy of iconoclastic hagiography have identified a number of characteristics that differentiate it from the iconophile tradition:[65] a lack of icons; no mention of the dispute regarding them; a leading role for the cross, which fulfils the functions of icons; an assessment of the saint not for who he is but for his acts; the social dimension of good works (meaning not only miracles but also acts of charity, compassion and mercy), which have a positive effect on all members of the community and an emphasis on the models of holiness from the Scriptures, and, in particular, the Old Testament, to the detriment of later saints and customs of the Church.

Precisely these characteristics are also found in the *vita* of Gregorios Dekapolites: in contrast to iconodule iconography, in which miracles and cures are performed by the intermediation of an icon – the *Vita of Stephanos the Younger* is a well-known case – Gregorios does not need

---

[62] *Vita of Gregorios Dekapolites* 73 = Dvornik p. 69,12–24.
[63] *Vita of Gregorios Dekapolites*, Proem., 18–24: Τοιοῦτον καὶ ὁ ἐν προφήταις καὶ βασιλεῦσι περιώνυμος Δαυὶδ εἰλικρινέστατον τὸν καθ' ἑαυτὸν βίον ὑπέφηνεν ἄγαλμα ἐκ πολυχρόου δαψιλείας τῆς τῶν πειρασμῶν νιφάδος θεοειδέστατον κάλλος ἠκριβωκὼς καὶ ὡραιότητι τῆς τούτων περιουσίας ὁσημέραι καλλυνόμενος. Ὃς καὶ τῆς καρδίας **θεοῦ εἰκόνα** ἑαυτὸν σκιαγραφήσας πρόκειται πᾶσιν ἀνθρώποις στήλη βιωφελὴς καὶ σωτήριος· ἔφη γὰρ ὁ θεὸς «Εὗρον Δαυὶδ τὸν τοῦ Ἰεσαὶ ἄνδρα κατὰ τὴν καρδίαν μου». Cf. also Act. 13,22; *Vita of Georgios of Amastris*, 37 (p. 57,1ff.).
[64] Alexander 1953; Anastos 1954; 1955; Alexander 1958b; Sansterre 1994; Magdalino 2015a.
[65] Ševčenko 1977a: 121–27; Auzépy 1992.

external elements to work wonders, and when he resorts to one, it is always the cross.[66] His deeds characterise him as a hero: Gregorios bears the blows a young man gives him for no reason and makes him reconsider (ch. 20); he has no fear when he encounters Slav pirates (ch. 21); he becomes the servant of another monk (ch. 22) and he takes pity on the hard-hearted tax collector Merkuras (ch. 23). The social dimension is also evident: poor men and women helped by Gregorios achieve prosperity (chs. 19 and 37), and he guarantees compliance with ecclesiastical regulations, unmasks a monk who pretends to be possessed exposing him as a liar (ch. 46), prevents a Stylite from fornicating (ch. 65) and convinces a prostitute to abandon her profession (ch. 28). Gregorios also helps maintain social order: he teaches a lesson to a monk who had been involved in embezzlement (ch. 38), guarantees the distribution of food to the destitute (ch. 45), rebukes a friend for leaving an unburied body in a roadside ditch (ch. 47), mediates in a neighbourhood dispute, helps a woman retain her house despite pressure from other monks (ch. 54), intercedes before the *archon* of Thessaloniki on behalf of an imprisoned *komes* condemned to death and achieves his release (ch. 48) and intercedes for the *protokankelarios* Georgios, who had been imprisoned by the *magistros* (ch. 52).[67] Finally, in the *Vita of Gregorios Dekapolites* we also see comparisons of its protagonist with the patriarchs of Israel (Abraham, Joseph, Moses and Jacob) and with King David, the prophet Elijah and even Job. The only non-Old Testament figure is the protomartyr Stephanos (ch. 20,7), who owing to his early date could be included among the Apostles.

In the 820s, Ignatios Diakonos wrote the *vita* of Georgios of Amastris (*BHG* 668), a work considered one of the few surviving examples of iconoclastic hagiography. Some of the variations from and similarities to the account of the life of Gregorios Dekapolites have already been noted,[68] but it is worth emphasising the differing treatment given the milieu of the two saints. Ignatios Diakonos insists that Georgios of Amastris was ordained by Tarasios, was a friend of Empress Eirene the Restorer, protected the iconodule Ioannes of Gotthia and inspired the writing of an iconodule story of the relics of St Euphemia,[69] that is, was part of a circle

---

[66] *Vita of Gregorios Dekapolites* 3,17–20 = Dvornik p. 48,15–16; *Vita of Gregorios Dekapolites* 7,12–13 = Dvornik p. 50,5–7; *Vita of Gregorios Dekapolites* 27,5–6 = Dvornik p. 56,22. Cf. also *Vita of Gregorios Dekapolites* 39,7–8 and 57,9ff.
[67] Kazhdan 1986: 161–62.
[68] Ševčenko 1977a: 120–26; Markopoulos 1979; Efthymiadis 1991a: 75–80; Auzépy 1992; Kazhdan 1999: 356–66. On the *vita* of Georgios of Amastris, see Chapter 6. On the iconodule conversion of Ignatios and his incorporation Methodios' circle, see Chapter 2.
[69] *Vita of Georgios of Amastris* 30,1–30; 52,3–54,8; Cf. Ševčenko 1977a: n. 87.

of important image worshippers. Gregorios Dekapolites had no relationship with any known iconodule, with the exception of his uncle Symeon: neither in his youth with the patriarchs who favoured venerating images, nor later on with any icon-venerating saint who opposed imperial policy nor with any layman whom we know to have been orthodox. His *vita* does not tell us this, but by tracing his movements, we have confirmed that he was in contact with prominent iconoclasts and with high-ranking officials at the court of Theophilos. Given this evidence, one may well wonder about the author's reasons for omitting these proper names.[70] Ignatios does not record the identity of many of the persons who played a role in Gregorios' biography, in the same way that he does not explain the reasons for his travels.

We know that when Gregorios returned to Thessaloniki from Italy, he was obliged to beg, until finally a woman offered him her protection and guaranteed his daily bread (ch. 36). According to the hagiographical *topos*, this was a well-to-do lady who was widely respected for her works of charity. If we assume that she existed, she probably belonged to one of Thessalonki's important families and might well have provided Gregorios with a means of approaching the iconoclast authorities in order to intercede later on behalf of the disadvantaged. But why not give her name, when persons such as Markos and Zacharias are identified? The situation is the same with the silence that shrouds Gregorios' consecration in ch. 69, since we know neither who ordained him nor in which monastery this took place, which is particularly striking since this is a key moment in the life of any monk. We can locate the Thessaloniki event after Gregorios' return from the Olympos in Bithynia. Although there is no mention of the date, the way the account develops and the distribution of his works and miracles before and after indicates that it occurred about the time he fell ill and shortly before his death, probably ca. 840.

An explanation for all these omissions can be found in the context in which the *vita* was written: the year was 843. The heretic Emperor Theophilos had died on 20 January of the previous year. Empress Theodora and her council of regents had repeatedly expressed a desire to re-establish the veneration of images. Despite the efforts to the contrary of

---

[70] The rhetoric regulations inherited, certainly, considered the lack of proper names to be a characteristic of epideictic rhetoric (the eulogy), see Delehaye 1926: 150–52; Russell and Wilson 1981. A good Middle Byzantine example is the funeral *Enkomion of Basileios I* that Leon VI dedicated to his father, in which all public figures are always mentioned in the form of periphrasis. Ignatios Diakonos, however, does not include any description or indirect allusion that enables to identify the individuals with whom the Dekapolites interacted.

Ioannes VII Grammatikos and his followers, multiple sectors of the Church pressed for the measure to be implemented: the monks of the Stoudios monastery, holy men such as Ioannikios and Hilarion of Dalmatos, the future patriarch Methodios from an advantageous position due to his close relationship to the court and others. In this scenario, the disciples of Gregorios Dekapolites decided to encourage the veneration of their spiritual father, who had recently died, and chose as the hagiographer a great writer whose iconoclast past had forced him into exile in the Bithynian Olympos (specifically the monastery of Antidion)[71] and would oblige him to spend the rest of his life in the monastery of Pikridion[72] (at the end of the Golden Horn) after the purge carried out by Methodios. Pikridion was deeply involved in the defence of icons, since its hegoumenos Theodosios signed the two epistles that Theodoros Stoudites sent to Pope Paschal in 817 (*epist.* 271 and 272).

It is unthinkable that in a context of extreme praise of now-triumphant iconoduly, a penitent (who was later to write with the fervour of the convert the highly iconophile *vitae* of the patriarchs Nikephoros and Tarasios) should omit pious elements of the saint he was to praise. It is similarly unthinkable that for stylistic reasons he omitted religious practices, personal contacts, the identities of benefactors and precise places at the risk of giving rise to misunderstandings. Moreover, the speed with which Gregorios' veneration was promoted meant that his disciples, direct witnesses to the events in question, were still alive. There can be no doubt that the followers of Gregorios who commissioned the *vita* were aware of details such as the circumstances of his consecration as a priest. As this took place so late, in fact, the great majority of them must have been present at it. If these omissions are not due to a lack of knowledge on the writer's part, therefore, they must be due to the protagonist: Gregorios' iconoclastic contacts compelled his biographer to keep silent and thus distort reality. The lack of precision in the hagiography is not due to a literary prohibition that forbade the mention of living persons[73] but to their deep involvement in the newly defeated iconoclast heresy. People and places commonly regarded as hostile to icons are systematically omitted. Despite these attempts, the text is in actual fact extremely revealing, but more because of what it leaves out than what it says.

---

[71] Janin 1975: 135–36; Ruggieri 1991: 218; see Section 2.2.2.
[72] Janin 1969: 403–4; Berger 1988a: 688; Ruggieri 1991: 195. For the periods that Ignatios spent there, see Mango and Efthymiadis 1997: 195–97 (*epist.* 43–47).
[73] As indicated at the end of *PmbZ* # 2486.

The fact that Gregorios was twice accused of being a traitor (προδότης) is particularly interesting. On the first occasion, it was by a youth in Ainos, who asked him who he was and what he was planning (ch. 20). On the second, it was by the inhabitants of Otranto, who accused him of having travelled to the town with the sole aim of betraying the Christians: ὡς ἐπὶ προδοσίαν χριστιανῶν ἥκειν (ch. 33). Owing either to an involuntary lapse on the part of the hagiographer or to a conscious desire to link these events, the resolution of the dispute includes a repeated textual component.[74] As nothing in these passages refers to the iconoclast crisis, we can conclude that the betrayal in question involved an alliance with the enemy. Precisely the only context in which a similar expression (betraying the Christians) is used in medieval Greek literature is the account of the treachery of Alexios Mouselé included in various versions of the chronicle of Symeon Logothetes.[75] According to the historiographical account, in about 838 Emperor Theophilos sent Alexios to Sicily as a duke (δοῦκα Σικελίας), but the islanders accused him of conspiring against the emperor and attempting to seal an alliance with the Arabs. As the *strategos* of Sicily, Alexios was one of the most important officials in the whole empire during this period, and it is easy to understand that there may actually have been an attempt at usurpation. A few years previously, during the reign of Michael II, the *tourmarches* Euphemios proclaimed himself emperor precisely in Sicily.[76] Through the archbishop of Syracuse, Theodoros Krithinos, Theophilos managed to have the usurper Alexios returned to Constantinople, where he was imprisoned.[77]

The textual similarity suggests an analogous reality that goes beyond the contacts between Alexios and Gregorios Dekapolites. His being mistaken for a traitor by a youth in Ainos and the death threat issued by the inhabitants of Otranto must be linked: perhaps the physical appearance of Gregorios (a native of Isauria) was similar to that of the new Arab enemy; this would also explain why the punishment initially imposed on him was the wearing of a turban.[78] The same thing occurred in the case of the youth of Ainos, who abandoned his violent attitude when Gregorios

---

[74] *Vita of Gregorios Dekapolites* 20,10–12: Ὁ δὲ νεανίας τούτων ἀκηκοώς, **τὸ ἀγριαῖνον** ἦθος ἀποβαλὼν ἱκέτης τῷ ὁσίῳ καθίσταται καὶ τὴν τοῦ πλημμελήματος ἐζήτει συγχώρησιν, cf. Ibid. 33,8–10: Ὁ δὲ ὅσιος ταῖς κατὰ διάνοιαν εὐχαῖς **τὸ ἀγριαῖνον** τῆς γνώμης τῶν κακοποιῶν ὑποχαλάσας οὐδὲν εἰς αὐτὸν πρᾶξαι παρέπεισεν.

[75] Symeon Logothetes 219: ὡς τὰ μὲν Χριστιανῶν τοῖς Ἀγαρηνοῖς προδίδωσιν; Ps-Symeon 668, 15–17.

[76] Michanian and Prigent 2003; Prigent 2006; 2017. For Euphemios, see *PmbZ* # 1701; *PBE* I: Euphemios 1.

[77] Signes Codoñer 1995: 449–59.   [78] Mango 1985: 637; for Makris it is a shroud.

affirmed that he was a Christian and the son of Christian parents.[79] This evidence, together with the saint's declaration that he had always travelled with 'the imperial seal of approval' (ch. 49,13), suggests that he was actually on a mission on behalf of Byzantine intelligence. To his Arab appearance can perhaps be added some knowledge of Arabic – let us remember that he was from Isauria and was concerned about the conversion of Saracens in Islamic territory, as we know from the historical account – which would have allowed him access to valuable information for the defence of the Byzantine province of the south of Italy.[80] This would explain his passing quickly through Syracuse and the generous aid of the bishop of Otranto, which included the punishment of his assailants. We can likewise also make sense in this way of Gregorios' attempt to cross the Arab border in secret to return to Thessaloniki when he was discovered by a Saracen enemy whom he had to confront (chs. 35–36), as well as his need to live under a false name in Thessaloniki, where he appears to have called himself Georgios instead of Gregorios until he was discovered by a man possessed by the devil.[81]

The work of Gregorios was vital for the survival of these Christian communities but had no place in the post-iconoclast pro-government movement that arose after the Triumph of Orthodoxy, which admitted the existence only of supporters of images and their detractors. This was the fate of Theodoros Krithinos, among others. This archbishop of Syracuse, with whom Gregorios probably had a meeting, was subject to an iconodule restoration attempt. The school of historians that begins with Symeon Logothetes affirms that after the arrest of Alexios Mouselé, Theodoros confronted the emperor for failing to keep his word. As a result, Theophilos ordered Theodoros imprisoned for his lack of respect, to which the chronicler adds that in fact this was due to the discovery that he venerated icons.[82] The iconoclasm of Theodoros Krithinos, however,

---

[79] *Vita of Gregorios Dekapolites* 20,9–10: Ὁ δὲ φησί «Χριστιανός, καὶ ἐκ τοιούτων γονέων γεγέννημαι, τῆς δὲ ὀρθῆς δόξης ἀντέχομαι».

[80] This open form of dialogue with the enemy explains the fact that Gregorios was invoked by the monk Petros (*PmbZ* # 6071) when he fell into Arab hands. Thanks to his (apparently posthumous) intermediation the monk logically managed to escape unhurt, see *Vita of Gregorios Dekapolites* 88.

[81] *Vita of Gregorios Dekapolites* 61,6–9: Οἱ δὲ τοῦτον γιγνώσκοντες τῷ δαίμονι ἔφασκον «Ἀκάθαρτον καὶ κακόδαιμον πνεῦμα, τὸν Γεώργιον Γρηγόριον καλεῖς;» Ὁ δὲ ἀπεκρίνατο «Ἐπλάσατο ἑαυτὸν κεκληκὼς Γεώργιον, ἐπεὶ Γρηγόριος ὀνομάζεται. Nothing suggests that Georgios was his birth name and he changed it for Gregorios when took the monastic habit, retaining only the initial of his name. This is a subsequent practice that seldom occurred in the ninth century, see Talbot and McGrath 2006.

[82] Symeon Logothetes 220, 13: ὁ δὲ βασιλεύς, ὡς ἐλεγχθείς, θυμῷ τε καὶ ὀργῇ ἀκατασχέτῳ κινηθεὶς τοῦτον τοῦ θυσιαστηρίου βιαίως ἐξήγαγεν, καὶ πληγὰς αὐτῷ οὐ μετρίας ἐπιθεὶς ἐξώρισεν, οὐ διὰ

was obvious to the ecclesiastical hierarchy, since Methodios did not hesitate to immediately expel him and replace him with Gregorios Asbestas. Theodoros was also included in fourth place after the iconoclast patriarchs in the anathemas proclaimed on the occasion of the Triumph of Orthodoxy. His anathema is repeated in the *kanones* no less than three times (!).[83]

In the face of a situation as complicated as the aftermath of the 843 restoration, it was necessary to protect the saint's memory and, more importantly, his disciples from possible accusations of sympathy for the now-defeated iconoclast cause. To achieve this, a hagiographer was chosen who could understand his situation and his repentance. It is impossible to know to what extent Gregorios and his circle accepted heresy. In any case, it appears that none of them did anything to defend the cause of images. For this reason, Ignatios proposed writing a *vita* reflecting tendencies that had been widely accepted by iconodules during the Second Iconoclasm, producing what Ševčenko has called a 'non-iconodule hagiography'.[84] To this subgenre belong texts such as the *vitae* of Georgios of Amastris, Leon of Catania, Philaretos and Eudokimos, in which neither icons nor the dispute are mentioned, seemingly indicating that their protagonists were not involved in it, as if they had lived in earlier times. In addition to these *vitae*, a non-iconodule account has survived (*Methodius ad Theodorum*) that was written at the court of the iconoclast Emperor Theophilos by a person as committed to the cause of the images as Methodios was.[85]

Clearly, neither Gregorios Dekapolites nor any of his disciples ever attacked an icon of Christ, the Theotokos or the saints. Nor did they take part in the persecution of those who venerated them. Moreover, if we consider the historical account by the Dekapolites that has survived, their monastic spirituality was likely based on a transcendental mysticism for which the matter of the images was irrelevant. On the other hand, their lack of involvement in defending the icons and their friendship with certain people could have caused them problems and discredited the memory of a holy man. Both dangers could be warded off by promoting veneration of their leader by recalling his origin and the family iconodule network that supported him in his youth. The ingenious proposal of Malamut, according to which the promotion of the cult of Gregorios

---

τὸ ἐλεγχθῆναι ὑπὸ τούτου μόνον, ἀλλὰ διὰ τὸ καταμαθεῖν αὐτὸν τὰς ἁγίας εἰκόνας τιμᾶν καὶ σέβεσθαι καὶ τὴν αὐτοῦ δυσσέβειαν κρυφαίως διαβάλλειν.

[83] *PG* 99, 1769A–D; 1773C; 1780A.   [84] Ševčenko 1977a: 127–29.
[85] Anrich 1913: vol. I, 140–50; Ševčenko 1977a: 125–26. See Section 2.1.1.

Dekapolites and the rapid composition of his hagiography aimed solely to retain the saint's relics at the monastery of Antipas and thus prevent their transfer to Thessaloniki, is unconvincing.[86] This would have meant silencing aspects of the saint's life in Thessaloniki and suppressing the name of the monastery where he spent many years and was consecrated a priest. But those interested in cultivating Gregorios' memory were his disciples, many of whom were established in Constantinople: Anastasios had moved there some years previously, but a large number of them went with him from Thessaloniki, since a man as seriously ill as he was needed constant care.

Indeed, the *vita* (following a well-known topos) describes how he was surrounded by his disciples when he died.[87] This same milieu commissioned the hagiography and informed its author regarding the saint's main characteristics and most memorable feats. From the account of the three informants (Symeon, Anastasios and Ioannes), Ignatios Diakonos constructs a text that reveals the perspective each man had of the saint: his uncle Symeon (deeply committed to the cause of icons) emphasises the iconoclast context in which Gregorios lived, while his disciples and companions Anastasios and Ioannes relate his everyday experiences, stressing the human dimension, the spirituality and the qualities of the Dekapolites as a prophet and an exorcist. Within this clear stratigraphy of testimonies collected by the hagiographer –chs. 62 and 63, for example, which interrupt the sequence of events to transmit the testimony of his disciple Ioannes and his uncle Symeon on Gregorios' capacity for bilocation–, the iconodule veneer concentrates on the formative stage of the saint by way of a response to the personality of the informant for the hagiographical text. Likewise, Ignatios interpolates an iconodule reflection (unconnected to prior or subsequent information) in the midst of a short *enkomion* of the personal virtues of his hero.[88]

3.2 The Milieu of Gregorios Dekapolites

The process of Gregorios' sanctification is similar to that of other important persons in the Second Iconoclasm who did not defend the veneration of images but managed to establish themselves as saints and models of

---

[86] Malamut 2004: 1214. On the monastery of Antipas, located adjacent to the cistern of St Mokios, see Janin 1969: 38.
[87] *Vita of Gregorios Dekapolites* 78,9–11: Καὶ κοιμᾶται μετὰ τῶν πατέρων αὐτοῦ τραφεὶς ἐν γήρᾳ καλῷ τῆς πνευματικῆς καὶ τελείας αὐξήσεως.
[88] *Vita of Gregorios Dekapolites* 73, cf. Malamut 2004: 1213.

virtue nonetheless. The best documented extreme cases are those of the entourage of Theophilos, which consisted of powerful men who stood out both politically and socially during the Second Iconoclasm without protecting the icons. Despite this, they came to be considered pious iconodules thanks to their subsequent commitment to the restoration of images. Indeed, the *Acta Davidis, Symeonis et Georgii* do not hesitate to praise their subjects and put them on the same level as the future patriarch Methodios, due to the support they gave him in the agreements prior to the Triumph of Orthodoxy.[89] Furthermore, some of the iconoclast emperor's closest collaborators ended up being venerated, such as the *magistros* Sergios Niketiates, who entered the *synaxaria* after his death during a campaign in Crete, when his body was moved to the monastery of the Theotokos of Niketiates, which he had founded in the Gulf of Nicomedia.[90]

For his part, Emperor Theophilos himself was the object of a politico-ecclesiastical restoration that used the creation of oral traditions that gradually took on written form and finally crystallised into independent texts such as *De Theophili imperatoris absolutione* (BHG 1732–34k) and *De Theophili imperatoris benefactis* (BHG 1735).[91] The episode of the conversion of Theophilos also entered the hagiography of the saints of Lesbos, where it is used to praise Symeon the Stylite as the only person responsible for this absolution, to the detriment of Empress Theodora and the future patriarch Methodios, whose divine visions and intercessions for Theophilos' soul are scorned.[92] In this operation, the resolution shown by those closest to the emperor was determinant, especially that of Empress Theodora. Although the differences from the case of Gregorios Dekapolites are considerable and their political connotations much less important, the part played by the entourage and the families of these persons can be regarded as similar. Let us therefore turn to the family and intimate circle of the Dekapolites to appreciate the extent to which its members may have collaborated in the process of his sanctification.

---

[89] *Acta of David, Symeon and Georgios* 245–46: Οἱ δὲ τοῦ Θεοῦ ἄνθρωποι Γεώργιος καὶ Μεθόδιος συμπαραλαβόντες Σέργιον τὸν Νικητιάτην, Θεόκτιστον, Βάρδαν καὶ Πετρωνᾶν, ἄνδρας ὀρθοδοξοτάτους καὶ τῆς συγκλήτου τυγχάνοντας πρώτους βουλῆς, οὐ διέλιπον ἀνενδότως ἐκλιπαροῦντες τὸν Συμεών καὶ ἐκμειλισσόμενοι συγκατανεῦσαι τῷ τῆς Αὐγούστης αἰτήματι καὶ μὴ παριδεῖν ἐν σκοτομήνῃ τὴν τοῦ Θεοῦ ἐκκλησίαν ὑπὸ τοῦ διαβόλου ἐλεεινῶς ἐκβακχευομένην. See Chapter 4.
[90] *SynaxCP* 777,5–78,16 (28 June). Cf. *PmbZ* # 6664; *PBE* I: Sergios 57.
[91] Markopoulos 1983; Vinson 1995; Afinogenov 1996a: 58–61; Markopoulos 1998; Afinogenov 1999a; 2004a. See Chapter 4.
[92] *Acta of David, Symeon and Georgios* 242,35–43,2; Karlin-Hayter 2006a. See also Timotin 2010: 143–49.

According to the *vita*, Gregorios' parents were Maria, a devout woman from a family of men of the Church,[93] and Sergios, who seems to have been quite the opposite, with no interest in spiritual matters.[94] They had at least one other son, whose name is not recorded.[95] They were a very well-to-do family, as can be gathered from the expensive clothes they wore[96] and the servants who attended Gregorios.[97] To these indications must be added the presence of a *grammatistes* (chs. 1, 9). Years later, Gregorios still had a servant, even when he decided to embrace asceticism in a cave.[98] The *archimandrites* Symeon was his maternal uncle.[99] Later relatives included the patriarch Euthymios (907–912),[100] as Arethas of Caesarea declared in his epitaph,[101] and a monk from his closest circle by the name of Epiphanios, who is said to have shared experiences with Gregorios and Symeon during the reign of Theophilos.[102]

3.2.1 The Archimandrites *Symeon and the Monastic Family*

According to the *Vita Gregorii Decapolitae*, in addition to being a hegoumenos, Gregorios' uncle Symeon was an *archimandrites*, that is, he was in charge of the monasteries of the Dekapolis in Isauria.[103] He undertook to take in Gregorios and initiate him into monastic life. The latter spent fourteen years under Symeon's protection,[104] and although he later adopted a hermit's way of life, he continued to ask his uncle for advice both via letters and in person.[105] Symeon's spirited defence of icons appears to have led Emperor Theophilos to order his imprisonment. In goal, he became aware that his nephew was seriously ill and asked Gregorios to visit him.[106] Gregorios' arrival coincided with Symeon's liberation.

---

[93] *PmbZ* # 4728; *PBE* I: Maria 7. On her piety, see *Vita of Gregorios Dekapolites* 1,6–8.
[94] *PmbZ* # 6638; *PBE* I: Sergios 58; *Vita of Gregorios Dekapolites* 1,5–6.   [95] *PmbZ* # 6638A.
[96] *Vita of Gregorios Dekapolites* 2,14–17: Ἔνδυμα δὲ ἦν αὐτῷ οὐκ ἐκ νημάτων Σηρῶν οὐδ' ὅσα πρὸς ποικιλίαν ὑφάνταις φίλον περιεργάζεσθαι, καί περ τούτοις τῶν γονέων σπευδόντων τὸν υἱὸν ἐναβρύνεσθαι.
[97] *Vita of Gregorios Dekapolites* 3,4–8.   [98] *PmbZ* # 11703.
[99] *PmbZ* # 7199 (who must be identified with *PmbZ* # 7214).
[100] Jugie 1913; *ODB* II, 755–56, s.v. 'Euthymios'.
[101] *Epitaphios for Euthymios* 84,24–27: Σελεύκεια μὲν αὐτὸν τιθηνεῖται, εἰς Γρηγορίου τοῦ θείου τὸ γένος ἀνάπτουσα, ὃν ἄλλον θαυματουργὸν ἡ μικρῷ πρὸ ἡμῶν ἠὐμοίρησε γενεά, τῆς τῶν Ἰσαύρων καὶ τούτου ὁρμώμενον Δεκαπόλεως . . . .
[102] *PmbZ* # 1589 and 21698; *Vita of the patriarch Euthymios* 59,21–29 and 61,28–30.
[103] *Vita of Gregorios Dekapolites* 5,12–13: Ὃν ἀρχιμανδρίτην εἶχε τηνικαῦτα τὰ πρὸς τῇ Δεκαπόλει συντελοῦντα σεμνεῖα. On the duties of the *archimandrites*, see De Meester 1949; Ruggieri 1991: 117–23.
[104] *Vita of Gregorios Dekapolites* 6.   [105] *Vita of Gregorios Dekapolites* 14–16.
[106] *Vita of Gregorios Dekapolites* 76–77.

Despite attempts to identify this Symeon Dekapolites with other champions of images of the same name, it seems clear that he is not the hegoumenos of Kyzikos called Symeon, the correspondent of Theodoros Stoudites, since the catechesis he sent him is dated between 821 and 826.[107] At that time, Gregorios' uncle led a community in Isauria, in which the young man was trained. We can likewise rule out identifying him with the Symeon Stylite mentioned in the *Synodikon of Orthodoxy* together with other iconodule leaders who supported the patriarch Methodios and the restoration of icons, such as Ioannikios, Hilarion of Dalmatos, Theodoros Stoudites and the miracle worker Isaakios.[108] The characterisation of Symeon as a Stylite is more in keeping with the protagonist of the *Acta Davidis, Symeonis et Georgii* (BHG 494).[109] The 'famous Symeon' (ὁ κλεινός Συμεών) found in a fragment of a homily of Methodios quoted by Niketas of Heraclea must be the saint of Lesbos. In a context similar to that of the *Synodikon*, the patriarch mentions Ioannikios, Hilarion of Dalmatos and Symeon as the leaders of the hegoumenoi, the ascetics and the stylites who shared his policy against the iconoclasts.[110] These three saints also appear as the major supporters of Methodios in his accession to the patriarchate in the *Vita of Ioannikios by Petros*.[111]

Our Symeon Dekapolites is the same man, however, as the friend of Methodios, with whom he overlapped in prison and who saw fit to commission from him the writing of a *vita* of Euthymios of Sardis. If we can believe Methodios, this Symeon was a charismatic leader,[112] since he is described as 'a man of God and angel of faithful Christians, oh Symeon, obedient by definition and a master of obedience for your disciples'.[113] The birth of Euthymios in Lycaonia (a region adjacent to Isauria) and his work as leader of the Sardis community seem to have been the origin of Symeon's interest in the life of this saint, whom he must have known personally.[114] The hagiographical sources allow us to reconstruct at least two moments of great tension in the iconoclastic persecution of Emperor

---

[107] *PmbZ* # 7195; Theod. Stoud., *epist.* p. 444*ff.; Efthymiadis 1995: 151–53.
[108] *PmbZ* # 3472; *PBE* I: Isaakios 11.
[109] *Synodikon of Orthodoxy* 53,132 and pp. 146–47; *Vita of Gregorios Dekapolites* 69, n. 5,10; *PmbZ* # 7178.
[110] Darrouzès 1966: 296, line 5; 1987: 54, line 12.
[111] *Vita of Ioannikios by Petros* 431A–B; Talbot 1998: 340–42.
[112] *PmbZ* # 7201. Methodios again refers to him, although not by name, in *Vita of Euthymios of Sardis* 9,166–67 and 48,957–59.
[113] *Vita of Euthymios of Sardis* 1,4–5: ἄνθρωπε τοῦ Θεοῦ καὶ ἄγγελε τῶν πιστῶν ναζηραίων, εὐχὰς ἐπικαλεσάμενος, ὦ Συμεών, τῷ ὄντι ὑπήκοε καὶ τῆς ὑπακοῆς παιδευτὰ τοῖς σοι προσανέχουσιν.
[114] Mango 1985: 645–46, n. 34.

Theophilos. The most important appears to have been in 833 or shortly afterwards, on the occasion of the edict against the iconodules. Shortly before this, however, Theophilos apparently promoted a less drastic, if equally violent measure, requiring all members of the clergy to follow the patriarch Antonios I in rejecting the veneration of images, under pain of exile. According to the *vita* of the patrician Niketas,[115] this ultimatum arrived in 830.

The same year saw the arrest of Ioseph of Thessaloniki and Euthymios of Sardis, although the hagiographer of the latter believes that the arrest represented a political conspiracy.[116] The prior imprisonment of Methodios also seems to have been due to political rather than religious considerations (specifically the affair of the pamphlets prophesying the death of Emperors Leon V, Michael II and Theophilos). Both causes do however coincide in time, making it possible that State and Church reasons overlapped. In this situation, those detained on the island of St Andrew contributed to the agitation against the sovereign and in favour of the new martyrs, disseminating Euthymios' testimony and sufferings. The *archimandrites* Symeon Dekapolites may also have been involved in these early events, providing reason enough for his co-religionist Methodios to take up his pen and write the *vita*. If he had not himself witnessed the torments of Euthymios, his position at the head of a considerable number of iconodules and their family ties with prominent hegoumenoi from Constantinople would have meant he was immediately informed of the events. In this situation, he must have hastened to ask a witness versed in writing, such as Methodios, to write about and disseminate news of this torment.

Theophilos' famous edict of 833 doubtless led to Symeon's arrest. It can be assumed that the conditions of his captivity were not arduous, since no sources mention any sadistic tortures meted out to him. He must have spent several years in confinement before hearing of the serious state of health of his nephew Gregorios Dekapolites and asking the latter to make him a final visit (however unlikely this may seem). Once he was set free, Symeon remained in Constantinople, where he came to prominence through his unconditional support of Methodios in his attempt to restore the veneration of icons. After the Triumph of Orthodoxy, the new patriarch did not forget Symeon's loyalty; to show his gratitude, Methodios appointed him *synkellos* and made him hegoumenos of the

---

[115] *Vita of Niketas the patrician* 327, ch. 4; Kazhdan 1999: 200.
[116] *Vita of Euthymios of Sardis* 41,274–43,410.

monastery of Sts Sergios and Bakkhos, an imperial foundation of Justinian that had been directed by Ioannes VII Grammatikos since 814.[117] This information has come down to us in a roundabout manner, since it became part of the dossier of the stylite Symeon of Lesbos, whose *vita* accumulates details in an uncritical manner.[118] The news that Symeon was appointed *synkellos* and received the monastery of Sergios and Bakkhos is a later interpolation, as the use of the title 'Augusta' to refer to Theodora reveals.[119] With his interest in literature, Symeon Dekapolites is historically closer to the profile required for a *synkellos* than Symeon the Stylite, a monk who led a life of sacrifice but had much less experience in matters of ecclesiastical governance.[120]

The confusion between the two men is easily understood, since they shared the same name and theological position and collaborated politically with Methodios. The matter can be cleared up, however, if we analyse the development of the monastery in Constantinople of Sergios and Bakkhos, which, under the administration of Ioannes Grammatikos (814–843), had become an iconoclast centre where Theophanes of Sigriane, Theodoros of Stoudios and Platon of Sakkoudion were interrogated. When Symeon was made its hegoumenos after the restoration of icons, this important patriarchal monastery was recovered for Orthodoxy. The establishment of Sergios and Bakkhos had in fact always been linked to the family and followers of Gregorios Dekapolites. According to the hagiographical account of Ioannes Diakonos, Ioseph Hymnographos stayed together with his master the Dekapolites in the monastery of Sergios and Bakkhos during his first visit to Constantinople (ca. 837) and established himself there permanently years later.[121]

---

[117] *Acta of David, Symeon and Georgios* 250, ch. 30,38–43: Τῇ δὲ πρώτῃ τῶν νηστειῶν κυριακῇ, ἐν τῇ τοῦ Θεοῦ ἁγιωτάτῃ συναθροισθέντες ἐκκλησίᾳ, Μεθόδιον μὲν τῷ ἀρχιερατικῷ καὶ ὑψηλῷ ἐνιδρύουσι θρόνῳ, τὸν δέ γε Συμεὼν σύγκελλον, νεύματι τῆς Αὐγούστης, τοῦ πατριαρχείου προεχειρίσαντο, τήν τε Σεργίου καὶ Βάκχου τῶν ἁγίων μονὴν πρὸς τὴν τῶν οἰκείων μαθητῶν καταγωγὴν καὶ ἀνάπαυσιν αὐτῷ προσδεδώκασι, τήν τε τῶν ἱερῶν ἀναστήλωσιν ὁμοῦ καὶ προσκύνησιν εἰκόνων ἐξέθεντό τε καὶ ἐδογμάτισαν. For the patriarchal monastery of Sergios and Bakkhos, cf. Janin 1969: 451–54, esp. 452; Efthymiadis 1995: 153.

[118] The *Acta of David, Symeon and Georgios* constitute a complex text that resulted from successive recreations of materials characteristic of the first half of the ninth century. For a stratigraphical analysis of its main textual components, see Chapter 6. On this hagiographical account, see Ševčenko 1977a: 117. Cf. Halkin 1959; Kazhdan 1984: 185–88; 1999: 200–202; Talbot 1998: 224–26; Karlin-Hayter 2004: 325–50.

[119] The empress enjoyed this title when she returned to the court ca. 862/863 and 867. During this period, the existing hagiography of Symeon of Lesbos was rewritten to include fresh data, see Chapter 6.

[120] *PmbZ* # 7178; *PBE* I: Symeon 13. On his work as *synkellos* of Methodios, see Chapter 2.

[121] *Vita of Ioseph Hymnographos* by Ioannes Diakonos 953A–B and 961B–C; *SynaxCP* 581–84,2. On the church of Sts Sergios and Bakkhos, see Janin 1969: 451–54; Mango 1975b; Bardill 2017.

This stay of the Dekapolites and his follower is impossible, since at the time the iconoclast patriarch Ioannes Grammatikos was head of the monastery. But it is likely true that Ioseph established himself there once Methodios transferred the management to Symeon Dekapolites. During the reign of Basileios I, the ascetic Ioannes of Galatia, a colleague of Ioseph Hymnographos, was appointed hegoumenos; it was he who miraculously discovered the relics of St Sergios.[122] The traditional commemoration of Sts Sergios and Bakkhos is complemented by another in May in Ruphinianai.[123] This must inevitably be related to the miraculous finding of the relics of Sergios by our Ioannes.[124] Years later, the emperor appointed him hegoumenos of the monastery of Diomedes, where he died on 15 March. This was the date when his liturgical commemoration began to be held under the advocation of Ioannes of Ruphinianai (ὁ ἐν Ῥουφινιαναῖς), because the complex of Sts Sergios and Bakkhos was located in this quarter of Constantinople.[125] In his honour, his friend Ioseph Hymnographos drew up a liturgical *kanon*[126] and a *Vita of Ioannes of Galatia*, of which we only have a translation into Georgian.[127] When Ioannes died, Emperor Leon VI offered the monastery of Sergios and Bakkhos to his spiritual father, the future patriarch Euthymios,[128] who, as mentioned, had blood ties with Gregorios Dekapolites. This was thus a measure to return one of their most valued monasteries to a family that was well established in the ecclesiastical world.

Sources other than the hagiography of Gregorios confirm the importance of his uncle Symeon and the existence of numerous disciples, including the monk Nikolaos,[129] who was miraculously saved by St Nicholas of Myra from dying in a terrible storm. As well as controlling

---

[122] *PmbZ* # 3266 and # 22779; *PBE* I: Ioannes 224; Krausmüller 2007c: 355–57.
[123] *SynaxCP* 709,53 (26 May); 713,6–7 (27 May).
[124] According to the *Vita of Ioannes of Galatia* 15: 'Bien plus à Constantinople, dans le sanctuaire de saint Serge, il découvrit lui-même les reliques cachées depuis de longues années, et que quelques hommes étourdis avaient cachées ainsi ignominieusement sous terre', see Kekelidze 1965: 66; Krausmüller 2019.
[125] *SynaxCP* 537/538,20–24 (15 March); 543/544,46–51 (16 and 17 March); *Typikon Messinense* 146,3 (18 April); *Menologion Basilii* 353C (15 March); *Georgian Calendar* 235 and 272–73; Follieri 1960–1966: vol. v/2, p. 169 and 175. On the monastery of Diomedes. see Janin 1969: 95–97.
[126] Tomadakes 1971a: 149, nr. 205.
[127] Van Esbroeck 1996. Kekelidze 1965 includes a French paraphrase of the content. The identification of its author, the *skeuophylax* Ioseph, with Ioseph Hymnographos is highly convincing despite the reticence of Stiernon 1973: 260–62.
[128] *Vita of the Patriarch Euthymios* 4,14–19. On the relationship between Leon VI and Euthymios, see Tougher 1997: 50–51; Timotin 2010: 194–207.
[129] *PmbZ* # 5591.

the monasteries of the Dekapolis in Isauria, Gregorios' family owned another monastery in Thessaloniki, according to the testimony of the *Vita Euthymii patriarchae* 58–60. The family's wealth had allowed the purchase in Thessaloniki of land for building a monastery that observed the discipline characteristic of disciples led by Symeon. This monastery, the name and location of which have been lost, seems to have housed Gregorios' community, which named him its hegoumenos,[130] thus forming a network of monasteries to guarantee the influence of Symeon Dekapolites. This is evidently a case of an expansion of the monastic network run by Symeon, not a later transfer, as is postulated by Malamut, although the difficulties experienced in Isauria may have been owing to the Arab threat of Al-Ma'mūn, which led to the movement of some members of the family.[131]

In all likelihood, the network that resulted depended on the same hegoumenos and followed the same rules, imitating the Stoudite model.[132] A dynastic element in their governance can be detected in the structure of the Dekapolitan monasteries: the *archimandrites* Symeon led those situated in Isauria, while his nephew Gregorios was in charge of the new monastery established in Thessaloniki, whose name is unknown.[133] Gregorios' early death from a serious illness kept him from inheriting management of the whole system, in which we must no doubt include an establishment in Constantinople, the capital of the empire. This was common practice among the influential provincial monasteries of the time. The hagiographer of the *vita* of Antonios the Younger (785–865), for example, relates how he accompanied his spiritual father from his monastery of Herakleion in Kios, Bithynia to the *metochion* of All Saints that they owned in Constantinople.[134]

3.2.2 The Disciples of Gregorios Dekapolites

Anastasios, the disciple of Gregorios in Thessaloniki and the informant of Ignatios Diakonos, settled into this establishment in the capital. According to the *Vita of Gregorios Dekapolites*, Anastasios was known for his piety and asceticism.[135] He was a disciple of Gregorios at St Menas in Thessaloniki

---

[130] *Vita of Gregorios Dekapolites* 50.   [131] Malamut 2004: 1212–13.
[132] On the monastic networks of this period and their dynastic model, see Introduction.
[133] *Vita of Gregorios Dekapolites* 50,2–3: τὸν αὐτοῦ καθηγεμόνα καὶ μέγαν Γρηγόριον.
[134] *Vita of Antonios the Younger* 4–6; *Vita of Antonios the Younger* (addit), pp. 204–9; *PmbZ* # 11651.
[135] *Vita of Gregorios Dekapolites* 52,1–2: Ἀναστάσιος δέ τις, μοναχὸς ἐπ' εὐλαβείᾳ καὶ ἀσκητικῇ πολιτείᾳ σεμνυνόμενος. On Anastasios, see *PmbZ* # 320 and *PmbZ* # 318.

until he was required to accompany the *protokankelarios* Georgios to Constantinople. After the vicissitudes mentioned above, both men reached the capital; Anastasios decided to remain there,[136] while Georgios returned to Thessaloniki after having been received by Emperor Theophilos, who appointed him *kandidatos*. Three months later, Gregorios resolved to visit the Bithynian Olympos, and in order to do so, he put in at Constantinople, where he stayed with Anastasios.[137] Due to a visit by one of his disciples from Thessaloniki and alerted to his arrival by his gift of clairvoyance, the saint cut short his stay on Olympos and returned to Constantinople. Clearly, the group must all have gathered at the same place. Despite the fact that the *Vita of Gregorios Dekapolites* does not name the location, the two *vitae* of Gregorios' disciple Ioseph Hymnographos contain the information: the first states that his disciple was waiting at the monastery of the martyr Antipas near the church of St Mokios,[138] while his later hagiographer, Ioannes Diakonos, maintained that it was the church of Sergios and Bakkhos.[139]

Although Anastasios did not act as hegoumenos, his influence should not be underestimated, since in all likelihood he was the same constant, hopeful man mentioned by Ignatios Diakonos in his *epist*. 40 addressed to the diakonos and *chartophylax* Nikephoros.[140] The allusion to Anastasios in this letter, drawn up apropos of a doctrinal formula that had initially been accepted and then revoked, can be better understood if we take into account the non-iconodule past of Anastasios, who was now in communion with Orthodoxy thanks to his constancy in the Lord (διὰ θεὸν ἐνστάσει). The information we have regarding Ioannes, another pious disciple of the Dekapolites who was an informant of Ignatios Diakonos,[141] shows that this monastery remained active years later, since after the death of his spiritual father, he settled there together with Ioseph

---

[136] *Vita of Gregorios Dekapolites* 52,29–30: Ἐν δὲ τῷ Βυζαντίῳ γενόμενοι ἐγὼ μὲν ἐν αὐτῷ μένειν ἔκρινα.
[137] *Vita of Gregorios Dekapolites* 53,1–3: Μηνῶν δὲ τριῶν παρῳχηκότων ἐκ Θεσσαλονίκης ἀπῆρεν ὁ ὅσιος καὶ πρὸς τὸ Βυζάντιον κατέπλει. Ἐν ᾧ ξενίζεται **παρ' ἐμοὶ** καὶ πρὸς τὰς τοῦ Ὀλύμπου προπέμπεται ἐξοχάς.
[138] *Vita of Ioseph Hymnographos by Theophanes* 5.
[139] *Vita of Ioseph Hymnographos by Ioannes Diakonos* 953A–B and 961B–C; *SynaxCP* 581–84,2.
[140] Ignatios Diakonos, *epist*. 40,22–23: Ἐπὶ δὲ τῇ τοῦ κοινοῦ ἀδελφοῦ Ἀναστασίου διὰ θεὸν ἐνστάσει καὶ ἥσθημεν καὶ πνευματικῆς θυμηδίας ἐπλήσθημεν. Concerning Nikephoros, the recipient of twenty-nine of the surviving missives of Ignatios, cf. *PmbZ* # 5306; *PBE* I: Nikephoros 71.
[141] *Vita of Gregorios Dekapolites* 62,1–2: Ἰωάννης δέ τις μαθητὴς ὢν τοῦ ὁσίου, ἀνὴρ ἐπ' εὐλαβείᾳ κοσμούμενος, σὺν πολλῇ πληροφορίᾳ ἡμᾶς ἐπιστώσατο. Cf. *PmbZ* # 3241; *PBE* I: Ioannes 244; Stiernon 1973: 260–62; Yannopoulos 2016.

Hymnographos when the latter returned from Crete.[142] Much as both men must have excelled in literary composition (if we take seriously the characterisation of them in the *vita* as having a way with words),[143] the only texts that survive are those of Ioseph Hymnographos, who probably had more influence than anyone else in the milieu of Gregorios Dekapolites. The nature of the relationship between the two saints is unclear. The former is never mentioned in the *vita* of Gregorios Dekapolites,[144] while in the *vita* of Ioseph Hymnographos the man praised as a disciple of the Dekapolites is Ioannes, Ioseph's companion. In fact, this Ioannes was venerated and entered the *synaxaria* not in his own right but merely as a disciple of Gregorios Dekapolites.[145]

(a) Ioseph Hymnographos

Born in Sicily ca. 808, where he lived until an Arab raid obliged his family to move to the Peloponnese,[146] Ioseph travelled at age fifteen to Thessaloniki to enter a monastery and devote himself to asceticism. His first biographer does not mention the monastery in question, but according to Ioannes Diakonos, it was the monastery of Latomos.[147] After the arrival of Gregorios Dekapolites in the city, Ioseph became one of his disciples, with the permission of the hegoumenos of the monastery. Ioseph Hymnographos accompanied Gregorios on his first journey to Constantinople and settled with him in the church of St Antipas, where they continued to lead lives of prayer and study of the Bible.[148] At some point, the iconodule leaders asked Gregorios to send Ioseph to Rome as an ambassador with a letter for the Pope requesting his assistance.[149] These events probably occurred during Gregorios' second journey to

---

[142] *Vita of Ioseph Hymnographos by Theophanes* 8: συμμεριστὴν τῶν πόνων Ἰωάννην ἔχων τὸν τοῦ θείου Γρηγορίου μαθητήν τε καὶ μιμητήν. *Vita of Ioseph Hymnographos by Ioannes Diakonos* 961C.

[143] *Vita of Ioseph Hymnographos by Ioannes Diakonos* 961C: Πολλὰς γὰρ εἶχε καὶ Ἰωάννης ἐπικαθημένας τῇ γλώσσῃ τὰς χάριτας.

[144] For Makris, there was no need for Ignatios Diakonos to mention him as he is Gregorios' 'well loved disciple' who receives a vision of God that reveals to him his master's holiness (*Vita of Gregorios Dekapolites* 57).

[145] *SynaxCP* 597/598,43 (11 April); 615,7–16,11 (19 April); *Menologion Basilii* 409D, 412A (18 April); *Typikon Messinense* 144,30 (18 April).

[146] On Ioseph Hymnographos, see *PmbZ* # 3454 and # 23510; *PBE* I: Ioseph 12; Costa-Louillet 1957: 812–23; Stiernon 1973: 254–55; *DS* VII, 1349–54.

[147] *Vita of Ioseph Hymnographos by Ioannes Diakonos* 945B. Concerning the monastery of Latomos, see Janin 1975: 392–94.

[148] *Vita of Ioseph Hymnographos by Theophanes* 5; *Vita of Ioseph Hymnographos by Ioannes Diakonos* 952C–53A.

[149] *Vita of Ioseph Hymnographos by Theophanes* 6; *Vita of Ioseph Hymnographos by Ioannes Diakonos* 953D–56A.

Constantinople to visit his uncle Symeon. As Malamut points out, the hagiographer's curious observation that 'the most happy Gregorios having received what he desired and having delivered what he had been requested to do, gives part and receives part of the unparalleled joy' must be interpreted as an agreement by which Methodios intervened to free Symeon, and in exchange Gregorios sent his disciple to Rome as a messenger.[150]

On the way, he passed through Patras, where he wrote a liturgical *kanon* dedicated to the Apostle St Andrew commissioned by the metropolitan of the see,[151] who wished to update the tribute by Theodoros Stoudites that had served them up to that time.[152] The epigram celebrated the triumph of Emperor Nikephoros I, who defeated the Slavs in Patras, as well as the promotion of the archbishopric of Patras by the emperor to a metropolitan see in 805/806 to coincide with this victory. Ioseph was unable to reach Rome, however, after this order, due to an Arab attack that destroyed his ship and left him hostage in Crete. Freed in early 843 after a ransom was paid,[153] Ioseph returned to Constantinople after the death of Theophilos, the death of his master Gregorios and the restoration of icons. After the death of Ioannes (ca. 850), with whom he had lived for some years as an ascetic in the monastery of Antipas, Ioseph moved to the monastery of St John Chrysostom.[154] Its founders had been extolled by Theodoros Stoudites in a single distich,[155] and the patron saint of the establishment was now sung by Ioseph.[156]

The Hymnographos remained there for five years, until there came to be so many disciples that a new monastery had to be founded on nearby land (855).[157] The foundation was dedicated both to his master Gregorios Dekapolites and to the Apostle St Bartholomew, whose relics had been

---

[150] *Vita of Gregorios Dekapolites* 77,4–6: Ἀπολαβὼν οὖν ὁ πανόλβιος Γρηγόριος τὸ ποθούμενον καὶ ἀντιδοὺς τὸ ζητούμενον ἀνεικάστου χαρᾶς μετεδίδου καὶ μετελάμβανε. For the interpretation, cf. Malamut 2004: 1215–6.
[151] Oikonomides 1996.
[152] Theod. Stoud., *epigram* LXXXVII (ed. Speck). At that time, 805/806, the monastery of Stoudios and Emperor Nikephoros were still on good terms, see Theod. Stoud., *epist.* 16,2–7; Cholij 2002: 45–47. For a comparison of the two eulogies of St Andrew and their political aims, see De Gregorio 2010.
[153] *Vita of Ioseph Hymnographos* by Theophanes 7; *Vita of Ioseph Hymnographos by Ioannes Diakonos* 960A–D.
[154] For the monastery of St John Chrysostom, see Janin 1969: 271–72; Stiernon 1973: 257–60.
[155] Theod. Stoud., *epigram* LXXXVII (ed. Speck): Εἰς τὸν ναὸν τοῦ Χρυσοστόμου / Τοῖς τὸν σὸν οἶκον παμπόθως ἐγηγερκόσιν / πρεσβευτικὴν πρόσνειμε δωρεάν, πάτερ. See Janin 1969: 271–72.
[156] Ioseph Hym., *Kanones* 266–88 (to St John Chrysostom).
[157] The dating has not been unanimous up to now. According to Tomadakes 1971a: 55 the foundation occurred in 850, for Stiernon 1973: 252–53 it was in 855, while Makris places it between 855 and 870, see *Vita of Gregorios Dekapolites* 29.

delivered to Thessaloniki by a pious nobleman.[158] The remains of the Dekapolites and the body of his friend Ioannes were moved there so that they could rest together.[159] This transfer was probably the pretext for Ioseph's production of many hymns dedicated to Gregorios, who is remembered on 20 November.[160] The deposition of the patriarch Ignatios in 858 meant that Ioseph became a victim of the Caesar Bardas, who exiled him to the Chersonesos in the Crimea. He returned and during the second patriarchate of Ignatios acted as the *skeuophylax* of Hagia Sophia, a post he maintained until the end of his life, even after Photios succeeded Ignatios to the patriarchal throne in 877. He died at the biblical age of seventy on 3 April 886. The dates of Easter for the year he died included in the *vita* indicate that it was 878 or 886.[161] The latter date is preferable, since Ioseph was already a priest when he began to follow Gregorios Dekapolites, according to the *Synaxarion of Constantinople*.[162]

No sooner had Ioseph died, than his disciple Theophanes, who succeeded him as the head of the monastery of Bartholomew, wrote a *vita* in his honour (*BHG* 944) for which the monks of his own community were an immediate audience. The cult of Ioseph became established thanks to this account and the *kanones* produced to celebrate his memory in the liturgy: the monk Euodios, who was also his disciple, penned a hymn to his master to be sung on 3 April.[163] Among others, Theophanes Sikelos also dedicated a poem to him,[164] and before long Ioseph had entered the

---

[158] *Vita of Ioseph Hymnographos by Ioannes Diakonos* 961D–64A. On the monastery of St Bartholomew, see Janin 1969: 57.

[159] *Vita of Ioseph Hymnographos by Theophanes* 9; *Vita of Ioseph Hymnographos by Ioannes Diakonos* 961C–D.

[160] Ioseph Hymnographos composed a *kontakion* (Tomadakes 1971a: 204, nr. 3) in addition to several *kanones* in memory of Gregorios Dekapolites. The end of the *kontakion* was edited by Pitra, *Analecta* I, 393. The complete text can be found in Mioni 1948: 180–82. As far as the liturgical *kanones* are concerned, three are catalogued in Tomadakes 1971a: 127–28, nr. 100–102. Migne includes a fragment in his *PG* 105, 1245A–48A. While two *kanones* are published in *AHG*, vol. III, 465–77: 'In sollemnis diei vigiliam praesentationis beatae Mariae Virginis et in sactos Dasium martyrem et Gregorium Decapolitam.' The second, edited in pages 478–88, is entitled 'In sanctum Gregorium Decapolitam' and was drawn up on the occasion of the transfer of his relics, see Section 3.2.2. Two other *kanones*, where he is praised along with the patriarch Proklos, remain unpublished, see *Tameion*, 99–100, nr. 253 and 256. On the function of these literary works, see Patterson Ševčenko 1998.

[161] *Vita of Ioseph Hymnographos by Theophanes* 14; *Vita of Ioseph Hymnographos by Ioannes Diakonos* 969D–72C.

[162] *SynaxCP* 581,9–12: ὅθεν καὶ τὴν τοῦ πρεσβυτέρου χειροτονίαν δέχεται καὶ μετὰ Γρηγορίου τοῦ Δεκαπολίτου τὴν Κωνσταντινούπολιν καταλαμβάνει.

[163] *AHG*, vol. VIII, 87–96 and 390f. On the relationship between them both, see Tomadakes 1971a: 57. On this disciple, see *PmbZ* # 1682; *PBE* I: Euodios 1. He is mainly known for having written version Z of the martyrdom of the forty-two saints of Amorion. See Chapter 6.

[164] Petit 1926: 125; Tomadakes 1971a: 99–102 and 242–72.

synaxaria.¹⁶⁵ A second, later hagiography, which provided less information, was written by Ioannes Diakonos, and two versions of it have come down to us (*BHG* 945 and 946).¹⁶⁶ Just as with the textual support of the cult of his guide Gregorios Dekapolites, none of these documents praises Ioseph Hymnographos for his commitment to the cause of icons, something barely mentioned in passing. The object of his journey to Rome in ca. 841 as a messenger of the iconodule leaders was allegedly to obtain the Pope's support.¹⁶⁷ But Ioseph was a mere courier in this venture, and it is not even clear that Rome was his real destination, since as soon as he set sail, he was captured by the Arabs. The final years of the reign of Theophilos were marked by confrontations with the Arabs. At this time, the emperor could not persecute iconodules, since he was busy on the eastern frontier, where the military pressure of the Abbasid Caliphate was causing serious problems for the Empire, a situation the Byzantines tried to counteract with a naval attack on the port of Antioch.¹⁶⁸

Ioseph Hymnographos did not suffer for the Orthodoxy of images and did not defend it publicly from the authorities, so that he can scarcely be considered a confessor. To the contrary, the model of holiness presented in his biography relies on more spiritual matters, and from the outset the hero's vocation stands out as strict asceticism: as a youth of fifteen, he entered a monastery in Thessaloniki, where he endured severe hardship.¹⁶⁹ So too when he met the Dekapolites and decided to join him, it was to share a life of asceticism and devotion, which continued in Constantinople, and to concentrate on Bible study, prayer and fasting.¹⁷⁰ After he was freed by his captors, Ioseph finally returned to the capital, not to celebrate the Triumph of Orthodoxy or help build the post-iconoclast Church but to live as a hermit together with his companion Ioannes, with whom he chose 'to share a life of seclusion'.¹⁷¹

---

¹⁶⁵ *SynaxCP* 581,19–84,20 (3 April); 581/582,32–583/584,39 and 585/586,34 (4 April); Halkin 1969: 947a and 947d.
¹⁶⁶ The identity of this author is not clear; some consider him to be Ioannes Doxopatres, who would have written it in ca. 917, see Costa-Louillet 1957: 814. About the *vitae* of Ioseph, see Kazhdan 1999: 341–42.
¹⁶⁷ *Vita of Ioseph Hymnographos by Theophanes* 6; *Vita of Ioseph Hymnographos by Ioannes Diakonos* 956A–60A.
¹⁶⁸ Signes Codoñer 2014: 328–33.
¹⁶⁹ *Vita of Ioseph Hymnographos by Theophanes* 3; *Vita of Ioseph Hymnographos by Ioannes Diakonos* 945A–48A. On the Christian virtues of Ioseph, see *Vita of Ioseph Hymnographos by Theophanes* 4.
¹⁷⁰ *Vita of Ioseph Hymnographos by Theophanes* 5 (installed at the church of Antipas adjacent to that of St Mokios); *Vita of Ioseph Hymnographos by Ioannes Diakonos* 952C–53A (in the church of Sts Sergios and Bakkhos).
¹⁷¹ *Vita of Ioseph Hymnographos by Theophanes* 8; *Vita of Ioseph Hymnographos by Ioannes Diakonos* 960D–61C.

Ioseph Hymnographos and Ioannes of Galatia, the hegoumenos of the monastery of Sts Sergios and Bakkhos and the protagonist of the miraculous discovery of the relics of Sergios, of whom we have already spoken,[172] are two more good examples of the ecclesiastical sector that operated on the fringes of the iconoclast dispute and about which we know very little owing to its silence. After the restoration of images, however, these men gradually became more involved in ecclesiastical affairs, first to promote the cult of their leader Gregorios Dekapolites and later to carve out a niche for themselves in the monasticism of Constantinople as champions of the legitimacy of the patriarchate of Ignatios. All this is apparent from Ioseph's literary production, which includes not only compositions in honour of his spiritual father and his companion Ioannes but also liturgical hymns celebrating some of the most outstanding iconodule saints.[173] The selection of heroes reveals two clear tendencies. One is the praise of contemporary saints with a very low profile in connection with images, such as Gregorios Dekapolites himself, the young Eudokimos,[174] the legendary St Andreas *en Krisei*[175] and the unknown hegoumenos of Pelekete named Hilarion, for whom neither a *vita* nor almost any other details survive.[176] The second tendency is a desire to praise figures close to the patriarchate, due either to their links to active resistance to Iconoclasm (e.g., Stephanos the Younger[177] or Ioannikios)[178] or to the special importance attached to them by various patriarchs, such as the veneration of the forty-two martyrs of Amorion promoted by the patriarch Methodios, in honour of whom Ioseph wrote two *kanones*.[179]

Ioseph's compositions gradually became more committed politically, and as a convinced Ignatian, he wrote a *kontakion* to commemorate the first anniversary of the death of the patriarch Ignatios,[180] together with a

---

[172] *PmbZ* # 3266 and # 22779; *PBE* I: Ioannes 224; Krausmüller 2007c: 355–57; Krausmüller 2019. See Section 3.2.1.
[173] The prolific work of Ioseph consists mainly of poetry in the form of hymns, see *PG* 105, 983–1426; Tomadakes 1971a; 1975; Armati 1986/1987.
[174] Tomadakes 1971a: 182, nr. 364; Theodorakopoulos 2004; Métivier 2012: 97.
[175] Tomadakes 1971a: 117, nr. 51; *Menaion* I: 444–51.
[176] Tomadakes 1971a: 152, nr. 219; *Menaion* IV: 198–203. On a possible attribution to Ioseph Stoudites, see Van de Vorst 1913a: 36. Hilarion of Pelekete apparently defended the veneration of icons at some time between the mid-eighth century and the beginning of the ninth. After his death, there was one miracle after another at his tomb, see *SynaxCP* 564,5–6 (27 March); 565,37 (27 March); 573,33 (30 March); *Menologion Basilii* 376A; *PmbZ* # 2587; *PBE* I: Hilarion 9.
[177] Tomadakes 1971a: 130, nr. 112; *Menaion* II: 307–15.
[178] Tomadakes 1971a: 123, nr. 79; *Menaion* II: 39–47.
[179] One is published in *Menaion* IV: 30–35, another in *AHG*, vol. VII: 99–107.
[180] Tomadakes 1971a: 204, nr. 2; Mioni 1948 doubts that Ioseph is the author, although his arguments are unconvincing.

kanon in his honour, in which he alluded to the plots of his opponents (verses 152–55), his usurpation (197–200), and his sufferings (115–19 and 143–46).[181] A similar intent can be seen in the poems Ioseph addressed to St Mokios[182] and St Menas,[183] whose cults were thriving at the time, thanks to the institutional support of the Emperor Basileios and the discovery of the relics of Menas, to the extent that the faithful kept vigil over Ignatios' body in this very church.[184]

Despite the traumatic changes ushered in by the appointment of the patriarch Photios after the death of Ignatios in 877, Ioseph Hymnographos continued to occupy his high position as the *skeuophylax* of Hagia Sophia, and during Photios' second mandate, he remained close to the patriarchal milieu.[185] Indeed, Theophanes, Ioseph's first hagiographer, exonerates Photios of any responsibility for the origin of the dispute with Ignatios, affirming that the sole party responsible for the scandal that shook the Church was the Caesar Bardas.[186] Theophanes also praises Photios when he describes his second patriarchate.[187] The *kanon* in which Ioseph extolled the placing of the garment of the Theotokos in the church of Blachernai thus makes sense.[188] This celebration on 2 July also commemorated the return to the church of the Virgin's garment, which had miraculously protected Constantinople from the Russian attack thanks to the procession organised by Photios.[189] In this piece by Ioseph, the Virgin is referred to as a περιτείχισμα (wall of circumvallation) for having acted as a protective wall and is praised for having saved the city. Two other hymns dedicated to the Virgin share the same imagery and praise her as the defender of the city.[190]

In the absence of any suffering or torture in defense of icons that might have allowed him to be presented as a confessor, Ioseph's hagiographers develop other characteristics to justify his holiness. Along with his ascetic

---

[181] Tomadakes 1971a: 119, nr. 60; ed. *AHG*, vol. II, 274–83, 436–37. The manuscript *Sinaiticus Gr.* 562, fol. 117–18, contains another unpublished hymn dedicated to Ignatios signed by a certain Theophanes, see *Tameion*, 64, nr. 124. This is perhaps the same disciple of Ioseph the Hymnographos who wrote his first *vita*.

[182] *Tameion*, 199, nr. 603.   [183] Tomadakes 1971a: 132, nr. 121; *Menaion* II: 443–48.

[184] *Vita of Ignatios* 76,3–10. On the church of St Menas, see Janin 1969: 333–35.

[185] On the relationship between Ioseph and Photios, see Tomadakes 1971a: 72–73.

[186] *Vita of Ioseph Hymnographos by Theophanes* 10,12–14.

[187] *Vita of Ioseph Hymnographos by Theophanes* 10,27–11,2.

[188] Tomadakes 1971a: 173–74, nr. 322; *Menaion* VI: 15–21.

[189] Vasiliev 1946; Wortley 1969/1970; Wortley 1977; Shoemaker 2008.

[190] Tomadakes 1971a: 186, nr. 385; *Menaion* VI: 552–59; *PG* 105, 1019–28 (the third of these *kanones*). For his part, Kazhdan 1996 considers that Ioseph could have been in Russia when the Russian attack occurred, hence his insistence on the protection of the Theotokos.

leanings, his two *vitae* stress his literary skills and his immense production of liturgical hymns, which led to him being known by the nickname Hymnographos.[191] His practice of praising saints of the Church is thus Ioseph's main asset for achieving holiness, as is also true of the two other most productive liturgical poets of Byzantine literature, Theophanes Graptos and Georgios of Nicomedia. The case of the latter is significant, for the *Synaxarion of Constantinople* only mentions him as having written *kanones*.[192] In the case of Ioseph, this is particularly relevant, since when he was cultivating this genre, he witnessed miraculous visions that confirmed him as a saint. After he founded the church dedicated jointly to the Apostle Bartholomew and Gregorios Dekapolites, for example, Ioseph wished to compose hymns in their honour but was unable to do so. After praying, he saw in a dream a man who took the Gospel, placed it on his chest and blessed him. From that moment on, he had a divine gift for writing liturgical poetry in praise of all manner of saints.[193]

(b) **The Dekapolitan Family Network**

The new cult of Gregorios Dekapolites set in motion by his disciples was established and recognised by the ecclesiastical institutions thanks to an extensive network of relatives and compatriots that had provided ample evidence of his piety and commitment to the defence of images throughout the previous generation. The new cult could be anchored in this iconodule substratum by means of a family with important ramifications capable of promoting it on all social levels. This is a well-known phenomenon during this period: the cult of St Eudokimos († 842), for instance, was promoted by his family, who took charge of transferring the young man's remains to Constantinople.[194] In addition to his uncle Symeon, the presence of other persons from the same region (the Dekapolis of Isauria)[195] as Gregorios is recorded and, more important, from his own

---

[191] *Vita of Ioseph Hymnographos by Theophanes* 1; *Vita of Ioseph Hymnographos by Ioannes Diakonos* 941A and 964C–65D.
[192] *SynaxCP* 356,20–22 (29 December): τῇ αὐτῇ ἡμέρᾳ μνήμη τοῦ ἐν ἁγίοις πατρὸς ἡμῶν Γεωργίου ἐπισκόπου Νικομηδείας τοῦ ποιητοῦ τῶν κανόνων.
[193] *Vita of Ioseph Hymnographos by Theophanes* 9–10; *Vita of Ioseph Hymnographos by Ioannes Diakonos* 964A–C.
[194] Costa-Louillet 1957: 783–88; Theodorakopoulos 2004; Métivier 2012. The case of Theodora of Thessaloniki (812–892) has also been studied, see Talbot 1996b; Kaplan 2013. On the Middle Byzantine phenomenon of family networks and their important impact on the strengthening of the aristocracy, cf. Gounaridis 2006; Flusin 2012; Settipani 2012; Varona Codeso and Prieto Domínguez 2013. See Chapter 4.
[195] On the Isaurian Dekapolis, see Hild and Hellenkemper 1990: 235–36. On Isauria in Roman and proto-Byzantine times, see Feld 2005.

small village, Eirenopolis. The small size of the place meant that it had limited, historical significance and little information has survived about it, making the mention of Eirenopolis all the more significant.

The first of these persons is Gregorios the *archimandrites* and hegoumenos of the monastery of Dalmatos in Constantinople.[196] He attended the Second Council of Nicaea (787), at which, under the presidency of the patriarch Tarasios, the veneration of icons was restored, and died in 806. Thanks to the *vita* of Hilarion of Dalmatos, we know that this Gregorios tonsured the young Hilarion in 788/789 and later consecrated him as a priest shortly before his own death.[197]

Gregorios had close links with his disciple (and probably nephew) Ioannes, who is known mainly for being the hegoumenos of Kathara.[198] The text of the *Synaxarion of Constantinople* (taken to be a summary of a lost *vita*) affirms that at the tender age of nine, Ioannes entered a monastery of Eirenopolis, where he was educated by Gregorios, who when the time came, took him to the Council of Nicaea and subsequently to Constantinople. The unusual name of Ioannes' mother, Gregoria,[199] makes us think that he and Gregorios the hegoumenos of Dalmatos were related on their mothers' side. Ioannes was born about 770, and once in Constantinople he was linked to the monastery of Dalmatos, as is natural, and to that of Stoudios, since he is mentioned in four letters of Theodoros Stoudites dated between 816 and 817.[200] Emperor Nikephoros I (802–811) consecrated him as the hegoumenos of the monastery of Kathara in Bithynia in 805, doubtless with the approval of Theodoros Stoudites, since during this period the centre belonged to the Stoudite congregation.[201] Perhaps Theodoros felt that Ioannes had betrayed his trust, since he mentioned him in one of his sermons among the iconodule hegoumenoi who accepted compromise solutions with the iconoclasts to prevent their monastery from being attacked.[202] During the reign of Leon V (813–820), Ioannes was persecuted, imprisoned and exiled. Michael II

---

[196] *PmbZ* # 2438; *PBE* I: Gregorios 165. On the monastery of Dalmatos, cf. Janin 1969: 82–84. On its founders, see Hatlie 2003.
[197] Matantseva 1993: 18–19; *SynaxCP* 731,47–34,60 (*BHG* 2177b); Kazhdan 1999: 341–42.
[198] *PmbZ* # 3139; *PBE* I: Ioannes 460; Costa-Louillet 1954/1955: 241–44; Stiernon 1970; Cheynet and Flusin 1990: 205–7.
[199] *SynaxCP* 631,41–34,38, here 631,43 (*BHG* 2184n).
[200] Theod. Stoud., *epist.* 267, 271, 272, 365. Ioannes of Kathara was, moreover, one of the signatories of the two missives sent to Pope Paschal I (*epist.* 271, 272) in favour of iconophilia. See Chapter 2.
[201] Stiernon 1970: 119–23; Speck 1978: 693, n. 111. On the monastery of Kathara, see Janin 1975: 158–60; Delouis 2005: 214–21.
[202] Theod. Stoud., *Parvae catecheseis* 92.

(820–829) allowed him to return, but the new religious policy of Theophilos had him confined to the island of Aphousia in the Sea of Marmara, where he died on 27 April, probably in the year 835.[203]

Although he has no apparent connections to Gregorios Dekapolites, we find another iconodule saint praised by the hagiography of the period, Prokopios Dekapolites.[204] The more we analyse Prokopios' *vita* and how it was produced, the more evident it becomes that he is another relative. According to the surviving hagiography,[205] Prokopios had a worldly education that reflected his inclination to arms, inherited from his father, and his love of God. When he decided to embrace asceticism, he took refuge in the mountains, where he encountered Basileios, an abbot who had fled from the prevailing iconoclasm and who acted as his teacher. This is corroborated by the *Synaxarion* and by the existence of two letters Basileios received from Theodoros Stoudites between 816 and 818, in which reference is made to Prokopios.[206] With Basileios, Prokopios suffered the iconoclast persecution of Leon V, and both men were beaten and imprisoned. Following the advice of his mentor, Prokopios shut himself away in an unnamed monastery. Three years later, he decided that cenobitic life was not in keeping with the Holy Scriptures, and in his fourth year at the monastery he accordingly asked the father superior about the truth of the Gospel. His fellow monks answered that no one could consistently follow the Word of God, which led Prokopios to abandon the monastery and retire to the forest, where he spent seven years. It was there that the gift of prophecy was bestowed upon him.

As more and more young men were joining him, he opened a monastery and tonsured and educated them. His anchoritic monasticism was so severe, that his monks were *monochitones* (μονοχίτωνες), having only one tunic. This was not enough for Prokopios, however, who decided to live as a hermit, appointed one of his monks abbot and departed to live in strict asceticism. He was finally arrested by imperial order, and after enduring prison, torture and exile, apparently died on 27 February in exile. For Efthymiadis, the editor of the *vita*, the text's internal chronology implies that Prokopios was an orthodox confessor under Theophilos, since he settled in the monastery where he spent four years after the Second Iconoclasm had already begun. To this figure must be added the seven

---

[203] *SynaxCP* 634,37. See Section 3.1.   [204] *PmbZ* # 6368.
[205] *Vita of Prokopios Dekapolites*; *SynaxCP* 491f., 493,11–26; Delehaye 1906.
[206] Theod. Stoud., *epist*. 317, in which he is not named, and Theod. Stoud., *epist*. 389,28–29 in which he is sent greetings (τὸν ἀδελφόν μου, τὸν κῦριν Προκόπιον, πλεῖστα προσειπέ). On this hegoumenos Basileios, see *PmbZ* # 924; *PBE* I: Basilios 130 and Prokopios 20.

years he spent in the forest before his arrest, which brings us to the year 826. For Senina, however, Prokopios' death must be dated in line with the epistles of Theodoros Stoudites, putting it in 818–820.[207] According to the *PmbZ*, Prokopios' arrest is related to the edict proclaimed by Theophilos in 833 that is often mentioned in the hagiographies.[208] The main dates of his biography would thus be: birth ca. 795, training with the hegoumenos Basileios ca. 815–818, monastic life 818–822, life as a hermit 823–830, foundation and management of his own monastery 830–833 and iconoclast persecution and death in exile post-842.

According to Efthymiadis, the editor of the *vita*, Prokopios Dekapolites is the monk praised together with the hegoumenos Basileios in the same entry of the *Synaxarion of Constantinople* for having been tortured with him.[209] In commemoration of this event, a certain Theophanes created two *kanones* honouring Prokopios and Basileios.[210] Although they have been attributed to Theophanes Graptos, the author may instead have been Ioseph's disciple, who later wrote his *vita*. The cult of Prokopios for its part developed to the point of having an independent hagiography (*BHG* 1583) and its own entry in the *Synaxarion* for 27 February.[211] This hagiography has another peculiarity: it represents the rewriting of three previous *vitae* of well-known saints, Theodoros Stoudites, Gregorios Dekapolites and Makarios of Pelekete. On the other hand, the lack of historical information regarding the iconoclastic persecution and the lack of originality present in Prokopios' *vita* have meant that this important link in the Dekapolites clan has up to now been neglected.

There can be no doubt that the hagiography in honour of Prokopios was deliberately written on the basis of previous ones. The prologue belongs to the *vita* B of Theodoros Stoudites produced by the monk Michael; chapter 4 is clearly based on ch. 3 of the *Vita of Gregorios Dekapolites*; and the following chapters appear to follow its example. The basic text for chs. 13–19 is the *vita* of Makarios of Pelekete.[212] This centonist practice of breaking down texts for use in new settings fits within the culture of the συλλογή described by Odorico[213] and is not uncommon in hagiography. It cannot be mere coincidence that the *vita* of the patrician and monk Niketas (who died in 836), which was written by an

---

[207] Senina 2015: 306–8.　[208] *PmbZ* # 6368.　[209] *SynaxCP* 493,11–27 (27 February).
[210] Eustratiadès 1936: 476, nr. 62–63; *PmbZ* # 8135.
[211] *SynaxCP* 491,32–92,36 (27 February); *SynaxCP* 489,51 (26 February).
[212] The correspondences have been pointed out by Efthymiadis in *Vita of Prokopios Dekapolites*, pp. 310–12.
[213] Odorico 1990; 2011.

anonymous author about two generations later, is also based on the *Vita of Gregorios Dekapolites*. Indeed, the surviving fragment copies several passages from the hagiography of the Dekapolites, three of them of considerable length.[214] Unfortunately, the incompleteness of the eulogy of Niketas precludes in-depth study of the relationship between the resultant *vita* and its models and of the meaning of this intertextual dialogue.

According to the *vita* of Prokopios, his biography clearly ran parallel to that of Gregorios in numerous aspects, despite the *loci communes*: both men were from the Dekapolis and from wealthy families; had a good education; combined living as a hermit and monasticism; fled their homes to devote themselves to God; spent years in a monastery, which they left after confronting their hegoumenos owing to (a lack of) discipline; lived some time alone; got the gift of prophecy from the Lord; were strict ascetics and founded their own monastery to organise their many followers. This is when the life of Prokopios diverges from that of Gregorios, as he is persecuted and exiled for his iconodule ideas. To reflect this aspect of his subject's story, the hagiographer used the account of Makarios of Pelekete, an iconodule hero who stands out both as a founder and hegoumenos and for his confrontation with the iconoclast leaders.[215] Finally, the hagiographer began the work by copying the prologue of *vita* B *of Theodoros Stoudites*, where he merely changed the name of the protagonist.[216]

The rewriting of these materials indicates that the author was a monk, probably a copyist with access to them, who wished to extol the memory of Prokopios for reasons unknown to us. Was Prokopios perhaps his teacher? Were they compatriots? Or did they share blood ties? In any case, we should not be surprised by the *vitae* the author selected. The choice of the *Vita of Gregorios Dekapolites* is due to the saints' common origin, and the choice of the other two must reflect the accessibility of these texts rather than their dissemination, since in contrast to the *Vita of Gregorios*

---

[214] *Vita of Niketas the patrician* 341, ch. 20 (= *Vita of Gregorios Dekapolites* 69, 12–27 (Dvornik)); *Vita of Niketas* 343, ch. 21 (= *Vita of Gregorios Dek.* 70, 3–4 (Dvornik)); *Vita of Niketas* 343, ch. 22 (= *Vita of Gregorios Dek.* 70, 9–12 (Dvornik)); *Vita of Niketas* 349, ch. 33 (= *Vita of Gregorios Dek.* 74, 6–15 (Dvornik)); *Vita of Niketas* 349–51, ch. 34 (= *Vita of Gregorios Dek.* 75, 2–8 (Dvornik)), see Ševčenko 1977a: 117, n. 26a.

[215] *Vita of Makarios of Pelekete*; *SynaxCP* 577–80; Van de Vorst 1913b. On the monastery of Pelekete in Bithynia, see Mango and Ševčenko 1973: 242–48; Janin 1975: 170–72; Ruggieri 1991: 224. See Section 1.3.3.

[216] *Vita* B *of Theodoros Stoudites* postdates 868, as it refers to Nikolaos Stoudites as μακαρίτης 'blessed' (296C) and mentions Gregorios of Syracuse (312D), who died after 861. We do not know its exact date, but in any case, it dates from the ninth century. See Section 1.2.2. For the successive rewritings of the hagiography of Theodoros, see Delouis 2011: 106–8.

Dekapolites, which we assume was widely distributed, judging by the fact that over thirty manuscripts survive, the *Vita of Makarios of Pelekete* appears only in *Parisinus Gr.* 548 (f. 136–54v). We can only assume that the author had access to it in the monastery of Pelekete itself. Given the links of several members of the Dekapolites family with the Stoudite circle, and, in particular, with its leader Theodoros (with whose blessing Gregorios was the hegoumenos of Dalmatos, and Ioannes that of Kathara), it is logical that our hagiographer was sent to Pelekete through the mediation of the Stoudite abbot. The relationship between the monastery of Pelekete and the network administered from Stoudios is difficult to pinpoint. But there can be no doubt that the former had fallen under the influence of the latter, given the epistolary correspondence between both hegoumenoi,[217] the reproduction of the Stoudite organisational system by several monasteries with common regulations (*typoi*)[218] and the fact that Makarios of Pelekete joined other pro-Stoudite leaders in signing the missive addressed to Pope Paschal I.[219]

But who is the protagonist of the *vita*? The vague portrait painted by the surviving texts tells us little about Prokopios Dekapolites. It is recorded, however, that he had links with the Stoudite circles through the monastery of Pelekete (as his *vita* proves) and that he originated from Dekapolis, as the title of the work indicates: Βίος καὶ πολιτεία τοῦ ὁσίου πατρὸς ἡμῶν Προκοπίου τοῦ Δεκαπολίτου. In contrast to other saints of the period, and even of the Dekapolitan milieu, the saint is not identified by the monastery where he was hegoumenos, as is the case of Hilarion of Dalmatos and Ioannes of Kathara. This way of identifying him is due to a conscious analogy that refers to the example of Gregorios Dekapolites: Βίος καὶ θαύματα τοῦ ὁσίου πατρὸς ἡμῶν Γρηγορίου τοῦ Δεκαπολίτου. We know that Gregorios never held any position in the Dekapolis area; he simply originated there. Nor does the strong inspiration the anonymous hagiographer found in the *Vita Gregorii Decapolitae* by Ignatios Diakonos seem fortuitous. Indeed, Ignatios undertook to praise his hero's uncle, the *archimandrites* Symeon, and his full brother (whose name is not recorded) along with his hero. Two full chapters are devoted to this pious individual: the first relates that when Gregorios was secluded in a cave and wished to

---

[217] Theod. Stoud., *epist.* 159, 230, 294, 362, 371. See Pratsch 1998: 238–41. See Section 1.3.3.
[218] *Vita of Makarios of Pelekete* 156,23–25: Καὶ τὸ μὲν ἔργον τέλος εἶχε τῶν ἑπομένων μοναζόντων, αὐτὸς δὲ τῆς ἐφέσεως ἐπιτυχών **τοὺς πάλαι τύπους τῆς μονῆς** ἐν τούτοις ἐνεούργει, ἐπίτασιν μᾶλλον ἢ ὕφεσιν τούτοις ἐπιτιθείς.
[219] They were the hegoumenoi of Pikridion, Paulopetrion, Agrou, Dalmatos and Kathara, see Theod. Stoud., *epist.* 267,30–31. See Chapter 2.

see his brother, a monk diligent in his ministries, he sent him a messenger. In his desire to practice asceticism, however, Gregorios' brother had changed his whereabouts, and the envoy failed to find him.[220] A later chapter narrates the emotional encounter between the two men.[221]

Although this is not made clear, everything points to the brother being no other than Prokopios Dekapolites. Moreover, the internal chronologies of both *vitae* place the encounter at the beginning of Gregorios' life as a hermit and at the end of that of Prokopios, shortly before the latter founded his own monastery. It is reasonable to suppose that the younger man sought the advice and greater experience of his elder brother in the faith and in monastic administration. Finally, the preservation of some of the relics of the martyr St Prokopios in a chapel of the church of St Menas, together with those of Gregorios Dekapolites, must have led to a 'devotional symbiosis' based on the fact that Prokopios the confessor and Gregorios were brothers.[222] This is not an isolated case. Although the phenomenon of the 'devotional symbiosis' during the Middle Byzantine era has not been studied in depth, we find clear examples from this period, such as the cult of St Elias the Younger based on that of the prophet Elijah and the veneration of Prince Konstantinos coinciding with the commemoration of Konstantinos I the Great.[223]

One more relative is mentioned in the hagiography of Gregorios Dekapolites: a brother of his mother Maria,[224] also a monk, who lived in a monastery near Eirenopolis at the time when Gregorios took monastic vows in 815.[225] This was thus a blood uncle and brother of the *archimandrites* Symeon. To this well-documented immediate family can be added the members of the Dekapolitan network who, although they hailed from Eirenopolis, made their fortune in Constantinople and in the milieu of Stoudios after participating in the Second Council of Nicaea. The hegoumenos Ioannes of Kathara belongs to the same generation as Symeon and Maria. Judging by his mother's name (Gregoria), he was likely related to the lineage of Gregorios Dekapolites. All these details make sense if we take him to be a brother of Symeon, Maria and the unnamed monk of Eirenopolis, and as such a nephew of the famous Gregorios of Dalmatos (see Figure 3.1), since this family connection would explain the high

---

[220] *Vita of Gregorios Dekapolites* 11,2–6. [221] *Vita of Gregorios Dekapolites* 13,1–10.
[222] On the preservation of the martyr Prokopios' relics in St Menas, see Janin 1969: 443–44.
[223] For this phenomenon see Chapters 4 and 6–7.
[224] On Maria, see *PmbZ* # 4728; *PBE* I: Maria 7. As for her husband, Gregorios' father, see *PmbZ* # 6638; *PBE* I: Sergios 58.
[225] *Vita of Gregorios Dekapolites* 4,7–9.

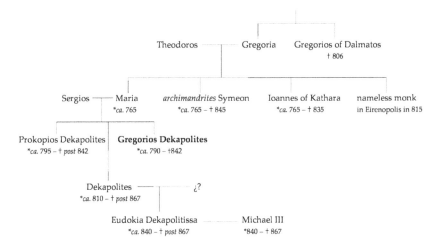

Figure 3.1 Family tree of the Dekapolitan network (*birth, †death)

position Symeon attained. After the presence at Nicaea of his uncle Gregorios and his considerable social progress as a consequence of being appointed hegoumenos of Dalmatos, he must have secured the necessary support for his nephews to achieve prominence in monastic affairs: Symeon became *archimandrites* of the Dekapolis, while Ioannes attained the hegoumenate of Kathara. This family tie also explains Gregorios Dekapolites' travels in the Prokonnesos region.[226] This was an unusual stopover to make on the way to Constantinople, but at the same time the island was frequently used as a place of exile for opponents of the imperial power. Ioannes of Kathara was detained there by orders of Theophilos, and Gregorios Dekapolites must have travelled there to visit his uncle.

When, years later, the Lord called his servant Gregorios Dekapolites to his bosom, the family network woven by his uncles had considerable support and enough favours to call in to allow the cult of the last saint of the family to be consolidated. With the Stoudite sector sufficiently involved through Gregorios of Dalmatos and Ioannes of Kathara, the *archimandrites* Symeon took advantage of his links with Methodios to have the budding patriarch not only approve the emergence of this cult, but even promote it, by involving as hagiographer the recognised man of

---

[226] *Vita of Gregorios Dekapolites* 19,1–13.

letters Ignatios Diakonos, who would shortly afterwards be commissioned to write the *vitae* of the patriarchs Nikephoros and Tarasios. Methodios' support for this family originating from Asia Minor earned him numerous sympathisers at the head of the patriarchate. At the same time, he limited the potential influence of the Stoudite sector by strengthening other independent groups that would end up supporting his consecration, such as the ones around Ioannikios, Symeon the Stylite and Hilarion of Dalmatos (probably the leader of the Dekapolitan faction). For their part, the disciples of Gregorios Dekapolites who had arrived from Thessaloniki assured themselves a privileged position in the new order, as well as guaranteeing that no one would ask awkward questions about their non-iconodule past. This strategy was successful for both parties: the ascetic Ioannes, for example, a faithful follower of Gregorios Dekapolites who never defended images, was well received in Constantinople, where he was allowed to continue his ascetic life and attained the privilege of being buried below his holy master. Methodios in turn multiplied the non-Stoudite centres of power and weakened the pressure the monastery of Stoudios might exert. The subsequent appearance of a hagiography of Prokopios Dekapolites must be understood in a similar context.

This situation continued during the first generation after the Triumph of Orthodoxy. Ioseph Hymnographos came to run his own monastery and to be appointed the *skeuophylax* of Hagia Sophia. We know little of the secular relatives of the Dekapolites family in a wider sense.[227] But no doubt they too were able to take advantage of the opportunities offered to them in the capital due to the fact that their relatives had previously attained prominent positions in the monastic hierarchy and now in important parts of the *Synaxarion*. We know of a descendant who settled in Constantinople and made his fortune. The sources record only his name (Dekapolites),[228] but his chronology suggests that he may have been a nephew of the renowned Gregorios Dekapolites. It is impossible to guess the degree of kinship (whether they were close or second-degree relatives, etc.). In any case, however, the vindication of their common origin by the members of this clan led to the consolidation of their family name. As the

---

[227] We should not count among them the holder of the seal published by Gray Birch 1898: nr. 17619. Although the inscription reads: Μιχαὴλ διοικητῇ Δεκαπόλεως, the person concerned is not from Dekapolis but an official who worked there. On the duties of the *dioiketes*, a provincial administrator or tax collector, see *ODB*, s.v. 'Dioiketes'. See also *PmbZ* # 5144; Winkelmann 1985: 135. For the few surviving seals from this province (among them two from a subsequent *dioiketes*), see McGeer et al. 1996: 19.

[228] *PmbZ* # 1274; *PBE* I: Dekapolites 1.

new Byzantine aristocracy gained importance, the use of surnames became more common.[229] The importance of the surname 'Dekapolites' and the high social standing of its members continue to be apparent in the mid-tenth century, in the person of Theodoros Dekapolites, a patrician and quaestor under Konstantinos VII (913–959) and a *magistros* in the time of Romanos II (959–963). He was also a jurist of note in Romanos' court who wrote several new ordinances or 'novels' related to agrarian law,[230] and his epitaph – he died after 961 – was written by the recognised poet Ioannes Geometres.[231]

By any reckoning, the member of the family who rose the highest in the imperial hierarchy was Eudokia Dekapolitissa, who is as obscure as her father.[232] Mentioned only in the chronicle of Symeon Logothetes, Eudokia was chosen by Empress Theodora and her counsellor Theoktistos to marry the young Emperor Michael III in 855. According to Symeon Logothetes, she was considered the ideal candidate to keep the allegedly dissipated heir away from his lover Eudokia Ingerina.[233] The wedding ceremony was performed in the church of St Stephen within the Palace of Daphne, from where the newly-weds travelled to the Magnaura. The bride was evidently of a known status and must have belonged to one of the best families of Constantinople with a presence at the court. We know virtually nothing about her, but we can assume that Theodora's choice was strengthened by the candidate's membership in a family known for piety and Orthodoxy (see Figure 3.1). This iconophile lineage was valued highly by Empress Theodora, who sought a young woman with deeply traditional values capable of seducing her dissolute son Michael with her discretion and prudence in keeping him away from undesirable company. Theodora thus achieved another important objective: being related to a family with impeccable religious credentials, which, because it lacked an iconoclast past, would strengthen the position of the Amorian dynasty as a bastion of Orthodoxy. The system was not a new one: some years previously, in 788, Empress Eirene chose as a wife for her son Konstantinos VI the young Maria of Amnia from Paphlagonia, whose

---

[229] On this phenomenon which began in the ninth century, cf. Patlagean 1984a; Kazhdan 1997; Cheynet 2006.
[230] Lemerle 1979: 98–100 and 116–26; Schmink 2005: 280–83; *PmbZ* # 27708; *ODB* III, p. 2043, s.v. 'Theodore of Dekapolis'.
[231] Ioannes Geometres, *poems*, pp. 317–23. It is likely that the owner of the seal nr. 121 published by McGeer et al. 1996: 153 belonged to this very family. The same applies to the two seals included by Seibt 2002: 130.
[232] For Eudokia, see *PmbZ* # 1631; *PBE* I: Eudokia 3. We do not know the name of his father; the sources only refer to him as Dekapolites.
[233] Symeon Logothetes 234, ch. 131,6; Ludwig 1997: 136–37.

main virtue was that she was a granddaughter of St Philaretos the Merciful, a rich man remembered for his works of charity in two versions of his *vita* (*BHG* 1511z; 1512).[234]

The pomp of the royal wedding between Michael III and Eudokia Dekapolitissa in the year 855 may well have coincided with the transfer of the relics of Gregorios Dekapolites and with the founding of a monastic complex in his honour.[235] The composition of a liturgical *kanon* by Ioseph Hymnographos[236] helped enhance a ceremony that sought not only to vindicate the saint's memory but also to emphasise the spiritual lineage of the future empress. This *kanon* stands out both for the abundance of biographical detail (taken over from the *vita* written by Ignatios Diakonos) it provides about the saint and for direct references to Gregorios in the prayers of the *theotokia* (verses 624–27). Nonetheless, the marital life of Eudokia Dekapolitissa was not easy, and her virtue was never attractive to Michael, who continued to prefer the company of Eudokia Ingerina. Far from having children with his legitimate wife, Michael frequented his former lover (now the legitimate wife of his favourite Basileios) to such an extent that Michael rather than Basileios might well have been the father of Eudokia Ingerina's children.[237] After a life as an *augusta* ignored by her husband, Eudokia Dekapolitissa's status as a widow beginning in 867 did not change her situation; the new Byzantine Emperor Basileios I ordered her to return to her father's house.[238]

3.3 Links between the Literary Circle of Gregorios Dekapolites and Other Iconodule Milieux

The process of the promotion of the cult of Gregorios Dekapolites occurs within a well-defined socio-ecclesiastical group, which, after the defeat of

---

[234] On Maria of Amnia, see *PmbZ* # 4727; *PBE* I: Maria 2. On Philaretos the Merciful, see *PmbZ* # 6136; *PBE* I: Philaretos 1. On his cult, see *SynaxCP* 269,28–70,33; 269/270,43–45 (1 December); 271/272,40–43 (2 December). For his *vita*, see Kazhdan and Sherry 1996. See Chapter 4.
[235] On this monastery of St John Chrysostom, see Janin 1969: 271–72; Stiernon 1973: 257–60. On the transfer of Gregorios' relics, see *Vita of Ioseph Hymnographos by Theophanes* 9; *Vita of Ioseph Hymnographos by Ioannes Diakonos* 961C–D.
[236] *AHG*, vol. III, 478–88, its title is 'In sanctum Gregorium Decapolitam' and presents the achrostidis: Λόγοις σε θείοις, παμμάκαρ, μέλπω, πάτερ· ὁ Ἰωσήφ. Verses 215–20 indicate that it was written to celebrate the transfer of his relics: Ὦ θαῦμα! Πῶς πηγάζει / εὐωδίας μύρον τὰ σὰ / ὀστέα φανεροῦντά σε Θεοῦ / εὐωδίαν ἀληθῆ / γεγενημένον, ἱερὲ / πάτερ Γρηγόριε! On the remainder of the liturgical poems produced by Ioseph Hymnographos in memory of Gregorios Dekapolites, see Section 3.2.2.a.
[237] On Eudokia Ingerina, see *PmbZ* # 1632 and 21754; *PBE* I: Eudokia 2. There is no agreement on the paternity of Leon VI: for Kislinger 1983, he is a son of Basileios I. For other scholars, he is the son of Michael III, see Mango 1973. Cf. also Karlin-Hayter 1991a; Tougher 1997: 42–67.
[238] Symeon Logothetes 252,14–16.

heresy, consisted of some of the iconodule bastions that, thanks to their contacts at the court and their political acumen, finally achieved the patriarchate and the Triumph of Orthodoxy. The Dekapolitan network clearly managed to join the right faction, earning it the protection of the future patriarch Methodios and of one of the most influential holy men in public life, Ioannikios. If we consider the complex network of interests among these persons, we can appreciate the links they shared, in particular, with the Methodian milieu and subsequently with the Ignatian milieu: rejection of iconoclastic imposition by imperial power, fierce opposition to the Stoudite movement, a vindication of anchoritic spirituality, strong political and religious ambition, etc. Clear evidence of their close collaboration is provided by the creation of a literary circle reflecting the existing political circle, which left a common imprint on the works produced by or for these persons, especially in their hagiographies.

We know that the *Vita Gregorii Decapolitae* was written by Ignatios Diakonos,[239] who chose to follow a non-iconodule model. This decision reflected not only the peculiarities of the saint, already discussed above, but also a tendency he knew well and aspired to emulate: the hagiographical texts written by Methodios in honour of Theophanes the Confessor and Nicholas of Myra paid no attention to the matter of images,[240] and the *Vita of Ioannikios* likewise does not portray its hero confronting the iconoclasts (with whom he had a good relationship) or suffering for defending Orthodoxy.[241] Moreover, many coincidences among these texts show that Ignatios Diakonos, before he came under the protection of the patriarch, got support and inspiration from both the hagiographies of Methodios and oral accounts that circulated regarding the holiness of Ioannikios, which shortly afterwards would be captured in a hagiography.

After moving to Constantinople from Sicily, Methodios entered the monastery of Chenolakkos[242] in Bithynia at the request of Euthymios of Sardis. There he studied, copied manuscripts and made a mark as a precious and affected writer. No doubt he also came to sympathise with a monasticism of the hermit type, which caused a confrontation with the Stoudite group long before conflict arose due to the choice of the patriarch

---

[239] On Ignatios Diakonos, see *PmbZ* # 2665. See Chapter 2.
[240] Ševčenko 1977a: 125–26; Kazhdan 1999: 367–79. Perhaps his situation at the court while writing it dissuaded him from treating controversial themes? See Yannopoulos 2007b.
[241] Two almost contemporary *vitae* of Ioannikios survive, one signed by the monk Sabas (see Section 7.1.1) and another by Petros (see Section 2.2.1). Cf. also Mango 1983; Kazhdan 1999: 327–40. On the relationship between Ioannikios and the iconoclasts, see Ringrose 1979: 146–48.
[242] *Vita of Methodios* 1245. See Janin 1975: 189–90; Ruggieri 1991: 211–12.

who restored images. Theodoros Stoudites had pronounced anchoritism and the miracles linked to it a form of religious life inferior to cenobitic monasticism, since the latter allowed the articulation of a joint effort subordinate to strong leadership in defence of Orthodoxy. His words in one of his *Parvae catecheseis* (821–826) question the work of Ioannikios in particular:

> Let Father Ioannikios and those of his class keep the desert and the mountain. You shall love obedience and the cell. He has not been persecuted, but you were persecuted by the law. He has not been imprisoned, but you were imprisoned by the Lord. He has not been beaten, but you were beaten by Christ. My lot was so much better than theirs![243]

Likewise, the hagiography (*Laudatio*) Theodoros Stoudites composed in honour of his uncle Platon of Sakkoudion († 814) presents his model of ideal holiness: the monk who lives in a community, cultivates humility and obedience, carries out the duties of hegoumenos satisfactorily and publicly professes his faith and is punished and exiled for doing so.[244]

However, the dialectic between the hermit and the cenobitic models is not that easy: Platon lived for some time as a *reclusus* inside the monastery, following an ancient habit attested, for instance, in the Palestinian desert at the time of Dorotheos of Gaza, whose *Doctrinae* were widely read at Stoudios. The model of Platon of Sakkoudion can be extrapolated to feminine holiness, as can be seen from the case of his mother Theoktiste († ca. 798), who was praised for abandoning her family and worldly life in favour of the convent and the defence of her faith. She did not suffer for defending images, but she did for confronting Konstantinos VI in the Moechian controversy. Together with other relatives, Theodoros' mother was imprisoned for three days.[245] In contrast to Stoudite austerity,[246] in his works, Methodios insists on his heroes' miracle-working to lay the foundations of a very different type of hagiography. A good example is the

---

[243] Theod. Stoud., *Parvae catecheseis* 38 (ed. Auvray, p. 141,45–50): Ἐχέτω οὖν ὁ πατὴρ Ἰωαννίκιος σὺν τοῖς ὁμοταγέσι τὴν ἐρημίαν καὶ τὴν ὀρεινήν· σὺ στέργε τὴν ὑποταγὴν καὶ τὴν ξενίαν· ἐκεῖνος ἐν τῷ νῦν καιρῷ οὐ δεδίωκται, σὺ δὲ δεδιωγμένος ἕνεκεν δικαιοσύνης· ἐκεῖνος οὐ πεφυλάκισται, σὺ δὲ ἐφυλακίσθης διὰ Κύριον· ἐκεῖνος οὐ τέτυπται, σὺ δὲ ἐτύφθης διὰ Χριστόν. Πόσῳ ταῦτα ἐκείνων βελτιώτερα! See Kazhdan 1985; Flusin 1993: 37–41.

[244] *ODB* III, 1684; Costa-Louillet 1954/1955: 230–40; Leroy 1958a; 2002. On the Stoudite model incarnate in Platon, see Van de Vorst 1914; Leroy 1958b: 329–58; see Section 1.1.2.

[245] Theod. Stoud., *Laudatio of Theoktiste* 896C–97A; Von Dobschütz 1909a: 60; Efthymiadis and Featherstone 2007. On Theoktiste, see *PmbZ* # 8023; *PBE* I: Theoktiste 3. For the feminine religious ideal established by Theodoros, see Guillard 1982; Abrahamse 1985: 53–54; Hatlie 1996a; Constantinou 2005. Cf. Connor 2004: 166–81; Delierneux 2014.

[246] Von Dobschütz 1909a; Delouis 2005: 308–15.

comparison between the *vita* of Theophanes the Confessor written by Methodios between 823 and 832 (*BHG* 1787z) and the panegyric Theodoros Stoudites devoted to him (*BHG* 1792b).[247]

Both texts were apparently composed independently, which means that we can observe the different concepts of holiness in them: while Theodoros Stoudites repeatedly insists on the sufferings of Theophanes and his attitude towards power (Moechian and iconoclast controversies), Methodios stressed his chaste marriage to his wife Megalo, his separation so that he could devote himself to God and the founding of the monastery of Megas Agros. For Theodoros Stoudites, Theophanes' condition as confessor is the most noteworthy element, since only this allows miracles to be performed – Καὶ τίς ἡ ἐξομολόγησις; Ἡ τῶν θαυμάτων ποίησις. 'What is confession? The performance of miracles.'[248] – while for the future patriarch, this ability is independent and a true sign of holiness. Theodoros therefore reduces the miracles performed by Theophanes to the odd healing and curing of those possessed by the Devil (ch. 17) and voluntarily limits himself to the posthumous miracles of Hiereia, as if the saint got his powers after his life devoted to confession was over.[249]

Methodios, on the other hand, details many more miraculous episodes in varied contexts, always far from the saint's sufferings[250] and includes the characterisation of a hermit as holy due to his gift of prophecy. The man in question is Gregorios of Sigriane,[251] a monk established in Bithynia who prophesied to Theophanes that the Emperor Leon IV and his father-in-law Leon would both die within three years. He also predicted that Theophanes himself would die a martyr's death.[252] The characterisation of this secondary personage[253] embodies all the clichés of the visionary saints praised by Middle Byzantine hagiography immediately afterwards.[254] Moreover, Gregorios is called ὁ διορατικώτατος,[255] and his words are treated as a true prophecy: ἡ προφητεία τοῦ γέροντος.[256] This

---

[247] Pargoire 1902. [248] Theod. Stoud., *Vita of Theophanes the Confessor* 17.
[249] Cf. Method., *Vita of Theophanes the Confessor* 37,20–38,18.
[250] He feeds the hungry: ch. 31, p. 20,6–15. He frees fifty-three people from a maritime danger: ch. 39, p. 25,6–15. He heals a man possessed by demons: ch. 33, pp. 21,7–22,10. He makes frogs croak or fall silent at will: ch. 34, p. 22,19–20. His posthumous miracles include the elimination of a plague affecting the livestock of Samothrace: ch. 54, p. 35,20–29. The elimination of a plague of locusts: ch. 60, p. 39,9–17. The elimination of a plague of worms: ch. 61, p. 39,18–28. The curing of a nun: ch. 62, pp. 39,29–40,27. Other healing episodes: ch. 59, pp. 38,28–39,8.
[251] *PmbZ* # 2406. [252] Method., *Vita of Theophanes the Confessor* 16, pp. 11,11–12,5.
[253] Method., *Vita of Theophanes the Confessor* 16, p. 11,15–18.
[254] Pratsch 2005: 290–97; Timotin 2010: 41–64.
[255] Method., *Vita of Theophanes the Confessor* 16, p. 11,22.
[256] Method., *Vita of Theophanes the Confessor* 16, pp. 12,4 and 13,28.

gift of clairvoyance also appears among the abilities of Theophanes described by Methodios, to the extent that Theophanes could predict where money would be found[257] or guess what guests would require.[258] For the patriarch, the qualities of the visionary are the result of his holiness and a habitual characteristic of those who support him, as, for example, Hilarion of Dalmatos, whom Methodios describes in his will as 'Hilarion, reputed for his visions'.[259] Further on in the account, moreover, since the saint is aware of God's will, he goes so far as to predict his own exile[260] and specify the time of his own death.[261]

These different paradigms of holiness lead to different ways of revealing God's benevolence to the saint. Theodoros Stoudites does not reject clairvoyance as an expression of holiness, but he plays down its importance and greatly restricts its presence in his hagiographical texts. Indeed, in his *enkomion* of Platon of Sakkoudion, he mentions Platon's ability to predict the future in passing, without relating any specific example.[262] Quite the opposite occurs in the *vitae* written by Methodios, who – due to his personal tastes and supposed clairvoyant abilities[263] – delights in the prophetic gifts of his protagonists. This is also the case in the account of Euthymios of Sardis (dated 832), in which Methodios devotes an entire chapter to the successive pamphlets that announced the death of the Emperors Leon V, Michael II and Theophilos,[264] repeating the prophecy in which the saint predicted his own death[265] and detailing the theology of prediction by analysing the prophet's visions of God.[266] At the same time as its concept of holiness differs, the *vita* of Euthymios of Sardis also reveals a deliberate opposition to the Stoudios leader, who is not mentioned at all, despite his important work in defence of images, while an unusual amount of attention is paid to his brother Ioseph of Thessaloniki, who is praised as a collaborator of Euthymios and mentioned three times.[267] The reason for this should perhaps be sought in the questioning to which Ioseph subjected his brother Theodoros, due to his extremism in the 'Ioseph affair'.

---

[257] Method., *Vita of Theophanes the Confessor* 32, pp. 20,24–21,6.
[258] Method., *Vita of Theophanes the Confessor* 38, p. 24,24–32.
[259] Darrouzès 1966: 296; *Synodikon of Orthodoxy* 123. The explanation can be found in his *vita* (still unpublished), which narrates how the Virgin appears to him, see Matantseva 1993: 29.
[260] Method., *Vita of Theophanes the Confessor* 48, p. 31,8–16.
[261] Method., *Vita of Theophanes the Confessor* 55, p. 36,3–8.
[262] Theod. Stoud., *Laudatio of Platon* 816B: Τίς γὰρ ἐκείνου τὸ μέλλον προβλέψαι στοχαστικώτερος;
[263] Treadgold 2004. This interest in the hereafter explains that some manuscripts attribute the edifying tale of the devil and hell (*BHG* 635x) to Methodios, see *DS* X, 1108.
[264] *Vita of Euthymios of Sardis* 13,249–72.   [265] *Vita of Euthymios of Sardis* 20, 404–8.
[266] *Vita of Euthymios of Sardis* 37, 772–89.
[267] *Vita of Euthymios of Sardis* 12, 243–47; 13,270–72; 15,300–304. Cf. Gouillard 1987: 8, n. 47.

After the synod of 809 restored Ioseph of Kathara, Theodoros condemned it as a new heresy.[268]

The type of the prophet-saint with a strong inclination towards life as a hermit is precisely that chosen by Ignatios Diakonos, a future member of the Methodian circle, to praise Gregorios Dekapolites. Emphasis is given to Gregorios' clairvoyance, which allows him to aid an impoverished woman in Thessaloniki (*Vita of Gregorios Dekapolites* 37), to intercede for a man condemned to death and obtain his freedom (ch. 48), to prophecy what will happen during the journey of the monk Anastasios (ch. 52) and to attend the gathering of disciples who awaited him in Constantinople (ch. 53). He is also capable of predicting the death of a stylite (ch. 43), an abbot (ch. 44) and various youths (chs. 45, 50 and 51). Moreover, the characteristics with which Methodios depicts Gregorios of Sigriane, an important secondary personage of his *vita* of Theophanes, appear again in the portrait painted by Ignatios of the *archimandrites* Symeon (who plays a similar prophetic role in the account, by announcing his future to the protagonist) as a true visionary capable of guiding the young saint. For Methodios, this is the main trait of Gregorios of Sigriane, and he does not hesitate to describe him as ὁ διορατικώτατος.[269] Ignatios Diakonos takes over this distinctive element to portray Symeon.[270] He also mirrors the evolution of the protagonist, who develops the gift of prophecy himself.[271] Ignatios Diakonos therefore decides of his own accord to follow the path of Methodios and uses the same criteria that the future patriarch treats as identifying a man as holy.

In addition to using the hagiographical models already established by Methodios as foundations, Ignatios Diakonos builds the holiness of Gregorios Dekapolites on the oral accounts circulating in 843 regarding two important monks, Ioannikios and Methodios himself. One sign of the holiness of the future patriarch was his sexual abstinence, which was ratified by the divine necrosis of his genitals, since (according to his own testimony) during his stay in Rome, St Peter helped him free himself from his carnal passions.[272] To judge by the importance Methodios attached to

---

[268] Gill 1968: 64–65. [269] Method., *Vita of Theophanes the Confessor* 16, p. 11,22.
[270] *Vita of Gregorios Dekapolites* 15,19–21: Ὡς οὖν δυναμένῳ ταῦτα καὶ κρίνειν καὶ διακρίνειν καλῶς **τῇ ἄνωθεν ἐλλαμπούσῃ σοι διορατικῇ χάριτι** πεφανέρωκα γνῶναι παρὰ σοῦ ἠλπικὼς τὸ τῆς ὄψεως σαφές.
[271] *Vita of Gregorios Dekapolites* 47,7–9: Ὁ δὲ διορατικῷ βλέμματι τὰ μέλλοντα τούτοις προθεώμενος; Ibid., 45,6: Ὁ δὲ τῷ λόγῳ μεστὸς γεγονὼς ἐκπλήξεως τὴν διορατικὴν τοῦ πατρὸς ἐπιστασίαν εἶχεν ἐν θαύματι.
[272] Theoph. Cont. IV, 10,19–39; Genesios 59,49–71; Ps-Symeon 652,14–21. On the figure of the holy eunuch in Byzantium, see Ringrose 1999; Tougher 2004.

chastity and virginity, as is made clear in his *enkomion of St Agatha* and his *Scholia on the Acta of St Marina*, written during his stay in Rome (ca. 815–821),[273] he must have thought his sexual impotence an advantage that brought him closer to God. What is more, this characteristic allowed him to expose the false accusation of fornication promoted by his enemies that he had to face shortly after his appointment as patriarch.[274] According to the historiographical sources, his accusers bribed the mother of Metrophanes, bishop of Smyrna in 857, to say that Methodios was the father of her son. The inclusion by Ignatios of a similar anecdote in the *Vita of Gregorios Dekapolites*, in which a figure resembling the mother of Gregorios Dekapolites appears to him to cut him near his navel to end his suffering,[275] thus constitutes a defence of the treatment as a gift from God[276] and brings his vision of a holy man in line with that of Methodios. Despite the hagiographical record in the story of Konon and the *Vita of Symeon the Fool*, the clearest and most immediate parallel to the action of a third party on a saint's genitals by God's will is the situation of Methodios.[277]

These literary connections with the circle that formed around the Dekapolites were not limited to Methodios and Ignatios Diakonos, even if they are particularly visible in their case, for instance, when the two writers extol the memory of Ioannikios, a close collaborator of Methodios in his rise to the patriarchate. Among the concerns they share is a clear interest in the gift of prophecy their hero enjoyed: Ioannikios is 'the prophet of our generation',[278] whom Emperors Staurakios and Leon V consult about the future[279] and is considered διορατικός or 'clairvoyant' following the path marked by Methodios.[280] In both texts, the *vita* of Gregorios Dekapolites and that of Ioannikios, the announcements of a forthcoming death is accompanied by a change in attitude by the recipient of the prophecy, who decides to distribute his possessions among the

---

[273] Mioni 1950; Krausmüller 1999; 2009. See Chapter 2.
[274] Theoph. Cont. IV, 10,1–19; Genesios 59,40–49; Ps-Symeon 652,10–14. The *Vita of Ioannikios* (produced not long after his death in 846) already mentions the event: τοὺς δέ γε βεβήλους ἐκείνους τοὺς κατὰ τῆς Σωσάννης γέροντας, συκοφάντας, ἀπελεγχθέντας ἐδίκω καὶ κανονικῇ ἐξορίᾳ τε καὶ ἀναθεματισμῷ παραδέδωκεν (*Vita of Ioannikios by Petros* 70, 432A).
[275] *Vita of Gregorios Dekapolites* 10–11.
[276] *Vita of Gregorios Dekapolites* 11,1–2: τὴν ἴασιν τοῦ πάθους θεόθεν δεξάμενος.
[277] For the story of Konon, see *Spiritual Meadow*, PG 87/3, 2856. For that of Symeon, see *Vita of Symeon the Fool*, p. 155.
[278] *Vita of Ioannikios by Petros* 35, 403C: Οὗτος ὁ σημειοφόρος καὶ τῆς καθ' ἡμᾶς γενεᾶς προφήτης. See also *Vita of Ioannikios by Petros* 2, 385C.
[279] Timotin 2010: 71–74.
[280] *Vita of Ioannikios by Petros* 53, 414C: Τῷ οὖν **διορατικῷ** τῆς καρδίας ὀφθαλμῷ.

needy.[281] Both hagiographers also explore the relevance conferred by Methodios on the appearances of the saint in his *vita* of Euthymios of Sardis,[282] as Gregorios Dekapolites and Ioannikios both appear in dreams to prisoners to announce that they will be freed.[283] Methodios is probably responsible as well for the increasing importance of the figure of the dragon as the incarnation of evil vanquished by the saint, a common motif in the characterisation of the iconoclast hero.[284] Methodios uses this image in his *scholia* (comments) on the *passio* of St Marina;[285] Ignatios Diakonos recovers the motif to describe the single combat of his hero Gregorios Dekapolites with evil,[286] and Ioannikios kills no less than seven dragons.[287] In the case of the two hagiographies of the latter saint, it is clear that at this point they develop a path marked out by the patriarch in his *kanon* in honour of Ioannikios, where we read that his only weapons against the dragons were the cross and the rod, not icons.[288]

The *vita* of Gregorios Dekapolites was composed four years before that of Ioannikios, but the legends circulating about the venerated ascetic were familiar to Ignatios Diakonos – who may even have known Ioannikios personally – since he lived for some years in the Bithynian monastery of Antidion.[289] This was the monastery where Ioannikios began his religious life and where he spent extended periods, as is shown by the fact that he received the parents of a prisoner of war who requested his intercession before the *koubikoularios* Agapetos and the *sakellarios* Leon there[290] and also where he expired and was buried. It was specifically the hegoumenos Ioseph[291] who commissioned the writing of a *vita* by Sabas (see Chapter 1), which made the monastery of Antidion the centre of the cult of Ioannikios. In addition to the elements already mentioned, the *vitae* signed by Sabas and Ignatios Diakonos share the characterisation of their respective heroes by invisibility: both Gregorios Dekapolites and Ioannikios make themselves invisible to evade people searching for them.

---

[281] *Vita of Gregorios Dekapolites* 58; *Vita of Ioannikios by Petros* 65, 427C and 67, 428B.
[282] *Vita of Euthymios of Sardis* 44.
[283] *Vita of Gregorios Dekapolites* 88; *Vita of Ioannikios by Sabas* 50, 378A–B. During his youth Gregorios Dekapolites also had several visions, see ch. 15,6–19.
[284] Gero 1978; Auzépy 2002.   [285] Method., *Scholia in honour of St Marina* 49,15–16.
[286] *Vita of Gregorios Dekapolites* 30.
[287] *Vita of Ioannikios by Petros* 29, 400C; 37, 405C–406A; 40, 407B–C; 46, 410C; 47, 412C; 54, 416A. See Kiessling 1970; Quacquarelli 1975; White 2008: 166–67.
[288] *AHG*, vol. III, 141–42, lines 181–85: Ἰοβόλων δρακόντων ἀνὰ μέρος σοὶ φανέντων, σταυρῷ καὶ ῥάβδῳ τούτους τῇ ἐν χερσί σου ἔκτεινας, μακάριε.
[289] Janin 1975: 135–36; Ruggieri 1991: 218.   [290] *Vita of Ioannikios by Sabas* 50, 378C–79A.
[291] *PmbZ* # 3453; *PBE* I: Ioseph 19. This hegoumenos was the recipient of *epist*. 33 by Ignatios Diakonos.

Gregorios goes unnoticed by his disciple Ioannes[292] and his uncle Symeon (ch. 63), while Ioannikios is invisible thrice: to the companions of Eustratios, to the monk Ioannes of Antidion and to the crowd that seeks him.[293] The close friendship between Methodios and Ioannikios for its part helps make better sense of the substantial overlap of their political and literary circles,[294] as does the fact that Methodios founded his own monastery near where Ioannikios was living.[295] No sooner had the anchorite died on 4 November 846, than the patriarch attempted to promote his cult by means of a religious *kanon* of his own making.[296]

Within this literary circle of common socio-political interests and reciprocal textual influences between different milieux, the clan of Gregorios Dekapolites attempted to play a leading role and to preserve and cultivate its own characteristics in order to ratify its position and thus reaffirm its own identity. As is shown in Chapter 2, Ignatios Diakonos maintained an intense literary relationship with the patriarch Methodios, who commissioned the *vitae* of the patriarchs Nikephoros and Tarasios from him.[297] By writing the *Vita Nicephori*, Ignatios Diakonos was likely trying to persuade Methodios not to include him in the purge of 843.[298] As in the case of the *vita* of Ioannikios signed by Petros, the anti-Stoudite nature of the *Vita of Tarasios* is clear. The personal rejection of its author and his confrontation with the patriarch of the time, Methodios, likely led him to create an opposing portrait to the Stoudite leader when describing Tarasios.[299] In about 843 (the year he also wrote the *Vita of Gregorios Dekapolites*), Ignatios penned the first of the two *vitae*, which does not omit prophetic elements such as Nikephoros' prediction to Bardas, the nephew of Leon V, warning him that observing the misfortunes of others should lead Bardas to better manage his own. Four years later, Bardas was blinded.[300] This mutilation probably took place in 820, when Michael II

---

[292] *Vita of Gregorios Dekapolites* 62. On this disciple Ioannes, see *PmbZ* # 3241; Yannopoulos 2016.
[293] *Vita of Ioannikios by Sabas* 50, 363B; 366B and 380B.
[294] *Vita of Ioannikios by Sabas* 46–48, 372B–76A; ch. 53, 381C–82C; *Vita of Ioannikios by Petros* 70–71; 432B–33A; *Vita of Michael the Synkellos* 102–5. See also Von Dobschütz 1909a: 93–100.
[295] It was the monastery of Elegmoi/Eleobomon, see Chapter 2. During his stay in Trichalix Ioannikios also received a visit from the former hegoumenos of this monastery of Elaiobomoi, named Antonios, and his administrator Basileios, whom he asked to take a message to Inger, the metropolitan bishop of Nicaea, see *Vita of Ioannikios by Sabas* 30, 360; *Vita of Ioannikios by Petros* 38, 406. This visit apparently took place in 820–824.
[296] *AHG*, vol. III, 134–45. see Chapter 2.
[297] Von Dobschütz 1909a: 54; Ševčenko 1977a: 123, 125 and n. 92; Efthymiadis 1991a: 83.
[298] Afinogenov 1996b: 89–90. The commissioning of the *Vita Tarasii* to Ignatios Diakonos was already noted by Von Dobschütz 1909a: 59; *Vita of Tarasios*, pp. 49–50.
[299] Speck 2003. [300] *Vita of Nikephoros* 201,19–20.

succeeded Leon V and crushed the members of his family. For its part, the *Vita of Tarasios* includes the prophetic vision of Leon V, in which the dead patriarch appeared in a dream to announce Leon's forthcoming murder at the hands of a certain Michael.[301]

The repeated presence of announcements of future events known to the saint thanks to divine inspiration is a topos characteristic of the literary group formed by Methodios and his followers and those of Ioannikios, of which the Dekapolitan network was also a part to some extent. A desire to adhere to this tradition would seem to be why the anonymous hagiographer of Prokopios Dekapolites, eager to follow the successful path of Ignatios Diakonos and his *Vita of Gregorios Dekapolites*, made the gift of prophecy the only miraculous feature of his hero.[302] The supernatural gift of prophecy is of course not confined to these authors but is a well-known hagiographical topos and a common element in the construction of holiness. But the particular importance it acquires for them, the common, characteristic treatment it receives and its use in similar contexts allows us to trace the links between the two writers, to analyse the progressive shaping of this group and to appreciate its subsequent ramifications. The rejection of the Stoudite school was accompanied by the promotion of a model of holiness different from that of its founder Theodoros Stoudites. The anchorite and prophetic dimension of the saints vindicated by Methodios' circle was therefore stressed.[303]

On the other hand, although Theodoros Stoudites, in his praise of Platon of Sakkoudion, establishes an alternative paradigm of holiness,[304] subsequent generations of Stoudites made this element of the Methodian circle their own, perhaps due to their more traditional nature, which was well established in Byzantine society. The most obvious case is Nikolaos Stoudites (793–868), who predicted the death of the Emperor Michael III and the Caesar Bardas in their expedition against the Arabs occupying Crete.[305] But we also know that two other members of the monastery of Stoudios stood out as prophets, since they announced the accession to the patriarchal throne of Euthymios; these are the hegoumenos Arkadios and the Stoudite monk Epiphanios.[306] The Stoudite hagiographical circle also produced an account of the *archimandrites* Hilarion of

---

[301] *Vita of Tarasios* 67,1–9 (p. 163). See Timotin 2010: 135–42.
[302] *Vita of Prokopios Dekapolites* 8, p. 315. [303] Timotin 2010: 182–94.
[304] On the specific case of Gregorios Dekapolites and the confrontation of the Stoudites with monks inclined towards hesychasm such as he, see *Vita of Gregorios Dekapolites*, ed. Dvornik, p. 17ff.
[305] *Vita of Nikolaos Stoud.* 913A and 917B. Cf. Delouis 2005: 331–37. For this figure, see *PmbZ* # 5576; *PBE* I: Nikolaos 26; see Chapter 5.
[306] *Vita of Euthymios* 10, 61, 1–2 and 22–23. For the Stoudite hegoumenos Arkadios, see *PmbZ* # 20565.

Dalmatos (775–845), a mainstay of Constantinopolitan monasticism against iconoclast heresy.[307] This *Vita of Hilarion of Dalmatos* (*BHG* 2177) was written by Sabas, the same author who produced the hagiographies of Ioannikios and Petros of Atroa. A personal friend of Theodoros Stoudites, who sent him at least one epistle[308] and promoted him to hegoumenos of the monastery of Dalmatos,[309] Hilarion is portrayed as a prophet capable of predicting the death of others. Indeed, in a passage of an abbreviated version of the *Vita* A of Theodoros of Stoudios, Hilarion predicts the death of Theodoros Stoudites himself.[310] The prophetic gifts of all these heroes, which testify to their holiness, are supported in the hagiographical text on Theodoros Stoudites, in which his clairvoyance is emphasised by means of two predictions announcing the death of their recipient.[311]

This is not a case of an innovation by the Stoudite milieu, but rather of the integration of elements characteristic of the Methodian group through an initial *Vita Theodori Studitae* (now lost) written by Methodios himself[312] and by the assimilation of saints who had supported the patriarchate of Methodios and his ecclesiastical policy, such as Hilarion of Dalmatos. Evidence for this can be found in the *Synodikon*, where the patriarch Methodios mentions Ioannikios, Hilarion and Symeon as leaders of the hegoumenoi, the ascetics and the stylites who share his anti-iconoclast policy.[313] These three saints also appear as the main supporters of Methodios' attempt to attain the patriarchate in the *vita* Petros composed in honour of Ioannikios.[314] It is therefore not unreasonable to assume that Hilarion of Dalmatos drew together a large portion of the followers of Gregorios Dekapolites.

At the same time as the Stoudite milieu was opening up to these manifestations of holiness, the circle of Methodios (and especially the heirs of the Dekapolitan clan) continued cultivating and encouraging them with praise of their most distinguished members and with special devotions. The cult of Ioannikios was strengthened by a *theotokion* Ioseph Hymnographos wrote in his honour, which was used during the *orthros*

---

[307] *PmbZ* # 2584; *PBE* I: Hilarion 1; Costa-Louillet 1957: 788–94; Kazhdan 1999: 341–42. See also *SynaxCP* 731–34 (*BHG* 2177b). See Chapter 7.
[308] Theod. Stoud., *epist*. 90: Ἱλαρίωνι ἀρχιμανδρίτῃ. Theodoros also mentions him in three other letters dated between 816 and 818, see Theod. Stoud., *epist*. 214; *epist*. 267; *epist*. 291.
[309] Theod. Stoud., *Magnae catecheseis* 89. Moreover, this catechesis is dedicated to Hilarion himself. Cf. Pratsch 1998: 149–50; Delouis 2005: 217–18 and 222–23.
[310] *Vita* A *of Theodoros Stoud*. 252–53. See also Matantseva 1996c: 151–52.
[311] *Vita* B *of Theodoros Stoud*. 272B–C; 300C–301C. Cf. Timotin 2010: 152–58.
[312] Krausmüller 2006: 144–50. See Section 2.1.4.
[313] Darrouzès 1966: 296, line 5; Darrouzès 1987: 54, line 12.
[314] *Vita of Ioannikios by Petros* 431A–B; Talbot 1998: 340–42.

of the saint's feast day (4 November).³¹⁵ This hymn is one of four dating to the ninth century that survive³¹⁶ and was probably definitive for the ratification of the cult of Ioannikios, since it was chosen to join the *Menaia*. Ioseph Hymnographos, as a disciple of Gregorios Dekapolites, praised other non-iconodule saints in addition to his master, since his writings include a *kanon* extolling the virtue and the miracles of Eudokimos.³¹⁷ But he also continued celebrations encouraged by patriarch Methodios' texts such as those honouring the forty-two martyrs of Amorion,³¹⁸ St Marina³¹⁹ and St Nicholas of Myra,³²⁰ Methodios' devotion for whom was shared by Ioannikios, who visited a chapel near the monastery of Balaiou in Bithynia dedicated to the bishop of Myra.³²¹

Although the Dekapolitan milieu never formed a lobby as important as that of the monks of Stoudios, their loyalty to Ioannikios' memory led them to side with the patriarch Ignatios in the disputes deriving from his conflict with Photios. Ioannikios' public prophecy that Ignatios deserved the patriarchate made him the only legitimate patriarch. According to Ignatios' hagiographer, after Methodios' death, the patriarchate was offered to Ignatios, who considered himself unworthy. After he rejected it, the empress consulted Ioannikios, who designated Ignatios again, as a consequence of which the latter finally accepted the position.³²² Their unconditional support for Ignatios meant that when he was deposed and exiled by Michael III in 858, the followers of the Dekapolites, such as Ioseph Hymnographos, also had to abandon Constantinople for the Chersonesos.³²³ Ignatios' reinstatement in 867 involved the promotion of Ioseph, who was appointed *skeuophylax* of Hagia Sophia. On the death of the patriarch Ignatios, his remains lay for a time in the same place those of Gregorios Dekapolites had, in the church of St Menas.

---

[315] *Menaion* II: 39–47.
[316] The other three are those signed by the patriarch Methodios, the abbess Theodosia and Georgios of Nicomedia, who was later to stand out as a friend of Photios but who at that time only held the post of *diakonos* or priest (cf. *PmbZ* # 2259 and 22083), see *AHG*, vol. III, 111–21. References to the cult of Ioannikios only appear in those of Theodosia and Ioseph Hymnographos, from which we can infer that they are later, see Topping 1986/1988: 388–90.
[317] *Menaion* VI: 271–76.
[318] He dedicated two *kanones* to them: one is published in *Menaion* IV: 30–35, another in *AHG*, vol. VII: 99–107. The *idiomelon* that Methodios composed in his honour can be found in *Menaion* IV: 29.
[319] *Menaion* IV: 144–52.   [320] Schirò and Gonzato 1960: 547.
[321] *Vita of Ioannikios* by Sabas 370C. Cf. Patterson Ševčenko 1998: 107–12. On the cult of Saint Nicholas in Byzantium, see Ahrweiler 1996; Kountoura-Galaki 2004; Magdalino 2015b.
[322] *Vita of Ignatios* 16, p. 22,8–11.
[323] *Vita of Ioseph Hymnographos* by Ioannes Diakonos 968–69. Concerning the presence of Ioseph in the Ignatian ranks, see Dvornik 1948: 238.

Ioseph Hymnographos again entered into the dynamics that have already been analysed and composed a *kontakion* and a *kanon* in his memory, in order to promote his veneration.[324] Likewise when Niketas David Paphlagon wrote the *Vita Ignatii* (a text clearly opposing Photios and the Emperor Basileios I), he chose to follow the model of the *Vita Tarasii* by Ignatios Diakonos,[325] preserving the hagiographical tradition of a literary circle linked to his hero with which he wished to establish a relationship.

The Dekapolitan network apparently remained vital for years after the death of its main point of reference, Gregorios Dekapolites; the choice of Eudokia Dekapolitissa as the wife of Michael III favoured this group, and we cannot rule out the possibility that the predilection of the monastery of Stoudios for the new Macedonian dynasty led by Basileios[326] sought to counteract the Dekapolitans' influence and prevent the religious control of the former imperial family, the Amorians. Although in the early tenth century its capacity for action and its socio-ecclesiastical relevance were reduced, however, the Dekapolitan identity remained clear. Perhaps the best example is the patriarch Euthymios, who claimed to descend from Gregorios Dekapolites and shared or exceeded many of his characteristics of holiness. A prophetic gift, for example, allowed the patriarch to serve Emperor Leon VI as a true political counsellor: Euthymios was not only διορατικός but also διορατικώτατος.[327] His clairvoyance led him to predict to the *basileopator* Stylianos Zaoutzes, the emperor's father-in-law, that he would fall from grace and die before Leon VI,[328] and to have a prophetic dream in which the dead patriarch Ignatios announced the future reconciliation of the two opposed sectors of the Church.[329] The passage of time thus did not erase the traces of Gregorios. To the contrary, even years later, the Dekapolitan family clan and literary milieu remained well established.

3.4 Conclusions

The group formed by Gregorios Dekapolites and his followers nicely illustrates the existence of an extensive socio-ecclesiastical sector during the years of the

---

[324] The *kontakion* was edited by Mioni 1948: 178–80. For the hymn, see Schirò and Gonzato 1960: 545.
[325] As has been shown by Timotin 2010: 173–81.
[326] For the strong links between the Macedonian dynasty and the monastery of Stoudios, on which it concentrated its patronage, see Delouis 2005: 374–431.
[327] *Vita of the Patriarch Euthymios* 3, 21,2–3. On his prophetic gifts, cf. also ch. 3, 15,6–8 and 17,24–26; Timotin 2010: 194–207.
[328] *Vita of the Patriarch Euthymios* 3, 15,6–8.   [329] *Vita of the Patriarch Euthymios* 21, 135,34–36.

restoration of icons about which the sources tend otherwise to be silent. The surviving literature is generally partisan and depicts a society polarised between a majority advocating the veneration of images and a heretical minority that got its hands on imperial power and used those institutions to persecute the champions of Orthodoxy. Once this situation changed, thanks to the intervention of Theodora, who listened to the defenders of icons, Byzantine writers took up the topic of the major representatives of both factions, describing violent social confrontations that in many cases must not have occurred and ignoring intermediate figures who moved with varying intensity back and forth between the two trends. The attempts of the disciples of Gregorios Dekapolites to find a place in the new post-iconoclast system led them to promote the veneration of their spiritual father by following the iconodule patterns in vogue. Thanks to their family history, which included figures of the stature of the *archimandrites* Symeon and Ioannes of Kathara, this was easy to accomplish. The influence of the milieu of the Dekapolites extended to disciples and relatives to such an extent that subsequent generations played an important role in governing the Empire thanks to their affinity with the ruling dynasty.

Despite the new prevailing fashion, however, the desire of Gregorios' followers to have him fit the rigid schema of the hegoumenos confessor who becomes a saint after having confronted the emperor in a dialectic *agon* fails to conceal the historical reality confirmed by his disciples Ioannes and Ioseph Hymnographos: the three men are considered iconodule saints despite not having spoken out in favour of the icons and not having suffered for the cause. Their desire to be closer to God led them to concentrate on hardship, the mortification of the flesh and study of the Bible, which was enough to make them worthy of veneration, although hagiographers attempt to give their holiness a veneer of commitment to iconophilia. In this endeavour, the followers of the Dekapolites decided to encourage a rapprochement (both literary and political) to the Methodian milieu, not only because it held ecclesiastical power but also because of its greater tolerance and leniency in such matters, unlike the iconodule stridency of the Stoudites. The result was a fruitful reciprocal influence between the Dekapolitans and members of the circle of the patriarch Methodios. Despite this, the obsession of some writers with the iconoclast crisis and the need to fit a pre-established social pattern show the extent to which the texts fail to reflect the richness and variety of individual sensitivities or how large the portion of the population was that professed a mitigated, low-density icon veneration, since their religiosity led them to pay scant attention to matters of ecclesiastical tradition such as the specific manner of worshipping the Godhead and the saints.

CHAPTER 4

The Secular Milieux and Their Rewriting of the Second Iconoclasm
The Aristocracy, the Army, the Court and the Imperial Family

The iconoclast crisis triggered in the year 726 became a salutary lesson in the writing of lives of saints, since one major response of authors and ecclesiastical authorities to the new threat to Orthodoxy was to produce or disperse accounts that extolled the attitude of icon worshippers and condemned the atrocities committed against them by false Christians (usually secular authorities). A clear example of this apologetic purpose is the *Vita of Stephanos the Younger*, which was written by the homonymous deacon of Hagia Sophia in 809, this is forty-four years after the saint's death in 765. This is the first extensive hagiography of a contemporary iconodule saint of Constantinopolitan origin that has come down to us and is very probably one of the first to be written.[1] It should be noted that not until the first restoration (787–815) did a work of these characteristics appear in Constantinople. Indeed, during the 'Dark Age' between ca. 670 and 787, the only text that can be attributed to a milieu of the capital is the *Miracles of St Artemios*.[2]

The literary genre of saints' lives apparently seemed the most appropriate not only for praising heroes involved in the events in this period but also for helping to create an official discourse of the events of the Second Iconoclasm. Throughout the ninth century, numerous hagiographies added to this objective more personal or partisan interests, be it promoting the veneration of a specific saint for family reasons, strengthening the situation of the monastery he had founded or consolidating the veneration of a specific saint in order to reinforce the role of specific monastic groups or even the patriarchate itself. Nor was there any shortage of attempts to flatter or win over important contemporary figures, such as the commissioner of the *vita*, the founder of the monastery, the aristocrat who

[1] Auzépy 1997.
[2] See Introduction. For the *Miracles of St Artemios*, see Sevcenko 1977a: 121–27; Kazhdan 1999: 27–35; Efthymiadis 2011a: 95–101; Haldon 2014.

provided his protection or the patriarch currently on the throne.[3] The revitalisation and cultivation of literature in the ninth century appears to represent an almost exclusively monastic phenomenon. Given that written production was dominated by monastic culture,[4] as well as the pious approach that gave rise to such works, it is easy to believe that ecclesiastical sectors were involved in the production and dissemination of hagiographies, and indeed of most literature regarding the recent past. Although this is what the (generally monastic) sources would have us believe, however, the historical phenomenon seems to have more complex roots, since it was linked to the revitalisation of the bureaucratic milieux that took place between Eirene's reign (780–802) and that of Nikephoros I (802–811). These secular bureaucratic milieux with strong links to the court are the same as those that, from the period of the reign of Eirene as sole ruler, gave rise to the renewal of iconodule monasticism. This was a true reforming dynamic, whose more visual aspect consisted of the adoption of minuscule script in book production.[5]

Although this was a minority process, we also have records of passages from monastic to secular life, as in the case of a Stoudite monk named Eulalios, a master of the art of writing who abandoned the monastery.[6] Secular groups were therefore not strangers to literature, nor did they necessarily live on the fringe of religious circles and their textual production. To the contrary, a certain communication and interchange went on between the different milieux. Moreover, it was Theophilos who founded an establishment of higher education at the expense of the imperial treasury and offered a position as teacher there to Leon the Mathematician, the future bishop of Thessaloniki.[7] Theophilos may well have been the dedicatee of the lost historical work on the Arab invasion of Sicily in 826 written by Theognostos,[8] who had previously dedicated his treatise *On Orthography* to the Emperor Leon V, Theophilos' godfather.

In view of the indissoluble combination of imperial power and the doctrines on images, the partisan advantage achieved by the imperial household from the restoration of Orthodoxy makes sense. It is worth considering, therefore, how literature was used in contemporary aristocratic and courtly

---

[3] See the examples given by Timotin 2012.
[4] To take the well-known expression of Kazhdan 1999: 167–407.
[5] Ronconi 2014. For the minuscule and the first manuscripts written in it, see Brubaker and Haldon 2001: 37–54 with previous bibliography.
[6] Theod. Stoud., *Magnae catech.* XLIII, p. 307. On this monk, see *PmbZ* # 1664; *PBE* I: Eulalios 3.
[7] Speck 1974c; Treadgold 1979b: 187; Markopoulos 2017. See Introduction.
[8] Treadgold 2013: 89. On Theognostos, see *PmbZ* # 8012; *PBE* I: Theognostos 7.

circles,[9] since – led by the imperial household itself – the presence of laymen in ninth- and tenth-century texts not only intended to record their role in the transformation of history.

4.1 The Aristocratic Milieu

4.1.1 Hagiography and Aristocracy in the Early Ninth Century: Philaretos and Eudokimos

Very little surviving hagiographical material goes back to the first half of the ninth century (i.e., before the restoration of icons), and even less to the eighth century. We will never know whether the literary purge carried out by the victors put paid to a large number of texts written by heretics, or whether the absence of material indicates (among other more eventful circumstances) the simple lack of interest in writing that some authors both Byzantine and modern attribute to iconoclasts. The reduction in manuscript production and circulation during the eighth century is not in doubt[10] – although it was deeply rooted in the social composition of the elites – since during the Isaurian period (with a tendency towards iconoclasm) the leaders were generally from a military rather than a bureaucratic background, being the administration the only sphere in which the transmission of written texts was continuously cultivated. At the same time, it is striking that in some works that claim to be hagiographical, it is difficult to appreciate the holiness of the protagonist, a fact probably due to their secular bias. In several of these cases, the connections of the new saint with political leaders rather than with powerful ecclesiastical communities explain their survival and, in all likelihood, also their composition.

Chronologically, the first example of this kind that has come down to us is the *vita* of Philaretos the Merciful (*BHG* 1511z–12b), a high-status rich landowner from Amnia in Paphlagonia known for his works of charity and for helping those in need.[11] The Arab raids and the confiscation of land by Philaretos' neighbours meant that he lost his fortune and his slaves,

---

[9] For an introduction to the main milestones of this phenomenon throughout the whole Byzantine millennium, see Carile 1998. The relationship between the emerging tenth-century aristocracy and other literary genres (poetry, epistolography and historiography) has been analysed by Andriollo 2014. For those concentrating on saints' lives, see Patlagean 1981 and Métivier 2018.
[10] Mango 1975a; Browning 1978; Mullet 1990; Brubaker and Haldon 2001: xxv–xxxvii.
[11] Rydén 2002, with an extensive bibliography. A good literary analysis can be found in Kazhdan 1999: 281–91, who considers this *vita* a secular hagiography, and Efthymiadis 2016. See also *SynaxCP* 269,28–70,33; 269/270,43–45 (1 December); 271/272,40–43 (2 December).

although he continued to be generous in adversity. His situation improved in 788, when his granddaughter Maria was chosen to participate in a bride-show,[12] which she won to become the fiancée of Emperor Konstantinos VI. The whole family benefitted from this marriage and moved to the capital, where Philaretos continued to give alms until he died in 792 at the age of ninety. He was buried in the convent of Krisis (also known as Rhodophyllion), where he had purchased a tomb.[13] Why he chose to rest forever in this convent is beyond us.[14]

Although he predicted his own death and prophesied the destiny of his grandchildren, Philaretos does not have the usual qualities of a Byzantine saint and even less so those of an iconodule martyr. Far from being an ascetic or a hermit, he was married with several children; he had no links with monasteries or churches, and his contact with them went no further than paying to be buried in a convent in Constantinople, like many wealthy men; despite his generosity with the needy, he wanted for nothing and came to enjoy the privileges of being related to the imperial family; his works of charity were accompanied by no pious deeds, and he never venerated icons or defended the practice.[15] His *vita* is unanimously regarded as a mixture of frivolous elements out of a storybook (the bride-show, the madman's reward, etc.) with biblical motifs (the personage of Job) and components characteristic of both a family chronicle and an edifying account.[16] The text did not aim to establish a religious cult or the adoration of the saint's relics. Nor does it increase the prestige of a monastic centre or the cohesion of a specific community with a shared devotion.

Although we know the year of its composition (821 or 822), the place (Karioupolis in the Peloponnese) and the author's identity (Niketas, a monk and a grandson of the saint),[17] we do not know why it was written. The fact that it coincides in time with the wedding of the iconoclast Emperor Michael II and Euphrosyne allows us to speculate that this event spurred Niketas to undertake a project that had probably been in his head since the death of his grandfather thirty years previously.[18] Now that he was in exile, he not only had the time for this, but he must have seen an

---

[12] Concerning Maria of Amnia, see *PmbZ* # 4727; *PBE* I: Maria 2. Regarding her grandfather Philaretos the Merciful, see *PmbZ* # 6136; *PBE* I: Philaretos 1.
[13] On the Constantinopolitan convent of Krisis, see Janin 1969: 28–31.   [14] Auzépy 1993.
[15] Ševčenko 1977a: 121–27; Auzépy 1992: 57–67.
[16] Poljakova 1973; Diller-Sellschopp 1982; Kazhdan and Sherry 1996; Ludwig 1997.
[17] *PmbZ* # 5434; *PBE* I: Niketas 8.
[18] Speck 1978: 206; Rydén 2002: 44–49; Kaplan 2015: 174–75.

opportunity to thus gain favour with the emperor. He may have achieved his aim and been recalled from exile after the work was written. But we do not know this, and we are also unaware of the reasons for his exile. In any case, either to facilitate the performance of the marriage or to celebrate it, in 821/822 Niketas put in writing in this *vita* the family history of Euphrosyne, the daughter of Emperor Konstantinos VI and great-granddaughter of St Philaretos the Merciful, thanks to whom her husband Michael II would found the new Amorian dynasty strengthened by the double legitimacy, both political and religious, that he obtained from his marriage. In the latter connection, we should not be surprised by the absence of Euphrosyne's grandmother, Empress Eirene, who later became a saint as a result of her decisive support of the return of iconoduly, but who is only mentioned once (line 378) in contrast to the absolute dominance of Philaretos, a saint who like his hagiographer and the new emperor felt no devotion for icons.

A similar case is that of the cult of St Eudokimos († ca. 842), which was promoted by his wealthy family, which produced a group of influential aristocrats in Asia Minor with important contacts at the court. Eudokimos was born in Cappadocia in the early ninth century to patrician parents who gave him a good education, which led to his being called to Constantinople to take up a position at court.[19] His good deeds and the help he offered others did not pass unnoticed by his hagiographers. Subsequently, Emperor Theophilos (829–842) granted him the rank of *kandidatos* and later appointed him *stratopedarches* of Cappadocia. After his major victories over the Arabs, service as a priest and aiding of the poor, widows and orphans generally, he died at the age of thirty-three in Charsianon, where he had established his residence. His charismatic character and his posthumous miracles explain the wish of the Cappadocian people to venerate him. But his family decided that this devotion should be based in the capital, and to this end, they attempted to move his relics. The people of Charsianon strongly opposed this – which is curious, since no evidence of his veneration has survived in Cappadocia, even among the frescoes of military saints that were habitually executed on a standard model[20] – and his mother Eudokia decided to entrust the monk Ioseph with the theft of the relics. Once this had been accomplished, new miracles occurred as the procession made its way to Constantinople, including the healing of the abbess of the convent of Mantineon in Asia Minor, who heard of the arrival of the saint's body in her region and ran to

---

[19] *PmbZ* # 1640; Costa-Louillet 1957: 783–38.   [20] Jolivet-Lévy 1991; Walter 2003.

meet it.[21] Beyond this information, we do not know who this abbess was, but the convent of Mantineon was well known owing to its founder, a young aristocrat named Anthousa.[22] Finally, Eudokimos' parents had a church built in the capital dedicated to the Theotokos,[23] so that they could deposit their son's coffin there once it had been coated with silver. It is perhaps no coincidence that the location chosen for this new temple was near the convent *en Krisei*, the resting spot of Philaretos the Merciful, who had bought himself a tomb there.

Numerous liturgical notices of the veneration of Eudokimos in the capital each year on 31 July have survived, with this being mentioned in the *Typikon* of the Great Church,[24] the *Synaxarion of Constantinople*[25] and the *Menologion* of Basileios II.[26] Eudokimos is also praised in a *kanon* composed in his honour by Ioseph Hymnographos.[27] Our main source for his biography is the metaphrastic *vita* of Eudokimos (*BHG* 607), which on any reckoning replaced a previous iconoclast *vita*, from which it does not appear to have varied greatly, since it coincides with other existing testimonies, including the much less informative thirteenth-century *Vita of Eudokimos* attributed to Konstantinos Akropolites (*BHG* 606). Auzépy's study showed that we are dealing with an iconoclast narrative, because it shares the characteristics of pre-iconodule hagiography also found in the *vitae* of Leon of Catania, Philaretos and Georgios of Amastris.[28]

Who the author of this initial biography was is unknown. But to judge by the insistence of the metaphrastic text on vindicating the family ties of Eudokimos (both their specific maternal-filial links and the paternal relationship established with God, 'the first father of all'),[29] its composition was likely commissioned by a relative, perhaps his mother, since we know she masterminded the theft, transfer and deposit of the saint's body in Constantinople. The narration goes into detail about the miracles that took place in Charsianon and during the journey of the relics but does not

---

[21] *Vita of Eudokimos* 22,1–13.
[22] *PmbZ* # 500; *PBE* I: Anthousa 2; *SynaxCP* 848,31–52,17 (27 July); Mango 1982; Ruggieri 1985; Talbot 1998: 13–19.
[23] Janin 1969: 177–78; Majeska 1984: 316–18 places it on the western periphery of Constantinople near the Golden Gate.
[24] *Typikon of the Great Church* I, 355.   [25] *SynaxCP* 857,2–26 (31 July).
[26] *Menologion Basilii* 565D–68B. Likewise we find Eudokimos celebrated every year on 31 July in the *Typika Dmitrievskij* I, 98; 477 and 861; III, 53; *Typicon Messinense* 173,1.
[27] Tomadakes 1971a: 182 (on Ioseph, see Sections 3.2.1.a and 5.2.3.a); Theodorakopoulos 2004; Métivier 2012: 97.
[28] Auzépy 1992. On the iconoclast account that gave rise to the metaphrastic *vita*, see Ševčenko 1977a: 116–17 and 127.
[29] *Vita of Eudokimos* 17,23–30.

mention any in the capital, from which it can be inferred that it was produced to celebrate solemnly their placement in the new church of the Theotokos, without the later addition of new healings or subsequent miracles. The *vita* affirms that when Eudokimos' mother opened her son's tomb, the body was intact and gave off a floral fragrance, despite the fact that eighteen months had passed since his death.[30]

The *Synaxarion* places Eudokimos as a contemporary of Theophilos and claims that his remains were transferred on 6 July.[31] Although the chronology is uncertain, it is generally accepted that the saint was born in 807 and died in 842. This reconstruction by Ch. Loparev is based on the identification of the monk Ioseph, who steals Eudokimos' body, with Ioseph Hymnographos and on the close collaboration of the saint and Theophilos on the Arab border.[32] If this time frame is correct, the transfer of the relics took place after the death of Theophilos, so that the original *vita* could no longer be iconoclast *sensu stricto*, although the original hagiographer may have been trained in iconoclastic literary trends and have had insufficient time to adopt the new conventions of iconodule hagiography. This has a second consequence as well: two years later, when the transfer was completed and Eudokimos' veneration was initiated in Constantinople (i.e., in 844), the defeat of iconoclasm and the Triumph of Orthodoxy forced the reshaping of the social and religious scene of the empire. If the dating must instead be brought forward a bit, the sanctification process took place during the final years of the reign of Theophilos. This is not particularly important, since this is not a religious sanctification by the faithful (whether iconodules or not), but a sanctification promoted by his family with other interests in mind.

Earlier studies have stressed the importance of Eudokimos' family in the establishment and promotion of his veneration.[33] As Talbot emphasises, in contemporary family cults, the veneration of women who were married or had been married was generally promoted by their relatives, while the memory of men was cultivated by their disciples.[34] In the case of Eudokimos (and that of Philaretos), however, the whole provincial family strove to give prominence to the saint related to them. It would appear to be no coincidence that just at the time when the Arab frontier at Charsianon was in the limelight and its administrative emancipation as a

---

[30] *Vita of Eudokimos* 18.   [31] *SynaxCP* 857,2–26 (31 July).
[32] Theodorakopoulos 2004: 129–31 considers the evidence insufficient to maintain these dates. However, the *PmbZ* (# 1640) accepts this dating, based on Eudokimos' brother, Konstantinos (*PmbZ* # 3948), from whom Michael Maleinos would descend.
[33] Theodorakopoulos 2004; Métivier 2012.   [34] Talbot 1996b; Kaplan 2013.

separate *thema* was being established,[35] the relatives of Eudokimos were encouraging his veneration as a saint in Constantinople. Although the hagiographical testimonies do not record the name of the aristocratic family to which Eudokimos belonged, there can be no doubt that they were ancestors of the Maleinoi, as it was they (together with their allies the Phokades) who appropriated his figure throughout the tenth century. In the *vita* of Michael Maleinos (*BHG* 1295) it is accordingly specified that his father was called Eudokimos, a name he received from his ancestor, the Cappadocian saint.[36]

4.1.2 Aristocratic Models of Feminine Holiness (Ninth-Tenth Centuries)

The ninth and tenth centuries witnessed a phenomenon of family sanctification, by which the aristocratic classes assumed the possession of holiness to justify their prerogatives and build new spheres of power. Many of the cults that arose after the disappearance of iconoclasm were therefore due not to spontaneous processes, in which anonymous believers gathered around an exceptional religious figure, but to advertising operations planned by powerful families in the pursuit of specific ends, generally the exercise of power and proximity to the imperial family.[37]

In contrast to other family cults, which are generally of provincial origin but transferred to Constantinople – this is the case of Theodora of Thessaloniki (*BHG* 1737) and Maria the Younger in Bizye (*BHG* 1164)[38] – Eudokimos' cult is genuinely Constantinopolitan, created and imposed from the capital as a system for legitimising his family's power over the region of Charsianon, the ultimate origin of their wealth and their influence at court.[39] To do so, his parents built a sanctuary of their own, which was a perfect way to promote veneration of their relative by means of a place devoted to the purpose. The husband of Maria the Younger and Emperor Leon VI followed this example and built sanctuaries in which to install the relics of their wives. Empress Theophano was deposited at the

---

[35] Oikonomidès 1972: 55; Métivier 2008: 448–51.
[36] *Vita of Michael Maleinos* 3, p. 551,18–21. See Laiou 1998, who emphasises in p. 403 how Leon Diakonos describes Nikephoros Phokas ('un soldat profondément pieux et au comportement d'ascète, un homme très juste') and its marked parallelism with Eudokimos. See also Métivier 2017.
[37] On the phenomenon of family networks and their considerable effect on aristocracy's strengthening in Middle Byzantium, see Gounaridis 2006; Flusin 2012; Settipani 2012; Varona Codeso and Prieto Domínguez 2013.
[38] Talbot 1996b: 65–67.   [39] Métivier 2012: 105–7.

church of All Saints in Constantinople,[40] while the husband of Maria the Younger, the *tourmarches* of Bizye, was also obliged to steal the relics of the saint with the help of forty men who made the transfer possible.[41]

The writing of the hagiographical texts that formed the basis of these family cults is also due to the will of their closest relatives. The case of Empress Theophano, the wife of Leon VI (886–912), is well known;[42] two *vitae* in her honour have survived, a contemporary one (*BHG* 1794) and a fourteenth-century revision by Nikephoros Gregoras (*BHG* 1795). The former hagiography is due to a family request rather than an imperial commission.[43] It is no accident that she belonged to the Martiniakoi family (a branch of the Martinakioi clan), who were obliged to convert the family home into a monastery in ca. 842, after Emperor Theophilos received an oracle.[44] The hagiographer was a close friend. His friendship with the father of the empress is mentioned in the *vita* that has come down to us,[45] along with his connection to the *artoklines* Martinos, who was an uncle of the saint and his close friend. The description of how Martinos appeared to the writer in dreams urging him to honour the memory of his niece with hymns is clear evidence of a literary commission.[46]

Outside the court, we find the same phenomenon of families united around one of their own liable to be recognised as a saint. The examples of Theodora of Thessaloniki and Thomaïs of Lesbos are well known.[47] According to her life history, Theodora of Thessaloniki (812–892) and her entire family were in favour with the heretic Emperor Theophilos; indeed, her convent flourished during his reign. This iconoclast stain, which explains the clergy's refusal to allow Theodora to be buried in a privileged manner apart from the other nuns in the common grave,

---

[40] Downey 1955/1956; Karlin-Hayter 1969; Majeska 1977; Dagron 1994; Featherstone 2010.
[41] *Vita of Maria the Younger in Bizye* 17, 698–99. English translation in Talbot 1996a: 239–89; Constantinou 2010. See also Peeters 1951; Bartikjan 1980; Pratsch 2004. On this new church, see Mango 1968b.
[42] On Theophano, see *PmbZ* # 8165 and # 28122; Loparev 1899; 1910: 63–73; Diehl 1908; Costa-Louillet 1957: 823–36; Rydén 1985; Garland 1999: 126–35.
[43] Flusin 2001: 30. Cf. Cesaretti 1988; Alexakis 1995a; Strano 2001; Cesaretti 2005; Kazhdan 2006: 54–55 and 105; Vukašinović 2015.
[44] Theoph. Cont. III, 27,1–10; Genesios III, 15, 49.74–86; Skylitzes 72,47–55. For Mango 1973: 20–21 these are distant relatives of Theophilos, cf. Tobias 2007: 473f.
[45] *Vita of the Empress Theophano* 1,12–13.
[46] *Vita of the Empress Theophano* 21,29–22,17. See also Alexakis 1995a. On Theophano's sanctification, see Dagron 1996: 159–68 and 209–10.
[47] On the *Vita of Thomaïs of Lesbos* (*BHG* 2454), see Costa-Louillet 1957: 836–39; Laiou 1989; Talbot 1994; 1996a: 291–322; Efthymiadis 2015. Cf. also *SynaxCP* 367/368,39–41 (3 January). On the Constantinopolitan Church at which her veneration was established, see Majeska 1984: 321–25.

affected all those belonging to the lineage. To correct this situation, after the restoration of Orthodoxy, the family initiated a marketing campaign that aimed to clear their name, the main characteristic of this being to encourage the cult of Theodora. To this end, they commissioned the writing of a *vita* of their holy relative, the *Vita of Theodora of Thessaloniki*.[48] Because the family's heretical past had not been forgotten in their city of origin (Thessaloniki), however, the *vita* insists on justifying the birth of the cult and the transfer of the relics, but throughout its pages also mentions her relatives as a pious orthodox family.[49] This same reason led the hagiographer to attach great importance in his account to the metropolitan of Thessaloniki, Antonios, who, as an ancestor of the saint, was also of her lineage. Antonios' iconodule credentials were faultless and undeniable, since he confronted Leon V the Armenian, suffered for the faith and became a confessor and was chosen by Methodios in 843 to replace Leon the Mathematician at the head of the see.[50] The establishment of a family cult patently gave its members an aureole that could be highly beneficial, especially when the holiness that extended to the family as a whole allowed it to remove iconoclast shadows.

Although it has been less studied, the veneration Theokleto enjoyed from her relatives is no less surprising: to honour her memory, her relatives spruced up her uncorrupted body every year on the anniversary of her death. They changed her clothes, combed her hair and cut her nails as they continued to grow. This saint of Theophilos' time stood out for her studies of the Holy Scriptures and for giving alms to the poor in the same way Eudokimos had. We know nothing about her attitude to icons. No *vita* of Theokleto survives but merely brief entries in *synaxaria* and *menologia* that report that she was born in the thema of the Optimatoi, predicted her own death and worked miracles posthumously but never during her lifetime.[51] These cults of pious lay women emerged in the ninth and tenth centuries and are known at all socioeconomic levels.[52] In addition to their social impact, the dynamic of the sanctification of a member of the lineage chosen for his or her virtues is important, since Eudokimos was known

---

[48] Patlagean 1984b. Talbot 1996a: 159–237 offers an English translation of this *vita*.
[49] Kaplan 2013.
[50] This is Antonios the bishop of Dyrrhachium, see *PmbZ* # 556; *PBE* I: Antonios 34; Paschalidis 1994a.
[51] *SynaxCP* 914,3–34; Prieto Domínguez 2016a.
[52] For the situation of women during the iconoclast period and their models of sanctity, see Kazhdan and Talbot 1991; Taft 1998: 73–74; Connor 2004: 166–81; Herrin 2006; 2013: 159, n. 90. On female cults in Byzantium, see Patlagean 1976; Wilson 1995; Delierneux 2014.

as The Just (ὁ δίκαιος). Unsurprisingly, the phenomenon occurs in the most powerful families, about which we know the most and which allow us to draw the most conclusions, although it sometimes remains hidden by the successive reinterpretations of Byzantine authors.

The case of Kassia (ca. 805–ante 867), that is, the poetess who could have been empress, is worthy of separate attention.[53] Some 1,300 of her verses survive, most of them in the form of *kanones* and liturgical hymns (almost 1,000 verses)[54], to which must be added her collection of sacred-profane *Sentences* (of which 4 different versions survive).[55] In her compositions, she gave great importance to female figures, from numerous women saints to the Virgin Mary herself as the Theotokos. Byzantine historians mention her participation in the bride-show to choose the new empress whom Theophilos would marry.[56] Indeed, Kassia was initially selected for her beauty, although the emperor finally opted for Theodora. The reason lay in the reply she gave to his comment 'Evil flows through women' (διὰ γυναικὸς ἐρρύη τὰ φαῦλα). Kassia replied 'But the best also emanates through a woman' (ἀλλὰ καὶ διὰ γυναικός πηγάζει τὰ κρείττονα).[57]

Once Kassia had been rejected by Theophilos, she founded her own convent, which must have been a small religious foundation, since it is scarcely mentioned in the sources.[58] She had previously received three epistles from Theodoros Stoudites himself, in which he praises her erudition and literary skills as similar to those of the Classical authors, despite her youth,[59] and describes her form of expression as 'more adorned and precious than any transitory charm'.[60] These stylistic assessments show how early our poetess began to compose verse. From earliest childhood, she had felt the call to take the veil; the hegoumenos of the monastery of Stoudios calls her 'bride of Christ' and 'maiden of Christ' (νύμφη Χριστοῦ, κόρη Χριστοῦ).[61] The letters also show Kassia's involvement in the anti-

---

[53] *PmbZ* # 3636 and # 3637; *PBE* I: Kassia 1 and 2; Rochow 1967; Lauxtermann 1998: 391–97.
[54] Rochow 1967: 32–58; Kazhdan 1999: 323–26; Lauxtermann 2003: 241–70; Prieto Domínguez 2019a with previous bibliography.
[55] Lauxtermann 2003: 248–51; Schönauer 2010.
[56] The historicity of imperial bride-shows has been much debated, see, e.g., Rochow 1967: 5–19, 73–76 and 194–201; Treadgold 1975; 1979a; Ludwig 1997: 104–45, esp. pp. 130–36; Vinson 2004; Signes Codoñer 2014: 73–74.
[57] Ps-Symeon 625.
[58] Rochow 1967: 26–29; Janin 1969: 102; Berger 1988a: 649–50; Prieto Domínguez 2019a: 19–21.
[59] Theod. Stoud., *epist.* 370,2–4: Οἷα ... ὁμοῦ μὲν σοφά, ὁμοῦ δὲ καὶ συνετά, ... κόρη ἀρτιφυεῖ τηλικαύτην γνῶσιν.
[60] Theod. Stoud., *epist.* 370,7–8: μάλιστα καὶ κόσμος σοι ὁ λόγος, πάσης ἐπικήρου εὐπρεπείας ὡραιότερος.
[61] Theod. Stoud., *epist.* 217,10 and 17.

iconoclast policy of the time: on the one hand, she sends alms and gifts to Theodoros, who had fallen out of favour for denouncing imperial heresy (*epist.* 217 and 370), while, on the other, she helps the Stoudite monk Dorotheos,[62] who had been imprisoned in 816 for defending the cult of icons during the persecution decreed by Leon V. The first two letters were written between 816 and 818, when iconodules were facing ever greater difficulties and signs of solidarity between the persecuted and their sympathisers multiplied. Kassia herself was whipped at least twice for her opposition to iconoclasm (*epist.* 370), and the hegoumenos Theodoros saw in her a perfect candidate for monastic life. Owing to this, he gave her advice about how to behave in public and exhorted her to take the veil.[63]

Despite Kassia's declaration of intentions, years passed and not even the religious tolerance of the reign of Michael II (820–829) led to her entering a convent. *Epistle* 539, which was sent between 821 and 826, shows that she continued to be a laywoman whose commitment to the veneration of images was no longer as intense as it had been. In addition, Theodoros Stoudites criticises her because as a pious woman she did not concern herself with saving the soul of a certain *strategos* 'in order that he would be found in the Orthodox communion' (ὥστ' ἂν εὑρεθῇ ἐν τῇ ὀρθοδόξῳ κοινωνίᾳ).[64] It is easy to imagine that the *strategos* in question was an iconoclast[65] and that in the eyes of the hegoumenos of Stoudios, he died a heretic, since he neither received the last rites from the hands of an iconodule priest nor had the opportunity to repent of his iconoclastic sins. Theodoros accordingly blames Kassia for not having shown 'true love' (ἀληθινῇ ἀγάπῃ)[66], which must be understood as Christian (iconodule) love, as opposed to family love. The key to interpretation of the remark is in the quotation 'I count all things but loss'[67] from St Paul's Letter to the Philippians,[68] in which the pre-eminence of faith in Christ is defended over Jewish lineage and blood ties.

Whether moved by the words of her spiritual father Theodoros or by her own desires, Kassia finally had herself tonsured and founded her own convent, in which she devoted herself to literary production in the peace of her cell. Despite the volume of her writings, the subject of icons is marginal in it: Kassia is indifferent to the new saints who have arisen from opposition to iconoclasm and praises none of them in her hymns. We may

---

[62] *PmbZ* # 1406; *PBE* I: Dorotheos 9. [63] Gouillard 1982. [64] Theod. Stoud., *epist.* 539,27.
[65] This *strategos* was very likely the husband of Kassia's sister, see *PmbZ* # 3636C; *PBE* I: Anonymous 682.
[66] Theod. Stoud., *epist.* 539,24.
[67] Theod. Stoud., *epist.* 539,26–27: τὰ ἄλλα πάντα σκύβαλα ἡγούμεναι. [68] Phil 3:8.

well wonder whether the main reason for this decision was the lack of women in this group (with the exception of the legendary *patrikia* Maria, of whom it would later be said that she died confronting Emperor Leon III for defending the icon of the Chalke Gate, which was eliminated in 726).[69]

The singularity of Kassia's work, part of which was intended to be sung at religious services, was used by her milieu as a basis for promoting her cult, as it could be presented as objective proof of her holiness. Together with the nuns of the convent, which was founded during the reign of the iconoclast Theophilos, her relatives focused on her defence of the veneration of icons, which the poetess includes in the fifth theotokion of her *Funeral Kanon*.[70] They also had the elements they needed to praise their hegoumene as another new confessor of the Church. The best evidence for this was furnished by the testimony of Theodoros Stoudites, who affirmed that Kassia had made donations to him, had helped an imprisoned iconodule monk and had even been whipped on two occasions.

Together with these undisputable facts, the account of Kassia's participation in the beauty contest to choose the new empress was adorned with some words in verse, which not only characterised the poetess as a defender of women's rights but also challenged the iconoclast emperor. This entire episode may have been extensively narrated in a lost hagiography of Kassia that served as a common source for both tenth-century historians and the compiler of the *Patria*.[71] The reworking of the dialogue between Theophilos and Kassia imposes an iconodule reading on the episode: the golden apple the emperor offers her symbolises iconoclast heresy and recalls the original sin into which Eve fell by accepting the apple from the snake.[72] The heroine rejects it and enters a theological debate to defend Orthodoxy. On affirming that the best emanates through a woman, Kassia reminded her interlocutor that it was thanks to the Theotokos (the Mother of God) that Christ, who would redeem the world, was born. In the last analysis, his wish to be made incarnate and make himself visible justified the veneration of icons.

As in the case of other iconodule hagiographies of the period, it can be assumed that this account in honour of Kassia also accused the iconoclasts

---

[69] Auzépy 1990.
[70] Τὸν υἱὸν τοῦ Θεοῦ, ἐκ γυναικὸς λαβόντα σάρκα, ἧς τὴν θέαν τιμῶμεν τοῖς πίναξιν, 'The son of God, who became incarnate from a woman, whose sight we honour in icons.'
[71] For the reconstruction of this *Vita Cassiae* and its possible relationship with the *Vita* of Empress Theodora see Lauxtermann 1998: 396–97.
[72] Gen 3.

of attacking the Theotokos.[73] What is certain is that they never attacked the Virgin systematically and that Theophilos in particular was devoted to her.[74] This leads to the conclusion that the conversation was at least partially altered after the triumph of the iconodules in 843, when numerous authors began to portray Theophilos in a negative light.[75] Most likely the story was not popularised immediately, since no ninth-century source reports the episode. This may have been out of respect for Empress Theodora, who did not come out well in it, since she appeared to be the sovereign's second choice.

In any case, the usefulness of this narrative for the nuns of Kassia's convent is clear: it allowed them to counteract the memory of the problematic relationship of the poetess with the iconoclast *strategos* of the testimony of Theodoros Stoudites, as well as controversial assertions such as that at the beginning of Kassia's hymn to St Christina, in which she affirms: 'Women also have abandoned the error of idolatry for the power of your cross'.[76] Taken out of context, these verses seem to extol the triumph of iconoclasm (the naked cross) compared with the idolatry of which the iconodules were accused. Although Kassia's holiness was not recognised at the time, and she appeared in no *synaxarion*, the account of her confrontation with the iconoclast Emperor Theophilos avoided criticism of her milieu and ensured it social prestige.

4.1.3 *The Political Meaning of the New Aristocratic Saint: Imperial Ideology*

The model of the promotion of a specific family cult, such as that of Eudokimos, must thus be analysed not in ecclesiastical or religious, but in political terms. Flusin has pointed out that the Macedonian emperors took charge of systematising saints' veneration in Constantinople, producing hagiographical material at the court and transferring relics (mainly from Old Testament figures) to the capital.[77] They favoured certain devotions of their own (Elijah, the archangels, etc.)[78] and were a source of holiness, although Patlagean regarded this as so *en mode mineur* (to a lesser

---

[73] Gero 1977: 144–46; Koutrakou 2005.
[74] Theoph. Cont. III, 3.1–4 and 9.62–64. Seals belonging to prominent iconoclast lay officials, moreover, used to ask for the intercession of the Theotokos since the eighth century, see Glynias 2017.
[75] Prieto Domínguez 2019b. See Section 4.4.
[76] Καὶ γυναῖκες κατήργησαν τὴν πλάνην τῆς εἰδωλομανίας δυνάμει τοῦ Σταυροῦ σου.
[77] Magdalino 1987; Flusin 2000; 2001; Gallina 2011. [78] Dagron 1996: 201–10.

degree).[79] Basileios I encouraged the veneration of his son Konstantinos but did not manage to establish it, perhaps because Konstantinos was confused in the liturgy with Konstantinos I the Great.[80] Leon VI did the same with his mistress Zoe Tzaoustaina (in vain),[81] his brother Stephanos and his wife Theophano. In the end, the Macedonian dynasty had to settle for having as saints the patriarch Stephanos and Theophano,[82] and it is clear that the success of these two sanctifications was due to the groups supporting the imperial enterprise, the patriarchate, in the first case, and Theophano's family, the Martiniakoi, in the second. In the same way, the cult of Eudokimos was only possible thanks to his family, the ancestors of the Maleinoi.

This family dimension means that attempts to re-read the biography of Eudokimos in search of elements characteristic of an iconodule saint will inevitably be unsuccessful. The sources, both the *synaxaria* and the metaphrastic *vita*, merely describe his piety, mercy and love of justice but never specify his works or what these noble sentiments actually came down to. Métivier emphasises that, just as the emperor imitates Christ, so Eudokimos imitates the emperor, which means that it is no coincidence that the monk in charge of transferring his body to the definitive tomb is called Ioseph (like Joseph of Arimathea, who took the body of Christ down from the cross); that he practices the virtues of the emperor par excellence (piety, charity and justice); that he sings the Psalms of King David and that the beneficiary of his first miracle was named Elijah, like the prophet who protected Basileios I.[83] Aristocratic holiness thus follows the imperial model. All these elements, however, could well have been, if not added, at least emphasised in the writing of the metaphrastic *vita* that belongs to the late ninth century.

Were they already in the original *vita* written on the occasion of the transfer of Eudokimos' relics ca. 842? It is impossible to say. But their presence does no more than update a process already latent in the original *vita*, which aimed to bring the saint (and his family) closer to the emperor. The anonymous metaphrast certainly makes no mention of Theophilos, who doubtless lived in the imperial palace when Eudokimos associated with him[84] and who showered him with honours such as the title of

---

[79] Patlagean 1989.
[80] Dagron 1996: 208–9. On the attempt, see *Vita of Ignatios* 94 and Ps-Symeon 692,20–93,11.
[81] Ps-Symeon 703,6–7. [82] *SynaxCP* 694,1–18; 689/690,54–55 and 714,4–5.
[83] Métivier 2012: 107–9. [84] *Vita of Eudokimos* 5,3–5.

kandidatos and the post of *stratopedarches* of Cappadocia.[85] Not for nothing was the father of Eudokimos the patrician Basileios,[86] who can be identified as a *strategos* of Charsianon mentioned by Syrian sources as an emissary of Theophilos to the Caliph Al-Mu'taṣim in 838 charged with negotiating the release of the prisoners of Amorion.[87] Byzantine historians tell us that it was impossible to reach an agreement,[88] but Syrian ones are more meticulous and report that Theophilos turned over two letters to his legate Basileios. The first was amicable and proposed that the captives be exchanged for gifts. Al-Mu'taṣim demanded, to the contrary, that two strong men of Theophilos be handed over to him: Theophobos (Nasr the Kurd) and the patrician Manuel. Basileios responded by presenting the second, more hostile letter.

The power of Eudokimos' family in Cappadocia, where the border with the Arabs was a matter of serious concern for Theophilos, was probably one reason why both he and his father were appointed the *strategos* and *stratopedarches* of the area. Like the main collaborators of Theophilos, if their religious beliefs placed them in the iconodule sector, they kept quiet about it. We have already noted that the author of the original *vita* characterises Eudokimos as an iconoclast saint and nowhere alludes to the crisis of images. In any case, if that *vita* was not iconoclast, the metaphrast felt that it was and not only purged the style but eliminated any details that might prove this. He therefore does not mention Theophilos or provide any date for Eudokimos, in contrast to the entries of the *Synaxarion*, which were no doubt included in the pre-metaphrastic *vita*. In fact, the religious affiliation of the saint and of the first hagiographer are of little importance. It does not matter whether the former was a committed iconoclast or whether the latter had had an iconoclast education that showed through in the writing of the *vita*, or whether they both fervently venerated icons and tried to keep up appearances and reconcile their personal vision with historical reality (as Theodorakopoulos would have it).[89] What is important is the relationship between the aristocracy and the religious phenomenon of holiness and its utilitarian use to achieve specific, quite mundane goals.

---

[85] *Vita of Eudokimos* 7,14–28. Concerning the positions of *kandidatos* and *stratopedarches* of Cappadocia, see Theodorakopoulos 2004: 131–32.
[86] *PmbZ* # 937.
[87] Michael the Syrian II, 501; Bar Hebraeus I, 138; Vasiliev 1935: vol. I, 174–75; *PmbZ* # 937 and # 932. The identification was proposed by Potache 1981: 110, n. 2.
[88] Theoph. Cont. III, 34,25–34; Genesios III 12, 46,87–95; Skylitzes 78,42–79,50.
[89] Theodorakopoulos 2004: 136.

The metaphrastic hagiographer wanted to make Eudokimos fit the new model of a saint that became fashionable after the restoration of icons: the ascetic iconodule monk who, in common with Niketas of Medikion and Petros of Atroa, suffered for Orthodoxy as a confessor or martyr. He does not hesitate to justify Eudokimos as an ascetic monk, but also as one of the world, whose miracles allow him to be compared with the few monks attaining the highest level of perfection.[90] But this attempt does not hide the true model that supports his sanctification process: military commanders included in the *synaxaria* who are noted above all else for their virginity and philanthropy.[91]

4.2 The Military Milieu

The period of the Second Iconoclasm thus saw the strengthening and development of a very specific type of holiness. The most distinguished example is the aristocratic military hero Eudokimos, of whom a complete *vita* survives. Eudokimos, however, is by no means the only sanctified great general of Theophilos' time: another well-known case is Kallistos, the Duke of Koloneia and the protagonist of one version of the popular *Passion of the 42 Martyrs of Amorion* (version Γ = *BHG* 1213), which is attributed to the well-known iconodule confessor Michael Synkellos.[92] The account describes how a large group of Byzantine officials taken prisoner by the Arabs in the capture of Amorion in 838 were transferred to the region of the Tigris, where they were tortured in an attempt to force them to reject Christianity. Since they refused, they were finally executed seven years later on 6 March 845.[93]

The hero of the *vita* of Michael the Synkellos (the aforementioned Kallistos) had a brilliant military career under Theophilos and is a perfect instance of the model of holiness already analysed. Kallistos[94] also stood out for his philanthropy and his virginity, as well as for singing the Psalms of King David whenever he had occasion to do so and for preferring a church to any other place.[95] When he arrived in Constantinople to

---

[90] *Vita of Eudokimos* 14,10–30. See also *Vita of Eudokimos* 1,11–12,8.
[91] For a general survey of the cult of military saints in Byzantium, see White 2013: 1–93.
[92] The story of the forty-two Martyrs of Amorion was very popular in the second half of the ninth century, as is apparent from the successive versions. On their hagiographical dossier, see Kotzambassi 1992. On the authorship of this text, parallel to an *idiomelon* of the patriarch Methodios and a *kanon* signed by Ignatios Diakonos, see Chapter 2.
[93] For an analysis of the successive surviving hagiographies (*BHG* 1209–1214) and their possible chronology, see Kazhdan 1986: 150–60; 2006: 206–9; Kotzambassi 1992; Kolia-Dermitzaki 2002; Métivier 2018: 180–84 and 187–90. On the later versions, see Section 6.3.6.
[94] *PmbZ* # 3606; *PBE* I: Kallistos 1 and Kallistos 2.
[95] *Passion of the 42 Martyrs of Amorion* (version Γ) 24,13–30.

continue his studies, Kallistos joined the imperial troops due to his physical strength and the renown of his family.[96] He held the position of Count *ton Scholon*, in which he distinguished himself for chastity and discipline,[97] but also for giving alms to the poor.[98] Shortly before he died, Theophilos named him Duke of Koloneia. As governor of that area of the *thema* of the Armeniakoi, Kallistos not only protected the poor from the powerful and refused to comply with the emperor's order to punish the monks of Pelekete[99] but also confronted the Paulicians, a Armenian sect now established in Tephrike that rejected worship of the Virgin and the saints and therefore also their icons.[100] These heretics ended up ambushing him, capturing him and delivering him to the caliph, who imprisoned him along with the generals arrested in Amorion. From then on, Kallistos' fate was linked to that of the group of future martyrs.

The *vita* that is the basis of their veneration is clearly iconodule, since it was written shortly after the Triumph of Orthodoxy by a distinguished representative of the literary circle of the patriarch Methodios. But the model of holiness Kallistos sets is in keeping with the earlier iconoclast pattern, in the same way that the dynamic of the establishment of his veneration repeats the strategies of family cults discussed above: Kallistos was from a famous Anatolian family.[101] This hagiographer gives no further details, but another version of the martyrdom (version Δ, written by Sophronios) affirms that Kallistos was one of the Melissenoi.[102] This family played an important role during the iconoclastic years, and it is easy to see that they attempted to use this hagiography to whitewash their past so as to maintain their social recognition and prestige.[103]

Both of Kallistos' parents appear in the narration performing pious deeds dear to the iconoclasts: his mother appears about halfway through

---

[96] *Passion of the 42 Martyrs of Amorion* (version Γ) 23,21–23.
[97] *Passion of the 42 Martyrs of Amorion* (version Γ) 23,23–24,12. Concerning the military career of Kallistos, see Haldon 1984: 187, 189f., 300, 324, 330–332, 463f., 601, 607.
[98] *Passion of the 42 Martyrs of Amorion* (version Γ) 24,13–25,19.
[99] *Passion of the 42 Martyrs of Amorion* (version Γ) 28, 26–37. Kallistos' refusal is along the same lines, see p. 25,27–31. On the Bithynian monastery of Pelekete, see Section 1.3.3.
[100] Garsoïan 1967; Astruc et al. 1970; Lemerle 1973; Barnard 1977; Ludwig 1998.
[101] *Passion of the 42 Martyrs of Amorion* (version Γ) 23,15–18.
[102] *Passion of the 42 Martyrs of Amorion* (version Δ = *BHG* 1209) 50,5–6: κατὰ τοὺς Μελλισσεινοὺς λεγόμενον. Winkelmann 1987: 152–53 is also of the same opinion. For Kazhdan 1986: 155, it is a textual error and Kallistos should not be identified with Melissenos but rather with a different *strategos*, as appears in Ps-Symeon 639,1–3. According to *PmbZ* # 4952, this Melissenos was named Theodotos.
[103] They failed, however, in this enterprise, because as of 880 we find no evidence of them (Settipani 2006: 501) and Kallistos in venerated in just one *synaxarion*: *Typika Dmitrievskij* 1, 53 (6 March). For the genealogy of the Melissenoi, see Settipani 2006: 77 and 492–505.

the *vita* distributing her possessions among the poor,[104] while his father is mentioned at the beginning as someone who stood out for his hospitality, temperance and intelligence. This meant that after his death he received the divine gift of healing the possessed and the sick.[105] It is worth pointing out that the performance of exclusively posthumous miracles is characteristic of iconoclast hagiographies. Kallistos' daily contact and great familiarity with Emperor Theophilos, together with the trust the latter placed in him, by granting him positions of power and taking the trouble shortly before his death to leave him financially secure, suggest a true affection between the two men that the iconodule hagiographer tried to play down, converting their encounters into a theological struggle. Indeed, Kallistos is tempted to abandon Orthodoxy by means of flattery from his family and friends.[106] This detail fits in well with his membership in the family of the Melissenoi, who included recognised iconoclasts, some of them as important as the patriarch Theodotos I Melissenos Kassiteras (815–821), a known collaborator of Leon V the Armenian.[107] According to Byzantine historians, Theodotos' intrigues allowed him to win Emperor Leon around to iconoclasm and then have him replace Nikephoros at the head of the patriarchate.[108]

The latent confrontation between Kallistos and Theodotos in the text – one suffers the intrigues, the other carries them out; one is an iconodule, the other an iconoclast – is most clearly seen in the hagiographer's conviction that Kallistos was so highly esteemed by pious men that he could have been appointed patriarch.[109] This comparison of the two figures is clear to the reader, since they are from the same family. A further detail to be taken into account when assessing the survival of this model of holiness, which reached its peak during the time of Theophilos, is the existence of a previous version of the martyrdom of Amorion by an anonymous author (version B = *BHG* 1212) that is clearly favourable to the iconoclast emperor. Version Δ by Sophronios, which relates the collective martyrdom by concentrating on the figure of another *strategos* of Theophilos, Theodoros Krateros, who faces the caliph in a dialectic duel (*agon*),[110] offers some praise of the victories of the last

---

[104] *Passion of the 42 Martyrs of Amorion* (version Γ) 28,21–26.
[105] *Passion of the 42 Martyrs of Amorion* (version Γ) 23,15–18.
[106] *Passion of the 42 Martyrs of Amorion* (version Γ) 28,3–15.
[107] *PmbZ* # 7954; *PBE* I: Theodotos 2; Lilie 1999: 148–55.
[108] Theoph. Cont. I, 11,17–44 and 15,17–16,19; Genesios I.9 (8.64–9.83), 13 (11.32–59).
[109] *Passion of the 42 Martyrs of Amorion* (version Γ) 26,30–32.
[110] On Theodoros Krateros, see *PmbZ* # 7679. On Sophronios and his account, see Section 6.3.6.

iconoclast emperor over the Arabs. The hagiographer of version B for his part not only fails to mention iconoclasm or to offer any apologetic element in defence of icons but also shows true sympathy for Theophilos, praising him as a great emperor who was both brave and effective.[111] Version B is one of the early ones, from before the year 846,[112] like version P (*BHG* 1214c), which belongs to the same period[113] and also omits the dispute over the images and praises Theophilos as well as his wife, the very pious Theodora.[114] We do not know who the authors of these two texts were, but they must have had links with the court, since they serve its interests in supporting the rehabilitation of Theophilos.

The senior military officials at the court of Theophilos included Petros of Galatia and Sergios Niketiates, whose entries in the *Synaxarion* reveal a cult that is a result of the same process.[115] Petros, also known as Petros the Thaumatourgos, was appointed *komes* of the *tagma* of the *exkoubitores* during the reign of Theophilos, when he was twenty-five years old.[116] He should not be confused with Petros the Patrician, who is celebrated on 1 July[117] and is the result of the assimilation of the domestic of the *scholae* who founded the monastery of Evandros in Constantinople before 811[118] and a disciple of St Ioannikios also named Petros, who after consolidating the monastic life of this foundation was celebrated annually by the monks.[119] Sergios Niketiates, for his part, was related to Theophilos by marriage, since he was from the family of Empress Theodora. He distinguished himself as a *strategos* in the Cretan campaign against the Arabs, during which he died on 28 June of an unknown year in the reign of Michael III. Soon after that, his body was transferred to the monastery of the Theotokos of Niketiates, which he had founded on the Gulf of Nicomedia.[120]

Another brilliant man of arms who triumphed during the reign of an iconoclast emperor and was sanctified and became the subject of a well-known *vita*, although he ultimately did not appear in the liturgical

---

[111] *Passion of the 42 Martyrs of Amorion* (version B) 11,22–31.   [112] Kotzambassi 1992: 126.
[113] Halkin 1986: 152–61.   [114] Halkin 1986: 154.
[115] *SynaxCP* 125,4–26,12 (9 October: Petros of Galatia); *SynaxCP* 777,5–78,16 (28 June: Sergios Niketiates).
[116] *PmbZ* # 6077 and 26426; *PBE* I: Petros 145.   [117] *SynaxCP* 792,35–94,3.
[118] *PmbZ* # 6046; *PBE* I: Petros 148. On the monastery of Evandros, see Janin 1969: 114; Ruggieri 1991: 190.
[119] Wortley 1980: 555–57.
[120] *PmbZ* # 6664; *PBE* I: Sergios 57; Grégoire 1933: 515–31; Guilland 1971: 51, nr. 11; Varona Codeso and Prieto Domínguez 2013. He is also briefly mentioned in the *Acta of David, Symeon and Georgios* 245,31.

calendars, was Antonios the Younger.[121] Unfortunately, his complete *vita* has not survived, although three fragments have come down to us by different means as the *Vita of Antonios the Younger* (*BHG* 142), the *Vita of Antonios the Younger* (*BHG* 142/addit) and one last fragment (*BHG* 143).[122] Antonios occupied the post of *ek prosopou* of the *thema* of the Kibyrrhaiotai during the reign of Michael II (820–829) and took part in this capacity in the campaigns against the rebel Thomas the Slav.[123] Thanks to the hagiographical account, we know that in this post he was known for his justice and philanthropy, which meant that he had no one whipped, and for his virginity, to the point that he never kissed a woman or a man without a beard in his life.[124] Antonios' youth thus reflects the same kind of military sainthood as that of Eudokimos, which would later be complemented by an iconodule model of holiness in keeping with his experiences after the Triumph of Orthodoxy in 843.[125]

A final case can be added of a *strategos* who triumphed in the service of an iconoclast emperor and whose sanctification was recognised with an entry in the *Synaxarion of Constantinople*.[126] This is Manuel the Armenian, who died on 27 July 838.[127] Manuel was *protostrator* under Michael I and *patrikios* and *strategos* of the *thema* of the Armeniakoi under Leon V. After he served for a while in the caliphate, Theophilos appointed him *magistros* and *domestikos ton scholon* so as to have him fighting at his side. In the campaign of 837, they took Zapetra, and on 22 July 838 the Battle of Anzes was fought on the plain of Dazimon. This was the 'true' battle of those associated with this site, since Byzantine historians narrate it on various occasions, creating confusion. In fact, a few days before the fall of Amorion to the troops of Al-Mu'taṣim, it was in this enclave that Theophilos confronted Amer, the emir of Melitene in the Cappadocian frontier, who was called 'Amr Ibn 'Abd Allah al-Aqta ('the One-

---

[121] *PmbZ* # 534; *PBE* I: Antonios 12.
[122] Unfortunately, the attempt of Godfrey Tanner, David Turner and Daniel Farrell to produce an overall edition of the *Vita of Antonios the Younger* by re-examining the manuscripts Vienna ÖNB Hist. Gr. 31, fol. 1a–17a (tenth century), the Brussels Bibliothèque Royale 8163-6931, fol. 2–16v, and the Athens EBE 2534, (twelfth century) was not implemented. See also Van den Ven 1910; Kazhdan 1999: 291–94; Métivier 2018: 191–93.
[123] For the biography of this person born in Palestine, see *PmbZ* # 534; *PBE* I: Antonios 12; Tanner 1997; Karlin-Hayter 2007; Signes Codoñer 2014: 183–99.
[124] *Vita of Antonios the Younger* 194,21–24; cf. Vinson 1998: 510.
[125] For the career of Antonios the Younger after the restoration of icons, see Section 4.3.2.
[126] *SynaxCP* 851,57 (27 July); Halkin 1954a: 9–11.
[127] Treadgold 1979b: 182ff. On Manuel the Armenian, see *PmbZ* # 4707; *PBE* I: Manuel 6; Grégoire 1933; Grégoire 1934. Cf. also Hirsch 1876; Bury 1912: 143f.; Vasiliev 1935: vol. I, 154f.; Signes Codoñer 1995: 461ff.; 2006; 2014: 83–102.

Handed').[128] In this battle, Manuel heroically saved the life of Theophilos at the price of serious wounds that caused his death five days later, according to the historians of the group of the Logothetes.[129] He was buried in his palace in the capital near the cistern of Aspar, where his veneration likely became established among the monks of Manuel's monastery.[130] As a great *strategos* of the iconoclast period, everything suggests that his sanctification was almost identical to that of contemporaries such as Eudokimos.

The sources mention another Manuel the Armenian; this second Manuel was an uncle of Empress Theodora and the tutor of Michael III who was a member of the regency council in charge of restoring the cult of icons. He was appointed *protomagistros* of the navy and died ca. 860, after saving the young emperor's life in another battle at Dazimon, as the other Manuel had done for his father Theophilos twenty years previously on the same spot. This is one of the famous 'doubles' of Byzantine historiography. The pattern of the hero who saves the emperor during a campaign against the Arabs is repeated no less than four times during this period: (1) Theophobos helps Theophilos;[131] (2) Manuel saves Theophilos;[132] (3) Manuel and Theophobos save Theophilos in Dazimon in 838;[133] (4) Manuel saves Michael III at the Battle of Anzes in Dazimon.[134] Grégoire has established that the account of the Battle of Dazimon in which Michael III is the protagonist was merely a doublet of the passage referring to the reign of his father Theophilos.[135] In his famous studies on Manuel the Armenian, Grégoire also proposed that this was a single historical person, a thesis many subsequent researchers have accepted uncritically. Grégoire believed that after his death in 838, Manuel was sanctified and honoured with an iconoclast *vita*, which the Logothetes and his followers used in their historiographical account, while Genesios and Theophanes Continuatus used another iconodule life that portrayed Manuel as a great defender of icons, a restorer of Orthodoxy and a pious man active until ca. 860.

In Grégoire's opinion, this second *vita* was a falsification of events produced in his own so-called monastery of Manuel with the assistance

---

[128] *PmbZ* # 8552; Bury 1909; Signes Codoñer 2014: 279–312.
[129] Ps-Symeon 636–37; Symeon Logothetes 130,28.
[130] Janin 1969: 320–21; Ruggieri 1991: 193. [131] Cont. Theoph. III, 22 and Genesios 42,71–79.
[132] Cont. Theoph. III, 24,12–35 and Genesios 43,4–27.
[133] Cont. Theoph. III, 31–33 and Genesios 48,30–73.
[134] Cont. Theoph. IV, 24 and Genesios 65,22–65.
[135] Grégoire 1933: 521; Grégoire 1934: 201; Varona Codeso 2010: 134–36 and 269–77.

of the monks of Stoudios, in an attempt to rehabilitate him and keep him from being remembered as a heretic.[136] To do so, they did not hesitate to 'bring back from the dead' the figure of Manuel and transform him into a champion of Orthodoxy: the wounds he received in battle were said to have healed completely due to the mediation of the monks of Stoudios in exchange for his commitment to restore icons, which he did before Theodora herself. But as this healing is generally dated to 843 as a prelude to restoration, are we to assume that Manuel's injuries had confined him to his bed since 838? Moreover, the link with the monastery of Stoudios through Helena, the wife of the patrician Manuel and supposedly a sister of Theophilos, is at odds with the chronological details at our disposal, since she was miraculously healed of an incurable disease by Nikolaos Stoudites in ca. 867/868.[137] Her miraculous healing is dated during these years in connection with what happened to Eudokia Ingerina, who was also healed by Nikolaos of Stoudios after the accession to the throne of her husband Emperor Basileios I.[138] At that time, her husband Manuel was still alive, since after this healing he himself fell ill and asked Nikolaos to tonsure him as a monk, so that he could regain his health. This is therefore a third Manuel.[139] The third Manuel is probably the *patrikios* and *logothetes of the dromou* to whom Metrophanes of Smyrna sent a letter denouncing the affronts to patriarch Ignatios.[140]

This view of things, which considers all events subsequent to 838 an invention combining hagiography and folk tales, continues to be accepted despite its many inconsistencies and general improbability.[141] Signes Codoñer has recently shown that Manuel's feats after 838 are historical fact, which means that there is no reason to think of the extraordinary influence of a fictitious hagiographical account that has not survived.[142] Despite the common acceptance of the thesis that the *magistros* Manuel who died in 838 and the *protomagistros* Manuel who was Theodora's brother were the same person, the arguments for this are unconvincing. The coincidence of the name, the post, the Armenian origin, the proximity to Theophilos and the confusion of Byzantine historians (who attribute identical heroic deeds to similar persons) have meant that the idea has not

---

[136] Grégoire 1933: 520–24; 1934.
[137] *Vita of Nikolaos Stoud.* 916B–C. On Helena, see *PmbZ* # 22569; *PBE* I: Helene 2.
[138] *Vita of Nikolaos Stoud.* 913D–16B, see *PmbZ* # 1632 and # 21754; *PBE* I: Eudokia 2.
[139] *PmbZ* # 24866.   [140] *PmbZ* # 24869; see Section 5.2.1.
[141] Dvornik 1953: 70; Treadgold 1979b: 182–83; *PmbZ* # 4707; *PBE* I: Manuel 6; Signes Codoñer 2006; Varona Codeso 2010: 269–84.
[142] Signes Codoñer 2013b.

been challenged until now. Although Grégoire's proposal is imaginative and in one sense compelling, it is better to consider all the information about Manuel the Armenian historical. We are thus no longer concerned with how to interpret the testimony of the group of the Logothetes, who place his death in 838, since this detail is corroborated by a liturgical source of seemingly little interest because it confuses the events: the *Synaxarion of Constantinople*. We must trust sources of all kinds and recognize the possibility that both men were remembered in two hagiographical accounts. Although the complete texts of these two *Vitae Manuelis* have not survived, studies such as Signes' have reconstructed their possible content through an analysis of their influence on contemporary historians.[143] We are therefore concerned with two different texts in memory of Manuel the Armenian, and recourse is needed to the habitual literary practices of the time, if we are to draw any conclusions.

After the restoration of icons in Byzantium, several common types of hagiographical rewriting modified details, situations, persons, the order of events, the role of the protagonists and the like. Beginning in the seventh century, we have evidence of multiple rewritings of the *vita* of Ioannes the Merciful,[144] and in the mid-ninth century the revision or composition of a new *vita* was not unusual, as the hagiographies of Petros of Atroa show.[145] By this time, the monastery of Stoudios had become an important centre for the reinterpretation of recent history due to the rewriting carried out there of the *vitae* of Niketas of Medikion, Ioannikios, Theodoros Stoudites and Nikolaos Stoudites.[146] In the same way, the *Synodicon vetus* presents a second, later version that gives a major role to the *magistros* Manuel and the Stoudites. In this context of collective 'reinvention', we even have a record of the process used at the Constantinopolitan convent of Krisis,[147] where the non-iconodule saint traditionally linked to the place – St Philaretos, mentioned at the beginning of this chapter – was replaced by the legendary St Andreas *en Krisei*, who was celebrated for having confronted Konstantinos V until he died defending icons.[148] For some

---

[143] Signes Codoñer 1995: 519–24, 532–34, 567–69; 2006 bases himself on the reconstruction of the lost sources by the trail they left in the extant work of historians and on the general characteristics of iconoclast hagiography indicated by Auzépy 1992.
[144] Déroche 2011.
[145] Both are signed by the same author: the monk Sabas, see *Vita of Petros of Atroa*, p. 11; *Vita retractata of Petros of Atroa*. About this holy man, see *PmbZ* # 6022; *PBE* I: Petros 34.
[146] Afinogenov 2004c; Delouis 2011.
[147] On the convent of Krisis, see Janin 1969: 28–31; Majeska 1984: 314–15 places it on the western periphery of Constantinople.
[148] On Andreas *en Krisei* and his accounts, see Costa-Louillet 1954/1955: 214–16; Auzépy 1993; Kazhdan 1999: 203.

scholars, the figure of Andreas *en Krisei* has a historical origin in the martyrdom of Andreas of Blachernai, who was beaten to death in 761/762 along with his companions Stephanos, Paulos and Petros.[149] The discovery of his allegedly miraculous relics gave the community excellent iconodule credentials and made it a site of pilgrimage. Due to this, a second version of the account of his life, the surviving pre-metaphrastic *Vita of Andreas en Krisei* (BHG 111), appeared in the years after the Triumph of Orthodoxy, at the same time that a *kanon* in his honour was commissioned from Ioseph Hymnographos, who mentions the convent of Krisis in a pun in which he compares Andreas to a lily (Greek κρίνον).[150] Although we know of other extreme cases in which a saint suspected of sympathising with iconoclasm was replaced by another, no completely new biography unconnected with the previous one for a saint already known and venerated was ever produced.

Taking all this into account, the most likely reconstruction in the case of Manuel the Armenian is the simplest: there were two different Manuels. The first was the iconoclast general who died in 838 and is remembered in the liturgical calendar of the Church of Constantinople; he was the subject of a *vita* modelled on that of Eudokimos, in keeping with the type of holiness of other great generals of Theophilos of the same period. The second Manuel is Theodora's uncle, on whom the empress relied during the regency and with whose help the restoration of the cult of icons was possible. In common with the other members of the restoring imperial family, such as Theoktistos, Petronas and Theodora herself, this Manuel also underwent a process of sanctification that had considerable repercussions among chroniclers.

The confusion between the two Manuels thus likely originated from an attempt by their contemporaries to identify the more recently deceased saint with an established saint by the same name. This dynamic is by no means new and belongs to the 'devotional symbiosis' very popular during this period, as is shown by what happened to Prokopios Dekapolites, whose cult was based on that of his brother Gregorios Dekapolites.[151] So too, the adoration of St Elias the Younger was widespread, owing to confusion with the prophet Elijah from the time of Leon VI, thanks to their homonymity and common character as seers,[152] while the veneration of Prince Konstantinos, the first-born son of Basileios I, was promoted on

---

[149] Krausmüller 2007a.
[150] *Menaion* I: 444–51. The metaphrastic *vita* (BHG 112) dates from the second half of the ninth century.
[151] See Chapter 3.
[152] Timotin 2010: 95. The devotion of Leon VI to the prophet Elijah was visible even in his bath and extended to the whole Macedonian dynasty, see Magdalino 1988b: 103–9. See Section 6.3.3.

his death in 879 by the patriarch Photios to coincide with the commemoration of Konstantinos I the Great.[153] This 'devotional symbiosis' of the two Manuels explains the presence of doublets in the accounts of the historians, who describe the same feats, attributing them first to the Manuel of the iconoclast period and then to the Manuel who took part in the restoration. It is scarcely believable that this confusion was shared by Theophanes Continuatus, Genesios and Skylitzes. More logically, their common source or the sources at their disposal voluntarily confused the two Manuels, as a result of which the achievements of the sanctified Manuel began to be attributed to the Manuel related to Theodora as well, making his veneration easier.

The monks of Stoudios play an important part in the merging of the two figures; they were entrusted with healing the *magistros* Manuel in exchange for his commitment to restoring images. This episode appears to be part of the *Vita Manuelis B* (the iconodule account) and in fact took place much later, as is shown by the *Synodicon vetus*. The *Synodicon vetus* offers a concise account of the history of the councils from Apostolic times until the late ninth century, and appeared in at least two versions, the first of which was written shortly after 887, to judge by its markedly anti-Photian character.[154] In it, the account of the restoration coincides with the testimony of Georgios Monachos, according to whom Theodora called a synod to depose Ioannes Grammatikos and consecrate Methodios, who would take charge of restoring icons.[155] In the tenth-century version, on the other hand, Manuel is the absolute protagonist: having recovered from his illness, he undertakes to persuade Theodora and thus trigger the restoration.[156] Mango believes that this pro-Stoudite version depends on the historiographical text of Genesios.[157] Be that as it may, the iconoclast *Vita Manuelis A* followed the principles of the sanctification of generals discussed in this chapter, and in the same way his veneration, once established in Constantinople, was probably encouraged by his family in order to affirm his proximity to Emperor Theophilos. What is more, Theophilos' family made a noteworthy attempt to ensure that its members received veneration and were included in the *synaxaria*. We do not know if the change of doctrine with regard to images was the main reason for this,

---

[153] Halkin 1954a; Grumel 1966; Karlin-Hayter 1966; Grumel 1967; Patlagean 1989: 356–57. See Chapters 6–7.
[154] Van Dieten 1980/1982.   [155] *Synodicon vetus*, 156.
[156] *Synodicon vetus*, appendix II, 156. Mango 1977: 133–34.
[157] Genesios 56,38–43. For the Stoudite influence of this version, see Karlin-Hayter 2001: 171–83; Varona Codeso 2010: 191–92 and 212–13.

although it seems clear that it helped trigger the pursuit of a religious justification for legitimizing their memory.

4.3 The Court Milieu: The Family and Collaborators of Theophilos in Post-Iconoclast Hagiography

Not only the collaborators of Emperor Theophilos but also his family found a place in the hagiography after the restoration of the cult of images. Because of their previous record as iconoclast heretics, their rehabilitation as public figures worthy of imitation inevitably involved rewriting their participation in these events and by extension the whole Second Iconoclasm. The success of this process was possible only due to vigorous efforts by a family network at court, which encouraged their veneration reciprocally with objectives that were not as pious as they might have been.

4.3.1 The Court of Theophilos and Its Post-Iconoclast Reinvention

This process took place even with Theophobos, another great military commander of Theophilos' milieu, who died shortly before the restoration. Many details of his biography overlap with that of Manuel the Armenian: Theophobos was of Persian origin and for this reason was chosen by the emperor to lead a *tagma* of special cavalry made up of Khurramite refugees.[158] He was appointed *patrikios* and married into the imperial family. According to some sources, he married a sister of Theophilos named Helena in a ceremony that took place in 843.[159] According to others, his wife was a sister of the empress, who must then be Theodora's third sister, whose name was ignored, along with that of her husband, in a kind of *damnatio memoriae* for having conspired against the emperor.[160] Theophobos fought alongside Theophilos at Zapetra (837) and even saved his life at the Battle of Dazimon (838).[161] An alleged conspiracy to place him on the throne led to his being accused of treason and condemned to death by Theophilos in 842. His body was deposited in the monastery of

---

[158] *PmbZ* # 8237; *PBE* I: Theophobos 1; Bunijatov 1959: 613–16, nr. 7; Rekaya 1974; Rosser 1974; Cheynet 1998; Letsios 2004; Signes Codoñer 2014: 153–72; Zuckerman 2017.
[159] Theoph. Cont. III, 21,6–10; Genesios 38,57ff.; Skylitzes 67,3–5; Ps-Symeon 626,2–3; *PmbZ* # 2547.
[160] Symeon Logothetes 130,8; Ps-Symeon 626,2–3. Mango 1977: 137–38; Treadgold 1988: n. 386; Signes Codoñer 1995: 483; Settipani 2006: 171–72; Varona Codeso and Prieto Domínguez 2013; Zuckerman 2017: 142–47.
[161] Theoph. Cont. III, 22.

Theophobia in the capital.[162] According to Grégoire, the monks of the community wished to make him a holy martyr and forged a legendary hagiography in which Theophobos was a committed iconodule who gave his life defending images. For Signes Codoñer, study of the historiographical works of the tenth century shows that two hagiographical accounts of Theophobos existed: as in the case of Manuel, a first iconoclast *vita* was followed by an iconodule one.[163] It is in fact plausible that the monastery of Constantinople in which the remains of one of the main figures of the Second Iconoclasm lay wished to update the image of its patron saint to fit the new socio-ecclesiastical situation. There can also be no doubt, however, that his relatives, the imperial family itself *lato sensu*, played a decisive role in this process.[164]

The case of Konstantinos Maniakes, also known as the Armenian, is similar.[165] Konstantinos arrived at the court of Theophilos as the Armenian ambassador and advanced in his career thanks to his innate abilities, which led the emperor to appoint him *droungarios* of the *arithmos* or of the *vigla*. Under Michael III, he was given the rank of *patrikios* and was appointed *logothetes tou dromou*. Although we do not know his stance regarding icons, we do know that, despite his familiarity with Theophilos, his followers tried to make him a champion of the restoration of Orthodoxy, and this is how he is portrayed in subsequent historiography. According to Genesios and Theophanes Continuatus, Konstantinos was entrusted by Empress Theodora with notifying the iconoclast patriarch Ioannes VII Grammatikos of his overthrow; the latter injured himself in order to discredit Konstantinos. This false accusation gave rise to a spirited defence of the Armenian that portrays him in glowing terms,[166] and the tone is maintained later on every time historians speak of him: when Konstantinos intervened to defend Theoktistos in an attempt to avoid his murder; when he opposed the appointment of Photios as patriarch; when he put himself at risk by taking food and consolation to the deposed Ignatios, who was shut up in the tomb of Konstantinos V; when he defended Michael III from the murderers of Bardas and when, after the

---

[162] Grégoire 1934; Janin 1969: 245–46; Ruggieri 1991: 199.
[163] Signes Codoñer 1995: 496–97 and 554–55.
[164] For Zuckerman 2017: 145, the parallel promotion of Manuel and Theophobos responded to a competition between two branches of the imperial family, rather than two opposing monasteries.
[165] *PmbZ* # 3962; *PBE* I: Konstantinos 41 and Maniakes 1; Markopoulos 1986.
[166] The vocative ὦ ἀκροαταί, characteristic of hagiography, marks the beginning of this part (Genesios 4,3,19 p. 58). It might be taken from the original source, that was none other than a *Vita Constantini*, see Karlin-Hayter 1971: 486, n. 4.

assassination of the Caesar, he calmed down several factions on the battlefield. If we abstract these details, the overall image of Konstantinos the Armenian is of a militant iconodule of the Ignatian party that included figures of the calibre of Theoktistos, an outstanding member of Theodora's group of counsellors. It is therefore unsurprising that some scholars have argued for the existence of a lost *Vita Constantini*, traces of which can be followed through the works of the historians who used it.[167] In any case, the family ties of Genesios and Konstantinos the Armenian mean that the possibility that the historian took the opportunity to praise his grandfather cannot be ruled out.

Regardless of the specific motives in each case, the retinue of Theophilos, which was made up of powerful men who stood out politically and socially during the iconoclast period without ever protecting icons, to a greater or lesser extent clearly underwent a process of sanctification by means of which they ended up being venerated and presented as models of virtue after the restoration of Orthodoxy. The *Acta of David, Symeon and Georgios* thus did not hesitate to praise Sergios Niketiates, Theoktistos, Bardas and Petronas or to place them on the same level as the future patriarch Methodios due to the support they gave him in the agreements prior to the Triumph of Orthodoxy.[168] The entry of Sergios Niketiates in the *Synaxarion* has already been mentioned. Apart from the hagiographical accounts and the processes of sanctification, only one other member of this group managed to find a place in the calendar of saints' days: Theoktistos.

Theoktistos was a eunuch who had a brilliant career under iconoclast emperors: after service as a member of the imperial guard of Leon V, he helped Michael II gain the throne.[169] The latter appointed him *patrikios* and *chartoularios tou kanikleiou*. Theophilos in turn made Theoktistos a *magistros* and *logothetes tou dromou* before appointing him a counsellor of Theodora during the regency of Michael III. Theoktistos' loyalty to Theodora cost him his life in 855, when Bardas and the young Michael wished to banish the empress from power. To his alleged great military successes (Crete in 843) must be added his decisive influence in ecclesiastical matters such as the appointments of Methodios and Ignatios to the patriarchate. According to the Logothetes, it was thanks to the suggestion

---

[167] Authors such as Karlin-Hayter 1971: 484–92 are convinced of the circulation of this *Vita Constantini*. Wasilewski 1971: 64 considers that this *vita* not only existed but was written by Ioseph Genesios himself and Skylitzes alludes to it in his preface. Cf. Kaldellis 1998: xv–xxi, who is more sceptical.
[168] *Acta of David, Symeon and Georgios* 245–46. See Section 6.3.7.
[169] *PmbZ* # 8050; *PBE* I: Theoktistos 3; Malyševskij 1887.

of Theoktistos that Theodora restored the cult of icons.[170] On this basis and due to the decisive role he played in the conversion of Theophilos by means of his *enkolpion* (a small devotional piece worn around the neck), Theoktistos began to be venerated after his death and entered the liturgical calendars, with his memory being celebrated on 20 November.

According to Halkin, his entry in a liturgical book was impossible before the second patriarchate of Ignatios (867–877), after the deaths of both his assassin, the Caesar Bardas, and Emperor Michael III, with whose acquiescence the Caesar had acted.[171] Although the *Synaxarion of Constantinople* is rather terse, it does include the term ἄθλησις 'martyrdom';[172] the calendar of saints' days contained in the manuscript *Parisinus Gr.* 1582 adds that Theoktistos was a martyr; and Nikodemos Hagiorites and the *Megas synaxaristês* of Doukakis specify that he was a ὁμολογητής 'confessor'. His imprisonment and murder at the hands of the ambitious Caesar Bardas likely allowed a pious interpretation of the end of his life. From this starting point, his followers may have gone so far as to make Theoktistos the subject of oral stories and even of a now-lost hagiographical account. The existence of this **Vita Theoctisti* was postulated some time ago by Karlin-Hayter as a necessary source for Theophanes Continuatus and other tenth-century historians such as Symeon Logothetes,[173] to judge by the extremely favourable portrayal of Theoktistos as a victim of the malicious intrigues of Bardas, whose lustful behaviour with his daughter-in-law he had previously criticised.

Theoktistos' new role as a champion of iconoduly, however, clashes not only with his extreme familiarity with the iconoclast emperors but also with his own past, in which he actively persecuted iconodules. This is recorded by the author of the *vita* of Euthymios of Sardis, who testifies that the saint was cruelly interrogated about his collaborators. Because he kept silent, Euthymios was whipped by three imperial envoys who had travelled to Cape Akritas. One of these was Theoktistos, who did not hesitate to torture Euthymios with a total of 130 lashes.[174] Eight days later,

---

[170] Symeon Logothetes 131,2 (232,5–6); Ps-Symeon 647,7–9. For the importance of the part played by Theoktistos, see Dvornik 1933: 34–45 and 88–92.

[171] Halkin 1954a: 11–14.

[172] *SynaxCP* 244,16–18: ἄθλησις τοῦ ἁγίου Θεοκτίστου πατρικίου. Τῇ θέσει εὐνούχου, ὃς ἦν ἐπὶ Θεοδώρας τῆς αὐγούστης.

[173] Karlin-Hayter 1971: 464ff. For the **Vita Theoctisti* as a source of the Logothetes, see Karlin-Hayter 1971: 455. Some recent scholars are reticent about all these lost *vitae*, like Zuckerman 2017: 129, who states that 'these biographies must be dismissed, therefore, as a figment of scholarly imagination'.

[174] *Vita of Euthymios of Sardis* 18–19, 339–81; Gouillard 1987: 40; *Synodikon of Orthodoxy* 126, n. 51; Sénina 2009.

The Court Milieu

the saint died of his injuries. The hagiographer –the future patriarch Methodios – vigorously condemns this abuse, describing the torturers as δείλαιοι or 'despicable' in a clear reference to their iconoclast sympathies.[175]

4.3.2 The Family of Theophilos and Theodora

This attempt to sanctify certain aristocrats also affected relatives of Empress Theodora: her brother-in-law Konstantinos Baboutzikos, the husband of Sophia,[176] took part in the disastrous defence of Amorion as army commander and was one of the forty-two martyrs executed by the Arabs.[177] This *patrikios* and *droungarios* was mentioned in the hagiographical narratives and named in hymns. It is even possible that a letter of condolence from the empress addressed to his children has been preserved.[178] It appears that this epistle was taken from a lost account of the martyrdom of the forty-two heroes of Amorion and subsequently included in the Georgian *vita* of St Konstanti Kaxay.[179] The latter was a Georgian nobleman put to death by the caliph in 846 (according to the Islamic dating given by the *vita*)[180] also in Samarra, like Konstantinos Baboutzikos.

The cases of Theodora's brothers Bardas and Petronas, two mainstays of the post-iconoclast Byzantine government whom the sources mention as supporting restoration, are similar.[181] Petronas served as a *droungarios tes viglas* under Theophilos, who appointed him *patrikios*.[182] After Petronas helped his brother Bardas overthrow Theodora, the new emperor, his nephew Michael III, appointed him *strategos* of the thema of Thrakesioi and later commander-in-chief of the fleet sent against the Arab emir of Melitene, whom Petronas defeated soundly at Poson (or Porson). He attained the post of *domestikos ton scholon* and became a *magistros* after the celebration of his triumph in Constantinople.[183] Killed in action

---

[175] *Vita of Euthymios of Sardis* 19,363.
[176] *PmbZ* # 6842; *PBE* I: Sophia 1; Varona Codeso and Prieto Domínguez 2013: 128–30.
[177] Theoph. Cont. III, 30,16–20; Skylitzes 75,39. *PmbZ* # 3932; *PBE* I: Konstantinos 30.
[178] As proposed by H. Grégoire in *Byzantion* 4 (1927) p. 801.
[179] Abashidze and Rapp 2004: 160–63.   [180] Abashidze and Rapp 2004: 159,29–30.
[181] *Acta of David, Symeon and Georgios* 245–46; Genesios IV 2, pp. 56,65–57,67; Skylitzes 82,37–39, who is mistaken on considering Petronas an uncle of Theodora (μητραδέλφων).
[182] *PmbZ* # 5929; *PBE* I: Petronas 5; *Vita of Antonios the Younger* (addit), pp. 187–210; Guilland 1970: 597–98; Treadgold 1979b: 175ff.
[183] On the Battle of Poson, see Huxley 1975; Haldon 2001: 83–84. On his campaigns on the Armenian frontier, see Dorfmann-Lazarev 2004: 59–63.

(865?), he was buried in a stone sarcophagus in the convent of Ta Gastria, specifically in the west wing of the church opposite the tomb of his sister Empress Theodora and his three nieces.[184] This location was clearly far from accidental: the family links between the two persons were complemented by a family cult promoted by their descendants.

In contrast to the case of Theodora, the process of the sanctification of Petronas or Konstantinos Baboutzikos did not achieve their inclusion in the *synaxaria*. But this does not mean that the efforts of their milieu were any less intense, given that *vitae* survive in honour of many saints of the period who similarly found no place in the calendars of saints' days. In a now-classic study, Patlagean confirmed the existence of a disparity or contradiction between hagiography and liturgy in the ninth and tenth centuries, in the sense that ecclesiastical recognition of cults was not always forthcoming.[185] Of the saints from the eighth to the tenth centuries analysed by Patlagean (a total of thirty-four, seven of whom were women), less than 15 per cent were celebrated in the first editions of the *Synaxarion of Constantinople*.[186] The liturgical calendar included in the manuscript *Patmiacus Gr.* 266 (P) mentions only Theophanes, Theodoros Stoudites and the patriarchs Nikephoros and Ignatios, while the *synaxarion* of the manuscript Jerusalem Hagios Stavros Gr. 40 (H) adds Nikephoros of Medikion and Empress Theophano.

There may well have been a historiographical account praising Petronas, as Karlin-Hayter postulated.[187] Regardless of whether this *Vita Petronae* was a source for the historian Genesios, there can be no doubt about the role played by Petronas as a protector of male saints, which finally allowed him to find his own place in hagiographical texts. The *Acta of David, Symeon and Georgios*, for example, describe how Petronas called on St Georgios of Lesbos to confess his sins and give him in compensation eight pounds of gold, three hundred tunics and three hundred blankets. Georgios interceded to forgive Petronas his sins and prophesied the future annihilation of the whole Arab army.[188] On any reckoning, this forecast is taken from the story of Antonios the Younger, either from his *vita* or through historians such as Theophanes Continuatus.[189] After hearing what had happened, Petronas' brother Bardas felt envious and also made

---

[184] *De ceremoniis* II, 647a; Grierson 1962: 27, n. 85. On the monastery of Ta Gastria, cf. Janin 1969: 67–68; Ruggieri 1991: 191.
[185] Patlagean 1981.   [186] Patlagean 1981: 103.   [187] Karlin-Hayter 1971: 494.
[188] *Acta of David, Symeon and Georgios* 252,15–22; Talbot 1998: 229–30; Karlin-Hayter 2004: 348.
[189] See Section 6.3.7. For Kazhdan 1984: 185–88, this prophecy allows the dating of the *Acta* as after 863.

a confession to the saint, giving him similar gifts. In return, Georgios predicted that Bardas would soon achieve the highest post, that he would occupy until his death.[190]

Better known is the appearance of Petronas in the *vita* of Antonios the Younger (*BHG* 142), the first part of which presents him as a military saint, a highly successful type during the iconoclast period, as noted above. During the persecution carried out by Theophilos, Antonios apparently took refuge on the Bithynian Mount Olympos and specifically at the monastery of Herakleion at Kios. This establishment was able to boast iconodule credentials, since it was led for a long time by abbot Ioseph, who attended the Second Council of Nicaea as a supporter of images, and because it provided training to Nikephoros, the future founder of Medikion.[191] The account of these years would have been contained in the text's lacunae, but clearly after the Triumph of Orthodoxy Antonios' adherence to the model of the cenobitic saint beloved of iconodule hagiographers was intensified. At that time, he had a vision that warned him that the problems in the bosom of the Church were not over but would reappear after an interval.[192] This is generally interpreted, following Halkin, as a prediction of the Photian schism due to the forced removal of Ignatios in order to place Photios in the patriarchal chair. Mango, on the other hand, takes the dispute between Methodios and the Stoudites to be in question.[193]

After begging the hegoumenos of the monastery to be allowed to retire to lead a contemplative life, Antonios was sent to a *metochion* in the capital owned by the monastery of Herakleion, the smaller monastery of Hagion Panton ('All Saints').[194] It was there in 855 that he met Petronas, who sought his blessing to overcome a serious illness. After the miraculous healing of his son Marianos shortly afterwards, such a strong link was established between the patrician and the saint, that Petronas was kept from withdrawing from the world and becoming a monk only by Antonios, his confessor from then on, who persuaded him that he could best serve God if he did not do this.[195] In 863, Antonios encountered his spiritual son Petronas when the latter was on his way to curb the Arab raids in Asia Minor. He accompanied him as far as the fortress of Plateia Petra and encouraged him to engage in combat even against the direct orders

---

[190] *Acta of David, Symeon and Georgios* 252,22–31; Talbot 1998: 230–31.
[191] *Vita of Nikephoros of Medikion* 408, nn. 3 and 5; Janin 1975: 152–53.
[192] *Vita of Antonios the Younger* (addit) 3–4.   [193] Halkin 1944: 207–8; Mango 1977: 139–40.
[194] *Vita of Antonios the Younger* (addit) 19, 222,7–28. Cf. also Janin 1969: 390.
[195] *Vita of Antonios the Younger* (addit) 10–12.

Petronas had received from the emperor, prophesising an overwhelming success.[196] That was precisely the outcome, the event in question being the famous Battle of Poson of 3 September 863. In gratitude, Petronas installed Antonios in his home in Constantinople.[197] At the age of eighty and feeling that his end was near, Antonios retired to the monastery of Leon Diakonos,[198] where he died on the same day as Petronas, 11 November 865.[199]

Theophanes Continuatus maintains that the saint predicted his own death and prophesied that Petronas too would die soon,[200] but a slightly different account appears in the historians: Ioannes was a famous monk established on Mount Latros near Ephesos, who was known for never leaving his cell. When he heard that Petronas was in the area, however, Ioannes approached him to announce that he had God's protection and that he should place the image of St John the Evangelist on his soldiers' shields to protect them. After the victory, Petronas praised the saint highly.[201] This is probably not a different person but Antonios the Younger himself, called Ioannes either in reference to his name prior to taking his vows or owing to confusion with his spiritual father Ioannes. It is less likely that the historians identified our saint with a later monk.[202]

The hagiographical text praising the saint is unusual, in that it makes a layman like Petronas a kind of joint protagonist in its final portion.[203] This *vita* was written by an anonymous hagiographer,[204] probably a monk from the *metochion* of All Saints, since he had as an informant his spiritual brother, another monk named Iakobos who shared a house with the saint for at least seven years.[205] We know that the *vita* was written at the instigation of a certain Klemes, whose invocation as 'ἄριστε τῶν πατέρων' and 'ὑμετέρα ὁσιότης' suggests that he was an abbot.[206] Since Halkin, this Klemes has been taken to be the man mentioned on three

---

[196] *Vita of Antonios the Younger* (addit) 15. [197] *Vita of Antonios the Younger* (addit) 16.
[198] Janin 1969: 306–7.
[199] *Vita of Antonios the Younger* (addit) 17–18. The chronology of the life of Antonios is according to Halkin 1944: 195–97, who takes the date of the saint's death as his starting point. This chronology has been widely accepted, see Tanner 1997, who includes a synoptic chart on page 157.
[200] Theoph. Cont. IV, 25,88–103.
[201] Theoph. Cont. IV, 25,21–33 and lines 40–103; Skylitzes 100,27–32.
[202] Such as the monks Ioannes *PmbZ* # 22966 or *PmbZ* # 23246.
[203] *Vita of Antonios the Younger* (addit) 10–18.
[204] *PmbZ* # 11651; *Vita of Antonios the Younger* 1, 187,5–24; 44, 216,17–25; *Vita of Antonios the Younger* (addit) 19.
[205] *PmbZ* # 2639; *PBE* I: Iakobos 6.
[206] *PmbZ* #3656; *Vita of Antonios the Younger* (addit) 204–6. On this Klemes, see also Section 5.2.2.a.

occasions in the correspondence of Theodoros Stoudites[207] and in the *vitae* of Ioannikios as paying a visit to the influential ascetic.[208] The abbot Klemes who accompanied into exile Paulos of Plousia,[209] with whom he was associated and who is honoured on 7 March or the following days, must be the same person. This bishop of Plousia, in the *thema* of Boukellarioi, attended the funeral of Niketas of Medikion[210] and, according to our hagiographer, invited Antonios the Younger to eat with him daily, which suggests that his friendship with Klemes played a part in the latter's decision to commission a biography of a man they both considered a saint. The commission likely dates from the four months of 868 when Klemes was the head of the monastery of Stoudios before his death.[211] He would thus have been almost ninety when he commissioned this *vita*, although some researchers regard the chronology as hampering identification with the abbot of Stoudios owing to his old age.[212]

This circumstantial evidence suggests in any case that we are concerned with a Stoudite composition from within the Ignatian party. This working hypothesis is confirmed by the vision of Antonios the Younger related to the Photian schism; by the fact that the only imperial figures of whom a positive image is offered are Prokopia (the mother of the patriarch Ignatios) and Petronas (the guarantor, together with Theodora, of Ignatios' attaining the patriarchate); by its total silence on the restoration of icons and the role of Methodios and by the commemoration of Antonios on 1 December although his death took place on 11 November (the feast day of Theodoros Stoudites, which forced its displacement).[213] The dating deduced by Halkin is supported by its Stoudite origin from within the Ignatian party, which confirms that the *vita* must have been written between 877 and 886 or at the time of the reconciliation of Photians and Ignatians made possible by Antonios Kauleas in 899.[214] Vinson, for her part, considers the death of Empress Theophano (897) the *terminus post quem* for the *vita*, since the hagiographer implicitly justifies the second marriage of Leon VI on showing the father of Antonios the Younger marrying again, despite already having male issue.[215] Her idea is persuasive, but Antonios' attitude and the fact that his siblings abandoned their father shows that they did not approve of

---

[207] *PmbZ* # 3653; Theod. Stoud., *epist*. 302,25ff; 433,46–47 and 538,59–60.
[208] *Vita of Ioannikios by Petros* 36, 404C–405C; *Vita of Ioannikios by Sabas* 28, 357B.
[209] *PmbZ* # 3654; *Vita of Petros of Atroa* 68,5, p. 197. For the commemoration of Paulos of Pluosia, see *SynaxCP* 518; 521; 524.
[210] *PmbZ* # 5853. [211] *PmbZ* # 23705. [212] Efthymiadis 1995: 148–49.
[213] *Vita of Antonios the Younger* (addit) 192–93. [214] *Vita of Antonios the Younger* (addit) 208.
[215] Vinson 1998: 483–85.

his new marriage, so that this text can scarcely have been written at the court of Leon VI. On the other hand, the hagiographer claims to have seen St Antonios shortly before his death. This detail, together with the slightly later death of abbot Klemes (in 868) and the complete lack of mention of any miracles or posthumous events, argue for an earlier composition, not long after 865.

The affiliation of the author of the *vita* remains unknown, but we know that one of his main informants (and the only one mentioned) was his spiritual brother the monk Iakobos,[216] a disciple of Antonios the Younger and a member of the monastery of All Saints, the *metochion* owned in Constantinople by the monastery of Herakleion (in Kios in Bithynia).[217] Iakobos had entered the monastery as a child and was associated with Antonios for many years, owing to which his testimony is generally thought reliable. As for the purpose of this hagiography, objectives characteristic of the Ignatian party and the Stoudite circle are associated with others characteristic of a family well established at the court, to which must be added a secondary wish to provide models of Christian masculinity aimed at a male audience.[218] The status of Petronas as the spiritual son of a saint, with their mystical union leading to death at the same moment, coincides with the process of general sanctification of the imperial family led by Empress Theodora. The benefits of this go beyond the legitimation of the family's memory and seem to involve specific goals involving worldly power. One of the people most favoured by the leading role played by Petronas in the account of the final years of Antonios the Younger is accordingly his son Marianos.[219] Although the hagiographer does not give his name, a son of Petronas (generally identified with Marianos) was miraculously healed by Antonios the Younger.[220] After his father's death in 867, Marianos was the *eparchos* of Constantinople and as such was in charge of announcing publicly in the forum that Basileios I was the new sole emperor.[221] He does not appear to have had any qualms about the fact that the arrival of the new sovereign involved the murder of his cousin Michael III or that his blood ties with the last member of the Amorian household had negative consequences for him, at least in the short term.

---

[216] *PmbZ* # 2639; *PBE* I: Iakobos 6. Cf. *Vita of Antonios the Younger* 9, 193,10–14; *Vita of Antonios the Younger* (addit) 19, 222,7–25.
[217] Janin 1969: 390.   [218] Vinson 1998: 502–3.
[219] *PmbZ* # 4769 and # 24956; *PBE* I: Marianos 5.   [220] *Vita of Antonios the Younger* (addit) 12.
[221] Symeon Logothetes 253,3–5 (132,3–5); Ps-Symeon 687,6ff.

4.4 The Imperial Couple in Post-Iconoclast Hagiography: Theophilos and Theodora

While three of the closest collaborators of the iconoclast emperor, the *magistroi* Sergios Niketiates, Manuel the Armenian and Theoktistos, ended up being venerated, as is borne out by their liturgical presence in the *synaxaria*, members of the imperial family such as Petronas featured in hagiographical accounts and were considered champions of iconoduly. So too in the case of the sovereign couple: if Empress Theodora enjoyed the sanctification reflected in the *vita* composed in her honour, Theophilos also underwent a political and ecclesiastical rehabilitation that overlooked his iconoclast past and was soon committed to writing. In both processes, the role played by the milieu and the remaining members of the imperial family was crucial.

Shortly after Theophilos' death, his widow Theodora initiated a gruelling campaign aimed at redeeming her husband from the charge of having been an iconoclast, avoiding his anathematisation and thus guaranteeing the legitimacy of her regency and the future position of her son Michael III. Both historiographical (Theophanes Continuatus; Pseudo-Symeon) and hagiographical sources (*Acta of David, Symeon and Georgios*; *Vita of Eirene of Chrysobalanton*) unanimously consider Theophilos' wife the main agent of his absolution due to the great love she bore him. Before proceeding to the restoration of icons, Theodora asked the religious representatives for her husband's pardon as a necessary condition for the Triumph of Orthodoxy.[222] The week from 4 to 11 March 843 was therefore devoted to prayers for the redemption of Theophilos, as had been agreed at the synod of 3 March at the Palace of the Kanikleion.[223] Given the ecclesiastical difficulties in granting absolution, Theodora invoked the repentance of her husband who, conscious of his error, had included among his final wishes the payment of sixty pounds of gold as compensation to ascetics and other victims of his persecution. The late emperor had also forsworn iconoclasm on his deathbed, when after great suffering, he finally saw the image of Christ that appeared on the *enkolpion* of Theoktistos.[224] This episode had a precedent in the conversion of the iconoclast patriarch Paulos IV (780–784), who, when he fell ill and saw his

---

[222] Theoph. Cont. IV, 4–5. Afinogenov 1996a: 58–61; Markopoulos 1998; Afinogenov 1999a; Varona Codeso 2010: 77–80 and 201–4; Prieto Domínguez 2019b.
[223] *Acta of David, Symeon and Georgios* 249ff.   [224] Ps-Symeon 651,11–13; Vinson 1995.

death was near, retired to the monastery of Phloros.[225] As he died repentant, he was not only pardoned by his contemporaries but also remembered by them liturgically each year on 31 August.[226]

In order to dispel any remaining doubts, the final proof that Theophilos had the grace of God was provided by the numerous posthumous miracles that interceded for his soul: Symeon of Lesbos, one of the main opponents to his rehabilitation, went so far as to abandon the synod for the restoration and the city of Constantinople, until he recalled a vision he had had in which immediately after his death Theophilos implored his assistance by saying three times: Καλόγηρε, βοήθει μοι!, 'Oh monk, help me!'[227] It is worth noting that in the hagiography of the saints of Lesbos, Symeon the Stylite is the only person responsible for this absolution, to the detriment of Empress Theodora and the future patriarch Methodios, whose divine visions and intercessions for Theophilos' soul are treated with disdain.[228]

Theodora for her part had a dream during the last few days of her husband's life, in which the emperor was tortured by a group of angels in the presence of the Theotokos and Christ. Amidst great suffering, Theophilos lamented his punishment and bitterly regretted having persecuted images.[229] This vision is characteristic of post-iconoclast writing, when 'dream literature' became fashionable,[230] and is narrated both in the *vita* of the empress and in a hagiographical account of the emperor, *De Theophili imperatoris absolutione* (*BHG* 1732–34k), in which, in Theodora's dream, her husband is brought before the supreme judge at the Chalke Gate.[231] As for the patriarch Methodios, after having led the prayers for the salvation of Theophilos' soul, he had a vision of a shining angel whose mission was to announce that the emperor had obtained God's forgiveness. This was effectively demonstrated by the miraculous disappearance of Theophilos' name from the list of iconoclast heretics the patriarch had drawn up in person and deposited at the high altar to make amends for the damage caused to icons.[232]

---

[225] Theoph. 457,14–17; *Vita of Tarasios* 8–11. On the monastery of the Theotokos of Phloros, see Janin 1969: 495–96.
[226] *SynaxCP* 933,53–54. About Paulos IV, cf. *PmbZ* # 5829; *PBE* I: Paulos 4; Lilie 1999: 50–56 and 271–76.
[227] *Acta of David, Symeon and Georgios* 242–46.
[228] *Acta of David, Symeon and Georgios* 242,35–43,2; Karlin-Hayter 2006a.
[229] *Vita of the Empress Theodora* 264–65 (ch. 8). See also Timotin 2010: 143–49.
[230] Dagron 1985: 47–51; Markopoulos 1998: 45.
[231] Afinogenov 2004a: 106 and 325. Contrary to the affirmation of Markopoulos 1998, the account of the angel deleting the name of the emperor from the roll does belong to this very period and not to a later context, see Prieto Domínguez 2019b: 222–23, n. 64.
[232] *Narratio de Theophili absolutione* 36–37.

Finally, the synod confirmed the redemption of the soul of the deceased in writing to the empress. The *vita* of Eirene of Chrysobalanton mentions the miracle that certified the rehabilitation of Theophilos, although it omits any mention of Methodios' action.[233] In any case, the superiority of ecclesiastical authority over imperial authority is evident, justifying the wish of the remaining relatives to achieve the redemption of the iconoclast emperor: only a solution such as those of the *oikonomía* of the Byzantine Church could cleanse his image and legitimise the dynasty in order to guarantee the young heir's right to the throne.

The imperial campaign to distinguish Theophilos from the iconoclast emperors included harsh persecution of the memory of figures such as Konstantinos V, whose remains were desecrated. At Methodios' request, Theodora ordered them burnt in a public square known as the Amastrianon, as Konstantinos had done with the relics and images of the saints. His ashes were thrown into the sea, according to the *Necrologium imperatorum et catalogus eorum sepulchrorum*.[234] A few years later, when Michael III had come of age and succeeded to the throne, he promoted the transfer to the church of the Holy Apostles in Constantinople of the body of Empress Eirene, the first restorer of icons (ca. 752/759–August 803).[235] By installing Eirene's body in the mausoleum of Justinian I to replace that of Konstantinos V, Michael was not only insulting the memory of the iconoclast emperor, whose religious programme had been roundly condemned, but also minimising the achievements of his mother, from whose influence and governance he tried to escape at all costs. Half a century before the Triumph of Orthodoxy in 843, another woman had already been able to restore the cult of images. No source dates this event. But we know from the *Vita of the Patriarch Ignatios* that in 861 the sarcophagus of green marble in which Konstantinos V had lain was still in the mausoleum of Justinian, since the deposed patriarch Ignatios was imprisoned in it after the Council.[236] We also know that the sarcophagus was used as construction material for the church of Pharos, which was consecrated in 864 by the patriarch Photios.[237] The measure was therefore implemented between 861 and 864. On the other hand, this transfer went against the interests of the young monarch, since far from weakening his mother's public image, it helped establish a new type of iconodule saint, the restoring empress.

---

[233] *Vita of Eirene of Chrysobalanton* 2,18–24.
[234] Grierson 1962: 53; Symeon Logothetes 248–49; Ps-Symeon 681.
[235] *De Ceremoniis* II, 42; version L of the *Catalogus sepulchrorum*. See Herrin 2013: 210–13, esp. nn. 14 and 15, for whom Theodora was in fact the responsible for this transfer.
[236] *Vita of Ignatios* 36,20–21.   [237] Phot., *Homily* X, pp. 180–81; Grierson 1962: 33–34, 53–55.

The main response to Michael's decision was the writing of a *vita* to honour the memory of Empress Eirene (*BHG* 2205).[238] By means of this hagiographical text, the nunnery of Prinkipos on the Sea of Marmara attempted to avoid the transfer to the capital of the remains of the founder and patron saint of their convent dedicated to the Theotokos.[239] It is here that not only Empress Eirene, but also Maria of Amnia, the first wife of Konstantinos VI, and other imperial ladies had taken the veil. In addition, the place was the destination of Megalo, the wife of the chronicler Theophanes.[240] The purpose of the *Vita of the Empress Eirene* is obvious, if we consider its insistence that the will of Empress Eirene was to rest there eternally. The hagiography of Eirene is a cento text assembled out of all the material on its protagonist included in the *Chronographia* of Theophanes. The *vita* therefore includes numerous negative details that undermined her proclamation as a saint: she was easily deceived by those around her, since she was a woman, and she had an excessive political ambition that led her to order the beating and forced tonsuring of the associates of her son Konstantinos VI, whom she actually blinded in order to continue to exercise imperial power.[241] Curiously, however, it omits the advice of Eirene to her son that he blind Alexios Mouselé, perhaps because this episode was less well known. The reasons for this negative presentation of the protagonist are unclear. Perhaps this was a convention of the genre, as hagiographies devoted to women were not presented like those of their male counterparts, and they were not attributed the same virtues, as is shown by the *vita* of Athanasia of Aegina (*BHG* 180), at no point in which is the saint presented as an iconodule heroine.[242] Or perhaps this was due instead to a lack of skill on the part of the author, who was more interested in describing Eirene's funeral in the place she had mentioned (at the Chapel of St Nicholas, in the left wing of the church dedicated to the Theotokos of the convent she had founded on the island of Prinkipos) than in producing an edifying and convincing hagiographical text.[243]

In any case, and despite the fact that it did not achieve its objective, since Eirene's body was finally taken to the capital, where in the tenth century it lay in the mausoleum of Justinian at the church of the Holy Apostles, the writing of a *vita* in honour of the first restoring empress

---

[238] Treadgold 1982; Halkin 1988; see also *SynaxCP* 877,56–57.
[239] On this convent of Prinkipos, see Mamboury 1920; Janin 1975: 69; Ruggieri 1991: 209–10.
[240] Theoph. 478–80 (AM 6295).
[241] *Vita of the Empress Eirene* 16,32–17,1; 17,18–29; 21,26. On her reign, see Speck 1978; Garland 1999: 73–94.
[242] Kazhdan and Talbot 1991: 394ff.; Delierneux 2014.   [243] Treadgold 1982: 244–51.

prepared the way for the sanctification of Theodora. Indeed, just as the hagiography of Eirene owes much to the historiographical work of Theophanes the Confessor, so too that of Theodora contains numerous historical details that had already appeared in the work of Georgios Monachos. Beyond the similarities in its composition, it is clear that the nuns of Prinkipos did a service to the memory of Theodora by reinforcing the veneration of the first restoring empress with a *vita*. Indeed, those in favour of the sanctification of Theodora subsequently relied on that phenomenon, as can be gathered from the manuscript transmission: the only surviving copy of the *Vita of the Empress Eirene* is included in the codex *Vaticanus Gr.* 2014, folios 122v–36, where it is followed by the hagiography in honour of Theodora (folios 136v–43) and the account of the rehabilitation of Theophilos (folios 143r–143v), which brings the manuscript to a close.[244] This is far from a coincidence: these three hagiographical accounts were copied together because a propaganda programme linked them to the Triumph of Orthodoxy in order to promote the veneration of its protagonists.

Before we consider the hagiography that praises Empress Theodora the restorer, let us examine the surviving texts that discuss the absolution of Theophilos. According to Markopoulos,[245] the rehabilitation of the iconoclast emperor involved the creation of oral traditions that little by little became part of written discourse and finally took the form of separate texts. One of these is the *De Theophili imperatoris absolutione*, which blames the patriarch Ioannes Grammatikos for the virulence of the iconoclast persecution to justify the emperor, and which had a rich manuscript tradition. Another is the *De Theophili imperatoris benefactis* (*BHG* 1735), a tribute to the emperor based on the same merits that were attributed to him by tenth-century chroniclers. These coincide to a large extent with the attributes of the saints of the Second Iconoclasm: he dispensed justice personally throughout the city; protected the poor, fortified the walls of Constantinople to benefit the community, refounded numerous religious buildings such as the church of the Blachernai, etc.[246]

De Theophili imperatoris benefactis post-dates the story of the absolution of Theophilos, not only because of the praise it contains (which proves that there was already a receptive audience for a positive image of the iconoclast

---

[244] Franchi de' Cavalieri et al. 1902: 14–15 date this manuscript to the eleventh century. For Ševčenko, it belongs to the twelfth century, see Treadgold 1982: 237, n. 2. Cf. also Canart and Peri 1970: 671.
[245] Markopoulos 1998: 37–49; Afinogenov 2004a; Prieto Domínguez 2019b.
[246] Theoph. Cont. III, 2–3; 7–8 and ch. 16; Skylitzes 50–51; 54–55; Laiou 1994: 151–53 and 162.

monarch), but because it mentions his rehabilitation as already achieved. In the same way, the hagiography of Theodora is of later date, since while *De Theophili imperatoris absolutione* is exclusively about the redemption of Theophilos, the *Vita Theodorae* presents this episode as one of a number of actions of Theodora as wife and empress; far from the whole account revolving around it, this is simply another successful achievement of the protagonist. Kazhdan's proposal,[247] according to which the *Vita Theodorae* predates the account describing the absolution of Theophilos, is thus difficult to accept.

The *Vita Theodorae* has not yet been dated with any certainty.[248] Its editors, Regel and Markopoulos, were inclined to think that it was written shortly after her death (post 867) and in any case before 871: Markopoulos places the composition of the chronicle of Georgios Monachos precisely in 871, judging that the common elements in the *vita* of the empress must be earlier.[249] In their opinion, the *vita* served as a source for the historian and must have been written in the first few years of the reign of Basileios I (867–886). Afinogenov later demonstrated, however, that Georgios Monachos wrote his work in 845–846, to judge by the long quotes he includes from the *Refutatio et eversio* of the patriarch Nikephoros, his rejection of Thomas the Slav and his ignorance of the fate of the forty-two martyrs of Amorion, who were executed in 845.[250] The *Vita Theodorae* is therefore later than the historiographical work. According to Afinogenov, shortly after the chronicle of Georgios Monachos was written, a series of texts were composed that revolve around the restoration of icons and the conversion of Theophilos, in order to justify his rehabilitation. The oldest of these and their common source must be the *Narratio historica in festum restitutionis imaginum* (*BHG* 1734), which already draws from the account of Georgios Monachos, although it adds some details, such as the fact that the martyrs of Amorion were transferred to Syria.[251] Finally, the *Vita Theodorae* was written with elements taken from the two previous works (Georgios Monachos and the *Narratio*), as a textual analysis makes clear.[252]

We can thus conclude that Empress Theodora, while still alive and supported by the patriarchate under first Methodios and later Ignatios, promoted the writing of hagiographical accounts that redeemed her

---

[247] Kazhdan 1986: 154.
[248] Markopoulos 1983. There is an English translation in Talbot 1998: 353–82.
[249] *Vita of the Empress Theodora* 251–56 (and ed. Regel 13).   [250] Afinogenov 1999b; 2004b.
[251] Afinogenov 1999a.   [252] Afinogenov 1997: 16; 1999b: 442–44.

husband and sanctified the rest of his family members, despite his iconoclast past. After her death, the process continued and she herself became the subject of veneration and sanctification because of her decisive role in the restoration of icons.[253] Her story is well known:[254] she was born in Paphlagonia in *ca*. 815 of Armenian descent, and married Emperor Theophilos in ca. 830, after having been chosen in a bride-show.[255] After her husband's death in 842, she assumed the regency of her son the minor Michael III and promoted the restoration of the cult of images, cancelling the previous iconoclast policy. She governed until she was deposed by Michael and her brother Bardas in 856, and shortly afterwards she entered the convent of Ta Gastria, where her body would be laid to rest alongside that of her mother Phlorina-Theoktiste, her brothers and sisters and her daughters.[256]

The date of her death is unclear; most sources affirm that she survived her son (who was assassinated in 867), but the *vita* reports that Michael was alive when his mother passed.[257] To overcome this difficulty, Karlin-Hayter proposes emending the text and takes the imperial couple prostrate in Theodora's bed to be Basileios I and his wife.[258] Although this idea is ingenious, it has not found much support among scholars. Among other reasons, it is difficult to explain away the incoherence of mentioning Basileios at the end of the *vita* as a pious man, when scarcely three pages before he is condemned as the assassin of the young Michael III on 23 September 867.[259] Given the presence of such an accusation in a text aimed at the general public rather than a closed monastic community, it seems likely that the monarch referred to was not Basileios and that it was not produced during his reign. By contrast, we can assume that the hagiography of Empress Theodora was written in the late ninth century during the reign of Leon VI (886–912), as Karlin-Hayter and Vinson believe;[260] the reference to Michael III as present at his mother's deathbed

---

[253] *SynaxCP* 458–60 (11 February); *BHG* 1731–35.
[254] *PmbZ* # 7286; *PBE* I: Theodora 2; Garland 1999: 95–108; Herrin 2001: 185–239.
[255] Treadgold 1975; 1979a; Rydén 1985; Nikolaou 1994; Vinson 1999. On the family interests and the Armenian circle that made this union possible, see Varona Codeso and Prieto Domínguez 2013.
[256] Grierson 1962: 57. On the transfer of the relics of Theodora, see Herrin 2001: 233–35; Herrin 2013: 213–14.
[257] *Vita of the Empress Theodora* 270–71 (ch. 12).   [258] Karlin-Hayter 1990.
[259] *Vita of the Empress Theodora* 268,14–16: Μιχαὴλ δὲ μόνος ἐκράτησε χρόνους ιδ' καὶ ἐσφάγη παρὰ Βασιλείου πατρικίου καὶ παρακοιμωμένου αὐτοῦ ἐν τῷ παλατίῳ τοῦ ἁγίου Μάμαντος, χρόνων ὢν εἴκοσι ἐννέα, 'Michael ruled alone for fourteen years and was murdered at the age of twenty-nine in the palace of St Mamas by his parakoimomenos, Basileios the patrikios.'
[260] Karlin-Hayter 1990: 208; Vinson 1998: 472; 2003.

makes perfect sense in this context. Leon VI vindicated not only his official father Basileios, in honour of whom he composed a famous funeral oration (*Enkomion of Basileios I*), but also the members of the previous dynasty, the Amorian, as part of his political programme and imperial propaganda.[261] Perhaps this was because Leon was in fact the son of Michael III,[262] as is suggested by the fact that Leon VI also encouraged the worship of the archangel Saint Michael.[263]

The *Vita of Theodora* praises the empress, who was probably Leon's grandmother, and celebrates the defeat of the iconoclast heretics, thus appropriating the restoration of Orthodoxy as a legitimate mainstay of her government and the Macedonian dynasty. Leon took charge not only of giving Michael III a decent burial after bringing his remains to Constantinople and giving him a state funeral with imperial honours,[264] but also of portraying him in a favourable light for posterity. To partially compensate for the slander spread against him by Basileios I, the *vita* describes Michael III as a devoted son who accompanied and comforted his mother during her final hours. This effected a partial correction of the negative image of the last Amorian sovereign, who, in order to seize power, had not hesitated to conspire with Bardas against his own mother, whom he shut away in the convent of Ta Gastria and deprived of her material assets. Understanding the *Vita of Theodora* as a piece of imperial propaganda lends particular relevance to a detail that has previously gone unnoticed: the presence of the wife of Michael III prostrate next to him at the foot of Theodora's bed. The details that we have regarding Eudokia Dekapolitissa are few in number,[265] but her appearance in the account makes sense if we assume she was related to St Gregorios Dekapolites, who was recognised as a saint by the iconodules after the Triumph of Orthodoxy. She was chosen to be Michael's wife by Empress Theodora herself. We should also take into account the important positions held at court by her descendants, some of whom were of the calibre of Theodoros Dekapolites, a patrician and quaestor under Konstantinos VII (913–959) and a *magistros* at the time of Romanos II (959–963).[266]

Although the *vita* of Empress Theodora was written later and clearly owes a debt to the texts that served to rehabilitate her husband Theophilos,

---

[261] Tougher 1994; Vinson 2003.
[262] There is abundant bibliography on the possibility that Michael III was the real father of Leon VI; see Mango 1973; Karlin-Hayter 1991a; Tougher 1997: 42–67.
[263] Magdalino 1987: 56, n. 26.   [264] Tougher 1997: 62ff.; Herrin 2013: 215.
[265] For Eudokia, see *PmbZ* # 1631; *PBE* I: Eudokia 3. See Section 3.2.2.b.
[266] On Theodoros Dekapolites, who was also an important jurist, see Section 3.2.2.b.

the surviving hagiography is merely the final example of a long tradition that arose as soon as she died. In her study of the two stories about the reign of Michael III, Karlin-Hayter argued that before this *Vita Theodorae* had been put down in writing, at least two biographical texts about her were in circulation: one was hagiographical, while the other was political and gave great importance to other members of her family, such as her siblings Eirene, Petronas and Bardas.[267]

The *Vita Theodorae* differs from standard hagiographical accounts, in that it is written more as a historical account that takes interest in the events that occurred, than as the life of a saint that serves to recall the latter's works. As a consequence, many scholars have seen it as an imperial panegyric (*basilikós lógos*). The lack of miracles is striking in an iconodule saint, unless we consider the repentance of Theophilos' iconoclast past on his deathbed to be one. The restoration of icons in 843 is narrated in detail, emphasising Theodora's part in it. But this cannot be considered a miracle, neither is the protection of Constantinople from a maritime attack from Arab troops.[268] This expedition, which seems to have taken place in 842, is not mentioned in any other source, whether Greek or Arabic, except for the chronicle of Georgios Monachos.[269] In all likelihood, it is an exaggeration that seeks to link iconoclasm with the defeat of Theophilos at Amorion in 838, so as to set it against the end of heresy sponsored by Theodora together with her victory over the Arab ships.[270] Finally, the omission of the gift of clairvoyance that historians attribute to Theodora (cursing Michael before he assassinated Theoktistos, the prophecy of Bardas' future, the prediction that Basileios I would be the ruin of the Amorian dynasty)[271] indicates that the hagiographer's intention was not so much to prove the empress' holiness, as to rewrite recent history. In order to do so, he praises Theodora within a historical context, of which he offers a partial and biased view in keeping with the interests of the new imperial household.

The authorship of this *vita*, transmitted as an anonymous work, remains a mystery. Its interest in legitimising imperial power, rehabilitating Michael III and appropriating the restoration of icons for the propaganda of Leon VI, show that the author belonged to the circle closest to this monarch. Despite the effervescent literary environment of Leon's court,

---

[267] Karlin-Hayter 1971: 495. The idea is accepted by the last editor of the *vita*; see *Vita of the Empress Theodora* 251.
[268] *Vita of the Empress Theodora* 265,4–8.   [269] Georgios Monachos II, 801,7–14.
[270] Vasiliev 1935: vol. I, 192, n. 1.   [271] Karlin-Hayter 1971: 495–96 with references.

where the production of homilies reached new heights,[272] few of the hagiographers we know of share the text's concerns.[273] Among them, Kosmas Vestitor and Anastasios Quaestor stand out; both men were in the emperor's direct service.[274] Kosmas cultivated biblical themes (*Oratio in Ioachim et Annam parentes deiparae* (*BHG* 828), two *Laudationes* of Zacharias (*BHG* 1881r–81s)) and venerated in particular St John Chrysostom, devoting no less than five *enkomia* to the transfer of his relics to Constantinople. For his part, Anastasios Quaestor or Balbos composed several *kanones* to celebrate the feast days of various ancient martyrs (Menas, Hermogenes and Eugraphos, Boniface and Susanna the Deaconess), in addition to an *enkomion* of St Agathonikos of Nicomedia (*BHG* 42) and another dedicated to St Catherine of Alexandria (*BHG* 32b).[275] He also wrote the funeral epigram of Metrophanes of Smyrna, the well-known defender of the patriarch Ignatios against Photios.[276]

In addition to his liking for saints who defended Orthodoxy and the literary genre of religious *enkomia*, he also paid considerable attention to iconoclasm; it is no accident that Anastasios presented Catherine as confronting the pagan emperor and contrasting the idolatrous cult of the statues of the emperors with the iconodule veneration of the icons representing the saints in Christ.[277] Although the former is false, the latter clearly is not. This concern to continue arguing, albeit indirectly, against the iconoclast heresy shows that the author of the *Vita Theodorae* was heavily involved in the defence of images, which makes Anastasios the best candidate. The current state of research does not allow us to be sure of this. But if this conclusion were corroborated by future studies, we would have a better understanding of the method used by the imperial family to achieve the sanctification of its predecessors, spreading their veneration among believers and thus reaffirming their own exercise of power.

4.5 Conclusions

During the Second Iconoclasm, a large proportion of written literature relating to the aristocracy sought to praise members of important families to achieve specific objectives directly linked to their interests. In this procedure, the importance of contemporary hagiography that was not

---

[272] Antonopoulou 1997; 1998 and 2017.   [273] Efthymiadis 2011a: 114–15.
[274] On Kosmas Vestitor, see *PmbZ* # 4125; *PBE* I: Kosmas 61. On Anastasios Quaestor, see *PmbZ* # 20297; Lauxtermann 1998: 401–5.
[275] Krausmüller 2009b.   [276] Edited by Mercati 1929/1930: 60.
[277] *Enkomion of St Catherine of Alexandria by Anastasios Quaestor* 249; Krausmüller 2009b: 312.

explicitly iconodule and deeply rooted in iconoclast tradition should not be undervalued: the secular and military saints 'canonised' under Theophilos, such as Eudokimos and Manuel the Armenian, were likely officially promoted by the regime as alternative role models to the iconodule monastic confessors. The presence of Eudokimos in the *Synaxarion*, together with Petros of Galatia and Sergios Niketiates, bears witness to the successful rivalry of these milieux faced with iconodule hegoumenoi. Their model of holiness was effectively disseminated and incorporated by hagiographical narratives or historical accounts with a hagiographical dimension, as in the cases of Kallistos, Theophobos and Konstantinos the Armenian.

The recourse to praising eminent generals as models of virtue similar to iconodule saints continued after the restoration of icons (as in the cases of Theoktistos and Petronas), although the models of holiness and the codes for their representation changed and were adapted to the new post-iconoclast tendencies. The resulting texts not only fulfilled an immediate function that affected the author and the protagonist and their milieu (family, monastery, etc.), but also gradually rewrote the events in question. The individual exoneration of many important civic leaders who held power during the Second Iconoclasm led to the construction of a general account that restricted the responsibility for heresy to emperors whose dynasties had disappeared and fanatical patriarchs who broke with tradition and ecclesiastical dogma (such as Ioannes Grammatikos), the guardians of which were to a large extent the monks sponsored precisely by the civic leaders who were the protagonists of these works.

Despite the fact that some extensive *vitae* facilitated and disseminated the cult of their protagonists, very few of these were accepted into the *Synaxarion of Constantinople*. When this occurred, moreover, there was generally only a brief mention of the person and not a full summary of his or her works and miracles. A good example is Empress Theodora herself, whose heroic re-establishment of Orthodoxy did not lead to a cult established by the people or monastic sectors; on the contrary, the court itself promoted her holiness. Her memory was only celebrated liturgically on the calendars of saints' days produced by the imperial government: the *Synaxarion of Constantinople*,[278] the *Menologion of Basileios II*[279] and the *Synodikon of Orthodoxy*,[280] none of which sources included any

---

[278] *SynaxCP* 458,27–60,8 (11 February); 455/456,53 (10 February). The *akoluthies* that survive in his honour are of a later date, see Petit 1926: 274–75.
[279] *Menologion Basilii* 308C–D; *Menologion of Basileios II*, fol. 392.
[280] *Synodikon of Orthodoxy* 93,768–9 and 97,801–2.

posthumous miracles. In addition, the main manuscript containing the *vita* of Theodora (the London *British Library Add.* 28270, a. 1111, fol. 1r–16v) affirms that it was read on the Sunday of Orthodoxy, that is, the first Sunday in Lent, when the return of the icons was celebrated. This feast day, as political and politicised as it was ecclesiastical, became a state affair that outlasted the Amorian dynasty and affected all subsequent emperors and their public image. For this reason, the same manuscript includes after the *vita* of Theodora two accounts that aimed to exonerate Theophilos: the *Narratio de Theophili imperatoris absolutione*, fol. 16v–22r, and *De Theophili imperatoris benefactis*, fol. 22r–25v.[281] Quite apart from any sentiments, fervour or popular devotion that might have existed towards the final iconoclast emperor, his successors (in particular Leon VI) continued to encourage texts that described the iconoclast crisis, well aware of the major role literature could play in guaranteeing their own legitimacy in the exercise of imperial power.

---

[281] An eschatological text follows, the *Vision of St Isaiah of Nicomedia* (*BHG* 2208), fol. 25v–27v, and a selection of hagiographical texts from the *Spiritual Meadow* and from saint's lives. On this codex, see Van de Vorst and Delehaye 1913: 271–72; Cataldi Palau 1992: 253–56.

CHAPTER 5

The Ignatian Milieu
The Management of Inherited Iconodule Literature

When the patriarch Methodios gave up his soul to the Redeemer on 14 June 847, he left behind a convulsed Church, which, despite being obliged to join forces to combat iconoclast heresy, experienced major internal disagreements, as the excommunication en masse of the monks from the Constantinopolitan monastery of Stoudios makes clear.[1] One result of these clashes was the lack of a clear candidate to replace Methodios as the head of Christendom in the East. The name of the archbishop of Syracuse, Gregorios Asbestas, who was in the capital at that time, was among those most often mentioned as a candidate for the position. A contemporary of the late patriarch and also from Sicily, a hotbed of oriental spirituality that gave Constantinople prestigious prelates in the ninth century,[2] his admiration for Methodios was well known, since by any reckoning he had become his official biographer,[3] and his candidacy was seen to ensure continuity. But Gregorios was not alone: the *vita* of the patriarch Ignatios indicates that there were many candidates,[4] while the historian Genesios names two of them, Basileios and Gregorios, sons of Emperor Leon V who had also become monks and were very virtuous.[5] In their case, their father's iconoclast past made their candidatures for the patriarchate impossible. The lack of a clear majority in favour of any candidate led Empress Theodora to settle the matter by imposing her choice, Ignatios I,[6] who was consecrated on 3 July, scarcely three weeks

---

[1] *Regestes*, nr. 435; See Chapters 1–2.
[2] Such as Theodoros Krithinos, the patriarch Methodios, Gregorios Asbestas and Ioseph Hymnographos, see *DS* VII, 2193–206; Cracco Ruggini 1980; Prigent 2017.
[3] On Gregorios Asbestas, *PmbZ* # 2480 and 22348; *PBE* I: Gregorios 26; Grumel 1940/1942; Dvornik 1948: 17–38; Karlin-Hayter 1977. Regarding the *vita* of Methodios that he produced, see Section 7.2.2.
[4] *Vita of the patriarch Ignatios* 16,1–3.
[5] Genesios IV, 18, pp. 70.86–71.93. About them, see *PmbZ* # 927 and 2474.
[6] On the patriarch Ignatios I, see *PmbZ* # 2666 and 22712; *PBE* I: Ignatios 1; *Dictionnaire de Théologie Catholique* VII/1, 713–22; Costa-Louillet 1954/1955: 461–78; *Bibliotheca Sanctorum* 7, 665–72.

after the death of Methodios. Contemporary sources provide little information regarding this choice,[7] the clearest evidence of the empress' support being provided by the *Vita of the Patriarch Ignatios*, echoed by the Byzantine historian Zonaras.[8]

According to Dvornik, the consecration as patriarch of this monk, a eunuch son of the Emperor Michael I Rhangabe (811–813),[9] satisfied the most fanatical ecclesiastical sector (the Zealots), since as a monk his vision of veneration was very close to theirs and he agreed that conclusive persecution of iconoclasts was necessary.[10] But according to Grumel and Karlin-Hayter, the true representative of the party most hostile to iconoclasts had been Methodios, so that the choice of Ignatios represented an attempt to curry favour with the old supporters of the rejection of images.[11] Regardless of how we interpret these events, the fact is that the new patriarch lost no time in making clear the party policy he intended to implement in his ministry; on the very day of his enthronement, he forbade Gregorios Asbestas to attend the ceremony. This irritated the archbishop and his followers, who threw the candles they were carrying to the ground and responded that the Church had been entrusted to a wolf rather than a shepherd.[12]

Shortly afterwards, Ignatios had a Constantinopolitan synod anathematise, excommunicate and depose Gregorios and his sympathisers Eulampios of Apamea, Petros of Syllaion and Petros of Sardis,[13] who appealed to Pope Leo IV (847–855) and Pope Benedict III (855–858), giving rise to the second schism in the recently reunified Church.[14] We do not know when this synod took place. Grumel maintains that it was not long after 848. Mansi gives the year as 854, while Dvornik suggests 852 or 853.[15] Regardless of when the synod was held, Gregorios Asbestas was deposed as archbishop of Syracuse, and the patriarch Ignatios appointed Theodoros in his place.[16] Gregorios' dismissal appears to have been motivated exclusively by his opposition to the patriarch.[17] The division within the Church was soon confirmed, and the patriarch Ignatios sought

---

[7] Ps-Symeon 657; *Vita of Nikolaos Stoud.* 904B.
[8] *Vita of Ignatios* 16; Zonaras XVI 4.30. This vision is defended by Afinogenov 1994: 59.
[9] For his figure and his brief reign, see *PmbZ* # 4989; *PBE* I: Michael 7; Sansterre 1996; Haldon 2017.
[10] Dvornik 1948: 36–38.　[11] Grumel 1939; Karlin-Hayter 1977.　[12] *Vita of Ignatios* 23,1–3.
[13] Concerning Eulampios, see *PmbZ* # 1672; *PBE* I: Eulampios 1. For Petros of Syllaion, see *PmbZ* # 6089; *PBE* I: Petros 33. On Petros of Sardis, cf. *PmbZ* # 6088; *PBE* I: Petros 74.
[14] *Regestes*, nr. 445 dates this event to late 847–848; Bernardakis 1903: 254–57; Grumel 1940/1942.
[15] On this synod, see *Vita of Ignatios* 22,20–24; Ps-Symeon 671. For Grumel's datation, see *Regestes*, nr. 445. Cf. Mansi XIV, 1028–32; Dvornik 1948: 20–22.
[16] *PmbZ* # 7730.　[17] *Vita of Ignatios* 24,10–14; Mansi XIV, 428B, nn. 14 and 16.

support among the Stoudite monks, who were brought back from exile to oppose the plots that began to be hatched at court. A very active part in these was played by one of the most powerful imperial officials, the *protoasekretis* Photios,[18] spurred on to a large extent by Gregorios Asbestas.

The first patriarchate of Ignatios lasted eleven years (847–858) and ended with a political argument that finally placed Photios on the patriarchal throne. Michael III claimed his state rights, depriving his mother of imperial power in 856. The *logothetes tou dromou* Theoktistos,[19] who according to some authorities was Theodora's uncle, was replaced by the new emperor's right-hand man, his maternal uncle Bardas,[20] who like him had been a victim of the regency organised by Theodora and Theoktistos. On 20 November 855, Theoktistos was assassinated in the imperial palace with the approval of Michael III, who was proclaimed emperor by the senate a few months later (in March 856). With Theodora removed from power, the patriarch Ignatios began to act as the queen mother's spokesman. He forbade access to Hagia Sophia to Bardas, who had recently been named Caesar by his nephew Michael III. The alleged reason was the incestuous relationship Bardas was supposed to have had with his recently widowed daughter-in-law. The historical veracity of this accusation has been analysed by Dvornik, who reviews the sources.[21] On Twelfth Night of the year 858, Bardas flouted the patriarchal order and attended the liturgy; Ignatios' response was to deny him communion. The Caesar reacted by blaming Theodora and asking the patriarch to tonsure her, which Ignatios refused to do.[22] Finally, Theodora and her daughters were shut away in the convent of Ta Gastria.[23] When a conspiracy to kill Bardas was discovered, the patriarch was the first to fall: he was deposed and exiled to the Island of Terebinthos on 23 November 858.[24]

The sources that describe the quarrel between Bardas and the patriarch Ignatios and his consequent fall from grace are relatively numerous: the *Libellus* of the *archimandrites* Theognostos (ca. 861), a letter from Metrophanes of Smyrna to the *logothetes* Manuel (post 869/870) and a letter from Stylianos of Neocaesarea addressed to Pope Stephen V (post 880). Thanks to them, we know that in fact the inflexibility of the

---

[18] *PmbZ* # 6253 and 26667; *PBE* I: Photios 1; Hergenröther 1867–1869; Lemerle 1971: 177–204; Varona Codeso and Prieto Domínguez 2013.
[19] *PmbZ* # 8050; *PBE* I: Theoktistos 3; Malyševskij 1887; see Chapter 4.
[20] *PmbZ* # 791; *PBE* I: Bardas 5; Dvornik 1966.   [21] *Regestes*, nr. 449; Dvornik 1966.
[22] Dvornik 1958: 11ff. On the sources about the fall of Theodora, see Karlin-Hayter 1971: 471ff.
[23] On Ta Gastria, see Janin 1969: 67–68; Ruggieri 1991: 191.
[24] *Vita of Ignatios* 17; *Vita of Nikolaos Stoud.* 908A.

patriarch Ignatios towards the new reign of Michael III and Bardas had been ably exploited by his opponents, who encouraged a rebellious attitude that finally compromised him and cost him his position. Ignatios' own biographer, Niketas Paphlagon, allows himself the observation that the ecclesiastical hierarchy was favourably disposed towards his possible abdication for the good of the Church. It seems to have been the insistence of the bishops and the imperial authorities that led Ignatios to invite his staunchest supporters to choose a new patriarch.[25] The candidate judged most satisfactory by all parties was Photios, who was not yet considered a creature of Bardas.[26] Despite the fact that Ignatian sources claim otherwise, Ignatios probably signed instruments of abdication that included conditions, a novel feature. Indeed, Photios appears to have signed an acknowledgement of the patriarchal dignity of Ignatios and of respect for his will, since had he not done so, Ignatios would have again become the legitimate patriarch.[27]

Irrespective of the price paid, the alliance between the Photian and Ignatian factions did not last long. Photios' desire to include Gregorios Asbestas among the bishops who consecrated him was considered a provocation. Indeed, Gregorios' presence at these proceedings was another point in the accusation submitted in Rome, where the case of the archbishop of Syracuse remained pending. All in all, Photios' attempt to reunify the Byzantine Church around him involved winning over the sympathisers of the archbishop of Syracuse and Gregorios himself, who was a clear link with the late patriarch Methodios, with whom Gregorios had collaborated closely and whose *vita* he was to write.[28] The need to legitimise his patriarchate by relying on that of the patriarch who restored Orthodoxy turned out to be a characteristic element of Photios' actions rather than a single, specific measure.

---

[25] Grumel 1939.
[26] According to Dvornik 1948: 12–13, Photios was chosen to be Ignatios' successor because: 'He seemed acceptable to both parties. As an intellectual he naturally sympathized with the moderates, but, up to then, he owed all his promotions, the professorship at the University, the post of First secretary of the Chancery and the membership in the Senate, to Theoctistus and to Theodora. His last public function, the embassy to the Arabs, had been entrusted to him by Theoctistus and Theodora. The marriage of his brother to Theodora's sister seemed also to have tightened the relationship of Photius' family with Theodora. Moreover, he could not be blamed for any partisanship in the overthrow for Theoctistus and Theodora, for it had happened while he was on his mission to the Arabs. As head of Imperial Chancery, Photius must have shown an extraordinary talent for practical administration. He was not only a fervent iconodule, but also well versed in theological lore.'
[27] *Regestes*, nr. 456; Stephanou 1952; 1955.   [28] Karlin-Hayter 1977: 141–45.

The Ignatian Milieu

The political situation became progressively more volatile, and despite some interventions in favour of the Ignatians,[29] Photios was considered responsible for the police repression against them promoted by Bardas and for the ill-treatment of Ignatios himself, who was first transferred to Hiereia, then shut away in the Noumera prison and finally deported to Mytilene by sea.[30] The defenders of the ex-patriarch declared that Photios was a perjurer and insinuated that he had attempted to get back the signed oath of loyalty. Ignatios was therefore once again the legitimate patriarch, although he was in exile.[31] In this situation, the only solution available to Photios was to call a synod in winter 860/861 to excommunicate Ignatios and require the secession of a dozen bishops and numerous hegoumenoi, among them Nikolaos of Stoudios.[32] This synod, which mended the division in the Byzantine Church, was held at the church of the Holy Apostles of Constantinople. Its conclusions were signed by a hundred and thirty bishops and the two papal legates, Rodoaldus of Porto and Zacharias of Anagni. Although they were destroyed by order of the anti-Photian Council of 869, we know that they omitted the Ignatian question by the express desire of Michael III and Photios, despite the fact that it was the main concern of the papal envoys.[33]

The patriarchate of Photios lasted for nine years (858–867), until the death of his patron and protector Michael III. No sooner had the new emperor, Basileios I, ascended the throne, then he decreed the reinstatement of Ignatios and the removal from office of Photios, who was condemned and exiled. The second patriarchate of Ignatios lasted ten years (867–877), and after his death, he was again succeeded by Photios. The second patriarchate of Photios lasted a further nine years (877–886), until Leon VI inherited the imperial throne and exiled Photios definitively, condemning him to oblivion.[34]

Much of the second half of the ninth century thus passed with the Byzantine Church polarised in two major parties around two supposedly legitimate patriarchs, one deposed and the other in power. From the outset, both parties called on Rome to mediate, which only made the conflict fester. Pope Nicholas I, advised by the Ignatian Theognostos and

---

[29] *Regestes*, nrs. 459; 460; 463. Phot., *epist*. 3, 4, 6 and 8.   [30] *Vita of Ignatios* 25,18–21.
[31] Stephanou 1955; Konstantelos 1989/1991.
[32] *Regestes*, nrs. 458; 461; 462. On the synod of 861, see Dvornik 1948: 70–90; Anastos 1990; Troianos 2012: 146–48; Ronconi 2018. For the appearance of Ignatios before this synod, see *Vita of Ignatios* 31.
[33] A summary of the minutes is offered by Von Glanvell 1905: 603–10.
[34] See Tougher 1997: 68–88.

deeply disappointed with the work of his legates, notified Emperor Michael III in spring 862 that he continued to consider Ignatios the legitimate patriarch.[35] The dissident faction was thus strengthened in its struggle against Photios.

5.1 The Patriarch Ignatios and His Attitude to Literature

In such a difficult situation, it is unsurprising that Ignatios, as head of the patriarchate, wished to maintain continuity, introducing himself as the natural successor of the great Methodios. The surviving sources provide very little information about the activities of Ignatios as patriarch; after narrating his accession to the Constantinopolitan throne, they describe in detail the confrontation with Gregorios Asbestas and go on to mention the confrontation with the Caesar Bardas, which would end in Ignatios' overthrow and exile. The limited details of the pastoral work of Ignatios that have come down to us reveal his strong bond with Empress Theodora and his commitment to the anti-iconoclastic discourse of the Church that arose after the restoration of Orthodoxy. We should probably restrict to his first patriarchate measures such as the profanation of the remains of Konstantinos V and Ioannes VII Grammatikos, who were removed from their coffins and taken to the hippodrome on race day to be beaten before being publicly burned in the square called Amastrianon.[36] The ashes of these heretics were then thrown into the sea. The date is not clear, but the general opinion is that it was ca. 852 and in any case before 856.[37] It may well be that Methodios long had the idea of exhuming the remains of Konstantinos V but that Theodora was obliged to wait a few years before putting it into practice, in order to avoid a violent reaction from the iconoclasts. The elimination of the remains of Konstantinos V from the Heroon of Justinian at the church of the Holy Apostles must have been approved by the patriarch Ignatios. When he was tortured in 861, while imprisoned in the green marble sarcophagus that had belonged to

---

[35] *MGH, epist.* VI, p. 450; Herbers 1993.
[36] Symeon Logothetes 248,15–49,2; Ps-Symeon 681,4–12; *De Cerimoniis* II, 645,1–9; Grierson 1962: 53. For the political significance of this measure, see Section 4.4.
[37] *PmbZ* # 2666; Rochow 1994: 138–39. It is mainly supported by Georg. Monachos Continuatus 834,17–35,3 who attributes the measure to Emperor Michael. According to the historian Kedrenos, the person responsible was Caesar Bardas, see Georgios Kedrenos, II, 18,18–21; Gero 1977: 164–5, n. 58. In contrast, Karlin-Hayter places this event during Methodios' patriarchate basing herself on the *Necrologium imperatorum et catalogus eorum sepulchrorum*, see Grierson 1962: 53; Karlin-Hayter 1991b: 116; 1991c: 382, n. 41.

Konstantinos V,[38] the measure was turned against him, explaining the vigorous condemnation of this outrage by Niketas David Paphlagon in his *vita*.

Along the same lines, the third recovery of the relic of St John the Baptist's head with the consent of the imperial household is clearly an anti-iconoclast propagandistic measure on Ignatios' part. These events were remembered in an anonymous hagiography, the *Sermo de capitis inventionibus* (*BHG* 841),[39] which was produced in the immediate milieu of Ignatios. This is clear from the indifference and coolness with which Methodios is treated, in contrast to the praise given to Ignatios. On this occasion, the head of John the Baptist was supposedly hidden in the town of Komana in Cappadocia to prevent its violation by the iconoclasts, who were accused of destroying the relics of saints in addition to their icons.[40] During his first patriarchate, Ignatios was blessed with a vision that revealed to him where the head was to be found, and on the patriarchate's initiative, a delegation was sent to Komana to find it and bring it to Constantinople, where it was deposited in a church belonging to the palace (τῷ ἐν βασιλείοις ναῷ).[41] The date was 25 May, and the head was received with great joy by the people of the capital, as if this were an imperial procession in which the patriarch shared the limelight with the emperor.[42] This celebration must have been particularly pleasing to the monks of Stoudios. It should not be forgotten that the saint to whom their monastery was dedicated was none other than John the Baptist the Forerunner, and that it celebrated the feast days in his honour with particular devotion, as the compositions of Theodoros Stoudites reveal: *Laudatio de capitis inventione* (*BHG* 842), *Oratio de nativitate* (*BHG* 843) and *Laudatio de decollatione* (*BHG* 864), as well as the *Parvae catecheseis* 15 (*BHG* 1394t). Shortly afterwards, under the patriarch Euthymios, the relic of the Forerunner's head ended up being kept at the very monastery of Stoudios.[43]

Despite the efforts made by members of his circle, Ignatios is mentioned only in version B of the *Synaxarion*, where he is erroneously referred to as one of the protagonists of the first two discoveries of the relics – occurred sometime before in the reign of Michael III – celebrated on 24 February.[44] On the correct third anniversary of their discovery (25 May), however, the

---

[38] *Vita of Ignatios* 35,7–11.   [39] Walter 1980; Wortley 2004: 145–53; Delouis 2005: 391–411.
[40] On this affirmation, so often repeated by iconodule authors, see Gero 1977: 152–65; Wortley 1982.
[41] *Sermo de capitis inventionibus* 734E.   [42] *Sermo de capitis inventionibus* 734F.
[43] *Vita of the Patriarch Euthymios* 59,18–61,20.
[44] SynaxCP 486,56–87,44. See also *Menologion of Basileios II*, vol. II: 420.

name of neither our patriarch nor the emperor is mentioned. Indeed, there are not even any references to the miracle performed by Ignatios.[45] Despite this, the personal bond established between the patriarch and the bishop of Komana Ioannes, a loyal Ignatian, continued even years later, since the latter is among the signatories of the letter that Stylianos of Neocaesarea sent to Pope Stephen V to deny Photios any legitimate claim to the patriarchate.[46]

Empress Theodora and her adviser Theoktistos must also have found strong support for their decision to marry off the young prince Michael III in 855 in the patriarch Ignatios, who owing to his position presumably officiated at the ceremony. The bride chosen was Eudokia Dekapolitissa,[47] who despite her charms was unable to effectively seduce Michael III. The wedding was held in St Stephen's church within the Palace of Daphne, and by means of it Theodora linked the imperial family, tainted with the stigma of iconoclast heresy owing to the behaviour of Theophilos, to a young lady of impeccable credentials and a collateral descendant of one of the new iconodule saints, Gregorios Dekapolites.[48]

The close collaboration between Ignatios and Theodora can even be traced in the fall from grace of the empress, when the patriarch refused to tonsure her, as Bardas and Michael desired.[49] The situation escalated, and Ignatios ended up being forced to abdicate, as noted above, in an openly hostile context. In this situation, Ignatios' need to reaffirm his position and to denounce the interference and abuse committed in the name of imperial interests led to him using all possible means to make his voice heard. He evidently lost no time in turning to literature as well. As he was outshone in this area by his predecessor Methodios and his rival Photios, however, his literary production and patronage have attracted practically no attention until now. It is true that very few writings assigned to him survive and that these attributions are generally not unanimous. This is the case of the *Stichoi on Lazarus*, a poem generally considered the work of Ignatios Diakonos, but which some authors have assigned to the patriarch Ignatios owing to the ambiguity of the *lemmata* in the manuscripts. In

---

[45] *SynaxCP* 707,8–17.
[46] For Ioannes of Komana, see *PmbZ* # 22826. On Stylianos of Neocaesarea, see *PmbZ* # 27409. It was also signed by the bishops Eusebios of Nazianzus (*PmbZ* # 21816) and Ioannes of Leontopolis (*PmbZ* # 22827).
[47] For Eudokia, see *PmbZ* # 1631; *PBE* I: Eudokia 3. See Chapter 3.
[48] On the wedding, see Symeon Logothetes 234, ch. 131,6; Georg. Mon. Cont. 816,7–14; Georg. Mon. Cont. (Muralt) 1037B; Georg. Mon. Cont. (Istrin) 4,30–36. For the political and religious significance of this event, see Section 3.2.2.b.
[49] *Vita of Ignatios* 17,11–32.

the late nineteenth century, the editor of the work considered it proven that it was written by the patriarch Ignatios, but this affirmation was later rejected by Wolska-Conus, who assigned these verses to Ignatios Diakonos, as is generally believed today.[50] Given the scarcity of texts by him and of information about them and their contents, we must conclude with Beck that Ignatios was outstanding neither as a theologian nor as a writer.[51] His literary production must have been very limited, if it existed at all.

The manuscript tradition ascribes to one Ignatios short poetic pieces for use in liturgy, and the later the manuscripts, the more often these pieces are said to be the work of Ignatios the patriarch. Most of them are merely attributed to an unspecified Ignatios, however, with no further clarification. As early as the nineteenth century, modern researchers took for granted that this was the patriarch, without considering other authors of the same name whose literary production is more in keeping with these *kanones*.[52] Without justification of any kind, scholars such as Émereau and Follieri in turn accepted these attributions.[53] But these *kanones* are in fact the work of a slightly older contemporary also called Ignatios, the Diakonos: namely, the *kanones* to the patriarch Nikephoros (13 March), Iakobos the Confessor (21 March), Ioannes Klimakos (30 March), Georgios of Mytilene (7 April), Lucillianos (3 June), Tatiana (12 January), Hilarion (6 June), Metrophanes of Constantinople (4 June) and the Theotokos.[54] In Chapter 2, we had the opportunity to analyse the meaning of these compositions within Ignatios Diakonos' production and how they were placed at the service of the post-iconoclastic propaganda orchestrated by the patriarch Methodios.

Even though nothing written by Ignatios appears to have survived, we know that he acted as patron to other men of letters and commissioned texts on iconoclasm, in particular, during his second patriarchate (867–877). At the council he called in 869/870, the so-called Eighth Oecumenical Council,[55] not only was Photios condemned, but a new

---

[50] Sternbach 1898: 156; Wolska-Conus 1970; Lauxtermann 2019: 237–41.
[51] Beck 1959: 603 confuses the enkomion in honour of Ignatios written by Michael (see Section 5.2.2. b) with a non-existent enkomion that was allegedly composed by the patriarch Ignatios in honour of St Michael. This error is repeated by Wolska-Conus 1970: 334, n. 28.
[52] Thus Papadopoulos 1890: 246, who gives no reason to justify this authorship.
[53] Émereau 1923: 433–34; Follieri 1960–1966: vol. v,1, p. 272.
[54] *Theotocarium Nicodemi Hagioritae*, Venezia 1898: 57. Cf. *AHG*, vol. xiii, 377. See Chapter 2.
[55] On the Council of 869/870, see Hergenröther 1867–1869: vol. ii, 7–166; Dvornik 1948: 196–229; 1973a; Stiernon 1967; 1973; Stephanou 1973; Peri 1976; Perrone 1990; Herbers 2008; *Council of Constantinople (869/870)*.

public repudiation of iconoclasm was signed by those attending, who also pronounced another anathema against Konstantinos V, Ioannes VII Grammatikos and the remaining iconoclast patriarchs who had been condemned earlier. This measure was extended by name to the current iconoclast heretics: Theodoros Krithinos, the former bishop of Syracuse; a certain Paulos; Theodoros Gastes; Stephanos Molites and Leon Laloudios.[56] The emperor's representative, Baanes, personally took charge of the interrogations during the eighth session, and the emperor himself appeared at the end to affectionately embrace three disciples of Krithinos who had renounced their master and forsworn heresy.[57] This blow to iconoclasm is accompanied by a council canon (the seventh), in which the Fathers encouraged the production of icons but only by individuals within the Church. This prohibition on making images applied to persons who had been anathematised (such as Photios and his supporters) aimed not only to deprive the illegitimate patriarch of his self-proclaimed restoration of icons, but also to identify the anathematised Photians with iconoclast heretics.[58]

One attendee at the Eighth Oecumenical Council was the pro-Ignatian bishop Theokletos of Lakedaimon[59] in the Peloponnese, in whose honour a highly conventional hagiography was composed. The *Vita of Theokletos of Lakedaimon* (*BHG* 2420) was written a century later by an anonymous author who knew little about the saint and provides very few biographical details, although it does echo the ecclesiastical conflict that ran through the Byzantine Church. The text states that Theokletos was temporally expelled from the bishopric by the secular authorities due to his differences with other clergymen, which unfortunately are not recorded. They regretted their decision afterwards, and the saint was reinstated.[60] This information, together with Theokletos' absence from the Photian Council of 879/880, when the bishop of Lakedaimon was a certain Antonios,[61] makes it reasonable to assume that he was a firm supporter of Ignatios. Although he is not mentioned in the *Synaxarion* of Constantinople, Theokletos

---

[56] For this new anathema, see Mansi XVI, 139–42 and 388–89; *Synodikon of the Orthodoxy* 57,175–76; Gouillard 1961a: 387ff.; Mango 1977: 135. About these individuals, see *PmbZ* # 7675 on Theodoros Krithinos; *PmbZ* # 5855 on Paulos; *PmbZ* # 7681 on Theodoros Gastes; *PmbZ* # 7071 on Stephanos Molites; and *PmbZ* # 4437 on Leon Laloudios.
[57] Dvornik 1953: 82–83. Concerning Baanes Angoures, cf. *PmbZ* # 719 and # 20716.
[58] Mansi XVI, 402ff., 164; Dvornik 1953: 84. See Chapter 6.
[59] *PmbZ* # 28035. His presence is confirmed by the Council acts, see Mansi XVI, 135A, 159D and 195C.
[60] *Vita of Theokletos* 11–12; Kislinger 2007: 28–29.   [61] Mansi XVIIA, 376D; *PmbZ* # 20484.

was venerated on 1 December, as is attested by the *Synodikon* of Lakedaimon.[62]

Ignatios' official hagiographer, Niketas David Paphlagon, places the building work he commissioned within his second patriarchate. During this period, Ignatios restored several churches where the Virgin, the Apostles and martyrs were celebrated on their feast days and also gave speeches. Indeed, Niketas Paphlagon includes an alleged example of the edifying sermons with which he addressed the faithful.[63] Moreover, Ignatios encouraged Emperor Basileios I to do the same, and it was on his suggestion that the latter replaced the icons of the interior of the church of Sts Sergios and Bakkhos, which had been destroyed during the patriarchate of Ioannes Grammatikos.[64] As we will see, during his second patriarchate, Ignatios began a propaganda campaign to legitimate his exercise of the patriarchate and to build links with the iconodule martyrs.

After his death on 23 October 877, the patriarch Ignatios was venerated in a particularly striking manner, since his supporters tried to identify him with the saints who confronted the iconoclasts and defeated the heresy, presenting his sufferings and torture as if they were similar to those of the iconodules who opposed the heretic emperors.[65] Indeed, Ignatios was included in the *Synodikon of Orthodoxy* among the patriarchs of Constantinople worthy of acclaim for having defended icons.[66] Ignatios' holiness was closely linked to iconodule circles, which had guaranteed his accession to the patriarchate. According to his official hagiographer, Theophanes the Confessor himself blessed Ignatios as patriarch on a visit to him when the latter was still very young.[67] Ioannikios' appreciation was similarly prophetic, since he answered Empress Theodora's question by naming Ignatios as a future patriarch.[68] Whether because of these connections with iconodule saints predating his patriarchate or because of the injustices he suffered during his pontificate, on his death the people venerated Ignatios with great devotion: as the ecstatic crowd drew near, anxious to obtain a relic of the new saint, both his shroud and his wooden coffin were cut into small pieces and shared out among them.[69] After vigil was kept over him in the Constantinopolitan church of St Menas,[70] his body was buried at his own monastery of St Michael of Satyros by the Bithynian Chalcedon.[71] The continuous healings and miracles that

---

[62] Jenkins and Mango 1961: 230.   [63] *Vita of Ignatios* 70–72.   [64] Skylitzes 162,20–25.
[65] Prieto Domínguez 2014b.   [66] *Synodikon of Orthodoxy* 51,110; 53,114–15; 103,881.
[67] *Vita of Ignatios* 14,28–34.   [68] *Vita of Ignatios* 16,8–11; Dvornik 1948: 17–18.
[69] *Vita of Ignatios* 76,3–7.   [70] Janin 1969: 333–35.
[71] Janin 1975: 42–43; Ruggieri 1991: 201.

followed there increased his fame to such an extent that it is said that Photios expelled the sick from the Church and had a ditch dug around the tomb to keep the faithful from touching it any longer.[72]

The annual celebration of Ignatios' memory is included in the *Menologion Basilii*[73] following his entry in the *Synaxarion* of *Constantinople* for 23 October, which omits some of the most problematic aspects of his patriarchate and the confrontation with the dissidents who supported Photios.[74] We know that he was celebrated at Hagia Sophia,[75] where a still-surviving mosaic representing Ignatios was added to the north wall. According to the *Synodicon vetus*, the proclamation of Ignatios as a saint and his inclusion in the diptychs began with Photios himself during his second patriarchate.[76] The revision of the *typikon* of Hagia Sophia, which includes the commemoration of Ignatios on 23 October,[77] probably dates from this time, strengthening the idea that the reconciliation signed publicly by Photios and Ignatios before his death was sincere. This reconciliation took place in about 876 and led to Ignatios appointing Photios as his successor.[78] According to Leon VI, it was his father Emperor Basileios who urged the two men to come to this agreement so as to re-establish the unity of the Church.[79] Even Photios himself described a scene of reconciliation, which allegedly took place in the imperial palace, in two ceremonial hymns: *Anthologia Barberina* 136 and 137.[80] Both are alphabetical poems and were sung publicly in the presence of Basileios, who is celebrated for restoring peace between Photians and Ignatians. These hymns seem to have been composed by Photios in 880 for performance during a liturgy in Hagia Sophia or the Nea Ekklesia.

Pro-Ignatian sources, on the other hand, deny the reality of this reconciliation,[81] but Ignatians such as Ioseph the Hymnographos were both admired and liked by Photios.[82] Indeed, even when he acknowledges their

---

[72] *Vita of Ignatios* 87,19–28. [73] *Menologion Basilii* 124C–D (23 October).
[74] *SynaxCP* 158,14–60,12 and 155/156,47–48. He should not be confused with the Ignatios celebrated on 6 December whose body lay at the church of the Blachernai, see *SynaxCP* 284,55–56; Janin 1969: 267. All that is known about this saint is that he was the founder and hegoumenos of a monastery at Kios in Bithynia and that he died in exile before 843, see Loparev 1910: 123; *Vita of Antonios the Younger* (addit), p. 210, n. 2 and p. 211.
[75] *Typikon of the Great Church* I, 76 (23 October).
[76] *Synodicon vetus* 164, p. 140. Cf. Dvornik 1958: 55–56; 1964: 101.
[77] *Typika Dmitrievskij* I, 15.
[78] Mansi XVIIA, 424; Theoph. Cont. V, 44,8–16; Hergenröther 1867–1869: vol. II, 315; Dvornik 1948: 198 dates the reconciliation in 876.
[79] *Enkomion of Basileios I*, pp. 63–65; Tobias 2007: 236–52 for Emperor Basileios' management of this dispute.
[80] Ciccolella 1998; Lauxtermann 2019: 53–56. [81] *Vita of Ignatios* 91,13–25.
[82] *Vita of Ioseph Hymnographos by Ioannes Diakonos* 969,30; Tomadakes 1971a: 71–73.

different points of view, Photios always proclaims the holiness of his rival, as, for example, in his brief treatise on episcopal and synodic matters generally known as *Synagogai*, despite the fact that it is structured with ten questions and answers (*erotapokriseis*).[83] Ioseph Hymnographos, a committed Ignatian, wrote a *kontakion* to commemorate the first anniversary of the death of Ignatios,[84] in addition to a *kanon* in his honour alluding to the machinations of his adversaries (verses 152–55), his usurpation (197–200) and his suffering (115–19 and 143–46).[85] Michael for his part composed an *Encomium Ignatii* (*BHG* 818), which was read at the great Photian Council of 879/880.[86] There is also an unpublished *kanon* paying tribute to the patriarch Ignatios on 23 October that survives in the codex *Sinaiticus Gr.* 562, fol. 117–18.[87]

The patriarch Ignatios was always more monk than pontiff, as later traditions bear out. The *vita* of Eirene of Chrysobalanton, for instance, includes a pious legend in which Ignatios receives three apples from Paradise,[88] while his successor the patriarch Euthymios considered him his lord and master. Indeed, according to his hagiographer, Euthymios had a vision of Ignatios in which the latter announced an end to the disputes within the Church, which was divided at the time by the matter of the fourth marriage of Emperor Leon VI:[89] 'For it was revealed to me this night, as I was in prayer, by my lord and master Ignatios, that in the tenth season of him who lately received the sceptre there will be perfect peace and calm; but do you, when this comes about, remember me in my humility.' The desire of Euthymios to identify with Ignatios in his aspirations to the patriarchal throne is a natural response to the desire of the patriarch Nikolaos Mystikos to vindicate Photios, his master and protector.

5.2 The Milieu of the Patriarch Ignatios

As one of the most powerful institutions of the Byzantine Empire, the patriarchate of Constantinople gathered together many major intellectuals

---

[83] Phot., *Synagogai*, 1229D-32A: πλείστους καθαιρεθέντας ἐπὶ ἐγκλήμασι παρὰ **τοῦ ἁγιωτάτου Ἰγνατίου** ἡμεῖς ἐδεξάμεθα, καὶ τοὺς ὑφ' ἡμῶν καθαιρεθέντας **ὁ ἐν ἁγίοις Ἰγνάτιος** ἐδέξατο. Cf. Darrouzès 1984.
[84] Tomadakes 1971a: 204, nr. 2; Mioni 1948: 94–95 and 177–80.
[85] Tomadakes 1971a: 119, nr. 60; ed. in *AHG*, vol. II, 274–83 and 436–47.
[86] See Section 3.2.2.a.   [87] *Tameion*, 64, nr. 124.
[88] *Vita of Eirene of Chrysobalanton* 13, p. 82,15–23.
[89] *Vita of the Patriarch Euthymios* 21, p. 140,33–36: «τοῦτο γάρ μοι ταύτῃ τῇ νυκτὶ ἀνήγγειλεν προσευχομένῳ ὁ κύριός μου καὶ δεσπότης Ἰγνάτιος, ὡς τῷ δεκάτῳ καιρῷ τοῦ ἄρτι τὰ σκῆπτρα λαμβάνοντος εἰρήνη τελεία καὶ βαθεῖα ἔσται κατάστασις. ὑμεῖς δέ, ταύτης γενομένης, μιμνήσκεσθέ μου τῆς χθαμαλότητος».

of the time. When Ignatios was consecrated as patriarch, there was already an active milieu surrounding his family, the Rhangabe. A good example of their literary impact is the chronicle known as *Scriptor incertus de Leone Armenio*, in which Michael I Rhangabe and his family are praised and the good works he carried out with his wife Prokopia, for which 'everyone glorified them', are emphasised.[90] This historical text, of which only two fragment survives, tends to be dated to the time of Michael II (820–829).[91] It is possible, however, that this date should be moved forward to the Triumph of Orthodoxy during the patriarchate of Methodios.[92] This would explain the access of an author as hostile to iconoclasm as the *Scriptor incertus* to the patriarchal archives,[93] something that seems improbable during the patriarchate of the iconoclast Antonios I (821–837). What there is no doubt about is that the writer is very much in favour of the iconophile clergy and the patriarch Nikephoros, who is referred to as having died († 828),[94] and at the same time a great detractor of Emperor Leon V, whom he fiercely attacks *inter alia* for ordering that Michael I's sons, one of whom was the future patriarch Ignatios, be castrated after his defeat.[95] Moreover, the *Scriptor incertus* stresses the piety and the monastic virtues of Michael I, praising him as a protégé of God.[96] This text was likely one of the sources used by Sabas to write his *vita* of Ioannikios during Ignatios' first patriarchate,[97] but its most substantial significance is as a demonstration of the existence of a literary milieu favourable to the new patriarch when he came to power.

For his part, Ignatios had already formed a consolidated monastic circle of his own before ascending the patriarchal throne of Constantinople. In his youth, he founded and led at least three monasteries on the Princes' Islands located between the capital and Chalcedon, at Terebinthos, Niandros and Plate.[98] To these must be added the establishment of the monastery of St Michael in Satyros (also known as Anatellon), which Ignation built in 873/874 during his second patriarchate on the

---

[90] *Scriptor incertus* 29,29. The chronicle survives in a single eleventh-century manuscript, *Parisinus Gr.* 1711, anno 1013. Treadgold 2002: 6–7; 2013: 90–99 identifies this chronicle with the lost historiographical text of Sergios the Confessor. The *Scriptor incertus*, accordingly, would be none other than Photios' father, which would constitute a true irony of fate. Cf. Mango 1977: 135–36; Nogara 1978; Phot., *Bibliotheca*, cod. 67.
[91] Markopoulos 1999: 262. Cf. also Browning 1965; Kazhdan and Sherry 1997.   [92] Sénina 2013.
[93] For the use of the patriarchal archives by the *Scriptor incertus*, see Markopoulos 1999: 259.
[94] *Scriptor incertus* 54,487–88: ἐν ὁσίᾳ τῇ μνήμῃ Γερμανὸν καὶ Ταράσιον καὶ Νικηφόρον.
[95] Genesios I,5. On the other hand, the *Scriptor incertus* does not mention explicitly Ignatios.
[96] *Scriptor incertus* 40,31–41.
[97] Mango 1983: 399–400. On this *vita* of Ioannikios, see Section 7.1.1.
[98] *Vita of Ignatios* 11,24–27; Pargoire 1901a: 56–91; Janin 1975: 63, 65 and 67; Ruggieri 1991: 209.

Bithynian coast, which faced his previous monasteries and whither he transferred the remains of his father Michael I Rhangabe.[99]

We have no record of any man of letters who belonged to these communities of the future patriarch Ignatios, which may be historical coincidence. The lack of information about writers linked to the patriarchate during the first patriarchate of Ignatios, by contrast, is much more striking. The truth is that very little is known about his first patriarchate: the surviving sources take pleasure in detailing the confrontations with his detractors, first Gregorios Asbestas and subsequently Photios. The dispute with Photios as to who was the legitimate patriarch monopolised the attention of both contemporary and later chroniclers and hagiographers, who disregard completely Ignatios' years at the head of the Constantinopolitan Church. The scanty information regarding his management between 847 and 858 shows that the Ignatian milieu, at least at its early stage, was not a learned one and that it was far from attaining the usual standards of the Patriarchate. The impression created, moreover, is that iconodule propaganda was not generated by the patriarchate during this period, but the opposite.

A good example is the *vita* of Niketas the patrician (*BHG* 1342b),[100] two versions of which are known: the first written by his nephew and successor as hegoumenos of the monastery of Katesia and the second by a monk from the latter place.[101] Although we lack definitive dates for both *vitae*, it is reasonable to think that the first was produced during this period, owing to the importance it attaches to Emperor Michael I and his image as a great patron of iconodule monasticism who did not hesitate to give the monastery of Chrysonike to the future saint and sponsor his entry into monastic life.[102] The initial part of the *vita* has been lost, but we are familiar with its content thanks to the summary given by the *Synaxarion A* (*BHG* 1342e). This is nonetheless an isolated work, in which some characteristics of post-iconoclast hagiography appear, but which was written for internal use within the monastery by one of its members in order that the feast day of its founder could be celebrated with greater pomp.

---

[99] *Vita of Ignatios* 11,27–32; Pargoire 1901a: 69–78; Janin 1975: 42–43; Ruggieri 1991: 201; Mango 1994: 347–50; Ricci 1998; 2012. The transfer of the body of Michael I is narrated by Theoph. Cont. I, 10,16–25.
[100] Kazhdan 1999: 200. On the patrician Niketas, cf. *PmbZ* # 5424; *PBE* I: Niketas 160; see also Section I.1. For his nephew and first hagiographer, see *PmbZ* # 5473. For his second and last hagiographer, see *PmbZ* # 11711.
[101] For the monastery of Katesia, see Janin 1975: 95; Ruggieri 1991: 222.
[102] *Vita of Niketas the Patrician* 325, ch. 2. On the monastery of Chrysonike, see Janin 1969: 541.

Hardly any works can be found representing a commission from the patriarchate or a composition by Ignatios' circle during his first patriarchate, with the exception of the account of the third finding and repatriation of the relic of St John the Baptist's head. On the other hand, after Ignatios' overthrow and exile, his supporters began a textual production designed to denounce the outrage suffered by their leader and to answer the arguments of Photios and his sympathisers justifying his accession to the patriarchal throne in 858. An example is the *libellus* the *archimandrites* Theognostos sent to Pope Nicholas I (in ca. 861), in which he reports the abuse of Ignatios and begins to issue anti-Photian propaganda.[103] During Ignatios' first patriarchate, Theognostos held the position of *exarchos* supervising provincial monasteries.[104] In the synod of 860/861, he was one of the few to remain loyal to Ignatios, and after its conclusion, which was the first ecclesiastical victory of Photios, he took refuge in Rome. There Theognostos tried to persuade the pope to mediate in the conflict and in favor of Ignatios. We know that when he reached Rome, he held the title of *archimandrites*,[105] and Pope Nicholas did not yield to the pressure of Michael III to have him extradited to Constantinople.[106] After the accession to the throne of Basileios I in 867, the restoration of Ignatios as patriarch appears to have been marked by the return of important Ignatians to the capital of the Byzantine Empire. In August 868, Theognostos returned as a legate of Pope Adrian II with a letter of recommendation in which the Pope emphasises his work to restore Ignatios as patriarch.[107]

As a reward for his efforts, Theognostos was appointed hegoumenos of the important monastery of the Theotokos tes Peges (of the Source) in Constantinople[108] and *skeuophylax* of Hagia Sophia.[109] This is mentioned

---

[103] On Theognostos, see *PmbZ* # 8018 and # 28010; Hergenröther 1867–1869: vol. I, 407–12; Dvornik 1948: 62–65, 76–85, 98–102, 138–42; Bernardakis 1903: 254–57.

[104] *MGH*, *epist.* VI, Nicolai I. *epist.*, nr. 88, p. 477,21f: Theognostum, et qui a fratre coepiscopo nostro Ignatio quasdam provincias exarchatus pondus accepisse dignoscitur. On the post of *exarchos*, see Darrouzès 1970: 127–31; Leontaritou 1996: 226–35; Koder 2013: 93.

[105] Stylianos of Neocaesarea, *epist.* 1, in *MGH*, *epist.* VII, 377,6–8 (= Mansi XVI, 429B). On the duties of the *archimandrites*, see De Meester 1949 (esp. p. 121 on Theognostos); Ruggieri 1991: 117–23.

[106] The year was 865, see Dölger, *Regesten*, nr. 464. For Theognostos' work in Rome, see Sansterre 1983: vol. I, 45 and 79–80.

[107] *MGH*, *epist.* VI, Hadriani II. *epist.* 37 and 38; *Liber Pont.* II 108, p. 180,11f.: qui Romae apud sanctissimum papam Nicolaum pro restituendo Ignatio sedulus intercessor extiterat.

[108] Janin 1969: 223–28; Majeska 1984: 325–26. This community gave rise to a rich hagiographical tradition on the miracles and healings that took place in its church, see Efthymiadis 2006/2007; Talbot 2012.

[109] For Theognostos and Ioseph the Hymnographos holding the post of *skeuophylax* at the same time, see Stiernon 1973: 262–64.

in a letter from Emperor Basileios I to Pope Adrian II in mid-871.[110] This appointment was likely part of the process of the renovation of the monastery undertaken by the emperor after the earthquake that struck Constantinople on 9 January 869 and damaged numerous buildings, including the church of the Holy Apostles and Hagia Sophia itself.[111] The quake was so violent that it was remembered in the *Synaxarion of Constantinople*,[112] and contemporary authors chose to interpret it as a message from God, who thus took sides in the dispute between Ignatios and Photios, and a mark of his will regarding the anti-Photian Council held in Constantinople from 5 October, which finally anathematised Photios on 29 October. Thus, the *Vita of the Patriarch Ignatios* interprets this earthquake, together with a terrible hurricane that occurred shortly afterwards, as a clear sign of God's rejection of Photios and his anger at mankind for not having punished him before, stating:[113]

> And after the synod a violent squall suddenly sprang up . . . . It was no accident that these signs occurred – they were clear indications of the chaos and confusion that was about to be set in motion once again in the Church by the Devil, maker of mischief. And it might never have happened if, as I have said, Photius's case had been judged in accordance with apostolic ordinance.

Photios himself sent two letters to the deacon and *chartoularios* Georgios Amasianos[114] about this earthquake, which he interpreted as punishment for the persecution of Photios. In the first, he laments the suffering of the city, describes the extent of the damage and explains the natural origin of earthquakes, while at the same time giving thanks to God for having freed him from being the patriarch at the time. He also explains the origin of earthquakes by referring to Aristotle to refute the idea that they are due to God's will.[115]

In this context, the decision of Emperor Basileios to rebuild the church of Peges, which he made more beautiful than it had ever been,[116] marked his faith in the Ignatian party. Moreover, the appointment of Theognostos

---

[110] Mansi XVI, 203C; Dölger–Müller, *Regesten*, nr. 488. See also *Epistle to Adrian II* by the patriarch Ignatios in Mansi XVI, 204E; *Regestes*, nr. 534.
[111] *Vita of Ignatios* 65,28–34; Ps-Symeon 688; Georgios Monachos Cont. 840; Downey 1955: 599; Ševčenko 1977a: 114; Dagron 1981: 93; Berger 1988a: 644–45; Berger 2013a: book III, 182.
[112] *SynaxCP* 380,19–23 (9 January).
[113] *Vita of Ignatios* 66: καὶ μετ' αὐτὴν ἐξαίφνης ἐπῆλθε πνεύματος σφοδρὰ καταιγίς . . . . οὐκ εἰκῆ δὲ ταῦτα παρηκολούθηκε τὰ σημεῖα, ἀλλὰ τῆς μελλούσης αὖθις ἀκαταστασίας καὶ ταραχῆς διὰ τοῦ ταραχοποιοῦ δαίμονος ἐπὶ τῆς ἐκκλησίας ἐνίστατο τεκμήρια σαφῆ, ἅπερ ἴσως οὐκ ἂν συνέπεσεν, εἰ μετὰ τὸν ἀποστολικόν, ὡς εἴρηται, τὰ κατ' αὐτὸν ἐκρίθη θεσμόν. English translation by Smithies.
[114] *PmbZ* # 11711; Phot., *epist*. 101–2.   [115] Vercleyen 1988: 168–69.
[116] Theoph. Cont. V, 80,5–8.

at the head of such an important monastery was a clear imperial support for Ignatios. It is to these years, when he was running a Marian establishment, that we can attribute with some degree of certainty one of the few literary compositions by Theognostos to survive: the *enkomion* of the dormition of the Holy Mother of God (*BHG* 1139k).[117] An encomium in honour of all the saints also survives (*BHG* 1617), together with an *akolouthia* on the divine participation (μετάληψις), which includes the author's name (Θεογνώστου) at the end of the acrostic.[118]

There can be no doubt that the *libellus* is Theognostos' most important work both for its historical implications and for the valuable information it contains in regard to the mentality of the Ignatian party. The *libellus* includes an account of the events that occurred in the Constantinopolitan see during Ignatios' last three years (858–861) to demonstrate the ill-treatment he suffered. Anxious for the Pope of Rome to intervene in the dispute, the deposed patriarch entrusted Theognostos with producing this text (*BHG* 818c), which was written in the first person, as if narrated by Ignatios, to be taken to Rome.[119] It not only contains a vivid description of the injustices committed, but also unfolds all the anti-Photian arguments on which would later be built the accusations that would lead to Photios' overthrow on two occasions. Of particular interest is the account of how at the synod Ignatios denied Photios any authority, affirming that he was among those excommunicated for being associated with Gregorios Asbestas, had been ordained by anathematised members of the clergy and had been appointed patriarch from lay official without even serving as an ecclesiastic.[120]

This final accusation ('that Photios was a state official and a layman, being made a pastor before he was a sheep')[121] is particularly relevant, since it was to have great influence on the literary production of the time and on the restoration of the fight against iconoclasm as the storyline of the new works. It is important to remember how Photios became prominent: he was a layman who ran the imperial chancery as *protoasekretis*. His good work and his family relations made him the perfect candidate for the patriarch to accompany Michael III on his accession to the imperial throne. In order to comply with canonical precepts, Photios went through

---

[117] Jugie 1918. [118] Jugie 1918: 171f.; Beck 1959: 544.
[119] *Libellus by Theognostos* 856C: προσωποποιηθείς ὑπὸ Θεογνώστου ... εἰς ὄνομα Ἰγνατίου τοῦ πατριάρχου.
[120] *Libellus by Theognostos* 856oD–61A; Dvornik 1948: 84, who also translates the passage.
[121] *Libellus by Theognostos* 861A: Ἕτερον δὲ, ταξεώτης ἦν καὶ ἐκ λαϊκοῦ τάγματος, καὶ πρὶν γενέσθαι πρόβατον, ποιμὴν ἐχρημάτισεν.

all levels of the ecclesiastical hierarchy, in that beginning 20 December, he was and over the course of five successive days appointed reader, subdeacon, deacon, priest and bishop, so that he could be consecrated as patriarch on Christmas Day of 858.

Aware that this rapid promotion was used against him by his detractors, Photios attempted to justify his accession to the Constantinopolitan throne as early as in the synodal epistle he sent to Pope Nicholas I in spring 860 to inaugurate his patriarchate.[122] This letter was taken to Rome together with another from Emperor Michael III by the *protospatharios* Arsaber.[123] In it, Photios declared that he had wanted to embrace monastic life since childhood but had been unable to do so until then due to the obligations he assumed as head of the *asekreteia* (lines 15–32). He also mentions the pressure applied to him to accept the position of patriarch (46–70). The reply from Pope Nicholas was short and to the point. He made no mention of Ignatios and simply expressed regret that the choice of Photios conflicted with canon law, which prohibited the rapid rise of laymen to episcopal rank.[124] In any case, the goal of the legates he sent to take part in the synod held to condemn iconoclasm was also to resolve the Ignatian question. The fact that these legates did not live up to Nicholas' expectations was another matter.[125]

After the synod, Photios sent a conciliatory reply to the Pope.[126] In this missive, he asks Nicholas I to excuse him and responds in detail to the objection that he came by the Constantinopolitan patriarchal throne in a manner contrary to the canons, alleging that the responsibility for his appointment was not his but of those who pressured him to accept the post (lines 123–31). He quotes the examples of Nikephoros and Tarasios, who also attained the patriarchate as laymen, since the canons mentioned by Pope Nicholas I did not exist then (154–84). In addition, he lists the biblical parallels of Abraham and Melchisedech (185–99),[127] who shared a common faith despite their different traditions, as well as the fact that the latter was not circumcised (200–40). Finally, he adduces the cases of Ambrosios and Nektarios, who were baptised at the same time as they were ordained priests (291–316).

---

[122] Phot., *epist.* 288. Hergenröther 1867–1869: vol. I, 407–11.
[123] *PmbZ* # 609; *PBE* I: Arsaber 20.　　[124] *MGH, epist.* VI, pp. 439–40; Dvornik 1948: 76; 1973a.
[125] Anastos 1990.
[126] Phot., *epist.* 290, sent in August–September 861, see Hergenröther 1867–1869: vol. I, 438–60; Dvornik 1948: 92–93; Konstantelos 1989/1991; Leserri 2005. The reply of Nicholas I of 18 March 862 has survived, see *MGH, epist.* VI, pp. 447–452; Mansi xv, 174B–78B.
[127] Gen 17:9–14, 23–24; Ex 4:24–26; Heb 7:1–3.

Photios offers to issue a synodal decree to the effect that no one could attain the patriarchate in the future without previously passing through the preceding ecclesiastical stages and states that, if there were any real hindrance to him taking the post, he would abandon it immediately (339–58). As proof of his good will, he will return to Rome the jurisdiction of the sees desired by the Pope, if the emperor will grant Photios' wish, as his legates will inform him (385–418).[128] In contrast to the previous epistle, Photios ends by asking Nicholas not to receive any priests without a letter of recommendation, since many fugitives resort to this stratagem. He also asks him to concern himself with the correct ecclesiastical order, laying the foundations on which he would later build the reasoning that would trigger the western schism of the *filioque* (437–80).

It is highly significant that when Photios in this letter of defence lists precedents to justify his choice as patriarch, he does not include Paulos III (688–693), who also attained the patriarchal throne of Constantinople from an official post as a *protoasekretis* and as a layman. Photios deliberately selects Tarasios and Nikephoros for ideological reasons. In common with Paulos III, the three of them had attained the patriarchate as senior imperial officials, but what at the time had been readily accepted now caused a scandal. The difference is in the fact that they both successfully confronted iconoclasm; for this reason, they are often part of the post-iconoclastic mentality. Photios' desire to legitimise his own patriarchate by referring to other patriarchs who fought against heresy is clear in a large part of the literary production of his circle, as will be seen in Chapter 6. This appropriation of Tarasios and Nikephoros by the Photians nipped in the bud any attempt by Ignatios to invoke them in his own defence. This can be seen when, in the first of the sessions of the synod of 860/861, Ignatios was accused of not having been chosen according to the canons after the relevant deliberations among ecclesiastics but of having been appointed arbitrarily by Theodora. Ignatios replied that Tarasios was also appointed by a woman, to which the emperor in person replied:[129] 'You should not say that he was raised by a woman, but that the lord Methodios and the lord Tarasios were appointed under a woman's rule.' With this comment, Michael III made it

---

[128] In his first letter to Michael III (*MGH*, *epist*. VI, pp. 433–39), Pope Nicholas I requested the return of the territories that the Byzantine emperor had snatched from the Roman see in the previous century and placed under Constantinopolitan jurisdiction, see Grumel 1951/1952; Anastos 1957; Bertolini 1959; Noyé 1998.

[129] Von Glanvell 1905: 605: Ignatius dixit: 'Dominus Tharasius pater a femina promotus est'. Imperator dixit: 'Ne dicas feminam. Etenim femina imperante factus est dominus Methodius et dominus Tharasius'. See Dvornik 1948: 81.

clear not only that the choice of these patriarchs had been canonical but also that the memory of the holy patriarchs who fought against iconoclasm could not be exploited by Ignatios, since they corresponded to Photios.

In his flight into exile in 858, Ignatios was not alone. Many monks loyal to him were not prepared to accept the new patriarch imposed by the emperor without following the canons and abandoned their monasteries. Bishops such as Metrophanes of Smyrna, who was considered one of the bastions of Ignatios by Pope Nicholas I in his letter to Emperor Michael III, were deposed from their sees by the new patriarch.[130] But it was especially monks, some of whom were highly cultivated and deeply respected Ignatios, who on his behalf suffered persecution, imprisonment or torture – an extreme case being that of the monk Blasios, who had his tongue cut out by Bardas[131] – or had to abandon Constantinople or its monasteries for an uncertain exile. Among them was the famous Ioseph Hymnographos, who moved to the Chersonesos in Crimea.[132] Another was the hegoumenos of Stoudios, Nikolaos Stoudites,[133] who remained a member of the Ignatian party, to the point that Pope Nicholas I, in his letter to Emperor Michael III of 28 September 865, offers to send him to Rome as a representative of the Ignatian cause.[134] Nikolaos was accompanied in his decision by numerous monks, such as his brother Titos, also a Stoudite monk, and his disciple Evarestos; they dispersed in small groups of two or three people.[135] Ultimately, most of these Stoudite monks must have met up again in a newly founded establishment in the quarter of Lips, named Kokorobion, which was run by Evarestos himself.[136] Evarestos was celebrated as a saint in late December by means of a *vita* and a homily in his honour.[137]

---

[130] *MGH, epist.* VI, *Nicolai epist.*, nr. 88, p. 482,5f. (= Mansi xv, 211A), see Mansi xvi, 416D; Dvornik 1948: 33; Neil 2006: 17. At the Ignatian Council of 869 Metrophanes was subsequently readmitted, but was exiled once again by the Photian Council of 879/880.

[131] *PmbZ* # 1015; *PBE* I: Blasios 1; Phot., *epist.* 3 and 6; *Vita of Ignatios* 25,21–25.

[132] *Vita of Ioseph Hymnographos* by Theophanes 12, p. 10,22–27; *Vita of Ioseph Hymnographos* by Ioannes Diakonos 968–69. On Ioseph's membership in the Ignatian ranks, see Dvornik 1948: 238, who affirms erroneously that he was the *synkellos* of the patriarch.

[133] *Vita of Nikolaos Stoud.* 908C–9B. About this person, *PmbZ* # 5576; *PBE* I: Nikolaos 26; see Section 5.2.2.a.

[134] *MGH, epist.* VI, *Nicolai epist.* 88, p. 482,4–7 (= Mansi xv, 211A–B); Dvornik 1948: 64–66.

[135] On Titos, see *PmbZ* # 8508; *PBE* I: Titos 1. On the pro-Ignatian stance of Evarestos, see *Vita of Evarestos of Stoudios* (BHG 2153) 13, pp. 306–7. Cf. *PmbZ* # 1618 and # 21752; *PBE* I: Evarestos 1; Dvornik 1948: 64–65; Krausmüller 2013c: 349–50.

[136] On the monastery of Kokorobion, built on land bought by a certain Samuel (*PmbZ* # 6504), see Janin 1969: 282–83; Ruggieri 1991: 192; *Vita of Nikolaos Stoud.* 909C.

[137] Antonopoulou 1998: 342. For his commemoration, see *SynaxCP* 345/346,55–58 (= *BHG* 2153c) and 347,1–48,25 (26 December); 353/354,34 (28 December); 353/354,49 (29 December); *Typikon of the Great Church* I, 159 (26 December).

The case of an anonymous copyist, to whom we owe one of the first minuscule manuscripts to contain homilies of St John Chrysostom, is similar. Thanks to the colophon, we know that the manuscript was written at the monastery of St Anna in Kios in Bithynia in 861/862 'during the exile of Ignatios the most holy patriarch'.[138] Whole communities even turned away from the new patriarch in a clear manifestation of anti-Photian resistance. In the region of Bithynia, moreover, the monastery of Pissadinoi on Olympos saw its hegoumenos Nikolaos and the senior monks leave out of loyalty to Ignatios.[139] This seems a sensible measure, if one takes into account the persecution carried out against Bithynian monks by certain followers of Photios, who did not hesitate to set fire to some cells at the foot of Mount Olympos. Although this version of events comes from Anastasius the Librarian,[140] whose prejudiced partiality and strong connections with the Ignatian milieu are well known, the disciplinary canons of the Photian synod of 860/861 corroborate the rejection of part of the clergy.[141] The situation is also mentioned in other hagiographical sources, such as the *vita* of Antonios the Younger.[142]

The return of Ignatios to the patriarchate in 867 brought about the return of many of those who had fled with him from Constantinople and would now support him in his opening up of the Byzantine Church to Rome. Despite his advanced age and fragile health, Nikolaos Stoudites was called for and reinstated as the hegoumenos of Stoudios.[143] The links between this important monastery and the Rhangabe family were thus strengthened once more. The good relationship between Ignatios and the Stoudites went back to the times when Theodoros Stoudites himself had been adviser to Ignatios' father Michael I[144]. As a reward for the participation of Theodoros in government affairs, the monastery of Stoudios had flourished in the final years of the iconodule interval (812–815).[145]

---

[138] This is the manuscript Meteora Metamorphoseos 591, see Bees 1913; Ronconi 2015a: 133. On this monastery, see Janin 1975: 135.

[139] Concerning this Nikolaos, see *PmbZ* # 5603; Lake 1909: 42. On the monastery of Pissadinoi, see Janin 1975: 172–74. The source for this information is the *Vita of Euthymios the Younger* 12, p. 24 (*ROC*, p. 176).

[140] Mansi XVI, 5.

[141] *Regestes*, nrs. 468 and 495; *Council of Constantinople of 861*, canon 15. See also Hergenröther 1867–1869: vol. 1, 397; Marin 1897: 201–5; Dvornik 1948: 65, n. 1 and p. 66; *Vita retractata of Petros of Atroa*, p. 29.

[142] *Vita of Antonios the Younger* (addit), 208 and 212.

[143] *Vita of Evarestos of Stoudios* 16, p. 309,1–5.

[144] Dobroklonskij 1913: vol. 1, 709–19; Alexander 1958a: 99–101, 220–21, 227; Treadgold 1988: 179–89; Pratsch 1998: 183–201; Cholij 2002: 52–44.

[145] Theoph. 494,33–95,15 (advice to Michael I on measures against the Paulicians); Theoph. 495,24–28 (advice on the war with Bulgaria); Theoph. 498,14–99,5 (on the prisoners of that war), see Rochow 1991: 308–9 and 312.

Metrophanes for his part recovered the bishopric of Smyrna, while Ioannes of Galatia was called by Basileios I to take charge of the important monastery of Sts Sergios and Bakkhos in Constantinople.[146] Not only did Ioannes miraculously find the relics of Sergios,[147] but he was also praised in a *vita* by Ioseph Hymnographos that has come down to us in a Georgian version.[148] The latter also returned in 867 and was offered the highest honours but only accepted appointment as *skeuophylax* of Hagia Sophia out of loyalty to Ignatios.[149] In addition to this important poet, Ignatios surrounded himself with other men of letters during his second patriarchate with the clear goal of counteracting the propaganda of the Photians, vindicating himself and linking himself to iconodule saints. Along with loyal authors such as Metrophanes of Smyrna appear others such as the prolific Michael Monachos, who joined the patriarchate's group as an inspiring figure and brilliant star.

5.2.1 Metrophanes of Smyrna

Metrophanes of Smyrna was one of the major champions of the cause of Ignatios and is known for denouncing the abuse committed by Photios. If Theognostos internationalised the conflict by informing the Pope of Rome, Metrophanes stands out for having been a mainstay of resistance within the empire and a point of reference for the whole Ignatian party.[150] We do not know whether his appointment as bishop of Smyrna was due to the patriarch Methodios or to Ignatios; in any case, Metrophanes' prominence began at the synod of 859. It was there that he vehemently defended Ignatios as the legitimate patriarch, leading to his imprisonment in the gaol of Noumera and his subsequent exile to Chersonesos.[151] In compensation, he was one of the first to be reinstated in his see by the Ignatian Council of 869/870,[152] and with the authority of this position, he played an active part in council sessions. The minutes include two long speeches of his[153] and the epistle he wrote to the *patrikios* and *logothetes tou*

---

[146] *PmbZ* # 3266 and # 22779; *PBE* I: Ioannes 224, see Chapter 3.   [147] Krausmüller 2019.
[148] Kekelidze 1965: 61–68. For the identification of its author, see Stiernon 1973: 260–62. The *Vita of Ioannes of Galatia* stands out for the help and protection of the archangel St Michael (chs. 2, 12, 19 and 24).
[149] *Vita of Ioseph Hymnographos* by Theophanes 12, p. 10,22–27; *Vita of Ioseph Hymnographos* by Ioannes Diakonos 968–69; *SynaxCP* 581–84,5–6 (*BHG* 947b).
[150] For Metrophanes' biography, see *PmbZ* # 4986 and # 25088; *PBE* I: Metrophanes 1.
[151] Mansi XVI, 416D; Dvornik 1948: 33.
[152] Mansi XVI, 18C; *Council of Constantinople (869/870)*, 35.
[153] Mansi XVI, 82B–83C, 344D–45A, 89C–92D, 349D–53C.

dromou, Manuel, in which he lists the reasons for the condemnation of Photios.[154] The Manuel addressed by Metrophanes is likely the same person as the patrician to whom Photios wrote a forceful epistle during this period, criticising him harshly (*epist.* 226): according to the patriarch, the eye of God can see the plotting of Manuel to kill him, and Photios reminds Manuel that the person who plans a death is a murderer even if there is no blood on his sword. If he does not change his attitude, he will be unable to avoid the trial he will face tearful and repentant, although Photios does not wish to see Manuel in this situation. Taking into account that in the initial sessions of the Ignatian Council the *logothetes tou dromou* was a certain Ioannes,[155] it seems likely that his replacement wished to gather information at first hand on the Photian conflict.

After Ignatios' death in 877, the return of Photios to the patriarchate did not mean that Metrophanes was deposed, despite the fact that the metropolitan of Smyrna always refused to recognise him as patriarch. Initially, Photios tried to win Metrophanes over by sending him a letter with gifts, which gave rise to a misunderstanding between Metrophanes, a friend of his and the patriarch. The food Metrophanes received arrived in poor condition, while his friend (who happened to be with him at the time) received a better gift from Photios. Photios' response survived; he expresses a wish for the return of peace and the re-establishment of good relations between them.[156] The friend accompanying Metrophanes was probably the metropolitan Stylianos of Neocaesarea,[157] another distinguished Ignatian who at the same time was addressed by Pope John VIII, urging him to recognise Photios as the legitimate patriarch.[158] Be that as it may, in November, at the start of the Photian Council of 879/880, Metrophanes was replaced by Niketas as the metropolitan of Smyrna.[159]

From this moment on, the leadership of the Ignatian cause passed to Stylianos of Neocaesarea, who rejected any form of obedience to Photios and sent several epistles to Pope Stephen V, in which he denounced Photios and his followers (such as Theodoros Santabarenos) for their authoritarian measures and their decisions on the jurisdiction of the

---

[154] Mansi XVI, 413E–20D. On Manuel, see *PmbZ* # 24869; Hergenröther 1867–1869: vol. II, 255ff.
[155] *PmbZ* # 22797. These nobles apparently attended the anti-Photian synod of 869 following an imperial order, cf. Mansi XVI, 18B; 309D; *Council of Constantinople (869/870)*, 34.
[156] Phot., *epist.* 282. Photios addresses him as φίλων ἄριστε 'the best of the friends' and τῇ σῇ ὁσιότητι 'your holiness'.
[157] *PmbZ* # 27409. For this identification, see Dvornik 1948: 238–40.
[158] *MGH*, *epist.* VII, *epist. Iohannis VIII*, nr. 210, p. 29,29–31. The recipients included not only Metrophanes and Stylianos but also Ioannes of Syllaion, see *PmbZ* # 22785.
[159] Mansi XVI A, 496C–501C. On this Niketas, see *PmbZ* # 25705.

monasteries. Two of these missives have survived, one of 886 and another of 891, this second letter signed by several bishops, such as Ioannes of Komana.[160] All these pro-Ignatian texts (the *libellus* of Theognostos, the *Epistle to Manuel* of Metrophanes, the letters of Stylianos, etc.), together with other papal documents, were gathered by an anonymous author firmly opposed to Photios in an appendix transmitted in the manuscripts after the Minutes of the Eighth Council. This is generally known as the 'anti-Photian Collection' and was copied during the period of Pope Formosus (891–896).[161] As well as offering a version of the overthrow of Ignatios and the promotion of Photios unanimously favourable to Ignatios, the Collection introduces a virulent tone and insults the patriarch.[162] Moreover, Stylianos did not recognise the successor of Photios, Stephanos I (18 December 886–17/18 May 893), because Photios had ordained him deacon.[163] Not until the end of the patriarchate of Stephanos was this schismatic sector publicly reconciled with the Photian Church.[164]

Metrophanes' relationship with Photios is in any case complex and confusing. A manuscript of Stoudite origin (the tenth-century *Vaticanus Palatinus Gr.* 216) in fact ascribes to Metrophanes the anti-Manichean corpus of Photios (*Libri contra Manichaeos* and *Mystagogia de spiritu sancto*).[165] There is no doubt that Metrophanes was a great theologian of the Ignatian party, as is borne out by his extensive written production,[166] which includes many exegetic works (commentaries on the General Epistles, on the Hexameron, on *Ecclesiastes*, fragments of a commentary on the Psalms, *Theognosia* [*CPG* 3223]) together with others of religious controversy (the epistle to the *logothetes* Manuel, a treatise against the Jews [*CPG* 7799], a Profession of Faith) and of course liturgical works both in prose (homilies on St John and St Matthew, an *enkomion* of St Polycarp of Smyrna [*BHG* 1563], an *enkomion* of the archangels Michael and Gabriel

---

[160] *MGH*, epist. VII, *epist. ad res Orientales*, nr. 2, pp. 375,7–80,12; nr. 4, pp. 381,21–82,26. On Ioannes of Komana, see *PmbZ* # 22826.
[161] Mansi XVI, 409–57. For its dating, see Dvornik 1948: 271–72. For the dissemination in Constantinople of the 'anti-Photian Collection' at that time, see Simeonova 1998: 48 and n. 92.
[162] Dvornik 1948: 232. For an analysis of the texts it includes, see Dvornik 1948: 168–69 and 216–36.
[163] On the patriarch Stephanos, brother of Emperor Leon V, see *PmbZ* # 27208; Kolias 1953. See Section 8.1.
[164] *Vita of the Patriarch Euthymios* 63,27f.; Nikolaos Mystikos, *epist.* 75,52–63; Grumel 1934; Dvornik 1948: 265–70.
[165] Lemerle 1973: 38–39; Polidori 2014.
[166] Beck 1959: 543–44; Van Deun 2008, with references to the editions of Metrophanes' works; 2017.

[*BHG* 1292], an *enkomion* of Euthymios of Sardis [*BHG* 2146]) and in verse (*kanones* dedicated to the Trinity and the Theotokos and a hymn to St Xena). The profession of faith attributed to him in the manuscript *Parisinus Gr.* 887 may be his, although it appears to be incomplete, and whether this was the text pronounced when he took possession of his see in Smyrna is uncertain.[167] As bishop of Smyrna, it is understandable that he wrote a tribute to the most important local saint, Saint Polycarp.[168]

Although we cannot specify the date of Metrophanes' death, the *terminus ante quem* is October 912, when his disciple Arsenios copied two epitaphs together with a hymn of his master's to the Trinity preserved in the manuscript Leiden Gronovii 12 (Geel nr. 8), sixteenth century, fol. 234r–v.[169] These two verse epitaphs were composed shortly after Metrophanes' death, one by Anastasios Traulos, also known as Quaestor, the other by Leon Choirosphaktes, who also dedicated a similar poem to the patriarch Photios.[170] Both poems praise Metrophanes as an example of ecclesiastical virtues, but whereas the former extols his wise freedom of speech,[171] the latter praises his work to end the schisms and unify the Church.[172]

A tradition in Metrophanes' biography links him directly and inescapably to iconoclasm: the connivance of his mother with the iconoclasts in an attempt to sabotage Methodios after the latter was chosen patriarch. Metrophanes' mother allegedly accepted a bribe from Ioannes VII Grammatikos and other iconoclasts in exchange for accusing the iconodule patriarch of having sexually abused her. This rape would have produced her son, who later occupied the see of Smyrna. This legend, mentioned by all the tenth-century chroniclers,[173] reproduces a rumour created to discredit Metrophanes himself. Methodios' honour was not affected by this episode, as the patriarch had withered genitals, which meant that the accusation was entirely without foundation. No hagiographical text mentions the rumour, despite the fact that the situation favoured its

---

[167] Neirynck and Van Deun 2018. [168] Van Deun and De Vos 2010. [169] *PmbZ* # 20604.
[170] The two poems have been published by Mercati 1929/1930: 60. On Anastasios Traulos, see *PmbZ* # 20297; Lauxtermann 1998: 401–5. Concerning Leon Choirosphaktes, see *PmbZ* # 24343. The poems he produced to Photios and the patriarch Stephanos have been published by Kolias 1939: 130–31.
[171] Anastasios Traulos, εἰς Μητρόφανην 7: ζήλωσον αὐτοῦ τὴν σοφὴν παρρησίαν.
[172] Leon Choirosphaktes, εἰς Μητρόφανην 11–12: τὸν ἐν χρόνῳ τε καὶ κρίσει ποιούμενον / τοὺς εἰς ἕνωσιν καὶ διάστασιν λόγους.
[173] Theoph. Cont. IV, 10,1–34; Genesios IV 5, pp. 59,40–60,83; Skylitzes 87,53–89,36; Ps-Symeon 652,13–53,2; Georg. Mon. Cont. (Istrin) 3,24–4,7; Zonaras XVI 384,17–87,2. Concerning the mother of Metrophanes, see *PmbZ* # 4986A and # 25088A; *PBE* I: Anonyma 21.

emergence. The *vita* of Ioannikios (written not long after his death in 846) refers to the machinations of the Stoudites against Methodios and hints at a sexual element.[174] But it would take time for details to be added and, most important, for the perjurer to be identified as the mother of Metrophanes of Smyrna. The dissemination of this slander was probably the work of the Photians, who were irritated by Metrophanes' fierce opposition to their leader.[175]

Metrophanes was not only discredited by this personal attack but was also portrayed as an unprincipled upstart capable of collaborating with heretics. This harsh accusation makes sense if we understand the bishop of Smyrna to also be the Metrophanes who composed a rhetorical panegyric in honour of Euthymios of Sardis,[176] following the literary trail blazed by the injured patriarch Methodios. In the eyes of his enemies, Metrophanes' hypocrisy had been revealed – no sooner had he slandered Methodios, than he imitated his hagiographical writings – and the objectives of his literary production were counteracted. This work by Metrophanes, dedicated to an important confessor of Orthodoxy, is described in the title as βίος σὺν ἐγκωμίῳ (Life with encomium) and is aimed at a monastic community that celebrated the saint on 26 December.[177] The editor of many of Metrophanes' writings regards the vocabulary and syntax of this encomium as different from that of the remainder of his works.[178] Its theme, however, is also different from those in Metrophanes' theological treatises, to which must be added that the model he followed was written by Methodios in a pompous style. Finally, an early date of composition, when the iconoclast dispute was at its height, during Metrophanes' youth, may explain the discrepancies in terms of expression from his mature work.

In fact, the text is no more than a *metaphrasis* of the *vita* in honour of Euthymios of Sardis written by the patriarch Methodios, which retains a lofty style but introduces important modifications to make it more readily understandable. Metrophanes shows awareness of the existence of a previous *vita* in honour of Euthymios:[179] 'it invites me today [to write] the

---

[174] *Vita of Ioannikios* by Petros 70, p. 432A: τοὺς δέ γε βεβήλους ἐκείνους τοὺς κατὰ τῆς Σωσάννης γέροντας, συκοφάντας, ἀπελεγχθέντας ἐδίκῳ καὶ κανονικῇ ἐξορίᾳ τε καὶ ἀναθεματισμῷ παραδέδωκεν.

[175] Dvornik 1948: 14–15.

[176] Papadakis 1970. For the identification of the two men named Metrophanes, see Beck 1959: 512; *PmbZ* # 4984.

[177] *Enkomion of Euthymios of Sardis* 1 and 4. On this iconodule martyred in 831, see Section 2.1.2.

[178] Neirynck and Van Deun 2018: n. 4.

[179] *Enkomion of Euthymios of Sardis* 2,3–5: ὃ ἡμᾶς τήμερον συγκαλεῖ τὸ τῆς ἡμέρας ὑπόμνημα. Τὰ γὰρ τῆς χθὲς πνευματορήτορές τινες καὶ φιλοσόφων οἱ πρόμοι πεφράδασι.

reminder of this day, for some of the spiritual rhetoricians and the foremost men [οἱ πρόμοι] of the philosophers declared that of yesterday'. Πρόμος, 'foremost man', is not a common word and is also found in a significant context clearly linked to the iconodule patriarchate, the poem included in a psalter created within the milieu of Methodios.[180] Likewise, the presence of a 'Christological cycle'[181] appears to be connected with interpolations from the patriarchal milieu added to the *Epistula ad Theophilum* to defend the interests of the patriarch.[182] This debt to Methodios directly links Metrophanes with the patriarchal milieu, as is confirmed by the Oxford Bodleianus, Laud Gr. 69, the only manuscript in which this encomium has been transmitted. This codex, from the late tenth or early eleventh century, contains a collection of hagiographical texts for the December feast days and presents for the 6th of that month a *vita* of St Nicholas of Myra written by Michael *archimandrites* (*BHG* 1348).[183] As will become apparent in Section 5.2.2, we are concerned here with the *metaphrasis* written by Michael Monachos based on the hagiography also produced by Methodios. The codex thus preserves two *metaphraseis* from significant texts by the icon-restoring patriarch.

Unfortunately, the final part of the manuscript has been lost and the account of Euthymios goes no further than the beginning of the reign of Michael II, which led the editor of the *Vita of Euthymios of Sardis* of the patriarch Methodios to harshly criticise the piece.[184] This means that the most important part of what survives is the confrontational dialogue between the hero and the iconoclast Emperor Leon V (ch. 18). We therefore lack the account of the saint's dialogue with Theophilos, his torture and his death. Despite this, Metrophanes' conception of monastic life as always at the patriarchate's disposal and dependent on it is visible. Metrophanes is the only source that affirms that Tarasios consecrated Euthymios.[185] By adding this detail omitted by Methodios, the re-worker

---

[180] Ševčenko 1965: 43.   [181] *Enkomion of Euthymios of Sardis* 18,149–56.
[182] For these Constantinopolitan elements, see Ševčenko 1979/1980: 735; Signes Codoñer 2014: 405–8. Concerning the iconographical cycles in this important apologetic epistle, see Walter 1997.
[183] Coxe 1853/1854: 552–54; Ehrhard 1936–1939: vol. I, 516–18. The feast days of the saints it celebrates indicate that a Stoudite origin is out of the question as it includes neither Theoktiste, the mother of Theodoros Stoudites, nor Blasios of Amorion, both celebrated on 20 December. Neither does it mention the hegoumenos of Stoudios, Evarestos, who is remembered on the 26th. See Introduction.
[184] Gouillard 1987: 37: 'Le panégyrique est un tissu de généralités édifiantes sur lequel brochent de rares traits historiques'.
[185] *Enkomion of Euthymios of Sardis* 13–14.

strengthens the image of the patriarchate, as does the dialogue between Tarasios and Euthymios he reproduces. In the latter, the humility and obedience of the new bishop is contrasted with the will of the patriarch, which must be obeyed.[186] In fact, the Ignatians' vindication of Euthymios makes sense, if we take into account that, according to Metrophanes, he was one of the candidates to succeed Theodotos on the patriarchal throne of Constantinople.[187]

Metrophanes was above all else a man at the service of the patriarchate and its interests, although he was more concerned with giving the tenures of Ignatios theological content than with becoming involved in propaganda. If we take the characterisation of Metrophanes as a monk presented by the title of the encomium (Μητροφάνους μοναχοῦ) to be historical and not simply a sign of humility, the work was written during his youth or in one of the periods he spent in exile for working for Ignatios' cause. In any case, in contrast to his co-religionist Michael Monachos, with whom he shares the compositional technique of the *metaphrasis*, he has no link with the Stoudites or with any other monastic community. He devoted himself entirely to serving the patriarchate, provided that Ignatios was its leader. This patriarch favoured the encouragement of cults to which he had a strong personal devotion. This is the case with archangel St Michael; it is no coincidence that the same name was borne by Emperor Michael I, the father of Ignatios. In common with other writers of his circle, Metrophanes also produced an encomium to the archangels Michael and Gabriel (*BHG* 1292) that has recently been published. Although the work does not mention the matter of images, archangels are described as 'simple images; plentiful participation in the eternal and divine resplendent light',[188] and Metrophanes asks them to root out the discord sown in the Church[189] and to appear in his circle and free him from the choices

---

[186] *Enkomion of Euthymios of Sardis* 7,13–16: ἐμοὶ μὲν ὦ δέσποτα τὸ ἄξιον ἱερουργίας ἡγήσασθαι καὶ τὸ τῆς ἀρχιερωσύνης τὰς ἡνίας ἑλέσθαι καὶ ταύτην πηδαλιουχῆσαι οὐκ ἄμεινον. Τοιούτων ἀρετῶν καὶ κατορθωμάτων οὐδὲν ἐμαυτῷ σύνοιδα. Tarasios replies to these humble words of Euthymios: Μή μου τὴν βούλησιν ἐλέγχων τὴν κλῆσιν ἀποτρέπου (ch. 7,21).

[187] *Enkomion of Euthymios of Sardis* 25,10–12: προκέκρικα οὖν σε πάντων, τοῦθ᾽ ἕνεκα εἰ βουληθῇς εὖ πρᾶξαι κατὰ τὸ ἐμοὶ δοκοῦν, τῇ ἐκκλησίᾳ ἀποκληρῶσαι, καὶ τῇ πατριαρχίᾳ δοξάσαι ὡς λόγου καὶ χάριτος μετέχοντα.

[188] *Enkomion of the Archangels Michael and Gabriel* 2,14–5: εἰκόνες ἁπλαῖ, καὶ μετουσίαι δαψιλεῖς τῆς ἀνάρχου καὶ θεουργοῦ φωταυγίας.

[189] *Enkomion of the Archangels Michael and Gabriel* 11,161–62: Ἐκτίλατε τὰ παρὰ τοῦ ἐχθροῦ σπαρέντα ζιζάνια ἐν τῷ τῆς ἐκκλησίας ἀγρῷ, καὶ καθαρὸν ἀποφήνατε τοῦ ἀληθινοῦ Δεσπότου καὶ Κυρίου τὸν σπόρον, 'Pluck out the tares seeded by the enemy in the field of the Church, and declare that the seed of the Master and the Lord is pure.'

(προαιρέσεις) of his spiritual enemies.[190] These pleas are quite ambiguous, as they may refer both to Photian adversaries and to iconoclast heretics (note the pun on the word προαίρεσις < αἵρεσις, 'heresy').

With this encomium, Metrophanes is part of the Ignatian milieu, as was later on Michael Monachos, who also penned a *laudatio* in honour of the two archangels (see Section 5.2.2). The only manuscript that has transmitted this encomium of Metrophanes is the twelfth-century parchment codex Oxford *Bodleianus, Auctarium* E.5.12, which contains a selection of ascetic and hagiographical texts. One is the *vita* of Nicholas of Myra written by the Stoudite Michael Monachos, which is habitually found in manuscripts containing works by Metrophanes: the piece by Metrophanes appears on folios 250–56v and that of Michael on folios 276v–94v.[191] This is probably not coincidence but rather another sign of the collaboration of the two men of letters in a common cause, that of the patriarch Ignatios.

5.2.2 Michael Monachos

The monk Michael has long remained in the shadows. The interest aroused by Michael Synkellos, the monk and cleric from Jerusalem who during the patriarchate of Methodios helped build the post-iconoclast Church from the hegoumenate of the monastery of Chora, first brought Michael Monachos to attention due to their homonymity and the similarity of the posts they held. The chronology indicates that the latter was a different person from a later generation, although this is no reason to postulate the existence of a third Michael Monachos, as Ehrhard does.[192] Study of the work of Michael Monachos makes it possible to reconstruct his biography and his close contact with the patriarchate.[193] We know that he was a Stoudite monk and a skilful rhetorician who flourished during the second half of the ninth century until he attained the post of *synkellos*

---

[190] *Enkomion of the Archangels Michael and Gabriel* 11,181–85: ἐξαιρεῖσθε πάσης κακοπραγίας καὶ πονηροβουλίας. Παρεμβάλετε κύκλῳ ἡμῶν, καὶ **τοὺς πολεμοῦντας ἡμᾶς ἀπὸ ὕψους** τῆς ἰδίας κακίας ἀποδιώκετε νοητοὺς δυσμενεῖς ἡμῶν. Ἀγαθύνατε τῶν πονηρευομένων ἀνθρώπων τὰς προαιρέσεις. Τῶν ἀπεχθανομένων καθ'ἡμῶν **διασκεδάζετε τὰς βουλάς**, 'Free us from every misdeed and malice. Take your place in our circle and chase away those who fight against us from the height of their own evil as our spiritual enemies. Reform the choices of men acting wickedly. Silence the counsels of those hateful to us.'
[191] Coxe 1853/1854: 659–61; Van De Vorst and Delehaye 1913: 364–65, nrs. 2 and 5.
[192] Ehrhard 1936–1939: vol. 1, 486, 489, 491, 510, 622, 680; Beck 1959: 503–5; Cunningham 1991: 36, n. 119; Kazhdan 1999: 257–59.
[193] *PmbZ* # 5121 and # 25099; *PBE* I: Michael 128.

under the patriarch Nikolaos Mystikos, as is attested by his epitaph in old-fashioned verse written for the monastery of Galakrenai in Bithynia.[194] The manuscripts ascribe to this Michael Monachos and *synkellos* two important hagiographies: the *Vita* B of Theodoros Stoudites (*BHG* 1754) and the *Vita* of Nicholas of Myra (*BHG* 1348), in addition to the following works, many of them still unpublished: *Encomium of Zacharias, Father of St John the Baptist* (*BHG* 1881n), two *Encomia of the Holy Angels* (*BHG* 127 and 129a), *Encomium of Daniel and the Three Youths in the Furnace* (*BHG* 488a), *Encomium of Eustratios* (*BHG* 646b),[195] *Encomium of the Archangels Gabriel and Michael* (*BHG* 1294a), *Encomium of St Mokios* (*BHG* 1298h), *Encomium of the Apostle Philip* (*BHG* 1530a),[196] *Encomium of St Ignatios, Patriarch of Constantinople* (*BHG* 818), *Encomium of St Isaakios and St Dalmatos* (*BHG* 956d) and *Oration on the Girdle of the Blessed Theotokos* (*BHG* 1147). The specific attribution varies in each manuscript: the humble monk Michael, the *synkellos* Michael, the monk and *synkellos* Michael, etc.[197]

Although these compositions are epideictic and highly rhetorical, and have no documentary purpose, some conclusions can be drawn from them regarding the life of their author, his career at the Constantinopolitan monastery of Stoudios and his membership in the milieu of the patriarch Ignatios. In the *Encomium of the Archangels Gabriel and Michael* (*BHG* 1294a), the author appears as a monk devoted to the art of the written word who considers himself a panegyrist[198] and is aware that the best offering he can make to the archangels is his literary work.[199] Perhaps even a qualified master in the monastery school with some rhetorical aspirations, his Greek reveals extensive training, even if his literary skills are far from sublime.[200] Despite the fact that his date of writing corresponds to the final third of the ninth century,[201] the matter of the icons continues to be topical for the author, who does not hesitate to defend the importance

---

[194] *PmbZ* # 25178; Ševčenko 1987; Lauxtermann 2003: 120.
[195] For the attribution of these last two pieces, see *BHG* III, 259.
[196] The strongest proof of his authorship is its preservation along with other works unquestionably by Michael Monachos, i.e., the *Encomium of the Archangels Gabriel and Michael* (*BHG* 1294a) and *Vita* B *of Theodoros Stoudites*, in the same manuscript, the *Vaticanus Gr.* 1669, see Section I.2.
[197] Émereau 1924: 411; Loenertz 1950: 103–7; *PmbZ* # 5096; Beck 1959: 603; Follieri 1960–1966: vol. v,1, p. 294; Krausmüller 2013a: 288–90.
[198] *Enkomion of the Archangels Michael and Gabriel* V,1.
[199] *Enkomion of the Archangels Michael and Gabriel* V,6.   [200] Matantseva 1996a: 116–17.
[201] Having ruled out a possible dating under Michael III (842–867), the emperor at the time was clearly orthodox, see Matantseva 1996a: 113.

of the veneration of icons and to justify it[202] and even to attack iconoclasts vehemently.[203]

Admitting that the archangel Michael was celebrated fervently throughout the empire and that he was doubtless venerated at the monastery of Stoudios,[204] his popularity clearly increased exponentially after the Triumph of Orthodoxy in 843. The reasons for this are unknown, but his homonymity with the young emperor whose mother Theodora was regent was supposedly put to good use. In the patriarchal milieu, a certain Pantoleon, a deacon and *chartophylax* of Hagia Sophia,[205] produced two texts in honour of archangel Michael: an extensive *Narratio miraculorum maximi archangeli Michaelis* (*BHG* 1285–88)[206] and an *Encomium of the Archangel Michael* (*BHG* 1289). This author, a contemporary of Michael III and Theodora,[207] also includes sporadic references in defence of Orthodoxy and pleas for heretics and the ungodly to be destroyed[208] in both writings, which he solemnly pronounced in a sanctuary of Constantinople dedicated to the archangel.[209] We do not know the exact relationship between these texts and the *Encomium of the Archangels Gabriel and Michael* by Michael Monachos (*BHG* 1294a), which appears to be inspired by them. But it is clear that the tenth-century entry of the *Synaxarion of Constantinople*,[210] which celebrates this archangel on 8 November, derives primarily from the text of Michael Monachos.[211]

What led Michael Monachos to write this piece is uncertain, but we know that private devotions (such as that of the patriarch Ignatios or Emperor Basileios) helped strengthen St Michael's celebration. Indeed, Ignatios built in Satyros a monastery dedicated to St Michael to honour the memory of his father, Michael I Rhangabe, whose remains were taken

---

[202] *Enkomion of the Archangels Michael and Gabriel* V; XI and XII.
[203] *Enkomion of the Archangels Michael and Gabriel* XII,1: Πιπτέτω φθόνος δεινὸς τῶν εἰκονομάχων, ἐμφραττέσθω τὰ στόματα τῶν λαλούντων κατὰ τῆς τοῦ Χριστοῦ καὶ θεοῦ ἡμῶν εἰκόνος ἀνομίαν ἐν ὑπερηφανίᾳ καὶ ἐξουδενώσει.
[204] Matantseva 1996a: 127–28.
[205] We know nothing about this author, and he does not appear in the prosopographies. For other possible writings of his, see Beck 1959: 453–57 and 636.
[206] Martin-Hisard 1994: 367–70.
[207] *Enkomion of the Archangel Michael* 454,20: Τὸ ἐν ἡμετέροις χρόνοις καταληφθὲν καὶ γέγονος θαῦμα εἰς Μαρκιανὸν ἐν τῷ Εὐσεβωνύμῳ ναῷ, ἐπὶ Μιχαὴλ ἄνακτος καὶ Θεοδώρας τῆς αὐτοῦ μητρός.
[208] *Enkomion of the Archangel Michael* 455,28: Ἔκτιλον τὰ παρὰ τοῦ ἐχθροῦ σπαρέντα ζιζάνια ἐν τῷ τῆς ἐκκλησίας ἀγρῷ. Ἀπόφηνον καθαρὸν τοῦ ἀληθινοῦ οἰκοδεσπότου καὶ κυρίου τὸν σπόρον. Καταπολέμησον καὶ καταίσχυνον καὶ διάλυσον τῶν κακοδόξων καὶ δυσσεβῶν τοὺς συλλόγους.
[209] The exact location of the sanctuary has not yet been specified, see Martin-Hisard 2014: 456. For the churches in his honour, see Janin 1969: 337–50.
[210] *SynaxCP* 203–4.   [211] Martin-Hisard 2014: 461–63.

there.[212] Coinciding with this foundation in 873/874, during the second patriarchate of Ignatios, Emperor Basileios I strongly encouraged the cult of St Michael, since he was under his protection, building numerous churches dedicated to him. It has been speculated that guilt for having murdered his predecessor Michael III led Basileios to this religious policy.[213] An inclusive solution for Michael's choice of subject must be sought: it is plausible that he was content to fit in with the devotion of the emperor and at the same time please two important religious groups in the capital, the Stoudites and the Ignatians. Perhaps this idea led him to produce another panegyric dedicated to Zacharias, the father of St John the Baptist (*BHG* 1881n). The devotion to this saint was shared by the monks of the monastery of Stoudios (dedicated to St John the Baptist) and the clerics surrounding the patriarch Ignatios. No doubt the patriarchal clergy looked favourably on the updating of this cult, already promoted by the patriarch Germanos, who also wrote a brief treatise on Zacharias (*BHG* 1881m = *CPG* 8028).[214] We know of the celebration of Zacharias in the monasteries of Stoudite tradition thanks to the *Synaxarion Evergetis*,[215] in which he is remembered on 5 September, the eve of the celebration of archangel St Michael, for the miracle he performed in Chonai.

Michael's Stoudite identity can be best appreciated in his writing of compositions full of meaning for the federation to which he belonged. One of these is the *Encomium of St Isaakios and St Dalmatos* (*BHG* 956d), the fourth-century founders of the monastery of Dalmatos in Constantinople.[216] We have already noted the strong links between this monastery and the Stoudite federation, of which he was a member at the time of its re-founding by Theodoros (see Section 3.2.2.b). After being under the authority of Ioannes of Kathara, *archimandrites* of Dalmatos after the Second Council of Nicaea,[217] and of Hilarion, who died on 6 June 845,[218] the monastery was run by a certain Meletios.[219] This is likely the Stoudite monk by the same name who received two epistles[220] from Theodoros Stoudites between 809 and 818. Meletios is mentioned in *epist.* 138 as one of the apostates who during the persecution of Leon V

---

[212] *Vita of Ignatios* 11,27–32. On this establishment and on the transfer of Michael I, see Section 5.2.
[213] Janin 1969: 337. On archangel Michael as the protector of Basileios I, see Magdalino 1987: 56 and 58 (c).
[214] The work remains unpublished in the manuscript *Messanensis Gr.* 30, anno 1307–8, fol. 11–15, see Beck 1959: 475.
[215] *Synaxarion Evergetis* I, 18–20.   [216] Janin 1969: 82–84.   [217] *SynaxCP* 632,46.
[218] *SynaxCP* 732,47–33,55. On Hilarion of Dalmatos and his *vita*, see Section 7.2.2.
[219] *PmbZ* # 4946.
[220] Theod. Stoud., *epist.* 218 and 327. See *PmbZ* # 4945; *PBE* I: Meletios 3; Pratsch 1998: 243–46.

briefly abandoned Orthodoxy; according to the testimony of the hegoumenos of Stoudios, he was exiled in the *thema* of Anatolikon while being presbyteros.[221] This Meletios is named together with his predecessor in the *Synodikon* of the Church of Rhodes, which means he must have fought in defence of Orthodoxy.[222]

Within the Ignatian party, Hilarion of Dalmatos, a point of reference for iconodule monasticism in the capital, became renowned owing to the legend that he prophetically warned the mother of the patriarch Photios that she bore in her womb 'the incarnation of Satan'.[223] As his worthy successor, Michael Monachos was hegoumenos of Dalmatos and faithful to the patriarch Ignatios. In the final invocation of his encomium in honour of the founders of the monastery, he reveals both the post he held and the place where he wrote the piece: the monastery of Dalmatos. He implores the saints here to protect and guide him so that he can lead the other monks competently.[224] Given that those who preceded him in the post of hegoumenos of Dalmatos were also *archimandritai*, the obvious conclusion is that Michael Monachos also held the position of *archimandrites*, that is, 'patriarchal exarch of all Constantinopolitan monastic communities'. This is confirmed by Michael's insistence on the duties of the founder of Dalmatos as *archimandrites*[225] and by the presence of this post in the title of one of his works.[226]

The best proof of Michael's adherence to the Stoudite federation is in any case his writing of the hagiographies of the two most important hegoumenoi of the Stoudite monastery in the ninth century: Theodoros Stoudites and Nikolaos Stoudites. The *Vita B of Theodoros Stoudites* was already discussed in Chapter 1 in our discussion of the Stoudite milieu

---

[221] Theod. Stoud., *Magnae catecheseis* 61.
[222] Ἱλαρίωνος καὶ Μελετίου, τῶν ὁσίων ἀρχιμανδριτῶν καὶ ἡγουμένων τῶν Δαλμάτων, αἰωνία ἡ μνήμη, ed. Cappuyns 1934: 198, nr. 21.
[223] Ps-Symeon 669,14–16: ἀλλὰ καὶ ὁ ὅσιος καὶ ὁμολογητὴς Ἱλαρίων ὁ τῆς Δαλμάτου εἴρηκέ μοι ὅτι σεσωματωμένον Σατανᾶν βαστάζεις.
[224] *Enkomion of Isakios and Dalmatos* 33: καὶ **ἐμὲ τὸν ἐλάχιστον ὑμῶν καὶ παρ' ἀξίαν ἐγκωμαστὴν** ἐκ τῶν ποικίλων παγίδων τοῦ ἐχθροῦ καὶ τῆς ὑμῶν ἐνθέου καταξιοῦντες εὐλογίας ἵν' ὑπ' αὐτῆς φρουρούμενος ἐν παντὶ καιρῷ καὶ τόπῳ καὶ πράγματι ἰθυνόμενός τε καὶ φωτιζόμενος ἀξίως διατεθείην τῆς κλήσεως ἧς προσκέκλημαι. ὁρᾶτε τὴν δυσχέρειαν ὅση ἦσαν ποτ' ἦσαν ὄλβιοι μηλίσιοι, νῦν δὲ τοὐναντίον ἅπαν. καὶ **εὐοδοθείην κατ' αὐτὴν λιταῖς ὑμῶν ἁγίαις εἰς τὸ εὐαρέστως Θεῷ κυβερνῆσαι τοὺς λογικοὺς ἄρνας φιλοπόνως** τέ καὶ διεγειγερμένως πρὸς νομὰς ζωηφόρους εὐπειθείας καὶ ταπεινώσεως ὡς ἂν καὶ τὸν μισθὸν εὕροιμεν οἱ ἀνάξιοι μετὰ πάντων τῶν θεοσεβῶς ὁμοῦ καὶ φιλαγίως ποιμανευσάντων ἐν τῇ τῶν οὐρανῶν βασιλείᾳ.
[225] *Enkomion of Isakios and Dalmatos* 28. Cf. the tenth-century *Life of Dalmatos*: Βίος καὶ πολιτεία τοῦ ἐν ἁγίοις πατρὸς ἡμῶν καὶ ἀρχιμανδρίτου Δαλμάτου (ms. Istanbul Hagia Trias 96, f. 130v–46v), Delehaye 1926: 27–28.
[226] 'Μιχαὴλ ἀρχιμανδρίτου', see Anrich 1913: vol. i, p. 113, apparatus.

during the iconoclast period. But it is worth stressing the great importance given throughout the narration to the patriarch Nikephoros, who is always portrayed favourably as having a good relationship with Theodoros and ironing out any old differences the Stoudites might have with the patriarchate.[227] It is also important that it became necessary to update the *vita* of this great hegoumenos so that every monk could benefit from reading it: the original text narrating the biography of Theodoros Stoudites appears to have been written by the patriarch Methodios in the final years of his life, that is, when iconoclasm had already been defeated.[228] At the same time, the patriarch may have dedicated a liturgical hymn to him.[229] Methodios' bombastic style, with its lofty theological digressions, its rhetoric and its recherché vocabulary, were too complex for an ordinary monk. Michael Monachos accordingly produced a *metaphrasis* that insisted above all else on formal matters, faithfully respecting the content of his model.[230]

At the request of the Stoudite community as a whole (τὸ κοινὸν τῆς ἀδελφότητος), Michael wrote this *Vita* B after the death of the hegoumenos of Stoudios, Nikolaos Stoudites, that is, after 868.[231] The exact date is unknown: Matantseva proposes the late ninth century, whereas Krausmüller suggests the early tenth,[232] although in an earlier article he affirms that 'the *Life* of Nicholas [of Stoudios] was written before the *Life* of Theodore'.[233] In any case, it was composed during the hegoumenate of Anatolios (the abbot of Stoudios between 886 and 916),[234] who was also the patron for the *vita* of Nikolaos Stoudites, as well as for the *menologion* preserved in the manuscript *Vaticanus Gr.* 1660. For this rewriting, Michael took the opportunity to add some details his predecessor had not mentioned, such as the miracles of Theodoros that Sophronios used to recall.[235] Sophronios was none other than the hegoumenos of the monastery of Stoudios, who appointed Nikolaos Stoudites as his successor in 849 during his ascetic retreat.[236] By the time this hagiography was produced, Sophronios had been dead some time (since 3 November 855), but

---

[227] Delouis 2005: 326–30. [228] Krausmüller 2006; 2013. [229] Pentkovskij 2001: 293–94.
[230] *Vita* B *of Theodoros Stoud.* 236A–B. On Methodios' style, see Krausmüller 2006; Hinterberger 2008: 132.
[231] Nikolaos Stoudites is mentioned as μακαρίτης 'blessed' (*Vita* B *of Theodoros Stoud.* 296C).
[232] Matantseva 1996a: 123–24; Krausmüller 2013a: 287. [233] Krausmüller 2006: 148, n. 11.
[234] *PmbZ* # 20347; *Vita of the Patriarch Euthymios* 159–61. For his efforts to create a specifically Stoudite hagiographical genre, see Delouis 2005: 305–73.
[235] For Sophronios as an oral source for Michael Monachos, *Vita* B *of Theodoros Stoud.* 308D, 309C, 312A.
[236] *PmbZ* # 6848; *PBE* I: Sophronios 1.

Michael's strong memory of him meant that he became one of the witnesses of his *Vita* B.[237]

(a) The *Vita* in Honour of Nikolaos Stoudites (*BHG* 1365)

For its part, the *vita* in honour of Nikolaos Stoudites (*BHG* 1365) seems to have been a commission from abbot Anatolios[238] to replace an earlier account that was not to his literary taste, although it had probably been written by Antonios Mauros, a direct disciple of the saint.[239] This lost *vita* 1 must date to shortly after the year 911. Fortunately, a translation into Old Church Slavonic survives, while the hagiography that has come down to us in Greek (*vita* 2) was written shortly afterwards in accord with the literary tastes of Anatolios, who had a highly developed aesthetic sense.[240] One characteristic it shares with the *vita* of another important Stoudite, Blasios of Amorion (*BHG* 278),[241] is the presence of an edifying account bearing virtually no relation to the main plot, in this case the story of the soldier Nikolaos (*BHG* 2311/1317h), who fought in Bulgaria under the orders of Emperor Nikephoros I (802–811).[242] Despite having been presented as an anonymous work, the recent idea that the author of the surviving *vita* of Nikolaos of Stoudios is Michael Monachos is as thought-provoking as it is convincing.[243] The proposal is confirmed both by the author's clear pro-Ignatian bias[244] and by the literary character of both works (the *vitae* of Nikolaos and of Theodoros of Stoudios) compared with the original texts they take as sources. In both cases, the major changes are restricted to formal matters, in a move towards a more direct and less Asiatic style, while the content is faithfully maintained, apart from slight omissions or modifications aimed at reaching a wider audience. This occurs, for example, in the narration of the Photian schism, which is toned down in *vita* 2 of Nikolaos Stoudites.[245]

---

[237] *PmbZ* # 5121 and # 25099; *PBE* I: Michael 128.
[238] Anatolios is mentioned in the *Vita of Nikolaos Stoud.* 893A. On Anatolios see Section 1.2.2.
[239] *PmbZ* # 20485. For this attribution, see Afinogenov 2001: 319–20.
[240] Afinogenov 2004c: 313–22. This scholar proposes that it was written before the year 920, see p. 314. See also Von Dobschütz 1909a: 70–72; Nissen 1936/1938; Heldt 1995; Efthymiadis 1998: 43–44; Kazhdan 1999: 235–36; 2006: 89; Delouis 2005: 331–37.
[241] On this individual and the *vita* produced in his honour, see the end of this Section (5.2.2.a).
[242] Clugnet 1902; Stephenson and Shilling 2012. In the *vita* of Blasios of Amorion it is the story of Euphrosynos the Cook (*BHG* 628), see Efthymiadis 1996: 62; Kazhdan 2006: 226.
[243] Krausmüller 2006: 144–45; 2013a: 286, n. 12, who bases himself on the repetition of unusual expressions: ἕτεροι τῶν τῆς ἐκκλησίας ἱερομυστῶν (*Vita* B *of Theodoros Stoud.* 233C,2–3), ἔνιοι τῶν τῆς ἐκκλησίας ἱερομυστῶν (*Vita of Nikolaos Stoud.* 900B3).
[244] *Vita of Nikolaos Stoud.* 905C: ὁ οὖν τοῦ θεοῦ ἀρχιερεὺς καὶ τοῦ θεοφόρου ἐπώνυμος, 908A: τὸν μέγαν Ἰγνάτιον, 913B: τῷ θεοφόρῳ Ἰγνατίῳ.
[245] *Vita of Nikolaos Stoud.* 905B–13C; Afinogenov 2004c: 318.

But who was Nikolaos of Stoudios? He was no doubt quite important, since he was the head of one of the most influential monasteries in the capital during the conflict between Ignatios and Photios. The reasons for his attaining this position must be sought in his committed defence of icons in his youth, which has a special meaning for the hagiographer. Nikolaos was born in 793 to a peasant family from Kydonia, a town in Crete.[246] At the age of ten, he was sent to Constantinople to continue his studies under his uncle Theophanes, a monk at the monastery of Stoudios.[247] There he learnt quickly and stood out both for his skill in tachygraphy[248] and his study of the Scriptures and saints' lives.[249] His work as a copyist is well known and is recorded in the *vita*.[250] His many manuscripts include outstanding works such as the Uspenskij Gospel, dated at 835, which is the oldest known example of a minuscule manuscript.[251] These skills may have made Nikolaos the personal secretary of Theodoros Stoudites, accompanying him in his defence of icons.

After having been tonsured as a monk by Theodoros Stoudites himself,[252] Nikolaos accompanied his hegoumenos into exile during the years 815–821 to the Fort of Metopa (in Bithynia) and then to Boneta (in the *thema* of Anatolikon). The conditions of exile became gradually more arduous, to the extent that Emperor Leon V sent an agent with orders to give each man 100 lashes and leave them to die of hunger.[253] A new document regarding these saints fell into the hands of the emperor, who had them punished again with such cruelty that they almost died.[254] They were imprisoned for three years until their transfer to Smyrna, where they were again tortured and put in chains for another twenty months until the

---

[246] *PmbZ* # 5576; *PBE* I: Nikolaos 26; Dobroklonskij 1913: vol. 2, 85–99; Costa-Louillet 1957: 794–812; Phytrakes 1968; Detorakes 1970: 219–33. For his birth in Crete, see *Vita of Nikolaos Stoud.* 865B–C.
[247] *Vita of Nikolaos Stoud.* 869A–C. For his uncle Theophanes, cf. *PmbZ* # 8127; *PBE* I: Theophanes 21.
[248] *Vita of Nikolaos Stoud.* 872A–B: ταχυγράφος ἀποφανθεὶς χρησιμώτατος. See Ronconi 2014: 414.
[249] *Vita of Nikolaos Stoud.* 872B.
[250] *Vita of Nikolaos Stoud.* 876B: καὶ μαρτυροῦσιν αἵ τε βίβλοι καὶ τὰ ἐκείνου πονήματα.
[251] Among the manuscripts attributed to him are the following: St Petersburg RNB Gr. 219 ('Tetraevangeliarium Uspenskij'); *Parisinus Coislin Gr.* 269, fol. 97r–296r; *Vaticanus Gr.* 2079; *Patmiacus Gr.* 742; Moskow GIM Sinod. Gr. 97; *Parisinus Gr.* 494. The bibliography on the subject is very extensive, see Leroy 1973; 1977; Aletta 2002/2003. On the first Stoudite minuscule manuscripts, all from this period, see Kavrus 1983, esp. 99–102; Perria 1993; Fonkitch 2000; 2010.
[252] *Vita of Nikolaos Stoud.* 872C.
[253] *Vita of Nikolaos Stoud.* 884B–85A; *SynaxCP* 443–44,8–10; *Vita B of Theodoros Stoud.* 296B–C. See Pratsch 1998: 250–59.
[254] *Vita of Nikolaos Stoud.* 885A–88C.

death of Leon V.[255] Michael Monachos drew information regarding the persecution, torture and confession of Nikolaos both from the data contained in the original *Vita Theodori Studitae*, which he reproduced in his *Vita* B,[256] and from the testimony of Theodoros' letters, who often mentions his future successor as hegoumenos of Stoudios and considers him his own companion in torment.[257] Theodoros mentions Nikolaos on many occasions in his letters and introduces him as an equal in his suffering for the Orthodoxy of images.[258] In fact, Nikolaos was 'his sole companion' in exile,[259] and after being freed in early 821, they remained together.[260]

The accession to the throne of Michael II meant the liberation of Theodoros and Nikolaos (probably in January 821).[261] The greater tolerance enjoyed by iconodules allowed them to travel to Chalcedon, where they lived for a time with the deposed patriarch Nikephoros, who expressed his admiration on seeing the marks of the torture they had faced to defend Orthodoxy.[262] Nikolaos likely accompanied Theodoros Stoudites and the patriarch Nikephoros during their meeting with Emperor Michael II regarding the need to re-establish the veneration of icons.[263] The remaining sources for their part restrict the attempts of the iconodules to persuade Michael II to restore icon veneration to an epistolary exchange.[264] As well as presenting Nikolaos as one of the leaders of the cause of images, the hagiographer insists on the 'hereditary' component of his holiness, and has him accompany Theodoros to St Tryphon monastery near Cape Akritas, where Nikolaos attended Theodoros during his last days until his death on 11 November 826.[265] We can assume that

---

[255] *Vita of Nikolaos Stoud.* 888C–89A; *SynaxCP* 444,10–16; *Vita* B *of Theodoros Stoud.* 300B.
[256] *Vita* B *of Theodoros Stoud.* 293A–D; 296A–D; 297B; 300B. Cf. Pratsch 1998: 250–59.
[257] Theod. Stoud., *epist.* 382,63: Νικόλαος ὁ συγκλειστὸς καὶ σύμπονος καὶ συστρατιώτης μου (spring 819).
[258] Theod. Stoud., *epist.* 41 (written in 809/811); *epist.* 81 (spring 816).
[259] Theod. Stoud., *epist.* 111,30: προσκύνει δουλικῶς ὁ ἀδελφὸς Νικόλαος, μόνος ἐγκαταλειφθείς μοι (winter 815/816 in exile); *epist.* 122, 123, 124, 125, 126, 128, 129, 150 and 151 (all from the summer of 816). They both suffered the same torture, see *epist.* 252, 288, 290 and 388 (whipped and imprisoned during winter 817/818). See also *epist.* 344, 349, 368, 384, 392, 405, in which he is mentioned, are also from the year 818. *Epist.* 381, 382, 402, 406 and 410 correspond to the following year (they both again received blows).
[260] Theod. Stoud., *epist.* 417, 421, 436.   [261] *Vita of Nikolaos Stoud.* 889B–C.
[262] *Vita of Nikolaos Stoud.* 889C–92A. *SynaxCP* 444,18–19; Theod. Stoud., *epist.* 475, 12–13; Pratsch 1998: 274ff.
[263] *Vita of Nikolaos Stoud.* 892A–93A.
[264] Theod. Stoud., *epist.* 418 and 429; *Vita of Nikephoros* 209,12–10,12; Theoph. Cont. II, 8,1–4; Lilie 1999: 144.
[265] *Vita of Nikolaos Stoud.* 900A; *SynaxCP* 444,22–23; Pratsch 1998: 271–91, esp. 290–91.

Nikolaos was also present during the transfer of the body to the Island of Prinkipos nearby, since after the funeral he decided to establish himself near the tomb of his spiritual father and become an ascetic. His fame as a saint and confessor of Christ became so great that would-be disciples began to arrive seeking his spiritual guidance, including prominent figures of the Senate and the capital.[266]

When Emperor Theophilos reactivated iconoclasm, Nikolaos was obliged to flee until he found refuge in Thrace in the *proasteion* of Phirmoupolis courtesy of a certain Eirene.[267] He decided to remain there after the Triumph of Orthodoxy in 843 and the restoration of the monastery of Stoudios, devoted to the contemplative life and asceticism.[268] The death of Naukratios on 18 April 848 meant that he was a unanimous choice as hegoumenos of Stoudios, a post he filled for only three years, before again retiring to Phirmoupolis in search of the spiritual peace Constantinople could not offer him.[269] The virtues of Nikolaos, which were as noble as those of his predecessors, justified his appointment.[270] He left Sophronios as a substitute, but the latter died four years later, and Nikolaos' brothers persuaded him to return as hegoumenos at the end of the year 853.[271]

The overthrow of the patriarch Ignatios in 858 led to the self-imposed exile of Nikolaos, whose principles did not allow him to come into contact with the new patriarch. The imperial authorities forbade him to establish himself in any property of the monastery of Stoudios and appointed the monk Achillas as head of the community.[272] After five years, in 863, Nikolaos was appointed archbishop of Nakoleia,[273] while in the Constantinopolitan Council of 879/880 we find him siding with the patriarch Photios.[274] Nikolaos wandered until he fell ill, and it was in this state that he was called to the palace to a meeting with Emperor Michael III in Constantinople. Like the iconodule heroes, he confronted the emperor with success, although he was confined to a Stoudios cell.[275]

---

[266] *Vita of Nikolaos Stoud.* 900B–C.
[267] *Vita of Nikolaos Stoud.* 901A–B. On the pious Eirene, see *PmbZ* # 1447; *PBE* I: Eirene 8. On the monastery of Phirmoupolis, see Janin 1969: 494–95; Ruggieri 1991: 194.
[268] *Vita of Nikolaos Stoud.* 904A.
[269] For his appointment, see *Vita of Nikolaos Stoud.* 904B–D; *Vita of Evarestos of Stoudios* 12, p. 306,3–8.
[270] *Vita of Evarestos of Stoudios* 12, p. 306,9–11.
[271] *Vita of Nikolaos Stoud.* 905A–B. On Sophronios, see *PmbZ* # 6848; *PBE* I: Sophronios 1.
[272] *Vita of Nikolaos Stoud.* 908B–9B; *Vita of Evarestos of Stoudios* 13, p. 307,6–8.
[273] *Vita of Nikolaos Stoud.* 912B.
[274] Mansi xviiA, 373C. On Achillas, see *PmbZ* # 75 and 20094; *PBE* I: Achillas 1.
[275] *Vita of Evarestos of Stoudios* 14, p. 307,32–8,4.

But the saint was tempted again, this time by the patriarch Photios, who tried to win him over to his cause while he was at the monastery of Kokorobion. This was a vain attempt, since Nikolaos fled with his brother to Prokonnesos, Mytilene and Xamelion in the Chersonesos.[276] Finally, he was taken to the monastery of Stoudios by order of Caesar Bardas, where he remained for two years (865–867) under the supervision of the new hegoumenos, Sabas, a disciple of Photios.[277]

After the accession to the throne of Basileios I in 867, however, Nikolaos recovered the hegoumenate of Stoudios. Despite his initial reticence, the emperor himself persuaded him to return to his post.[278] There can be no doubt that Basileios I greatly improved Nikolaos' opinion of him, given the miraculous healing in the same period of his wife, Empress Eudokia Ingerina, who was thought to be beyond recovery until she had a vision of a monk – Nikolaos Stoudites himself – who would cure her.[279] The good relationship of the monastery of Stoudios with the worldly powers was strengthened by another no less miraculous healing by Nikolaos: that of Helena, the wife of the patrician Manuel, who was allegedly a sister of Theophilos.[280] Her husband Manuel was probably the *patrikios* and *logothetes tou dromou* who two years later received a letter from Metrophanes of Smyrna asking that he explain why Photios had been dismissed from the patriarchal see. It is easy to understand the reasons that led Michael Monachos to record this specific episode, given his collaboration with the Ignatians and the close relationship they shared with the monastery of Stoudios.[281]

Only a few months later, Nikolaos died in Stoudios on 4 February 868 at the age of seventy-five.[282] His *vita* takes pleasure in the saint's healing miracles and the many prophecies that would later form the basis for his sanctification.[283] More details are found in the hagiography of his disciple Evarestos, who describes how Nikolaos fell ill when he was visiting the community of Kokorobion. Knowing that his end was near, he expressed a desire to be buried on the spot, but the monks persuaded him to return to

---

[276] *Vita of Nikolaos Stoud.* 912A–B. These travels are omitted by the *Vita of Evarestos* 15–16, despite the fact that it contains a narrative very similar to that of the *Vita of Nikolaos*.
[277] *Vita of Nikolaos Stoud.* 912C–13A; *Vita of Evarestos of Stoudios* 16, pp. 308,34–9,1. Concerning this Sabas, see *PmbZ* # 6451; *PBE* I: Sabas 6. See Section 7.2.
[278] *Vita of Nikolaos Stoud.* 913B–C; *Vita of Evarestos of Stoudios* 16, p. 309,1–10; *SynaxCP* 444,30–33.
[279] *Vita of Nikolaos Stoud.* 913D–16B. On Eudokia Ingerina, see *PmbZ* # 1632 and 21754; *PBE* I: Eudokia 2.
[280] *Vita of Nikolaos Stoud.* 916B–C. On Helena, see *PmbZ* # 22569; *PBE* I: Helene 2. See Section 4.2.
[281] *PmbZ* # 24866 and # 24869.   [282] *Vita of Nikolaos Stoud.* 921C; *SynaxCP* 444,33–37.
[283] *Vita of Nikolaos Stoud.* 913C–16D (miraculous healings); 916D–17B and 921C–D (prophecies).

Stoudios to die, which he did after appointing Evarestos hegoumenos of Kokorobion.²⁸⁴ At Stoudios, after addressing his brothers and nominating Klemes as his successor, he expired.²⁸⁵ Klemes' tenure was brief, since he died on 17 July and was replaced by Hilarion.²⁸⁶

The process of Nikolaos' sanctification began immediately after his death, since he was buried on the right-hand side of the church of St John Prodromos of the monastery of Stoudios alongside his predecessors as heads of the community, Naukratios and Theodoros, who were already liturgically venerated on a regular basis.²⁸⁷ Nikolaos' miracle-working capacity was also clear from the first, as three days after his death a prophecy by him was fulfilled: a cargo of grain arrived to ease a scarcity of food, earning him high praise from the new hegoumenos Klemes.²⁸⁸

Some anonymous verses (a distich in iambic trimeters) in Nikolaos' honour survive from this initial stage of his veneration.²⁸⁹ There is no doubt, however, that the main evidence, along with the *vita* by Michael Monachos, is the entry in the *Synaxarion of Constantinople*.²⁹⁰ As generally, the *Synaxarion* summarises the *vita*. In doing so, it emphasises the main elements of the subject's holiness, which in Nikolaos' case have to do with his defence of icons, despite the time that had passed since these events. This bias is such that the *Synaxarion* gives the impression that the only thing Nikolaos did throughout his life was confront iconoclastic heresy and suffer for defending Orthodoxy until the coming to power in 867 of Basileios I, who reinstated him as head of Stoudios shortly before his death. In fact, the *synaxaristes* pretends that the twenty-four years of iconodule government that followed the Triumph of Orthodoxy had no effect on the biography of the saint and also omits the dispute with the patriarch Photios.²⁹¹ As Nikolaos is an iconodule hero, the *Synaxarion* mentions the torture he suffered and his close relationship with two figures of reference of the resistance already recognised as saints, Theodoros Stoudites and the patriarch Nikephoros.²⁹² In this way, the new cult of Nikolaos was established on the basis of strong traditions and following a

---

²⁸⁴ *Vita of Evarestos of Stoudios* 17–18, pp. 309,19–10,22.
²⁸⁵ *Vita of Nikolaos Stoud.* 921B, which specifies that it was on his deathbed; *Vita of Evarestos of Stoudios* 18, p. 310,27–37. Concerning this Klemes, see *PmbZ* # 23705; *PBE* I: Klemens 4.
²⁸⁶ *Vita of Nikolaos Stoud.* 924A–B; *PmbZ* # 22601; *PBE* I: Hilarion 4.
²⁸⁷ *Vita of Nikolaos Stoud.* 921B–C.   ²⁸⁸ *Vita of Nikolaos Stoud.* 921D–24A.
²⁸⁹ Detorakes 1970: 233: Ἔδοξε τῷ στήσαντι μέτρα τῷ βίῳ / καὶ Νικόλαον ἐκμετρῆσαι τὸν βίον.
²⁹⁰ *SynaxCP* 443,33–44,37 (4 February); *Typikon of the Great Church* I, 227 (4 February).
²⁹¹ *SynaxCP* 444,27–33.
²⁹² *SynaxCP* 444,3–4 and 22–23 (exile with Theodoros Stoudites); *SynaxCP* 444,16–19 (conversation with the patriarch Nikephoros).

strategy already apparent in the *vita*: identifying the new confessor with the saints who preceded him, such as Theodoros Stoudites and Platon of Sakkoudion, alongside whom he was buried. This was done in imitation of the model of holiness that Theodoros had proposed for his uncle Platon, in which the reading of *vitae* is one of the religious practices that characterise him as a saint.[293] Michael Monachos emphasises this same custom when writing the hagiographies of the Stoudite heroes Theodoros, Nikolaos and, in all probability, Blasios of Amorion.[294]

It remains impossible to identify the author of the *vita* of Blasios of Amorion (*BHG* 278), but he was clearly a Stoudite monk.[295] The possibility that this writer was the Michael Monachos who wrote the *vita* of Nikolaos Stoudites has already been recognized by a number of scholars,[296] and the narratological construction of the text supports it, as pointed out earlier. This *vita*, which survives only in the tenth-century codex *Parisinus Gr.* 1491, was commissioned by a certain Loukas,[297] a disciple of the saint who was the hagiographer's main informant. Blasios was ordained a deacon by the patriarch Ignatios in Constantinople at Hagia Sophia, where his elder brother was already a priest.[298] After living in Rome for eighteen years at the monastery of St Caesarius, he returned to Constantinople and established himself at the monastery of Stoudios (ca. 897). Shortly afterwards, he decided to retire to Mount Athos, but he returned to Stoudios to die in 912, after having established a good relationship with Emperor Leon VI.[299]

(b) Texts Associated with the Patriarchate and the *Encomium of Ignatios* (*BHG* 818)

The rewriting of pre-existing texts is characteristic of the literary production of Michael Monachos: some of the texts that place him within the Ignatian milieu are of precisely this type. A good example, in addition to those already examined, is the *Enkomion of St Mokios* (*BHG* 1298h),[300]

---

[293] Theod. Stoud., *Laudatio of Platon* 824C.
[294] *Vita* B *of Theodoros Stoud.* 245A; *Vita of Nikolaos Stoud.* 872B; *Vita of Blasios* 663F. See Efthymiadis and Kalogeras 2014: 262, n. 48. The reading of hagiographies also appears in the *Vita of Eirene of Chrysobalanton* 5, p. 16,17–25 as a sign of holiness. This fact, along with the dedication to the archangel Gabriel of the church of Chrysobalanton and Eirene's vinculation with Chalkoprateia (ch. 21), further proves the pro-Ignatian bias of the work.
[295] *Vita of Blasios* 669A–D; *PmbZ* # 31283.
[296] Grégoire 1929: 413–14; Afinogenov 2001: 318; 2004c: 322.   [297] *PmbZ* # 24759.
[298] On Blasios of Amorion, see *PmbZ* # 21177.   [299] Tougher 1997: 17–18, 116 and 121.
[300] Delehaye 1912: 176–87 and 226–27. For Mokios' veneration, Wortley 1999: 363–68; Berger 2013b.

The Milieu of the Patriarch Ignatios

which is no more than a stylistic *metaphrasis* of the *passio* that already existed (*BHG* 1298) and provides no new information. The production of the text is probably linked to the magnificent restoration of the church of St Mokios, which contained his remains, by Emperor Basileios I after it collapsed in 869 to such an extent that not even the altar could be saved.[301] Michael ends the composition by alluding to the feast day of the restoration of the building, mentioning Basileios by name and insisting on the annual celebration of the saint's memory.[302] If the rebuilding was as splendid as historians claim, it is logical to assume that the patriarch Ignatios was present at its inauguration.

Another representative case is the stylistic rewriting of an original by Methodios, since together with masterpieces of Stoudite hagiographical literature, Michael also wrote a *metaphrasis* of the *vita* of Nicholas of Myra (*BHG* 1348), which took as a model the one written by the patriarch (*BHG* 1352y).[303] This hagiographical undertaking is to a large extent a doublet of the *vita* by Methodios, but in a much more readable style and with a new prologue and epilogue. It suggests that Michael Monachos had access to the patriarchal texts and probably the patriarchal library and above all else indicates his good relationship with members of the circle of the patriarch Ignatios. One of these must have been Leon, who commissioned him to write the piece as an order (ἐπίταγμα) and who is the recipient of Michael's *metaphrasis*.[304] Traditional attempts to identify this Leon with persons by the same name close to Theodoros Stoudites have been inconclusive due to the amount of time that separates the two men.[305] Most likely he lived in the second half of the ninth century, and he may have been one of the senior dignitaries who took part in the sessions of the Ignatian Council of 869/870 at which Photios was deposed and excommunicated.[306] Unfortunately, no definitive conclusion can be reached.

---

[301] Theoph. Cont. V, 81,1–5. See also Georgios Kedrenos II, 239,9–11. On the future monastery of Mokios, see Janin 1969: 354–58; Berger 2013b.

[302] *Enkomion of Mokios by Michael Monachos*, p. 187,17–24.

[303] Anrich 1913: vol. II, 264–73; Kazhdan 1999: 378. On its author, see *PmbZ* # 5089; Krausmüller 2006: 145–46. On the *vita* of Nicholas of Myra that Methodios dedicated to one Theodoros, see Section 2.1.1. For the relationship between both texts, see Ševčenko 1977a: 119, n. 46; Magdalino 2015b; Krausmüller 2016.

[304] *PmbZ* # 4441; *Vita of Nicholas of Myra* (*BHG* 1348) 114,8 and 139,1; Anrich 1913: vol. II, 270–72.

[305] A correspondent of Theodoros Stoudites, the *patrikios* and *sakellarios* Leon, see *PmbZ* # 4417. For the *patrikios* Leon mentioned in the epigrams of Theodoros, see *PmbZ* # 4432. Maybe we are facing the *hypato* (consul) Leon who appears in the *vitae* of Theodoros of Stoudios, see *PmbZ* # 4421.

[306] Like the two Leones *patrikioi* and *anthypatoi*, see *PmbZ* # 24324; *PmbZ* # 24326. Or perhaps the *patrikios* and *Domestikos ton Exkubiton* Leon, see *PmbZ* # 24325. The last candidate, who was present at the council sessions, is the *hypatos* Leon, who was called as a witness so that he could

Definitive evidence for Michael's membership in the Ignatian party is found in the writing of two *encomia*: one dedicated to the deposition of the girdle of the Theotokos (*BHG* 1147), another to honouring the patriarch Ignatios. Almost all the manuscripts attribute the former to Michael Synkellos, but the thirteenth-century Venetian codex *Marcianus Gr. Z* 362, fol. 207v–13v interestingly claims that the author was Niketas Paphlagon.[307] This is easy to understand, given Niketas' well-known, controversial attacks on Photios. Indeed, the encomium makes perfect sense as one more element in the dispute between the two patriarchal parties: it might well have been seen as an attempt by the Ignatian milieu to counteract the propaganda of Photios, who, after defending the city from the Russians in summer 860 via the assistance of the garment or robe of the Theotokos (*maphorion*), made the feast day of its deposition at the church of Blachernai on 2 July an ideological element, as is apparent from the texts written by several Photians: the *Enkomion of the Robe of the Virgin* of the *synkellos* Theodoros (*BHG* 1058) and the *kanones* for this feast day by Georgios of Nicomedia.[308] In a similar manner, the exaltation of a parallel celebration recalling the transfer of the girdle (*zone*) of the Virgin to the church of Chalkoprateia on 31 August[309] was a clever move by Ignatios' followers during his second patriarchate. In fact, Ioseph Hymnographos devoted a hymn to the Deposition of the Girdle, to be sung at Chalkoprateia.[310] It is significant that in the second half of the ninth century the Lord is replaced by the Theotokos in the formulae of invocation of the seals; this phenomenon appears related to the changing social status of women and may have been strengthened by the veneration of this Marian relic[311] but is perhaps also to be connected to the defeat of iconoclasm, which allegedly rejected the cult of the Virgin.[312] In fact, the iconodules revitalised the devotion of the Virgin to make her more maternal and protective, labelling her *Meter Theou* in addition to the previous Theotokos.[313]

The second encomium signed by Michael the monk, *presbyteros* and *synkellos*, is an enthusiastic display of loyalty to Ignatios. This panegyric was read at the Photian Council of 879/880, in the minutes of which it has

---

retract, as in the past he had declared against Ignatios under threat, see Mansi XVI, 151 (ninth session: 12 February 870); *Council of Constantinople (869/870)*, 289; *PmbZ* # 24327; Hergenröther 1867–1869: vol. II, 116–17.

[307] Mioni 1985: nr. 362. [308] See Section 6.3.4. Cf. Baynes 1955a; 1955b; Wortley 2005.
[309] *SynaxCP* 935,2–36,4; Shoemaker 2008; Krausmüller 2011.
[310] *PG* 105, cols 1009D–17D. The church of Chalkoprateia is explicitly mentioned in col. 1013A (ode 5.3).
[311] Kazhdan and Talbot 1991: 403. [312] Kazhdan 1999: 148–49; Cunningham 2015.
[313] Pentcheva 2006: 61–103; Connor 2016: 110–11.

survived (albeit in fragmentary condition) as a eulogy of the deceased patriarch and a symbol of the reconciliation between the two factions.[314] A close reading of the surviving fragment of the *Encomium Ignatii* in relation to the latest *Vita of the Patriarch Ignatios* (*BHG* 817) by Niketas David Paphlagon shows the extent to which Michael Monachos laid the foundations for the subsequent sanctification of the patriarch. When Niketas David, the bishop of Dadybra in Paphlagonia, wrote his *Vita Ignatii*,[315] his main motivation seems to have been profound hatred for the patriarch Photios, the rival of the hero of his narrative. On the other hand, besides including all kinds of sources, legends and rumours that denigrated his adversary and allowed him to create an anti-Photian political pamphlet, Niketas also followed in a rather literal fashion the model Michael provided him for constructing Ignatios' holiness.

In his *Encomium Ignatii*, Michael begins by relating the lineage of his hero, in which holiness was abundant on both his father's and his mother's side.[316] After emphasising Ignatios' links to imperial power, Michael recalls how, when he was appointed patriarch, he received the *omophorion* (bishop's pallium) of the Apostle James, brother of the Lord, with whom he was buried.[317] In his youth, Ignatios had to confront Leon the Armenian, and despite the latter's cruelty, he stood so firm in defense of Orthodoxy that iconodule heroes of the stature of Ioannikios and Theophanes the Confessor prophesied his destiny as a patriarch.[318] When Methodios died, therefore, Empress Theodora gathered together the Church institutions, and both the senate and the monks as a whole chose Ignatios.[319] Michael categorically affirms that the only person to blame for the overthrow, torture and exile of Ignatios is Caesar Bardas (τὸν κράτιστον τὸν καίσαρα λέγω Βάρδαν), who was reacting against the patriarch's criticism of his incestuous relationship with his daughter-in-law. For the author, however, the true reason for Bardas' action was political, since Ignatios refused to tonsure Theodora and her daughters.[320]

The affront to Ignatios ended thanks to Basileios I, who achieved divine justice by reinstating him on the patriarchal throne with full honours and

---

[314] Dvornik 1948: 80; Kazhdan 1999: 258–59.
[315] This is a well-known *vita* due to its great importance, see Costa-Louillet 1954/1955: 461–78; Featherstone 1981; Paschalidis 2004; Kazhdan 2006: 97–102. As for its dating, Jenkins 1965 places the writing of the *Vita Ignatii* 'in about 910'; Tamarkina 2006 proposes that it post-dates the death of Emperor Basileios I (886) and predates the patriarchate of Nikolaos Mystikos (901).
[316] *Enkomion of Ignatios* (*BHG* 818) 292B–C; *Vita of Ignatios* 2.
[317] *Enkomion of Ignatios* 292C; *Vita of Ignatios* 75.
[318] *Enkomion of Ignatios* 292C–D; *Vita of Ignatios* 3–5; 14,28–34 (a prophecy of Theophanes); 16,8–11 (a prophetic appointment by Ioannikios).
[319] *Enkomion of Ignatios* 292D–E. [320] *Enkomion of Ignatios* 292E–93A; *Vita of Ignatios* 17.

great veneration, something the remaining patriarchs accepted with great joy.[321] After many years (ἐπὶ χρόνοις) in the patriarchate – Michael never specifies how many or what happened during them – Ignatios died on the day of St James, brother of the Lord, and was laid to rest in the monastery of St Michael he had founded in Satyros.[322] The deceased patriarch then performed the following miracle: there was a terrible storm at sea, and it was impossible to transport his body. Suddenly, however, the sea became completely calm, and the people were all able to take part in the funeral and the transfer of the body to Satyros.[323] Michael adds another miracle that Ignatios performed while still alive: while he was exiled in Mytilene, the River Lykos burst its banks and became a lake that could not be waded across. Ignatios raised his hands to heaven to pray and its volume was reduced.[324] His signs and miracles were as numerous as the grains of sand in the desert; the hagiographer compares him with the angels and praises him for having had visions. On this note, he brings the text to a close with a reflection on the appearances of saints and the position of the Church regarding the writings attributed to Athanasios of Alexandria: 'if anyone says that saints do not appear to us, but angels in their place, he should be anathematised'.[325]

Perhaps this mention of Pseudo-Athanasios, who in the early eighth century affirmed 'the visions and apparitions which take place in temples and sepulchres do not take place through the saints' souls, but through angels who assume the saints' form',[326] is related to Photios' reading of the treatise of Eustratios of Constantinople.[327] An author of the second half of the sixth century, Eustratios attacked the theory of the 'inactivity' of the soul after death, explicitly denying that any divine force took on the appearance of the souls of the saints. We should not be surprised that an intellectual like Michael Monachos shared concerns with Photios, whom he exonerates from any blame in his praise of the deceased patriarch. Michael's political interests in the reconciliation of the two ecclesiastical

---

[321] *Enkomion of Ignatios* 293A–B; *Vita of Ignatios* 53,18–29.
[322] *Enkomion of Ignatios* 293B; *Vita of Ignatios* 74 (death of Ignatios); 76,23–27 (funeral in Satyros).
[323] *Enkomion of Ignatios* 293C; *Vita of Ignatios* 76,14–22.
[324] *Enkomion of Ignatios* 293C. This is the only information not included in the *Vita of the Patriarch Ignatios*.
[325] *Enkomion of Ignatios* 293D–E: Οὕτω γράψασα· εἴ τις οὐκ αὐτοὺς λέγει τοὺς ἁγίους ἡμῖν ἐπιφαίνεσθαι, ἀλλὰ τοὺς τῶνδε, φησίν, ἀγγέλους, ἔστω ἀνάθεμα.
[326] Pseudo-Athanasios, *Questions to the Duke Antiochus* 26 (*PG* 28,614B): Αἱ ἐν τοῖς ναοῖς καὶ σωροῖς τῶν ἁγίων γινόμεναι ἐπισκιάσεις καὶ ὀπτασίαι οὐ διὰ τῶν ψυχῶν τῶν ἁγίων γίνονται, ἀλλὰ δι' ἀγγέλων ἁγίων μετασχηματιζομένων εἰς τὸ εἶδος τῶν ἁγίων. For the date of the work, see Thümmel 1992: 246–52. On this passage, see Dagron 1991a: 32; Krausmüller 1998/1999.
[327] Phot., *Bibliotheca*, cod. 171, 117b.41–18a.5. Cf. Eustratios of Constantinople, *Refutation*, pp. XLVIII–LII; Dal Santo 2012.

sectors, along with the Photian context in which the encomium of Ignatios was to be read, led him to relieve the current patriarch of blame. For this reason, Michael pulls no punches when seeking the person responsible for his hero's misfortunes, who is Bardas rather than Emperor Michael III or Photios. Indeed, the lack of reference to the rule of Ignatios avoids some thorny issues. The silences of the author aside, however, the important point is that this strengthens the image of Ignatios as an iconodule confessor. This is the main feature of the holiness of Ignatios that justifies immediate veneration of him and is what we find in the *Vita Ignatii*, which Niketas David concludes by praising the deceased patriarch as 'in truth the new confessor of the faith and bearer of God's message'.[328]

Evidence available to date does not allow anything specific to be said about the personal relationship between the two Ignatian writers, Michael Monachos and Niketas David Paphlagon.[329] It is hard to say whether they knew each other, and if so, what kind of relationship they had. If Flusin is correct, and a fragment survives of a lost *vita* in honour of Niketas David written by a pupil of his, Niketas David was imprisoned in the monastery of Dalmatos.[330] This would have been a reprisal for having rejected an offer from Emperor Leon VI, but we do not know when this happened, how long Niketas remained there, or – more important – whether Michael Monachos was still the hegoumenos of the monastery and thus his supervisor. Be that as it may, and irrespective of whether it was in Dalmatos that Niketas had access to Michael's writings, his great debt is evident in the *Vita of the Patriarch Ignatios* (as we have seen), but also in encomia such as the one dedicated to the prophet Daniel and the three youths (*BHG* 488b) based on that of Michael (*BHG* 488a). Above all, Niketas David Paphlagon and Michael Monachos share the passionate identification of their common hero, the patriarch Ignatios, with the holy confessors of the iconoclast period.

5.2.3 Other Hagiographical Texts of the Ignatian Milieu

(a) Acta of the Ten Martyrs of Constantinople (BHG 1195)

The *Passio et inventio X martyrum Constantinopolitanorum* (*BHG* 1195)[331] is a paradigmatic example of the way in which the patriarch Ignatios and

---

[328] *Vita of Ignatios* 97, p. 132,2–4: τοῦ ἐν ἁγίοις πατρὸς ἡμῶν Ἰγνατίου ἀρχιεπισκόπου Κωνσταντινουπόλεως, τοῦ νέου ἀληθῶς ὁμολογητοῦ καὶ θεοφόρου.
[329] For the biography of Niketas David Paphlagon, see *PmbZ* # 25712; Paschalidis 1999.
[330] Flusin 1985: chs. 25–26, pp. 125,22–27,56: εἰς τὴν ἱερὰν τοῦ Δαλμάτου καταδίκην αὐτίκα κατεδίκασεν.
[331] *AASS*, Aug. II: 428–48; *SynaxCP* 877,24–80,13 (9 August).

his followers tried to establish links and become identified with the heroes of the first iconoclast period. This work was written in 869 on the occasion of the discovery of the relics of the New Martyrs who supposedly confronted Emperor Leon III in 730 to prevent him from destroying an icon of Christ located at the Chalke Gate at the entrance to the palace.[332] The text displays clear historiographical aspirations and a well-defined three-part structure: the first part describes the origin of the iconoclast heresy, introduces the milieu in which the saints lived and offers a portrait of the antagonist, Emperor Leon III the Isaurian, who is the true instigator of the action and is to trigger the confession and defence of Orthodoxy by the protagonists.[333] The second part features, as sole protagonist, the patriarch Germanos, who passionately defends icons at the palace before Leon III, justifying his theology with the characteristic reasoning of the resistance to Second Iconoclasm. The emperor ignores Germanos' words and, in order to be rid of him, accuses him of conspiracy. Before resigning, Germanos prophesies to his *synkellos* and successor in the patriarchate, the iconoclast Anastasios, what will happen to him fifteen years later.[334]

The third part of the text is its core, since it describes the martyrdom of the defenders of the image at the Chalke Gate and how they refused to accept heresy despite the emperor's threats and punishments, due to which they were finally condemned to death. Their bodies were buried near the monastery of Aninas, near that of Mokios,[335] until the vision of the patriarch Ignatios allowed their recovery and a burial matching their importance.[336] It is in the final part of the account that prodigious events abound: the appearance to Ignatios in his dreams of a beautiful woman who declared herself of the martyrs of the Christ of the Chalke Gate (the patrician Maria)[337] and told him the exact place where she was buried together with her companions; a second vision in response to the forgetfulness of the patriarch, in which the angry martyrs threatened to depose him, if he did not heed their words;[338] the end to natural disasters while

---

[332] *Vita of Stephanos the Younger* 100–1 and 193–94; Theoph. 405 (pp. 545–46); Stein 1980.
[333] *Acta of the Ten Martyrs* 435A–37C.
[334] *Acta of the Ten Martyrs* 440D–42E. On the iconoclast patriarch Anastasios (730–754), see *PmbZ* # 285; *PBE* I: Anastasios 2; Lilie 1999: 22–29.
[335] For the location of the nearby monastery of Aninas, see Janin 1969: 34–35. *SynaxCP* 877,53–53 affirms that they lay in the monastery of Mokios.
[336] *Acta of the Ten Martyrs* 443C–47B.   [337] *PmbZ* # 4724.
[338] The finding of relics thanks to a prophetic dream was a very popular *topos* in the second half of the ninth century: this was not only how the remains of the martyrs of the Chalke were found but also those of Menas, Hermogenes and Eugraphos, likewise in the reign of Basileios I, *SynaxCP* 470,19–40 (17 February); Maraval 1989.

Ignatios talked to the faithful congregated at Hagia Sophia of the Martyrs; the fragrance of the uncorrupted bodies of the saints and the miraculous liquid that flowed from their new tomb. In all these situations, Ignatios was present, acting as a direct intermediary between God and his people, since he not only promoted the discovery of these martyrs but also led all the prayers and liturgies to give thanks to God.

As Auzépy has shown, the events surrounding the destruction by Leon III of the icon of Christ that watched over the Chalke Gate are all a propaganda fiction gradually created by the iconodules during the interlude of 787–815, with new additions after the Triumph of Orthodoxy in 843.[339] In the *Passio et inventio X martyrum Constantinopolitanorum*, the author has combined sources such as the chronicle of Theophanes with the *vita* of Stephanos the Younger (also a literary product from the patriarchal milieu), to which he has added new details to create a narrative that fits his needs.[340] These needs included promoting Ignatios and affirming him as the head of the patriarchal see, in which he had been enthroned for scarcely two years (since 867) after returning from exile and replacing the deposed Photios. As already noted, the irregular rise of Photios to the patriarchate and the resistance he encountered led him to make a legitimising speech that rested on the precedents of the great iconodule patriarchs Tarasios and Nikephoros, who like him had been raised to the throne from simple laymen, owing to which he presented himself as a martyr of the Second Iconoclasm.

The patriarch Methodios, the restorer of images, had been a controversial figure. Worse still, he had left powerful enemies among the Stoudites, with whom Ignatios had a good relationship and whose support he wished to retain. Tarasios and Nikephoros had also had public disagreements with the Stoudites. It was therefore necessary to look further back and vindicate the figure of Germanos, who had attracted less attention and was free of connotations of any kind. This approach fit the anathemas recited for the first time at the council of 869 against the Isaurian dynasty and iconoclasts of the First Iconoclasm (730–787), which were then added to the *Synodikon of Orthodoxy* in its second phase of composition.[341] At the same time, it was necessary to praise Germanos' work as head of the patriarchate and give it more importance. The hagiographer accordingly devotes considerable space to praising him, showing his authority to believers and his firmness to the emperor, as when

---

[339] Auzépy 1990. This text was also discussed by Loparev 1910: 47–55; Mango 1959: 116–18.
[340] Auzépy 1990: 460 and 466–72; Kazhdan and Talbot 1991: 393–94; Auzépy 1999: 193–94 and 298–300 (on the relationship with the *vita* of Stephanos the Younger); Brubaker 1999b; Brubaker and Haldon 2001: 219–20.
[341] Lauritzen 2017.

Germanos gathers the people together at Hagia Sophia and incites them against the imperial iconoclastic policy.[342] By this means, the author sought to create a reading with a contemporary perspective on these past events, and there can be no doubt that passages that treat the differences between the patriarch and imperial power that would finally lead to his overthrow are perfectly valid for both Germanos and Ignatios. (It should be remembered that if Leon III had the help of Anastasios as his henchman and accomplice, Michael III had that of Bardas.) After the patriarch opposed the imperial will and aroused the emperor's anger, he was subjected to ambushes such as those plotted by Herod against St John the Baptist.[343]

The veneration of the ten martyrs did not catch on in any case with the Stoudites, either due to its considerable pro-patriarchal bias or because of its lack of direct involvement in the interests of the Stoudite confederation. The Stoudite *menologion* for the month of August (ms. *Vaticanus Gr.* 1671) therefore omits this celebration,[344] and the *synaxaria* of Stoudite tradition, like the *Synaxarion Evergetis*, also fail to commemorate the *inventio* of these relics.[345] In fact, the centre of the whole hagiographical composition is the patriarchate as an institution about which the narrative development revolves. Worldly power appears as a counterpoint and progressively loses importance: once the confrontation with Germanos, by means of which the latter was strengthened morally and socially, is over and the emperor has played his role as the villain condemning the martyrs to death, he disappears and is not mentioned again. The result is a concentration on the patriarchate and Ignatios, to the greater glory of whom the text was written. Indeed, despite the fact that the discovery occurred under an Orthodox emperor, and despite the full pageantry given to the solemn burial of the relics, Basileios did not take sides in these celebrations, and the final chapters are exclusively about Ignatios. It was he who had the prophetic dreams and who administered and valued the relics. It was also Ignatios who was the blessed with the prodigious ending of natural disasters as he was speaking about the ten martyrs in Hagia Sophia.[346] It is also worth noting the similarity of this miracle with the

---

[342] *Acta of the Ten martyrs* 440F-41A.
[343] *Acta of the Ten martyrs* 440E: Ἐπὶ τούτοις πάνυ χολάσας ὁ τύραννος, ἐνεῖχε τῷ μακαρίῳ Γερμανῷ, ὥς ποτε Ἡρώδης τῷ προδρόμῳ, καὶ ἐν κρυφῇ τοῦτον παγιδεῦσαι ἐνήδρευεν, ἵνα ὡς φρατριαστήν, καὶ οὐχ' ὡς ὁμολογητὴν αὐτὸν ἐξωθήσῃ τοῦ θρόνου.
[344] Ehrhard 1936–1939: vol. I, 673–76.   [345] *Synaxarion Evergetis* II, 240–42.
[346] *Acta of the Ten Martyrs* 446F: Παράδοξον δὲ τεράστιον κατ' αὐτὴν τὴν ὥραν γεγένηται ... μετὰ τῆς αἰτήσεως, ὁ μὲν φοβερὸς κλόνος τῆς γῆς κατεπαύθη παραχρῆμα· ὁ δὲ σφοδρότατος χειμὼν ἀνεστάλη.

one which, according to Michael Monachos and Niketas David, was performed by Ignatios immediately after his death, when a terrible storm prevented his funeral, but he made it die down. Finally, the hagiographer omits any reference to the first patriarchate of Photios, giving the impression that from the death of Methodios to the reign of Basileios I, the only patriarch during the whole time was Ignatios.[347]

But who was the hagiographer? The text had been transmitted as anonymous, although it is clearly by a contemporary who lived through the earthquake of January 869 and shortly afterwards wrote the piece during the second patriarchate of Ignatios.[348] It has been proposed that Ignatios himself commissioned it.[349] The author is certainly part of the patriarch's circle and enjoys a close relationship with him; he does not hesitate to reproduce two dialogues of Ignatios, one with the archdeacon Leon and the other with the *skeuophylax* Ioseph.[350] Leon is the first person the patriarch tells of the miraculous appearances; he also asks him about the existence in Constantinople of a monastery dedicated to St Aninas. Leon can confirm that the place exists, but knows nothing of the martyrs who may lie there. It is Ioseph who provides the missing information, and as he has venerated them personally, his testimony is invaluable.[351] One of these two persons has long been thought to be the author of the work.[352]

We know little of this Leon, who in the final third of the ninth century held the post of archdeacon. The surviving seals indicate that he also was a *gerokomos*, that is, he ran a hospice for the elderly (*gerokomeion*)[353] and was perhaps the archdeacon to whom the epistle sent in 878 by the monk Theodosios was addressed, which would mean that he came from southern Italy or held a post there.[354] This Leon should not be confused with the deacon of the same name who took part in the Ignatian Council of 869/ 870. The latter, having been ordained by Methodios, became a follower of Photios, which meant that during the second session (7 October 869) the

---

[347] *Acta of the Ten Martyrs* 445B: εὐσεβῶν δὲ βασιλέων καὶ ἀρχιερέων τιμίων τὸν θρόνον ἀνεπιλήπτως ἰθυνόντων, ψήφῳ θείᾳ ἐγχειρίζεται τὰ τῆς ἀρχιερωσύνης πηδάλια Ἰγνάτιος ὁ μακαριώτατος καὶ θεοφιλέστατος, μετὰ τὴν ἔνθεον κοίμησιν τοῦ ὁσίου καὶ ὁμολογητοῦ καὶ τῆς ἀληθείας προμάχου Μεθοδίου, ἐπὶ τῆς εὐτυχοῦς βασιλείας τοῦ ὀρθοδόξου καὶ εὐσεβοῦς Βασιλείου, συνέβη ... σεισμὸν γενέσθαι σφοδρότατον.
[348] *Acta of the Ten Martyrs* 445; Ševčenko 1977a: 114, n. 6.   [349] Auzépy 1990: 467.
[350] *Acta of the Ten Martyrs* 446D–E and 447A. On the archdeacon Leon, see *PmbZ* # 24319. For the *skeuophylax* Ioseph, see *PmbZ* # 3454 and 23510.
[351] *Acta of the Ten Martyrs* 446E.   [352] Ostrogorsky 1930: 241, n. 1 first proposed it
[353] Zacos and Nesbitt 1984: vol. II, nr. 833: Λέοντι βασιλικῷ ἀρχιδιακόνῳ καὶ γηροκόμῳ. Cf. Leontaritou 1996: 97 (nr. 75); 121 (nr. 8); 140 (nr. 6). See *PmbZ* # 4513 and 24348.
[354] Lavagnini 1959–1960: 276; Rognoni 2010. On Theodosios Monachos, see *PmbZ* # 27892. For the Leon recipient of this epistle, see *PmbZ* # 24330.

penitence of being suspended from his post until Christmas Day was imposed on him.[355]

We have more information about the *skeuophylax* Ioseph, a disciple of Gregorios Dekapolites and an important writer better known as Ioseph Hymnographos.[356] Ioseph's production consists mainly of liturgical poems, many of which are dedicated to iconoclast confessors[357] and to the archangel Michael.[358] He scarcely seems to have written longer prose texts, with the possible exception of the double encomium in honour of the Apostle St Bartholomew (*BHG* 232 and 232b) some manuscripts attribute to him[359] and the *vita* of Ioannes of Galatia that survives in a Georgian version. Indeed, the account of the miraculous discovery of the relics of the Early Christian saint Sergios by Ioannes during the same period has interesting similarities to this text, since Sergios' relics too had also been forgotten and buried by the ungodly for many years without being venerated.[360] The important role Ioseph plays in the *Passio et inventio X martyrum Constantinopolitanorum* suggests that he wished to record his participation in these events: not only did he inform Ignatios precisely of the location of the monastery of Aninas and the saints who rested there, but he also played an active part in the exhumation. Pious men and monks had descended to seek them, but the martyrs demanded that Ioseph bring up the relics of their.[361]

The excessively laudatory treatment given to Ioseph[362] makes it hard to believe that he is the author of the piece. The humility of Byzantine monks led them to portray themselves in a much more modest way. It appears instead that the writer wished to praise Ioseph openly to gain his sympathy and that of his patron, the patriarch Ignatios. On the other hand, it is unlikely that, if Ioseph described the finding of the relics of the martyrs, he

---

[355] Mansi XVI, 42f.; *Council of Constantinople (869/870)*, 80; *PmbZ* # 24319; Hergenröther 1867–1869: vol. II, 84.
[356] *PmbZ* # 3454 and # 23510; *PBE* I: Ioseph 12; Van de Vrost 1920; Colonna 1953; Costa-Louillet 1957: 812–23. See Section 3.2.2.a.
[357] Tomadakes 1971a; Stiernon 1973: 243–66; Kazhdan 1999: 270–71. See Chapter 3.
[358] Ioseph Hym., *Kanones* 103–71.
[359] These are the codices *Vaticanus Gr.* 984 (a. 1354, a palimpsest, with a ninth-century *scriptura inferior*); *Vaticanus Gr.* 1667 (tenth century); *Parisinus Gr.* 1219 (eleventh century); *Vaticanus Gr.* 655 (sixteenth century). Translation into Latin in *PG* 105,1421–26; Stiernon 1973: 259.
[360] Kekelidze 1965: 66; Krausmüller 2019:56–60.
[361] *Acta of the Ten Martyrs* 447A. Krausmüller 2019: 53–56.
[362] *Acta of the Ten Martyrs* 446E: Ἰωσὴφ ὁ εὐλαβέστατος μοναχός, καὶ τῆς μεγάλης ἐκκλησίας τὴν φροντίδα ἀναδεδεγμένος τῶν ἱερῶν κειμηλίων; 447A: τὸν εὐλαβέστατον σκευοφύλακα Ἰωσὴφ ... ὡς εὐλαβείᾳ πολλῇ ὑπερκείμενον.

did not dedicate a liturgical hymn for their commemoration,[363] especially when we know that the earthquakes he experienced throughout his life – perhaps that of 869 in particular? – and the panic they generated constituted a reason for producing a poem. The *Canon in terrae motus periculo* represents an impassioned plea to God to have mercy, to take pity on men and to prevent earthquakes, or at least to end them immediately once they begin, so as to avoid calamities. The whole piece, which is quite monotonous, is an entreaty to God to be merciful and curb his anger towards men.[364]

Although these considerations suggest that Ioseph was not the author of this *Passio*, the *skeuophylax* Ioseph's knowledge of the monastery and his contemplation of the martyrs years before, when the church collapsed during the time of Theophilos,[365] neatly coincide with Ioseph Hymnographos' brief stay with his master Gregorios Dekapolites in the monastery of St Antipas near that of St Mokios, in the same area where the monastery of Aninas stood.[366] At the moment, therefore, we have no firm evidence to declare with any confidence that the archdeacon Leon, informed in detail by Ioseph, wrote the account of the ten martyrs of Constantinople, although this seems more than likely.

(b) Lazaros the Painter

Among the New Martyrs of iconoclasm, saints such as Lazaros the Painter stand out; his sanctification cannot be separated from his membership of the Ignatian party. The polarisation of the post-iconoclast Byzantine Church between the followers of Photios and the defenders of Ignatios had a determinant effect of praising members of both groups as confessors of icons. Lazaros was a monk of Khazar origin with outstanding pictorial abilities.[367] A sympathiser of the cause of Ignatios, he was sent to Rome in 855 to persuade Pope Benedict III to depose Gregorios Asbestas.[368] Despite the magnificent gifts Lazaros brought, the Pope made no

---

[363] As he seems to have done with St Eudokimos, in whose honour Ioseph Hymnographos composed a *kanon*, see Tomadakes 1971a: 182, nr. 364; *Menaion* VI: 271–76. As Loparev suggests, Ioseph might be the monk (*PmbZ* # 3452) who helped Eudokia, the mother of Eudokimos, to recover his body, see *Vita of Eudokimos* 19,5–30; 21,8–9; *Vita of Eudokimos by Konstantinos Akropolites* 15–16, 215,33–17,10; *Vita of Eudokimos* (*BHG* 607e) 231,18–26 and 231,36–232,1.
[364] Tomadakes 1971a: 119, nr. 62; Latin translation in *PG* 105, 1416–21. In the acrostic we read: Ὦ Χριστὲ τῆς γῆς τὸν κλόνον παῦσον τάχος Ἰωσήφ.
[365] *Acta of the Ten Martyrs* 446E.
[366] *Vita of Ioseph Hymnographos by Theophanes* 5. For the location of Antipas, see Janin 1969: 38.
[367] *PmbZ* # 4234; *PBE* I: Lazaros 2; Cicognara 1807; Hatlie 2007a: 404–6; Calahorra Bartolomé 2018.
[368] *Liber pontificalis* II, 147; Dvornik 1948: 19 and 25; Davis 1995: 186; *Regestes*, nr. 448.

declaration to this effect and Lazaros had to lead a second embassy at some point after 865, when Pope Nicholas I sent an epistle to Michael III in which he recognised Lazaros (whom he refers to as presbyteros and monk) as loyal to Ignatios.[369] A surviving missive that denounces the difficulties a certain Georgios caused his mission may be from Lazaros.[370] The letter is dated winter 870. Around this time, or perhaps a little later, Lazaros died in Rome.

Both Lazaros' patron Ignatios and his co-religionists must have seen in him a perfect opportunity to give their faction the iconodule record that would legitimate their power. The body of Lazaros was brought to Constantinople and buried at the monastery of Evandros across the Golden Horn in Galata, where his memory was celebrated liturgically on 17 November every year. According to the *Synaxarion*, this monastery was founded before 811 by the domestic of the *scholae* Petros Patrikios, who was honoured there each year on 1 July.[371] Indeed, Stylianos of Neocaesarea is the first to call Lazaros *Homologetes* (confessor).[372] During the second patriarchate of Ignatios, the legend of Lazaros was encouraged with a double aim: making it easier to justify his veneration and serving the interest of the patriarch Ignatios more efficiently. Although the entry in the *Synaxarion of Constantinople* offers few details, therefore, it insists both on the torture Lazaros suffered for defending images and on his two embassies in Rome.[373] It is likely that during the promotion of this new cult the followers of Ignatios told pious stories, subsequently gathered together by tenth-century historians. These tales offered more details of the tortures inflicted on Lazaros and the virtues that justified his sanctification.[374] According to Theophanes Continuatus, the monk continued to paint icons despite the prohibition decreed by Emperor Theophilos. Even after his imprisonment, Lazaros persevered with his creation of saints' images, which led to his being brutally condemned and his hands burnt with red-hot iron to prevent him from painting again. Through the mediation of

---

[369] *MGH, epist.* VI, *Nicolai epist.*, nr. 88, p. 482,5f. (= Mansi xv, 211A): *Lazarus presbyter et monachus, qui dicitur Chazaris.*

[370] Raasted 1981; *PmbZ* # 4235.

[371] *SynaxCP* 792,35–94,3. On Petros Patrikios, see *PmbZ* # 6046; *PBE* I: Petros 148. His liturgical figure is in fact the result of the combination of the domestic of the *scholae* with a disciple of St Ioannikios, also named Petros, who after consolidating the monastic life of this foundation was celebrated annually by the monks, see Wortley 1980: 555–57. On the monastery of Evandros, see Janin 1969: 114; Ruggieri 1991: 190.

[372] Mansi xvi, 428C.   [373] *SynaxCP* 231,9–34,7 (17 November).

[374] Theoph. Cont. III, 13; Skylitzes 60,20–61,45; Kedrenos II 113,6–14,7; Zonaras XV 27,6–10, 364,16–65,11. These sources have been analysed by Brubaker and Haldon 2001: 72–73; Brubaker and Haldon 2011: 427–28; Brubaker 2012: 121–22.

Empress Theodora, Lazaros was freed and took refuge at the monastery of the Prodromos tou Phoberou, where he painted an icon of John the Baptist that performed healing miracles.[375] No less miraculous is the production by this monk (according to Theophanes Continuatus) of the icon of Christ at the Chalke Gate after the death of Theophilos,[376] as the injuries to his hands ought to have prevented him from painting again. The historian even links Lazaros with Empress Theodora: when she sought his support to achieve her husband's absolution, the painter monk replied that God in his justice forgot neither the suffering withstood in his name nor the emperor's hate.

This tradition, which gives particular importance to Theodora and helped consolidate the model of holiness of the restoring empress, originated during the second patriarchate of Ignatios, who tried to defend and promote the image of Empress Theodora despite the fact that she had been ostracised. The oral legends that were spread also included the one of the restoration of the icon of the Christ of the Chalke Gate by Lazaros. This not only shows the piety of the painter-monk but also directly linked (once again) the Ignatians with the martyrs of the First Iconoclasm. The saints who had given their lives to defend the image were not only vindicated and venerated by the circle of the patriarch Ignatios, but one of their members – someone deeply involved in the dispute with Photios – had also been in charge of restoring the icon from the Chalke Gate in order to do justice to these martyrs and promote Ignatios' cause. Even more meaningful in this context is the revelation of the thirteenth-century pilgrim Anthony of Novgorod,[377] according to whom Lazaros took part in the decoration of the apse of Hagia Sophia, the inauguration of which was used by Photios as a key element in his official propaganda.

5.3 Conclusions

This chapter has revealed the attitude of the patriarch Ignatios and those who surrounded him towards literature in general and images in particular. Despite Ignatios' apparent initial lack of interest in written expression, the patriarchate of Constantinople as an institution was still obliged to administer existing literature regarding the iconoclast dispute. His first patriarchate (847–858) saw the repatriation of the head of St John the Baptist from Komana and the creation of a text to transmit these events and the decisive

---

[375] On the monastery of the Prodromos tou Phoberou, see Janin 1954: 70–3; Cormack 1977a: 41.
[376] Mango 1959: 125–26.   [377] Mango and Hawkins 1965: 144–45.

part the patriarch played in them. The changes in the imperial household and the arrival of Photios radically changed the Byzantines' attitude to recent history due to his vindication of a past as a confessor hero. This situation and the serious difficulties Ignatios faced in defending his right to the title of patriarch meant that active propagandising patronage of iconodule texts could be apparent only after his return to the patriarchal throne of Constantinople (867–877). In contrast to Photios, Ignatios could not allege that he had played a part in the conflict. His official biographer Niketas David Paphlagon can only adduce that during the persecution Ignatios fasted and mortified the flesh, that he baptised children and that he occasionally lodged defenders of icons.[378] For this reason, during his second patriarchate, he had collaborators interested in (re)writing the parts of the Second Iconoclasm that had not been appropriated by Photios, such as the *vitae* of the Stoudite hegoumenoi or of marginal saints such as Lazaros the Painter and Antonios the Younger,[379] intimately linked to Petronas.

Due to a lack of charisma and training or an inability to administer the human resources at his disposal, the patriarch Ignatios did not create as powerful and united a literary circle as the other leaders discussed. However, he had renowned men of letters espousing his cause, such as Metrophanes of Smyrna and Michael Monachos, who were accompanied by anonymous writers including the individual responsible for the *Passio et inventio X martyrum Constantinopolitanorum*, in their common objective of vindicating Ignatios. To do so, they did not hesitate to link him to the martyrs of the First Iconoclasm, who had confronted Emperor Leon III, and to the early iconoclasts now anathematised at the anti-Photian Council of 869/870 and included in the *Synodikon of Orthodoxy*.[380]

To judge by its results, this propaganda was successful, since a work such as the *Synodicon vetus* echoes its discourse. The *Synodicon vetus* aspires to be an official and precise catalogue of all the Councils celebrated by the Church until the year 887, despite the pro-Ignatian sectarianism of its compiler. He goes as far as to invent details or add data that are not always historical,[381] although he uses some reliable sources, such as the *Ecclesiastical Histories* of Eusebios, Socrates, etc. To be precise, for the iconoclast period (chs. 147–56) this author mainly follows the Chronicle of Theophanes the Confessor.[382] If we leave to one side the problem of the

---

[378] *Vita of Ignatios* 13–14.
[379] Concerning this saint, see *PmbZ* # 534; *PBE* I: Antonios 12. His *vita* has come down to us in three separate fragments, see Section 4.2.
[380] Lauritzen 2017.   [381] *Synodicon vetus*, p. xv; Van Dieten 1980/1982.
[382] Markopoulos 1978: 111.

historicity of the information he cites, the chapters including the synods held during the patriarchates of Ignatios and Photios are very significant.[383] One can see in them the typically hagiographical manner in which the author portrays Ignatios, the negative image he offers of Photios as his adversary and the narrative of the suffering of the patriarch Ignatios, which is characteristic of that faced by iconodule confessors during the Second Iconoclasm.

---

[383] *Synodicon vetus* 132–38 (chs. 157–62).

CHAPTER 6

The Photian Milieu
Rewriting and Updating Iconodule Literature

As seen in Chapter 5, Photios rose to the patriarchate apparently thanks to the will of the young Emperor Michael III and his advisers, rather than to a desire for change emanating from the Church. In its early period, the Ignatian patriarchate was weak and its links with the Roman Pope far from satisfactory. This led to unease in many ecclesiastical sectors, which saw in the new imperial interference not only an expression of the views of a group hostile to the current patriarch but also a transgression of canonical tradition and an insult to the dignity of the legitimate patriarch Ignatios and by extension all those he represented. Photios' need to respond to criticisms of being an upstart, to persuade the members of the Church that he was not the emperor's puppet and to strengthen his leadership by giving himself a legitimacy he in fact lacked, obliged him to deploy all kinds of dialectical and propaganda resources adapted to his individual interlocutors. In regard to the literature on iconoclasm, Photios and his followers appropriated this identity legacy to present themselves as the legitimate heirs of the confessors who confronted iconoclast heresy and as the true instigators of its defeat and the Triumph of Orthodoxy. By various means, they linked themselves directly to many of these New Martyrs and retold their stories, giving them a double reading that updated the iconoclast conflict in the light of the new controversy that was shaking the Church and rewriting them from a different perspective.

6.1 The Inevitable Topicality of Iconoclasm

The establishment of an annual liturgical celebration to commemorate the defeat of iconoclasm, which consisted of a ceremonial procession through the streets of Constantinople in which all the institutions of the empire took part, together with a Eucharist in which the symbol of the faith and the anathemas against the main iconoclast leaders were publicly proclaimed,[1] amounted to a periodic revival of the iconoclastic conflict. Although there may initially have been a danger of the supporters of heresy forming a common front with the aim of checking the iconodule advance, it was progressively warded off and finally eliminated in such a way that the multiple condemnations of iconoclasm that recur throughout the second half of the ninth century have a more ideological than real meaning. They contribute to the creation of the new imperial discourse of the Macedonian dynasty and its propaganda[2] but also help reaffirm the legitimacy of the patriarch who again sanctions these anathemas. Such is the case of Photios, whose attacks on iconoclasm constitute more an argumentative resource than a genuinely controversial perspective.[3] Authors such as Dvornik or Schreiner believed that the iconoclast party must have been a real threat, which led Photios to try to neutralise it by all possible means.[4] More accepted is the idea developed by Mango, that this risk did not exist and was only one of the pillars on which the patriarch established his power and legitimated his governance.[5]

Iconoclasm continued to be a subject for debate at all councils of the second half of the ninth century. After two Photian synods limited to Constantinople, Michael III called the synod of 860/861 to ratify the condemnation of iconoclast heresy; we assume that he did so at the request of the patriarch Photios. This is shown by the answer offered by the Pope,[6] the comment included by Anastasius the Librarian in his *Liber Pontificalis*[7] and the contemporary discussion in the *Synodicon vetus* of this council, which states that Photios' objective was to completely eradicate iconoclasm while also condemning Ignatios.[8] Photios was particularly proactive in his implementation of an iconodule policy, encouraging the creation of icons or mosaics with images of the saints, as, for example, the apse mosaic of Our Lady at Hagia Sophia, which was solemnly inaugurated in 867 in the presence of Emperor Michael III and Caesar Basileios, already associated

---

[1] On the feast day of the Sunday of Orthodoxy and its creation, see Gouillard's study in *Synodikon of Orthodoxy*. Cf. *Regestes*, nr. 418. The ceremonial, with the procession from the church of Blachernai to Hagia Sophia, where the patriarch held a banquet in the *sekreton*, is detailed in the *Kletorologion* of Philotheos (Sept. 899), see Bury 1911; Oikonomides 1972: 65–235, esp. 165–66; *De ceremoniis* I, 156–60, 190–1 and II, 551–52; *Narratio historica in festum restitutionis imaginum* 715–43; Afinogenov 1999a.
[2] Speck 1984.   [3] Gouillard 1961a; Thümmel 1981; Rochow 1983.
[4] Dvornik 1953; Schreiner 1988: 400–2; Kaplan 1997: 74–80. The traditional vision of Photios' relationship with images was defined by Hergenröther 1867–69: vol. III, 562–67.
[5] Mango 1977.
[6] *MGH, epistolae* VI, 433ff.; cf. Phot., *epist.* 290,359–65. On this synod, see *Regestes*, nrs. 467 and 468; Dvornik 1948: 70–90; 1958: 21–25.
[7] *Liber Pontificalis* II, 154ff.; Neil 2006: 115–17.   [8] *Synodicon vetus* 134.

with the throne.⁹ Also in the summer of 867, Michael III and Basileios, along with Photios, held a synod in the church of the Holy Apostles that reprobated and deposed Pope Nicholas and included a condemnation of iconoclasm.¹⁰ The end of the synod was marked by the proclamation of a homily to celebrate this new repudiation of iconoclasm entitled 'Of the same [Patriarch Photios], Homily delivered from the Ambo of Hagia Sophia, when the triumph over all the heresies was proclaimed by our orthodox and great Emperors, Michael and Basil'.¹¹

Ignatios shared this concern; it should not be forgotten that the Council of 869 that he presided over in Constantinople at the church of Hagia Sophia not only reprobated Photios and his followers but also validated anew the canons issued at the Second Council of Nicaea regarding the theology of images and once more anathematised iconoclast heretics by name, both those who were alive (Theodoros Krithinos, a certain Paulos, Theodoros Gastes, Stephanos Molites and Leon Laloudios) and the iconoclast leaders who were already dead (such as Konstantinos V and Ioannes Grammatikos).¹² Unsurprisingly, this was one of the main concerns of the synod of 843 promoted by Theodora, as is apparent from the *Horos* of this synod.¹³ But the new anti-iconoclast anathema was also accompanied by the seventh canon of the council, which encouraged the production of icons only by those within the Church. This limitation applied to individuals such as Photios and his supporters, who had been anathematised, thus denying the alleged Photian restoration of images, as well as identifying the condemned Photians with iconoclasts.¹⁴

Ten years later, after Ignatios had died, the great Photian council of 879/880 ratified the success of the ecclesiastical policies of Photios and also offered the appropriate condemnations of iconoclasm, since it was here that the decisions of the Second Council of Nicaea (787) were ratified.¹⁵ Despite the significant differences that existed between the two sees, the patriarch's negotiations with Rome allowed this restoration council to name him 'supreme minister' and yielded the West's official recognition

---

⁹ Dvornik 1935; Mango 1997: 140. On the mosaic of Our Lady at Hagia Sophia, see Mango and Hawkins 1965: 115–51; Oikonomides 1985.
¹⁰ We know little of this synod, see *Regestes*, nr. 482; Dvornik 1948: 120–31; Sansterre 1973.
¹¹ Phot., *Homily* XVIII, trans. Mango 297–315; Dvornik 1953: 93–96.
¹² Stephanou 1973; Perrone 1990; Herbers 2008; Lauritzen 2017. For this new anathema, see Mansi XVI, 389C–D; Gouillard 1961a: 387ff.; Mango 1977: 135. See Section 5.1.
¹³ *Synodikon of the Orthodoxy*, Appendix 1, 296,104.
¹⁴ Mansi XVI, 402ff., 164; Dvornik 1953: 84.
¹⁵ It was during the fifth session (26 January 880), see Mansi XVII, 493–512; Dvornik 1948: 192–94.

of the second meeting at Nicaea as the seventh oecumenical council.[16] In this way, Photios established a comparison between himself and his predecessor Tarasios and had his alleged (i.e., anachronistic) success acknowledged in the fight to restore images.

6.2 Iconoclasm in the Work of the Patriarch Photios

Photios' personal interest in these condemnations of iconoclasm was corroborated by his composition of an apologetic tract on the theology of icons.[17] This brief treatise shows clear continuity with the thought of the patriarch Nikephoros and that of Theodoros Stoudites, who developed the positions defined in the minutes of the Second Council of Nicaea (787). Photios goes still further, however, and develops the postulates on the theory of images after Aristotle in a manner parallel to the Neoplatonic thought developed by Ioannes Damaskenos.[18] He had similar influence on the wording of chapter 22 regarding iconoclasm of the *Panoplia dogmatica* by Euthymios Zigabenos.[19] Although Photios' reaction to a heresy that had already been defeated is striking and may seem unnecessary, his example was imitated by his closest followers, such as Arethas, the future bishop of Caesarea, who similarly wrote a treatise *Against Iconoclasts* (*Pros eikonomachous*). The text is intended for the *asekretis* Nikolaos, and in it Arethas compares the different ethnic representations of Christ with the different languages and alphabets in which the Scriptures are written. The difference is that, compared with the texts, the images need no translation.[20] The hostile references to iconoclasts that Arethas includes elsewhere in his work,[21] together with the writing of this treatise, have led some scholars to take these as signs of the reality of this vision of Christianity as late as the tenth century.[22]

What is certain is that iconoclast doctrine is a recurrent theme in the work of the patriarch, revealing that one of Photios' obsessions was portraying himself as the victor over iconoclasm. Not only did he give theological content to his opposition to this heresy (in his *Amphilochia* and *Homilies*), but he also

---

[16] For the Council of 879/880, cf. Hergenröther 1867–1869: vol. II, 379–551; Grumel 1930; 1938: 357–72; 1967: 336–37; Jugie 1938; Haugh 1975: 123–30; Meijer 1975; Boojamra 1982; Gallagher 2007; Troianos 2012: 149–50.
[17] Thümmel 1981; 1983.
[18] On Photios' interest in ancient philosophy, see Ronconi 2011 with previous bibliography.
[19] Barber 2007: 151–56.
[20] Dvornik 1953: 96–97; Crostini 2013: 123;. On the *asekretis* Nikolaos, see *PmbZ* # 25938. He was son of Gabriel, see *PmbZ* # 22021. Concerning Arethas of Caesarea, see *PmbZ* # 20554; Flusin 2017.
[21] Westerink, *Arethae Scripta minora* I, 101, 114 and 115.   [22] Laourdas 1954; Rochow 1983: 102.

sponsored the representation of Christ, the Virgin and the saints in images. At the same time he used his letters to build up a group awareness in his followers supported by the principles of orthodox resistance used by Theodoros Stoudites. By means of this process, in which literature plays a vital role, as analysed in this chapter, Photios managed to set himself up as the victor over iconoclasm and the new patron of the arts, as he himself affirms in the inauguration of the mosaic of the Virgin of the apse of Hagia Sophia on 29 March 867: 'If one called this day the beginning and day of Orthodoxy (lest I say something excessive), one would not be far wrong. For though the time is short since the pride of the iconoclastic heresy has been reduced ... this too is our ornament.'[23] In addition, at the beginning of the same sermon, Photios attributes the initiative for suppressing of iconoclasm to himself: 'For even if it is we who have sown and first ploughed with much toil the fallow land, yet that too was not independent of imperial zeal and co-operation.'[24]

The presence of discussion of iconoclasm in the patriarch's homilies was analysed in detail by Dvornik in a classic article.[25] In a desire to link the genre of homilies to the daily ups and downs of the Church, Photios devoted two compositions to the analysis of the Arian heresy and its similarities to iconoclasm (*Homilies* XV and XVI) and a third to the icon of the Theotokos of Hagia Sophia (*Homily* XVII), in which he does not hesitate to tackle the theology of icons, to celebrate the Triumph of Orthodoxy and to attack the iconoclast ideas 'of the Isaurians'.[26] The figure of the patriarch Ioannes Grammatikos attracts the full attention of Photios, who draws up a historical portrait of him in an attempt to understand the course of his life. According to Photios, Ioannes was an Orthodox young man who venerated images and even learnt the technique of painting icons[27] but fell into heresy. Illness led him to reflect, and Ioannes wrote a piece of repentance in addition to approaching the iconodule patriarch Nikephoros. Despite this, he not only ended up repeating his error but even became the leader of iconoclasm.[28] The

---

[23] Phot., *Homily* XVII, 168: Ταύτην τὴν ἡμέραν εἴ τις ὀρθοδοξίας ἀρχὴν καὶ ἡμέραν, ἵνα μηδὲν ὑπέρογκον εἴπω, καλέσειεν, οὐκ ἂν ἁμάρτοι τοῦ δέοντος· καὶ γάρ, εἰ καὶ βραχὺς ὁ χρόνος, ἐξ οὗ τῆς εἰκονομαχικῆς αἱρέσεως ἀπηθαλώθη ... ἐμὸν καὶ τοῦτο καλλώπισμα, trans. Mango 291. Cf. also Mango 1997: 140.

[24] Phot., *Homily* XVII, 165, trans. Mango 287; *Synodikon of Orthodoxy* 137–38.

[25] Dvornik 1953: 87–92. To this pioneering work on the patriarch's sermons should be added Mango, *The Homilies of Photius*, especially pp. 239–43, 264–66, 282–85, 289–91, 294–95; Jenkins and Mango 1956; Mango and Hawkins 1965; Tsironis 1998: 311–12; Bevegni 1999; Kazhdan 2006: 31–34.

[26] Phot., *Homilies* XV–XVII, 139–72; trans. Mango 244–96. See also Kustas 1964; Cameron 1994.

[27] Phot., *Homily* XV, 140.25–27.

[28] On the historical figure of Ioannes Grammatikos, see *PmbZ* #3199 and #3304. See Introduction.

Tenth Homily, delivered ca. 864, is dedicated to the inauguration and refurbishment of the palatine church of Pharos, the flagship of the iconodule renovation. Not only was it full of icons and mosaics, it had also been erected on the site of an iconoclast church built under Konstantinos V.[29]

Opposition to iconoclasm also left its mark on Photios' *Bibliotheca*, in which he reviews over 300 classical texts, none of them written by an iconoclast author.[30] On the contrary, the patriarch includes in it writers who could be used to defend icons,[31] condemns the iconoclastic interpretation of the doctrine of Pseudo-Leukios Charinos[32] and in *codex* 67 repeats the censure of Konstantinos Kopronymos for his impiety that included the chronicle of Sergios the Confessor.

The same is true of the *Amphilochia*, a collection of brief treatises in the form of *erotapokriseis* (question-answer) on varied matters generally of a theological or philosophical nature, which Photios dedicated to his good friend Amphilochios, the bishop of Kyzikos between 863 and 877 and later the bishop of Nicaea.[33] Due to the fact that almost half of the corpus of the private letters of Photios was included in the *Amphilochia*, the two corpora have been transmitted and edited together. Thanks to the study of Louth, which takes a detailed look at the sources and influences on the patriarch's writing, we can recognize the main post-Chalcedonian Christological postulates, as well as the doctrines regarding the Trinity and the incarnation of the Son that appear in the *Amphilochia*.[34] In addition to including an explicit reference to the work against iconoclasts written by the patriarch himself,[35] this collection includes many of the answers given by Photios in letters to friends or ecclesiastics regarding difficulties brought to light by iconoclast propaganda and for which no universally valid solution had been found. A later section devoted to the collection of letters will analyse the role of iconoclasm as a structuring element of Photios' personal relations with his followers.[36] An example is

---

[29] Janin 1969: 232–36; Ruggieri 1991: 162 and 198–99; Jenkins and Mango 1956; Connor 2016: 127–36.
[30] Treadgold 1980: 26–27 on the matter of icons. For the composition of the *Bibliotheca* and its dating see Ronconi 2015b with abundant previous bibliography.
[31] Phot., *Bibliot.*, cod. 29, 6a; cod. 52, 13a: cod. 110, 89b; cod. 119, 93b; cod. 160, 103a.
[32] Phot., *Bibliot.*, cod. 114, 91a, lines 4–5.
[33] On Amphilochios of Kyzikos, see *PmbZ* # 223 and # 20278; *PBE* I: Amphilochios 1. Most of Photios' letters to him discuss theological matters, see Phot., *epist.* 137, 162, 163, 178, 198, 207 and 253.
[34] Louth 2006. See also Leserri 2006; 2007. [35] Phot., *Amph.* 1,925–27.
[36] See Section 6.2.3. The main *Amphilochia* dealing with the subject of images are *Amph.* 87: Διὰ τί βοῶν καὶ λεόντων καὶ ἀετῶν καὶ ἀνθρώπων μορφαῖς αἱ τῶν χερουβὶμ ὄψεις τοῖς προφήταις ἐδείκνυντο = *epist.* 157; *Amph.* 111: Τὰ εἴδωλα τῶν ἐθνῶν ἀργύριον καὶ χρυσίον, ἔργα χειρῶν

epist. 37 and 38, in which he attacks iconoclasm as a response to the concerns raised by the *spatharios* Ioannes Chrysocheir,[37] and which were included in the *Amphilochia* as numbers 196 and 197 and entitled Τῷ αὐτῷ περὶ εἰκόνων. The first epistle affirms that the Hellenes, the Jews, the Manicheans and all those who reject the images of Christ are accomplices of the iconoclasts. The second mentions the biblical figure Simon Magus and the Gnostic Carpocrates, who despite their impiety did not renounce the images of Christ,[38] meaning that iconoclasts are worse than they were.

Visual language is not neglected in Photian propaganda and its attempt to portray the patriarch as the victor over iconoclasm and the patron of images. This is made clear by the iconographical programme he designed for the church of Hagia Sophia after iconoclasm officially ended,[39] which was dominated by a mosaic in the apse of the exalted Virgin with the baby Jesus in her arms that he describes in *Homily* XVII.[40] In the north tympanum there was a reproduction of St Gregorios the Illuminator, the founder of the Armenian Church, whose relics had recently been miraculously located in Constantinople and given importance by Photios.[41] Not only public buildings, however, were used. The patronage of images developed by Photios also includes the illumination of manuscripts. We know that in order to fête Emperor Basileios, the patriarch also commissioned in about the year 880 the codex *Parisinus Gr.* 510, an illuminated manuscript of the homilies of Gregorios of Nazianzus.[42] This is an extraordinary artefact, with large miniatures and a meticulous technique that is very rare in medieval Greek manuscripts. Its large size shows that it was made to be exhibited rather than to be read. In the margins of the text of Gregorios of Nazianzus, *Parisinus Gr.* 510 develops a complex iconographical programme with a clear political aim that seeks to flatter Basileios and to build an ideology of its own for the Macedonian dynasty.

Another testimony to this private use of illuminations belongs a few years earlier, in 867, when some of the emperor's men confiscated a number of books from Photios, one of which stood out because it

---

ἀνθρώπων = *epist.* 214; *Amph.* 119 = *epist.* 249, sent to Emperor Basileios I in 873, see Laourdas 1950; *Amph.* 205: Περὶ διαμορφώσεως καὶ χαρακτῆρος τῶν ἁγίων εἰκόνων = *epist.* 65; *Amph.* 217: Περὶ διαφορᾶς εἰκόνων = *epist.* 134.

[37] On Ioannes Chrysocheir, see *PmbZ* # 3340; PBE I: Ioannes 448. For other recipients of *Amphilochia* dealing with iconoclasm, see Dvornik 1953: 86.
[38] Acts 8:13.   [39] Cormack 1977a; 1981; 1986; Brubaker 1999a: 236–67.
[40] On this mosaic, see Mango and Hawkins 1965; Oikonomides 1985: 111–15.
[41] Mango and Hawkins 1972: 38–39; Greenwood 2006a; 2006b; Lourié 2011; Dorfmann-Lazarev 2016.
[42] Brubaker 1985; 1999a: 201–38, 412–14.

contained a striking iconographical programme: a colour image accompanied each of the seven Acts of a synod held against Ignatios with an allusive text that attacked the ex-patriarch.[43] According to the author of the *Vita Ignatii*, the man commissioned to paint these images, Gregorios of Syracuse, had been a loyal friend of Photios.[44] If this book really existed, the way in which it identified the patriarch Ignatios with the iconoclasts in order to show him as a heretic, a second Simon Magus, the Antichrist or the Devil himself make us think of Photios as the intellectual author of this programme, with Gregorios Asbestas, metropolitan of Syracuse, as his accomplice and, in all likelihood, the book producer. This is particularly so, given that Photios' predecessor in the patriarchate, Methodios, was responsible for a similar iconographical cycle in which the iconoclast conflict was treated as a visual accompaniment to the text of the Psalms, although on that occasion to praise his predecessor, the patriarch Nikephoros, for defending Orthodoxy.[45] According to Niketas Paphlagon, Photios had two copies of this illuminated codex with the cycle of malicious miniatures that attacked, condemned and denigrated the patriarch Ignatios: one preserved in his private library and the other sent to the Frankish Emperor Louis II (846–879) along with other gifts intended to internationalise the conflict and pressure the Pope of Rome to recognise Photios as the legitimate patriarch and anathematise Ignatios.[46]

6.2.1 *Photios and the Iconodule Patriarchs: Tarasios, Nikephoros and Methodios*

Since the first defeat of iconoclasm, the praise of the patriarchs who faced heresy became a constant element that allowed the uniting of the orthodox party around an acknowledged leader whose example not only fostered piety but also constituted a model of behaviour to imitate, first in the resistance during the Second Iconoclasm and subsequently in the reaffirmation of the veneration of images after the triumph of 843. The vindication of the previous patriarchs also became part of the official propaganda of the patriarchate, since the new patriarch reaffirmed his

---

[43] Crostini 2013: 109–12; Mango 1997: 140.
[44] *Vita of Ignatios* 54, p. 80,14–34. On Gregorios Asbestas, the metropolitan of Syracuse to whom Photios sent epistles 112 and 257, see *PmbZ* # 2480 and # 22348; *PBE* I: Gregorios 26; Karlin-Hayter 1977; Prigent 2017: 159–63.
[45] These are the psalter Moskow GIM Khludov 129D, the *Parisinus Gr.* 20 (incomplete) and the *Pantokrator* 61, see Section 2.1.4.
[46] *Vita of Ignatios* 57,24–28; Crostini 2013: 111, n. 26.

legitimacy and strengthened his power through it. We have already examined the case of Methodios, who evoked the memory of Tarasios and Nikephoros to gather round him both the radicals who called for more severe treatment of iconoclasts and those in favour of less onerous solutions to reintegrate them into the Church.

Photios also converted the vindication of his predecessors into an ideological element of his patriarchate, since it was they who legitimated his own governance of the Church: Nikephoros and Tarasios both for having attained the patriarchal see while being simple laymen, like Photios himself, and Tarasios also for having been a direct relative. One major objection of Photios' detractors was that he was a layman raised to the patriarchate and therefore appointed in an irregular manner against the canons. His enemies referred to him as a 'half-Hellene' upstart and ridiculed the promotion of a layman to patriarch in only five days. (Recall that in order to be consecrated a patriarch on Christmas Day 858, Photios had to pass through all the stages of the ecclesiastical hierarchy. On five successive days, he was therefore named reader, sub-deacon, deacon, priest and bishop.) We find Photios' response to these objections in the missive he sent to Pope Nicholas in August/September 861 (*epist.* 290), in which he alleges that before him Paulos III (in 687), his great-uncle Tarasios (in 784) and Nikephoros (in 806) had attained the patriarchate as laymen and senior imperial officials (*protoasekretis*) but that what had been readily accepted then was now causing a scandal.[47] In fact, it appears that the followers of both parties were rather unstable and that the day-to-day situation in Constantinople was that the man holding power at each moment was followed in a somewhat acritical manner.[48]

The cultivation of the memory of Tarasios (who also was Photios' πατρόθειος or great-uncle)[49] and of Nikephoros is well established in Photios' collected letters, in which he claims to consider them points of reference for his generation[50] as well as champions of Orthodoxy.[51] His interest in the figure of Tarasios went further than a desire to identify himself with the patriarch who defeated iconoclasm and restored Orthodoxy by means of the Second Council of Nicaea, since he also saw

---

[47] Phot., *epist.* 290,154–71; Hergenröther 1867–1869: vol. I, 438–60; Dvornik 1948: 92–93; Konstantelos 1989/1991; Leserri 2005. See Chapter 5.
[48] Morris 1995: 11–15 and 90–93.
[49] Phot., *epist.* 2,265–67; 290,311; 291,362–63. For the correct interpretation of πατρόθειος as 'great-uncle' instead of '(first) uncle', see Mango 1997: 137.
[50] Phot., *epist.* 290,157–58: οἱ τῆς καθ' ἡμᾶς γενεᾶς ἀειφανεῖς λαμπτῆρες.
[51] Phot., *epist.* 114,2–3; *epist.* 290,156ff., 165–66 and 299–301.

him as an inspirational model for ecclesiastical matters: if Tarasios had to face the hatred of the Stoudites due to his allegedly illegal appointment, Photios similarly had to fight against the Ignatians. The surviving letter from Photios to Nikolaos, the hegoumenos of the monastery of St Tarasios where the remains of his great-uncle lay,[52] specifically reflects Photios' use of the figure of Tarasios to reaffirm himself as the legitimate patriarch during the years he was removed from the see of Constantinople (867–877). Likewise, the iconographic programme of Hagia Sophia, which represented in the south-east vestibule the patriarchs Germanos, Tarasios, Nikephoros and Methodios, must be related to Photios' activities.[53] This propaganda project was very successful, and in some later sources Photios was even renamed 'Tarasios' after his great-uncle, as, for example, in the *Nomocanon* of Manuel Malaxos and the iambic verses included in the service in the patriarch's honour.[54]

As for the patriarch Nikephoros, Photios aims to identify himself with him because he too attained the patriarchate on Easter Sunday (12 April) in 806 as a layman,[55] but mainly due to his opposition to iconoclasm and how he suffered to defend Orthodoxy. When Basileios I came to the throne in 867, he immediately deposed Photios and imprisoned him under harsh circumstances. Photios wrote Basileios a letter imploring him to relieve his sufferings in exile in Skepe (material and spiritual deprivation: a loss of friends, servants, etc.) and put an end to them either with death or some form of consolation.[56] He affirms that of all the punishments the emperor imposed on him, the worst was the prohibition of books, a cruelty that not even Leon V the Armenian inflicted on Nikephoros when he exiled him.[57] With this comparison, Photios not only denigrates Basileios, by comparing him to his iconoclast predecessor, but also characterises himself as a new martyr who suffers unjustly. As will become apparent, Photios portrays himself elsewhere in his letters as persecuted for iconodule Orthodoxy during the Second Iconoclasm because of the great devotion of

---

[52] Phot., *epist.* 250. The letter consists of a theological exegesis of the Pauline phrase: 'now and forever Christ will be glorified in my body by my life or by my death' (Phil 1:20). It became, accordingly, part of his collection of *erotapokriseis* as Phot., *Amph.* 120: Τί δηλοῖ τὸ ἀποστολικὸν ῥητὸν τὸ 'πάντοτε καὶ νῦν δοξασθήσεται Χριστὸς ἐν τῷ σώματι μου' καὶ ἑξῆς; For the hegoumenos Nikolaos, see *PmbZ* # 5606; *PBE* I: Nikolaos 76. On the monastery of Tarasios, see Janin 1969: 481–82; Berger 1988a: 706ff.; Ruggieri 1991: 202–3.
[53] Cormack and Hawkins 1977: 222–28 and pp. 237–47 (on Photios' involvement).
[54] Pitsakis 2009.
[55] For the rapid promotion of Nikephoros and his ordination as a patriarch, see Alexander 1958a: 68–71.
[56] Phot., *epist.* 98; Leserri 2004. For the location of the monastery of Skepe, cf. Janin 1969: 455.
[57] Moreover, according to Photios, Leon V guaranteed his well-being, see Phot., *epist.* 98,41–44.

his parents. But he also takes advantage of this situation to identify himself with patriarchs and bishops who were unjustly exiled by the emperor in the fourth and fifth centuries, even if none of them were deprived of their possessions or their books: Athanasios of Alexandria, Eustathios of Antioch, Paulos the Confessor (whose *vita* was reviewed by Photios himself in *codex* 257 of his *Bibliotheca*), John Chrysostom, Flavian of Constantinople and Nestorios.[58] The subsequent canonisation of these exiles, mainly for political reasons, proved both their innocence and the error of the emperors who sentenced them. In this process, their holiness was strengthened by their suffering, making them martyrs of Orthodoxy, the most recent such figure being the patriarch Nikephoros. The vindication of Nikephoros' memory by Photios is clear in all his fields of action: he praises Nikephoros in the *Bibliotheca* and mentions his own high regard for Nikephoros' historiographical works when reviewing the *Short History*.[59] Indeed, Photios tends to rely on the theological postulates noted by Nikephoros to construct his rhetoric against the iconoclasts. This is the case with the comparison of the iconoclast heretics with the Arians initiated by Nikephoros in his *Antirrheticus* and fully developed by Photios in his *Homilies*.[60]

Photios' epistles include not only repeated eulogy of this great champion of the defence of Orthodoxy but also a letter indicating Photios' direct involvement in encouraging Nikephoros' cult. As in the case of the hegoumenos of the monastery of Tarasios, the patriarch wrote to the abbot of the monastery where Nikephoros had originally been buried: this was the monastery of Theodoros, which was founded by Nikephoros himself under that dedication but which had changed its name shortly afterwards due to the fame of its founder.[61] This is *epistle* 159, usually placed during Photios' first patriarchate (859–867), in which Photios replies to a missive of the hegoumenos Nikolaos[62] recommending a man to him, by affirming that he will act justly and equitably. As well as being a magnificent example of the clientelism by which the monasteries were related to the patriarchate (given its insistent appeals to reciprocal friendship), this document testifies

---

[58] Dagron 1974: 425–33; Vallejo Girvés 2000.　[59] Phot., *Bibliot.*, cod. 66, 164AB.
[60] Nikeph., *Antirrheticus* 244D; 561A–B; 796C; Phot., *Homilies* 239–43 and 246–47; Gwynn 2007.
[61] Janin 1975: 27; Ruggieri 1991: 203. It should be identified perhaps with the monastery of Batalas mentioned in some sources of the second half of the twelfth century, see Janin 1975: 16. It cannot be the monastery of Medikion, as it is never mentioned under the name of its founder Nikephoros. This phenomenon has also been attested in the case of Photios, since after his death, the monastery of the Armenianoi, where he had been exiled, took his name, see Janin 1975: 84–85; Ruggieri 1991: 189.
[62] On this hegoumenos of the monastery of St Nikephoros, see *PmbZ* # 5605; *PBE* I: Nikolaos 75.

to the good relationship between Photios and the Bithynian community of St Nikephoros, where the memory of the martyr patriarch was certainly cherished, his feast days in particular celebrated and his veneration encouraged. As seen in Chapters 2 and 5, a major role was played in the dissemination of this cult by the *vita* in honour of Nikephoros written by Ignatios Diakonos, a distinguished representative of the Methodian circle. During the patriarchates of Photios, the promotion of the veneration of Nikephoros meant spreading this *vita*, which was so successful that it was even the basis for a funeral inscription of the year 882 in the Thracian city of Panion in the area of the Propontis opposite the Prokonnesos.[63] The first half of the inscription (8 lines) is reasonably faithful to the start of the preface to the *vita* of Ignatios Diakonos, appropriating its words to commemorate the recent death of another ecclesiastic whose name is not given.

In this process of the propagandistic identification of the patriarch Photios with his precursor Nikephoros, new monasteries were created by Photios in imitation of Nikephoros' foundations. What is more interesting is that Photios purchased and re-founded monasteries of undeniably iconodule credentials. This was the case of the monastery of Hagia Trias on Chalki Island,[64] allegedly founded by Photios. In fact this establishment played an important part during the Second Iconoclasm, when it was run by Ioannes Chalkitos.[65] This hegoumenos was a correspondent of Theodoros Stoudites, for whom Ioannes provided lodging when he was exiled during the Moechian controversy.[66] Ioannes' friendship with Nikephoros of Medikion led him to supply the wood used to build his coffin.[67] Persecuted for defending icons, Ioannes was praised as a saint after his death in early 826 by Theodoros Stoudites in one of his *Catecheseis*, which offers a detailed account of his final words.[68]

Likewise, in his desire to identify himself with the revered New Martyrs of the Second Iconoclasm, Photios purchased the monastery of Manuel located near the cistern of Aspar in Constantinople.[69] Founded ca. 830 by the *magistros* Manuel, the regent of Theodora and a supporter of the

---

[63] Bees 1916.   [64] Metr. Athenagoras 1921; Janin 1975: 72–74; Mellas 1984: 327–28.
[65] *PmbZ* # 3194; *PBE* I: Ioannes 453.
[66] Theod. Stoud., *epist.* 76, 197, 268, 298, 318 and 320, sent between 816 and 818.
[67] *Vita of Nikephoros of Medikion* 18,18–20
[68] Theod. Stoud., *Parvae catech.* 13; Theod. Stoud., *epist.* 542,12–13, where he quotes Ioannes Chalkitos along with Michael of Synada and Athanasios of Paulopetrion.
[69] For this monastery, see Janin 1969: 320–22; Ruggieri 1991: 193; Magdalino 1996: 63–64, 67, 73 and 75.

restoration of icons, the establishment had been seriously damaged by the great earthquake of 867. The patriarch Photios had it fully renovated in such a way that some time later his great-nephew and successor of the patriarchate, Sergios II, transferred his remains there.[70] Moreover, the monastery of Ta Agathou, which was founded by Nikephoros, was bought by one of Photios' relatives, Leon Katakalon or Katakoilas.[71] If we believe Niketas David Paphlagon, this Leon was a staunch follower of Photios who did not hesitate to cruelly persecute supporters of his rival Ignatios.[72] During the patriarchate of his uncle Photios, Katakalon acquired the Bosphorus monastery where Nikephoros had passed part of the exile imposed on him by the iconoclasts. In 886, Leon VI not only decreed Photios' overthrow and exile but also ordered that he be accompanied by his closest collaborators, such as Theodoros Santabarenos and Leon Katakalon, whose possessions were confiscated. The fact that these included the monastery of Ta Agathou[73] shows the extent of the dissemination of Photian propaganda, in which numerous members of his circle were heavily involved.

Photios' relationship with Methodios, the patriarch who officially put an end to iconoclasm, was complex. At no time did Photios attempt to identify himself with him; he hardly mentions Methodios, and the general impression is that Photios aims to replace him, in order to be considered the true instigator of the end of heresy. In the elaborate official propaganda that issued from the patriarchate, Methodios is systematically ignored, even though he was buried alongside the tomb of Nikephoros in the church of the Holy Apostles, close to that of St John Chrysostom.[74] It is true that Photios composed a long *kanon* of 252 verses to celebrate liturgically the memory of the patriarch Methodios[75] in imitation of the *kanon* written by the latter to encourage veneration of Ioannikios.[76] But

---

[70] Varona Codeso and Prieto Domínguez 2013: 146–47.
[71] *PmbZ* # 24329; *PBE* I: Leon 119; *Vita of the Patriarch Euthymios* 161–62. According to the *Vita of Ignatios* 91, p. 124,30–31, he held the post of *droungarios* of the *vigla*. On his important family links, see Varona Codeso and Prieto Domínguez 2013: 141–44; Signes Codoñer 2015: 164–69.
[72] *Vita of Ignatios* 91, p. 126,1–6.
[73] *Vita of the Patriarch Euthymios* 4, 27,21f. and 29,29–33; Janin 1975: 16, 23 and 27; Ruggieri 1991: 199. In actual fact, the expropriation of the monastery of Ta Agathou by Leon VI returned it to patriarchal hands, since he donated it to Euthymios (907–912).
[74] Konstantinos Porphyrogennetos, *De Ceremoniis* 69,22–29.
[75] *AHG*, vol. X, 50–62; Tessari 2014: 415–42 stresses the superior style of this *kanon* compared with the remainder of the hymns produced by Photios. Another *kanon* dedicated to Methodios has been edited by Spanos 2010: 238–39 and 409. For the many manuscripts that contain it, see *Tameion*, 219, nr. 668.
[76] For this hymn and the friendship between Methodios and Ioannikios, see Chapter 2.

Photios wrote this during his youth, shortly after Methodios' death ca. 847 (see verses 40–45), long before he ascended the patriarchal throne and had to draw up a legitimising ideological programme.[77] This period also saw the production of the two *stichera idiomela*, brief compositions with an original musical rhythm intended to be sung among the Psalms of the liturgy of the Hours, which Photios dedicated to Methodios again with the aim of praising him and promoting his liturgical commemoration year after year.[78] These compositions show that in his youth, Photios sympathised with the postulates of the patriarch Methodios, whom he had probably met at the court of Theophilos long before the Triumph of Orthodoxy and the rise of Methodios. Thus, the silence of Photios the patriarch concerning Methodios' vital role in the restoration of icons is all the more significant.

Similarly, Photios' only mention of Methodios in the whole of his abundant prose corpus is found in an *Amphilochium* postdating his final, definitive exile in 886.[79] *Amphilochium* 324 is a brief essay in which Photios speaks of the dedications with which the churches are consecrated and of the holiness of the relics and the veneration they should receive: tradition has sanctified them to the extent of considering them purveyors of holiness.[80] The patriarch adds the example of Kyrillos of Alexandria and the veneration he inspired after his death. This practice has continued to be imitated to this day, Photios affirms, given that the patriarch Methodios recognised the holiness of his predecessor Nikephoros and blessed the monastery where he died, converting it into a place of veneration and pilgrimage.[81]

Although Photios takes great care not to praise Methodios expressly, he acknowledges his encouragement of the cult of the patriarch Nikephoros and approves its aims. Photios goes further down the path opened up by Methodios, not only in his vindication of the patriarch Nikephoros but also in his emulation of his predecessor, whom he seeks to replace to some extent in the collective memory as the restorer of images and whose pastoral work he imitates on more than one occasion in order to do so. Another paradigmatic case is that of the treatment of repentant heretics. Like Methodios, Photios supervised these procedures and drew up the abjuration formulae to receive iconoclasts into the Orthodox Church after

---

[77] The acrostic says Μεθοδίῳ Φώτιος ὕμνον προσφέρω. In contrast to Methodios, Photios includes neither title nor post, probably due to his youth and the fact that he was not yet a patriarch.
[78] Tessari 2014: 443–76.   [79] Phot., *Amph.*, vol. IV, p. X and XXI–XXII.
[80] Phot., *Amph.* 324,17–19. See Seventh Canon of the Second Council of Nicaea; *Nomocanon* 580.
[81] Phot., *Amph.* 324,30–34.

they were defeated in 843;[82] he also drew up abjuration formulae for dissidents, heretics and infidels. We are familiar with his concern to readmit repentant Paulicians, Jews and Arabs into the post-iconoclast Church.[83] It is reasonable to assume that the Ignatian clergy had to face similar public tests to rejoin the Photian Church.

If Photios continued and developed many aspects of Methodios' patriarchal administration, his real aim was to be identified with the patriarch Nikephoros, a true iconodule martyr during the Second Iconoclasm. To judge by the testimony of Arethas, this complex process of identification was successful, since in the epitaph he dedicated to the patriarch Euthymios, Photios is mentioned together with Nikephoros, as both famous for the persecution they suffered and their death in exile.[84] His vindication of his great-uncle Tarasios and the promotion of his veneration serve the same aim and promote the legitimacy as a patriarch that Ignatios' supporters denied Photios.

6.2.2 *Photios, His Family and Their Presence in the Literature on Iconoclasm*

In order to improve his reputation and public image, Photios made every attempt to link himself to the martyrs of the Second Iconoclasm, as can be seen in the way he identifies his sufferings with those of the patriarch Nikephoros. Although he could not appropriate the figures of the great heroes of iconoduly (such as Theodoros Stoudites), who were already vindicated by their disciples, with many of whom (such as the Stoudites) he was on bad terms, he could reproduce their procedure. If Theodoros Stoudites had disseminated the holiness of his mother, establishing her veneration and laying the foundations for a holy lineage, Photios could do no less with his own mother. Indeed, the patriarch's entire family was subject to the same literary process of the creation of a family of saints who suffered to defend the veneration of icons. The ultimate aim of all these endeavours was not only to legitimate Photios in the patriarchate, but to cause his own holiness to be recognized.

Throughout his collected letters, Photios tells us that his parents were persecuted by the iconoclasts: both died early in exile. His father, a direct

---

[82] Grumel 1935; Darrouzès 1987: 16–18; Arranz 1990. See Section 2.1.3.
[83] Lemerle 1973: 39–47; Eleuteri and Rigo 1993: 41–50 and 90; Tobias 2007: 95–114; Prieto Domínguez 2014a: 296–97.
[84] Arethas, *Epitaphios for Euthymios* 92,28–29: μετὰ Νικηφόρου καὶ Φωτίου τῶν ἀοιδίμων τοῖς διωγμοῖς καὶ θανάτοις συνδοξαζόμενε.

relative of Tarasios, received the title of confessor and was remembered liturgically, according to the *Synaxarion of Constantinople*.[85] His name was Sergios, and he held the rank of *spatharios* and was a well-established member of the Constantinopolitan imperial aristocracy.[86] A brief historiographical text (Στηλευτικόν τῶν εἰκονομάχων) that was a source for the reign of Michael II for Theophanes Continuatus is generally attributed to him.[87] Photios affirms that his father lost his wealth and his position due to his Orthodoxy[88] and that for this same reason both his parents died in exile when still young.[89] The patriarch does not miss an opportunity to mention that he himself was also persecuted for his iconoduly, as he had to share the punishments imposed on his parents.[90] Indeed, he goes so far as to say that just as his father and his great-uncle Tarasios were anathematised by the iconoclasts, so he too had been anathematised by 'all heretic synods and all iconoclast councils' (πᾶσα σύνοδος αἱρετικὴ καὶ πᾶν εἰκονομάχων συνέδριον), in reference to the Ignatian councils of 847, 859, 863 and 869.[91] Likewise, at the council of 879/880 that restored Photios to the patriarchal see, in expounding the piety of Photios, the official spokesman also mentions his great-uncle Tarasios, 'who converted many heretics', and his parents, of whom he says that they 'died in their struggle for the faith'.[92]

Despite the fact that Photios never mentions his parents by name, the chronicle of Pseudo-Symeon tells us that his father's name was Sergios and that he had some personal relationship with important saints of the Second Iconoclasm such as Michael of Synada and Hilarion of Dalmatos, who prophesied his son's future.[93] Like them, Sergios was venerated after his death; the torture and the exile he suffered in the times of Theophilos for defending images were remembered every 13 May, when Eirene, his wife and the mother of Photios, was also mentioned.[94] His memory is also celebrated in the *Menologion* of Basileios II, which erroneously places the

---

[85] *SynaxCP* 682,9–20; 681/682,57–83/684,40. Although the attention paid to patriarch Photios' family, some issues remain unresolved, see Bury 1890; Ahrweiler 1965; Mango 1977; Nogara 1978; Chrestou 1992; Treadgold 2002; Varona Codeso and Prieto Domínguez 2013.
[86] On Sergios, the father of Photios, see *PmbZ* # 6665; *PBE* I: Sergios 16.
[87] Barišić 1961: 260–66; Signes Codoñer 1995: 212; Treadgold 2013: 90–99 identifies Sergios with the *Scriptor incertus*, see Section 5.2.
[88] Phot., *epist.* 289,52–57. *Vita of Ignatios* 21,30–33 confirms that Photios' family was noble and wealthy.
[89] Phot., *epist.* 234,57–61.   [90] Phot., *epist.* 234,51–54.
[91] Phot., *epist.* 114,2–4. Cf. Mango 1977: 137; Varona Codeso and Prieto Domínguez 2013: 107–8.
[92] Mansi xviiA, 460B: ὁ πατὴρ καὶ ἡ μήτηρ ὑπὲρ εὐσεβείας ἀθλοῦντες ἐναπέθανον.
[93] Ps-Symeon 668,20–69,22; Gouillard 1971: 398–99.
[94] *SynaxCP* 682,9–20; 681/682,57–83/684,40.

persecution in the reign of Leon V instead of under Theophilos.[95] The identification of this pair of confessors with the parents of Photios was due to Papadopoulos-Kerameus and has been accepted by most researchers.[96] In addition to his entries in the Constantinopolitan *synaxaria*, a hymn in Sergios' honour survives.[97]

Another relative of Photios venerated due to his defence of the veneration of images was Sergios Niketiates,[98] a maternal uncle of the patriarch.[99] This kinship explains the confusion in some sources between the two uncles of Empress Theodora who assisted her during the restoration of icons: Sergios Niketiates (her maternal uncle) and Manuel the Armenian (her paternal uncle). But it is in any case clear that the holiness of Photios' family was accepted and assumed by the next generation, despite the *damnatio memoriae* issued against him by Emperor Leon VI. The cult of Photios was encouraged by, among others, the patriarchs Nikolaos Mystikos and Michael of Alexandria, as well as Arethas of Caesarea and Zacharias of Chalcedon, who recalled at the eighth synod the virtues of Photios, his many works of charity with the poor and his great apostolic work with the Slavs.[100] Nikolaos Mystikos, a patriarch of Constantinople on two occasions (901–907 and 912–925) and a disciple of Photios, in his letters describes his teacher as a saint whose life's work was worthy of admiration and remembrance.[101] Leon Choirosphaktes, an important diplomat at the court of Leon VI,[102] dedicated a poem of twelve iambic verses to him, in which he regrets the passage of time and the loss of such an illustrious mind; in his title, he showed that he considered the patriarch to be a holy person.[103]

---

[95] *Menologion Basilii* 453C–D.
[96] Papadopoulos-Kerameus 1899: 656, n. 2; Dvornik 1948: 387; Tomadakes 1977. For his part, Nogara 1978 considers that Sergios the Confessor and Sergios the father of Photios were two different individuals.
[97] *AHG*, vol. IX, 168–75 (text) and 396–97 (commentary).
[98] *SynaxCP* 777,5–78,16 (28 June). Cf. *PmbZ* # 6664. On the process of the sanctification of Sergios Niketiates, see Section 4.2.
[99] Mango 1997: 135; Settipani 2006: 174. This means that the patriarch Photios and Empress Theodora were cousins.
[100] Hergenröther 1867–1869: vol. II, 718–20; Papadopoulos-Kerameus 1899; Jugie 1922/1923; Dvornik 1948: 386–89; Chrestou 1991; Paschalidis 1994b.
[101] Nikolaos Mystikos, *epist.* 139, 49–52; *epist.* 75, 52–58; *epist.* 2, 17–25.
[102] This Leon Choirosphaktes (sometimes confused with Leon the Mathematician) was born in ca. 824 and lived until the year 919, see *PmbZ* # 4527 and # 24343. His philosophical-didactic poem *Theology in a Thousand Lines* stands out among his surviving literary production, while his epistles number just over twenty.
[103] Στίχοι ἰαμβικοὶ εἰς Φώτιον Πατριάρχην τὸν ἐν ἁγίοις, ed. Kolias 1939: 130 (appendix).

Photios' holiness was shared with and inherited from his father, together with whom he fought for iconoduly, as is confirmed in the *Vita of St Euthymios the Younger* from the early tenth century:[104] 'Photios ... who from the very cradle had been consecrated to Christ, for whose icon he suffered confiscation and banishment in common with his father; whose life was admirable and whose death was agreeable, as God has confirmed by miracles.' The author of the text, the metropolitan Basileios,[105] wrote this brief eulogy of Photios in such a way that the miracles with which God is said to ratify someone's holiness might refer to either his father or Photios himself. If the reference is to Photios, the author may have been thinking of the miraculous salvation of Constantinople, which was besieged in 860 by the Russians but suffered no damage thanks to the procession organised by Photios; in this he carried an icon of the Theotokos to accompany the garment of the Virgin kept in the church of Blachernai. Perhaps Basileios also considered that the conversion of the Russians was a miracle.[106]

So too for Arethas of Caesarea, the holiness of the patriarch was that of his whole family (τὸ γένος).[107] These same postulates were likely defended by Arethas in a poem he dedicated to the patriarch, which has unfortunately been lost. We know of its existence thanks to the codex *Vaticanus Barberini Gr.* 310, which originally contained this poem entitled Ἀρέθα ἀρχιεπισκόπου εἰς Φώτιον τὸν Πατριάρχην. Although the folios that included it have not survived, the index of the manuscript did come down to us.[108] In any case, the rapid process of the sanctification of Photios reflected the wishes of at least a part of Byzantine society that had positive memories of him. Over time, this positive evaluation of the patriarch became the majority view, and the name of Photios was included in the *Synaxarion of Constantinople* to be remembered on 6 February and in the *Synodikon of Orthodoxy*.[109] The spokesmen of this line of thought were none other than the disciples who during the years of his patriarchates were

---

[104] *Vita of Euthymios the Younger* 179,5–10: Φώτιος γὰρ ἦν ὁ μακάριος, ὁ φωτὸς ἀκτίσι φερωνύμως τοῦ ὀνόματος, πλήθει διδασκαλιῶν καταλάμψας τὰ πέρατα, ὁ ἐξ αὐτῶν σπαργάνων ἀφιερωθεὶς τῷ Χριστῷ, ὡς ὑπὲρ τῆς αὐτοῦ εἰκόνος δημήσει καὶ ἐξορίᾳ, τούτοις δὴ τοῖς ἀθλητικοῖς ἐκ προοιμίων ἀγῶσι, συγκοινωνήσας τῷ γεννήτορι, οὗ καὶ ἡ ζωὴ θαυμαστὴ καὶ τὸ τέλος ἐπέραστον, ὑπὸ Θεοῦ τοῖς θαύμασι μαρτυρούμενον.
[105] *PmbZ* # 20858; Papachryssanthou 1974.
[106] Vasiliev 1946; Wortley 1977: 111–26; Markopoulos 1979: 75–82; Paschalidis 1994b: 372–76.
[107] Arethas, *Opus* 5, in Westerink, *Arethae Scripta minora* I, 52,19–21: ὁ [i.e., Photios] χθές τε καὶ πρώην ἱερὸς μὲν τὸ γένος, ἱερώτερος δὲ τὴν σοφίαν, ὅση τε θεία καὶ ὅση ἡ κατ' ἀνθρώπους λογίζεται.
[108] Gallavotti 1987: nr. 28; Kougeas 1913: 5, n. 2 and pp. 95–96.
[109] *SynaxCP* 448,19–20; *Synodikon of Orthodoxy* 53,112–13; 103,883; 297,120.

part of Photios' circle and took part in his creation of an official ideology in which the iconoclastic controversy was retold and inevitably rewritten.

6.2.3 The Epistles of Photios and the New Orthodox Discourse

The identification of the members of the patriarchal circle during the tenures of Photios is possible thanks to the testimony of his collected epistles. After the collection of Theodoros Stoudites, that of Photios' letters is the largest that has survived from the ninth century: almost 300 missives catalogued and published during the patriarch's lifetime, if not by him personally, then by someone from his milieu who had his explicit approval.[110] Photios was obviously familiar with the collected letters of Theodoros Stoudites, and in editing his own, he pursued the same ends: offering his followers a unifying point of reference, in which arguments and proof of his model behaviour as patriarch were given, which they could use to refute the accusations of the Ignatians; leaving a testimony of his fight for Orthodoxy and of the sufferings, periods of exile and tortures this caused him[111] and building an image of himself as a confessor, which after his death could support the establishment of a cult in his honour.

An insistence on the holiness of his lineage is a key element in this, together with a catalogue of his many sufferings: Photios was persecuted by Emperor Basileios, unjustly accused by a sector of the Church and of course exiled in his youth along with his father by the iconoclasts. Moreover, as the anathemas and the excommunications were in his opinion unjust, they help to demonstrate his Orthodoxy, according to *epist.* 114 and 116, which were written after his anathematisation on 29 October 869 at the Ignatian synod. In these letters, Photios claims that this is an unlawful conviction and that although an anathema against heretics is a terrible thing, when it occurs against the defenders of Orthodoxy, as is the case here, it is null and void and the pious prefer it to having to associate with those who hate Christ.

All this constituted precious textual material, as Photios himself was aware,[112] for the writing of a future hagiography in his honour. This *vita* has not survived. But taking into account that after the Triumph of

---

[110] On Photios' collected letters, see Laourdas 1951; Wittig 1989/1991; Salvemini 1997; Wilson 2000; Cortassa 2003; Kazhdan 2006: 25–36; Schamp 2008.

[111] In his own words, along with the lack of books, the greatest suffering for Photios was hearing of the violation of the churches he had consecrated, Phot., *epist.* 86, 98, 174, 183 and 188.

[112] On letter collections as autobiographies, see Gibson 2013. A case in point is that of Gregorios of Nazianzus' collected letters, see Storin 2017; 2019, esp. 1–25.

Orthodoxy practically all the patriarchs of Constantinople had one produced for them and that this constituted a hagiographical sub-genre,[113] and given that we do have poems praising Photios, everything points to the existence of at least one *Vita Photii Patriarchae Constantinopolitani*. The candidates for the author are numerous, as the disciples and friends of Photios included a large number of intellectuals, as we shall see in Section 6.3. That Photios referred to himself in his writings as an iconodule martyr is not unknown in Byzantine literature.[114] The immediate reference Photios had in mind was probably *epist*. 41 of Theodoros Stoudites, which contains a large amount of hagiographical material that subsequently appeared in the *vitae* that praise the hegoumenos of Stoudios.

The collection of letters also offers a vivid portrait of the alliances Photios established with other persons and how he tried to keep his followers united even in times of persecution when the Ignatians were in power. Imitating the discourse of Theodoros Stoudites, Photios gathered around himself his most faithful disciples and identified his enemies with the enemies of Orthodoxy (i.e., the new iconoclasts), reaffirming his supporters in the faith and promising them the spiritual rewards and triumphs of iconodule martyrs. A good example of this Photian rhetoric is *epist*. 126, which Photios sent to his loyal metropolitans Euschemon of Caesarea in Cappadocia and Georgios of Nicomedia[115] after hearing of their behaviour in the sessions of the anti-Photian council of 869. Both men were interrogated in the hope that their testimony could harm Photios, but Euschemon always declared in favour of the patriarch.[116] After addressing them as 'friends, sons and brothers',[117] Photios uses the example of the devotion of St Job to exhort them to continue in the attitude of true disciples of Christ, since they will someday be rewarded with prizes and gifts:[118] 'As we have done up to now, we will continue to demonstrate for ever that these are the true and main disciples of the Lord,

---

[113] *Vita of Tarasios*, pp. 3–6.   [114] Hinterberger 2000: 139–64.
[115] Regarding Euschemon of Caesarea, see *PmbZ* # 1728; *PBE* I: Euschemon 5. On Georgios of Nicomedia, cf. *PmbZ* # 2259 and # 22083; *PBE* I: Georgios 223.
[116] Euschemon declared in the sixth and seventh sessions (24 and 29 October 869, Mansi XVI, 84C, 86D and Mansi XVI, 98D, 99B, respectively), the second time in the presence of Photios himself. His name erroneously appears as Euthymios in Anastasius' translation of the Acts (Mansi XVI, 86D) and in the Greek text (Mansi XVI, 348C), see *Council of Constantinople (869/870)*, 167.
[117] Phot., *epist*. 126,6.
[118] Phot., *epist*. 126,11–14: ὥσπερ μέχρι νῦν, οὕτω καὶ διὰ παντός, τουτουσὶ τοὺς ἐκείνου γνησίους καὶ κορυφαίους μαθητὰς ὀδυρομένους καὶ ἀμηχανοῦντας ἐπιδείξωμεν. Καὶ γὰρ, ὡς καὶ ὑμεῖς συνεπίστασθε, τῶν εἰς τέλος ἀγωνιζομένων ἐστὶ τὰ βραβεῖα καὶ οἱ στέφανοι.

the long-suffering and the needy. It will be then, as ye also know, that the prizes and the crowns will come for those who have fought to the end.'

Correspondingly, those in the Photian ranks who defected to the party of Ignatios were treated as heretics and as precursors of the Antichrist, as is apparent from the letter Photios sent to the monk Euthymios for having joined the Ignatians.[119] This was also the case with the monk Metrophanes,[120] who is defined in the *intitulatio* of several letters as an apostate (Μητροφάνει μοναχῷ ἀποστατήσαντι). *Epist.* 66–67 and 104 were sent during the first patriarchate of Photios, with the aim of persuading Metrophanes to repent and again support Photios. This monk is probably the same as the addressee of *epist.* 149, who, during the years when Photios was being persecuted, had taken up a hesychastic lifestyle and remained loyal to the exiled patriarch. As in the case of the heroes of the resistance against the Second Iconoclasm, his sufferings and his virtues are admired to such an extent that his combats and the trophies and the blessing obtained in the name of Christ constitute the subject of conversations and accounts written in his honour.[121]

The identification between the supporters of the patriarch Ignatios and the iconoclast heretics is made clear in the missive Photios sent to the deacon and *chartoularios* Gregorios Amasianos[122] from exile (869–872) to expose the offer of peace made by the Ignatians. The accession to the throne of Emperor Basileios had led some Photians to cherish hopes of an agreement.[123] But Photios warns them that this peace is against Christ, since the Ignatians 'fight against Christ' (Χριστομαχοῦσιν),[124] using the verb Χριστομαχοῦσιν deliberately, since during the iconoclast crisis it

---

[119] Phot., *epist.* 69 (Εὐθυμίῳ μοναχῷ παραπεσόντι); *PmbZ* # 1859; *PBE* I: Euthymios 18.

[120] According to Hergenröther 1867–1869: vol. I, 647; vol. II, 45 and 724, this would be the Metrophanes who arrived in Constantinople along with Basileios, Zosimas and others to implore Photios' help against Pope Nicholas I (Phot., *epist.* 2,327–30), see *PmbZ* # 4985 and # 4987; *PBE* I: Metrophanes 2 and Metrophanes 3.

[121] Phot., *epist.* 149: Μέγα μὲν τὸ ἄλγος ὑπὲρ τῶν ἐκκλησιῶν τοῦ θεοῦ, εἰς γὰρ τὴν οἰκουμένην ἐχύθη τὸ κακόν· μείζων δὲ ἡ χαρά, ἐν γὰρ τῇ ὑφηλίῳ θαυμάζεται ὑμῶν τὰ ἄθλα καὶ ἡ ἀρετή, καὶ παντὸς στόματός ἐστιν ἀντὶ παντὸς ἄλλου διήγημα οἱ λαμπροὶ ὑμῶν ἀγῶνες καὶ τὰ τρόπαια καὶ ὁ πολὺς ἐκεῖνος καὶ ἄξιος τῶν ὑπὲρ Χριστοῦ παθημάτων μακαρισμός. 'The greater the grief for the churches of God after evil spread through the ecumene, the greater the joy, because under the sun your sufferings and virtue are admired and your brilliant combats, the trophies and that great and praiseworthy celebration of suffering in Christ's name are worthy of all oral discourse and not of any other account.'

[122] For Gregorios Amasianos, see *PmbZ* # 22085, who erroneously calls him Georgios.

[123] Dvornik 1948: 163; Tobias 2007: 236–52.

[124] Phot., *epist.* 100,6–7: ἴστωσαν ὅτι Χριστομαχοῦσιν, ὑπὸ τῷ τῆς εἰρήνης ὀνόματι τὴν κατ' αὐτοῦ πολιορκίαν ἀνιστῶντες, 'so that they know they are fighting against Christ, in the name of peace, to repel its siege'.

specifically defined those who persecuted images.[125] In his homilies as well, the attacks and the condemnations Photios directs at all heretics, including dissidents from the true dogma, create the impression that he considered among the latter his personal enemies, the Ignatians.[126] Perhaps for this reason, every time that someone repented of belonging to the party of Ignatios, Photios expressed his joy in a way similar to Theodoros Stoudites' reaction to the conversion of an iconoclast.

This was the case when the elderly bishop of Eriste in Bithynia broke away from the schismatic faction and contritely asked to be accepted among Photios' supporters. The exact location of Eriste is unknown, although it is recorded that it belonged to the diocese of Nicomedia. According to Janin, it stood at the foot of the Bithynian Mount Olympos in the region of Atroa.[127] The monastic communities in this area clearly supported Ignatios.[128] But Photios had also devout collaborators there, such as the hesychast Athanasios, whose virtue in a hostile land is stressed by Photios in *epist.* 93, where he is compared to a palm tree that grows in salty ground, or the obstinate Ignatios, the bishop of Lophoi, who must never have been a convinced Photian.[129] A letter survives in which the patriarch acknowledges the role of the hesychast monk Athanasios as mediator in this process.[130] The patriarch sent him at least five letters (Phot., *epist.* 20, 26, 27, 93 and 212), in which it is obvious that Athanasios supervised the monasteries around the Bithynian Mount Olympos and that Photios granted him the power to appoint the hegoumenoi (*epist.* 26). We also know about Athanasios' intervention at the monastery of Symboloi,[131] where the monks, who belonged to the Stoudite federation, had revolted against their hegoumenos (probably a Photian) and had asked Athanasios to intercede for them and name a new superior. But Photios categorically condemns their sedition, saying that it is as if horses rose up against the charioteer, sheep against the shepherd or sailors against the captain. Ecclesiastical canons also made no provision for any kind of voting by the monks, which meant that those at Symboloi had to accept the hierarchs chosen for them.[132]

---

[125] It is used in this way by the main iconodule authors, see Theod. Stoud., *epist.* 358,16–17; Nikeph., *Refutatio et eversio* 160,12–14; *Vita of Gregorios Dekapolites* 3,11–13; Phot., *epist.* 2,367–69.
[126] Phot., *Homily* XVI,13 and 162,5–8, trans. Mango 276.
[127] Janin 1975: 129–30. On the aforementioned bishop of Eriste, see *PmbZ* # 12006; *PBE* I: Anonymus 618.
[128] Dvornik 1948: 65–68. [129] Phot., *epist.* 23 and 70.
[130] Phot., *epist.* 20, written at the end of the first patriarchate (May 866/September 867). For this monk, see *PmbZ* # 684; *PBE* I: Athanasios 18.
[131] About this monastery, see Janin 1975: 181–83; Ruggieri 1991: 87–88.
[132] Phot., *epist.* 27,8–24.

352   The Photian Milieu

The conditions of admission imposed by the Photians gradually became stricter, until they were similar to those required of the iconoclast clergy after the Triumph of Orthodoxy. The long missive Photios sent to Paulos, the archbishop of Thessaloniki[133] between 883 and 885, amounts to a pastoral treatise on how to treat Ignatians returning to the Church. The first part calls for severity for those repenting now after five years of peace in the Church and affirms that whether the conversion is sincere or hypocritical should be carefully considered.[134] The second part is more compassionate and describes the situation of those returning and the fact that they must endure unjust suspicion and isolation;[135] they must accordingly be received in a merciful fashion. A difficult letter in which Photios speaks of the marks left by sin may also belong to this context. This is *epist.* 43, addressed to the monk Sophronios (of whom we know nothing),[136] in which the patriarch notes that just as wounds leave marks on the body, so the scars of sin never disappear. Indeed, even after the sin has been corrected, the wounds leave the subject's soul prone to this sin again. Photios' words may refer to the impossibility of some penitents ever completely severing their links with the Ignatian faction. In his attempt to identify his cause with that of iconoduly, Photios also converted reconciliation with the Ignatian clergy into a matter of utmost seriousness, which he discusses at several points in his letters. That is the case with *epist.* 281,56–58, written in the same period (880–886) for his friend Theophanes, who had just been appointed archbishop of Caesarea.[137] Photios had also been concerned about the rehabilitation of the Ignatians many years previously, as *epist.* 174, which was sent from exile in 868/869 to the bishops loyal to him, makes clear. Although Photios was said to have considered receiving the Ignatians, or at least some of them, into communion, he flatly denies this.[138]

Photios builds several more epistles around the theme of iconoclasm, for example, *epist.* 37, 38, 39 and 134, in which he attacks iconoclasm in response to the concerns voiced by the *spatharios* Ioannes Chrysocheir.[139] In the first of these missives, he affirms that the Hellenes, the Jews, the Manicheans and all those who reject images of Christ are accomplices of

---

[133] On Paulos, see *PmbZ* # 5858 and 26314. He was consecrated in February 880, as on 3 March he attended the Eighth Council, that of the triumph of Photios (Mansi XVIIIA, 513B).
[134] Phot., *epist.* 283,2–177.   [135] Phot., *epist.* 283,178–535.
[136] *PmbZ* # 6849; *PBE* I: Sophronios 3.   [137] *PmbZ* # 28076, see Section 6.3.3.
[138] Phot., *epist.* 174,295–301. On his relationship with the Ignatians, see *epist.* 56; 100 and 252.
[139] For Ioannes Chrysocheir, who became *protonotarios tou dromou*, see *PmbZ* # 3340, *PBE* I: Ioannes 448.

the iconoclasts; in the second, he asserts that not even Simon Magus and Carpocrates renounced the images of Christ, which makes the iconoclasts worse than them; and in the third, he explains that these two heretics are a good example of the fact that the representation of images is contemporary with Christianity. In the longer *epist.* 134, Photios offers a detailed argument for the falseness of iconoclasm and develops the theology of icons, explaining that when it is said that Christ is the true image of the Father and that man is the image of God, it is not postulated that artificial representation is false, but rather that the existing differences are accentuated. In the same manner, the light of the sun is not invalidated by affirming that Christ is the true light.[140] If this Ioannes really is the recipient of *epist.* 57 and 80, he was a poor follower of the patriarch, since he attempted to betray him and ultimately went over to the opposite faction, which was a great disappointment to Photios. If we believe that Ioannes was related to the leader of the Paulician heretics, who was also named Chrysocheir, Photios' reasons for writing him to define the true dogma are apparent. Chrysocheir died in the attack on Tephrike of 872.[141]

Epist. 65, which was sent to the hegoumenos of Stoudios, Theodoros Santabarenos,[142] towards the end of his first patriarchate (864–865), responds to the malicious question of the iconoclasts as to which is the true image of Christ: the Roman, the Indian, the Greek or the Egyptian? Photios concludes by echoing the postulate that the icon is merely a vehicle to honour the representation. His reasoning presents the following clichés: (1) The question itself shows that the cult of images extends throughout the world; (2) Iconoclast postulates force us to doubt the text of the Gospel, which gives various details in different languages; (3) What type of cross is similar to the original? Should we not pray before the other types, with or without inscriptions? (4) What liturgical form is appropriate? (5) Is the fight against Christ concealed by the controversy over images?[143]

---

[140] These letters went on to become part of the *Amphilochia*: Phot., *epist.* 37 and 38 = *Amph.* 196 and 197: Τῷ αὐτῷ περὶ εἰκόνων; *epist.* 134 = *Amph.* 217: Περὶ διαφορᾶς εἰκόνων.

[141] *PmbZ* # 1153 and # 21340, *PBE* I: Chrysocheres 2; Lemerle 1973; Tobias 2007: 95–114.

[142] For Theodoros Santabarenos, see *PmbZ* # 7729 and # 27619; *PBE* I: Theodoros 174. He collaborated closely with Photios and in gratitude was granted the metropolitan see of Euchaita in 877. In the surviving letters (Phot., *epist.* 65, 142, 143, 203 and 205, all from his period as head of Stoudios) the patriarch enlightens him about iconoclast heresy and on biblical matters such as the death of Abel in Gen 4:8 (*epist.* 203) and the meaning of circumcision in Gen 17:9–14 and 23–27 (*epist.* 205, following Rom 2:29; 1 Cor 2:7 and Heb 2:14). Theodoros was doubtless versed in ancient literature and for this reason Photios includes the story of King Anios, which belongs to the Trojan cycle (*epist.* 142), and a fable of Aesop's also collected by Diogenes Laërtius (*epist.* 143, cf. Diogenes Laërtius I, 69).

[143] *Epist.* 65 = *Amph.* 205: Περὶ διαμορφώσεως καὶ χαρακτῆρος τῶν ἁγίων εἰκόνων.

Finally, *epist.* 214 is an exposition of the theology of images that takes the exegesis of Psalm 134:15 as a pretext: 'Pagan idols are silver and gold and the work of man.'[144] According to the patriarch, these words cannot be applied either to the sacred images or to Christian liturgical objects. In the first place, this is because they are inspired things, and secondly, because of the use to which they are put. (An altar of God takes the same form as one for devils; it is their function that distinguishes them.) Moreover, the tradition of icons starts with the Apostles themselves (lines 22–30). The recipient of the letter was a certain Stephanos, who remains unidentified. In contrast to what is said by the German prosopography (which follows the text's editor, Westerink),[145] this Stephanos was not a former iconoclast who had converted but quite the opposite. The *intitulatio* of the letter makes this clear: Στεφάνῳ ὀρθοδοξήσαντι, 'to Stephanos who (previously) was orthodox'. In the text, Photios addresses him twice: in the second, he alludes to his 'paternal piety';[146] while in the first, he includes the vocative εἰκονομάχε (iconoclast), which was a serious insult at the time.[147]

It is difficult to believe that after the intense purge carried out by Methodios and the years that had passed since the first patriarchate of Ignatios, anyone could convert to iconoclasm. It is also strange that Photios did not insist on rescuing Stephanos from heresy and that he did not make him a public element of his official anti-iconoclast propaganda. All this, together with the lack of specific or personal details about the man, raise the possibility that he may be a fictitious person created as a rhetorical measure to structure the exhibition, make it more persuasive and stress its apologetic nature. Be this as it may, Photios' preoccupation with iconoclasm is part of his vindication as a guarantor of official Orthodoxy issuing from the patriarchal throne. This is also the context of *epist.* 55, the recipient of which was the patriarch's brother Sergios.[148] Here Photios categorically affirms that the correct interpretation of Matthew 7:6 ('Do not give unto dogs what is holy or throw your pearls before swine, lest they trample upon them and turn upon you and tear you to pieces.') is that we are obliged to defend Orthodoxy from the threats of heretics and infidels.[149]

---

[144] *Epist.* 214 = *Amph.* 111: Τὰ εἴδωλα τῶν ἐθνῶν ἀργύριον καὶ χρυσίον, ἔργα χειρῶν ἀνθρώπων.
[145] *PmbZ* # 7087.   [146] Phot., *epist.* 214,31–32: τὴν προγονικὴν εὐσέβειαν.
[147] Phot., *epist.* 214,16.
[148] For Sergios, who held the rank of *protospatharios*, see *PmbZ* # 6672; *PBE* I: Sergios 107.
[149] *Epist.* 55 = *Amph.* 200: Τοῦ κυρίου λέγοντος 'μὴ βάλλετε τοὺς μαργαρίτας ὑμῶν ἔμπροσθεν τῶν χοίρων' καὶ ἑξῆς, πῶς δεῖ διδάσκειν τοὺς ἀπίστους; On Photios' characterisation of the heretics, stressing their madness, see Salvemini 2000.

6.3 The Milieu of Photios

Listing the intellectuals who gathered around Photios during his two patriarchates is an arduous and delicate task: many are mere names, others are difficult to identify and most are never mentioned.[150] The successive anathemas and the need to reinvent themselves after the two crushing overthrows and periods of exile of Photios made individuals who were not obliged to share the sad fate of their master keep silent. Despite everything, we can identify some of these men due to the importance they attained in the patriarch's lifetime or the following generation: Arethas of Caesarea; Gregorios Asbestas, the archbishop of Syracuse; Niketas Byzantios; Theodoros of Laodicea; Euschemon of Caesarea in Cappadocia; Zacharias of Chalcedon; Georgios of Nicomedia; the monk and philosopher Nikephoros and the patriarch Nikolaos Mystikos. The case of Konstantinos Sikelos is curious; he abandoned the circle of Leon the Mathematician, the bishop of Thessaloniki accused of iconoclasm, to join the disciples of Photios.[151]

To go into detail about the written production of each of these men and the many others who worked under the orders or following the inspiration of the patriarch Photios is beyond the scope of this monograph. Theodoros, the *synkellos* and *presbyteros* of Hagia Sophia, for example, wrote an *Enkomion of the Robe of the Virgin* preserved in the church of Blachernai (*BHG* 1058)[152] to praise Photios following the example that the patriarch set down in his *Homily* IV, in which he narrates the siege of Constantinople by the Russians.[153] That homily was delivered in early July, probably on the 2nd, to coincide with the feast day of the deposition of this relic of the Theotokos at the church of Blachernai.[154] The identity of this Theodoros Synkellos is unclear.[155] Perhaps he should be identified with Theodoros Santabarenos, as Wortley suggests.[156] Or perhaps we are concerned with the *metropolites* of Patras whom Photios sent to the island of Plate in ca. 863 to purify an altar that had been consecrated by Ignatios after it was destroyed in the

---

[150] Phot., *epist.* 290,64–81, written to Pope Nicholas I in August/September 861. On this 'school' run by the patriarch, see Dvornik 1973b; Treadgold 1981; Canfora 1998a; 1998b; Canfora et al. 2000; Kazhdan 2006: 37–41; Schamp 2011; Ronconi 2015b.
[151] On Konstantinos Sikelos, see *PmbZ* # 23741; Spadaro 1971. See Introduction.
[152] Wortley 1977: 111–26. Cf. Baynes 1955a; 1955b; Wortley 2005; Cunningham 2015.
[153] Phot., *Homily* IV, 40–52, trans. Mango 95–110.
[154] *SynaxCP* 793,1–94,8; Wortley 1969/1970: 199–203; Shoemaker 2008: 56–60.
[155] *PmbZ* # 27616.   [156] Wortley 1977: 116, n. 23. On Theodoros Santabarenos, see n. 142.

Russian attack of 860.[157] From Sections 6.3.1–6.3.7, we shall concentrate mainly on authors and works that discuss the iconoclast crisis, rewriting it in accord with the interests of Photios' circle.

6.3.1 The Interpolation of the Vita of Georgios of Amastris

One of the works born of the image controversy that served the Photian milieu is the *vita* of Georgios of Amastris.[158] This was written by Ignatios Diakonos in the 820s and is considered one of the few surviving examples of true iconoclastic hagiography.[159] Georgios was a bishop who was well placed at court, due to his friendship with Empress Eirene the restorer, and had been ordained by Tarasios the bishop of Amastris (the area from which he originated)[160] ca. 790 despite the opposition of Emperor Konstantinos VI, who had his own candidate for the post. Despite the more or less legitimate aspirations of the emperor, the hagiographer defends the patriarch's action.[161] He was the protector of the iconodule Ioannes of Gotthia, one of the signatories of the anti-iconoclast precepts of the Second Council of Nicaea[162] and inspired the composition of the account of the relics of St Euphemia by Konstantinos of Tios.[163]

In its early stages, the cult of Georgios of Amastris had the unconditional support of both the patriarch Tarasios and Emperor Nikephoros I, who preserved the saint's clothes with great devotion and wore them because he considered them the talisman that guaranteed his power.[164] However much this iconodule environment surrounded the hero of the

---

[157] *Vita of Ignatios* 47; *PmbZ* # 7728; *PBE* I: Theodoros 132. In this enterprise, he was accompanied by Amphilochios of Kyzikos and Pantoleon Bothros, *PmbZ* # 283; *PBE* I: Amphilochios 1; *PmbZ* # 5707; *PBE* I: Pantaleon 6.

[158] Ševčenko 1977b: 150–73; Markopoulos 1979; Efthymiadis 1991a. Its date of composition has been much discussed: Vasilevskij, Ševčenko and Treadgold consider that it dates from 820/842, see Treadgold 1988/1990: 132–44. For his part, Kazhdan believes that it was written in the late tenth century or even later, see *Dumbarton Oaks Hagiography Database*, s.v. 'George of Amastris'.

[159] Ševčenko 1977a: 120–26; Markopoulos 1979; Efthymiadis 1991a: 75–80; Auzépy 1992; Kazhdan 1999: 356–66. Ignatios Diakonos' authorship of this hagiography was rejected by Costa-Louillet 1940/1941; Wolska-Conus 1970.

[160] *PmbZ* # 2183; *PBE* I: Georgios 2; Costa-Louillet 1954/1955: 479–92.

[161] *Vita of Georgios of Amastris* 18.

[162] *PmbZ* # 3118; *PBE* I: Ioannes 6; Halkin 1948: 80–83; Huxley 1978: 161–69; Kazhdan 1999: 199–200; Auzépy 2000; 2006. The *Vita of Ioannes of Gotthia* was produced during the Second Iconoclasm and specifically followed the rules dictated by Theodoros Stoudites to praise the hegoumenos who is involved in politics and must become a confessor, which meant that he began to be venerated after his death. Georgios of Nicomedia wrote the only surviving *kanon* in his honour, see Section 6.3.4.

[163] *Vita of Georgios of Amastris* 30,1–30; and 52,3–54,8; Cf. Ševčenko 1977a: n. 87.

[164] *Vita of Georgios of Amastris* 56.

story, the *vita* avoids any controversy involving the iconoclasts and does not attack them. What is more, Ignatios Diakonos' closeness to contemporary iconoclasts can be seen in the intertext he includes from a passage of the patristic anthology of 754.[165] The element that has attracted most attention from readers and scholars is a Russian attack on Byzantine lands, which is generally considered the first attested in the sources.[166] Georgios had distinguished himself in his leadership of the defence of the town of Amastris against an Arab raid on Paphlagonia.[167] According to Vasilevskij, this is the invasion led by Harun al-Rashid in 797, which took Saphrad and reached the town of Amorion, but Costa-Louillet wonders whether it was instead the expedition of 811, in which the Arabs seized Euchaita.[168]

After his death in February 806,[169] the relics of Georgios of Amastris continued to perform miracles. Prominent among his post-mortem miracles is the miraculous conversion of the Russians, who had violently invaded the province. When they entered the church and tried to open the saint's sepulchre, they were unable to do so, due to divine intervention.[170] They were so amazed at this that they embraced the Christian faith. As Markopoulos demonstrated in a now classic study, this part of the work stands out from the rest, since its style is characteristic of Photios.[171] Taking this into account, the Russian attack mentioned must be the one of summer 860, during which the patriarch was able to stand out in his own right, since the emperor was at the head of the army on the eastern frontier and the fleet was fighting the Arabs in the Mediterranean in reprisal for the plunder of the Cyclades; the city of Constantinople was defended only by the authority of the patriarch.[172] The immediate objective of the interpolation is to contribute to the greater glory of Photios, who converted the Russians and made of this one of his major pastoral achievements at the head of the patriarchate, as is apparent in his *Homilies* III and IV and in his *Encyclica ad sedes orientales* (*Epist.* 2,277–316), in which he expresses his joy at the conversion of this people and their acceptance of a bishop in

---

[165] Mansi XIII, 300AB, cf. *Vita of Georgios of Amastris* 24,5–9. See also Morini 1979.
[166] Vasiliev 1946; Vernadsky 1949; Sorlin 1961: 320f.; Ahrweiler 1971.
[167] *Vita of Georgios of Amastris* 24 and 25.   [168] Costa-Louillet 1954/1955: 486.
[169] The year was established by Costa-Louillet, but the exact day is not clear. According to the *vita* it was 8 February while the *synaxaria* commemorate it on 21 February, *SynaxCP* 481,44–82,28 (*BHG* 668e); *Typikon of the Great Church* I, 237.
[170] *Vita of Georgios of Amastris* 43–46, pp. 64,3–69,17. The conversion is also described by the historians Theoph. Cont. IV, 33; Ps-Symeon 674,20–23; Georgios Mon. Cont. 827,3–5; Symeon Logothetes 241,5–8.
[171] Markopoulos 1979.
[172] Grégoire 1933: 531–34; Peri 1988/1989; Havlikova 1993; Hurbanic 2005; Majeska 2005.

Kiev. The addition is also connected to the official propaganda that sought to portray the patriarch as an iconodule saint. In effect, this interpolation in a *vita* of the iconoclast period[173] created a surreptitious equation between Photios and Georgios of Amastris, since both accomplished the peaceful conversion of the cruel Russians.

6.3.2 The Vita *of Michael the Synkellos and the Monastery of Chora*

We have already seen that when Michael Synkellos was the head of the monastery of Chora, he played an active part in the propaganda programme of the patriarch Methodios and that the *vita* of the founder of that monastery, Theodoros, is due to his influence if not written personally by him (*BHG* 1743). The death of Michael Synkellos on 4 January 846 was followed by his canonisation, which Methodios must have enthusiastically approved, if his hagiographer is correct to mention the close friendship and great affection between the two men. It was probably at this initial stage of his cult that the first version of the *Vita of Michael the Synkellos* was produced; it was subsequently rewritten in the form of the surviving premetaphrastic hagiography (*BHG* 1296). The *post quem* date of its composition is the death in 847 of Methodios, who is mentioned as already deceased.[174] As Ševčenko has pointed out, the *ante quem* date is 867, given that Michael III is praised as a living emperor.[175] We do not know the author's identity, but his extensive treatment of the monastery of Chora in the final part shows that he was a monk from there.[176] His own words indicate that he was not particularly familiar with his hero.[177]

The textual strata of the work tell us that the initial concerns of its (first) author included praising the Amorian dynasty. Only in this way can we explain the salvational presence of Empress Euphrosyne, the daughter of Konstantinos V and granddaughter of St Philaretos, and the founder of the Amorian dynasty together with Michael II. In the hagiography, she aids Michael when he is imprisoned in the Praitorion in 836 by bringing him

---

[173] Indeed the *vita* of Georgios of Amastris survives only in the tenth-century manuscript *Parisinus Gr.* 1452, which also contains the *Vita of Tarasios* (also by Ignatios Diakonos) and several texts on Agatha, the Sicilian saint to whom the patriarch Methodios was so devoted, cf. Halkin 1968: 161–62.

[174] *Vita of Michael the Synkellos* 116,12–13: τὸν ἐν ἁγίοις καὶ μέγα πατριάρχην Μεθόδιον. See Chapter 2.

[175] Ševčenko 1977a: 116, n. 19.   [176] Cunningham 1991: 5.

[177] *Vita of Michael the Synkellos* 128,10–13.

The Milieu of Photios

food and clothing.[178] The representation of his mother as the patron of an iconodule saint mitigates the cruelty of Theophilos, increases the piety of the imperial family, and strengthens the model of holiness represented by Empress Theodora, the restorer of icons. There are numerous highly favourable mentions of the ruling dynasty and its Orthodoxy, such as the account of the enthronement of Michael III and his mother Theodora along with the restoration of icons, since Theodora is in charge of calling a synod to depose Ioannes VII Grammatikos and choose the new patriarch.[179] Other examples are the list of gifts they made to the monastery of Chora[180] and the detailed description of the imperial family's emotional farewell to the saint when his death was imminent, during which they fell at his feet to request his intercession.[181] These eulogies place us during the rule of Michael III, that is, before his murder in 867. It would have been difficult to write thus under Basileios I, who made the *psógos* (blame) of his predecessor a mainstay of his reign.

All these reasons, together with the dating of the death of Michael Synkellos by means of the year of the reign of Michael III and Theodora (as in the first texts on the martyrs of Amorion),[182] indicate initial writing during the first patriarchate of Ignatios or the first patriarchate of Photios.[183] The definitive form of the *vita*, the version that has come down to us, is slightly later. As Sode demonstrated, this hagiography owes a debt to the *enkomion* in honour of Theodoros Graptos, an alleged disciple of the saint, which was composed by Theophanes of Caesarea during the second patriarchate of Photios.[184] In the form in which it has reached us, the *Vita of Michael the Synkellos* reflects deep concern for the matter of the *filioque*, which was not part of public or private debate until Photios' second patriarchate (877–886).[185] The author, wishing to make

---

[178] *Vita of Michael the Synkellos* 74,9–16. For the identification of Euphrosyne, see Treadgold 1979b: 188, n. 139. On this empress, cf. *PmbZ* # 1705 and 1708; *PBE* I: Euphrosyne 1; Treadgold 1975: 338–40.
[179] *Vita of Michael the Synkellos* 100,7–16; 100,28–29; 102,3–4.
[180] *Vita of Michael the Synkellos* 116,17–18.
[181] *Vita of Michael the Synkellos* 122,13–17: τὸν ὀρθόδοξον καὶ θεόστεπτον ἄνακτα Μιχαὴλ ἀνελθὼν καὶ τὴν αὐτοῦ θεοφιλῆ μητέρα, Θεοδώραν λέγω τὴν ὀρθόδοξον καὶ μεγάλην βασίλισσαν ... οἱ δὲ πιστότατοι καὶ ὀρθόδοξοι βασιλεῖς. According to Cunningham 1991: 170, n. 213, the order of words suggests that Theodora continued to exercise imperial power due to the minority of Michael III.
[182] *Vita of Michael the Synkellos* 112,25–29.
[183] This was the opinion of most authors following the thesis of Ševčenko, see Featherstone 1980: 97; Cunningham 1991: 6, n. 16; Auzépy 1999: 204, n. 95 specifies that it was produced in 847–858 during Ignatios' patriarchate; Auzépy 2001: 313, n. 73.
[184] Sode 2001: 49–94; 2004: 188. On this *enkomion*, see Section 6.3.3.
[185] Borgolte 1980; Sode 2001: 163–202.

Michael Synkellos a precursor of the fight against the dogmatic deviation of the *filioque* and the error of the Franks, affirms that an anonymous Pope of Rome asked Thomas the patriarch of Jerusalem to help combat this dogmatic fault. His reply was to send the eloquent Michael and the monk Iob together with their disciples, the Graptoi brothers, in 813.[186] This legendary explanation of how the Palestinian saints reached Constantinople – they were on the way to Rome, but had to remain to fight iconoclasm – is supported by the inclusion of the Graptoi in the hagiography of the *synkellos*, as pilgrims with no special link to him who are praised to strengthen the main account and Michael's alleged mission.

Photios' second patriarchate is also the most likely context for the copying of manuscript *Parisinus Gr.* 923, a lavishly illuminated codex containing an important religious *florilegium* of Palestinian origin (the PML[b]). Its production has been attributed to the monastery of Chora, and its addressee has been identified with the Emperor Basileios I himself.[187] The interest of the monks of Chora in pleasing this emperor and providing him with books and intellectual resources was along the lines of Photios' policy. Likewise, the rewriting of the *Vita of Michael the Synkellos* under Photios' patriarchal aegis explains its author's use (and abuse) of the *vita* of St Stephanos the Younger, whose veneration and hagiographical account was promoted by the patriarch Nikephoros, with whom (as noted above) Photios wished to be identified by all possible means. In her edition of the *vita* of St Stephanos the Younger, Auzépy has also noted the major textual debt to this hagiography of the work dedicated to Michael Synkellos.[188] Chapter 28 of the *vita* of Michael the Synkellos also overlaps to a considerable extent with the chapters of the *vita* of Theodoros of Chora devoted to the history of this monastery.[189] This shows that the text already existed for Loparev, the editor of the *vita* of Theodoros of Chora, and was copied when the *vita* of Michael the Synkellos was produced.[190] For Mango, the two *vitae* draw independently from a common source, which was probably not a hagiographical account but a narrative describing the foundation of the monastery of Chora.[191]

---

[186] Cunningham 1991: 9–13; *Vita of Michael the Synkellos* 6, 54–59.
[187] Declerck 2017. Chora continued to be an important cultural centre where manuscript production also flourished, as is apparent from the codex *Parisinus Coislin Gr.* 303, copied in this very monastery in the tenth century, see Binggeli 2018: 272–73.
[188] Auzépy 1999: 195. We find re-uses taken from numerous chapters of the *vita* of Stephanos the Younger (chs. 11, 29, 30, 34, 35, 40, 44, 45, 55, 66, 74 and 77), but the repetition of a long passage in the epilogue of the *vita* of Michael the Synkellos stands out (*Vita of Stephanos the Younger* 78).
[189] *Vita of Michael the Synkellos* 28, pp. 106,9–8,19 = *Vita of Theodoros of Chora* 23–25 and 27.
[190] This opinion is shared by Auzépy 1994: 211, n. 199; 2001: 313.   [191] Mango 2009: 189.

Regardless of whether such an account existed, the presence of both texts in the only two manuscripts that present these *vitae* tell us of an 'edition' of the *menologion* produced in Chora, paying particular attention to the saints who lay within its walls.[192] In this same 'edition' of the *menologion*, a place was found for the *vita* of the patriarch Germanos (715–730), the first leader who confronted iconoclasm (*BHG* 697).[193] The *vita*, which is highly legendary, has been transmitted as anonymous and has given rise to much speculation as to its date of composition.[194] That this hagiography insists that the monastery of Chora was the place of the eternal rest of Germanos;[195] that it owes a considerable debt to the *vita* of Stephanos the Younger, like the texts previously discussed[196] and that it ignores the martyrdoms caused by the destruction of the Chalke Gate icon at the end of the patriarchate of Germanos,[197] confirms that this was the context of its composition. The hagiographer, closer to the milieu of Photios, encourages Germanos' veneration by failing to mention what happened at the Chalke Gate, the saints of which had been vindicated and used by Ignatios and his followers.[198] This silence is as eloquent as his words and reveals his affiliation.

6.3.3 *Theophanes of Caesarea and His* Enkomion *of Theodoros Graptos*

The Graptoi brothers are intimately linked to the monastery of Chora and related by tradition to Michael Synkellos; their remains ended up in the same place in the monastery. Of the two Palestinian brothers, Theodoros was the one chosen as the protagonist of a eulogy of his defence of icons written by a close collaborator of the patriarch Photios, Theophanes of Caesarea.[199] Also known as Theophanes Sphenodaimon, this imperial

---

[192] These are the codices Genoa Urbani 33, tenth-eleventh century, and Pantokrator 13, twelfth century, which contain a version of the January *menologion* that includes the *vita* of Michael the Synkellos, to be read on the 4th, and the *vita* of Theodoros of Chora, corresponding to 5 (in the Genoa ms.) or 8 January. For these manuscripts, see Ehrhard 1936–1939: vol. I, 544–45; vol. II, 208–9 and vol. III, 196; Cataldi Palau 1996: 127–28; Mango 2009: 186.
[193] Lamza 1975: 200–40.
[194] It has been proposed that it dates from the eighth century (Beck 1959: 506), or the ninth century (Halkin in *AnBoll* 93 (1975): 423; Garton and Westerink 1979: v, n. 1; Auzépy 1999: 194 and 204, n. 95). According to Kazhdan 1999: 55–56, the text goes back to the late tenth century, while its editor considered that it belonged to the eleventh century (Lamza 1975: 39). Even the early twelfth century has been proposed by Ševčenko 1977a: 114, n. 4.
[195] *Vita of Germanos* 31,519–20; *SynaxCP* 677,20–80,5 (12 May).
[196] As it replaces chapters 5 and 55 of the *Vita* of Stephanos the Younger.
[197] *Vita of Germanos* 21–23; Lemerle 1971: 89–96.   [198] See Chapter 5.
[199] *PmbZ* # 28076, which quotes Photios' *epist*. 241 among its sources but forgets to mention his titles of *diakonos* and *protonotarios*; *PBE* I: Theophanes 22.

priest (κληρικὸς βασιλικός) already appears in the minutes of the Ignatian Council of 869/870 as one of the accomplices of Photios who helped him falsify a *libellus* against Pope Nicholas I.[200] Despite this, during Photios' exile, he was kept active and thanks to his wisdom, he enjoyed a certain degree of intimacy with Emperor Basileios I, which allowed him to help the deposed patriarch. In this way, he acted as a go-between for the two men ca. 873, putting to Photios in the emperor's name a series of biblical questions concerning the kings of the Old Testament.[201] We do not know to what extent Theophanes' role was determinant, but authors opposing Photios relate that he took part in the conspiracy orchestrated by the patriarch in exile to win the favour of Basileios I and return to Constantinople. According to them, the ex-patriarch forged a book that Theophanes hid in the imperial library and then pretended to find.[202] Allegedly, only the wisdom of Photios could interpret its obscure content regarding an epic genealogy of the emperor and a series of prophecies about the glorious future of his family. The satisfied emperor rewarded Theophanes by appointing him archbishop of Caesarea in Cappadocia and allowed Photios to return to the court.

As unlikely as this story may seem, a letter survives in which Photios forgives Theophanes' betrayal and affirms that he considers him a true friend (*epist.* 84). Was this perhaps gratitude for services rendered? In fact, there had clearly been tension between Photios and Theophanes because the latter had turned away from the patriarch during his exile, as is clear from the long prologue of *epist.* 241, which is full of reproaches, and the closing section, in which Theophanes is warned that he is close to Hell.[203] Whatever the relationship between the two clerics we know that Theophanes went from being *diakonos* and *protonotarios* to leading the diocese of Caesarea in 880. It was Photios himself who installed him in this important post – Caesarea was the first metropolis of the Constantinopolitan patriarchate, which meant that the metropolitan at its head lived in Constantinople and was *protothronos* (chairman) of the synod.[204] – Another epistle Photios sent on various ecclesiastical matters also testifies how close the two men became: this is *epist.* 281, in the first part of which the patriarch encourages Theophanes to be optimistic, since God is protecting him and has saved him from slander.

---

[200] Mansi XVI, 445C.
[201] Phot., *epist.* 241 on 1 Kings 5:10–11 and 1 Sam 16:13. This letter entered the collection of theological treatises as Phot., *Amph.* 115: Πῶς ἐσοφίσατο Σολομὼν ὑπὲρ πάντας ἀνθρώπους καὶ ὑπὲρ Γαιθὰν τὸν Ἰσραηλίτην; cf. Hergenröther 1867–1869: vol. II, 253–54; Prieto Domínguez 2014a: 297–98.
[202] *Vita of Ignatios* 90; Ps-Symeon 689,5–90,3; Moravcsik 1961: 66–69; Treadgold 2004.
[203] Phot., *epist.* 241,4–23 and 98–101. [204] Beck 1959: 158; *Vita of the Patriarch Euthymios* 208.

The Milieu of Photios 363

Photios urges Theophanes to devote himself completely to his work as a priest and gives him various administrative instructions referring to the general of the *thema*, the process of reconciliation with the Ignatians, the punishment of bishop Xyraphios and the choice of his substitute as bishop of Dasbentos.[205] The composition of the *enkomion* of Theodoros Graptos reflects the collaboration and understanding between the two men. Despite the long time that he had spent in the Photian ranks, Theophanes was able to win over the new Emperor Leon VI, and when the latter deposed Photios, it was Theophanes who consecrated the new patriarch Stephanos (886–893), the emperor's younger brother.[206] Theophanes likely continued to lead the diocese of Caesarea in Cappadocia until his death, which occurred before 902, by when we know that Arethas held the same post.

Theophanes' literary production also includes, in addition to the aforementioned *enkomion*, two *Laudationes* that remain unpublished: one in honour of the prophet Elijah (*BHG* 577c), the other dedicated to the saints Menas, Hermogenes and Eugraphos (*BHG* 1271d).[207] All these pieces are perfectly in keeping with the interests of the Byzantine court during the second patriarchate of Photios. We have already mentioned the special devotion Emperor Basileios professed for Elijah, to whom he dedicated the church of Nea that was consecrated by Photios in 880.[208] On the other hand, the alleged discovery of the relics of St Menas during those years gave rise to the production of several texts in honour of the saint[209] and of the emperor, as the party ultimately responsible for finding and liturgically enhancing Menas' remains.[210] Although this material is certainly legendary, its creation is in keeping with the splendour the church of St Menas acquired during this period.[211] Not only did the alleged relics of its holy patron saint reach there, but the church is mentioned in the new accounts of the passion of St Menas and was even chosen for the temporary resting place of the body of the patriarch Ignatios immediately after his death.[212]

If we concentrate on the *Enkomion of Theodoros Graptos* (*BHG* 1745z),[213] it is apparent that the text is the first in the written tradition

---

[205] *PmbZ* # 28455.   [206] Theoph. Cont. VI, 2, 354,5–7.   [207] Featherstone 1980: 95–96.
[208] The feast day of Elijah (20 July) was ostentatiously celebrated by the imperial family at the church of Nea, see Magdalino 1987; 1988a; 1988b; Brubaker 1999a: 170; Gallina 2011.
[209] Beck 1959: 561; Delehaye 2010.
[210] *SynaxCP* 470,19–40 (17 February). See Delehaye 2010: 142.
[211] Janin 1969: 333–35; Delehaye 2010: 146–50.   [212] *Vita of Ignatios* 76,3–14.
[213] Featherstone 1980; Sode 2001: 49–94. For Theodoros Graptos, see *PmbZ* # 7526; *PBE* I: Theodoros 68.

regarding the Graptoi brothers and Michael Synkellos. Theophanes of Caesarea affirms this.[214] The *enkomion* also does not include details that were later added by tradition, as is shown by the fact that it mentions that the brothers were punished by tattooing but not the twelve iambic verses printed on them (*BHG* 1746a).[215] This type of addition is characteristic of the gradual procedure of hagiographers, who, in their desire to praise and magnify the feats of the iconodule heroes, resorted to exaggeration to guarantee an increase in their veneration. In fact, not much more than one word was likely tattooed on the Graptoi brothers.[216] The process of progressive exaggeration by successive iconodule authors is well documented,[217] and the *Enkomion of Theodoros Graptos* thus predates the *vita* of Michael the Synkellos and served as a source for it.[218]

In contrast to the *vita* of Theodoros' alleged teacher Michael Synkellos, who affirms that Theodoros survived to witness the Triumph of Orthodoxy and attended the official restoration of icons, the *enkomion* maintains the opposite: the saint died while Theophilos was alive (in December 841) in exile in Apamea in Bithynia, where his funeral took place and where his relics were subsequently transferred to a monastery in Chalcedon through the mediation of his brother Theophanes.[219] The first of these two traditions is in keeping with Empress Theodora's desire to rehabilitate her husband implying Theophilos' forgiveness and is the one chosen by later historians such as Theophanes Continuatus.[220] The second is the version followed by the chroniclers of the Logothetes group. In fact, Pseudo-Symeon tells us that the monastery in which the remains of Theodoros were laid was called Michaelitzes after its founder, a certain Michael.[221] If we see in the pious Michael, who receives the saint's relics in his foundation, a reflection of Emperor Michael III, it is easy to

---

[214] *Enkomion of Theodoros Graptos* 5, 108,3–6.
[215] *Enkomion of Theodoros Graptos* 36–37, 144–45. This information appears in the remainder of the surviving hagiographical dossier devoted to Michael Synkellos and the Graptoi brothers: *Vita of Michael the Synkellos*; the metaphrastic *Vita of Theodoros Graptos* by Symeon Metaphrastes himself; *Vita of Theophanes Graptos* of the thirteenth-century Theodora Raoulena Paleologina (Rizzo Nervo 1991); *Vita of Michael the Synkellos* by Nikephoros Gregoras from the fourteenth century (Guilland 1926: 173–77). See Chapter 2.
[216] Sode 2001: 86–89; 2004: 187–88.
[217] Schreiner 1976: 166–70; 1988: 484–92; Auzépy 1990: 445–51; Hatlie 2007a: 412, n. 16.
[218] Contrary to traditional consensus. See Featherstone 1980: 97–103; Efthymiadis 1995: 142.
[219] *Enkomion of Theodoros Graptos* 39–41, 146–48; *Vita of Theodoros Graptos* 680–84. For the various traditions of Theodoros Graptos' death, see Sode 2001: 247–49.
[220] *Narratio de Theophili absolutione* 32,4; *Narratio amplior de Theophili absolutione* 32,8; *Narratio historica in festum restitutionis imaginum* 3,31; Theoph. Cont. IV, 11; Skylitzes 89,17ff.
[221] Ps-Symeon 643,8–10. On the monastery of Michaelitzes in Chalcedon, see Janin 1975: 34; Ruggieri 1991: 201. About its founder, see *PmbZ* # 25126.

understand the success of this version of the end of Theodoros Graptos (as opposed to the one that serves the interests of his mother) enthusiastically spread by the followers of the young ruler.

In any case, Theodoros ended up resting in the monastery of Chora alongside Theophanes Graptos. There Theophanes of Caesarea saw both bodies buried along with that of Michael Synkellos, the author of the *vita* of the latter, since he affirms that Theodoros was interred in Chora along with his teacher and friend Michael Synkellos.[222] We have no information regarding when Theodoros' relics were transferred from Chalcedon to Chora, but we can accept the death of Theodoros in exile and his initial burial at Chalcedon as historical fact. Taking into account that the *enkomion* Theophanes of Caesarea wrote in his honour was proclaimed in Constantinople, as internal references show,[223] it is reasonable to believe that it represents a response to the arrival of the remains of Theodoros Graptos at his new destination or the first liturgical celebration in his memory there.[224] This explains why Theodoros was chosen as the protagonist of this work rather than his brother, who already rested in Constantinople and was regularly venerated there. Moreover, the extensive written production of Theodoros – a letter to Ioannes, a controversial compendium against iconoclasts (*Kynolykos*), *enkomia* honouring saints, etc. – provided valuable textual material. Theophanes does not mention his sources on Theodoros, which must have been meagre, to judge by the large number of commonplaces and edifying reflections introduced into the account. He adduces only oral testimony when he describes the first funeral of the saint in Apamea (contrary to the imperial order of Theophilos prohibiting his burial), reporting that an old man said that a miracle took place as an angelic voice was heard.[225]

According to Theophanes of Caesarea himself, his aim was to celebrate the saint's feast day, but also to propose him as a model of virtue and have his example followed by the faithful.[226] This desire to recover saints from the iconoclastic period in order to promote their veneration is characteristic of the Photian party, which vindicated many of these New Martyrs and appropriated their memory, consolidating and disseminating their veneration. In this context, the memory of the Graptoi, pious pilgrims

---

[222] *Vita of Michael the Synkellos* 31. See Chapter 2.
[223] *Enkomion of Theodoros Graptos* 14, 120,15–16 and 18, p. 124,19–20. See Featherstone 1980: 97.
[224] *Enkomion of Theodoros Graptos* 14, 120,17–19. More details were probably given on this third and final transfer at the end of the eulogy, which unfortunately has been lost.
[225] *Enkomion of Theodoros Graptos* 39, 147,2–6. See Sode 2001: 92, n. 182.
[226] *Enkomion of Theodoros Graptos* 1–3, 104–7.

with no particular support from any institution who were said to have defended icons, became a legitimating element for an important Constantinopolitan sector whose interests were linked to the monastery of Chora. This process connects with the work carried out by Photios to depict the new emperor, Basileios I, as a pious and orthodox sovereign, who, despite not being responsible for the restoration of icons, was the guarantor of their maintenance, as was clear from his concern to invigorate the cult of the saints that made it possible. To be precise, a comparison of Theodoros Graptos with the prophet Elijah, the holy protector of Basileios I, twice underlines the hagiographer's wish to make the emperor party to the cult of the iconodule hero.[227] This is the origin of the new versions of the story of the protagonists of the restoration. Moreover, this enterprise favoured the interests of the new emperor, who wished to consolidate his dynasty at the cost of the previous one, strengthening his image as Orthodox by exaggerating the bad reputation of Theophilos as an iconoclast, whose sins contaminated his entire family. As well as attacking Theophilos for his impiety (again on two occasions),[228] therefore, the writer mentions neither Theodora nor Michael III when he describes the defeat of the iconoclast heresy, creating the fiction that the restoration of icons was a spontaneous event unconnected with imperial power.[229]

The connection of the *Enkomion of Theodoros Graptos* with the patriarchal circle led by Photios is apparent not only from the author's personal connections and the objectives he pursued with his work but from the text itself. On the one hand, its content is clearly indebted to the *Vita Nicephori* Ignatios Diakonos was commissioned to write by Methodios. Whether it be a common compositional resource or a personal, voluntary tribute, Theophanes was inspired by it to construct Theodoros Graptos' long theological dispute with Theophilos, which strikingly recalls the passage in which the patriarch Nikephoros confronts Emperor Leon V.[230] The pompous final *synkrisis*, in which Theodoros is compared to various biblical personages and to Christ himself, also follows a model similar to the close of the *Vita Nicephori*.[231] There is no need to insist on Photios' desire to identify himself with this predecessor and to propose works about him written within the patriarchal milieu as productive literary models.

---

[227] *Enkomion of Theodoros Graptos* 11, 118,2–4 and 19, 126,19–20.
[228] *Enkomion of Theodoros Graptos* 25, 131,4–5 and 27, 133,15–17 (comparing Theophilos with Pontius Pilate).
[229] *Enkomion of Theodoros Graptos* 41, 147.
[230] *Enkomion of Theodoros Graptos* 27–35, 133–44; *Vita of Nikephoros* 169,23–88,22.
[231] *Enkomion of Theodoros Graptos* 42, 148–50; *Vita of Nikephoros* 210,26–13,18.

On the other hand, the manuscript in which the *enkomion* is preserved confirms this. This is a *codex unicus*, Istanbul, Patriarchal Library, Hagia Trias 88, a late ninth-century *menologion* for the month of December and therefore contemporary with Theophanes of Caesarea.[232] The works contained in this manuscript include the *vita* of Euthymios, the metropolitan of Sardis (*BHG* 2145), fol. 227v–52v, which is intended to be read on 26 December immediately before the *Enkomion of Theodoros Graptos*, fol. 255–79v, which belonged to 28 December. In the two folios that separate the two *vitae*, St Stephanos the Protomartyr is celebrated (27 December); his name gave rise to confusion (perhaps voluntary) with Stephanos Sabaites, a martyr of Palestine origin to whom the monks of Chora were particularly devoted.[233] The same codex preserves a summary of the *vita* of St Lucia (*BHG* 995e), fol. 112v–13,[234] to whom her fellow Sicilian, the patriarch Methodios, was devoted, and two texts by Michael Monachos: the *vita* of Nicholas of Myra (*BHG* 1348), which he wrote following that of Methodios, and the *enkomion* of the prophet Daniel and the three youths in the furnace (*BHG* 488a). The combination of all these texts, which are closely connected to the patriarchate of Constantinople and the liturgy it promoted, indicates that the constitution of this *menologion* derives from there and likely dates to the second patriarchate of Photios, when it may well have been copied together. The most recent text must be that of Theophanes of Caesarea, which stresses the importance attached by the post-iconoclast Church to the iconodule saints of the Second Iconoclasm, such as Euthymios of Sardis and Theodoros Graptos, and indirectly reveals the service Photios was rendered at the end of his tenure by hagiographers who were well placed in the patriarchate, such as Michael Monachos, Theophanes of Caesarea and the patriarch Methodios himself.

6.3.4 Georgios of Nicomedia

Georgios was a *chartophylax* of Hagia Sophia[235] whose friendship with Photios is well documented in the patriarch's collected letters, eleven of which were sent to him.[236] Six of these are biblical exegeses later included in the collection of *Amphilochia*,[237] while the remaining five testify to

---

[232] Delehaye 1926: 19, nr. 23; Ehrhard 1936–1939: vol. I, 509–12.   [233] Auzépy 1994: 207–9.
[234] Halkin 1956.   [235] *PmbZ* # 2259, # 2273 and # 22083; *PBE* I: Georgios 223.
[236] Phot., *epist.* 26, 126, 156, 164–66, 169, 199, 201, 216, 248 and 277.
[237] Phot., *epist.* 156 = *Amph.* 86: Τί σημαίνει τὸ 'ἐγκομβώσασθαι' παρὰ τῷ ἀποστόλῳ Πέτρῳ ἐν ταῖς καθολικαῖς ἐπιστολαῖς εἰρμένον; *Epist.* 164 = *Amph.* 91: Τί ἐστιν 'οὐ θέλω ὑμᾶς ἀγνοεῖν, ἀδελφοί, ὅτι πολλάκις προεθέμην ἐλθεῖν πρὸς ὑμᾶς καὶ ἐκωλύθην ἄχρι τοῦ δεῦρο; An excerptum of this

Georgios' erudition,[238] his philological interests[239] and his closeness to Photios, whom he frequently consulted regarding the administration of the metropolitan see of Nicomedia, at the head of which Photios placed him in 860/861.[240] Georgios' loyalty to the patriarch led to his participation in the council for the reinstatement of his patron in 879/880.[241] Among the men of letters of Photios' milieu, Georgios stood out for his production of homilies – nine Marian sermons for the main feast days of the Virgin and a tenth homily written in honour of the medical saints Kosmas and Damian (*BHG* 381)[242] – but above all for his hymnographical work, to the extent that the composition of liturgical *kanones* is the main justification for his holiness in the succinct entry in the *Synaxarion of Constantinople*.[243] Although his cult is not attested outside the capital, his canonisation is highly significant, since it follows the pattern already analysed, in which a man of letters who works to establish and promote the cult of more or less contemporary heroes ends up subject to similar veneration.

Apart from the *enkomion* he wrote in honour of Nicholas of Myra (*BHG* 1364b), the hymns composed by Georgios of Nicomedia include several pieces that reveal his concern for current events, in which he helps spread the official patriarchate propaganda of Photios and his other collaborators.[244] A good example is the *kanon* Georgios dedicated to the deposition

---

matter is developed in *Amph*. 284: Τί ἐστιν τὸ 'καὶ ἐκωλύθην ἄχρι τοῦ δεῦρο, ἵνα καρπόν τινα σχῶ; *Epist*. 165 = *Amph*. 92: Πῶς ῥητόρων ἰδέαις αἱ τοῦ ἀποστόλου ἐπιστολαὶ σχηματίζονται, καὶ πῶς ἐκεῖνος ἰδιώτην αὐτὸν καλεῖ; *Epist*. 166 = *Amph*. 93: Ζητήματα διάφορα τοῦ ἀποστόλου διὰ κ' καὶ ζ' κεφαλαίων ἐπιλυόμενα; *epist*. 216 = *Amph*. 112: Τί ἐστιν τὸ 'ηὐχόμην αὐτὸς ἀνάθεμα εἶναι ὑπὲρ τῶν ἀδελφῶν μου τῶν συγγενῶν μου τῶν κατὰ σάρκα; *Epist*. 248 = *Amph*. 118: Διὰ τί περιετμήθη ὁ Χριστός;

[238] Phot., *epist*. 169, from which we know that Georgios used to compare Photios to Hippocrates and Galen for their medical knowledge; Phot., *epist*. 277 enlightens him on drunkenness by using one of Aesop's fables (otherwise unknown) in which Dionysius had three grapes: he kept the first for himself, he gave the second to Aphrodite and the third to Licentiousness (Ὕβρις). Their owners (Dionysius, Aphrodite and Licentiousness), accordingly, correspond to the various stages of drunkenness: effusiveness, love and lack of temperance, see Grumel 1951; Perry 1953.

[239] Phot., *epist*. 156 concerning the verb ἐγκομβώσασθαι used in Peter's first letter (1 Pet 5:5), which Georgios considered a barbarism (βαρβάρου φωνῆς). Photios replied that the word was perfectly attic and attested in authors such as Epicharmos and Apollodoros of Carystus, see Baldwin 1986; Anastasi 1988.

[240] Phot., *epist*. 26 encourages him to remain in the post of metropolitan. Phot., *epist*. 199 approves Georgios' decision to reprimand Petronios (*PmbZ* # 5938). Phot., *epist*. 201 comforts him in various ways after the death of a priest ordered by Georgios who had died while the patriarch was in exile.

[241] Mansi XVIIA, 373B; 500D.

[242] On the literary technique of Georgios' homilies, Tsironis 1998; Kazhdan 2006: 38–41; Shoemaker 2011.

[243] *SynaxCP* 356,20–22 (29 December): τῇ αὐτῇ ἡμέρᾳ μνήμη τοῦ ἐν ἁγίοις πατρὸς ἡμῶν Γεωργίου ἐπισκόπου Νικομηδείας τοῦ ποιητοῦ τῶν κανόνων.

[244] For the facet of Georgios of Nicomedia as hymnographer, see Follieri 1964; Papaeliopoulou-Photopoulou 1994/1995; Spanos 2010: 81–83.

of the garment of the Theotokos in the church of Blachernai,[245] a feast day celebrated on 2 July that recalled the return to the church of the dress of the Virgin that miraculously protected the city from the Russian attack thanks to the procession organised by Photios.[246] During Photios' second patriarchate, Georgios also composed a large number of pieces for the celebrations held in the church of Chalkoprateia, assuming control of feasts previously promoted by the Ignatians, such as the deposition of the Virgin's girdle.[247]

A verse regarding internal disagreements within the Church in a *kanon* in honour of St Mokios and the anniversary of the foundation of Constantinople should also be understood as linking liturgical feast days to the present. It was common to take advantage of this second anniversary to praise the Theotokos as well, as the patron and protector of the Byzantine capital.[248] The innovation of the metropolitan of Nicomedia lies in including references only explainable in light of the iconoclast question and the Photian schism. According to him, after the city of Constantinople turns its back on the troops of iconoclasm and internal strife, it proceeds to venerate the Virgin and her golden icon.[249]

The production of Georgios not only addresses the interests of the hard core of the patriarchal milieu, as is apparent from the hymn he penned to honour Stephanos the Younger,[250] a devotion maintained throughout the ninth century by the patriarchate as an institution, but also connects to the interests of Emperor Basileios. Basileios doubtless approved of the hymnographer, writing a piece in praise of the prophet Elijah, his own patron,[251] and another dedicated to St Menas, whose veneration had been invigorated by the discovery of his relics during the reign of Basileios.[252]

Of the extensive catalogue of pieces attributed to Georgios, relatively few celebrate iconodule saints, which makes his selection significant. The patriarch Tarasios, the first restorer of Orthodoxy and a paternal uncle of

---

[245] Papaeliopoulou-Photopoulou 1994/1995: 465–71; *Tameion*, 237, nr. 730.
[246] *SynaxCP* 793,1–94,8. A similar *kanon* for this same celebration was composed by Ioseph Hymnographos, Tomadakes 1971a: 173–74, nr. 322. This hymn is edited in *Menaion* VI: 15–21; Kazhdan 1996.
[247] *Menaion* VI: 558; Krausmüller 2011: 232–34, who includes the editions of these sermons and *kanones* of Georgios of Nicomedia.
[248] Papaeliopoulou-Photopoulou 1994/1995: 456–63.
[249] Papaeliopoulou-Photopoulou 1994/1995: 461: ᾠδὴ ζ'. Εἰκόνος χρυσῆς / Ὑψαύχενα νοῦν, / πολεμίαν καὶ θρασεῖαν πᾶσαν φάλαγγα / καὶ ἐμφυλίους στάσεις, ἄχραντε, / καὶ πᾶσαν βίου δυσχέρειαν / ἡ ἀνατεθεῖσά σοι πόλις / ἐκτρεπομένη δοξάζει σε / ἐγκαινισμῷ τῶν διὰ σοῦ καλῶν ἑκάστοτε.
[250] *Tameion*, 109, nr. 292.   [251] *Tameion*, 250, nr. 776.   [252] *Tameion*, 122, nr. 338.

Photios, is the protagonist of one of the *kanones*[253] and the patriarch Nikephoros of another.[254] Several of the iconodule saints promoted by Methodios were also the subject of liturgical pieces penned by Georgios, including Ioannikios, a point of reference of the resistance to iconoclasm and Bithynian hermit life,[255] the forty-two martyrs of Amorion[256] and Georgios of Mytilene, who is celebrated together with his brother Symeon of Lesbos.[257] It is striking that, along with these famous saints with extensive hagiographical and liturgical dossiers, Georgios also writes of other, seemingly much less successful cults. This is the case with Hilarion,[258] an iconodule hegoumenos of Pelekete of for whom no *vita* survives, and of whom we in fact know almost nothing except what is found in his entry in the *Synaxarion*.[259] Another example is the marginal saint Ioannes of Gotthia, whose *vita* (*BHG* 891) was produced outside the most productive centers in Constantinople and Bithynia, probably in Amastris, and whose veneration seems to have been very limited. Although he has an entry in the *Synaxarion of Constantinople*,[260] the only surviving *kanon* dedicated to him also honours the sixth-century abbot David of Thessaloniki, who has the same feast day.[261]

Georgios of Nicomedia also encouraged other devotions with substantial ideological content, as is shown by his *kanon* in honour of abbot Dios, an ascetic of Syrian origin who laid the foundations for Constantinopolitan monasticism.[262] He thus followed the example of Theodoros Stoudites, who had praised Dios in one epigram,[263] and of his contemporary Ioseph Hymnographos,[264] making Georgios too part of a distinct

---

[253] *Menaion* III: 665–70.
[254] *Tameion*, 165, nr. 488; Follieri 1964: 317. An *akolouthia* for this patriarch also survives in the codex Lesbos *Leimonos* 11, see Spanos 2010: 160–69 and 396–97.
[255] This hymn, which was sung on 4 November, was edited in *AHG*, vol. III, 111–21 and 569–70. On Ioannikios, see Sections 2.2.1 and 7.1.1.
[256] *Tameion*, 173, nr. 518, see also nrs. 519–20.
[257] *Tameion*, 192–93, nr. 582. Arbitrarily and without any evidence, this poem is attributed by Eustratiadès 1936: 538 to Theophanes Graptos.
[258] *Tameion*, 181, nr. 546. Ioseph Hymnographos also dedicated him a *kanon*, see Tomadakes 1971a: 152, nr. 219; *Menaion* IV: 198–203. See Chapter 3.
[259] *SynaxCP* 564,5–6 (27 March); 565,37 (27 March); 573,33 (30 March). See Section 1.4.
[260] *SynaxCP* 772,21–74,4 (26 June).
[261] This *kanon*, which has a lacuna, has been preserved only in the manuscript Lesbos *Leimonos* 11, see Spanos 2010: 68–70, 339–41 and 419–21. For the authorship of Georgios of Nicomedia, see *Tameion*, 227, nr. 699, n. 602.
[262] This *kanon* is still unpublished, see *AHG*, vol. XI, 605. At least two testimonies of it survive: *Sinaiticus Gr.* 627, fol. 67–69 and Meteora Metamorphoseos 150, fol. 154–56, see Krausmüller 2007b.
[263] Theod. Stoud., 'On Dios' (nr. 84), ed. Speck 239.   [264] Tomadakes 1971a: 178, nr. 343.

6.3.5 The Monk and Philosopher Nikephoros

We are familiar with the monk Nikephoros primarily thanks to the letters of the patriarch, who sent him eight missives from exile.[265] The letters suggest that the two men were close friends, since the patriarch insists that Nikephoros come and visit him,[266] despite the fact that Nikephoros had a moment of doubt when his loyalty appeared to waver out of fear of losing the favour of Emperor Basileios.[267] The letters also show that the monk was extremely interested in literary matters and harboured hagiographical pretensions, as a result of which he asked Photios for advice on more than one occasion.[268] There can be no doubt that Nikephoros was a true intellectual, as is apparent from the title that the patriarch gives him in every one of his letters, Νικηφόρῳ φιλοσόφῳ μονάζοντι. The denomination 'philosopher' is infrequent in this period and is awarded only to persons who stand out for their intellectual capacity, such as Leon the Mathematician, Niketas Byzantios and Konstantinos-Kyrillos the evangelist of the Slavs, or in the seventh century, Maximos the Confessor and Doctor Theophilos.[269] A distinguished hagiographer contemporary with Photios was also referred to thus: Niketas David Paphlagon, the author of the *Vita Ignatii*.[270] In the late nineteenth century, Norden identified this Nikephoros with the philosopher and rhetor of the same name who wrote various *vitae*,[271] of which an *enkomion* of the patriarch of Constantinople Antonios II Kauleas, who died on 12 February 901, survives (*BHG* 139).[272] The latter text includes references to the theology of images[273] and a succinct mention of the defeat of iconoclasm.[274] Nikephoros also

---

[265] Phot., *epist.* 204, 217, 235, 237, 238 and 242–44. All were written shortly before 875, when he returned to the Constantinopolitan court, see Hergenröther 1867–1869: vol II, 271–77; Brokkaar 1995.
[266] Phot., *epist.* 217, 237 and 238. On Nikephoros, see *PmbZ* # 25544.
[267] Phot., *epist.* 242–44, esp. *epist.* 243,96–98.   [268] Phot., *epist.* 204, 235 and 242.
[269] On the meaning acquired by the terms φιλόσοφος and φιλοσοφία during the medieval period, see Dölger 1953; Ševčenko 1956; Rigo 2006: 161; Papaioannou 2012. For Leon the Mathematician, see Introduction and Section 3.1. For Niketas Byzantios, see *PmbZ* # 5505, # 25703 and # 25713. On Konstantinos-Kyrillos, see *PmbZ* # 3927. Regarding Maximos the Confessor, see *PmbZ* # 4921; *PBE* I: Maximos 10. For the doctor Theophilos, see *PmbZ* # 8236.
[270] *PmbZ* # 25712; Paschalidis 1999: 95–99.   [271] Norden 1898: vol. I, 371–73; Brokkaar 1995.
[272] Leone 1989; Kazhdan 2006: 89–90.
[273] *Enkomion of Antonios II Kauleas* 5, 415,121–23 and 11, 420,277.
[274] *Enkomion of Antonios II Kauleas* 3, 414,68–69.

concerns himself with topical matters such as the Photian schism, the resolution of which he attributes to Emperor Leon VI.[275] If we accept that the two Nikephoroi are the same man, some twenty-eight years previously he asked Photios to supervise some of his hagiographical texts.

This is attested in *epist*. 204, in which Photios answers an earlier, now lost missive from Nikephoros by assuring him that the work he has sent contains no grammatical or syntactic errors and no rhetorical ones either, although it did need the odd amendment the patriarch has included. The assistance Photios provides goes beyond a positive assessment, since the patriarch takes an active part in correcting the literary text. The fact that at the end of the letter he forecasts a bright future for Nikephoros[276] shows that the latter cannot have been a bad writer. The rhetorical deficiencies of Nikephoros' prose can be surmised from another letter, *epist*. 235, in which Photios assesses his hagiographical work in more detail and regrets not having sent the rhetorical resources the monk had requested but justifies himself by claiming not to know exactly what was required.[277] As the earlier missive of Nikephoros has not survived, we cannot know exactly what the situation was: perhaps the patriarch promised Nikephoros a copy of an ancient rhetorical text or of part of the *Bibliotheca*, given his interest in rhetorical technique, or perhaps even a lost work on the subject. When speaking of his teaching dialectics in *Amphilochia*, in fact, Photios mentions a treatise that was available to his students.[278] Be all that as it may, Photios passes judgement on Nikephoros' style, which he characterises as improvised, hackneyed and full of imprecise vocabulary.[279]

These criticisms create the impression that Nikephoros was a rather careless man of letters, but he persevered until in *epist*. 242 Photios reproached him for precisely the opposite: a style that is too Asiatic and pompous. Perhaps this is an ironic comment, although it is clear that the patriarch's opinion refers to a different text referred to as 'the work of your fertile genius on the female martyr' (τὸ εἰς τὴν μάρτυρα τῆς ὑμῶν εὐφυΐας φιλοπόνημα).[280] We do not know who this saint is, although if we understand Photios to be punning, she might be St Euphemia, whose relics were repatriated and vindicated by the iconodules. Due to iotacism, the colloquial pronunciation of εὐφυΐας and of Εὐφημίας must have been very similar. Euphemia of Chalcedon was martyred in 303, and her

---

[275] *Enkomion of Antonios II Kauleas* 12, 421,307–11. See Grumel 1934: 283.
[276] Phot., *epist*. 204,6–7: εἴης αὐτὸς διὰ σεαυτοῦ λαμπρὸν φέρων τὸ εὐδόκιμον, 'May you also be a bearer of outstanding honour on your own merits.'
[277] Phot., *epist*. 235,8–10.   [278] *Amph*. 78, 97–102; Ronconi 2015b: 220.
[279] Phot., *epist*. 235,3–5.   [280] Phot., *epist*. 242,9.

remains had been venerated in Constantinople since antiquity, until the iconoclast Emperor Leon III desecrated them and had them thrown into the sea. Her body apparently remained uncorrupted, albeit in pieces, and her coffin finally reached the island of Lemnos, where Empress Eirene discovered her whereabouts in a vision. The official hagiographer of these events was Konstantinos of Tios, who, at the request of his ecclesiastical superior Georgios of Amastris, a close friend of the Empress, described them in *On the Relics of St Euphemia* (*BHG* 621), in which he also tries to justify the fact that the uncorrupted body of the saint by that point consisted of a collection of dry bones.[281]

Photios also wrote an *enkomion* in honour of a Palaeo-Christian saint, St Thekla (*BHG* 1721), and Nikephoros may well have been following his example with this composition. In the case of Euphemia, however, his choice would also have reflected an important ideological element, since, in addition to continuing to promote a figure to whom the iconodules had given a special meaning, the monk Nikephoros followed the official policy of the patriarchate, which presented itself as the victor over heresy against the claims of the monastic communities. Tarasios as patriarch had presided over the translation of St Euphemia's relics with great ostentation, showing that his patriarchal authority was responsible for this iconodule triumph. The spectacular ceremony took place in 796 and was organised to coincide with the saint's feast day, which was when the blood kept in a reliquary miraculously liquefied. All Byzantine society was present, according to Theophanes the Confessor, who also attended the event with Tarasios. The celebration also had a political dimension, and the authorities took advantage of this to again fill the church of St Euphemia near the hippodrome, which had been desecrated by the iconoclasts, with icons.[282]

We do not know whether the text by Nikephoros was an elaborate and extensive piece such as an epitaph, an *enkomion*, or a *vita* or simply a bit of reportage to be placed in some kind of *synaxarion*.[283] Indeed, some scholars have postulated that during his second patriarchate, Photios promoted a project that anticipated the great tenth-century hagiographical

---

[281] Mango, review in *JThSt* 17 (1966) 485–8; *AASS*, Sept. v, 274–83 (*BHG* 619–24n); Theoph. 607–8 (AM 6258 = 765/756); Berger 1988b: 318–20. For Konstantinos of Tios, see *PmbZ* # 3878.
[282] Naumann and Belting 1966; Janin 1969: 120–30; Majeska 1984: 142 and 148; Ruggieri 1991: 190; Mango 1999: 79–87; Goldfus 2006.
[283] Although the compilation of the *synaxaria* as we know them did not occur until the tenth century, earlier precedents did exist that allow their existence to be taken back to the seventh century, see Rapp 1993: 178, n. 48; Mango 1999. For the traditional view, see Luzzi 1999: 77–79.

collections.[284] In any case, in Photios' observations it is apparent that Nikephoros had a natural gift for literary composition (εὐφυΐα) and offered an accurate critical judgement of his own work:[285]

> After we have examined in accord with your assessment the work of your fertile genius on the martyr, we have seen it as a pure descendant of the Asian seed (as one might say without using the name of the Muses, but also in Asiatic style). We have not noticed any errors, with the exception of the occasional defect in the syntax. Although the terms are beautiful, however, they need improving, and the beauty of the text as a whole has been corrected toward its natural form.

Nikephoros himself had probably told the patriarch that the main fault of the text was its excessively Asiatic style. As well as agreeing with him, Photios is ironic about this lofty tone, since he consciously uses a bombastic expression.[286] As in previous cases, Nikephoros has made almost no grammatical or lexical errors, although he has been carried away by his Asiatic model while magnifying its characteristics, so that the result obtained is the opposite of the one that was sought: the work gives the impression of being less fine than it is (καλὸν ὄν, ὅμως ὑστερεῖν ἐδόκει). Photios therefore suggests that Nikephoros replace these grandiose forms with more common ones. The patriarch intentionally chooses the word καλλονή to designate the over-elaborate beauty of Nikephoros' style. This is a pedantic and perhaps ironic reference, since καλλονή is an unusual form of κάλλος that is rarely used before the ninth century.[287]

6.3.6 *The Forty-Two Martyrs of Amorion Again: Sophronios and Euodios*

We have already discussed the cult of the forty-two martyrs of Amorion, the Byzantine officials captured after the taking of the town in 838 who refused to yield to torture and instead confessed Christian Orthodoxy. Although they were transferred to the region of the Tigris, where

---

[284] Patterson Ševčenko 1998.
[285] Phot., *epist.* 242,9–15: Τὸ δὲ εἰς τὴν μάρτυρα τῆς ὑμῶν εὐφυΐας φιλοπόνημα κατὰ τὴν σὴν ἀξίωσιν ἐπελθόντες, τῆς μὲν Ἀσιανῆς σπορᾶς (ὡς ἄν τις εἴποι μηδὲ τῷ Μουσῶν ὀνόματι χρώμενος, ἅμα δὲ καὶ ἀσιανίζων) γνησίαν γονὴν κατειλήφαμεν· σφαλμάτων δὲ οὐδέν, πλὴν εἴ πού τι περὶ σύνταξιν, καὶ τοῦτο σπάνιον, ἐπεσημηνάμεθα. εἰ δέ τι πρὸς τὴν ἄλλην καλλονὴν τῶν ῥημάτων, καλὸν ὄν, ὅμως ὑστερεῖν ἐδόκει, καὶ τοῦτο πρὸς τὴν συγγενῆ μορφὴν τὸ ὅλον τοῦ λόγου κάλλος μεθηρμόσατο.
[286] Phot., *epist.* 242,10–12: τῆς μὲν Ἀσιανῆς σπορᾶς (ὡς ἄν τις εἴποι μηδὲ τῷ Μουσῶν ὀνόματι χρώμενος, ἅμα δὲ καὶ ἀσιανίζων) γνησίαν γονὴν κατειλήφαμεν. Bombastic Asianism is also the main characteristic of the *enkomion* of the patriarch Antonios II Kauleas, see Leone 1989: 407.
[287] See *LSJ* and *TLG*, s. v. καλλονή.

efforts at persuasion were redoubled, they did not renounce Christianity and were decapitated by the Arabs in 845. This took place specifically on 6 March, when their annual celebration was established in the *Synaxarion* of Hagia Sophia.[288] The great popularity of these New Martyrs and their promotion by various institutions meant that throughout the second half of the ninth century there were numerous accounts and hymns to them.[289]

In addition to the texts discussed in Chapters 2 and 4 regarding the forty-two martyrs of Amorion, another that relates their collective martyrdom by concentrating on Theodoros Krateros, one of Theophilos' generals, requires discussion. This is the version Δ (= *BHG* 1209), written by Sophronios, which stands out for the dialectic duel (*agôn*) of Krateros with the caliph.[290] Theodoros was a eunuch who prospered at court, assuming the titles of *protospatharios* and *strategos* of Boukellarioi.[291] His skill in the hippodrome during a mounted battle against Saracen prisoners earned him Theophilos' admiration.[292] Theodoros took part in the defence of the town of Amorion, where he was captured and required to renounce his faith and convert to Islam. His unsurprising refusal to cooperate led to his decapitation. The decision to make him the martyrs' leader was probably related to the significant social success of the family of the Krateroi in the mid-ninth century.[293] We know that a certain Krateros was the *strategos* of Anatolikon in the time of Theodoros Stoudites, owing to which Krateros had to supervise the latter's exile in 817/818 and punish him for encouraging iconoduly among priests of Asia.[294] When an anti-iconoclastic epistle of Theodoros Stoudites fell into the hands of Emperor Leon V, probably in 819, this Krateros had him cruelly whipped.[295] Under Michael II, Krateros was the *strategos* of the Kibyrrhaiotai and defeated the Arabs who had occupied Crete, although after the initial victory, he was captured

---

[288] *SynaxCP* 516,3–21.
[289] For the first versions and their chronology, Kotzambassi 1992; Kazhdan 2006: 206–9. See Chapter 4.
[290] *Passion of the 42 Martyrs of Amorion* (version Δ) 46,27–48,12; Kazhdan 1986: 157–59.
[291] *PmbZ* # 7679; *PBE* I: Theodoros 67. The surviving seal of the *basilikós mandator* Theodoros may belong to him, cf. *PmbZ* # 7679,1.
[292] Theoph. Cont. III, 23,11–35; Kolia-Dermitzaki 2002; Signes Codoñer 2014: 135–36; 279–312.
[293] Winkelmann 1987: 163 and 216, n. 797; Efthymiadis 1995: 158–60; Métivier 2018: 180–84 and 187–90.
[294] *PmbZ* # 4158; *PBE* I: Krateros 2. For the episode of the two priests converted to the veneration of icons, *Vita* B *of Theodoros Stoud.* 292B–C; *Vita* C *of Theodoros Stoud.* 47, 286; *Vita* A *of Theodoros Stoud.* 193C–96C.
[295] *Vita* B *of Theodoros Stoud.* 296B; *Vita* C *of Theodoros Stoud.* 50, 288; *Vita* A *of Theodoros Stoud.* 200A–B; Theod. Stoud., *epist.* 382.

and murdered by his enemies.[296] A seal of a Krateros who was *basilikós spatharios* and *strategos* of the *thema* in the same period has also survived.[297]

The importance of this family of the military aristocracy explains the interest of Sophronios – whose specific degree of kinship or relationship to them is unknown to us, although it was probably very close – in praising, by means of a new account of the passion of the forty-two martyrs of Amorion, the member of the Krateroi family who had best proven his Orthodoxy. This not only placed this wealthy family within the context of orthodox liturgy, but counteracted previous accusations against certain relatives who under iconoclast emperors had attacked saints such as Theodoros Stoudites. The text of Sophronios is similar to other writings in the hagiographical dossier of these forty-two saints, but version Δ stands out for its pro-Theophilos bias. Sophronios not only makes no mention of images, but also stresses Theophilos' victories over the Hagarenes, saying that he attacked the most important towns, among them that of the ruling household, whence he brought back plundered gold and silver and many slaves.[298] The Emir's vengeance took the form of attacking Amorion, the home town of Emperor Theophilos. This gives the hagiographer an opportunity to include praise of the town, showing how fond of it Theophilos was, since he considered Amorion the second finest place in the empire.[299] With this brief note, Sophronios humanises the emperor, who decided to send his best men to protect it, with the sad result that they ultimately fell in battle or were captured and then martyred in Samarra.

Before we consider the author, let us first analyse the date of his account in comparison to the plethora of similar texts that throughout the second half of the ninth century praised these new heroes of Orthodoxy. The *ante quem* date is the year 890, when Anastasios copied the manuscript *Parisinus Gr.* 1476, which contains this text along with other hagiographical writings of the summer semester (March–August) of the *menologion*.[300] The text post-dates August 847, since it mentions the caliph Al-Wathiq as already dead, and we know that he died that month.[301] In the epilogue, when the hagiographer speaks in the first person to invoke the saints and implore their protection, he introduces

---

[296] *PmbZ* # 4159; *PBE* I: Krateros 1. On his model of holiness, see Chapter 4.
[297] *PmbZ* # 4157; *PBE* I: Krateros 3. This Krateros is quite possibly one of the foregoing.
[298] *Passion of the 42 Martyrs of Amorion* (version Δ) 40,24–42,1.
[299] *Passion of the 42 Martyrs of Amorion* (version Δ) 42,4–6.
[300] Anastasios is also the author of the codex *Parisinus Gr.* 1470, see D'Agostino 1997.
[301] *Passion of the 42 Martyrs of Amorion* (version Δ) 44,27–28. On the caliph Al-Wathiq, see Turner 2013.

The Milieu of Photios

several references to current events that allow us to further specify the period: earthquakes, attacks by barbarians, famine and plague and conflicts that had torn the Church apart.[302] It seems obvious that the final reference is to the disputes between Ignatios and Photios,[303] which yields a date after 858. Earth movements were not infrequent during these decades, but along with the one of 869, the earthquake of 863 was especially remembered for its devastating effects.[304] The barbarian invasion par excellence in this period is that of the Russians, who camped at the gates of Constantinople in 860. Despite Photios' proclaimed triumph in his defence of the city, he could not prevent the destruction of the crops, which must have caused famine and plague in subsequent years. All these references point to a date of composition of approximately 862/863. A final point corroborates this conclusion: the chronology of the martyrdom is limited to the reign of Michael III, his mother Theodora and his sister Thekla.[305] As Kotzambassi rightly points out, the encomiastic aim of this mention – like that of Theophilos and his military capacity – was to flatter Theodora, which means that the text was written while she had some degree of imperial power. It is difficult to imagine that this praise would have been offered during the sole rule of Michael III and even less so during that of Basileios I.[306] The regency of Theodora continued until 856, when her son took over imperial power. We know, however, that ca. 862/863 Theodora returned to the court with the title of Augusta until the death of her son on 23 September 867.[307] It must thus have been during this final period of the first patriarchate of Photios that Sophronios produced his version of the fate of the martyrs of Amorion.

But who was this Sophronios, who was sensitive to the interests of Empress Theodora, in favour of the rehabilitation of Theophilos and prepared to write this piece near the end of the empress' life? The name is unusual, and the prosopographies include a very small number of individuals who bear it. In the mid-ninth century, there is mention of a

---

[302] *Passion of the 42 Martyrs of Amorion* (version Δ) 54,9–12.   [303] Kazhdan 1986: 153.
[304] A vivid description of this earthquake of early August is given by Niketas David Paphlagon in his *Vita of Ignatios* 39. Scholars disagree as to the exact year; for Vercleyen 1988: 169 it was in 861. According to Downey 1955: 599 and the editors of the *Vita of Ignatios* (p. 149, n. 110) it took place in 862. For Dagron 1981: 96, n. 65 it was in 863.
[305] *Passion of the 42 Martyrs of Amorion* (version Δ) 52,7–9.
[306] Kotzambassi 1992: 126–27. She is however wrong in affirming that the text was written before 856, when Michael III shut away his mother and sisters in a monastery to be emperor on his own.
[307] Bury 1907: 434; Herrin 2001: 228 and 293, nn. 99 and 100. Theodora receives the title of Augusta in the epistle Pope Nicholas I sent to her on 13 November 866, see *MGH, epist.* VI, nr. 95, pp. 547,18–48,38.

378 The Photian Milieu

Sophronios who was the successor of Nikolaos Stoudites at the head of the monastery of Stoudios from 849 until his death in 853.[308] Onomastics prove that this was a well-established name among the members of the Stoudite federation: its leader Theodoros mentions in his letters a monk named Sophronios,[309] while the abbot of Sakkoudion who held the post before Akakios was called this as well.[310] The chronology excludes the possibility that Sophronios the hegoumenos of Stoudios was our hagiographer. As he was active during the final part of the first patriarchate of Photios, it is tempting to think that he was the recipient of *epist.* 43.[311] From Photios' words, we can infer that the monk Sophronios was very concerned about the rehabilitation of sinners. In his missive, Photios explains that in the same way that wounds leave a mark on the body, so the scars of sins never disappear. Indeed, although the sin has been corrected, it leaves the soul prone to it in the future. The patriarch does not specify the question to which he is responding, but it is easy to believe that it referred to those who abandoned Ignatios to join the Photian party. We have already seen that Photios required a careful examination of each case to confirm whether the conversion was sincere.[312] Did the concern of the monk Sophronios involve Theophilos' repentance after his iconoclast sin? If so, we have a good candidate for the author of version Δ of the martyrdom of the forty-two martyrs of Amorion.

After 867, when Ignatios recovered the throne of Constantinople, all the individuals named Sophronios that we know of are linked to Photios. A deacon by that name was called before the Ignatian Council of 869/870 and accused of having come into contact with Photios.[313] He had been ordained as a priest by Methodios or Ignatios, as a consequence of which he was given a minor punishment that allowed him to regain his status in less than two months.[314] The two bishops Sophronioi who supported the reinstatement of Photios as patriarch at the Council of 879/880 were also professed Photians.[315] Although it is unlikely that all these mentions are to different Sophronioi, we have no evidence that allows us to link them to a single person. Most likely, an author related to the court came into contact with Photios during the second part of his first patriarchate, this cost him a public accusation at the Ignatian Council of 869, and in reward for his

---

[308] *PmbZ* # 6848; *PBE* I: Sophronios 1; *Vita of Nikolaos Stoud.* 904D–5A.
[309] Theod. Stoud., *epist.* 41,9; *PmbZ* # 6845; *PBE* I: Sophronios 2.   [310] *PmbZ* # 6846.
[311] *PmbZ* # 6849; *PBE* Sophronios 3. See 6.2.3.   [312] Phot., *epist.* 283,2–177.
[313] *PmbZ* # 27156.   [314] Mansi xvi, 42f.
[315] They are Sophonios the bishop of Apamea in Bithynia (*PmbZ* # 27157; Mansi xviiA, 373D) and Sophonios the bishop of Adrianoupolis (*PmbZ* # 27158; Mansi xviiA, 377A).

loyalty, Photios consecrated him a bishop in order to be able to count on his support at the Council of 879/880. If this was the case, was he the bishop of Apamea or of Adrianoupolis? Regardless of which Sophronios wrote version Δ of the account of the forty-two martyrs, the text clearly dates to the end of Photios' first patriarchate.

The next well-attested stage of this hagiographical dossier is also related to the patronage of Photios and involves the monk Euodios, the author of version Z of the hagiography of the saints of Amorion (*BHG* 1214). We do not have as much information about the monk Euodios as we would like.[316] We know that he lived in the second half of the ninth century and that he wrote at least two equally important pieces, in addition to the hagiographical account of the forty-two martyrs of Amorion: a liturgical *kanon* in honour of Ioseph Hymnographos, who was probably his teacher,[317] and a *Refutation of the Koran*,[318] which is actually a more user-friendly abbreviation of the work by the same title written by his contemporary Niketas Byzantios. The latter was a theologian well known for his collaboration with Photios in bringing the Armenians governed by King Ašot I into contact with Constantinople and the Chalcedonian creed, abandoning monophysite postulates.[319] Euodios and Niketas Byzantios may actually have known each other personally, since they shared an interest in anti-Islam controversy and both had extensive theological knowledge of Muslim beliefs and practices beyond the typical comments common to all authors.[320]

Euodios' account of the forty-two martyrs of Amorion is one of a number of texts that from early on spread the cult of these Byzantine officials, who had been considered saints since their execution by the Arabs on 6 March 845. In comparison with earlier compositions from the end of Methodios' patriarchate, which were more encomiastic, Euodios' work has a more narrative style and denser theology. In the second part of the prologue, he accordingly links the origin and expansion of Islam first to the affirmation of monothelite heresy and second to iconoclasm.[321] To do

---

[316] *PmbZ* # 1682; *PBE* I: Euodios 1.
[317] To be sung on 3 April, see *AHG*, vol. VIII, 87–96 and 390f. On the personal relationship between these two men, see Tomadakes 1971a: 57.
[318] Rigo 2006: 164–82.
[319] For Niketas Byzantios, see *PmbZ* # 5505, # 25703 and # 25713; Adontz 1934: 246; Khoury 1969: vol. II, 110–62; Dorfmann-Lazarev 2004: 86–87; Greenwood 2006a: 181–89; Rigo 2006. Niketas Byzantios' written production consists of *Answers to Two Letters of the Arabs*; *Refutatio of the epistle of Ašot king of Armenia*; *Refutatio of the Qurʾān*; *Twenty-four Syllogistic Chapters on the Procession of the Holy Spirit*.
[320] Krausmüller 2004; Rigo 2006: 177, n. 66.
[321] *Passion of the 42 Martyrs of Amorion* (version Z) 11, 64,29–65,3 and 39, 76,19–26.

so, he follows a pattern similar to the one expounded in his *Refutation of the Koran*.[322] This attention to the past, together with the correlation Euodios establishes between Arab-Byzantine relations and the internal religious situation of the Byzantine Empire – each time the Byzantines abandon Orthodoxy, the Arabs launch powerful raids inside their borders[323] – is a significant novelty introduced by him in the hagiographical dossier of the forty-two martyrs. Others are the visit of the traitor of Amorion to the saints when they are still imprisoned, as well the literary treatment of the men, whose passion is described as that of a single individual, since they always reaffirm their faith in unison. On this point, the *vita* of Euodios is followed faithfully by version A (*BHG* 1211), which is a summary of Euodios' text. The same is true of versions K and M, which belong to the second wording of the *Imperial Menologion*, dated to 1034–41.[324] In the conversations between the martyrs and the envoys of the caliph, finally, Euodios recalls information found in the work of Niketas Byzantios.[325]

The text of Euodios is not dated precisely. It must post-date 855/856, which is the date generally given for the writings of Niketas Byzantios, and it predates the tenth century, since Symeon Metaphrastes and the Continuator of Theophanes use it as a source. Kazhdan suggested that it was written at the same time as the *vita* of Theodoros of Edessa (*BHG* 1744), that is, ca. 900.[326] But the introduction of the iconoclast dispute as an element of the account is more in keeping with the literary tendency established by Photios, with whose ideological programme it is closely involved. The defeat of iconoclasm was a recurring theme not only within the official ideology of the patriarchate but also in that of the new Macedonian reigning dynasty. In this context, it makes sense for Basileios I to dedicate a chapel to the forty-two martyrs of Amorion at the Palace of the Sources (*en Pegais*)[327] alongside those he erected to Konstantinos I the Great and to the prophet Elijah and his disciple Elisha. With this measure, Basileios not only censured the previous imperial household, since Theophilos' failures led his men to martyrdom, but also introduced himself once more as an Orthodox emperor in whose dominions there was no place for iconoclast heresy. The inauguration of

---

[322] Rigo 2006: 175.   [323] *Passion of the 42 Martyrs of Amorion* (version Z) 4–11, 62,19–65,3.
[324] Kotzambassi 1992: 151–53 (version K) and 129–51 (version M). On the acrostic of version K spelling out 'ΜΙΧΑΗΛ Π', see Detorakes 1990; D'Aiuto 2012; Patterson Ševčenko 2013.
[325] *Passion of the 42 Martyrs of Amorion* (version Z) 15–36, 66–76,2.   [326] Kazhdan 1986: 155.
[327] Theoph. Cont. V, 91,15–18; Vasilevskij and Nikitin 1905: 279; Janin 1969: 486; Connor 2016: 61–62.

The Milieu of Photios

this church seems to have been a perfect excuse for Ioseph Hymnographos to compose a *kanon* in honour of the martyrs, and also – why not? – for the monk Euodios to follow his example and produce his own hagiographical account.

If this is the case, we can date the text of Euodios by the consecration of these sanctuaries, which appear to have been founded after the earthquake of 869 that caused serious damage to the area south of the capital's walls. After this natural catastrophe, Basileios also repaired the church of the monastery of the Theotokos tes Peges (of the Source), beautifying it as it had never been before. In this action, Basileios followed the example of the iconodule Empress Eirene, who had improved the monastery buildings some years previously.[328] The shadow of Photios inevitably falls on these events: not only had he converted the defeat of iconoclasm into an element of his ideology, but he encouraged among his entourage a reworking of this recent period in the history of the empire. This was the case with Euodios.

On the other hand, in ca. 872/873, Photios was recalled from exile to Constantinople by Emperor Basileios himself, who gave him a place in the imperial palace and put him in charge of the education of the crown princes Leon and Alexandros, in addition to allowing him to resume work as a teacher.[329] Basileios doubtless saw in Photios the ideologue he needed to legitimise his accession to the throne after the murder of his predecessor Michael III and to establish a new dynasty.[330] The part played by ecclesiastical foundations in this dynamic is clear: Konstantinos I the Great was the emperor of Constantinople par excellence, and three Anacreontic hymns survive, written by Photios in honour of Basileios, in which the new unity of the Church is celebrated, while in the court ceremonial the emperor is compared with Konstantinos the Great and the Old Testament Kings David and Solomon.[331] The prophet Elijah was the holy protector of Basileios, who professed particular veneration of him, and the story of the martyrs of Amorion justified the rift with the previous dynasty by

---

[328] Theoph. Cont. V, 80,5–8; Perger 1901: 260,5; Janin 1969: 224.
[329] Theoph. Cont. V, 44–48; Dvornik 1948: 162; Blysidou 1991: 113–21. Anti-Photian sources affirm that Photios resorted to magic practices in order to recover Basileios' favour, see *Vita of Ignatios* 91, p. 122,5–10; Ps-Symeon 694.
[330] On the imperial ideology created by Basileios, or rather for Basileios, and the undeniable part played by Photios, see Moravcsik 1961; Der Nersessian 1962; Brubaker 1985; Magdalino 1987; Maguire 1988; Anagnostakis 1989; Agapitos 1989; Markopoulos 1992; 2013; Tougher 1997: 70–73; Brubaker 1999a: 147–238; Schminck 2000; Prieto Domínguez 2014a.
[331] Markopoulos 1994. On these Anacreontic hymns, made up of Ionic dimeters catalectic or hemiambs of eight and seven syllables respectively, see Ciccolella 1998. Basileios I repaired many churches built by Konstantinos I and promoted his cult and representation along with his mother St Helena, see Brubaker 1994: 142–43; Connor 2016: 94–95.

accusing it of being iconoclast and heretical. In this connection, it is important to note the severity of Euodios' attack on Theophilos, in which Euodios claims that Theophilos' name (literally 'he who loves God') is mere imposture and insists that his iconoclast policy was the cause of the military successes of his adversaries.[332] Apart from its religious value, Euodios' account served this socio-political aim and also the private interests of Emperor Basileios efficiently and forcefully.

6.3.7 *The* Acta of David, Symeon and Georgios *(BHG 494)*

This text, officially known as *Acta Graeca ss. Davidis, Symeonis and Georgii Mytilenae in insula Lesbo*, is a genuine hermeneutic challenge within the literature arising in connection with iconoclasm after its defeat. In the form in which they have come down to us, the *Acta* describe the life and works (extending over almost 150 years) of three supposed brothers from Lesbos, who attained holiness in different ways but whose remains ended up together, as a consequence of which the three began to be venerated as a group.[333] The relics of Symeon and Georgios already lay in the same sarcophagus in Mytilene and were joined by those of their alleged elder brother David.[334] If we take into account the existence of liturgical hymns that venerate only the brothers Symeon the Stylite and Georgios, it is easy to conclude that the transfer of David occurred rather late. We have a *kanon* in honour of the two brothers written by Georgios of Nicomedia, as well as an eleventh-century *akolouthia*,[335] and the *Acta* in fact contain evidence of the well-established cult of only the two brothers.[336]

The only manuscript that preserves the *Acta* is relatively recent (Florence, *Laurentianus Plut.* 9.21, fourteenth century). This, together with the fact that the text includes contradictions and references to events much later than the iconoclast crisis, as well as omissions unthinkable for any contemporary, has led some to believe that it is so far removed from the ninth century that it deserves no credence.[337] In some parts of the *Acta*, however, a well-informed source is apparent, which points to a writer

---

[332] *Passion of the 42 Martyrs of Amorion* (version Z) 11, 64,30 and 65,1–2.
[333] *Acta of David, Symeon and Georgios* 37, p. 259,5–10.   [334] *PmbZ* # 1248; *PBE* I: David 13.
[335] *Tameion*, 192–93, nr. 582 (*kanon*). For the *akolouthia*, see Phountoules 1961; Kotzambassi 2015: 138–39.
[336] *Acta of David, Symeon and Georgios* 11, p. 222,10.
[337] Ševčenko 1977a: 117–18: 'As they stand now, the Acta are of late making and their precision is spurious'; Halkin 1954b: 23: 'ne mérite guère de confiance .... Vie fantaisiste'; Halkin 1959: 468–69.

contemporary with the restoration of icons. These portions of the text have led other scholars to posit an early date of composition: their editor believed that they were written ca. 900, since the hagiographer was able to obtain a good deal of information about the saints' disciples.[338] The fact is that the author of the *Acta* was a compiler who brought together several pre-existing hagiographies dating from the Triumph of Orthodoxy.[339] Using a method of composition similar to that of historians, he combined several sources, adapting a *vita* of each brother and following it faithfully in subsequent chapters, adding information from other sources in order to fill out and explain the events. He thus includes events that do not directly affect the lives of his heroes, such as the uprising of Thomas the Slav and the attacks by ships originating from Africa that plundered the islands.[340] This desire to give an overall view of the iconoclast crisis means that he lists the individuals exiled by Leon V and where they were sent[341] and mentions the main iconodule leaders in a gratuitous manner, since they have nothing to do with the evolution of his story.[342] Moreover, the brothers Graptoi are emphasised, perhaps as a pattern to be followed, since Theodoros and Theophanes Graptoi were full brothers whose remains were in the same place and who were venerated together.[343]

This author does not seem to have analysed the historicity of his sources conscientiously, since he accepts legendary details created by later tradition, as, for example, the verses allegedly engraved on the faces of the Graptoi, which as mentioned are not included in the tradition until the tenth century,[344] and even clearly non-historical data, for instance, placing Ioannikios and other famous ascetics in Constantinople before the restoration of images.[345] This legendary tradition can be found in only two texts: the *Vita Theodorae* and the *De Theophili imperatoris absolutione*.[346] The opposite is stated in the two *Vitae of Ioannikios*, which the writer appears not to know, since he also places Ioannikios and Methodios together alongside Ioannes Katasambas (or Kakosambas), who was harshly attacked by Ioannikios' hagiographers for being allied with the

---

[338] *Acta of David, Symeon and Georgios* 210. For other scholars it is contemporary, cf. Grégoire 1933: 517–18; Kazhdan 1984: 185–88; 1999: 200–202.
[339] Talbot 1998: 147; Karlin-Hayter 2004: 325–50.
[340] *Acta of David, Symeon and Georgios* 17–18, pp. 231,22–33,3.
[341] *Acta of David, Symeon and Georgios* 16, p. 229,4–13.
[342] *Acta of David, Symeon and Georgios* 19, p. 233,15–24 (Niketas of Medikion); 22, p. 238,5–16 (Euthymios of Sardis); 23–24, p. 239,3–18 and p. 241,8–10 (the Graptoi).
[343] *Acta of David, Symeon and Georgios* 23, p. 239,3–4.
[344] *Acta of David, Symeon and Georgios* 23, p. 239,3–16.
[345] *Acta of David, Symeon and Georgios* 27, p. 245,17–19.   [346] Darrouzès 1987: 17.

Stoudites.[347] We also find repetitions of the same event, as when a single miracle is performed by both brothers separately,[348] or when the compiler twice narrates the overthrow of Ioannes Grammatikos, the consecration of Methodios as patriarch and the feast day of Orthodoxy.[349] There is a clear difference between these two versions of the restoration of icons: the first includes the holding of the synod called by the empress, which is omitted in the second.[350]

What mid-ninth-century material was found in each of the original *vitae*, and what form these **vitae* took, is difficult to say.[351] The first nine chapters, however, correspond to the **vita* of David, which is clearly separated from the remainder of the work. This section contains only two brief references to iconoclasm,[352] which were perhaps introduced by the compiler of the *Acta* in an attempt to lend unity to the work as a whole. David's model of holiness concentrates in any case on his numerous visions, his humility and his defence of the importance of official monasticism after Theodoros Stoudites. Then come the chapters of the **vita* of Symeon the Stylite, the main themes of which, as in the **vita* of Georgios, are the fight against iconoclast heresy and the administration of the Triumph of Orthodoxy. Symeon's holiness is based on the lifestyle of hermits, to be precise of the Stylites, on his sacrifice and on his leadership in restoring the cult of images. These chapters also contain references to regulated monasticism, such as the fate of the disciple healed by St Symeon, Phebronia, who founded a convent, or the distribution of bread to all members of the community during his exile in Aphousia.[353]

The **vita* of Georgios, meanwhile, with its very different style, also contains elements of a hermit's hagiography based on his humility and at the same time his enormous physical sacrifice and dedication to others, as when in imitation of St Sabas he leaves firewood at the doors of the needy.[354] Although each of the three heroes offers a different model of

---

[347] *Vita of Ioannikios* by Petros 69–70, 431–32.
[348] Such as the miracle against the famine in *Acta of David, Symeon and Georgios* 13, pp. 224,12–25,11 (Georgios) and 24, pp. 240,21–41,10 (Symeon); the expulsion of demons in ch. 11, pp. 222,30–23,14 (Georgios) and ch. 24, pp. 239,17–40,11 (Symeon); or the miracle of the wine in ch. 32, pp. 254,18–55,7 (Georgios) and ch. 20, p. 236,15–26 (Symeon).
[349] *Acta of David, Symeon and Georgios* 29–30, pp. 248,22–50,24.
[350] Talbot 1998: 225, n. 407; Lilie 1999: 221, n. 169; Varona Codeso 2010: 199–202.
[351] Karlin-Hayter 2004: 332 affirms that the compiler of the *Acta* combined *vitae* of (at least) five different individuals to shape the personality of the three brothers.
[352] *Acta of David, Symeon and Georgios* 7, pp. 216,30–17,2 and 9, p. 219,12–14.
[353] *Acta of David, Symeon and Georgios* 19, pp. 234,3–36,3; 24, pp. 240,21–41,10. It is impossible to determine whether these are passages from the original hagiography or later interpolations.
[354] *Acta of David, Symeon and Georgios* 11, p. 222,17–22.

holiness, the *vita of Symeon and the *vita of Georgios are more closely related, both because of the events of iconoclasm in which they are involved and their recurrent themes. One of these is forgiveness. This is understood to be a pious virtue, since Symeon in his holiness is portrayed as accustomed to forgive, and this virtue is often repaid generously by others, making it seem a miracle of God. This is the case when, after Symeon absolves his brother Georgios for having given away the monastery's food and even the donkey that carried it, two donkeys loaded with bread, wine and cheese miraculously appear, causing the other monks to realise their mistake and ask forgiveness for having censured him. Five days later, moreover, a ship arrives from Smyrna with a cargo of flour, vegetables and gold accompanied by a request for Symeon's blessing and forgiveness.[355]

This interest of the *vitae in forgiveness can be explained because the rehabilitation of Emperor Theophilos was an important theme in them. Indeed, just before the account of Theophilos' death, there is a parallel case that announces to the reader the happy end of this episode: an important dignitary named Hesychios, *protonotarios ton Thrakesion*,[356] requests in writing that Georgios, the head of the monasteries of Lesbos founded by Symeon, redeem him from his sins.[357] The saint returns the papyrus unopened with its seal intact, and upon unrolling it, Hesychios sees that the text has miraculously disappeared, signifying that God has forgiven him. This story is a variant of the miracle by which Methodios finally grants forgiveness to Theophilos, according to the *De Theophili imperatoris absolutione* (*BHG* 1732) and the *vita* of Eirene of Chrysobalanton (*BHG* 952).[358] The forgiveness in the *Acta*, on the other hand, is due to the visions of Symeon himself, indicating that the parallel of Hesychios is a later creation modelled on other tenth-century texts. According to the *Acta*, Emperor Theophilos appeared in a dream to Symeon on the night of his death imploring him three times: 'O monk, help me!'[359] When Theodora expressed the wish that her husband not be condemned for his iconoclasm, Symeon rejected this and left the meeting angrily. Some days later, however, he remembered that vision and agreed to his

---

[355] *Acta of David, Symeon and Georgios* 13, p. 225,8–18.
[356] *PmbZ* # 2575; *Acta of David, Symeon and Georgios* 25, pp. 241,35–42,14.
[357] This form of communication is characteristic of Hesychios, since he also corresponded with Theodoros Stoudites, see Theod. Stoud., *epist.* 500.
[358] *Narratio de Theophili absolutione* 36,1–37,3; *Vita of Eirene Chrysobalanton* 2,18–24.
[359] *Acta of David, Symeon and Georgios* 26, pp. 242,32–43,2. See Markopoulos 1998; Karlin-Hayter 2006a; Prieto Domínguez 2019b.

absolution by the Church.[360] This version of events must have been taken directly from the *vita of Symeon, which, in order to praise his hero, remains silent about the visions of Empress Theodora and the future patriarch Methodios. According to other sources, they helped make the rehabilitation of Theophilos possible: Theodora saw in a dream how her husband was judged by God at the Chalke Gate,[361] while a shining angel appeared to Methodios to tell him that God had forgiven the emperor. His name subsequently disappeared from the list of iconoclasts deposited at the altar of Hagia Sophia.[362]

This concern with the emperor's forgiveness is a striking characteristic of some of the original materials with which the compiler of the *Acta* worked. To this one might add the pious image the compiler transmits of Theodora, who intercedes with her husband Theophilos on behalf of the iconodule leaders, preventing them from being hurled into the sea[363] and who relates her husband's repentance on his deathbed.[364] The young Michael III is also portrayed in a very favourable light, since it is said that when barely three years old, he was aware of the evil of the patriarch Ioannes Grammatikos, whom he had removed from his presence, while he was happy to be with Symeon of Lesbos, whom he had never met before.[365] Indeed, the iconoclast patriarch is actually blamed for Theophilos' evil deeds.[366] This accumulation of flattery indicates that the original author was sensitive to the interests of the imperial family, perfectly aware of the propaganda line created after Methodios' accession to the patriarchate and eager to support it. Methodios is praised in particular, since it is affirmed that he was the only iconodule who suffered persecution during the reign of Michael II.[367] It can accordingly be concluded that the original work that formed the basis of these chapters was written within the Methodian milieu, since it responds to the concerns of the restoring patriarch and Theodora's political demands in return for suppressing iconoclasm: absolution for her husband and protection for her son, insisting on their piety and Orthodoxy, so as to legitimise the dynasty and prevent the boy's rule from being questioned.

---

[360] *Acta of David, Symeon and Georgios* 28, p. 246,5–11.
[361] *Narratio de Theophili absolutione* 33–35; Afinogenov 2004a: 106, 325.
[362] *Narratio de Theophili absolutione* 36–37. See Section 4.4.
[363] *Acta of David, Symeon and Georgios* 23, p. 238,18–26.
[364] *Acta of David, Symeon and Georgios* 27, p. 244,7–21.
[365] *Acta of David, Symeon and Georgios* 29, p. 247,1–18, cf. Grégoire 1933: 517–18.
[366] *Acta of David, Symeon and Georgios* 23, p. 238,20–23.
[367] *Acta of David, Symeon and Georgios* 22, p. 237,4–26, esp. lines 4–6.

The link between the *vita of Symeon and the circle of the patriarch Methodios is also confirmed by the account of the injuries Ioannes VII Grammatikos inflicted upon himself in order to unjustly accuse the iconodules.[368] This story, which became popular among tenth-century historians,[369] originates in the account of the transfer of the relics of the patriarch Nikephoros, written by the hegoumenos Theophanes during Methodios' patriarchate[370] and appears in no other hagiographical work. It is therefore likely that the *vita of Symeon the Stylite was written shortly after the subject's death, in 844, by a man of letters who worked for or had important contacts with the patriarchate of Constantinople and who wished to extol the memory of this confessor.

By this time, there was already a well-established cult in honour of Georgios, the bishop of Mytilene and alleged monastic brother of Symeon.[371] This veneration was supported by the creation of a *vita* of Georgios in which he was the sole protagonist and was celebrated for his friendship with the patriarch Nikephoros, who predicts to Georgios the coming of the Second Iconoclasm as a stage of anger (ὀργή) within the Church. The saint was also praised for having confronted iconoclast heresy, which implied his death in exile.[372] Georgios' passing occurred under Leon V in 821, and after the Triumph of Orthodoxy, Methodios repatriated his relics, promoting his veneration to the extent that Georgios of Mytilene appeared on his own in the *Synaxarion of Constantinople*.[373] Everything seems to indicate that there must also have been a *vita of Georgios in which the confessor survived the defeat of heresy, supported the restoration of images and in gratitude was appointed bishop of Mytilene after rejecting the diocese of Ephesos. This second *vita of Georgios must be the one used by the compiler as the core of the *Acta*.[374] As Kazhdan pointed out on the basis of two prophecies made by the saint, the text was written between summer 863, the date of the victory of Petronas, and early 865, when Bardas was murdered, because the

---

[368] *Acta of David, Symeon and Georgios* 30, pp. 249,23–50,10.
[369] Genesios 57–58; Ps-Symeon 648,10–49,3; Theoph. Cont. IV, 3,6–11.
[370] *Translation of the Patriarch Nikephoros* 8, p. 123,16–17.
[371] *PmbZ* # 2160; *PBE* I: Georgios 134. See also *PmbZ* # 2110 and 2161; *PBE* I: Georgios 248; Halkin 1959: 464–69; Talbot 1998: 165–66, n. 119.
[372] *Vita of Georgios of Mytilene* 33–43. For his close relationship with the patriarch Nikephoros and his prediction, see 37,5–19. This *vita*, preserved in the tenth-century manuscript *Patmiacus Gr.* 254, was probably written shortly after the Triumph of Orthodoxy to coincide with the transfer of Georgios' relics.
[373] *SynaxCP* 589,5–90,6 (7 April) and 687,11–27 (16 May).
[374] *Acta of David, Symeon and Georgios* 31, pp. 250,29–52,31.

author would otherwise have ridiculed his hero for having Georgios predict 'a safe end' for Bardas when he was in fact murdered by Basileios.[375]

The dating of this material to the first patriarchate of Photios is corroborated and specified by a textual element: the title of 'Augusta' given to the empress. Not until Michael III allowed her to return to the court ca. 862/863 did Theodora begin to use this title. It is understandable that the first hagiographer, who was close to the saint but also to the court, wished to record not only the predictions made to Petronas and Bardas but also the new status of their sister as dowager empress.[376] In the description of the encounters prior to the restoration of Theodora and the iconodule leaders, there is a passage that affirms that the following were also present: 'Sergios Niketiates, Theoktistos, Bardas and Petronas, highly orthodox men who happened to be leaders of the senate.'[377] It is curious that the empress is referred to as 'Augusta' on no less than four occasions in this chapter.[378] It does not appear to be coincidence that on the two occasions when these members of the imperial family are mentioned, Theodora is given this title. Instead, both passages likely come from the same source, which was rewritten and altered by the compiler of the *Acta*, who extended the use of this title to new contexts as a reworking sign. Thus, in the chapter on the Graptoi brothers, for example, the empress is referred to as 'the Augusta' before adding the verses tattooed on the foreheads of the confessors.[379]

Although there are probably more, the next distinguishable compositional layer corresponds to the time of the compilation, when the *Acta* were given their final form. The exact moment is difficult to specify, although it was certainly late (probably well into the tenth century or even later). The compiler's objective in presenting the biographies of these three New Martyrs is clear: their relics lay in the same tomb in Mytilene, where miracles were performed,[380] and it was necessary to explain the confessors' feats to the faithful. This tendency is characteristic of subsequent literature, where the centre of interest is displaced from Constantinople to the provinces and much of the action accordingly occurs on the island of Lesbos. The compiler's repeated insistence that Mytilene was the

---

[375] Kazhdan 1984: 185–88; Kazhdan 1999: 200–202. For her part, Karlin-Hayter 2004: 326 places the production of the *Acta* later in the reign of Basileios I (867–886).
[376] *Acta of David, Symeon and Georgios* 31, p. 252,2 and 32, p. 253,5.
[377] *Acta of David, Symeon and Georgios* 28, pp. 245,31–46,2.
[378] *Acta of David, Symeon and Georgios* 28, pp. 245,20–46,30.
[379] *Acta of David, Symeon and Georgios* 23, p. 238,25.
[380] *Acta of David, Symeon and Georgios* 37, p. 259,9–10.

fatherland of the saints indicates that he was from there.[381] Although he is very interested in Lesbos, however, he also knows Constantinople intimately: indeed, this is the only source that specifies the exact place where Emperor Leon V was murdered, the Chapel of St Stephanos the Protomartyr in the Palace of Daphne.[382] The hagiographer also appears to address an audience that is from the capital, hence the need to locate Lesbos precisely by stating at the beginning that 'It is an island, one of the Cyclades, being part of the Aegean Sea, not far removed from the Hellespont, closer to the Asian continent than to the European. On this island is situated the city of Mytilene ....'[383]

Another peculiarity of the compiler is the attention he pays to family values and a religious family life. Five siblings in total decided to devote their lives to God.[384] The eldest, Symeon, exerts his authority over Georgios, whom he supervises and guides, as well as over his sister Hilaria when she decides to shut herself away in a cell. Symeon tonsures her as a nun and later heals her from the effects of a devil, while Georgios provides her with food and guides her spiritual growth.[385] Insistence on the family ties of the saints is an obsession for the compiler, who goes as far as to compare the tomb where the relics of the three lay with the mother's womb that bore them.[386] Is this excess a sign that these proclaimed blood ties did not actually exist and that it was therefore necessary to exaggerate the familial relationship of the monastic brothers?

6.4 Conclusions

The defeat of iconoclasm in 843 was a turning point around which the Byzantine Church continued to revolve during the following decades. The

---

[381] In many passages he insists on the saints' love of their homeland, see e.g., *Acta of David, Symeon and Georgios* 31, pp. 251,25–52,7.

[382] *Acta of David, Symeon and Georgios* 16, p. 229,20–23.

[383] *Acta of David, Symeon and Georgios* 2, p. 212,25–27: Λέσβος ἐστὶν νῆσος μία τῶν Κυκλάδων, τῷ Αἰγαίῳ λαχοῦσα πελάγει, οὐ πολὺ τῆς Ἑλλησπόντου ἀπέχουσα, τῇ Ἀσιάτιδι μᾶλλον ἢ τῇ Εὐρωπαίᾳ γειτνιάζουσα γῇ. Ἐν ταύτῃ πόλις ἵδρυται Μιτυλήνη, ἡ ....

[384] *Acta of David, Symeon and Georgios* 2, pp. 212,29–13,1. On the family aspects of the work, see Kazhdan 1999: 200–202.

[385] *Acta of David, Symeon and Georgios* 12, p. 223,16–23. On this Hilaria, cf. *PmbZ* # 2580.

[386] *Acta of David, Symeon and Georgios* 37, p. 259,6–9: τὸ τοῦ μεγάλου Δαβὶδ ἀπὸ τῆς Ἴδης ἐπὶ τὴν Λέσβον ἀνακομισθὲν λείψανον σὺν τοῖς δυσὶν ἀδελφοῖς ἐν μιᾷ καὶ αὐτὸ κατετέθη τῇ λάρνακι, ὡς ἄν, οὓς μία γαστὴρ ἡγιασμένη ἐν κόσμῳ ἐκυοφόρησε, τοὺς αὐτοὺς καὶ εἷς θαυματόβρυτος ἀναδεικνύηται τάφος ἐπιφερόμενος, 'the remains of the great David were also transferred from Ida to Lesbos and placed in one coffin with his two brothers, so that the same men whom one sanctified womb had brought into the world, one miracle-abounding tomb might also display'.

continuing topicality of iconoclasm demonstrated the need for a heresy to allow the Orthodox to reassert themselves dogmatically. Both the patriarch and the emperor needed to able to oppose the heterodox and to try to convert them in order to demonstrate their own great piety. In fact, we know of the existence of a ceremonial hymn (now lost) honouring Basileios I for his dialectical confrontation with the iconoclasts.[387]

Although the iconoclasts had been defeated some years ago, Photios and his circle continued to cultivate their memory, keeping the sacrifices of iconodules topical in order to legitimise their own exercise of patriarchal power and, when they were exiled, their right to recover it: these sufferings are compared with those inflicted upon them by the iconoclasts, with whom Photios compares his enemies as well as the supporters of Ignatios. In support of this new rhetoric dictated by Photios, who attempts to portray himself as the victor over iconoclasm, authors in his circle again narrated the life and works of confessors who had lived through those convulsed times and had supposedly defended icons, such as Georgios of Amastris, Michael Synkellos, Theodoros Graptos, the forty-two martyrs of Amorion and the brothers of Lesbos. Collaborators of his, such as Theophanes of Caesarea, Georgios of Nicomedia and the humble philosopher monk Nikephoros, were part of this enterprise, which aimed not only to provide justice for those who had fallen defending Orthodoxy but also to appropriate their credentials to support the man these authors considered the legitimate patriarch: Photios.

---

[387] *Anthologia Barberina* 124. Its existence is proven by the ancient index of the ms. *Vaticanus Barberini Gr.* 310, see Lauxtermann 2019: 53. Since Photios is the author of other poems dedicated to Basileios in the same collection (Ciccolella 1998), it is tempting to assume that the patriarch also composed this one.

CHAPTER 7

Mobility between Milieux
The Hagiographer Sabas, from the Bithynian Olympos to the Constantinopolitan Milieux

Literature is a human function that acquires its full meaning by becoming collective when it touches another individual who is influenced by the text. Up to this point, we have emphasised the literature of the iconoclast period and immediately afterwards, which continued to rewrite the history of iconoclasm and the changing participation in these events of many people in authority. This process of defining society and creating a Middle Byzantine identity was only possible thanks to the work of writers. Once we have analysed how they were organised, interacted with each other within the different milieux and devoted themselves to their patron's interests, the focus should be on the authors themselves. The conventions of the time meant that they remained anonymous and rarely claimed the attention they deserved. The scarcer the surviving information, therefore, the more important it is to investigate the role of these men, the reasons they wrote and what they achieved. At the end of this study, it will be enlightening to examine in detail the biography of one of the main hagiographers under iconoclasm in order to make sense not only of his geographical and social mobility but also of the evolution of his life coordinates and his own rise due to his involvement in the ideological enterprise of the iconodules. This individual treated here is the hagiographer Sabas.

Several authors named Sabas are known from the mid-ninth century, all of whom wrote about the contemporary situation with new martyrs as their protagonists. Sabas is the name of the writers of the *vita* of Makarios of Pelekete, the second *vita* of St Ioannikios, the two texts on the life and posthumous miracles of Petros of Atroa and the hagiography of Hilarion of Dalmatos. Although the surviving historical evidence is far from negligible, its dispersal and complexity have meant that these persons have previously all been considered in isolation. An army has thus arisen of authors with the same name and the same literary concerns writing at the same time. The prosopographies (*PmbZ*, *PBE*, etc.) generally include each piece of preserved information in a different entry and thus distorts reality by creating the impression that they were all of limited importance and artificially multiplying the number of persons named Sabas. Even if we imagine more individuals answering to the name Sabas than those that are explicitly vouched for, prosopographic studies show that this was never a fashionable or popular name in Constantinople and its hinterland in comparison to others such as Ioannes, Michael or Theophanes. (This may be due to its Syrian origin.) A contextualised analysis of all these works and of the information we have about the authors allows us to separate a Sabas who produced the *vita* of Makarios of Pelekete[1] from the remainder, who can all be identified as a single man. By paying attention to the life and literary activities of this second hagiographer, we gain insight into the social and geographical mobility of a writer during the Second Iconoclasm and the opportunities his literary abilities afforded him.[2] As will become apparent, Sabas played a key role in the work carried out by the Stoudite network and at the same time acted as a link between the patriarchate and the main iconodule sectors that reaffirmed their position after the Triumph of Orthodoxy in 843. His collaboration with these power groups and the literary products he created give us a better idea of the chronology of his main works. At the same time, this analysis allows reflection on the standing of writers in the Middle Byzantine period and answers some questions about who was writing in the mid-ninth century and why.[3]

7.1 Youth in Bithynia and First *Vita* of Petros of Atroa (*BHG* 2364)

To date, the only attempt to establish the date of birth of Sabas, who was a contemporary of Ioannikios (762–846) and a follower of Petros of Atroa (773–837), has been that of Van den Gheyn, who proposed 815 as a *terminus post quem*.[4] In his edition of the two texts on

---

[1] *PmbZ* # 6445; *PBE* I: Sabas 11.
[2] For the complex situation of the literary production in the period, see Karlin-Hayter 1993; Criscuolo 1994b; Auzépy 2004a; Odorico 2014. For contemporary hagiography, see Odorico and Agapitos 2004; Efthymiadis 2011a: 101–14; Bréhier 1916.
[3] The concern to define the status of the man of letters of the period within this literary genre has recently attracted a great deal of attention, see Odorico 2002; Efthymiadis and Kalogeras 2014; Hinterberger 2014b; Papaioannou 2014; Pizzone 2014; Kaplan 2015; Rapp 2015.
[4] *Vita of Ioannikios by Sabas* 375, note 's'. It was based on the description of Methodios as the first orthodox patriarch of his generation given in the *Vita of Ioannikios by Sabas* 372B. See *PmbZ* # 6447; *PBE* I: Sabas 1.

Petros of Atroa,[5] Laurent places Sabas' birth at the beginning of the ninth century, his reasoning being as follows: 'Quand saint Pierre mourra (en 837), son biographe nous apparaîtra en pleine force, fier du long commerce qui le mit en contact avec son héros'.[6] The autobiographical evidence Sabas includes in the account of his teacher, however, suggests setting the date slightly later. He affirms that he was initiated into monastic religious life by the saint.[7] His literary education and the lack of any mention of the company of Petros of Atroa during his childhood suggest that he spent this period with his parents in the capital. His Constantinopolitan origin is well documented,[8] and the tasks he performed at the monastery (never particularly arduous)[9] may indicate a background that was far from humble.

The reference to the Arab threat that forced the monks of Petros of Atroa to disperse is a useful means of better defining the chronology of our author.[10] Concerned for his safety, Sabas considered taking refuge in the mountains, but was unable to do so.[11] In his own words, the reason for this was neither ill-health nor being unaccustomed to walking, as a young man from a well-to-do family, but his physical status as ἀνίσχυρος, that is, 'weak, lacking strength'. The hagiographer was thus presumably still a teenager and had not yet attained a young man's strength. He must have been about thirteen years old at the time. The date of the Arab raid is thus a reliable way to establish when Sabas was born. In the first half of the ninth century, few attacks by the caliph's men constituted a real threat to the Bithynian monasteries. The chief exception is the plundering that took place throughout Asia Minor around 831, which ended with the involvement of Emperor Theophilos, who led the Byzantine troops to victory over the Arabs at Charsianon.[12] The same attacks are mentioned in another contemporary hagiographical text, the *vita* of Eudokimos.[13] If we take this event as a reference point, Sabas must have been born around 818.

---

[5] *BHG* 2364 and *BHG* 2365; Dujcev 1966; Markopoulos 2016. Regarding this holy man, see *PmbZ* # 6022; *PBE* I: Petros 34.
[6] *Vita of Petros of Atroa*, p. 11.
[7] *Vita of Petros of Atroa* 1,25. On Bithynian spirituality, its rich monastic life and the relationship with Constantinople, see Lefort 1995; 1996; Talbot 2001; Auzépy 2003a; Belke 2009; 2013; Grünbart 2013.
[8] *Vita of Petros of Atroa* 48,15.   [9] *Vita of Petros of Atroa*, p. 10–11.
[10] *Vita of Petros of Atroa* 48.   [11] *Vita of Petros of Atroa* 48,7–8.
[12] Theoph. Cont. III, 23,1–5; Skylitzes 68,44–48; Georgios Kedrenos 123,16–20. Cf. Vasiliev 1935: 98–124; Ahrweiler 1962; Métivier 2008: 448–51.
[13] *Vita of Eudokimos* 8.

Sabas' religious life began in the monastic federation led by Petros of Atroa, with whom Sabas was associated until his death in 837. Sabas spent his youth in the monasteries of St Zacharias and Hagios Porphyrios, which means that he should not be confused with the author by the same name who in around 840 wrote the *vita* of his teacher Makarios of Pelekete after succeeding him as hegoumenos.[14] The first work that can be securely attributed to our Sabas is the biography of his mentor Petros of Atroa, commissioned by the superior of the monastery of St Zacharias in Atroa, Iakobos,[15] who was the nephew of both his predecessor Paulos[16] and its founder Petros of Atroa himself. This *vita* appears to have been produced in about 847, given that Ioannikios was already dead when Sabas took up his pen;[17] it was based on the author's own experiences and on the testimony of various witnesses. This work put Sabas' spiritual father and his monastic federation on the map amidst the ecstatic atmosphere that followed the Triumph of Orthodoxy in 843, when the cults of any heroes who had confronted the defeated heresy were encouraged. At the same time that he extolled the memory of Petros of Atroa, Sabas gave his brother monks a common reference capable of keeping together the large number of foundations in Bithynia that shared the same monastic rule: the monasteries of St Zacharias, Hagios Porphyrios, Balaiou and Balentia, the convent of Lydia and the chapels of Kalonoros and Hippos.[18] The *vita* contains very little information, however, about the life of Sabas himself, who appears as merely another member of the community, who was present at the saint's miracles and was miraculously cured.[19] His tendency to locate events in which he was personally involved at the monastery of Hagios Porphyrios shows that he spent much of his time there, and this may accordingly have been where he wrote the *vita*.[20] If so, the monastery must have had some form of infrastructure characteristic of a *scriptorium*.[21]

---

[14] *PmbZ* # 6445; *PBE* I: Sabas 11; *Vita of Petros of Atroa*, p. 16–17; Van de Vorst 1913b. For the monastery of Pelekete in Bithynia, see Mango and Ševčenko 1973: 242–48; Janin 1975: 170–72; Ruggieri 1991: 224. See Section 1.3.3.

[15] *Vita of Petros of Atroa*, prol. 15–16. Cf. *PmbZ* # 2634; *PBE* I: Iakobos 4; *Vita of Petros of Atroa* 64–65 and *Vita retractata of Petros of Atroa*, p. 35–36.

[16] *PmbZ* # 5839; *PBE* I: Paulos 26.

[17] *Vita of Petros of Atroa*, p. 14–15. See also Kazhdan 1999: 336–40.

[18] *Vita of Petros of Atroa*, p. 35–47 and *Vita retractata of Petros of Atroa*, intr. 44–45. Cf. Delouis 2005: 228–30.

[19] *Vita of Petros of Atroa* 21; 48; 55; 71; 72. For the healing of Sabas' fevers, see *Vita of Petros of Atroa* 58. See also *Vita of Petros of Atroa*, p. 9–13. Cf. *PmbZ* # 6447; *PBE* I: Sabas 1.

[20] *Vita of Petros of Atroa*, p. 13–15; p. 40, n. 6; p. 65, n. 3.

[21] For the monastic workshops of manuscripts in Bithynia, see Hutter 1995; Brubaker and Haldon 2001: 37–52; Sietis 2018.

To judge by the title of the work, Sabas was still a simple monk when it was produced, despite his erudition.[22]

7.1.1 The Vita of Ioannikios (BHG 935)

Some years later (ca. 855), Sabas was commissioned to write a hagiography of St Ioannikios. Like all Bithynian monks, Sabas was familiar with this important follower of Methodios and in fact knew him personally, since he notes in the *Vita of Petros of Atroa* that Ioannikios informed him of the death of his teacher and of a vision in which Petros of Atroa had been raised to heaven by angels.[23] The same incident is summarised in the *Vita of Ioannikios* (ch. 44), where Sabas refers the reader to his earlier biography.[24] This definitive proof of the identity of our hagiographer supports the attribution to Sabas Monachos in the title.[25] This text as well offers little information about its author, and despite the fact that the names are the same, our hagiographer is not to be identified with the monk of Agauroi who in about 810 helped Ioannikios establish himself on Mount Trichalix,[26] witnessed one of his first miracles[27] and accompanied him to the lands of the Thrakesioi.[28]

Sabas' production of this *vita* in honour of Ioannikios was a response to repeated requests by Ioseph, the hegoumenos of the monastery of Antidion where Ioannikios died.[29] No sooner had the famous saint passed, than a monk named Petros Monachos wrote a *vita* of him on the orders of Eustratios, a close follower of Ioannikios who had become the superior of the monastery of Agauroi, also located at the foot of the Bithynian Mount Olympos.[30] The account stands out for its hostility to the Stoudite milieu, which Ioannikios did not hesitate to attack in order to favour Methodios, whose candidature to the patriarchate he vehemently supported.[31] But everything points to the fact that this text did not fully satisfy Ioseph, who had accompanied the saint in his final years, officiated at his funeral and afterwards taken charge of maintaining his cult and attending to the pilgrims who visited his tomb in Antidion. Ioseph

---

[22] Σάβα μοναχοῦ εἰς τὸν βίον τοῦ ὁσίου Πατρὸς ἡμῶν καὶ θαυματουργοῦ Πέτρου τοῦ ἐν τῇ Ἀτρώᾳ.
[23] *Vita of Petros of Atroa* 81.   [24] *Vita of Ioannikios by Sabas* 371A.
[25] Βίος καὶ πολιτεία [καὶ θαύματα] τοῦ ὁσίου πατρὸς ἡμῶν [καὶ θαυματουργοῦ] Ἰωαννικίου συγγραφεὶς παρὰ Σάβα μοναχοῦ.
[26] *Vita of Ioannikios by Sabas* 14, 345A–B.   [27] *Vita of Ioannikios by Petros* 13, 390B–C.
[28] *Vita of Ioannikios by Petros* 10, 389C. See *PmbZ* # 6443; # 6444; *PBE* I: Sabas 10.
[29] On Ioseph, cf. *PmbZ* # 3453; *PBE* I: Ioseph 19. See Section 2.2.1.
[30] For the *vitae* of Ioannikios by Petros and that of Eustratios of Agauroi (*BHG* 645), see Chapter 2.
[31] Von Dobschütz 1909a; Talbot 1998: 249.

therefore decided to promote the writing of a new *vita* and chose Sabas for the task.

Sabas was no doubt not chosen at random, since Ioseph was well aware of the abilities of another great ninth-century hagiographer: Ignatios Diakonos, who had by then already written the four major hagiographies that have come down to us.[32] An example of the close relationship of the two men is the epistle Ignatios sent to Ioseph.[33] A major influence on abbot Ioseph's decision was likely his knowledge of Sabas' earlier *vita* of Petros of Atroa, since this saint (like Ioannikios) does not fit the model of holiness most praised by iconodules, that of great monastic leaders who confronted heretics tenaciously, such as Theodoros Stoudites and Niketas of Medikion. In fact, Petros (and Ioannikios) correspond to the ancient model of miracle-working monks more concerned with spiritual matters than ecclesiastical ones. Probably for this reason Sabas emphasises the personal relationship of the two saints: Petros of Atroa did not want to die before visiting Ioannikios,[34] and Petros may already have accompanied him for a time together with Sabas and a certain Antonios.[35] The hermit saint in turn heard of the death of Petros thanks to a vision he had precisely when Petros was expiring on 1 January 837. In it, Ioannikios saw that the saint of Atroa had been raised to heaven by angels and ran to tell Sabas, who was with him.[36]

The resultant *vita* makes clear that Sabas sought to update the hagiographical text to bring it into line with the new political and ecclesiastical situation after Ignatios ascended the patriarchal throne in 847. He accordingly suppresses the enmity with the Stoudites (who were staunch defenders of the cause of Ignatios); revises the controversial figure of Ioseph of Kathara, who had officiated at the adulterous marriage of Konstantinos VI; tones down Ioannikios' desertion from the army; offers a harsher portrait of Emperor Theophilos' persecution of the iconodules and defence of iconoclasm, since he generally attaches more importance to the iconoclastic dispute, which had been played down in the previous *vita* of Ioannikios by Petros. Whereas Petros Monachos declared that the saint's links with heretics went no further than a certain unnamed brother-in-law of deeply

---

[32] Namely, the hagiographies of Ioannes of Gotthia, of Gregorios Dekapolites and of the patriarchs Tarasios and Nikephoros, see Efthymiadis 1991a. See Chapters 2–3.
[33] Mango and Efthymiadis 1997: 92–96 (*epist*. 33). For the monastery of Antidion, see Janin 1975: 135–36; Ruggieri 1991: 218.
[34] *Vita of Petros of Atroa* 80.
[35] *Vita of Ioannikios by Petros* 10,389C. For Antonios, see *PmbZ* # 560; *PBE* I: Antonios 32. Cf. *PmbZ* # 6073.
[36] *Vita of Ioannikios by Sabas* 44; *Vita of Petros of Atroa* 81.

iconoclast convictions, for example, Sabas admits that Ioannikios was an iconoclast in his youth, during his military service, thus following in the footsteps of his parents, who were committed iconoclasts.[37]

More attention is also paid to Michael I Rhangabe, the father of the patriarch Ignatios: whereas Petros Monachos merely mentions his fight against the Bulgarians,[38] Sabas describes the ascension to the throne of the iconoclast Leon V, presenting Michael as the victim of deception.[39] His desire to present the imperial family from which Ignatios came in a favourable light led Sabas to use as source for his *vita* of Ioannikios the *Scriptor incertus* chronicle, which praises Michael I and introduces him as a protégé of God.[40] The impious Leon, the *strategos* of Anatolikon, had apparently deserted deliberately in order to trigger the disaster of 22 June 813, which allowed his rise to power. Albeit in a less explicit manner, this vision appears already in the first hagiography of Sabas, in which Michael I is presented as a calm individual (εἰρήναρχος Μιχαήλ) who transfers power to Leon in order to avoid a confrontation.[41] Sabas also includes a note regarding the end of the imperial family, whose members were forced to separate and take monastic vows, which should be read in the light of the new situation of the patriarchate after Methodios' death. This is clearly an attempt by Sabas to ingratiate himself with Ignatios by means of an empathetic account of the calamities suffered by his father Michael I, who had been removed from power by a conspiracy that brought forth the iconoclast Leon V.

Sabas introduces a striking correction when he discusses Theophanes the Confessor. His predecessor Petros Monachos calls Theophanes Isaac in his *vita* of Ioannikios,[42] in the tradition imposed by Methodios, who declared that the name Isaac had been awarded by Konstantinos V.[43] But Sabas prefers the name used by Theodoros Stoudites, who in his *enkomion* affirms that some people called Theophanes by his father's name (Isaac), although both his proper and his Christian name was Theophanes.[44] Sabas' interest in shaping the figure of Theophanes of

---

[37] *Vita of Ioannikios by Petros* 35; *Vita of Ioannikios by Sabas* 2 and 5. For a comparison between both hagiographies, see Von Dobschütz 1909a: 94–100; Mango 1983; Sullivan 1994; Afinogenov 1996b: 84–88; Kazhdan 1999: 327–36.
[38] *Vita of Ioannikios by Petros* 16, 392C.   [39] *Vita of Ioannikios by Sabas* 16, 347B–C.
[40] *Scriptor incertus* 40,31–41; Mango 1983: 399–400; see Section 5.2. Sabas also used other historiographical source, the so-called *Chronicle of 811*, a brief text describing the hapless invasion of Bulgaria led by Emperor Nikephoros I, see Wortley 1980; Markopoulos 1999; Stephenson 2006.
[41] *Vita of Petros of Atroa* 12. Cf. Ostrogorsky 1952: 162.   [42] *Vita of Ioannikios by Petros* 405.
[43] Method., *Vita of Theophanes the Confessor* 2, p. 3,6–13.
[44] Theod. Stoud., *Vita of Theophanes the Confessor* 9, 276.

Sigriane in accord with Stoudite conventions may ultimately be due to the fact that he was himself the author of a *vita* in honour of the chronicler (different from the versions in the *BHG*) that survives only in a translation into Old Church Slavonic. This text is signed by a certain Sabas Monachos and was part of the lost Byzantine pre-metaphrastic prototype of the Slavonic reading *menologia* for March, being read on 12 March.[45]

The purpose of all these changes is clear: to bring the followers of Ioannikios closer to the most extreme sectors of the Constantinopolitan Church, by avoiding any attack on the Stoudite monks and their milieu, to emphasise Ioannikios' fight in favour of images and to play down the defence of the iconoclast Emperor Theophilos. The latter's spiritual absolution – endorsed by the influential Ioannikios – had been imposed by the empress to guarantee the success of the return to icon veneration and the survival of the dynasty. But it now appeared excessive, unnecessary and as contrary to traditional ecclesiastical discipline. The monastery of Stoudios, in other words, was thus kept happy, since its main hobby-horses continued to be the attack on iconoclasm, the supervision of imperial power and the *psógos* (condemnation) of Theophilos.

Sabas' compositional technique deserves attention. The pre-existence of a *vita* of the same saint conditions his approach to the literary event: the commissioner of the new *vita* of Ioannikios was clearly familiar with that of Petros Monachos and wished to introduce changes. (Were this not so, he would merely have commissioned a copy of the existing text.) It was therefore necessary to modify this account, but also to respect its content and record the main events; it should not be forgotten that the monk Petros could draw not only on his personal experience but also on the testimony of Eustratios, the inseparable companion of Ioannikios for 50 years. Sabas is thus a *remanieur* writer, who initiates a dialogue with literary tradition and the work of another author, while at the same time pursuing his own interests and those of his group. Which group was this? The commission Sabas received from the hegoumenos Ioseph suggests that he had moved to the monastery of Antidion, from where he worked for Orthodoxy as was understood in the Bithynian monasteries.

For Laurent,[46] the manner in which Sabas expresses the hagiographical commissions he was given shows that he was now a member of the community of St Zacharias led by Iakobos, and not that of Antidion:

---

[45] Loparev 1910: 92–95; Kazhdan 1999: 340; Afinogenov 2006: 131; Helland 2007: 64, nr. 17.
[46] *Vita of Petros of Atroa*, p. 12.

the former 'ordered him to do so' concerning the *Vita of Petros of Atroa*,[47] while the latter 'urged him on many occasions' with regard to the *Vita of Ioannikios*.[48] But the differences in expression may be due to the character of the two abbots, one more demanding, the other more persuasive and benevolent, not to the fact that the author had a different relationship with the two men. Further evidence in favour of Antidion as Sabas' environment when he wrote the *vita* can be found in his addition of an event that occurred when Ioannikios was ninety-two years old (ca. 844–845) involving Epiphanios of Balaiou. This appears to indicate that Sabas drifted apart, at least temporarily, from the brothers of the federation founded by Petros of Atroa. In fact, Epiphanios together with other monks confronted Ioannikios, who was forced to flee from his cell in Balaiou to seek refuge in Antidion.[49] The monastery of Balaiou was one of the series of centres led by Petros of Atroa and his successors; this is confirmed by the fact that it was the main monastery in charge of caring for the place where the saint died in the Oratory of St Nicholas and for his remains, which were preserved *in situ* for at least a year.[50] The Constantinopolitan origin of Sabas and his confirmed presence in the capital in around the year 831, finally, suggest considerable freedom and geographical mobility. These reasons may well have favoured his joining the milieu of the followers of Ioannikios, who were better organised and more influential than the monks organised around the memory of Petros of Atroa.

7.1.2 *Sabas' Monastic Days and Bithynian Heremitic Life*

On a personal level, his production of the new *vita* of the popular Ioannikios must have lent Sabas more prestige in Bithynian monasticism. This was combined with the sympathy he aroused in the capital as a result of his re-reading of the confrontation between the saint and the Stoudites. The surviving manuscripts also testify to a successful link between Sabas' *vita* of Ioannikios and the monastery of Stoudios.[51] Sabas was thus in an excellent position to receive more important commissions when in 858 the overthrow of Ignatios followed the promotion to the patriarchate of Photios, events that triggered the well-known ecclesiastical schism.[52]

---

[47] *Vita of Petros of Atroa*, prol. 15–16: προσταγείς βίον συντάξασθαι θεόληπτον παρά τοῦ μικροῦ (lege μετὰ μικρὸν) καθηγουμένου ταύτης τῆς ποίμνης ὁσιωτάτου πατρὸς Ἰακώβου.
[48] *Vita of Ioannikios by Sabas* 1, 333A: ὑπὸ τῆς τοῦ πατρὸς Ἰωσὴφ ἀγάπης πολλάκις εἰς τοῦτο προτετραμμένος.
[49] *Vita of Ioannikios by Sabas* 51, 379C–80B. On Epiphanios, cf. *PmbZ* # 1585; *PBE* I: Epiphanios 46.
[50] *Vita of Petros of Atroa*, p. 45–46.   [51] Delouis 2011. For the Stoudite *menologia* see Introduction.
[52] Grumel 1939; 1940/1942; Karlin-Hayter 1977.

During the final years of iconoclast persecution, Ignatios seems to have actively supported the victims of Theophilos' henchmen, especially in Bithynia,[53] thus allegedly converting the region into an important centre of anti-Photian resistance. Anastasius the Librarian, in fact, affirms that monks were persecuted there by the followers of Photios, who set fire to some cells at the foot of Mount Olympos.[54]

One example of the anti-Photian resistance is the monastery of St Anna in Kios, whose affiliation to the Ignatian party is supported by the manuscript Meteora Metamorphoseos 591.[55] Another well-known case, thanks to the hagiography, is that of Nikolaos, the superior of the monastery of Pissadinoi on the Bithynian Mount Olympos, where Euthymios the Younger grew up in the faith.[56] According to the *vita* of the latter, both the hegoumenos and the chief monks decided to abandon the monastery out of loyalty to Ignatios and to avoid coming into contact with Photios.[57] We know that the post of hegoumenos was occupied by a monk familiar with the situation in the area who was named Sabas[58] and who after repenting and doing penance (evidently for having sympathised with the Ignatian cause rather than for having had an iconoclast past, which would have made his appointment impossible) joined the new patriarch. He was not the only such person, since the influence of Photios on the Bithynian monasteries is well documented, although his authority was often implemented by an intermediary, as in the case of the hesychast monk Athanasios,[59] who lived on the Bithynian Mount Olympos near the monastery of Symboloi and had great personal *auctoritas*, allowing him to return the schismatic bishop of Eriste to the Photian faction.

A rumour reached Photios, however, that Sabas' repentance was insincere and that he had begun to plot against him, which led to the patriarch sending a warning letter.[60] In it, he expresses sadness at the possibility of deceit and the existence of these rumours and compares Sabas to a leprous

---

[53] *Vita of Ignatios* 12.   [54] Mansi XVI, 5. See Chapter 5.
[55] Janin 1975: 135. For the manuscript Meteora Metamorphoseos 591, see Bees 1913. See Section 5.2.
[56] On Nikolaos, see *PmbZ* # 5603; Lake 1909: 42. On the monastery of Pissadinoi, see Janin 1975: 172–74.
[57] *Vita of Euthymios the Younger* 12,24 (*ROC*, p. 176).
[58] The seal preserved in Athens, possession of the *kathegoumenos* Sabas, perhaps corresponds to this period, see Konstantopoulos 1906: 86, nr. 253b: Σάβα καθηγουμένου. Cf. *PmbZ* # 6455; *PBE* I: Sabas 8.
[59] On the hermit Athanasios, see *PmbZ* # 684; *PBE* I: Athanasios 18. See Section 6.2.3.
[60] Phot., *epist.* 15. See Hergenröther 1867–1869: vol. I, 397; *Regestes*, nr. 495. Cf. *PmbZ* # 6449; *PBE* I: Sabas 12.

sheep that the good shepherd (in this case Photios) must care for.[61] The patriarch's solution was to rapidly dismiss Sabas from his post; the latter reverted to being a simple monk and probably had to leave the monastery. He then chose to live as an ascetic, perhaps in one of the remote cells in the Mount Olympos area; Photios took advantage of this situation to maintain communication with Bithynian monasticism. In order to do so, he put aside any potentially problematic ecclesiastical matters and sent Sabas at least two letters with theological content regarding the correct interpretation of a pair of Johannine verses.[62] The *intitulatio* of these missives (Σάβᾳ πρεσβυτέρῳ καὶ ἡσυχαστῇ) reveals that the addressee continued to have the ecclesiastical obligations of a *presbyteros*.[63] By sending these exegetic epistles in the middle of his first patriarchate, Photios maintained contact with an important member of Bithynian monasticism and was thus able to assess more accurately the extent of support for the Ignatian cause outside the capital.

The internal chronology of the biography of the hagiographer Sabas allows him to be identified as the recipient of Photios' letters during the turbulent years of his first patriarchate. If this is right, during the period following his dismissal as hegoumenos of Pissadinoi, Sabas turned to asceticism,[64] and although we do not know what contacts he maintained with the various Bithynian milieux, he certainly did not forget his spiritual father, Petros of Atroa, whose memory continued to be celebrated regularly at the church of St Zacharias.[65] On this feast day, a public reading

---

[61] Phot., *epist.* 15,18–21: Πάντως δὲ δεῖ με ἀνιᾶσθαι· τῆς ἐμῆς γὰρ καὶ Χριστοῦ ποίμνης, κἂν μὴ βούλωνται, καὶ τὰ λεπρωθέντα· καὶ περὶ αὐτῶν μετὰ Παύλου διαμεριμνῶμεν, κἂν μὴ θέλωσι συναισθάνεσθαι, 'Indeed I must needs be distressed, as unfortunately the sheep of Christ's flock and mine are leprous and we must take heed and concern ourselves about them together with Paul (see 2 Cor 11:28).'

[62] Phot., *epist.* 176 and 177. The first comments on verse John 14:28 ('for my Father is greater than I'), while the second is an explanation of John 14:2–3 ('In my Father's house are many mansions, if it were not so, I would have told you. I go to prepare a place for you.'). Both epistles were also consecutively included in the corpus of theological matters dedicated to Amphilochios, the metropolitan of Kyzikos: *Amph.* 95: Πρὸς τίνα λύσιν ἀναφέρεται ἡ τοῦ υἱοῦ φωνὴ ἡ λέγουσα 'ὁ πατήρ μου μείζων μού ἐστι'; *Amph.* 96: Πῶς οὐ μάχεται τὸ τοῦ εὐαγγελίου ῥητὸν τὸ 'ἐν τῇ οἰκίᾳ τοῦ πατρός μου μοναὶ πολλαί εἰσιν' τοῦ 'ἐὰν πορευθῶ ἑτοιμάσω ὑμῖν τόπον'. Due to their location within the collection of letters and their links with the *Amphilochia*, the two epistles certainly predate the beginning of Photios' second patriarchate in 877, see Prieto Domínguez 2008: 261–65. On the collection of *Amphilochia*, see Louth 2006.

[63] Hergenröther 1867–1869: vol. II, 196; *PmbZ* # 6450; *PBE* I: Sabas 13.

[64] In this period an anchorite named Sabas prophesised a bright future for Ioannes of Galatia as head of a monastery in Constantinople. According to the chapter 16 of the *Vita of Ioannes of Galatia* that survives in Georgian, the prediction came true and Ioannes ended up running the monastery of Sts Sergios and Bakkhos during the reign of Basileios I, see Kekelidze 1965: 62. On Ioannes of Galatia, *PmbZ* # 3266 and # 22779; Krausmüller 2007c: 355–57. About this Sabas, *PmbZ* # 6459. The lack of data does not allow us to identify him with the hagiographer Sabas definitely.

[65] *Vita retractata* of Petros of Atroa 98,1–2.

took place of the hagiography Sabas had written, allowing him to observe the audiences' reaction to the narrative.[66] The cult of Petros of Atroa was well known for attracting pilgrims,[67] and Sabas, convinced of the edifying nature of the lives of saints, did not miss an opportunity to encourage it among believers of all sorts, stressing the universality of the healing achieved by his intercession both for priests and for public officials, women, children and the like.[68] In fact, the many miraculous healings by the saint awakened the faith of the most sceptical.[69] Wishing therefore to complete his account of the miracles that had been greatly increased by posthumous healing episodes, Sabas decided to rewrite his own hagiography, adding with new data or slightly modifying the version he had given of some events a few years previously. This was the origin of the *Vita retractata* of Petros of Atroa, which is discussed in detail in Section 7.1.3.[70] By this means, Sabas became a key figure in the main monastic groups that influenced contemporary public life.

7.1.3 The Vita Retractata *of Petros of Atroa (BHG 2365)*

The aim of the stylistic differences between the *Vita of Petros of Atroa* and the *Vita retractata* – the addition of *hápax legomena*, alliteration, word play, etc. – is to modestly raise the tone of the original text without making it less accessible to the reader.[71] The modifications of content are more ambitious. As Sabas declares in the prologue, his objective is no less than extolling the memory of his hero and offering him as a life model to achieve the holiness characteristic of his success. In this way, he hopes to encourage the believer, whether monk or layman, to engage in spiritual combat.[72] This pragmatic declaration is completed in the first chapter of those Sabas adds dealing with posthumous miracles, in which he reveals his plan to convince iconoclast heretics by showing them the miracle-working power of a true man of God.[73] This is doubtless one of the main

---

[66] *Vita retractata of Petros of Atroa* 98,4–6. On the type of reception of Middle Byzantine hagiography at that time, see Rapp 1995: 42–44; Efthymiadis 1996; Efthymiadis and Kalogeras 2014; Papavarnavas 2016.
[67] *Vita retractata of Petros of Atroa* 87,11.
[68] *SynaxCP* 42,4–19 (13 September); *Typikon of the Great Church* I, 27 (13 September) and 35 (15 September). For the veneration given to Petros of Atroa, see *Vita of Petros of Atroa*, p. 51–56; *Vita retractata of Petros of Atroa* 49–54.
[69] *Vita retractata of Petros of Atroa* 58; 104; 107; 112.   [70] Efthymiadis 2006: 160–70.
[71] These have already been noted by Laurent in *Vita retractata of Petros of Atroa*, p. 22–26; Ševčenko 1981.
[72] *Vita retractata of Petros of Atroa*, p. 77–78.
[73] Chapter 86bis, see *Vita retractata of Petros of Atroa* 135,12–17.

innovations of the second version, since the first *vita* made no reference to the survival of iconoclasm and even attempted to deny its existence.[74] The *Vita retracta*, by contrast, stands out for its apologetic intentions,[75] which led to the inclusion of a long doctrinal *excursus* in ch. 12 with a profession of Trinitarian faith, a theological statement in defence of images and a condemnation of the persecution of Leon V the Armenian.[76] It thus gave the federation of monasteries of this confessor the essential iconodule credentials to play a key role in the Church that arose after the Triumph of Orthodoxy.

The anti-iconoclast revision of the *vita* of Petros of Atroa is in keeping with that Sabas had produced himself some years previously in regard to St Ioannikios.[77] On that occasion, Sabas touched up the work of another author, and here he did the same to his own. In both cases, he made use of the reactions and comments of the audience that listened to the work – both texts were read aloud during the *orthros* of the feast day of the corresponding saint – and that after the Triumph of Orthodoxy expected new saints to have been champions against heresy.[78] These expectations were combined with the new ecclesiastical tendency promoted by Photios ever since he attained the patriarchate, which aimed to eliminate any iconoclast echoes in order to condemn their memory once again, an approach with which our hagiographer identifies himself. This is apparent, for example, in the two homilies of Photios against the Arians belonging to his first patriarchate, which are full of attacks on the iconoclasts.[79] Between 860 and 865, there were numerous attempts, since the enemies of icons seemed to have reorganised themselves to take advantage of the internal disputes between Ignatians and Photians after Photios' accession to the throne.[80] This agitation constitutes the background to the extended version of the *vita*,[81] the composition of which can be ascribed to approximately 863/864, provided we accept as a contemporary event the

---

[74] *Vita of Petros of Atroa*, p. 7 and 14. [75] *Vita retractata of Petros of Atroa* 86bis, p. 29.
[76] *Vita retractata of Petros of Atroa*, p. 96–103.
[77] *Vita of Ioannikios by Sabas* 376–78. Some common terms, in fact, appear in these dogmatic supplements, e.g., τῶν αὐτοῦ Σατᾶν ὑπασπιστῶν (*Vita of Ioannikios by Sabas* 334B), cf. τῶν ὑπασπιστῶν αὐτοῦ ἀγωνιζομένων (*Vita retractata of Petros of Atroa* 12,82).
[78] Auzépy 2004b; Cunningham 2011.
[79] Phot., *Homilies* XV and XVI, p. 236–43; Dvornik 1953: 67–97; Mango 1977; Gwynn 2007. For the Photian policy on iconoclasm, Kaplan 1997: 74–80; see Chapters 5–6.
[80] On a possible return of iconoclasm, see *Vita retractata of Petros of Atroa*, p. 47–49. The survival of iconoclast sectors twenty years after its official defeat is unsurprising, because fifty years later it was still a real danger in areas of Cappadocia, as Arethas of Caesarea attested, see Kougeas 1913: 42 and 51, n. 2; Dvornik 1953: 97; Laourdas 1954.
[81] *Vita retractata of Petros of Atroa*, p. 29–30 and 48–49.

confrontation with the Bulgarians during which one of the final miracles recorded by Sabas, the rescue of the *scholarios* Konstantinos from the waters of the River Hebros, occurs.[82] This campaign probably coincided with the confrontations that according to the *De administrando imperio* took place between Bulgaria and Croatia (31,60ff.) and Bulgaria and Serbia (32,44ff.). After the Byzantine victory, the khan Boris seemingly accepted Orthodox baptism in 864.[83]

All the modifications noted up to this point confirm Sabas' close relationship with two important Bithynian monastic circles: that formed by the followers of Ioannikios and that established around Petros of Atroa. We have likewise noted Sabas' affinity with the ecclesiastical policy dictated from the patriarchate first by Ignatios and subsequently by Photios. It is worth noting the minor but significant alteration introduced regarding Michael I and his son Theophylaktos, who pass from being styled Μιχαὴλ καὶ Θεοφυλάκτου τῶν πανενδόξων δεσποτῶν ('highly glorious') to being called τῶν πανορθοδόξων δεσποτῶν ('highly orthodox');[84] this is doubtless a reference to the Ignatian faction, which continued to denounce the overthrow of its leader as anti-canonical. Finally, the treatment of Theodoros Stoudites is striking and may be due to an attempt to strengthen existing links with the well-known group of his disciples. The first version of the *vita* presented him in chs. 37–38 as the great judge of the Byzantine Church. According Sabas in these chapters, the serious illness of the wife of a *hypatos* (consul) led to his asking several bishops and hegoumenoi for help. The only person capable of healing her, however, was Petros of Atroa, which gave rise to numerous cases of slander.

Taking advantage of Theodoros Stoudites' stay at the monastery of Kreskentios during his exile on the Gulf of Nicomedia, Petros visited him at the end of 821 to ask him to intervene in his defence, offering his opinion on the slander he was being subjected to. For over 15 years, Petros of Atroa had refrained from bread, cheese, wine and oil and had only eaten vegetables and herbs. He even refused water for long periods. The historicity of the accusation and the encounter with the Stoudite abbot is corroborated by all versions of Theodoros' *vita*.[85] After Theodoros

---

[82] *Vita retractata of Petros of Atroa* 111. For the Byzantine-Bulgarian confrontation of 863/864, see Petrov 1966: 47, n. 23; p. 49; Zlatarski 1918.
[83] Theoph. Cont. IV, 14,20–15,34. Cf. also Laskaris 1933; Schreiner 1987; Vaillant and Kyriakis 1993: 130–31 and 207–11; Speck 2000; Varona Codeso 2010: 102–5.
[84] *Vita of Petros of Atroa* 12,2–5.
[85] *Vita B of Theodoros Stoud.* 59, 316C–17A; *Vita A of Theodoros Stoud.* 117, 220C–D; *Vita C of Theodoros Stoud.* 71, 299. Cf. also *Vita of Petros of Atroa*, p. 19 and 27–28.

studied the issues, his verdict was conclusive: however much resentment Petros' zeal in fasting and mortifying his body might create, far from being a fraud (γόης), he performed miracles in response to God's will, and this fact should be recognised by the Church as a whole. To this end, Theodoros sent a letter to Petros' detractors, reproaching them for their behaviour and exhorting them to receive Petros with courtesy under penalty of anathemisation.[86]

In Sabas' revision, these two chapters are retained in full, but more emphasis is given to the presentation of the hegoumenos of Stoudios, which was already positive in the first version. Thus 'the great confessor Theodoros' (ὁ μέγας ὁμολογητὴς Θεόδωρος)[87] becomes 'the highly perspicacious great confessor Theodoros' (ὁ διακριτικώτατος ἐκεῖνος καὶ μέγας ὁμολογητὴς Θεόδωρος). Moreover, Sabas includes a second visit to Theodoros Stoudites by his hero, which appears to have taken place two years later (in 823) and confirms the good relationship between the two men and how they collaborated to revive iconodule monastic life after the murder of Leon V the Armenian.[88] Unfortunately, only the beginning of the chapter survives, since two pages of text have been lost. But this is enough to show that the Bithynian monasteries emulated the Stoudite organisational system. Theodoros recommends that Petros impose the behaviour and fundamentals of Stoudios' rules on his monks.[89] (The need for a reorganisation of the communities of Mount Olympos after their dispersal in reaction to the successive threats of the iconoclastic persecution of Leon V and the attacks of the partisans of Thomas the Slav is also apparent.)[90] By adding this second encounter, Sabas stresses the links between the great monastic federations of the period, emphasising the close personal relationship of Petros of Atroa and Theodoros Stoudites and thus that between the members of the circles that formed around the two men, who shared the same motivations, interests and objectives.

7.2 Transfer to Constantinople

As a result of the preceding, it comes as no surprise that shortly afterwards we can trace the steps of the hagiographer Sabas in Constantinople, and to be precise, at the monastery of Kallistratos, where he appears to have

---

[86] *Vita of Petros of Atroa* 38,18–20.   [87] *Vita of Petros of Atroa* 37,41.
[88] *Vita of Petros of Atroa* 41bis.
[89] *Vita retractata of Petros of Atroa* 41bis,7–12; *Vita retractata of Petros of Atroa*, p. 42–44.
[90] *Vita of Petros of Atroa* 41. Cf. *Vita of Petros of Atroa*, p. 44, n. 5; *Vita retractata of Petros of Atroa*, p. 41–42.

introduced the cult of St Ioannikios, whose memory was celebrated on 3 or 4 November.[91] According to the sources, Kallistratos was one of the few establishments in Constantinople that Konstantinos V destroyed or sold.[92] The monastery is mainly known for having accommodated the writer Epiphanios of Kallistratos, the author of a *Vita of the Virgin* (*BHG* 1049) and another of the Apostle Andrew (*BHG* 102), in the first half of the ninth century.[93]

Sabas took charge of the famous monastery of St John of Stoudios in 865 with the consent of Photios, who was forced to replace his faithful friend Theodoros Santabarenos due to the Stoudite monks' disapproval of his leadership. Since the initiation of the Photian schism, the Stoudite superiors had given Ignatios unconditional support both in their strict interpretation of the canons and in their gratitude to the patriarch who had recalled them from exile and readmitted them to the Church after their confrontation with Methodios.[94] Indeed, the hegoumenos of the monastery in 858, Nikolaos Stoudites, abandoned it in order to avoid betraying the legitimate patriarch.[95] This gave rise to a series of abbots named by the court and the patriarchate, which only served to increase the monks' discontent: Achillas, Theodosios, Eugenios and Theodoros Santabarenos.[96] A turning point came with Sabas,[97] whose appointment as superior of Stoudios meant the return home of Nikolaos Stoudites. The subsequent return of Ignatios to the patriarchate in 867 led to the return of Nikolaos to the hegoumenate of Stoudios, although his early death meant that his tenure lasted for only a few months. Nikolaos was followed by Klemes,[98] who also died prematurely, on 7 July 868. Hilarion then led the monastery of Stoudios continuously during the second patriarchate of Ignatios and the second of Photios, until the year 886.[99]

The *vita* of Nikolaos Stoudites offers little information about the hegoumenos Sabas but clearly states that he came from the monastery of Kallistratos, was a disciple of Photios and supervised the confinement of

---

[91] *SynaxCP* 189,47–48 = 193,8–9: Τελεῖται δὲ ἡ αὐτοῦ (i.e., Ioannikios) σύναξις ἐν τῇ μονῇ τῶν Καλλιστράτου. For the monastery of Kallistratos, see Janin 1969: 275–76; 1975: 432 and 438.
[92] Theoph. 443 (destroyed); Nikeph., *Antirrhetici* III,64: 493D (sold).
[93] *PmbZ* # 1581,1; Beck 1959: 513; Kazhdan 1999: 307 and 396; Cunningham 2019.
[94] Dvornik 1948: 49. On the Stoudite schism, see Chapters 1–2.
[95] *PmbZ* # 5576; *PBE* I: Nikolaos 26. For his continuous membership in the Ignatian party, see Chapter 5.
[96] Delouis 2005: 333–36. For Achillas, see *PmbZ* # 75; *PBE* I: Achillas 1. For Theodosios, see *PmbZ* # 7887; *PBE* I: Theodosios 43. On Eugenios, see *PmbZ* # 1659; *PBE* I: Eugenios 6. For Theodoros Santabarenos, see *PmbZ* # 7729 and 27619; *PBE* I: Theodoros 174.
[97] *PmbZ* # 6451; *PBE* I: Sabas 6.   [98] *PmbZ* # 23705; *PBE* I: Klemens 4.
[99] *PmbZ* # 22601; *PBE* I: Hilarion 4

Nikolaos during the two years of his rule (865–867).[100] His previous presence at the monastery of Kallistratos has already been mentioned, together with the theological instruction he got from Photios, which has been preserved in the form of *epist.* 176 and 177. We can assume that upon his arrival at Stoudios, Sabas had considerable support among the members of the community, who were grateful to have recovered the company of their beloved leader Nikolaos. We do not know to what extent the mediation of Sabas was crucial in this process, which must have smoothed the matter over between the patriarch and the influential monastery in the capital. The choice of Sabas was certainly not a coincidence by any means, since he was a sympathiser with the Ignatian cause who had nonetheless maintained a dialogue with the patriarch Photios, just as he had in the past shown support for the Stoudite circle, favouring its interests through his rewriting of hagiographical works. It is also likely that during the years before he ran the monastery of Stoudios (or perhaps immediately afterwards), he continued this '*pratique remanieuse*', as his reworking of the *vita* of Hilarion of Dalmatos (*BHG* 2177) shows. The title of the manuscript indicates that Sabas was a monk.[101] This notice (also found in the *vitae* of Petros of Atroa and Ioannikios) does not imply that our hagiographer never went on to a higher positions, as Laurent supposed.[102] In fact, these biographical notes appear to refer only to the moment when the work in question was composed, as can be seen in the case of Ignatios Diakonos, who, after having filled the honourable posts of metropolitan of Nicaea and *skeuophylax* of Hagia Sophia, signed his *vita Tarasii* with a simple Ἰγνατίου μοναχοῦ.[103]

7.2.1 The Vita *of Hilarion of Dalmatos* (BHG 2177)

Hilarion the Younger (775–845) was a mainstay of Constantinopolitan monasticism against iconoclast heresy.[104] The *archimandrites* and hegoumenos of the monastery of Dalmatos in the capital of the empire, he spent the years 806–807 in the monastery of Kathara, which lay within the *thema* of Opsikion, which included the Mount Olympos area. During this

---

[100] *Vita of Nikolaos Stoud.* 912C–13A.
[101] Βίος ἤτοι πολιτεία τοῦ ὁσίου πατρὸς ἡμῶν καὶ ἀρχιμανδρίτου Ἰλαρίωνος ἡγουμένου μονῆς τῶν Δαλμάτου, συγγραφεὶς παρὰ Σάβα μοναχοῦ.
[102] *Vita of Petros of Atroa*, p. 13.
[103] For Ignatios Diakonos, see *PmbZ* # 2665; *PBE* I: Ignatios 9. See Chapters 2–3.
[104] *PmbZ* # 2584; *PBE* I: Hilarion 1. For the hagiography produced by Sabas, see Costa-Louillet 1957: 788–94; Kazhdan 1999: 341–42.

period, the establishment was part of the Stoudite confederation,[105] due to which the monastery of Stoudios was proud of his consecration as hegoumenos of Dalmatos in 807. We also know that Theodoros Stoudites played a vital role in this appointment and dedicated a catechesis to Hilarion himself.[106] Indeed, Hilarion agreed to join the other pro-Stoudite leaders in signing the missive in defence of iconoduly that Theodoros Stoudites sent to Pope Paschal I in 817.[107] Between 807 and 815, Hilarion was the head of the monastery of Dalmatos,[108] but the arrival of Leon V led to his imprisonment for defending images. One confrontation with imperial power after another followed until the death of Theophilos, when Empress Theodora brought Hilarion back to the monastery of Dalmatos from exile in Aphousia. He died in June 845 at the biblical age of seventy according to the *Synaxarion of Constantinople*[109] and at the age of seventy-seven according to the surviving *vita*.

Theodoros Stoudites wrote Hilarion at least one epistle in 816.[110] He is also mentioned in three other letters dated between 816 and 818.[111] These connections are sufficient to explain why the members of the monastery of Stoudios wished to preserve a version of his biography. This has come down to us in the manuscript *Vaticanus Gr.* 984, fol. 203v–6,[112] by Sabas Monachos. Following classic works such as that of Beck,[113] some prosopographies give this Sabas a separate entry,[114] but as we shall see, he is identical with our hagiographer Sabas. We owe the identification of this author with that of the *vitae* of Petros of Atroa and Ioannikios to Matantseva, who argues on the basis of his characteristic vocabulary.[115] Kazhdan believed that the profile of the hero (Constantinopolitan, an active defender of icons, persecuted and imprisoned, etc.) did not fit what he called 'the Bithynian cycle' or 'Mount Olympos school', which was less concerned with political matters than were hagiographers such as Ignatios

---

[105] Stiernon 1970: 119–23; Speck 1978: 693, n. 111. On the monastery of Kathara, see Janin 1975: 158–60; Delouis 2005: 214–21.
[106] Theod. Stoud., *Magnae catecheseis* 89. For the date of this appointment, see Alexander 1958a: 84–85; Stiernon 1970: 114–15; Niavis 1987: 150–51; Pratsch 1998: 149–51; Delouis 2005: 217–18 and 222–23.
[107] This is *epist.* 271. On the relationship between Theodoros Stoudites and the Pope, Van de Vorst 1913c.
[108] For this monastery, see Janin 1969: 82–84; Ruggieri 1991: 114–15.
[109] *SynaxCP* 731/732,47–733/734,54 (6 June = *BHG* 2177b).
[110] Theod. Stoud., *epist.* 90: Ἱλαρίωνι ἀρχιμανδρίτῃ.
[111] Theod. Stoud., *epist.* 214; *epist.* 267; *epist.* 291.
[112] Franchi de' Cavalieri 1920: 107–10; Ehrhard 1936–1939: vol. I, 652 and 657; Turyn 1964: 149–50; Canart 2008b: 76. See Introduction.
[113] Beck 1959: 558.   [114] *PmbZ* # 6446.   [115] Matantseva 1993.

Diakonos and the historians.[116] The conclusions of the sociological analysis put forward here, however, are supported by the codicology and the history of the transmission of the texts, as noted in the related section of the introduction.

As one might expect, Sabas Monachos was part of the hagiographical enterprise based at this important monastery that aimed to rewrite the role of its leader Theodoros Stoudites and by extension of the whole of the community during the Second Iconoclasm and the initial period after the Triumph of Orthodoxy. Particular attention in this connection ought to be paid to the *vita* of Niketas of Medikion, which was rewritten by the Stoudites in such a way that at the end Theodoros Stoudites has pride of place to the detriment of the saint who is the protagonist.[117] Hilarion had been one of Methodios' great supporters, as is apparent from the *Synodikon*, in which the patriarch mentions Ioannikios, Hilarion of Dalmatos and Symeon as the leaders of the hegoumenoi, the ascetics and the Stylites who shared his policy against the iconoclasts.[118] These three saints also appear as strongly backing Methodios as a candidate for the patriarchate in the *vita* of Ioannikios,[119] and Hilarion of Dalmatos probably also was accompanied by a large proportion of Gregorios Dekapolites' followers. What is important here is that the unconditional support of these men for Methodios also endorsed his ecclesiastical policy, which had important anti-Stoudite aspects. By means of the *vita* written by Sabas, the monastery of Stoudios appropriated the figure of Hilarion, stressing the aspects of his actions that agreed with Stoudite thought, such as Hilarion's opposition to the rehabilitation of Theophilos in contrast to Methodios' inclination to grant a posthumous pardon to the iconoclast emperor.[120] This meant that no opponent could use the figure of Hilarion against the Stoudites, who began to regard him as a saint of their own commemorated on 5 June.[121]

The *vita* of Hilarion produced by Sabas remains unpublished. Thanks to Matantseva's work,[122] however, we understand its relationship to the extensive information about the same saint preserved in the *Synaxarion of*

---

[116] Kazhdan 1999: 341.   [117] Delouis 2011.
[118] *Synodikon of Orthodoxy* 53,130f.; Darrouzès 1966: 296, line 5; 1987: 54, line 12.
[119] *Vita of Ioannikios by Petros* 431A–B; Talbot 1998: 340–42.
[120] *Vita of Hilarion of Dalmatos* 22.
[121] *Synaxarion Evergetis* II, 144. The *Synaxarion of Constantinople* celebrates him on the same date (*SynaxCP* 731,6–7), although many other calendars of saints' days celebrate his memory on the following day, on 6 June (*SynaxCP* 731/732,39–45), or even the following month on 5 July (*SynaxCP* 799/800,52).
[122] Matantseva 1993.

Constantinople. The characteristics of both texts imply that they are rewritings that summarise an earlier hagiography. Matantseva suggests that we ought to reconstruct two separate sources for each text, *VHil(Sab)** and *VHil(Syn)** respectively. The simplest and the most likely explanation, however, is that a single hagiographical account has been interpreted in different ways by the two authors (*synaxaristes* and hagiographer) according to their specific interests. Sabas' work offers more extensive and precise information regarding its subject. Its other differences from the *Synaxarion* are not striking, although there has been a significant alteration in the chronology of the *vita*, with the life of the saint extended by seven years, probably to lend him greater moral authority for his appointment as hegoumenos of Dalmatos. Such utilitarian alterations in the chronology of the protagonist are habitual in Sabas, who has no qualms about changing the date and place of historical events to make his message more effective. The most striking and best studied example is the *vita* of Ioannikios.[123] By this means, the hagiographer avoided potential criticism and defused any malicious interpretation of Theodoros Stoudites' reference to Hilarion's youth in his *Magnae catecheseis*.[124]

7.2.2 The Vita *of the Patriarch Methodios* (BHG 1278)

It is easy to imagine that when Nikolaos took charge of the monastery of Stoudios again, Sabas became a simple monk. He likely returned to being an ascetic, but for him living in solitude did not mean living in isolation. Indeed, the opposite was true: being part of the Stoudite circle led him to write a final work that represents the height of the policy of rewriting hagiographical texts sponsored by the monastery of Stoudios and was widely resented. Once again, and according to his custom, Sabas rewrote an existing text: the *Vita s. Methodii patriarchae Constantinopolitani*.[125]

As we know from the mention of the manuscript *Vaticanus Gr.* 825 deciphered by Allatius,[126] the original hagiography was written by Gregorios the archbishop of Syracuse, also known as Asbestas.[127] He was

---

[123] Mango 1983. [124] Matantseva 1993: 25–6.
[125] *AASS* June II, pp. 960ff., and III, pp. 442–43; *SynaxCP* 749–50; Costa-Louillet 1954/1955: 453–61; Kazhdan 1999: 367–79. For the historical figure of Methodios, see *PmbZ* # 4977; *PBE* I: Methodios 1; Gouillard 1987: 11–16; Lilie 1999: 183–260. On his literary work, see Chapter 2.
[126] Gouillard 1961a: 374, n. 4.
[127] On this metropolitan, see *PmbZ* # 2480 and 22348; *PBE* I: Gregorios 26. See Chapters 5–6. A treatise survives of his own making on the appropriateness of receiving Jewish converts in baptism. In it Gregorios' profound knowledge of canon law is apparent, see Dagron 1991b.

a major supporter of Photios, who took charge of making him a patriarch and apparently did not hesitate to attack in his work both the detractors of Methodios (mainly the Stoudites) and his own (the followers of the patriarch Ignatios, among whom the monks of Stoudios stood out once again). We know of Gregorios' antagonism towards Theodoros Stoudites and his monks as a result of an episode included in the *Vita* B of Theodoros Stoudites,[128] in which two disciples of Gregorios Asbestas are said to have criticised and mocked the liturgical poems of Theodoros in the presence of the saint's hagiographer. Gregorios' enmity with the patriarch Ignatios began when Methodios was still alive.[129] Although this hagiography honouring the patriarch Methodios has not come down to us, a brief passage survived inserted in the twelfth-century *Thesaurus orthodoxae fidei* of Niketas Choniates.[130] There can be no doubt that this is an extract of the *vita* written by Gregorios, given the title, which has survived: Gregorios' authorship was so well known that the copyist of the codex Athens EBE 991 (second half of the sixteenth century) assigns the surviving *Vita of the Patriarch Methodios* to him in fol. 95v–101.[131] Given the impossibility of carrying out a comparative study, the relationship between the two *vitae* is unclear. In their pioneering studies, Beck (on Byzantine religious literature) and Ševčenko (on ninth-century hagiography) have pointed out that Sabas' hagiography is a summary.[132] The lack of both self-referential elements and declarations of direct knowledge of the hero have led some to consider it much later than the death of Methodios, although its origin in the Stoudite milieu has always been clear.[133] A further argument for attributing this *vita* to Sabas is codicological, since the Stoudite manuscript that transmits it to us, the *Vaticanus Gr.* 1667, also preserves the *vita* of Ioannikios written by Sabas.

The hagiographical dossier of Methodios is limited: in addition to the *vita* edited by Migne, the first manuscript of which is the early tenth-century *Vaticanus Gr.* 1667, fol. 148v–56v, and the information we have regarding the lost *vita* by Gregorios Asbestas, only a hymn in his honour,

---

[128] *Vita* B *of Theodoros Stoud.* 56, 312D–13A.
[129] *Vita of Ignatios* 22–24. For this confrontation, cf. Grumel 1939; 1940/1942. On his openly pro-Photian position, Dvornik 1948: 17–38; Karlin-Hayter 1977; Grabar 1984: 185–86, 196ff.; Dagron 1993: 169–86.
[130] *PG* 140, cols. 281D–84A.
[131] *PG* 140, 281D: Γρηγόριος ἀρχιεπίσκοπος Σικελίας, ὁ τὸν βίον τοῦ ἐν ἁγίοις Πατρὸς ἡμῶν Μεθοδίου πατριάρχου Κωνσταντινουπόλεως συγγραψάμενος.
[132] Beck 1959: 558. Ševčenko 1977a: 116 and n. 22.
[133] Von Dobschütz 1909a: 52ff.; Afinogenov 1996a: 62–63; Lilie 1999: 184.

written by Photios shortly after Methodios' death, survives.[134] Given the lack of other sources, some scholars have postulated that the information about Methodios offered by tenth-century historians comes from the hagiography Gregorios dedicated to him. The false accusations of fornication made against Methodios by a woman[135] thus originate in this *vita*, according to Hirsch and Gouillard.[136] The latter is inclined to believe that there was a connection between this plot against the patriarch and his conflict with the Stoudites.[137] This idea was already put forward by Von Dobschütz, for whom it is a conciliatory version of the conflict, since the *magistros* Manuel had strong links with the monastery of Stoudios.[138] The *vita* of Ioannikios by Petros (written shortly after the death of the former in 846) already includes the event, which is associated with the machinations of the Stoudites.[139] According to the historiographical sources, Methodios' accusers bribed the mother of Metrophanes, the metropolitan of Smyrna in 857, to say that Methodios had fathered her son. When Asbestas produced his hagiography, he must have used this event to attack also enemies of Photios such as Metrophanes, the bishop of Smyrna since 858, since his mother had been the false accuser and he himself was therefore an impostor who claimed to be an illegitimate son of Methodios.[140]

The surviving *vita* should in fact be considered not so much a summary as a diluted rewriting. After the fashion of Sabas when he worked on the text of Petros to produce his hagiography of Ioannikios, his work on Methodios maintains some of the structure and the contents of Gregorios' work but neutralises, eliminates or touches up other portions. This literary process is particularly noticeable if we compare the fragment included by Niketas Choniates in his *Thesaurus orthodoxae fidei* with the corresponding part of the account of Sabas. This text has traditionally been considered 'a rather sketchy biography',[141] 'poor in information',[142] and the like. But it is a valuable source of information if it is taken in its context and if we understand the implications of the details he offers, as well as those he

---

[134] This *kanon* (of considerable length as it consists of 252 verses) presents the acrostic 'Μεθοδίῳ Φώτιος ὕμνον προσφέρω,' see *AHG*, vol. x, 50–62. For the circumstances of its composition, see Varona Codeso and Prieto Domínguez 2013.
[135] Theoph. Cont. IV, 10,1–19; Genesios 59,40–49; Ps-Symeon 652,10–14.
[136] Hirsch 1876: 154–55; Gouillard 1961a: 375; Varona Codeso 2010: 90–94.
[137] *Synodikon of Orthodoxy* 129.
[138] Von Dobschütz 1909a: 46; Afinogenov 1996a: 66. See Chapters 2 and 4.
[139] *Vita of Ioannikios by Petros* 70, 432A.
[140] *PmbZ* # 4986 and 25088; *PBE* I: Metrophanes 1. For his major role in defence of Ignatios, see Bury 1912: 190–91; Dvornik 1948: 41–59 and 27–240; Karlin-Hayter 1991a: 108, n. 53. On his written production, see Van Deun 2008; see Chapter 5.
[141] Efthymiadis 2011a: 109.   [142] Kazhdan 1999: 370.

omits. In fact, this is a true political weapon that can only be understood within the faction that encouraged its composition and tended to use it. The undeserved lack of attention this text has received to date means this aspect is worth considering.

From its very beginning, the *vita* written by Sabas seems to presuppose the existence of an earlier hagiography from which he keeps his distance. This may be why the title the manuscript gives to this work is not Βίος καὶ πολιτεία or ἐγκώμιον, but ὑπόμνημα.[143] As a summary similar to the *vita* of Hilarion of Dalmatos, it omits the vivid, richly detailed miraculous stories Sabas included in the hagiographies he dedicated to Ioannikios and Petros of Atroa. The preface praises Methodios and expresses the curious wish that angels might help men, so that with their assistance someone with the class and dignity of Methodios might be commissioned to write a biography in his honour. Unfortunately, no such man (μηδεὶς τῶν τοιούτων ἀνδρῶν) has yet done so.[144] Logically for an Ignatian such as Sabas, the testimony of someone like Gregorios Asbestas was untrustworthy and unworthy even of consideration, obliging him to take up his pen himself to prevent Methodios' feats from falling into oblivion.[145]

As on other occasions, an order served as the catalyst for Sabas' literary activity, although we do not know who commissioned the work.[146] The end of the prologue contains a declaration of intentions in which, as a *topos humilitatis*, Sabas declares that he will write an account like one by an amateur, as if he were a young man learning to write, which will be both brief and truthful.[147] According to the surviving passage from Asbestas, his *Vita of the Patriarch Methodios* was in keeping with those of the patriarchs

---

[143] For this literary 'sub-genre', see Schiffer 2004; Gribomont 2012.
[144] *Vita of Methodios* 1244B–45A: εἰ μηδεὶς τῶν τοιούτων ἀνδρῶν μέχρι τοῦ νῦν τῷ πανευφήμῳ Μεθοδίῳ τοιοῦτόν τινα λόγον προκατεβάλετο, 'if none of these men has yet produced a similar text for the famous Methodios'.
[145] *Vita of Methodios* 1245A: Ἆρά γε ἀνιστόρητον πάντη τοσαύτην ἀνδρὸς ἀρετήν, εἰ καὶ ἐλάχιστοι, καταλείψομεν, καὶ οὐκ ἀναγγελοῦμεν τὰς θεόθεν δι' αὐτοῦ γεγενημένας εὐεργεσίας, 'Shall we leave such great virtue of the man completely unrecorded, even if we are insignificant, and shall we not proclaim the benefactions that have been worked by God through him?'.
[146] *Vita of Methodios* 1245A: καὶ πότε δὴ γνησιώτερον τὴν κελεύουσαν πατέρα τιμᾶν πληρώσομεν ἐντολήν, 'and when in that case will we comply with the order that urges us to honour the truly genuine father?'.
[147] *Vita of Methodios* 1245A–B: ἀλλ' ὃν τρόπον οἱ ἄρτι εἰς διδασκάλους φοιτῶντες τοὺς μὲν ἀρχετύπους τῶν γραμμάτων χαρακτῆρας ἀπομιμοῦνται, οὐκ ἐφικνοῦνται δὲ τῆς ἀκριβοῦς ἐμφερείας αὐτῶν, ὡς τὰ αὐτὰ τοῖς αὐτοῖς ἐοικέναι, οὕτω καὶ ὁ ἡμέτερος λόγος, ψελλίσει μὲν ἴσως διανοίας ἀτέχνου προβεβλημένος, τἀληθῆ δὲ καὶ συντόμως λέξεται κατὰ δύναμιν, 'However, in the way in which the students of the time before their teachers faithfully imitate the archetypal shapes of the letters and do not attain their exact likeness to the point that the latter resemble the former, in this way too our text will on the one hand probably stammer as being projected by an artless mind and on the other hand will briefly tell the truth according to its abilities.'

Tarasios and Nikephoros written by Ignatios Diakonos: long-winded, detailed texts written in a lofty and meticulous style. This is very different from the work of Sabas, who is certainly not a pretentious author and produces much shorter works than those of the men mentioned above. The programmatic affirmation that its pages contain the truth is curious and makes sense only if it is understood as a forceful denial of falsehoods previously related about his hero. By any reckoning, this falsehood just lied in the actions carried out against Stoudite interests.

If Sabas manages to defend the image of the monks of Stoudios without lying, this is thanks to the numerous omissions in his work. After indicating the rich Syracusan origins of Methodios and his transfer to Constantinople to follow a civil career (*PG* 100, 1245B), the *vita* relates his arrival at the Bithynian monastery of Chenolakkos[148] (*PG* 100, 1245D), where he witnessed the establishment of the iconoclast heresy in 815 and the overthrow of the patriarch Nikephoros (*PG* 100, 1248A). From Chenolakkos, the young Methodios travelled to Rome[149] (*PG* 100, 1245B), where he continued his training until, after the murder of Leon V, he returned to Byzantium to present Michael II with the definitions of Orthodoxy from the Pope in the hope that he would reinstate Nikephoros in the patriarchal chair.[150] Michael had him whipped, however, and imprisoned on St Andrew's Island, where he remained for nine years for refusing to forswear images, until an imperial decree granted him his freedom (*PG* 100, 1250B). When Theophilos' government became established, the new emperor called Methodios into his presence to invite him to renounce icons; after a verbal confrontation, the future patriarch was again whipped and imprisoned.[151] As a third attempt, Theophilos decided to fête Methodios in order to convince him: he had him installed in the

---

[148] Janin 1975: 189–90 places this monastery in the Bithynian region of Mount Olympos, but Ruggieri 1991: 211–12 locates Chenolakkos near the capital. According to the *Synaxarion of Constantinople*, this establishment was founded by a certain Stephanos under Leon III the Isaurian (717–741), *SynaxCP* 392,1–94,4 (14 January).

[149] For the youth of Methodios, see Pargoire 1903a. On his stay in Rome and the work as a copyist he carried out there, see Canart 1979; 2008a. In Rome, he apparently wrote a book from which the copyist Anastasios copied the manuscripts *Parisinus Gr.* 1476 and 1470; the latter contains the *vita* of the Apostle Bartholomew penned by Theodoros Stoudites (*BHG* 230), see Prato 1986; 2000; Perria 1991.

[150] *Vita of Methodios* 1248C: τόμους δογματικούς, ἤτοι ὅρους ὀρθοδοξίας, παρὰ τοῦ πάπα λαβών, ἀνέρχεται πρὸς τὸν διάδοχον Λέοντος, ἐλπίσας τοῦτον ἄξαι πρὸς τὴν ὀρθοδοξίαν, καὶ ἀποκαταστῆσαι τὸν ἐν ἁγίοις Νικηφόρον τῷ ἰδίῳ θρόνῳ, 'after collecting some dogmatic volumes from the Pope, in actual fact the definitions or Orthodoxy, he approaches Leon's successor in the hope that he would embrace Orthodoxy and restore saint Nikephoros on his own throne'.

[151] *Vita of Methodios* 1252B. See Pargoire 1903b.

palace and made him his friend. Methodios took advantage of the situation to work for Orthodoxy and convert many of those close to the emperor and even managed to persuade Theophilos to abandon his intransigence (*PG* 100, 1252C). The death of the emperor meant the passing of heresy.

At this point we are halfway through the *vita*, which has a clear bipartite structure, with the struggle of the iconodule confessor separated from the administration of the restoring patriarch. In this first part, numerous details are omitted, including those of Methodios' monastic career. We know from a letter of Theodoros Stoudites that before Methodios left the Byzantine Empire for Rome, he was already a hegoumenos.[152] That he was archdeacon of the patriarch Nikephoros[153] explains his interest in returning and interceding for him, as well as his diplomatic mission appealing to the Pope to mediate in defence of icons.[154] With his reply, Pope Paschal I dealt with the requests of Methodios and the patriarchate, while at the same time confirming his disdain for the demands of Theodoros Stoudites, who had proclaimed himself a champion of Orthodoxy and the representative of the iconodule monastic faction in Rome, as is apparent from two letters he sent to Paschal I in favour of iconophilia.[155]

The original version of Gregorios Asbestas presumably made use of these events of the life of Methodios to stress the superiority of the patriarchate and the importance of hierarchy, which were disagreeable subjects for the Stoudites. This is especially so in this case, since they were personified in Nikephoros, whose confrontation with Theodoros Stoudites as a result of the Moechian dispute is well known: the second marriage of Emperor Konstantinos VI in 795 was strongly opposed by Platon and Theodoros of Stoudios, who confronted the remainder of society and the Church (even the patriarchate), leading to the exile of both hegoumenoi on two occasions, between 796 and 797 and between 809 and 811.[156] Theodoros Stoudites' strictness towards Ioseph of Kathara, who was finally pardoned by the patriarch, had intensified a conflict in which Methodios doubtless sided against the Stoudites. The close relationship of Methodios and Nikephoros (who supported his monastic career) was uncomfortable for the official version issued by the monastery of Stoudios, and Sabas accordingly conceals it by any means possible. The same happens with

---

[152] Theod. Stoud., *epist.* 274: Μεθοδίῳ τῷ εὐλαβεστάτῳ ἡγουμένῳ. He likely was not the superior of the monastery of Chenolakkos, where he had initiated religious life, but of the monastery he founded at the foot of the Bithynian Mount Olympos named Elegmoi/Eleobomon, see Section 2.1.4.
[153] *Acta of David, Symeon and Georgios* 22, 237,6; Lilie 1999: 191–95.
[154] Genesios IV,5, 59,55; Skylitzes 87,79ff.   [155] Theod. Stoud., *epist.* 271 and 272.
[156] Henry 1969; Fuentes Alonso 1984; Pratsch 1998: 83–115 and 147–80.

relationships with Rome: even when the facts favour a pro-Stoudite interpretation and the missive of Paschal I could be presented as a diplomatic success of Theodoros, the *vita* makes no mention of it.

The imprisonments of Methodios resulting from his public defence of images are treated for their part as normal events in the *vita*. In fact, the hagiographer has considerably toned down the public profile of the future patriarch's actions. From the *Acta of David, Symeon and Georgios* we know that the reign of Michael II was particularly permissive regarding icons and that the only person who suffered reprisals was Methodios,[157] a fact to be understood as due to his political position rather than his religious one. This explains the harshness of Methodios' captivity and the fact that he shared a cell with a man imprisoned for attempted usurpation.[158] Nor does Sabas mention the important hagiographical work carried out by Methodios in this period, such as the *vita* of Euthymios of Sardis he wrote during his imprisonment. But some elements can be traced that indicate that Gregorios Asbestas mentioned the literary activities of his hero on St Andrew's Island. The sophisticated etymological wordplay with which Methodios initiates his *Vita Euthymii* (Εὐθυμίας φερώνυμον μάρτυρα, τὸν προθυμίας ἱεράρχην αὐτόχειρα, ἐν ἀθυμίας καιροῖς ... 'The martyr named after encouragement [εὐθυμία], the high-priest who accomplished courage [προθυμία] in the moment of discouragement [ἀθυμία] ...') was probably a characteristic stylistic element in the chapter of the biography produced by the archbishop of Syracuse. Years later, Sabas found inspiration in this passage of Gregorios' account of Methodios when he included first a note on the persecution of the patriarch in his *Vita Ioannicii*[159] and subsequently described his imprisonment in the *Vita Methodii* itself.[160] In

---

[157] *Acta of David, Symeon and Georgios* 22, 237,1–8. The religious freedom decreed by Michael II for the whole Empire, except the capital, is confirmed by *Vita B of Theodoros Stoud.* 317D. See Chapter 3.

[158] *Vita of Methodios* 1248C: ἐν ᾧ τάφῳ καὶ ἕτερος ἐπὶ τυραννίδι κατακέκλειστο, 'a tomb in which another man had already been imprisoned for attempted usurpation'. On Methodios' production of several pamphlets prophesising the death of various emperors, see Lilie 1999: 212–13; Treadgold 2004; Kaplan 2006: 202–5; Timotin 2010: 122–27.

[159] *Vita of Ioannikios by Sabas* 46, 372A: Μεθόδιος, ὁ κόσμου φυγὰς καὶ πλούτου ἀπὸ νεότητος, ὁ διαπρέψας ἀσκήσει καὶ ἁγνείᾳ σὺν **προθυμίᾳ**, καὶ ὑπὲρ τῆς εἰς Χριστὸν εὐσεβείας διωγμοὺς πολλοὺς καὶ ἀποδημίας ἐνέγκας, ὁ πρὸ ὀλίγων ἐτῶν ἐκ Ῥώμης ἐλθὼν καὶ ὑπὸ τῶν δυσσεβῶν ἐπὶ ἐννέα χρόνους ἐν μνημείῳ κατακλεισθείς.

[160] *Vita of Methodios* 1248C–49A: ἔπειτα δὲ ἔν τινι τάφῳ εἰς τὸ τοῦ Ἀποστόλου Ἀνδρέου νησίον κατέκλεισεν, ἐν ᾧ τάφῳ καὶ ἕτερος ἐπὶ τυραννίδι κατακέκλειστο, ὡς πᾶσαν αὐτῷ **ἀθυμίαν** πανταχόθεν ἐγγίνεσθαι, ἀπὸ τῶν πληγῶν, ἀπὸ τοῦ ἀθεράπευτον εἶναι, ἀπὸ τοῦ καταδικασθέντος ἀγροίκου ἀνδρός, ἀπὸ τῆς τοῦ τάφου στενοχωρίας, καί, τὸ δεινότερον, ἀπὸ τοῦ ἀφεγγοῦς σκότους. 'He then imprisoned him in a tomb on St Andrew's Island, in which tomb another man had already been imprisoned for attempted usurpation. On all sides he was overcome

each rewriting, however, he chose different components (*Vita Ioannic.*: προθυμία; *Vita Methodii*: ἀθυμία) in order to remove the etymological wordplay in the texts. There is also no mention of the traditions preserved by historians according to which Methodios had the friendship and support of important confessors such as the Graptoi brothers[161] and Michael Synkellos[162] or those explaining Methodios' arrival at the court as due to the help he gave Theophilos, who ended up taking him on campaigns against the Arabs.[163] These modifications and omissions eliminate Methodios' political position, his aggressive confrontation with imperial power and his hagiographical work in memory of a confessor of the calibre of Euthymios of Sardis. The resulting image is that of a low-profile monk, so that any confrontation he might have been involved in with the Stoudites becomes less significant.

The second part of the *Vita of the Patriarch Methodios* begins with the power vacuum regarding the patriarchal throne after Theophilos' death and the immediate overthrow of Ioannes VII Grammatikos and all his clergy (*PG* 100, 1253A). Although all outstanding men are considered, Methodios is appointed patriarch, since he surpassed everyone else in asceticism, in knowledge of the Scriptures, in his way with words for sermons, in his suffering in the face of trials and tribulations, in his moderation of thought and in his easy manner and conversation.[164] It is noted, for example, that Methodios copied seven complete psalters in a week of fasting, during which he refused even water (*PG* 100, 1253B–C). After a public speech in which he asked those who attacked Orthodoxy to rejoice at the end of heresy and which appears to correspond in time to his enthronement (*PG* 100, 12453C–56D), the hagiographer briefly recalls some major milestones of Methodios' patriarchate, although in fact he condenses them into a single episode: the end of iconoclasm involved the renewal of many ecclesiastical posts, although not all those appointed were worthy of the confidence Methodios placed in them (*PG* 100, 1257A). Envy arose, and the need for an assessment prior to the ordinations led to a

---

by a complete lack of spirit [***athymia***]: due to the blows, the lack of medical attention, the rough man who had been judged, the narrowness of the tomb and his terror in the darkness.'

[161] Ps-Symeon 642–43, Zonaras XV, 28.33–37. [162] *Vita of Michael the Synkellos* 24, 98,13–24.
[163] Genesios III 21 (53,8); Ps-Symeon 643–45; Theoph. Cont. III, 24,3–4; Skylitzes 69; Zonaras XV 28,38–39. The textual parallels between Genesios and the Continuator confirm the existence of a common source, which was probably none other than the *Vita Methodii* of Gregorios Asbestas.
[164] *Vita of Methodios* 1253B: πολλῶν τοίνυν μεγάλων καὶ ἁγίων ἀνδρῶν προβεβλημένων, μόνος προκρίνεται καὶ καθίσταται ὁ ἀθλοφόρος Μεθόδιος, ἀσκήσει πάντας ὑπερβάλλων καὶ γραφῶν ἐμπειρίᾳ καὶ προφορᾶς εὐγλωττίᾳ καὶ ἄθλων ὑπομονῇ καὶ φρονήματος μετριότητι καὶ συναναστροφῇ καὶ συνουσίᾳ χαριεστάτῃ.

schism, but the will of the patriarch was corroborated by the imperial verdict (*PG* 100, 1257B–D). By the will of God, Methodios began to suffer from dropsy and in his humility forgave those who had rebelled against his authority as patriarch (*PG* 100, 1260A–B). The final two chapters laud his holiness by means of a series of parallels with biblical figures and Fathers of the Church (*PG* 100, 1260C–61B) and conclude by requesting the assistance and intercession of the saint in the difficulties of everyday life (*PG* 100, 1261B–C).

Once again Sabas has made a conscientious selection of pre-existing material regarding his hero. In the first place, he offers a simplified account of the process of choosing Methodios as patriarch,[165] omitting the important support he enjoyed from members of the monastic clergy, such as Michael Synkellos[166] and Ioannikios,[167] along with the sympathy he had at the imperial court from Theodora and Theoktistos.[168] He also notably omits the remaining candidates, including one clearly supported by the Stoudite sector: Ioannes Kakosambas.[169] The speech Sabas puts in the mouth of Methodios (which has not survived in any other form) summarises the process of the restoration of Orthodoxy, which was no doubt extremely detailed in the work of Gregorios Asbestas. The *vita*'s interest in the purging of the iconoclastic clergy[170] probably corresponds to the attention given this matter in the original *Vita Methodii*, as well as to the interests of the Stoudites. Indeed, in its tone and its concern for the legality of the ordinations, which must be preceded by an examination, we can recognise the canonist facet of Gregorios when he produced the treatise *On the Baptising of Jews*.[171]

As Sabas tells the story, the devil caused a confrontation among the Orthodox, which was resolved in favour of the patriarch's authority. By means of this simple statement, he avoids mentioning Methodios' conflict with the Stoudites, whom he required under penalty of excommunication to anathematise any text that attacked Tarasios or Nikephoros, which meant rejecting some of the work of Platon of Sakkoudion and of Theodoros of Stoudios himself. In fact, our hagiographer has fused two

---

[165] On the selection process of Methodios as a patriarch, see Afinogenov 1996a; Lilie 1999: 216–30; Karlin-Hayter 2001; 2006b.
[166] Cunningham 1991: 26–27.   [167] *Vita of Ioannikios by Sabas* 46; *Vita of Ioannikios by Petros* 69.
[168] Leon Gramm. 228; Ps-Symeon 647, 651; Georg. Mon. Cont. 811; Theoph. Cont. II, 8; IV, 3; IV, 6; *Vita of Ignatios* 15; *Vita A of Theophylaktos of Nicomedia* 18; *Vita of Nikolaos Stoud.* 901C; Zonaras XVI 1,11.
[169] *PmbZ* # 3219; *PBE* I: Ioannes 240.   [170] Lilie 1999: 231–47.
[171] *Vita of Methodios* 1257C.

clearly separate processes together, in order to avoid having to mention the scandal of the false accusation of fornication, which was already present in Gregorios' account and was well developed later by historians. Sabas himself shows signs of familiarity with the episode, and seems to recognise the injustice of the accusation and consider Methodios' sexual impotence proof of his holiness, as can be seen in the hagiography's final imprecations.[172] The writer confines himself to acknowledging that Methodios was the object of envy that ultimately bore no fruit.[173] Sabas likely had in mind the narrative technique used by Petros in his *Vita Ioannicii*, in which even after the Triumph of Orthodoxy the devil attempts to sow discord within the Church. In addition to omitting any reference to the Stoudites, he also leaves out the veiled allusion introduced by Petros (who clearly blames these monks) by means of the comparison with St Athanasios of Alexandria.[174] The story must have been popular in ninth-century Byzantium, and Photios was able to take advantage of this, as the numerous references in his homilies to parallel episodes indicate.[175]

The insistence on the magnanimous pardon Methodios granted to anyone who had offended him while he was alive[176] is clearly of interest to the monastery of Stoudios, since it sanctions the *oikonomía* that allowed healing of the open wounds between the patriarchate and the monastery. Among other episodes of Methodios' work as patriarch, Sabas omits the conversion of Zelix and his followers,[177] which we know of thanks to the surviving fragment of the lost *vita* of Gregorios Asbestas and to the historians who recycled the passage (Theophanes Continuatus and Genesios). The relevance it is given in surviving sources – the *kanon* of Methodios practically places Zelix on the same level as Ioannes VII Grammatikos[178] – indicates that this was no minor matter. But the lack of Stoudite intervention in the process must explain its omission in Sabas' account.

---

[172] *Vita of Methodios* 1261A.   [173] *Vita of Methodios* 1257B.
[174] *Vita of Ioannikios by Petros* 70, 431B–32A.
[175] Phot., *Homilies* XV, pp. 142,19–43,16 (mention of the episode, narrated by Theodoretos of Cyrrhus, according to which the Arians bribed a prostitute to accuse the pious Eustathios of Antioch of having a son with her); 144,10–24 (a prostitute accuses Athanasios of Alexandria of having deflowered her); 147ff. (a prostitute is sent by the Arians to seduce Bishop Euphrates).
[176] *Vita of Methodios* 1260A–B.
[177] For this person, see *PmbZ* # 8642; Gouillard 1961a: 373–75; Varona Codeso 2010: 96 and 217–18.
[178] The absence of Zelix in the *Synodikon*, where one would expect to find him among the anathematised on the occasion of the triumph of iconoduly, proves that his conversion occurred at a later date during the patriarchate of Methodios and not in its early days, see Archimandrite Ephrem 2006.

Two prevailing tendencies can thus be seen in Sabas' creation of this *vita*: a concern for matters in which members of the community of Stoudios were involved, which means that the remaining episodes are omitted because they were of no interest to his readers, and a wish to tone down the image of the monastery and its contemporary supporters, such as the patriarch Ignatios. The demonisation of Ignatios, considered the Antichrist (as if he were a new Ioannes Grammatikos), is largely due to Gregorios Asbestas, and for Gouillard the origin of these attacks lies in the lost *Vita Methodii*.[179] To achieve this objective, Sabas follows a procedure as simple as it is effective: omitting passages or complete episodes to create a new historical record through the hagiographical text. By means of the *vitae* of other saints (even at times those opposed to their monastery), the Stoudites wished to erase any confrontation with the patriarchate and elevate their leader Theodoros Stoudites to the category of one of the patriarchs who fought against iconoclasm (e.g., Tarasios and Nikephoros) in order to form a holy trio, as if Theodoros himself had also been a patriarch and had never confronted the institution. Given the system used and its efficiency in avoiding opposing reactions, silence appears to have been the best narrative strategy for the pro-Stoudite version.

The date of the surviving *Vita of the Patriarch Methodios* is uncertain. Kazhdan considered that 'probably, it was written long after 847' and used as dating elements two passages at the end of the *vita* in which the author requests the intercession of the saint 'to hold the attacks of the barbarian nations ... award to the Emperors the palms of victory' (ἐπισχεῖν τῶν βαρβάρων ἐθνῶν τὰς ἐφόδους ... τοῖς βασιλεῦσι βραβεῦσαι τὰ νικητήρια).[180] Although these are timeless desires expressed in a stereotyped formula,[181] Kazhdan wondered whether the plural βασιλεῦσι may refer to Romanos I and his sons (920–944), in which case the barbarians might be the Bulgarians led by King Simeon. Apart from the fact that the text lacks any specific references, since this is a general expression of desire, this identification is difficult to accept if we heed the codicological evidence, which puts the first surviving copy of the *vita* in the early tenth century. Indeed, *Vaticanus Gr.* 1667 is a pre-metaphrastic *menologion* that was part of a collection of manuscripts that also includes *Vaticanus Gr.* 1660, which is dated precisely to the year 916.[182]

---

[179] *Vita of Ignatios* 22–24 and 54, p. 80,14–34; Gouillard 1971.
[180] *Vita of Methodios* 1261B–C; Kazhdan 1999: 368.   [181] Bréhier 1916: 364.
[182] For the dating of the manuscript *Vaticanus Gr.* 1667, see Giannelli 1950: 410–15; Canart 1982: 22, nn. 8 and 9. See Introduction.

The date of the writing of the *Vita Methodii* can thus be narrowed down to the early years of the second patriarchate of Ignatios (867–877), after Photios had been deposed. A fierce attack was mounted not only on Photios himself but on the whole of his pastoral work, which was subject to a drastic attempt to eliminate it that included the destruction of churches he had consecrated.[183] Photios was unable to respond, and his detractors initiated a powerful smear campaign against him that led to the convening of the anti-Photian council of 869/870 inaugurated in Constantinople on 5 October 869, which concluded with Photios' excommunication and anathematisation.[184] Only slightly more than a hundred Ignatian bishops took part in the sessions, where Photios refused to testify. His followers were also anathematised and suspended, although some of them remained loyal to Photios.[185] The purge of Photios' supporters must have created a lack of human capital in the sees, forcing Ignatios to appoint simple laymen as ecclesiastical hierarchs,[186] contrary to resolutions issued at his own council. Ignatios rapidly became involved in a bitter dispute with the new Pope John VIII, who not only disapproved of this pastoral work but also did not allow Ignatios to ratify the proposal from Bulgaria to deprive Rome of its jurisdiction over the Balkans. Pamphlets were also circulated in Constantinople that seriously damaged the image of the ex-patriarch, including the letter from Metrophanes of Smyrna to the *logothetes* Manuel stating the reasons for Photios' condemnation[187] and the 'anti-Photian collection', in which an anonymous author gathered together various texts attacking Photios from the moment of his consecration and praising Ignatios, including the *libellus* of the *archimandrites* Theognostos (ca. 861) aimed at Pope Nicholas.[188]

Attribution of the *vita* to this pro-Ignatian stage, in which an attempt was made to demolish the order established by Photios, is supported by the new foreign policy announced by Basileios I in an attempt to smooth matters over with the Pope of Rome. In order to make this rapprochement possible, the emperor not only deposed Photios and reinstated Ignatios but

---

[183] Phot., *epist.* 98 to Emperor Basileios I; *epist.* 112 to Gregorios Asbestas; *epist.* 174,44–94 to the bishops in exile; *epist.* 183 to the presbyteros and hesychast Arsenios; and *epist.* 188 to the persecuted bishops. Cf. Stratoudaki White 1974; Leserri 2004.
[184] Mansi XVI, 18; Hergenröther 1867–1869: vol. II, 76; Dvornik 1948: 132–58; Stephanou 1973; Perrone 1990.
[185] Dvornik 1948: 162; Blysidou 1991: 113–21.   [186] *MGH, Epist.* 6,762.
[187] Mansi XVI, 416. See Section 5.2.1.
[188] For its contemporary dissemination in Constantinople, see Simeonova 1998: 48 and n. 92.

also encouraged veneration of the Apostle Peter, the predecessor of the Pope and protector of the see of Rome.[189] The success of this religious policy extended even outside the capital, as the foundational inscription of the church of Skripou (Boeotia) shows.[190] Sabas seems to have played an active part in this policy, given the positive mentions of the Roman Apostles Peter and Paul that stud the text[191] and the location in Rome of the miracle performed by St Peter on the lower abdomen of Methodios to eliminate his corporal passions and allow him to grow in holiness.[192] During this period, moreover, in which Photios sent numerous recriminatory letters to false friends and traitors, *epist.* 91 to Sabas makes good sense. Although the prosopographies give him a different entry,[193] Hergenröther[194] long ago identified this recipient with Sabas the presbyteros and hesychast, to whom Photios dedicates the two letters of theological content discussed above.[195] Although no attempt has been made to date to pinpoint the chronology of this missive, both its content and its use of the term ἀποστάτης in the *intitulatio* indicate that it is contemporary with the anti-Photian council of 869/870. In *epist.* 91, Photios laments the fact that Sabas, who had given the impression of being a friend, has passed over to the group of his enemies and acted consistently against him:

> Πόθεν ἡ πρὸς πάντα σου κίνησις βραδεῖα καὶ νωθὴς εἰς τὴν καθ' ἡμῶν κατέστη συσκευὴν ὀξεῖα καὶ σφοδρά; ἢ δῆλον ὡς ἐν οἷς μὲν ἔπραττεν ὁ λογισμὸς κατὰ φύσιν, κἂν οὐκ ἦν αὐτῷ τάχος ἔμφυτον εἰς ἀντίληψιν τῶν καλῶν, ὅμως οὐδὲ ἀκρατῶς εἴα πρὸς τὰ φαῦλα φέρεσθαι καὶ ἀνενδότως τὴν ὁρμήν· ἐπεὶ δὲ καὶ αὐτῶν ἐξέπεσε τῶν κατὰ φύσιν, συνεξηνέχθησαν αὐτῷ καὶ αἱ κινήσεις πᾶσαι καὶ αἱ πράξεις εἰς τὸ στασιῶδες ἦθος καὶ ἐμμανές. ἡμᾶς δὲ γίνωσκε λίαν αἰσχύνεσθαι καὶ ὑπεραλγεῖν, οὐχ ὅτι νῦν πάντας κύβους καθ' ἡμῶν ἀναρριπτεῖς, ἀλλ' ὅτι καὶ αὐτὸς εἷς ἐδόκεις πάλαι τῶν φιλούντων ἡμᾶς.
>
> Since when has your slow and deliberate movement with regard to everything gone sour and vehement in your disposition towards us? It is clear that in those in whom reasoning worked according to nature, although there is no inborn speed in them to apprehend the good things, nothing allowed them to be brought uncontrollably towards perverse things and inflexibly to this irrational impulse. Since you have turned away from your own nature, all your actions and movements also contributed towards a

---

[189] Von Falkenhausen 1988. [190] Oikonomidès 1994: 489–93; Prieto Domínguez 2013.
[191] *Vita of Methodios* 1257B; 1257D; 1261A.
[192] Genesios IV,5 (59,55–60,64); Ps-Symeon 652,16–21; Theoph. Cont. IV, 10,19,32; Zonaras XVI, 1,29–32; cf. Lilie 1999: 199.
[193] *PmbZ* # 6450; *PBE* I: Sabas 13. [194] Hergenröther 1867–1869: vol. II, 196.
[195] Phot., *epist.* 176–77 = Amph. 95–96.

conspiratorial and furious nature. You must realise that we are truly ashamed and hurt, not because you now throw all the dice into the air against us, but because you seemed of old to be one of our friends.

The emphasis the deposed patriarch gives to betrayal and conspiracy (συνεξηνέχθησαν αὐτῷ καὶ αἱ κινήσεις πᾶσαι καὶ αἱ πράξεις εἰς τὸ στασιῶδες ἦθος καὶ ἐμμανές ... νῦν πάντας κύβους καθ' ἡμῶν ἀναρριπτεῖς) allows the letter to be placed in the months before and after the anti-Photian council of 869. It may well have been sparked by the writing of Sabas' *Vita Methodii*, which in Photios' eyes added Sabas' active involvement in the Stoudite conspiracy against him to the treachery of a supposed ally, who had preferred to defend the Ignatian cause. Indeed, the *intitulatio* of the epistle (Σάβα ἡσυχαστῇ μετὰ τῶν ἀποστατῶν γεγονότι) stresses the addressee's defection to the ranks of the patriarch Ignatios. Photios' epistolary style is characterised by the use of the words ἀποστάτης and ἀποστατέω to refer to the dissidents who have abandoned him.[196] It is also typical of the patriarch to consider those who left to work for the faction of Ignatios precursors of the Antichrist.[197]

Several other letters with similar content to *epist.* 91 have been dated to this period, such as *epist.* 175, in which the patriarch denounces the unfaithfulness of Paulos, who had been archbishop of Caesarea and was now an apostate in his eyes.[198] After having been ordained by Photios, Paulos attended the synod of 860/861 and helped condemn Ignatios. But Ignatios himself affirms in a letter addressed to Pope Nicholas that Paulos ultimately refused to endorse the accusations,[199] which meant that he was replaced as head of the see of Caesarea by Euschemon.[200] Likewise, in *epist.* 120 Photios reproaches the *praipositos* Theophilos for hating him, while Photios shows concern for Theophilos. The ex-patriarch concludes that the result is radically different for the two of them, since Theophilos' behaviour elevates Photios by obliging him to practise Christian virtues, whereas Theophilos is condemned for all eternity. According to the minutes of the council, this Theophilos, *protospatharios* and *praipositos*,

---

[196] Phot., *epist.* 7: Παύλῳ μοναχῷ ἀποστατήσαντι (*PmbZ* # 5866); *epist.* 66: Μητροφάνει μοναχῷ ἀποστατήσαντι (*PmbZ* # 4985; *PBE* I: Metrophanes 3); *epist.* 175: Παύλῳ γεγονότι ἀρχιεπισκόπῳ Καισαρείας καὶ ἀποστατήσαντι (see n. 199).
[197] Phot., *epist.* 69: Εὐθυμίῳ μονάζοντι παραπεσόντι (*PmbZ* # 1859; *PBE* I: Euthymios 18). See Section 6.2.3.
[198] Phot., *epist.* 175,4–5: κακὸς ἐγένου φίλοις καὶ θείου προδότης δόγματος καὶ τῆς σῆς ὁμολογίας πολέμιος, 'you have behaved badly to your friends, a traitor of God's dogma and an enemy of your own confession'.
[199] Mansi xvi, 49CD and 51B. For this individual, see *PmbZ* # 5865; *PBE* I: Paulos 85.
[200] Phot., *epist.* 126,6.

was in charge of introducing the Photian metropolitans at the session of 24 October 869 of the Ignatian synod.[201]

Also dating to this period are the numerous letters sent to Theodoros, the metropolitan of Laodicea in Phrygia, in which Photios expresses hopes that the rumour that Theodoros has deserted the Photian ranks is untrue (*epist.* 88), advises Theodoros not to act hastily (*epist.* 194) and fails to mention Theodoros' disloyalty, after reminding him that he has been his protector (*epist.* 251). In addition, the patriarch sent Theodoros *epist.* 41, in which he reminds him that worldly life is a testing ground and not a podium of awards; *epist.* 71, in which he warns that the current situation obliges Theodoros to show himself as a defender of the truth or be called a traitor; *epist.* 72, which declares that the height of bad behaviour is to boast of what one should cause shame; *epist.* 139 (= *Amph.* 220), which contains a comment to Matthew 5:28; *epist.* 140, in which Photios encourages Theodoros to show strength and defend his brothers; *epist.* 141, which declares that the situation requires only the noble to go down to the stadium; *epist.* 171, in which Photios affirms that it does Theodoros no good to forgive his own sins and *epist.* 252, which warns that Theodoros must show his repentance with deeds and not with words only.[202] We are very familiar with the betrayal of Theodoros, since it was public: he was one of the Photian bishops who, during the session of 7 October at the anti-Photian council of 869/870,[203] publicly repented and were accepted by Ignatios within the new ecclesiastical order Emperor Basileios had favoured.[204]

Given that we have no subsequent information about the hagiographer Sabas, it can be assumed that he died shortly after Ignatios' triumph.

7.3 Conclusions

Hagiographical textual production was designed first of all for the veneration of saints. But it also served to praise the founder of a monastery, to applaud the piety of the hegoumenos who commissioned the *vita*, to unite the monastic community around a point of reference and principles portrayed as worthy of admiration and imitation and to strengthen the

---

[201] Mansi XVI, 84C and 345D. Concerning Theophilos, see *PmbZ* # 28138 and 28140; *PBE* I: Theophilos 48.
[202] On Theodoros, see *PmbZ* # 5867 and 27620; *PBE* I: Theodoros 175.
[203] Mansi XVI, 37–42; 320–21.
[204] For the desertion at this time of important lay figures from the group of Photios' followers to that of Ignatios, see Prieto Domínguez 2013: 189, n. 70.

political position of the monastery and thus its social perception and influence. The figure of the author of this type of text is complex and no doubt depended in the last analysis on individual personality. The case of Sabas is paradigmatic, since like the famous Ignatios Diakonos, he was able to use his literary capacity as *remanieur* to promote both his spiritual father, by encouraging his liturgical commemoration, and the establishment of his cult but also to promote himself, by coming into contact with and being part of several major contemporary networks, one based on the memory of St Ioannikios and another on the epicentre of the monastery of Stoudios in Constantinople.

In his first stage, during the first patriarchate of Ignatios, Sabas produced his first version of the *Vita Petri Atroae* with the aim of praising his teacher and rewrote the *Vita Ioanicii*, which Petros Monachos had previously penned, and the *Vita Petri Atroae* that Sabas himself had written some years earlier. His goal was clear: to combine the forces of the Stoudite and Bithynian monks, mainly the circle of hermits that remained loyal to Ioannikios (to which end Sabas tones down the confrontation between their leader and the Stoudites) and the federation of monasteries founded by Petros of Atroa (which Sabas reminds of his teacher's good relationship with Theodoros Stoudites, while at the same time granting it excellent anti-iconoclast credentials). This is in keeping with the later writing of the *Vita Hilarionis Dalmatis*, the subject of which was a fanatic of the Stoudite regime that had trained him, although he supported Methodios in his accession to the patriarchate and was a predecessor of the group run by Gregorios Dekapolites (whose followers were firmly established in the Methodian milieu, which had such good relations with Ioannikios).

The difficult relationship of Sabas and Photios provides an explanation for the second part of his life, which we can contextualise thanks to the patriarch's surviving correspondence. The overthrow of Ignatios triggered a mass desertion of hegoumenoi and bishops on the Bithynian Mount Olympos, leaving vacant the post of the superior of the monastery of Pissadinoi, which Sabas occupied henceforth. The epistles he was sent by Photios (*epist*. 176–77 and *epist*. 15) reflect a progressive lack of understanding and help us to understand his move to the capital. His work there at the monastery of Stoudios was determinant in shaping the basis of the *menologia* that transmitted the official ideology of the community. The analysis of the surviving manuscripts carried out in the introduction allows us to better understand the process of the creation of political ideology through daily liturgy and to securely attribute to our Sabas an essential text on the defeat of iconoclasm and the creation of a new orthodox society, the *vita* of the patriarch Methodios (*BHG* 1278). The benefits to the Stoudite community of the toned-down versions of the *vitae* of Ioannikios and the patriarch Methodios are clear; Sabas was aware of this and also of the importance of establishing the *menologia*, if his vision of history was to prevail. Not for nothing, one of Methodios' feats he recalls is that he copied seven complete psalters during a week of fasting, during which he did not even drink any water.[205] This information is highly significant, because Methodios had probably also compiled *menologia*,[206] which means that the hagiographer identified himself with the saint.

Sabas' life story also allows us to reflect on literary patronage after the Dark Age.[207] This is a reality that the Byzantines themselves discreetly conceal, since when Sabas acknowledges that he was commissioned to write a work, he presents this as part of the obedience due a monastic superior. Such is the situation with the *vitae* of Petros of Atroa and Ioannikios, which are written in response to direct orders from the hegoumenoi of St Zacharias and Antidion. The hagiographical composition devoted to the patriarch Methodios satisfies an 'order that urges him' (τὴν κελεύουσαν ... ἐντολήν),[208] although we do not know who issued it. The *Vita retractata of Petros of Atroa*, by contrast, appears to respond to a spontaneous impulse on the writer's part. It is true that in around 863, when he wrote this, Sabas had been dismissed as head of the monastery of Pissadinoi and was living as a simple ascetic. It was precisely now that he received several epistles from Photios, thanks to whom before 865 Sabas had established himself in Constantinople in the monastery of Kallistratos, after which he ran that of Stoudios. Although nothing survives to justify a cause-effect relationship, the impression created is that the positive presence of Theodoros Stoudites in the *Vita retractata* was magnified in order to gain the sympathy of Sabas' future community. Either we believe in

---

[205] *Vita of Methodios* 1253B–C: ἐπειδὴ δὲ ἀσκήσεως καὶ εὐφυΐας ἐμνήσθημεν τοῦ ἀνδρός, ἓν αὐτοῦ κατόρθωμα εἰρηκότες, περὶ τῶν λοιπῶν ὑμῖν διανοεῖσθαι παραχωρήσωμεν. ἑπτὰ τοίνυν ψαλτήρια πλήρη ὁ σοφὸς Μεθόδιος ἔγραφε, καθ' ἑκάστης τὸ ἓν ἑβδομάδος νήστης ἀποπληρῶν· οὐδὲ γὰρ ὕδατος ἀπεγεύετο, πλὴν Σαββάτου καὶ Κυριακῆς. τοιαύτη, ὡς ἐν συντόμῳ εἰπεῖν, τοῦ ὁσίου ἡ ἄσκησις· τοιοῦτον ἐκ πολλῶν τοῦ ἀθλητοῦ τὸ μαρτύριον· αὕτη καὶ τῆς ἀρχιερωσύνης ἡ προεδρία. 'As we have recalled the asceticism and the intelligence of the man, we shall tell of one of his exploits, leaving you to reflect on the others. The sage Methodios thus wrote seven full psalters, completing them for each [of the days] of the week while fasting as he did not even take water except on Saturdays and Sundays. This was briefly the asceticism of the saint. This was, among many others, the martyrdom of the champion. It was also the privilege of the patriarchate.'

[206] Ehrhard 1936–1939: vol. I, 22–23; Rapp 1995: 33, n. 10.

[207] Scholarship on Byzantine patronage usually focuses on later periods, see Mullett 1984; Morris 1995: 9–142; Lauxtermann 2003: 34–36; Jeffreys 2009; Bernard 2014: 291–333.

[208] *Vita of Methodios* 1245A.

chance or we reconstruct a relationship (probably through intermediaries) due to which the patriarch Photios ended up thanking the writer for the services he rendered and the loyalty he showed.[209]

Texts are often the result of patronage but reveal no details about the promises made by the patron or the reward the author hopes to achieve by producing them. The clearest example of literary patronage in the ninth century is actually a failed effort – which is perhaps why we know about it. The *asekretis* Konstantinos, on behalf of an important superior, had commissioned Ignatios Diakonos to write an iambic iconodule propaganda poem to extol how both the Empress Theodora and her precursor Eirene suffered to restore Orthodoxy.[210] But the composition was not approved, and Ignatios had to correct it; he accordingly decided to invite Konstantinos to supervise his labour. The result would then hopefully be to the taste of their common patron and a third correction could be avoided. Either this did not occur or the effort was unsuccessful, since it seems that the poem never saw the light of day.

Although the practice of literature was evidently in the hands of writers, they were often artisans in the service of a patron who used them to achieve his own objectives. Using and controlling literature was thus a way of wielding power. This was vital in an empire characterised by an extensive use of religious confrontations as an instrument to underpin (or undermine) all kind of secular and ecclesiastical governments.

---

[209] On Photios as a literary patron, see Magdalino 2017.
[210] Ignatios Diakonos, *epist.* 32; Mango and Efthymiadis 1997: 186–87.

CHAPTER 8

Final Remarks

8.1 Literature under Iconoclasm and the Exercise of Power

There can be no doubt that literature magnified the historical importance of the iconoclast controversy, giving it a new social-political dimension and a validity that would extend over time. Although the matter did not always have much effect on daily life, the literature to which the controversy gave rise ultimately made it a major episode in collective memory and a key element of Byzantine identity. The *vitae* of the iconodule heroes deliberately invite the reader to magnify the seriousness and the consequences of this controversy and to assume that it was the main concern of the emperors of the period. In spite of the external threats the empire faced (from the Arabs and the Bulgarians) and the major achievements in domestic policy (economic recovery, legal reform, the development of the *themata* system, etc.),[1] the dispute over images was the most important chapter for creating its world vision. Iconoclasm made a splash in all fields, some of them very prominent, such as the ecclesiastical consequences for Orthodoxy, and others more elusive albeit still decisive (especially from a social point of view), due to the clear confrontation produced between some parts of the monastic world (supported by various social groups and families) and a particular imperial attitude incarnated by the State. Literature and written production would seem to have initially disappeared in the social and religious crisis, when economic difficulties were compounded by imperial heresy. In fact, literature followed some of the major intellectuals of the period, who took refuge behind monastery walls.

For an author such as Theodoros Stoudites, the iconoclast conflict clearly represented a dispute about the exercise of power. In this struggle, the iconoclast emperors had unlawfully imposed their heretical will on

---

[1] Bryer and Herrin 1977; Brubaker and Haldon 2001; 2011; Auzépy 2007; Brubaker 2012; Kaplan 2017.

society as a whole, blatantly interfering with the powers of a Church in charge of dogma and liturgical matters such as the veneration of images. The result of this Church-State confrontation was the temporary victory of the worldly powers, which decreed the exile and persecution of the iconodule patriarchs and the main monastic leaders. During the years of iconoclasm, the emperors promoted iconoclasts to the major bureaucratic and ecclesiastical posts and thus won numerous allies over to their cause.

One of the few channels available to the iconodules for counteracting this power and issuing counter-propaganda was literature, which they seem virtually to have appropriated. Early Christian models provided many examples of loyal believers who confronted the emperor to defend their faith. The new situation intensified the popularity of such literature as a weapon against imperial power and contributed to the creation of a well-organised opposition to iconoclast emperors. Despite a common cause, resistance was not a monolithic organisation, well-structured and strongly cohesive, but very much the opposite. It represented the sum of various small factions organised around charismatic leaders whose influence did not generally extend beyond the limits of their monasteries: Theodoros of Stoudios, Platon of Sakkoudion, Nikephoros and Niketas of Medikion, Makarios of Pelekete, etc. In this way, influential groups of intellectuals sharing political goals and literary resources arose. These networks formed part of milieux whose members promoted not only the reading, but also the copying and dissemination of their textual production.

In Theophilos' time (829–842), iconoclasm had changed its tune and was focused on the imposition of imperial authority in Constantinople and the surrounding areas (probably the original goal of Isaurian emperors). Despite the persecution, however, its opponents were better organised and armed at this stage, even if cohesion was not always strong. The main resource of monastic resistance was literature, which was used both to unite the monks and to attack their enemy. The success they achieved on both fronts meant that they took possession of literature to such an extent that almost all contemporary written work had iconodule content and was in keeping with the interests of image venerators. At the same time, because the events of the time were described from the monastic perspective of those who later proved victorious, the iconoclast sectors that led lay institutions felt no need to resort to literature and thus lost the battle of writing by failing to engage. Literature accordingly became specialised and was put in the service of iconodules, who after the Triumph of Orthodoxy continued to monopolise it. Despite the attempts of the aristocracy and the court to make use of the written word, it appeared to belong to the patriarchal circles that followed each other in power and provided spokesmen when the traditional monastic circles were in difficulty. This situation did not change until the accession to the throne of Leon VI (886–912). The milieux that formed around Methodios, Ignatios and Photios persisted and developed the literary fiction of the heroic monk who sacrifices himself to defend Orthodoxy. In fact, the decisive agents in the defeat of iconoclasm were the bishops, who exercised more effective power within the Church. But literature followed other paths, away from political reality, and the surviving textual representations of the period create the impression that everything was managed by the monks. They were not so much responsible for bringing about change, as for describing it, and in this way they appropriated its achievements, presenting themselves as the restorers of icons, when in fact they had much less room for manoeuvre, since they had much less power.

Iconodule sources associate iconoclastic bishops with imperial error and evil deeds. They clearly present the Second Iconoclasm as an opposition between the orthodox saints, who were essentially monks, and the secular clergy, represented by priests and bishops who are initially considered iconoclasts, that is, corrupted by political power, in the hagiographies. In contrast to the First Iconoclasm (726–787), which falls within a context of fiery theological debate, the Second Iconoclasm (815–843) was essentially a conflict over power. By rejecting images, the emperor actually denounced iconodule attempts to limit his prerogatives and keep him away from Church matters. According to authors such as Kaplan,[2] the true dispute was about authority and was a matter of clarifying whether the emperor had the right to intervene in Church matters, and whether the authority of the person with the final say was imposed on everyone else. The rejection of iconoclasm, and with it the defence of images, became in this context an act of political disobedience, a protest against imperial authority that the regent Theodora was only able to put an end to in 843, after restoring the cult of icons. There are numerous examples of this, as shown in the previous chapters, since almost all *vitae* of the period include some kind of *agôn* (dialectical struggle) in which the iconophile saint faces up to the emperor or his representative, whether a high lay official or the iconoclast patriarch Ioannes VII Grammatikos himself.

This model of protest against established power was maintained after the Triumph of Orthodoxy and continued to be productive for some authors linked to the monastic milieux even later on. This is the case with

[2] Kaplan 1999; 2006; Sterk 2004: 219–46; Moulet 2011.

the attacks on Caesar Bardas found in the *vita* of Eirene of Chrysobalanton, in which the saint warns that Bardas will die by the same hand as Emperor Michael III.³ It should not be forgotten that Eirene of Chrysobalanton was a sister-in-law of Bardas, who had legitimately married her sister Theodosia.⁴ Despite the fact that the *vita* (written as early as the late tenth century) does not explicitly mention either that this Theodosia was disowned by her husband (as in fact occurred) or that there was any conflict between them, the prophecy of the abbess aggressively questions completely the Caesar's authority to act against the canonical tradition in his bedroom intrigues. In the same way, the *Vita of Eustratios of Agauroi* (post 868) attacks Bardas for having ignominiously disowned his wife when he was already the Caesar in 862.⁵ By stressing the good relationship between St Eustratios and Theodosia, the hagiography transmits the idea that religious power always supervises events, which redounds to the justification of its superiority.⁶

One main objective of the hagiographies of both Eirene of Chrysobalanton and Eustratios of Agauroi was to unite the members of their respective communities. At the same time, these works sought to strengthen the monastic power and authority over lay institutions, and they unsurprisingly try to give them the best possible iconodule credentials. The narrator of the *vita* of Eirene, for example, does not hesitate to report that during her journey to Constantinople, she had a meeting with Ioannikios, the point of reference of the defence of Orthodoxy, who in addition to giving her his blessing, predicted that she would be the superior of the convent of Chrysobalanton.⁷ Eustratios of Agauroi for his part is presented as having close links with Ioannikios in the account of which he is the protagonist: as well as being one of Ioannikios' faithful disciples, he received a prophecy from the saint to the effect that he would attain the post of hegoumenos.⁸ We know that Eustratios commissioned a monk of his monastery, Petros, to write the first *vita* in honour of Ioannikios and

---

³ *Vita of Eirene Chrysobalanton* 38–39.
⁴ On Eirene of Chrysobalanton, see *PmbZ* # 1452 and # 21617; Connor 2004: 166–81. On her sister Theodosia, *PmbZ* # 7792.
⁵ *Vita of Eustratios of Agauroi* 33, 389, 16–20. For the monastery of Agauroi near Prousa, see Janin 1975: 132–34; Hergès 1898/1899.
⁶ Dagron 1996. Cf. the critical discussion by Kaldellis 2015. The allegations about 'bedroom intrigues' are formally due to the fact that the civil law concerning marriages and divorces – starting from the *Ekloga* – is directly influenced by the canons of the councils. This was anyway not just the proof of the political strength of the Church, but first of all the attitude of Emperor Leon to take control over the Church.
⁷ *Vita of Eirene Chrysobalanton* 8–11.   ⁸ On Eustratios, *PmbZ* # 1824; *PBE*: Eustratios 19.

that he was his main informant.[9] We have already looked in detail at the operation of this dynamic, by which literature was used by various iconophile sectors to strengthen private groups, creating personal networks and reinforcing the structures of government benefitting their interests.

The end of iconoclasm in 843 meant the failure of the attempt to subject the Orthodox Church to imperial power. It is true that the Byzantine Church never attained the freedom Theodoros of Stoudios and the Zealots called for;[10] to the contrary, the state-ecclesiastical system of Byzantium continued to be characterised by close collaboration between the two great organs of power, normally in the form of extensive protection given by the State to the Church (*symphonía*). The highest levels of independence were probably attained during the patriarchates of Photios (858–867 and 877–886), whose management as head of the Church and whose way of drawing together about him a pressure group capable of reinterpreting the triumph of the iconodules allowed a spectacular reinforcement of ecclesiastical authority, to the extent that the hierarchical order in imperial celebrations was altered. In the desire to reproduce an organisational scheme of celestial inspiration, the court ceremonial was classified in the *taktiká* (tables of rank) handled by the officials in charge of organising imperial banquets.[11] The order of priority within the administrative hierarchy reflected a higher level in the social hierarchy. While the *taktikón* Uspenskij, which was drawn up under Michael III and Theodora (845–856), includes no ecclesiastical posts,[12] the *taktikón* of Philotheos (*Kletorologion*), which was drawn up in the late ninth century (September 899), places the patriarch of Constantinople between the emperor and the Caesar, his future successor.[13] This novelty indicates that the post of patriarch, the leader of the Church, had merged with those of the civil authorities who governed the empire. This innovative hierarchical precept faithfully reflected the changes occurring in society during the two patriarchates of Photios, since the *taktikón* merely registers the new situation, in which the Caesar was below the patriarch and thus further from the emperor in the ceremonial hierarchy.

It is worth stressing how Photios replaced Emperor Basileios I in his duties by presiding over the Council of 879/880 (the eighth Oecumenical

---

[9] For Petros, *PmbZ* # 6075; *PBE*: Petros 126. See Section 2.2.1.
[10] Thomas et al. 2000: vol. I, 67–83; Hatlie 2007a: 255–440. [11] Barker 1957; Haldon 2008.
[12] Benechevitch 1926; Oikonomidès 1972: 41–63.
[13] Bury 1911; Oikonomidès 1972: 65–235; Winkelmann 1985.

Council of Constantinople).[14] Alleging that the emperor was in mourning for his first-born son Konstantinos, whom Photios had just sanctified,[15] the patriarch took charge of the synod and achieved a great personal triumph. Not only in ecclesiastical contexts, but also on other occasions Photios acted as spokesman for the imperial family, as when he sent *epistle* 287 to the khan Boris of Bulgaria to notify him of the death of Basileios I on 29 August 886. Thus strengthened, and with the unanimous support of the Church behind him, Photios was able to write his *Eisagogé* (*Introduction to Law*), in which he gives legal form to his wish to place the power of the patriarch on the same level as that of the emperor.[16]

Titles I–III of the *Eisagogé* of Photios represent the culmination of a lengthy process by means of which the Church as a whole (from simple monks to eminent patriarchs, through different milieux sharing a final objective, although their immediate interests sometimes clashed) tried by any means possible to deny the emperor's prerogatives over the Church, preventing him from interfering in matters of doctrine. Literature played an essential role in this process, since in his attempt to check this change and retain power, the emperor tried to expropriate the exclusive use of literature, which was a definitive weapon in the struggle, from the religious leaders. From the tenth century on, therefore, the emperors undertook previously unparalleled cultural enterprises intended to balance the importance attained by ninth-century monastic authors. But the appropriation of the defeat of iconoclast heresy by the patriarchate also implies the subjugation of the figure of the emperor: it is no coincidence that emperors decreed the First and Second Iconoclasms. A patriarch with a political programme as ambitious as that of Photios accordingly did not hesitate to describe himself in an official (although unpromulgated) text as 'the living icon of Christ'.[17]

The entire official discourse after the Triumph of Orthodoxy falsely suggests a strict binary division between iconodules and iconoclasts and makes the restoration of icons appear to be the work of the monastic and

---

[14] Indeed, Basileios only took part in the closing ceremony on 10 March 880, see Halkin 1954a: 16; Grumel 1967; Patlagean 1989: 356–57.
[15] Grumel 1966; 1967; Karlin-Hayter 1996; Luzzi 1996. On Prince Konstantinos, see *PmbZ* # 23742. In his honour the emperor erected a church devoted to him, see Janin 1969: 296. To please Basileios, Photios allegedly exorcised the spirit of the dead Konstantinos with the assistance of Theodoros Santabarenos, see Symeon Logothetes 132,120–22; Ps-Symeon 692,20f.; Tobias 2007: 249–51. See Section 6.2.3.
[16] Bompaire 1982; Schminck 1985; Signes Codoñer and Andrés Santos 2007: 84–100.
[17] Phot., *Eisagogé* III, 1: Ὁ Πατριάρχης ἐστὶν εἰκὼν ζῶσα χριστοῦ καὶ ἔμψυχος, δι' ἔργων καὶ λόγων χαρακτηρίζουσα τὴν ἀλήθειαν.

patriarchal sectors, although we know they did not always agree and that this was not a monolithic process in which they worked in unison. Quite the opposite: the different immediate objectives and biased writings of the different groups examined here show the diversity of milieux that existed within the Church and which implemented their own appropriation of iconoduly (Methodians, Dekapolitans, Ignatians, Photians, Stoudites, etc.). It is no less true that all these religious factions – occasionally at loggerheads with one another, as each sought to create a version of history in keeping with its own aspirations – continued to exploit the rhetoric of domination and superiority over imperial power, in which different sensitivities existed when they rewrote their iconoclast past. But the literature of the period also testifies to the lay authorities winning at least one battle: the rehabilitation of Theophilos, who had redeemed himself by his alleged final repentance, which also meant the absolution of imperial power from whatever sins against Orthodoxy it had committed.

Now that the former iconoclasts had forsworn their error and the great doctrinal struggles in Byzantium were over, the emperor needed new spiritual enemies to confront. Once again it was Photios, the great ideologue of the imperial household who proclaimed himself the champion of Orthodoxy, who provided a solution. The forced conversion of the Jews by Basileios I in 873/874 was in keeping with this need, as was the propaganda regarding the persecution of the Paulicians he created.[18] Firmly established in Tephrike on the upper Euphrates, these Christians rejected veneration of the Virgin and the saints and therefore also their icons.[19] Photios wrote a brief apologetic treatise against them to the hegoumenos of Hieron Arsenios[20] entitled *Against the Manicheans* (Κατὰ τῆς τῶν Μανιχαίων ἀρτιφυοῦς πλάνης Ἀρσενίῳ τῷ ὁσιωτάτῳ μοναχῷ, πρεσβυτέρῳ καὶ ἡγουμένῳ τῶν Ἱερῶν).[21] This missive follows the arguments of the *Refutation of Manichaeism* of Petros Sikeliotes, who also identifies Paulicianism with this ancient heresy in his six treatises against the Manicheans.[22]

The figure of Petros perfectly exemplifies the change the post-iconoclast Church was forced to undergo. In the final years of iconoclasm, Petros was a hesychast at the monastery of Herakleion in Bithynia.[23] After the

---

[18] Garsoïan 1967; Lemerle 1973: 1–144; Tobias 2007: 95–114.   [19] Barnard 1977; Ludwig 1998.
[20] *PmbZ* # 20598. The patriarch also sent him four letters: Phot., *epist.* 60, 183, 231 and 236.
[21] Perhaps because it belongs to the period of Photios' exile (years 871/872), this epistle was never part of his collected letters, disseminated under the supervision of the patriarch himself.
[22] Only two of these six treatises have been published completely in *PG* 104, 1305–50.
[23] *PmbZ* # 6076; # 6089; # 26431; *PBE* I: Petros 1; Petros 33; Petros 127.

Triumph of Orthodoxy, however, his compatriot Methodios appointed him the metropolitan bishop of Syllaion. Petros' participation in ecclesiastical policy is well known, since he demonstrated his commitment to icons by visiting Ioannikios[24] and his support for Photios by meeting other detractors of the patriarch Ignatios at his home.[25] As a consequence, Petros was anathematised together with Gregorios Asbestas and Eulampios of Apamea during the patriarchate of Ignatios in 852/853. Years later, we find Petros Sikeliotes as hegoumenos; he was sent on a diplomatic mission to Tephrike by Emperor Basileios to negotiate an exchange of prisoners with the Paulicians. The nine months he spent there during this mission allowed him to gather information to write his apologetic work against the Manicheans.[26] This work, which served the interests of the emperor and also of Photios, who used its arguments, perfectly illustrates the recycling of the Methodian old guard, forged in the fight against iconoclasm but with the passage of time in need of rewriting its own history and finding a new adversary so as to continue demonstrating its piety.

This open door to the legitimation of imperial authority meant that, with the accession to the throne of Leon VI, matters could change along with the very nature of literature. Emperor Leon expropriated the monopoly of literature enjoyed by religious circles, and put it at the service of his private interests and those of the imperial household,[27] initiating a process brought to its culmination by his son Konstantinos VII Porphyrogennetos (913–959) in his great enterprise as literary patron.[28] In an article on knowledge in authority and authorised history, Magdalino affirms that Leon and Konstantinos monopolised historical knowledge, which could involve a threat to the imperial court and its interests and indeed all knowledge generally.[29] This process consisted of the same three stages as the codification of law: the selection and reorganisation of material, rewriting and correction and supervision and composition of new material as necessary.

As an example of the new dynamic on which the shadow of iconoclasm continued to fall, when the brother of Leon VI, the patriarch Stephanos (886–893), died at age twenty-five, he was buried not in the church of the

---

[24] *Vita of Ioannikios* by Sabas Monachos 43; *Vita of Ioannikios* by Petros 68.
[25] Ps-Symeon 671,7–11.   [26] Lemerle 1973: 1–11; Speck 1974b; Ludwig 1987.
[27] Mango 1960; Odorico 1983; Magdalino 1988b; Tougher 1994; Antonopoulou 1997; 2017; Tougher 1997: 110–32; Kazhdan 1999: 53–65; Riedel 2018.
[28] Toynbee 1973; Huxley 1980; Schminck 1989; Kazhdan 1999: 133–84; Koutava-Delivoria 2002; Magdalino 2017.
[29] Magdalino 2013.

Holy Apostles, alongside other patriarchs, but at the monastery of Sykeon,[30] one of the few buildings damaged during the first iconoclast persecution. According to the testimony of the *vita* in honour of Theodoros of Sykeon, Konstantinos V had burnt the chapel of the church of Georgios of Sykeon because the relics of the hermit Theodoros were venerated there by believers attracted by his miracle-working. In response to popular protests, the same emperor had to agree to rebuild the chapel he had destroyed and make it even more magnificent.[31] The monastery was likely under imperial patronage from that point on, and that fact, together with its strong symbolic value as an example of the Triumph of Orthodoxy and the defeat of the iconoclast emperors, explains why the patriarch Stephanos was buried there, contributing to the spreading of his veneration as a saint.[32] This period saw a new 'updating' of the figure of Theodoros of Sykeon by the *skeuophylax* Nikephoros: his *enkomion* in memory of the saint involves him in the debate on fasting going on at that time.[33] Such cases show the extent to which the rewriting of the iconoclast dispute continued to be important in subsequent decades.

During the Second Iconoclasm, the iconodules had been so successful in their effort to keep alive the memory of their heroes and thus offer their version(s) of events that the generation that restored Orthodoxy and its descendants continued to rewrite the dispute over images during the following centuries. A desire to relate historical facts in a way that served political objectives or legitimated private interests led the various preexisting milieux within the Church to continue to produce texts on iconoclasm. This appropriation of literature by the restorers of icons was not exclusive: following the pattern initiated by the Stoudites, other milieux disputed their monopoly of the biased narration of events. Literature was the weapon of power par excellence for those in favour of images, but they were not always unanimous in their views. We know that different networks disputed the command of the written word and that, driven by their individual interests, they sometimes came together and sometimes clashed. In the final analysis, there was also a struggle between them to achieve a monopoly on 'truth'.

---

[30] Theoph. Cont. VI, 2, p. 354, 5–8. On Stephanos I, see *PmbZ* # 27208; Kolias 1953.
[31] *Vita of Theodoros of Sykeon* (*BHG* 1748), vol. I, chs. 49–51, pp. 270–71. For the monastery of Georgios of Sykeon, see Janin 1969: 77–78; Kaplan 1993b; Hatlie 2002: 218–25.
[32] *SynaxCP* 694, 1–18 (18 May); 714, 4–5 (27 May); 689/690, 54–56 (17 May); 159/160, 35; *Menologion Basilii* 464A–B (17 May); 605B (25 August); *Typikon of the Great Church* I, 300, 1–7 (27 May).
[33] Krausmüller 2003; Kaplan 2015: 181–84.

But the reflection of historical truth in the surviving texts is always mediated by their authors, and no clear victor can thus be identified in this struggle, which new combatants constantly joined. The continuous updating of the iconoclast crisis meant that great leaders, intellectuals and men of letters later looked back on this period again and again.[34] This practice ultimately made the controversy about the veneration of images one of the main identity elements of Byzantine society and accordingly also of its literature.

8.2 Literature and Social Change: The Role of Writing Production under Iconoclasm and the Literary Milieux

During the iconoclast period and the following years, the image crisis became the dominant theme in the political, religious and intellectual life of the Byzantine Empire. Iconoclasm inevitably also became the driving force of literary production, by transmitting self-seeking versions of historical reality.[35] The opposition to iconoclasm even served to justify civil wars,[36] and literature was used as a missile in this dispute, as a consequence of which a large proportion of the texts that have come down to us have a more or less marked apologist nature. Despite the power enjoyed by the iconoclasts, the surviving literature is eminently iconodule. But we should not make the mistake of putting blind faith in the sources, since, as this study has revealed, iconoclasm was also partly an ideological product constructed by the victors of the confrontation and to a large extent based in Constantinople. Although we know very little about the implementation of iconoclasm in the provinces,[37] in the Peloponnese, the attitude towards the heresy was ambiguous,[38] while Byzantine Italy was not paticularly fond of it,[39] and in the oriental provinces, icon veneration coexisted with quotidian aniconic practices.[40]

In fact (as shown in Chapter 3), a large part of the population all over the empire and even in Constantinople was mostly indifferent to the iconological question. The daily life of the anonymous individual

---

[34] On the impact of iconoclasm in later Byzantine literature, see Schukin 2008; Lukhovitskij 2013; 2016 Boeck 2015: 144–81.
[35] Karlin-Hayter 1993; Criscuolo 1994b; Auzépy 2004a; Odorico 2014.
[36] Magdalino 1993: 22–23; Treadgold 2012.   [37] Ahrweiler 1977.   [38] Konti 1999.
[39] Guillou et al. 1983: 207–11; Carile 1986; Von Falkenhausen 1989; Dell'Acqua and Gantner 2019. See Chapter 3.
[40] For the dissemination of iconoclasm in Palestine and the Orient, see Griffith 1985; Auzépy 2001: 305–14; Signes Codoñer 2013a; Reynolds 2017. For its situation in Anatolia, see Signes Codoñer 2014: 20–25.

continued on the fringe of these major matters of state, which is apparent in literature and explains why some hagiographical works were out of keeping with the official iconodule discourse and had other reasons for the literary celebration of saints in the ninth century. Examples include the *Vita of St Andrew the Apostle* by Epiphanios of Kallistratos, which was highly successful and has survived in a number of manuscripts; the cult of St Nicholas promoted by Methodios with several texts[41] and the uninterrupted textual devotion of the Virgin Mary.[42] Likewise, the continuing debate about the powers of saints after death,[43] which was also echoed by Methodios, shows that the iconoclast controversy was not the only motivating factor for contemporary writing. Iconoclasm was definitely the main factor, however, and had the greatest impact. It is clear that private devotion also existed, along with family cults handed down from parent to child, feast-days of local patron saints and the like. But it is the communal macro-enterprise of major literary milieux that subsequently gave iconoclasm its dimension when writing and rewriting its history and going back over it and its heroes, creating a new Byzantine identity that decisively changed society and its members.

This book may at some points resemble a history of the literature of the iconoclast period, given its detailed survey of texts and authors. But its larger aim is to reflect the literature of the social changes of the eighth and ninth centuries and how the texts represent an attempt – often successful – to redefine and change society irreversibly. A void has long existed in Byzantine studies, leaving us without a vision of writings not as sources of data, but as literary works with their own codes and readership. Despite the existence of fine detailed studies of specific texts, we need an overall vision if we are to understand who these texts were written for, how they were disseminated and how their sources were rewritten and why. As has recently been pointed out,[44] academic approaches that go no further than establishing a canon of the major authors of Byzantine literature have become obsolete, among other reasons because they cannot explain the literary event or the literariness of a text.

Attempting to understand the operation of literature during the Byzantine Revival after the Dark Age makes us aware that a long hagiographical text written in a lofty style and a much shorter and more humble

---

[41] Magdalino 2015b.
[42] Baynes 1955a; 1955b; Koutrakou 2005; Wortley 2005; Pentcheva 2006: 61–103; Krausmüller 2011; Cunningham 2015; 2019.
[43] Krausmüller 1998/1999; 2015; 2018; Dal Santo 2012.   [44] Agapitos 2015.

liturgical hymn intended only for the monastery in which it was produced, share the same guiding principles. Levels of expressive excellence, which have traditionally been considered literature, were provided by specific individuals within a specific framework with a clear horizon of expectations for the reader/listener. In this dynamic, the role of books or codices was essential, since only inclusion in them and the never random selection of materials give full meaning to individual texts, as is apparent from the works integrated in the different *menologia* discussed here. The somewhat artificial taxonomies that divide literature up by literary genre, and of course the Manichean division between poetry and prose, also do not increase our knowledge of what Byzantine literature really is and was. The literature produced under Iconoclasm and in its aftermath is by no means dead or simply continuist, but a living thing that must reinvent itself in response to the new needs of its surroundings and in order to play a prominent role in its world. As a result of this reinvention, new ideological and aesthetic codes in the production of texts were established and the socio-political framework was redesigned. Literary mileux were thus strengthened, extended and increased, as more and more writers clustered around a prominent patron. The result was the creation of a cultural heritage and identity that survived until the final days of Byzantium.

Map 1 Constantinople: Principal monasteries in Middle Byzantium

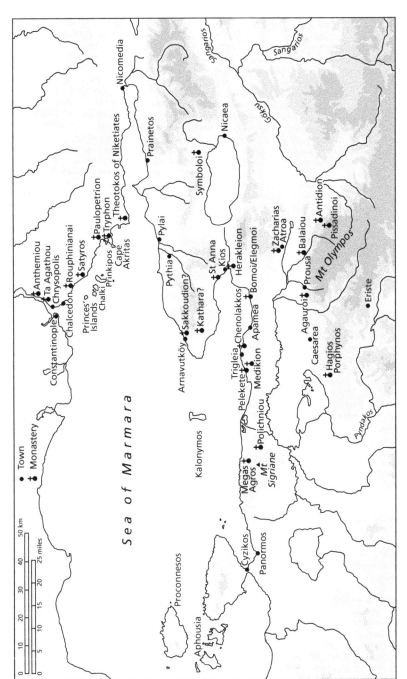

Map 2 Bithynia: Principal monasteries in Middle Byzantium

APPENDIX A

Chronology of the Patriarchs, Emperors, Popes and Hegoumenoi of Stoudios from 787 to 896

Chronology of the Patriarchs, Emperors, Popes and Hegoumenoi of Stoudios from 787 to 896

Hegoumenos of Stoudios	Patriarch of Const/nople	Emperor of Byzantium	Pope of Rome
Sabas (in 787)	Tarasios (784–806)	Konstantinos VI (780–797)	Adrian I (772–795)
Theodoros Stoudites (798–815)		Eirene (797–802)	Leo III (795–816)
	Nikephoros I (806–815)	Nikephoros I (802–811)	
		Staurakios (811)	
		Michael I Rhangabe (811–813)	
Leontios (815–820)	Theodotos (815–821)	Leo V (813–820)	Stephen V (816–817)
Theodoros Stoudites (820–826)	Antonios I (821–837)	Michael II (820–829)	Paschal I (817–824)
			Eugenius II (824–827)
Naukratios (826–848)			Valentine (827)
	Ioannes VII Grammatikos (837–843)	Theophilos (829–842)	Gregory IV (827–844)
	Methodios (843–847)	Theodora (as regent 842–858)	Sergius II (844–847)
Nikolaos Stoudites (848–851)	Ignatios (847–858)		Leo IV (847–855)
Sophronios (851–855)			

444

Nikolaos Stoudites (855–858)		Benedict III (855–858)
Achillas (858–863)	Photios (858–867)	Michael III (858–867)	Nicholas I (858–867)
Theodosios (863–864)			
Eugenios (864)			
Theodoros Santabarenos (864–865)			
Sabas (865–867)			
Nikolaos Stoudites (867–868)	Ignatios (2nd time) (867–877)	Basileios I (867–886)	Adrian II (867–872)
Klemes (868)			
Hilarion (868–886)			
	Photios (2nd time) (877–886)		John VIII (872–882)
			Marinus (882–884)
			Adrian III (884–885)
Anatolios (886–916)	Stephanos I (886–893)	Leo VI (886–912)	Stephen VI (885–891)
	Antonios II Kauleas (893–901)		Formosus (891–896)

APPENDIX B

Network Chart of Writers and Their Literary Relations under Iconoclasm and in Its Aftermath

Network Chart of Writers and Their Literary Relations under Iconoclasm and in Its Aftermath

Bibliography

PRIMARY SOURCES

Acta of David, Symeon and Georgios (*BHG* 464), ed. J. van den Gheyn, 'Acta Graeca ss. Davidis, Symeonis et Georgii Mitylenae in insula Lesbo', *AnBoll* 18 (1899): 211–59.

Acta of Davidis, Symeonis and Georgios (*BHG* 464), trans. D. Abrahamse and D. Domingo-Forasté, 'Life of Sts David, Symeon, and George of Lesbos', in *Byzantine Defenders of Images*, A. M. Talbot, ed. Washington. 1998: 143–241.

Acta of the Ten Martyrs of Constantinople (*BHG* 1195), in *AASS*, Aug. II: 428–48 (Text: 434–47).

Arethas of Caesarea, *Against Iconoclasts*, ed. L. G. Westerink, *Arethae archiepiscopi Caesariensis Scripta minora*. Leipzig. 1968. Vol. I: 75–81.

Arethas of Caesarea, *Epitaphios for Euthymios, Patriarch of Constantinople* (*BHG* 652), ed. L. G. Westerink, *Arethae archiepiscopi Caesariensis scripta minora*. Leipzig. 1968. Vol. I: 82–93.

Bar Hebraeus, Gregory. *Chronography*, trans. E. A. W. Budge. London. 1932.

Council of Constantinople (Synod of 861), Canons, ed. F. Lauritzen, *The Great Councils of the Orthodox Churches: From Constantinople 861 to Moscow 2000*, A. Melloni, ed. Turnhout. 2016. Vol. IV/1: 1–22.

Council of Constantinople (the Eighth Ecumenical Council: 869/870), eds. C. Leonardi and A. Placanica, *Gesta sanctæ ac universalis octavæ synodi quæ Constantinopoli congregata est Anastasio bibliothecario interprete*. Florence. 2012.

Council of Constantinople (Council of 879–880), Definition (Horos) and Canons, ed. F. Gemeinhardt, *The Great Councils of the Orthodox Churches: From Constantinople 861 to Moscow 2000*, A. Melloni, ed. Turnhout. 2016. Vol. IV/1: 23–40.

Council of Nicaea, Second (787)

Council of Nicaea, Second (787) Canons, in Mansi. Vol. XII: 951–1154; Vol. XIII: 2–820.

Council of Nicaea, Second (787) Concilii actiones. Acta conciliorum oecumenicorum. Series Secunda. Volumen III: Concilium universale Nicaenum secundum, ed. E. Lambertz. *Pars I: Concilii actiones I–III*. Berlin-New York. 2008. *Pars II: Concilii actiones IV–V*. Berlin-New York. 2012. *Pars III: Concilii actiones VI–VII*. Berlin-Boston. 2016.

Christodoulos, *Iambic Verses for the Graptoi Brothers* (BHG 1746a), ed. I. Van den Gheyn, *AnBoll* 18 (1899): 239. Trans. in *The Life of Michael the Synkellos*, M. B. Cunningham, ed. Belfast. 1991: 86–87.

Encyclica de obitu Theodori Studitae (BHG 1756) by Naukratios, ed. F. Combefis, *Historia haeresis monothelitarum sanctae in eam sextae synodi actorum vindiciae etc*. Paris. 1648: 855–88 (repr. in *PG* 99: 1825–49).

Enkomion of St Catherine of Alexandria (BHG 32b) by Anastasios Quaestor, ed. G. Metallenos, 'Ἀναστασίου πρωτασεκρῆτις ἐγκώμιον εἰς τὴν ἁγίαν Αἰκατερίνην', *Ἐκκλησιαστικὸς Φάρος* 54 (1972): 237–74.

Enkomion of the Patriarch Antonios II Kauleas (BHG 139), ed. P. L. M. Leone, 'L'Encomium in patriarcham Antonium II Cauleam del filosofo e retore Niceforo', *Orpheus* 10 (1989): 404–29.

Enkomion of Basileios I by the Emperor Leon VI, in *Leonis VI Sapientis Imperatoris Byzantini Homiliae*, ed. T. Antonopoulou. Turnhout. 2008 (CCSG 63): 195–218 (nr. 14).

Enkomion of Basileios I by the Emperor Leon VI, ed. and Fr. trans. A. Vogt and I. Hausherr, *Oraison funèbre de Basile I par son fils Léon VI le Sage*. Rome. 1932.

Enkomion of the Archangel Michael (BHG 1289) by Pantoleon, ed. and Fr. trans. B. Martin-Hisard, 'Hagiographie et Liturgie. Pantoléon et l'*Enkômion* pour l'archange Michel (BHG 1289)', in Σύναξις καθολική: *Beiträge zu Gottesdienst und Geschichte der fünf altkirchlichen Patriarchate für Heinzgerd Brakmann zum 70. Geburtstag*, D. Atanassova and T. Chronz. Münster-Berlin, eds. 2014: 451–76.

Enkomion of the Robe of the Virgin (BHG 1058) by the *synkellos* Theodoros, in *Graecolatinae Patrum Bibliothecae Novum Auctarium*, F. Combefis, ed. Paris. 1648. Vol. II: 751–86.

Enkomion of Theodoros Graptos (BHG 1745z) by Theophanes of Caesarea, ed. M. Featherstone, 'The Praise of Theodore Graptos by Theophanes of Caesarea', *AnBoll* 98 (1980): 93–150.

Enkomion of Theophanes the Confessor of Megas Agros (BHG 1792) by Theodoros Daphnopates, ed. K. Krumbacher, 'Ein Dithyrambus auf den Chronisten Theophanes', in *Sitzungsberichte d. philos.-philol. u. hist. Cl. d. Königl. Bayer. Akad. d. Wiss*. Munich. 1896: 583–625.

Epigram in Honour of Theodoros of Stoudios (BHG 1758), in *PG* 99: 105–8 and ed. S. Eustratiadès, Κατάλογος τῶν ἐν τῇ μονῇ Βλατέων (Τσάους-μοναστήρι) ἀποκειμένων κωδίκων. Thessaloniki, 1918: 47–48.

Epigram in Honour of Theodoros Stoudites (BHG 1758d) by Dionysios, ed. and trans. P. Speck, *Theodoros Studites: Jamben auf verschiedene Gegenstände: Einleitung, Kritischer Text, Übersetzung und Kommentar*. Berlin. 1968: 307–9.

Eustratios of Constantinople, *Refutation to Those Who Say That the Souls of the Dead Are Not Active*, ed. P. Van Deun, *Eustratii Presbyteri Constantinopolitani De statu animarum post mortem* (CPG 7522). Turnhout-Leuven. 2006 (CCSG 60).

Genesios, *Chronography*, Iosephi Genesii Regum Libri Quattuor, ed. A. Lesmueller-Werner and I. Thurn. Berlin-New York. 1978 (CFHB 14).

Genesios, *Chronography*, trans. and ed. A. Kaldellis, *Genesios: On the Reigns of the Emperors*. Canberra. 1998.

Georgian Calendar, ed. G. Garitte, *Le calendrier palestino-géorgien du Sinaïticus 34 (Xe s.)*. Brussels. 1958.

Georgios Kedrenos, *Chronography*, ed. I. Bekker, *Georgius Cedrenus Ioannis Scylitzae ope*. Bonn. 1838–1839.

Georgios Monachos, *Chronicle*, ed. C. De Boor, *Georgii Monachi Chronicon*. Leipzig. 1904. 2 vols. (repr. Stuttgart. 1978, with correc. P. Wirth).

Georgios Monachos Continuatus, ed. I. Bekker, *Theophanes Continuatus, Ioannes Cameniata, Symeon Magister, Georgius Monachus*. Bonn. 1838: 763–924.

Georgios Monachos Continuatus, ed. E. Muralt, *Chronicon breve quod e diversis annalium scriptoribus et expositoribus decerpsit concinnavitque Georgius Monachus cognomine Hamartolus*. Saint Petersburg. 1859 (repr. in *PG* 110: 980–1193).

Georgios Monachos Continuatus, ed. V. I. Istrin, Хроника Георгия Амартола в древнем славянорусском переводе. Т. 2. а) Греческий Текст «Продолжения Амартола»; б) Исследовани [*Cronicle of Georgios Hamartolos in Old Slavonic translation. a) Greek text of the Continuation of the Hamartolos. b) Study*]. Saint Petersburg. 1922 (repr. Munich. 1972).

Georgios of Nicomedia, *Enkomion of Nicholas of Myra* (BHG 1364b), ed. G. Anrich, *Hagios Nikolaos: Der Heilige Nikolaos in der Griechischen Kirche*. Leipzig-Berlin. 1913. Vol. I: 92–96 and Vol. II: 162.

Georgios of Nicomedia, *Homily in Honour of Cosmas and Damian* (BHG 381), in *PG* 100: 1504–28.

Georgios of Nicomedia, *Marian Homilies*, in *PG* 100: 1333–504.

Georgios Synkellos, *Chronography*, ed. A. A. Mosshammer, *Georgii Syncelli Ecloga chronographica*. Leipzig. 1984.

Chronography, trans. in *The Chronography of George Synkellos: A Byzantine Chronicle of Universal History from the Creation*, W. Adler and P. Tuffin, eds. Oxford. 2002.

Gregorios Dekapolites, *Sermo historicus*, in *PG* 100: 1201–12.

Gregorios Dekapolites, *Sermo historicus*, trans. in D. J. Sahas, 'What an Infidel Saw That a Faithful Did Not: Gregory Dekapolites (d. 842) and Islam', *GOTR* 31 (1986): 47–67.

Gregorios Dekapolites, *Sermo historicus*, Fr. trans. in ed. A. J. Festugière, *Ste Thècle, Saints Côme et Damien, Saints Cyr et Jean (Extraits), Saint Georges: Collections, grecques de miracles*. Paris. 1971: 294–307.

Ignatios Diakonos

Alphabetical Poem, ed. C. F. Müller, 'Ignatii Diaconi acrostichon alphabeticum', *Rheinisches Museum, N. F.* 46 (1891): 320–23.

Epistles, ed. and Eng. trans. C. Mango and S. Efthymiadis, *The Correspondence of Ignatios the Deacon*. Washington. 1997 (CFHB 29, DOT 11).

Kanon in Honour of the 42 Martyrs of Amorion, ed. V. G. Vasilevskij and P. Nikitin, *Skažanija o 42 amoriiskikh mučenikhax*. Zapiski Imper. Akademij Nauk VII/2. Saint Petersburg. 1905: 262–64.

Vita of Georgios of Amastris (BHG 668), ed. V. Vasilevskij, *Russko-vizantijskie issledovanija*. St Petersburg. 1893. Vol. II: 1–73 (repr. in V. Vasilevskij ed., *Trudy 3* [1915]: 1–71).

Vita of Georgios of Amastris (BHG 668), trans. by Jenkins et al., http://library.nd.edu/byzantine_studies/documents/Amastris.pdf.

Vita of Gregorios Dekapolites (BHG 711), ed. and Germ. trans. G. Makris, *Ignatios Diakonos und die Vita des hl. Gregorios Dekapolites*. Stuttgart-Leipzig. 1997.

Vita of Gregorios Dekapolites (BHG 711), Fr. trans. F. Dvornik, *La vie de s. Grégoire le Décapolite et les Slaves macédoniens au IXe siècle*. Paris. 1926.

Vita of Nikephoros, Patriarch of Constantinople (BHG 1335), ed. C. De Boor, *Nicephori archiepiscopi Constantinopolitani opuscula historica*. Leipzig. 1880 (repr. New York. 1975): 139–217.

Vita of Nikephoros, Patriarch of Constantinople (BHG 1335), trans. E. A. Fisher, 'Life of the Patriarch Nikephoros I of Constantinople', in *Byzantine Defenders of Images*, A. M. Talbot, ed. Washington. 1998: 25–142.

Vita of Tarasios, Patriarch of Constantinople (BHG 1698), ed. and trans. S. Efthymiadis, *The Life of the Patriarch Tarasios by Ignatios the Deacon*. Aldershot. 1998.

Ioannes Geometres, *Poems*, ed. É. M. Van Opstall, *Jean Géomètre: Poèmes en hexamètres et en distiques élégiaques*. Leiden-Boston. 2008.

Ioannes of Sardis, *Commentary on the Progymnasmata of Aphthonius*, ed. H. Rabe, *Ioannes Sardianus: Commentarium in Aphthonii Progymnasmata*. Leipzig. 1928.

Ioannes Scylitzes, *Chronography*, ed. H. Thurn, *Ioannis Scylitzae Synopsis historiarum*. Berlin-New York. 1973.

Ioannes Scylitzes, *Kanones*, ed. P. Toma, *Joseph the Hymnographer: Kanones on Saints according to the Eight Modes*. Münster. 2018.

Ioannes Scylitzes, *Vita of Ioannes the Ascetic* (Georgian version), ed. K. Kekelidze, *Studies in the history of Ancient Georgian Literature (in Georgian)*. Tiflis. 1955. Vol. III: 251–70.

Kanon on the Restoration of the Holy Icons, in *PG* 99: 1768C–80B.

Kassia, *Hymns and Sentences*, ed. and trans. A. Tripolitis, *Kassia: The Legend, the Woman and Her Work*. Nueva York. 1992.

Kassia, *Hymns and Sentences*, ed. and Span. trans. O. Prieto Domínguez, *Casia de Constantinopla: Poemas*. Madrid. 2019.

Kassia, *Hymns and Sentences*, ed. and Russian trans. T. A. Senina, *Sv. Kassija Konstantinopol'skaja: Gimny, kanony, epigrammy*. Saint Petersburg. 2015.
Konstantinos Porphyrogennetos, *De ceremoniis aluae Byzantinae*, ed. J. Reiske. Bonn. 1829. 2 vols.; ed. A. Vogt, *Le livre des cérémonies*. Paris. 1935–1940. 2 vols.
Konstantinos of Tios, *On the Relics of St Euphemia* (*BHG* 621), ed. F. Halkin, *Euphémie de Chalcédoine: Légendes byzantines*. Brussels. 1965: 84–106.

Leon Choirosphaktes

Epistles, ed. and Fr. trans. G. Kolias, *Léon Choerosphactes, magistre, proconsul et patrice*. Athens. 1939.
Epistles, ed. and Ital. trans. G. Strano, *Leone Choirosphaktes, Corrispondenza: Introduzione, testo critico, traduzione e note di commento*. Catania. 2008.
Enkomion of the Patriarch Photios, ed. G. Kolias, *Léon Choerosphactes, magistre, proconsul et patrice*. Athens. 1939: 130 (Appendix).
Theology in a Thousand Lines, ed. and trans. I. Vassis, *Leon Magistros Choirosphaktes: Chiliostichos Theologia*. Berlin-New York. 2002.

Letter to Pope Stephen V by Stylianos of Neocaesarea, in Mansi XVI: 425–46.
Liber Pontificalis by Anastasius the Librarian, ed. and Fr. trans. L. Duchesne, *Liber pontificalis: Texte, introduction et commentaire*. Paris. 1886–1892. 2 vols (repr. 1955).
Menaion, in Μηναῖα τοῦ ὅλου ἐνιαυτοῦ. Rome. 1888–1901. 6 vols.
Menologion Basilii, in *PG* 117: 20–613.
Menologion of Basileios II, in *Il Menologio di Basilio II (Cod. vaticano Greco 1613)*. Torino. 1907.
Menologion imperiale, ed. B. Latyšev, *Menologii anonymi Byzantini saeculi X quae supersunt, Fasciculus prior: Februarium et Martium menses continens; Fasciculus alter: Menses Iunium, Iulium, Augustum continens, sumptibus Caesareae Academiae scientiarum e codice Hierosolymitano S. Sepulcri 17*. St Petersburg. 1911–1912. 2 vols. (repr. Leipzig. 1970).

Methodios, Patriarch of Constantinople

Diataxis for the Admission of Heretics, in M. Arranz, 'La "Diataxis" du patriarche Methode pour la réconciliation des Apostats', *OCP* 56/2 (1990): 283–322.
Enkomion of St Agatha (*BHG* 38), ed. E. Mioni, 'L'encomio di S. Agata di Metodio patriarca di Costantinopoli', *AnBoll* 68 (1950): 58–93.
Enkomion of St Nicholas of Myra (*BHG* 1352z), in *Hagios Nikolaos: Der Heilige Nikolaos in der Griechischen Kirche*, G. Anrich, ed. Leipzig-Berlin. 1913. Vol. I: 153–82.
Epigram on the Icon of Christ above the Bronze Gate, ed. L. Sternbach, 'Methodii patriarchae et Ignatii patriarchae carmina inedita', *Eos* 4 (1898) 150–63: (text, 150–51).

Epistle to Sergios, Patriarch of Jerusalem, ed. J.-B. Pitra, *Monumenta* II: 355–57. A fragment is edited in *PG* 100: 1292C–93.
Formulae for the Admission of Heretics, in *PG* 100: 1308–17.
Kanon in Honour of Ioannikios, in *Analecta hymnica graeca*, I. Schiro and A. Kominis, eds., vol. III (Novembris): 134–45 and 569–72.
Kanon in Honour of Nicholas of Myra, ed. J.-B. Pitra, *Monumenta* II: 363–64.
Idiomelon on St Constantine and St Helena, in *Anthologia Graeca carminum christianorum*, W. Chris and M. Paranikas, eds. Leipzig. 1871: 99.
Passio of St Dionysios the Areopagite, Rusticus and Eleutherios (*BHG* 554d), ed. J. C. Westerbrink, *Passio S. Dionysii Areopagitae, Rustici et Eleutherii, uitgegeven naar het Leidse Hs*. Vulcanianus 52. Alphen. 1937: 44–62 and in *PG* 4: 669–84.
Refutation of the Iconoclasts (Contra Iconomachos), in *PG* 100: 1233–34.
Scholia in Honour of Sts Kosmas and Damian (*BHG* 377a), ed. L. Deubner, *Kosmas und Damian*. Leipzig. 1907: 41–42.
Scholia in Honour of St Marina (*BHG* 1167m), in *Festschrift zur fünften Säcularfeier der Carl-Ruprechts-Universität zu Heidelberg*, H. Usener, ed. Bonn. 1886: 48–53.
Speech about the Holy Icons, in *Čtenija v obščestve ljubitelej duchovnago prosveščenija*, E. Arsenij, ed. Moscow. 1893: Nov.–Dec., sec. III: 1–23; Pitra, *Monumenta* II: 357–61.
Vita of Euthymios of Sardis (*BHG* 2145), ed. and Fr. trans. J. Gouillard, 'La vie d'Euthyme de Sardes (†831), une oeuvre du patriarche Méthode', *TM* 10 (1987): 1–101.
Vita of Nicholas of Myra (*BHG* 1352y) '*ad Theodorum*', in *Hagios Nikolaos: Der Heilige Nikolaos in der Griechischen Kirche*, G. Anrich, ed. Leipzig-Berlin. 1913. Vol. I: 140–50; Vol. II: 546–56.
Vita of Theophanes the Confessor of Megas Agros (*BHG* 1787z), ed. B. Latysev, 'Methodii, patriarchae Constantinopolitani, Vita s. Theophanis confessoris e codice Mosquensi no. 159', *Mémoires de l'Académie des Sciences de Russie* 13/4 (1918): 1–44.

Metrophanes of Smyrna, *Enkomion of Euthymios of Sardis* (*BHG* 2146), ed. A. Papadakis, 'The Unpublished Life of Euthymius of Sardis: *Bodleianus Laudianus Graecus* 69', *Traditio* 26 (1970): 63–89.
Metrophanes of Smyrna, *Enkomion of the Archangels Michael and Gabriel* (*BHG* 1292), ed. P. Van Deun and E. Gielen, 'The Invocation of the Archangels Michael and Gabriel Attributed to Metrophanes Metropolitan of Smyrna (*BHG* 1292)', *BZ* 108/2 (2015): 653–71.
Metrophanes of Smyrna, *Letter to the logothetes Manuel*, in Mansi XVI: 416.

Michael Monachos

Enkomion of Ignatios, Patriarch of Constantinople (*BHG* 818) by Michael Monachos, in *PG* 105: 292–94; J. Hardouin, *Acta Conciliorum*. Paris. 1715. Vol. V: 1009–12; M. Raderus, *Acta Sacrosancti concilii octavi*.

Ingolstadt. 1604: 196–200; Ph. Labbe, *Sacrosancta Concilia.* Paris. 1671. Vol. VIII: 1260–64.

Enkomion of Mokios (*BHG* 1298h) by Michael Monachos, ed. H. Delehaye, 'Saints de Thrace et de Mésie', *AnBoll* 31 (1912) 161–300: (text, 176–87 and 226–27).

Oration on the Girdle of the Blessed Theotokos (*BHG* 1147), ed. F. Combefis, *Graeco-latinae patrum bibliothecae novum auctarium.* Paris. 1648. Vol. II: 790–802.

Vita of Nicholas of Myra (*BHG* 1348), a *metaphrasis* of the *vita* (*BHG* 1352y) written by the patriarch Methodios, in *Hagios Nikolaos: Der Heilige Nikolaos in der Griechischen Kirche*, ed. G. Anrich. Leipzig-Berlin. 1913. Vol. I: 113–39.

Vita B of Theodoros of Stoudios (*BHG* 1754) by Michael Monachos, in *PG* 99: 233–328.

Michael Synkellos

Anacreontic Verses on the Triumph of Orthodoxy, in C. Crimi, *Michele Sincello: Per la restaurazione delle venerande e sacre immagini.* Rome. 1990.

Enkomion in Honour of Dionysios the Areopagite (*BHG* 556), in *PG* 4: 617–68; R. Loenertz, 'Le panégyrique de S. Denys l'Aréopagit par S. Michel le Syncelle', *AnBoll* 68 (1950): 94–107 (repr. in *Byzantina et Franco-Graeca.* Rome. 1970: 149–62).

Enkomion of Isakios and Dalmatos (*BHG* 956d), ed. and trans. P. Hatlie, 'The Encomium of Ss. Isakos and Dalmatos by Michael the Monk (*BHG* 956d): Text, Translation and Notes', in *EUKOSMIA. Studi miscellanei per il 75° di V. Poggi S. J.*, V. Ruggieri and L. Pieralli, eds. Catanzaro. 2003: 275–311.

Enkomion of the Deposition of the Girdle of the Theotokos (*BHG* 1147), in *Graeco-latinae patrum bibliothecae novum auctarium*, F. Combefis, ed. Paris. 1648. Vol. II: 790–802.

Enkomion of the Archangels Michael and Gabriel (*BHG* 1294a), ed. T. Matantseva, 'Eloge des archanges Michel et Gabriel par Michel le Moine (*BHG* 1294a)', *JÖB* 46 (1996): 97–155.

Libellus on the Orthodox Faith, in *Bibliotheca Coisliniana*, ed. B. de Montfaucon. Paris. 1715: 90–93.

Greek Syntax, ed. D. Donnet, *Le traité de la construction de la phrase de Michel le Syncelle de Jérusalem.* Brussels-Rome. 1982.

Passio of the 42 Martyrs of Amorion (*BHG* 1213 = version Γ), eds. V. G. Vasilevskij and P. Nikitin, *Skažanija o 42 amoriiskikh mučenikhax.* Zapiski Imper. Akademij Nauk VII/2. Saint Petersburg. 1905: 22–36.

Translation of the Dogmatic Epistle to the Armenians Written in Arabic by Theodore Abū Qurrah, in *PG* 97: 1504–21.

Michael the Syrian, *Chronique*, ed. and Fr. trans. J. B. Chabot. Paris. 1901.

Narratio miraculorum maximi archangeli Michaelis (*BHG* 1285–88) by Pantoleon, in *PG* 140: 573–92

Narratio de Theophili absolutione (*BHG* 1732), in *Analecta Byzantino-Russica*, W. Regel, ed. St Petersburg. 1891: 19–39, col. I.
Narratio amplior de Theophili absolutione (*BHG* 1733), in *Analecta Byzantino-Russica*, W. Regel ed. St Petersburg. 1891: 19–39, col. II.
Narratio historica in festum restitutionis imaginum (*BHG* 1734), in *Bibliotheca Patrum Graeco-Latinae Auctarium Novum*, F. Combefis, ed. Paris. 1648. Vol. II: 715–43.
Narratio historica in festum restitutionis imaginum (*BHG* 1734a), ed. F. Halkin, 'Deux impératrices de Byzance, II: L'impératrice sainte Théodora († 867)', *AnBoll* 106 (1988): 28–34.
Narratio de Theophili imperatoris benefactis (*BHG* 1735), in *Analecta Byzantino-Russica*, W. Regel, ed. St Petersburg. 1891: 40–43.
Narratio de sanctis patriarchis Tarasio et Nicephoro (= *De schismate Studitarum*) (*BHG* 1757), in *PG* 99: 1849–53.

Niketas Byzantios

Answers to Two Letters of the Arabs, ed. K. Förstel, *Niketas von Byzanz: Schriften zum Islam*. Würzburg-Altenberge. 2000: 156–98.
Refutatio of the Epistle of Ašot king of Armenia, in *PG* 105: 587–666.
Refutatio of the Qurʾān, ed. K. Förstel, *Niketas von Byzanz: Schriften zum Islam*. Würzburg-Altenberge. 2000: 2–152.
Twenty-Four Syllogistic Chapters on the Procession of the Holy Spirit, in *Monumenta graeca ad Photium ejusque historiam pertinentia*, J. Hergenröther, ed. Regensburg. 1869: 84–138.

Nikephoros, Patriarch of Constantinople

Antirrheticus adversus Constantinum Copronymum, in *PG* 100: 205–534.
Against Eusebium, ed. and Fr. trans. A. Chryssostalis, *Contra Eusebium de Nicéphore de Constantinople (introduction, édition, traduction, notes)*. Paris. 2016.
Apologeticus pro sacris imaginibus, in *PG* 100: 534–850.
Refutatio et Eversio, ed. J. M. Featherstone, *Nicephori Patriarchae Constantinopolitani Refutatio et Eversio Definitionis Synodalis Anni 815*. Leuven. 1997 (CCSG 33).
Short History, Eng. trans. C. Mango, *Nikephoros Patriarch of Constantinople, Short History: Text, Translation, and Commentary*. Washington. 1990 (CFHB 13, DOT 10).

Nikolaos Mystikos, Epistles, ed. and trans. R. J. H. Jenkins and L. G. Westerink, *Nicholas I Patriarch of Constantinople: Letters*. Washington. 1973 (CFHB 4; DOT 2).
Passion of the 42 Martyrs of Amorion (*BHG* 1209 = version Δ) by Sophronios, ed. V. G. Vasilevskij and P. Nikitin, *Skažanija o 42 amoriiskikh mučenikhax*. Zapiski Imper. Akademij Nauk VII/2. Saint Petersburg. 1905: 38–56.

Passion of the 42 Martyrs of Amorion (*BHG* 1211 = version A), ed. V. G. Vasilevskij and P. Nikitin, *Skažanija o 42 amoriiskikh mučenikhax*. Zapiski Imper. Akademij Nauk VII/2. Saint Petersburg. 1905: 1–7.
Passion of the 42 Martyrs of Amorion (*BHG* 1212 = version B), ed. V. G. Vasilevskij and P. Nikitin, *Skažanija o 42 amoriiskikh mučenikhax*. Zapiski Imper. Akademij Nauk VII/2. Saint Petersburg. 1905: 8–21.
Passion of the 42 Martyrs of Amorion (*BHG* 1214 = version Z) by the monk Euodios, ed. V. G. Vasilevskij and P. Nikitin, *Skažanija o 42 amoriiskikh mučenikhax*. Zapiski Imper. Akademij Nauk VII/2. Saint Petersburg. 1905: 61–78.
Passion of the 42 Martyrs of Amorion (*BHG* 1214 = version Z) by the monk Euodios, ed. and Mod. Gr. trans. S. Efthymiadis, Εὐωδίου Μοναχοῦ οἱ σαρανταδύο μάρτυρες τοῦ Ἀμορίου. Nea Smyrne. 1989.
Passion of the 42 Martyrs of Amorion (*BHG* 1214c = version P), ed. F. Halkin, *Hagiologie byzantine*. Brussels. 1986: 153–61.
Petros Sikeliotes, Refutation of Manichaeism, in *PG* 104: 1305–50 (partial edition of two of his six treatises).

Photios, Patriarch of Constantinople

Against the Manicheans, ed. W. Conus-Wolska in C. Astruc et al., 'Les sources grecques pour l'histoire des Pauliciens d'Asie Mineure: texte critique et traduction', *TM* 4 (1970): 1–227: (text, 181–183).
Amphilochia, ed. B. Laourdas and L. G. Westerink, *Photii patriarchae constantinopolitani Epistulae et Amphilochia*. Leipzig. 1983–1987. Vols. 4–6/1.
Bibliotheca, ed. R. Henry, *Photius: Bibliothèque*. Paris. 1959–1977. 8 vols.
Bibliotheca, partial Eng. trans. N. G. Wilson, *The Bibliotheca: A Selection Translated with Notes*. London. 1994.
Bibliotheca, Ital. trans. in *Fozio: Biblioteca* (introduzione di L. Canfora), N. Bianchi and C. Schiano, eds. Pisa. 2016.
Eisagogé, in *Jus Graecoromanum*, J. D. Zepos, ed. Athens. 1931. 2 vols. (repr. Aalen. 1962).
Eisagogé, Span. trans. J. Signes Codoñer and F. J. Andrés Santos, *La "Introducción al derecho (Eisagogé)" del patriarca Focio*. Madrid 2007.
Enkomion of St Thekla (*BHG* 1721), ed. B. Laourdas, Φωτίου Ὁμιλίαι, ἔκδοσις κειμένου, εἰσαγωγὴ καὶ σχόλια. Thessaloniki. 1959: 181–86.
Epistles, ed. B. Laourdas and L. G. Westerink, *Photii patriarchae Constantinopolitani epistulae et Amphilochia*. Leipzig. 1983–1987. Vols. 1–3.
Homilies, ed. B. Laourdas, Φωτίου Ὁμιλίαι, ἔκδοσις κειμένου, εἰσαγωγὴ καὶ σχόλια. Thessaloniki. 1959.
Homilies, Eng. trans. C. Mango, *The Homilies of Photius, Patriarch of Constantinople*. Cambridge. 1958.
Nomocanon, in Σύνταγμα τῶν θείων καὶ ἱερῶν κανόνων, eds. G. A. Rhalles and M. Potles. Athens. 1852–1859 (repr. 1966).

On the Icons, in *Monumenta graeca ad Photium ejusque historiam pertinentia*, J. Hergenröther, ed. Regensburg. 1869: 53–62.
Synagogai, in *PG* 104: 1219–32.

Pseudo-Symeon, *Chronography*, ed. I. Bekker, *Theophanes Continuatus, Ioannes Cameniata, Symeon Magister, Georgius Monachus*. Bonn. 1838 (CSHB 33).
Regestes of the Byzantine Empire in F. J. Dölger, *Regesten der Kaiserurkunden des Oströmischen Reiches von 565–1453. I. Teil: Regesten von 565–1015*. Munich-Berlin. 1924 (repr. Hildesheim. 1976).
Regestes of the Byzantine Empire (867–1025), in *Regesten der Kaiserurkunden des Oströmischen Reiches von 565–1453. 2. Halbband: Regesten 867–1025*, F. Dölger and A. E. Müller, eds. Munich. 2003.
Regestes of the Patriarchate of Constantinople, in V. Grumel, *Les regestes des actes du Patriarcat de Constantinople. Vol. I. Les Actes des Patriarches. Fasc. II et III: Les Regestes de 715 a 1206*, 2nd ed. Paris. 1989 (rev. J. Darrouzès).
Scriptor incertus, ed. F. Iadevaia, *Scriptor incertus*, 2nd ed. Messina. 1997.
Sermo de capitis inventionibus (*BHG* 841), ed. Ch. Dufresne Du Cange, *Traité historique du chef de saint Jean-Baptiste*. Paris. 1666: 229–54. The last part is reproduced in *AASS*, Iunii iv. Antwerp. 1708: 731–35.
Stichelegeia (στιχελεγεῖα) (*BHG* 1756a), in *Parvae catecheseis*, E. Auvray, ed. Paris. 1891: lxvi.
Suidae lexicon, ed. A. Adler. Leipzig. 1928–1938. 4 vols.
Symeon Logothetes, ed. S. Wahlgren, *Symeonis Magistri et Logothetae chronicon*. Berlin-New York. 2006.
Synodicon vetus, ed. and trans. J. Duffy and J. Parker, *The Synodicon vetus*. Washington. 1979 (DOT 5; CFHB 15).
Synodikon of Alexios Stoudites (1025–1043), ed. F. Lauritzen in *The Great Councils of the Orthodox Churches. From Constantinople 861 to Moscow 2000*, A. Melloni, ed. Turnhout. 2016. Vol. iv/1: 375–94.
Synodikon of Orthodoxy (*BHG* 1392), ed. and Fr. trans. J. Gouillard, 'Le Synodikon de l'Orthodoxie. Édition et commentaire', *TM* 2 (1967): 1–316.

Theodoros of Stoudios

Epigrams, ed. and Germ. trans. P. Speck, *Theodoros Studites: Jamben auf verschiedene Gegenstände: Einleitung, Kritischer Text, Übersetzung und Kommentar*. Berlin. 1968.
Epistles, ed. G. Fatouros, *Theodori Studitae Epistulae*. Berlin. 1992. 2 Vols. (CFHB 31).
Epistles, ed. J. Sirmond, in *PG* 99/1: 903–1680.
Laudatio S. Arsenii Anachoretae (*BHG* 169), ed. Th. Nissen, 'Das Enkomion des Theodorus Studites auf dem heiligen Arsenios', *BNJ* 1 (1920): 246–62; *PG* 99: 849–81.

Laudatio of Platon of Sakkoudion (BHG 1553) by Theodoros of Stoudios, in *PG* 99: 804–50.
Laudatio of Theoktiste (BHG 2422) by Theodoros of Stoudios, in S. Efthymiadis and J. M. Featherstone, 'Establishing a Holy Lineage: Theodore the Stoudite's Funerary Catechism for His Mother *(BHG* 2422)', in *Theatron: Rhetorische Kultur in Spätantike und Mittelalter*, M. Grünbart, ed. Berlin. 2007: 13–51.
Magnae catecheseis, ed. A. Papadopulos-Kerameus, *Theodori Studitae Magna Catachesis.* St Petersburg. 1904: 1–931. Partial edition by J. Cozza-Luzi, *Nova Patrum Bibliotheca.* Vol. 9/2 (Cat. 1–77); Vol. 10/1 (Cat. 78–111). Rome. 1888–1905. (a new edition is being prepared by O. Delouis and V. Déroche for the collection *Sources chrétiennes*)
Parvae catecheseis, ed. E. Auvray, *S.P.N. et Confessoris Theodori Studitis Praepositi Parva Catachesis.* Paris. 1891; Fr. trans. in A. M. Mohr, *Petites catéchèses* (= *Les Pères dans la foi 52*). Paris. 1993.
Refutation of the Iconoclasts, in *PG* 99: 436–77.
Rule (Hypotyposis), in A. Mai and J. Cozza-Luzi, *Nova patrum bibliotheca.* Rome. 1849. Vol. 5: 111–25 (repr. in *PG* 99: 1704–20).
Rule (Hypotyposis), trans. T. S. Miller, 'Stoudios: Rule of the Monastery of St John of Stoudios in Constantinople', in *Byzantine Monastic Foundation Documents: A Complete Translation of the Surviving Founders' Typika and Testaments*, J. Thomas et al.. eds. Washington. 2000 (DOS 35). Vol. 1: 84–115.
Testament (Diathêkê) (BHG 1759), ed. J. de la Baume, *Sancti Theodori Studitae Epistolae aliaque scripta dogmatica.* Paris. 1696. Vol. 5: 80–88 (repr. in *PG* 99: 1813–24).
Testament (Diathêkê), trans. T. S. Miller, 'Theodori Studitae testamentum', in *Byzantine Monastic Foundation Documents: A Complete Translation of the Surviving Founders' Typika and Testaments*, J. Thomas et al., eds. Washington. 2000 (DOS 35). Vol. 1: 67–80.
Vita of Theophanes the Confessor of Megas Agros (BHG 1792b) by Theodoros of Stoudios, ed. and Fr. trans. S. Efthymiadis, 'Le panégyrique de S. Théophane le Confesseur par S. Théodore Stoudite *(BHG* 1792b). Edition critique du texte intégral', *AnBoll* 111 (1993): 259–90 with an addition in *AnBoll* 112 (1994): 104.

Theognostos, *Enkomion of the Dormition of the Holy Mother of God (BHG* 1139k), ed. M. Jugie *Patrologia Orientalis.* Paris. 1922. Vol. XVI: 457–62.
Theognostos, *Enkomion in Honour of All the Saints (BHG* 1617), in *PG* 105: 849–56.
Theognostos, *Libellus for the Pope Nicholas I (BHG* 818c), in Mansi XVI: 296–301 (= *PG* 105: 856–61).
Theophanes the Confessor, *Chronography*, ed. C. De Boor, *Theophanis chronographia.* Leipzig. 1883–1885. 2 vols.
Theophanes the Confessor, *Chronography*, trans. by C. Mango and R. Scott, *The Chronicle of Theophanes Confessor: Byzantine and Near Eastern History AD*

284–813. Oxford. 1997. Partial translation by H. Turtledove, *The Chronicle of Theophanes (A.D. 602–813)*. Philadelphia. 1982.
Theophanes Continuatus, *Chronography*, Books I–IV, ed. and trans. M. Featherstone and J. Signes-Codoñer, *Chronographiae quae Theophanis Continuati nomine fertur libri I–IV*. Berlin. 2015 (CFHB 53).
Theophanes Continuatus, *Vita Basilii*, Book V, ed. and trans. I. Ševčenko, *Chronographiae quae Theophanis Continuati nomine fertur liber quo Vita Basilii imperatoris amplectitur*. Berlin. 2011 (CFHB 42).
Theophanes Continuatus, *Chronography*, Book VI, ed. I. Bekker, *Theophanes Continuatus, Ioannes Cameniata, Symeon Magister, Georgius Monachus*. Bonn. 1838 (CSHB 33).
Translation of Nikephoros, Patriarch of Constantinople (BHG 1336–37b) by Theophanes Presbyteros, ed. Th. Ioannou, *Mnemeia hagiologika*. Venice. 1884 (repr. Leipzig. 1973): 115–28; *PG* 100: 159–68.
Translation of Theodoros of Stoudios and Ioseph of Thessaloniki (BHG 1756t), ed. Ch. Van de Vorst, 'La translation de s. Théodore Studite et de s. Joseph de Thessalonique', *AnBoll* 32 (1913): 27–62.
Typika Dmitrievskij, ed. A. Dmitrievskij, *Opisanie liturgičeskich rukopisej, chranjaščichsja v bibliotekach pravoslavnago vostoka*. St Petersburg. 1917 (repr. Hildesheim. 1965).
Typikon of the Great Church, ed. J. Mateos, *Le Typicon de la Grande Église. Ms. Sainte-Croix no 40, Xe siècle*. Rome. 1962–1963. 2 vols. (OCA 165, 166).
Typikon Messinense, ed. M. Arranz, *Le Typicon du monastère du Saint-Sauveur à Messine: Codex Messinensis gr. 115 A. D. 1131, introduction, texte critique et notes*. Rome. 1969 (OCA 185).
Vita of the Apostle Andrew (BHG 102) by Epiphanios of Kallistratos, ed. A. Dressel, *Epiphanii monachi et presbyteri edita et inedita*. Paris-Leipzig. 1843 (= *PG* 120: 185–260).
Vita of Andreas en Krisei (BHG 111), in *AASS*, vol. VIII (Oct.): 135–42.
Vita of Andreas en Krisei (BHG 112), in *AASS*, vol. VIII (Oct.): 142–49; *PG* 115: 1109–28.
Vita of Antonios the Younger (BGH 142), ed. A. Papadopoulos-Kerameus, Συλλογὴ παλαιστίνης καὶ συριακῆς ἁγιολογίας (= *Pravoslavnij Palestinskij Sbornik* 57). Saint Petersburg. 1907. Vol. I: 186–216 (repr. in *Syllogê Palaistinês Syriakês Hagiologias*. Thessaloniki. 2001).
Vita of Antonios the Younger (BGH 142/addit), ed. F. Halkin, 'Saint Antoine le Jeune et Pétronas le vainqueur des Arabes en 863 (d'après un text inédit)', *AnBoll* 62 (1944): 210–25 (repr. in F. Halkin, *Saints moines d'Orient*. London. 1973. Ch. VIII).
Vita of Antonios the Younger (BGH 143), in P. Euergetinou, Συναγωγὴ τῶν θεοφθόγγων ῥημάτων καὶ διδασκαλιῶν τῶν θεοφόρων καὶ ἁγίων πατέρων. Constantinople. 1861: 116–18.
Vita of Antonios of Ruwah (Arabic version), ed. I. Dick, 'La Passion arabe de S. Antoine Ruwah, néo-martyr de Damas (25 déc. 799)', *Le Muséon* 74 (1961): 109–33.

Vita of Athanasia of Aegina (*BHG* 180), ed. L. Carras, 'The Life of St Athanasia of Aegina', in *Maistor: Classical, Byzantine and Renaissance Studies for R. Browning*. Canberra. 1984: 199–224.
Vita of Athanasia of Aegina (*BHG* 180), trans. L. Sherry, 'Life of St Athanasia of Aegina', in *Holy Women of Byzantium*, A. M. Talbot, ed. Washington. 1996: 137–58.
Vita of Anthousa of Mantineon (*BHG* 2029h), in *SynaxCP*, 848–52.
Vita of Anthousa of Mantineon (*BHG* 2029h), trans. A. M. Talbot, 'Life of St Anthousa of Mantineon', in *Byzantine Defenders of Images*, A. M. Talbot, ed. Washington. 1998: 13–19.
Vita of Blasios of Amorion (*BHG* 278), in *AASS*, Nov. 4: 657–69 (rev. Grégoire, *Byzantion* 4 (1927/1928): 805–8).
Vita of Eirene Chrysobalanton (*BHG* 952), ed. and trans. J. O. Rosenqvist, *The Life of St Irene Abbess of Chrysobalanton*. Uppsala. 1986.
Vita of the Empress Eirene (*BHG* 2205), ed. F. Halkin, 'Deux impératrices de Byzance, I: La Vie de l'impératrice sainte Irène et le second concile de Nicée en 787', *AnBoll* 106 (1988): 5–27.
Vita of Eudokimos (*BHG* 606) by Konstantinos Akropolites, ed. I. Taxidis, 'L'éloge de Saint Eudocime par Constantin Acropolite (*BHG* 606)', *Parekbolai* 3 (2013): 5–44.
Vita of Eudokimos (*BHG* 607), ed. Ch. Loparev, 'Βίος τοῦ ἁγίου καὶ δικαίου Εὐδοκίμου', *Pamjatniki drevnej pis'mennosti* 96 (1893): 1–23.
Vita of Eudokimos (*BHG* 607e), ed. B. Latyšev, *Menologii anonymi*, vol. II: 228–32.
Vita of Eustratios of Agauroi (*BHG* 645), ed. A. Papadopulos-Kerameus, Ἀνάλεκτα ἱεροσολυμιτικῆς σταχυολογίας. St Petersburg. 1891–1898. Vol. 4: 367–400; Vol. 5: 408–10.
Vita of Euthymios, Patriarch of Constantinople (*BHG* 651), ed. and Eng. trans. P. Karlin-Hayter, *Vita Euthymii patriarchae*. Brussels. 1970 (previously published in *Byzantion* 25/27 (1955/1957): 1–172 and 747–78).
Vita of Euthymios the Younger (*BHG* 655), ed. L. Petit, 'Vie et office de saint Euthyme le Jeune', *ROC* 8 (1903): 155–205 and 503–36 (repr. in *Bibliotheca Hagiographica Orientalis*. Brussels. 1904: 14–51).
Vita of Euthymios the Younger (*BHG* 655), ed. and Eng. trans. A. Alexakis and A. M. Talbot, 'Life of Euthymios the Younger', in *Holy Men of Mount Athos*, R. P. H. Greenfield and A. M. Talbot, eds. Cambridge, MA. 2016 (DOML 40): 1–126.
Vita of Evarestos of Stoudios (*BHG* 2153), ed. C. Van de Vorst, 'La Vie de s. Evariste, higoumène à Constantinople', *AnBoll* 41 (1923): 288–326.
Vita of Evarestos of Stoudios (*BHG* 2153c), in *SynaxCP*, 345/346,55–58.
Vita of Georgios of Amastris (*BHG* 668e), in *SynaxCP*, 481,44–82,28.
Vita of Georgios of Mytilene (*BHG* 2163), ed. I. M. Phountoules, 'Οἱ ἅγιοι Γεώργιοι, ἀρχιεπίσκοποι Μυτιλήνης', in Λεσβιακὸν ἑορτολόγιον. Athens. 1959. Vol. 1: 33–43.
Vita of Georgios of Mytilene, in *SynaxCP*, 589–90 and 687.

Vita of Germanos, Patriarch of Constantinople (BHG 697), ed. L. Lamza, *Patriarch Germanos I von Konstantinopel*. Wuzburg. 1975.

Vita of Hilarion of Dalmatos (BHG 2177) by Sabas Monachos, in T. Matantseva, 'La Vie d'Hilarion, higoumène de Dalmatos, par Sabas (BHG 2177)', *RSBN* 30 (1993): 17–29.

Vita of Hilarion of Dalmatos (BHG 2177b), in *SynaxCP*, 731–34.

Vita of Ioannes of Gotthia (BHG 891), ed. and Fr. trans. M. F. Auzépy, 'La vie de Jean de Gothie (BHG 891)', in *La Crimée entre Byzance et le Khaganat khazar*, C. Zuckérmann, ed. Paris. 2006: 69–85.

Vita of Ioannes of Kathara (BHG 2184n), in *SynaxCP*, 631–34.

Vita of Ioannes of Galatia by Ioseph Hymnographos, Fr. trans. M. van Esbroeck, 'La Vie de Saint Jean higoumène de Saint-Serge par Joseph le Skevophylax', *Oriens christianus* 80 (1996): 153–66.

Vita of Ioannes Psichaites (BHG 896), ed. P. Van den Ven, 'La vie grecque de s. Jean le Psichaïte, confesseur sous le règne de Léon l'Arménien (813–820)', *Le Muséon* 21 (1902): 97–125.

Vita of Ignatios, patriarch of Constantinople (BHG 817), in *PG* 105: 488–574; Eng. trans. A. Smithies, *Nicetas David, the Life of Patriarch Ignatius* (notes by J. M. Duffy). Washington. 2013 (DOT 13; CFHB 51).

Vita of Ioseph Hymnographos (BHG 944) by Theophanes, ed. A. Papadopoulos-Kerameus, *Sbornik greceskich i latinskich pamjatnikov, kasajuscichsja Fotija patriarcha* (= *Monumenta graeca et latina ad historiam Photii patriarchae pertinentia*). St Petersburg. 1901. Vol. II: 1–14.

Vita of Ioseph Hymnographos (BHG 946) by Ioannes Diakonos, in *PG* 105: 939–75.

Vita of Ioannikios (BHG 935) by Sabas Monachos, in *AASS* Nov. II,i, J. Van den Gheyn, ed. Brussels. 1894: 332–83.

Vita of Ioannikios (BHG 936) by Petros Monachos, in *AASS* Nov. II,i, J. Van den Gheyn, ed. Brussels. 1894: 384–435.

Vita of Ioannikios (BHG 936) by Petros Monachos, trans. D. Sullivan, 'Life of St Ioannikios', in *Byzantine Defenders of Images*, A. M. Talbot, ed. Washington. 1998: 243–351.

Vita of Kostanti Kaxay, ed. and trans. M. Abashidze and S. H. Rapp Jr, 'The Life and Passion of Kostanti-Kaxay', *Le Muséon* 17/1–2 (2004): 137–73.

Vita of Leon of Catania (BHG 981), ed. A. Acconcia Longo, 'La Vita di S. Leone vescovo di Catania e gli incantesimi del mago Eliodoro', *RSBN* 26 (1989): 80–98.

Vita of Leon of Catania (BHG 981b), ed. and trans. A. G. Alexakis, *The Greek Life of St Leo Bishop of Catania*. Brussels. 2011.

Vita of Makarios of Pelekete (BHG 1003) by Sabas Monachos, ed. J. Van den Gheyn, 'S. Macarii Monasterii Pelecetes Hegumeni, Acta Graeca', *AnBoll* 16 (1897): 142–63.

Vita of Maria the Younger in Bizye (BHG 1164), in *AASS*, Nov. 4. Brussels. 1925: 692–705.

Vita of Maria the Younger in Bizye (*BHG* 1164), trans. A. Laiou, 'Life of St Mary the Younger', in *Holy Women of Byzantium: Ten Saints' Lives in English Translation*, A. M. Talbot, ed. Washington. 1996: 239–89.

Vita of Methodios, Patriarch of Constantinople(*BHG* 1278), in *PG* 100: 1243–62.

Vita of Michael Maleinos (*BHG* 1295), ed. L. Petit, 'Vie de saint Michel Maléinos', *ROC* 7 (1902): 543–94 (repr. in *Bibliothèque hagiographique orientale* 4. Paris. 1903: 7–26).

Vita of Michael of Synada (= *BHG* 2275), in Theod. Stoud., *Parvae catecheseis* 21, ed. E. Auvray: 76–79.

Vita of Michael of Synada, in *SynaxCP*, 793–94.

Vita of Michael of Synada (*BHG* 2274x), in Μέγας συναξαριστής, K. X. Doukakis, ed. Athens. 1891–1896. Vol. 5: 411–22.

Vita of Michael the Synkellos (*BHG* 1296), ed. and trans. M. B. Cunningham, *The Life of Michael the Synkellos*. Belfast. 1991.

Vita of Michael the Synkellos (*BHG 1297*) by Nikephoros Gregoras, ed. F. Schmit, 'Kachrie-Dzami', *IRAIK* 11 (1906): 227–59.

Vita of Nikephoros of Medikion (*BHG* 2297–98), ed. F. Halkin, 'La Vie de Saint Nicéphore, fondateur de Médikion en Bithynie (d. 813)', *AnBoll* 78 (1960): 396–430.

Vita of Nikephoros of Medikion, in F. Halkin, 'S. Nicéphore de Médikion d'après un synaxaire du mont Sinai', *AnBoll* 88 (1970): 13–16.

Vita of Niketas of Medikion (*BHG* 1341) by Theosteriktos, in *AASS*, April I (3rd ed.): XVIII–XXVII.

Vita of Niketas of Medikion (*BHG* 1342) by Ioannes Hagiolites, in Μέγας συναξαριστής, K. X. Doukakis, ed. Athens. 1891–1896. Vol. 3: 36–51.

Vita of Niketas of Medikion (Slavonic version), in *Velikija Minei ceti: sobrannyja vserossijskim mitropolitom Makariem*, Aprel, tetr. I, dni 1–8. Moscow. 1910: 42–102.

Vita of Niketas the Patrician (*BHG* 1342b), ed. and Fr. trans. D. Papachryssanthou, 'Un confesseur du second Iconoclasme: La vie du patrice Nicétas (836)', *TM* 3 (1968): 309–51.

Vita of Nikolaos of Stoudios (*BHG* 1365), in *PG* 105: 864–925. Cf. the *enmendationes* by Nissen, in *BNJ* 14 (1928): 331–39.

Vita of Petros of Atroa (*BHG* 2364) by Sabas Monachos, ed. and Fr. trans. V. Laurent, *La vie merveilleuse de Saint Pierre d'Atroa († 837)*. Brussels. 1956.

Vita retractata of Petros of Atroa (*BHG* 2365) by Sabas Monachos, ed. and Fr. trans. V. Laurent, *La vita retractata et les miracles posthumes de Saint Pierre d'Atroa*. Brussels. 1958.

Vita of Petros of Galatia, in *SynaxCP*, 125–26.

Vita of Petros the Patrician (*BHG* 2365u), in *SynaxCP*, 792–94.

Vita of Philaretos the Merciful (*BHG* 1511z) by Niketas the monk, ed. and trans. L. Rydén, *The Life of St Philaretos the Merciful Written by His Grandson Niketas*. Uppsala. 2002.

Vita of Philaretos the Merciful, in *SynaxCP*, 269–70.

Vita of Prokopios Dekapolites (*BHG* 1583), ed. S. Efthymiadis, 'La vie inédite de s. Procope le Décapolite', *AnBoll* 108 (1990): 307–19.
Vita of Prokopios Dekapolites, in *SynaxCP*, 491–92.
Vita of Sabas (*BHG* 1608), ed. E. Schwartz, *Kyrillos von Skythopolis*. Leipzig. 1939: 85–200.
Vita of Sabas (*BHG* 1608), trans. in R. M. Price and J. Binns, *Cyril of Skythopolis: The Lives of the Monks of Palestine*. Kalamazoo. 1991: 93–209.
Vita of Sergios Niketiates, in *SynaxCP*, 777–78.
Vita of Stephanos the Younger (*BHG* 1666) by Stephanos Diakonos, ed. and Fr. trans. M. F. Auzépy, *La Vie d'Étienne le Jeune par Étienne le Diacre: Introduction, édition et traduction*. Aldershot. 1997.
Vita of Stephanos, Patriarch of Constantinople, in *SynaxCP*, 694.
Vita of Symeon the Fool (*BHG* 1677), ed. L. Rydén, *Das Leben des heiligen narren Symeon von Leontios von Neapolis*. Stockholm. 1963.
Vita of Thaddaios of Stoudios (Slavonic version and Eng. trans.), D. E. Afinogenov, 'The Church Slavonic Life of St Thaddaios the Martyr of the Second Iconoclasm', *AnBoll* 119 (2001): 313–38.
Vita of the Empress Theodora (*BHG* 1731), ed. A. Markopoulos, 'Βίος τῆς αὐτοκράτειρας Θεοδώρας (*BHG* 1731)', *Symmeikta* 5 (1983): 249–85 (repr. in *History and Literature of Byzantium in the 9th and 10th Centuries*. Aldeshot. 2004).
Vita of the Empress Theodora (*BHG* 1731), in *Analecta Byzantino-Russica*, W. Regel, ed. St Petersburg. 1891: 1–19.
Vita of the Empress Theodora (*BHG* 1731), trans. M. Vinson, 'Life of St Theodora the Empress', in *Byzantine Defenders of Images*, A. M. Talbot, ed. Washington. 1998: 353–82.
Vita of the Empress Theodora, in *SynaxCP*, 458–60.
Vita of Theodora of Thessaloniki (*BHG* 1737), ed. and Mod. Gr. trans. S. A. Paschalidis, Ὁ Βίος τῆς ὁσιομυροβλύτιδος Θεοδώρας τῆς ἐν Θεσσαλονίκῃ. Διήγηση περί τῆς μεταθέσεως τοῦ τιμίου λειψάνου τῆς ὁσίας Θεοδώρας (Εἰσαγωγή, κριτικό κείμενο, μετάφραση, σχόλια). Thessaloniki. 1991.
Vita of Theodoros Graptos (*BHG* 1746) by Symeon Metaphrastes, in *PG* 116: 653–84.
Vita of Theodoros Graptos (*BHG* 1746e), in *SynaxCP*, 352,4–54,3.
Vita of Theodoros of Sykeon (*BHG* 1748), ed. and Fr. trans. A. J. Festugière, *Vie de Théodore de Sykéôn*. Brussels. 1970.
Vita of Theophanes Graptos (*BHG* 1793) by Theodora Raoulena Paleologina, ed. A. Papadopoulos-Kerameus, *Analecta Ierosolymitikes Stachyologias*. Saint Petersburg. 1897. Vol. IV: 185–223 (repr. Brussels. 1963).
Vita of Theodoros of Chora (*BHG* 1743), ed. C. Loparev, 'De S. Theodoro monacho hegumenoque Chorensi', *Zapiski Klassicheskago otdelniia imperatorskago russkago arkeologischeskago obschestva* 1 (1904): 1–16.
Vita A *of Theodoros of Stoudios* (*BHG* 1755) by Theodoros Daphnopates, ed. V. Latysev, 'Zitie prep. Theodora Studita v miunhenskoj rukopisi nº 467', *VV* 21 (1914): 222–54.

Vita B *of Theodoros of Stoudios* (*BHG* 1754) by Michael Monachos, in *PG* 99: 233–328.
Vita C *of Theodoros of Stoudios* (*BHG* 1755d), ed. V. Latysev, 'Vita S. Theodori in codice Mosquensi musei Rumianzoviani 520', *VV* 21 (1914): 258–304.
Vita of Theodoros of Stoudios (*BHG* 1755f = *Vita* D), ed. T. Matantseva, 'Un fragment d'une nouvelle vie de saint Théodore Stoudite, vie D (*BHG* 1755f)', *BF* 23 (1996): 151–63.
Vita of Theodoros of Stoudios (*BHG* 1755m) by Stephanos Meles, ed. and Fr. trans. O. Delouis, 'La Vie métrique de Théodore Stoudite par Stéphane Mélès (*BHG* 1755m)', *AnBoll* 132 (2014): 21–54.
Vita of Theokletos of Lakedaimon (*BHG* 2420), ed. and trans. A. Kaldellis and I. Polemis, *Saints of Ninth- and Tenth-Century Greece*. Cambridge, MA. 2019 (DOML 54): 163–255.
Vita of the Empress Theophano (*BHG* 1794), ed. E. Kurtz, *Zwei griechische Texte über die hl. Theophano die Gemahlin Kaisers Leo VI*. St Petersburg. 1898: 1–24.
Vita of the Empress Theophano (*BHG* 1794), Mod. Gr. trans. A. Alexakis et al., 'Βίος καὶ Πολιτεία τῆς Ἁγίας καὶ Ἐνδόξης Θαυματουργῆς Αὐτοκρατείρας Θεοφανώς (*BHG* 1794)', *Bella, Epistemonike Epeterida* 4 (2007): 147–227.
Vita of the Empress Theophano (*BHG* 1795) by Nikephoros Gregoras, ed. E. Kurtz, *Zwei griechische Texte über die hl. Theophano die Gemahlin Kaisers Leo VI*. St Petersburg. 1898: 25–45.
Vita A *of Theophylaktos of Nicomedia* (*BHG* 2451) by Theophylaktos, ed. A. Vogt, 'S. Théophylacte de Nicomédie', *AnBoll* 50 (1932): 67–82.
Vita B *of Theophylaktos of Nicomedia* (*BHG* 2452), ed. and Fr. trans. F. Halkin, *Hagiologie byzantine*. Brussels. 1986: 170–84.
Vita of Theophylaktos of Nicomedia (*BHG* 2452c), in *SynaxCP*, 519–22.
Vita of Thomaïs of Lesbos (*BHG* 2454), in AASS, Nov. 4. Brussels. 1925: 234–42.
Vita of Thomaïs of Lesbos (*BHG* 2454), Eng. trans. by P. Halsall, 'Life of St Thomais of Lesbos', in *Holy Women of Byzantium: Ten Saints' Lives in English Translation*, A. M. Talbot, ed. Washington. 1996: 291–322.
Zonaras, *Chronography*, eds. M. Pinder and T. Büttner-Wobst, *Ioannis Zonarae epitomae historiarum libri XVIII*. Bonn. 1841–1897. 3 vols.

SECONDARY SOURCES

Abashidze, M., and Rapp, S. H. Jr. (2004) 'The Life and Passion of Kostanti-Kaxay', *Le Muséon* 17/1–2: 137–73.
Abrahamse, D. de F. (1982) 'Magic and Sorcery in the Hagiography of the Middle Byzantine Period', *BF* 8: 3–17.
  (1985) 'Women's Monasticism in the Middle Byzantine Period: Problems and Prospects', *BF* 9: 35–58.
Acconcia Longo, A. (1989) 'La Vita di S. Leone vescovo di Catania e gli incantesimi del mago Eliodoro', *RSBN* 26: 3–98.
Adontz, N. (1933) 'L'âge et l'origine de l'empereur Basile Ier', *Byzantion* 8: 475–500 (repr. in *Études arméno-byzantines*. Lisbon. 1965: 47–109).

(1934) 'L'age et l'origine de l'empereur Basile Ier (867–886) (suite)', *Byzantion* 9: 223–60.
Afinogenov, D. E. (1991) 'Predstavlenija Georgija Amartola ob ideal'nom imperatore', in *Vizantiskie Očerki: Trudy sovetskikh uchenykh k XVIII mezhdunarodnomu kongressu vizantinistov* Moskow: 163–83.
(1994) 'Κωνσταντινούπολις ἐπίσκοπον ἔχει: The Rise of Patriarchal Power in Byzantium from Nicaenum II to Epanagoga', *Erytheia* 15: 55–65.
(1995) 'Patriarch Photius As Literary Theorist: Aspects of Innovation', *BSl* 56: 339–45.
(1996a) 'Κωνσταντινουπόλις ἐπίσκοπον ἔχει II: From the Second Outbreak of Iconoclasm to the Death of Methodios', *Erytheia* 17: 43–71.
(1996b) 'The Great Purge of 843: A Re-Examination', in *Λειμών: Studies Presented to L. Rydén*, ed. J. O. Rosenqvist. Uppsala: 79–91.
(1997) 'The Bride-Show of Theophilos: Some Notes on the Sources', *Eranos* 95: 10–18.
(1999a) 'Imperial Repentance: The Solemn Procession in Constantinople on March 11, 843', *Eranos* 97: 1–10.
(1999b) 'The Date of Georgios Monachos Reconsidered', *BZ* 92/2: 437–46.
(2001) 'The Church Slavonic Life of St Thaddaios the Martyr of the Second Iconoclasm', *AnBoll* 119: 313–38.
(2004a) *Повесть о прощении императора Феофила' и торжество православия* ('Tale of Forgiveness of the Emperor Theophilus' and the Triumph of Orthodoxy). Moscow.
(2004b) 'Le manuscrit grec *Coislin*. 305: La version primitive de la *Chronique* de Georges le Moine', *REB* 62: 239–46.
(2004c) 'Rewriting a Saint's *Life* in the Monastery of Studiou: Two *Lives* of St Nicholas the Studite', in *The Heroes of the Orthodox Church: The New Saints, 8th–16th c.*, ed. E. Kountura-Galaki. Athens: 313–22.
(2006) 'Did the Patriarchal Archive End Up in the Monastery of Stoudios? Ninth Century Vicissitudes of Some Important Document Collections', in *Monastères, images, pouvoirs et société à Byzance*, ed. M. Kaplan. Paris: 125–34.
(2010) 'The Story of the Patriarch Constantine II of Constantinople in Theophanes and George the Monk: Transformations of a Narrative', in *History As Literature in Byzantium*, ed. R. Macrides. Farnham: 207–14.
(2018) 'Integration of Hagiographic Texts into Historical Narrative: The Cases of the Lives of St Stephen the Younger and Niketas of Medikion', in *Byzantine Hagiography: Texts, Themes and Projects*, ed. A. Rigo. Turnhout: 325–40.
Agapitos, P. A. (1989) "Ἡ εἰκόνα τοῦ αὐτοκράτορα Βασιλείου Α' στὴ φιλομακεδονικὴ γραμματεία 867–959', *Hell* 40: 285–322.
(2004) 'Mortuary Typology in the Lives of Saints: Michael the Synkellos and Stephen the Younger', in *Les vies des saints à Byzance: Genre littéraire ou biographie historique?*, eds. P. Odorico and P. A. Agapitos. Paris: 103–35.
(2015) 'Contesting Conceptual Boundaries: Byzantine Literature and Its History', *Interfaces: A Journal of Medieval European Literatures* 1: 62–91.

Ahrweiler, H. (1962) 'L'Asie Mineure et les invasions arabes (VIIe–IXe siècles)', *Revue Historique* 227/1: 1–32 (repr. in *Études sur les structures administratives et sociales de Byzance*. London. 1971. Ch. ix).
  (1965) 'Sur la carrière de Photius avant son patriarcat', *BZ* 58: 348–63.
  (1971) 'Les relations entre les Byzantins et les Russes au IXe siècle', *BIC* 5: 54–56.
  (1977) 'The Geography of the Iconoclast World', in *Iconoclasm: Papers Given at the Ninth Spring Symposium of Byzantine Studies*, eds. A. A. Bryer and J. Herrin. Birmingham: 21–27.
  (1996) 'Le culte de saint Nicolas', *Transversalités* 57, janvier–mars: 147–53.
Aletta, A. A. (2002/2003) 'Un nuovo codice del copista Nicola (sec. X in.): l'Athen. B. N. 2651', *BBGG* 56–57: 63–76.
Alexakis, A. (1994) 'A Florilegium in the Life of Nicetas of Medicion and a Letter of Theodore of Studios', *DOP* 48: 179–97.
  (1995a) 'Leo VI, Theophano, a Magistros Called Slokakas and the Vita Theophano (BHG 1794)', in *Bosphorus: Essays in Honour of C. Mango*, eds. C. Rapp et al. Amsterdam. (= *BF* 21: 45–56.
  (1995b) 'A Ninth Century Attestation of the Neighbors' Pre-Emption Right in Byzantine Bithynia', *Erytheia* 16: 73–79.
  (1996a) *Codex Parisinus Graecus 1115 and Its Archetype*. Washington.
  (1996b) 'Addendum to the Article "A Ninth Century Attestation of the Neighbors' Pre-Emption Right in Byzantine Bithynia"', *Erytheia* 17: 41–42.
  (2011) 'Some Remarks on Dogmatic Florilegia Based Mainly on the Florilegia of the Early Ninth Century', in *Encyclopedic Trends in Byzantium?*, eds. P. Van Deun and C. Macé. Leuven: 45–55.
Alexander, P. J. (1940) 'Secular Biography at Byzantium', *Speculum* 15: 194–209 (repr. in *Religious and Political History and Thought in the Byzantine Empire*. London. 1978. Ch. i).
  (1953) 'The Iconoclastic Council of St Sophia (815) and Its Definition (Horos)', *DOP* 7: 35–66.
  (1958a) *The Patriarch Nicephorus of Constantinople: Ecclesiastical Policy and Image Worship in the Byzantine Empire*. Oxford.
  (1958b) 'Church Councils and Patristic Authority: The Iconoclastic Councils of Hiereia (754) and St Sophia (815)', *HSCPh* 63: 493–505.
  (1977) 'Religious Persecutions and Resistance in the Byzantine Empire in the Eighth and Ninth Centuries: Methods and Justifications', *Speculum* 52/2: 238–64.
Anagnostakis, E. (1989) 'Τό ἐπεισόδιο τῆς Δανιηλίδας: Πληροφορίες καθημερινοῦ βίου ἤ μυθοπλαστικά στοιχεῖα', in *Ἡ καθημερινή ζωή στό Βυζάντιο*, ed. C. G. Angelidi. Athens: 373–90.
Anastasi, R. (1988) 'L'epistula 156 di Fozio', *StFB* 4: 41–54.
Anastos, M. V. (1954) 'The Ethical Theory of Images Formulated by the Iconoclasts in 754 and 815', *DOP* 5: 151–60.
  (1955) 'The Argument for Iconoclasm As Presented by the Iconoclastic Council of 754', in *Late Classical and Mediaeval Studies in Honor of A. Matthias Friend, Jr.*, eds. K. Weitzmann et al. Princeton: 177–88.

(1957) 'The Transfer of Illyricum, Calabria and Sicily to the Jurisdiction of the Patriarchate of Constantinople in 732–733', in *Silloge bizantina in onore di Silvio Giuseppe* Mercati. Rome: 14–31.
(1990) 'The Papal Legates at the Council of 861 and Their Compliance with the Wishes of the Emperor Michael III', in Αρμός: Τιμητικός τόμος στον Καθηγητή Ν. Κ. Μουτσόπουλο για τα 25 χρόνια πνευματικής του προσφοράς στο Πανεπιστήμιο Θεσσαλονίκης. Thessaloniki: 185–200 (repr. in M. V. Anastos, *Aspects of the Mind of Byzantium*. London. 2001. Ch. VI).
Anderson, J. C. (1994) 'The Palimpsest Psalter, *Pantokrator Cod*. 61: Its Content and Relationship to the Bristol Psalter', *DOP* 48: 199–220.
(1998a) 'Further Prolegomena to a Study of the Pantokrator Psalter: An Unpublished Miniature, Some Restored Losses and Observations on the Relationship with the Chludov Psalter and the Paris Fragment', *DOP* 52: 305–23.
(1998b) 'The Content of the Marginal Psalter Paris. gr. 20', *RSBN* 35: 25–35.
(2006) 'The Creation of the Marginal Psalter', in *Ritual and Art: Byzantine Essays for Christopher Walter*, ed. P. Armstrong. London: 44–65.
Andreou, G. (2005) 'Alcune osservazioni sul menologion del lezionario Paris Gr. 382 (X sec. ex)', *BBGG* III serie 2: 5–16.
(2008) 'New Evidences Relating to the Studite Rite', *BBGG* serie III, 5: 27–40.
Andriollo, L. (2014) 'Aristocracy and Literary Production in the 10th century', in *The Author in Middle Byzantine Literature: Modes, Functions and Identities*, ed. A. Pizzone. Boston-Berlin: 119–38.
Angelidi, Ch. (2004) 'Les Vies des saints ne sont pas seulement des Vies saintes', in *Les vies des saints à Byzance: Genre littéraire ou biographie historique?*, eds. P. Odorico and A. Agapitos. Paris: 73–86.
(2012) 'Translationes Agathae: Note sur le culte d'une sainte entre Byzance et la Sicile normande', *Nea Rhome* 9: 123–52.
Angold, M. (1998) 'The Autographical Impulse in Byzantium', *DOP* 52: 1–17.
Anrich, G. (1913) *Hagios Nikolaos: Der Heilige Nikolaos in der Griechischen Kirche*. Leipzig-Berlin.
Antonopoulou, T. (1997) *The Homilies of the Emperor Leo VI*. Leiden.
(1998) 'Homiletic Activity in Constantinople around 900', in *Preacher and Audience: Studies in Early Christian and Byzantine Homiletics*, eds. M. B. Cunningham and P. Allen. Leiden: 317–45.
(2017) 'Emperor Leo VI the Wise and the "First Byzantine Humanism": On the Quest for Renovation and Cultural Synthesis', *TM* 21/2: 187–233.
Armati, A. (1986/1987) 'Giuseppe Innografo negli Analecta Hymnica Graeca', *Diptycha* 4: 141–48.
Arranz, M. (1990) 'La "Diataxis" du patriarche Methode pour la réconciliation des Apostats', *OCP* 56/2: 283–322.
Astruc, C. et al. (1970) 'Les sources grecques pour l'histoire des Pauliciens d'Asie Mineure: texte critique et traduction', *TM* 4: 1–227.
Athenagoras (Metr.) (1921) Αι ιστορικαί μοναί της νήσου Χάλκης: Η Μονή της Αγίας Τριάδος. και παράρτημα: Ο τόπος εξορίας και του θανάτου του μεγάλου Πατριάρχου Φωτίου. Constantinople.

(1927) 'Ὁ θεσμὸς τῶν συγκέλλων ἐν τῷ οἰκουμενικῷ πατριαρχείῳ', *EEBS* 4: 3–38.
Aufhauser, J., ed. (1913) *Miracula S. Georgii*. Leipzig.
Auzépy, M. F. (1988) 'La place des moines à Nicée II (787)', *Byzantion* 58: 5–21.
  (1990) 'La destruction de l'icône du Christ de la Chalcé par Léon III: Propagande ou réalité?', *Byzantion* 60: 441–92 (repr. in *L'histoire des iconoclastes*. 2007).
  (1992) 'L'analyse littéraire et l'historien: L'exemple des vies de saints iconoclastes', *BSl* 53: 57–67.
  (1993) 'De Philarète, de sa famille et de certains monastères de Constantinople', in *Les saints et leur sanctuaire à Byzance: Textes, images et monuments*, eds. C. Jolivet-Lévi et al. Paris: 117–35.
  (1994) 'De la Palestine à Constantinople (VIIIe–IXe siècles): Étienne le Sabaïte et Jean Damascène', *TM* 12: 183–218 (repr. in *L'histoire des iconoclastes*. 2007).
  (1995) 'L'évolution de l'attitude face au miracle à Byzance (VIIe–IXe siècle)', in *Miracles: Prodiges et merveilles au moyen âge*. Paris: 31–46.
  (1997) *La Vie d'Étienne le Jeune par Étienne le Diacre*. Aldershot.
  (1998) 'Manifestations de la propagande en faveur de l'orthodoxie', in *Byzantium in the Ninth Century: Dead or Alive?*, ed. L. Brubaker. Aldershot: 85–99.
  (1999) *L'hagiographie et l'iconoclasme byzantin*. Aldershot.
  (2000) 'Gothie et Crimée de 750 à 830 dans les sources ecclésiastiques et monastiques grecques', *MAIET* 7: 324–31 (repr. in *L'histoire des iconoclastes*. 2007: 199–207).
  (2001) 'Les Sabaïtes et l'iconoclasme', in *The Sabaïte Heritage in the Orthodox Church from the Fifth Century to the Present*, ed. J. Patrich. Leuven: 305–14 (repr. in *L'histoire des iconoclastes*. 2007: 209–20).
  (2002) 'Constantin, Théodore et le dragon', in *Toleration and Repression in the Middle Ages: in memory of L. Mavrommatis*, ed. K. Nikolaou. Athens: 87–96.
  (2003a) 'Les monastères', in *La Bithynie au Moyen Âge*, eds. B. Geyer and J. Lefort. Paris: 431–58.
  (2003b) 'Un modèle iconoclaste pour le psautier Chludov?', in *Byzantium, State and Society, in memory of N. Oikonomides*, eds. A. Avramea et al. Athens: 11–29 (repr. in *L'histoire des iconoclastes*. 2007).
  (2004a) 'Controversia delle immagini e produzione di testi', in *La cultura bizantina*, ed. G. Cavallo (*Lo Spazio letterario del Medioevo, III. Le culture circostanti*, vol. 1). Rome: 149–82.
  (2004b) 'Les saints et le triomphe de l'Orthodoxie', in *The Heroes of the Orthodox Church: The New Saints, 8th–16th c.*, ed. E. Kountura-Galaki. Athens: 17–29.
  (2006) 'La vie de Jean de Gothie (*BHG* 891)', in *La Crimée entre Byzance et le Khaganat khazar*, ed. C. Zuckermann. Paris: 69–85.
  (2007) *L'histoire des iconoclastes*. Paris (Bilans de recherche 2).
  (2012) 'Le rôle des émigrés orientaux à Constantinople et dans l'Empire (634–843): Acquis et perspectives', *Al-Qanṭara* 33/2: 475–503.

et al. (2005) 'À propos des monastères de Médikion et de Sakkoudiôn', *REB* 63: 183–94.
Baguenard, J. M. (1990) *Les moines Acémètes: Vies des saints Alexandre, Marcel et Jean Calybite.* Abbaye de Bellefontaine.
Baldwin, B. (1986) 'A Literary Debate between Photius and George of Nicomedia', *Aevum* 60: 218–22.
Barber, Ch. (1999) 'Writing on the Body: Memory, Desire, and the Holy in Iconoclasm', in *Desire and Denial in Byzantium*, ed. L. James. Aldershot: 111–22.
  (2007) *Contesting the Logic of Painting: Art and Understanding in Eleventh-Century Byzantium.* Leiden.
Bardill, J. (2017) 'The Date, Dedication, and Design of Sts Sergius and Bacchus in Constantinople', *Journal of Late Antiquity* 10/1: 62–130.
Barišić, F. (1961) 'Les sources de Génésios et du Continuateur de Théophane pour l'histoire du règne de Michel II (820–829)', *Byzantion* 31: 257–71.
Barker, E. (1957) *Social and Political Thought in Byzantium, from Justinian I to the Last Palaeologus.* Oxford.
Barnard, L. (1977) 'The Paulicians and Iconoclasm', in *Iconoclasm: Papers Given at the Ninth Spring Symposium of Byzantine Studies*, eds. A. A. Bryer and J. Herrin. Birmingham: 75–82.
Bartikjan, R. M. (1980) 'Razmyslenija o zitii sv. Marii Novoj', in *Moyen Age Bulgare: Recueil bulgaro-soviétique rédigé en l'honneur du prof. Ivan Dujcev*, ed. V. T Gûzelev. Sofia: 62–64.
Baynes, N. H. (1955a) 'The Finding of the Virgin's Robe', in *Byzantine Studies and Other Essays*, ed. N. H. Baynes. London: 240–47.
  (1955b) 'The Supernatural Defenders of Constantinople', in *Byzantine Studies and Other Essays*, ed. N. H. Baynes. London: 248–60.
Bevegni, C. (1999) 'Le due omelie di Fozio sull'eresia ariana: Motivi e spunti di ricerca', in *Lingua e teologia nel Cristianesimo greco*, eds. C. Moreschini and G. Menestrina. Brescia: 271–97.
Beck, H. G. (1959) *Kirche und theologische Literatur im byzantinischen Reich.* Munich.
Bees, N. A. (1913) 'Un manuscrit des Météores de l'an 861–2 (avec une étude sur les manuscrits grecs datés de IXe siècle)', *REG* 26: 53–74.
  (1916) 'Zu einer byzantinischen Inschrift aus Panion vom Jahre 882', *RhM* 71: 285–88.
Belke, K. (1996) *Tabula Imperii Byzantini (TIB IX: Paphlagonien und Honorias).* Vienna.
  (2009) 'Heilige Berge Bithyniens', in *Heilige Berge und Wüsten. Byzanz und sein Umfeld*, ed. P. Soustal. Vienna: 15–24.
  (2013) 'Bithynien: Historische und geographische Beobachtungen zu einer Provinz in byzantinischer Zeit', in *Neue Funde und Forschungen in Bithynien*, eds. P. Winter and K. Zimmermann. Bonn: 83–109.
Benechevitch, V. N. (1926) 'Die byzantinischen Ranglisten nach dem Kletorologion Philothei und nach den Jerusalemer Handschriften', in *BNJ* 5: 97–167; 6 (1928): 143–45.

Berger, A. (1988a) *Untersuchungen zu den Patria Konstantinupoleos*. Bonn.
  (1988b) 'Die Reliquien der heiligen Euphemia und ihre erste Translation nach Konstantinopel', *Hell* 39: 311–22.
  (2013a) *Accounts of Medieval Constantinople: The Patria*. Cambridge, MA-London.
  (2013b) 'Mokios und Konstantin der Große: Zu den Anfängen des Märtyrerkults in Konstantinopel', in *Antecessor: Festschrift für Spyros N. Troianos zum 80. Geburtstag*, eds. V. A. Leontaritou et al. Athens: 165–85.
Bernard, F. (2014) *Writing and Reading Byzantine Secular Poetry, 1025–1081*. Oxford.
Bernardakis, P. (1903) 'Les appels au Pape dans l'Église grecque jusqu'à Photius', *EO* 6: 30–42, 118–25 and 249–57.
Bertolini, O. (1959) 'Longobardi e Bizantini nell'Italia meridionale ... (774–888)', in *Atti del 3º Congresso internazionale di studi sull'alto Medioevo*. Spoleto: 103–24.
Beševliev, V. (1992) 'Die protobulgarische Inschrift von Direkler (Philippoi)', *JÖB* 42: 233–45.
Binggeli, A. (2018) 'La réception de l'hagiographie palestinienne à Byzance après les conquêtes arabes', in *Byzantine Hagiography: Texts, Themes and Projects*, ed. A. Rigo. Turnhout: 265–84.
Bithos, G. P. (2009) *Saint Methodios of Constantinople. A study of His Life and Works*. Rollinsford.
Blake, R. P. (1939) 'Note sur l'activité littéraire de Nicéphore Ier, patriarche de Constantinople', *Byzantion* 14: 1–15.
Blysidou, B. N. (1991) Ἐξωτερική πολιτική καί ἐσωτερικές ἀντιδράσεις τήν ἐποχή τοῦ Βασιλείου Αʹ: Ἔρευνες γιά τόν ἐντοπισμό τῶν ἀντιπολιτευτικῶν τάσεων στά χρόνια 867/886. Athens.
Boeck, E. N. (2015) *Imagining the Byzantine Past: The Perception of History in the Illustrated Manuscripts of Skylitzes and Manasses*. Cambridge.
Boissevain, J. (1974) *Friends of Friends: Networks, Manipulators and Coalitions*. Oxford.
Bompaire, J. (1982) 'Réflexions d'un humaniste sur la politique: le patriarche Photius', in *La Notion d'autorité au Moyen Âge, Islam, Byzance, Occident*, eds. G. Makdisi et al. Paris: 45–55.
Boojamra, J. L. (1982) 'The Photian Synod of 879–880 and the Papal Commonitorium (879)', *ByzSt* 9: 1–23.
Borgolte, M. (1980) 'Papst Leo III., Karl der Grosse und der *Filioque* Streit von Jerusalem', *Byzantiná* 10: 403–27.
Bréhier, L. (1916) 'L'hagiographie byzantine des VIIIe et IXe siècles, hors des limites de l'Empire et en Occident', *Journal des savants* 14 (Août): 358–67 and (October): 450–65.
Bremmer, J. (2008) 'Iconoclast, Iconoclastic, and Iconoclasm: Notes toward a Genealogy', *CHRC* 88: 1–17.
Brokkaar, W. G. (1995) 'De Brieven van Photius aan Nicephorus'. Unpublished PhD thesis. University of Amsterdam.

Browning, R. (1965) 'Notes on the "Scriptor incertus de Leone Armenio"', *Byzantion* 35/2: 389–411.
  (1978) 'Literacy in the Byzantine world', *BMGS* 4: 39–54.
Brubaker, L. (1985) 'Politics, Patronage, and Art in Ninth-Century Byzantium: The "Homilies" of Gregory of Nazianzus in Paris (B. N. gr. 510)', *DOP* 39: 1–13.
  (1989a) 'Byzantine Art in the Ninth Century: Theory, Practice, and Culture', *BMGS* 13: 23–93.
  (1989b) 'Perception and Conception: Art, Theory and Culture in Ninth-Century Byzantium', *Word and Image* 5/1: 19–32.
  (1994) 'To Legitimize an Emperor: Constantine and Visual Authority in the 8th and 9th centuries', in *New Constantines: the Rhythm of Imperial Renewal in Byzantium, 4th–13th centuries*, ed. P. Magdalino. Aldershot: 139–58.
  (1999a) *Vision and Meaning in Ninth-Century Byzantium*. Cambridge.
  (1999b) 'The Chalke Gate, the Construction of the Past, and the Trier Ivory', *BMGS* 23: 258–85.
  (2000) 'Greek Manuscript Decoration in the Ninth Century: Rethinking Centre and Periphery', in *I manoscritti greci tra riflessione e dibattito, Atti del V Colloquio internazionale di paleografia greca*, ed. G. Prato. Florence. Vol. 2: 513–33.
  (2003) 'Text and Picture in Manuscripts: What's Rhetoric Got to Do with it?', in *Rhetoric in Byzantium*, ed. E. Jeffreys. Aldershot: 255–72.
  (2012) *Inventing Byzantine Iconoclasm*. London.
Brubaker, L., and Haldon, J. (2001) *Byzantium in the Iconoclast Era, c. 680–850: The Sources, an Annotated Survey*. Cambridge.
  (2011) *Byzantium in the Iconoclast Era, c. 680–850. A History*, Cambridge.
Bryer, A. A., and Herrin, J. (1977) *Iconoclasm: Papers Given at the Ninth Spring Symposium of Byzantine Studies*. Birmingham.
Bunijatov, Z. M. (1959) 'Babek i Vizantija', *Doklady Akademii Nauk Azerbajdžanskoj SSR* 15: 613–16.
Bury, J. B. (1890) 'The Relationship of the Patriarch Photius to the Empress Theodora', *EHR* 5: 255–58.
  (1907) 'The Ceremonial Book of Constantine Porphyrogenetos', *EHR* 22: 209–27 and 417–39.
  (1909) 'Mutasim's March through Cappadocia in A.D. 838', *JHS* 29: 120–29.
  (1911) *The Imperial Administrative System in the Ninth Century with a Revised Text of the Kletorologion of Philotheos*. Oxford (repr. Cambridge. 2015).
  (1912) *A History of the Late Roman Empire from the Fall of Eirene to the Accession of Basil I (802–867)*. London.
Calahorra Bartolomé, A. (2018) 'Lázaro de Constantinopla: Monje y pintor durante el periodo iconoclasta', *Estudios Bizantinos* 6: 1–36.
Calisi, A. (2013) *Teodoro lo Studita, Antirrheticus Adversus Iconomachos: Confutazioni contro gli avversari delle sante icone*. Bari.
Cameron, A. (1992) 'The Language of Images: The Rise of Icons and Christian Representation', in *The Church and the Arts (Studies in Church History 28)*, ed. D. Wood. Oxford: 1–42.

(1994) 'Texts As weapons: Polemic in the Byzantine Dark Ages', in *Literacy and Power in the Ancient World*, eds. A. Bowman and G. Woolf. Cambridge: 198–215.

Canart, P. (1970) *Codices Vaticani graeci 1745–1962*. Vaticano.

(1979) 'Le patriarche Méthode de Constantinople copiste à Rome', in *Paleographica, Diplomatica et Archivistica: Studi in onore di Giulio Battelli*. Rome: 343–53.

(1982) 'Cinq manuscrits transférés directement du monastère de Stoudios à celui de Grottaferrata?', in *Bisanzio e l'Italia: Raccolta di Studi in memoria di A. Pertusi*. Milan: 19–28.

(2008a) 'Additions et corrections au Repertorium der Griechischen Kopisten 800–1600', in *Vaticana et Medievalia, Etudes en l'honneur de L. Duval-Arnould*, ed. J. Martin. Florence: 41–63.

(2008b) 'Les palimpsestes en écriture majuscule des fonds grecs de la Bibliothèque Vaticane', in *Libri palinsesti greci: Conservazione, restauro digitale, studio*, ed. S. Lucà. Rome: 71–84.

Canart, P., and Peri, V. (1970) *Sussidi bibliografici per i manoscritti greci della Biblioteca Vaticana*. Vaticano.

Canfora, L. (1998a) 'Le "cercle des lecteurs" autour de Photius: Une source contemporaine', *REB* 56: 269–73.

(1998b) 'Il "reading circle" intorno a Fozio', *Byzantion* 68: 222–23.

et al. (2000), *Fozio: Tra crisi ecclesiale e magistero letterario*. Brescia.

Cappuyns, N. (1934) 'Le Synodicon de l'Église de Rhodes au XIIIe siècle', *EO* 174: 196–217.

Carile, A. (1986) 'L'Iconoclasmo fra Bisanzio e l'Italia', in *Culto delle immagini e crisi iconoclasta*. Palermo: 13–54.

(1998) 'Santi aristocratici e santi imperatori', in *Oriente Cristiano e Santitá. Figure e storie di santi tra Bisanzio e Occidente*, ed. S. Gentile. Carugate: 35–44.

Cataldi Palau, A. (1992 [1994]) 'Manoscritti greci originari dell'Italia meridionale nel fondo "Additional" della "British Library" a Londra', *BBGG* 46: 199–261 (repr. in *Studies in Greek Manuscripts*. Spoleto. 2008 (Testi, Studi, Strumenti 24). Vol. 1: 347–410).

Cesaretti, P. (1988) 'Some Remarks on the *Vita* of the Empress Theophano (*BHG* 1794)', *Svenska kommittén för bysantinska studier*. Bulletin 6: 23–27.

(2005) 'Un leitmotiv narrative tra la vita di santa Theophano (*BHG* 1794) e il *Menologio di Basilio II* (cod. Vat. gr. 1613)', *Nea Rhome* 2: 115–51.

Ceulemans, R., and Van Deun, P. (2017) 'Réflexions sur la littérature anthologique de Constantin V à Constantin VII', *TM* 21/2: 361–88.

Cheynet, J. C. (1998) 'Théophile, Théophobe et les Perses', in Η Βυζαντινή Μικρά Ασία (6os–12os αι.) (= *Byzantine Asia Minor (6th–12th c.)*, ed. S. Lampakes. Athens: 39–50.

(2006) 'Aristocratic Anthroponymy in Byzantium', in *The Byzantine Aristocracy and Its Military Function*, ed. J. C. Cheynet. Aldershot. Ch. III.

Cheynet, J. C., and Flusin, B. (1990) 'Du monastère Ta Kathara à Thessalonique: Théodore Stoudite sur la route de l'exil', *REB* 48: 193–211.

Cholij, R. (2002) *Theodore the Stoudite: The Ordering of Holiness*. Oxford.
Chrestou, P. (1991) "Ἡ μνήμη τοῦ ἱεροῦ Φωτίου", *Kleronomia* 23: 129–54.
 (1992) "Ἡ οἰκογένεια τοῦ ἱεροῦ Φωτίου", *ΕΕΘΣΠΘ* 2: 22–25.
Chris, W., and Paranikas, M. (1871) *Anthologia Graeca carminum christianorum*. Leipzig.
Chryssostalis, A. (2009) 'La reconstitution d'un vaste traité iconophile écrit par Nicéphore de Constantinople (758–828)', *Semitica et Classica* 2: 203–15.
Ciccolella, F. (1998) 'Three Anacreontic Poems Assigned to Photius', *OCP* 64: 305–28.
 (2000) *Cinque poeti bizantini: Anacreontee dal Barberiniano greco 310, testo critico, introduzione, traduzione e note*. Alessandria.
Čičurov, I. S. (1981) 'Feofan ispobednik: Publikator, redaktor, avtor?', *VV* 42: 78–87.
Cicognara, L. (1807) *Vita di S. Lazzaro, monaco e pittore*. Brescia.
Clugnet, L. (1898) 'Les Offices et les dignités ecclésiastiques dans l'église grecque', *ROC* 3: 142–50, 260–64, 452–57; 4 (1899) 116–28.
 (1902) 'Histoire de saint Nicolas soldat et moine', *ROC* 7: 319–30.
Colonna, M. E. (1953) 'Biografia di Giuseppe Innografo', *Annali della Facoltà di Lettere e filosofia della Università di Napoli* 3: 105–12.
Conca, F. (2010) 'Giorgio Monaco, tra ortodossia e cronaca', *RSBN* 47: 119–40.
Congourdeau, M. H. (2009) 'L'enfant immolé: Hyper-réalisme et symbolique sacrificielle à Byzance', in *Pratiques de l'eucharistie in les Églises d'Orient et d'Occident (Antiquité et Moyen Age)*, eds. N. Bériou et al. Paris: 291–307.
Connor, C. L. (2004), *Women of Byzantium*. New Haven-London.
 (2016) *Saints and Spectacle: Byzantine Mosaics in Their Cultural Setting*. Oxford.
Constantelos, D. J. (1968) *Byzantine Philanthropy and Social Welfare*. New Brunswick.
Constantinou, S. (2005) *Female Corporeal Performances: Reading the Body in Byzantine Passions and Lives of Holy Women*. Uppsala.
 (2010) 'A Byzantine Hagiographical Parody: Life of Mary the Younger', *BMGS* 34/2: 160–81.
Cormack, R. (1977a) 'The Arts during the Age of Iconoclasm', in *Iconoclasm: Papers Given at the Ninth Spring Symposium of Byzantine Studies*, eds. A. A. Bryer and J. Herrin. Birmingham: 35–44.
 (1977b) 'Painting after Iconoclasm', in *Iconoclasm: Papers Given at the Ninth Spring Symposium of Byzantine Studies*, eds. A. A. Bryer and J. Herrin. Birmingham: 147–63 (repr. in *The Byzantine Eye: Studies in Art and Patronage*. London. 1989. Ch. IV).
 (1981) 'Interpreting the Mosaics of S. Sophia at Istanbul', *Art History* 4: 131–149 (repr. in *The Byzantine Eye: Studies in Art and Patronage*. London. 1989. Ch. VIII).
 (1986) 'Patronage and New Programs of Byzantine Iconography', in *The 17th International Byzantine Congress: Major Papers*. Washington: 609–38 (repr. in *The Byzantine Eye: Studies in Art and Patronage*. London. 1989. Ch. X).

Cormack, R., and Hawkins, E. J. W. (1977) 'The Mosaics of St Sophia at Istanbul: The Rooms above the Southwest Vestibule and Ramp', *DOP* 31: 175–251.
Corrigan, K. (1992) *Visual Polemics in the Ninth-Century Byzantine Psalters*. Cambridge.
Cortassa, G. (2003) 'Lettere dell'uomo di lettere', *Humanitas* 58/1: 123–39.
Costa-Louillet, G. da (1940/1941) 'Y eut-il des invasions russes dans l'Empire Byzantin avant 860?', *Byzantion* 15: 231–48.
  (1954/1955) 'Saints de Constantinople aux VIIIe, IXe et Xe siècles', *Byzantion* 24: 179–263 and 453–511.
  (1957) 'Saints de Constantinople aux VIIIe, IXe et Xe siècles (*suite*)', *Byzantion* 25–27: 783–852.
  (1959/1960) 'Saints de Sicile et d'Italie méridionale aux VIIIe, IXe et Xe siècles', *Byzantion* 29/30: 89–173.
  (1961) 'Saints de Grèce aux VIIIe, IXe et Xe Siècles', *Byzantion* 31: 309–69.
Coxe, H. O. (1853/1854) *Catalogi codicum manuscriptorum Bibliothecae Bodleianae I, Recensionem Codicum Graecorum continens*. Oxford (repr. with handwritten corrections by R. Barbour and N. Wilson as *Bodleian Library Quarto Catalogues I: Greek Manuscripts*. Oxford. 1969).
Cracco Ruggini, L. (1980) 'La Sicilia tra Roma e Bisanzio', in *Storia della Sicilia*. Naples. Vol. III: 1–96.
Crimi, C. (1990a) *Michele Sincello: Per la restaurazione delle venerande e sacre immagini*. Rome.
  (1990b) 'Aspetti dell'imitatio nell'anacreontea di Michele Sincello di Gerusalemme', in *Metodologie della ricerca sulla Tarda Antichità: Atti del I Convegno dell'Associazione di Studi Tardoantichi*, ed. A. Garzya. Naples: 317–27.
  (1998) 'L'"Epitafio di Atanasio di Metone" (*BHG* 196) di Pietro vescovo d'Argo: Note al testo e all'interpretazione', in *ALPHEIOS: Rapporti storici e letterari fra tra Sicilia e Grecia (IX–XIX sec.)*, ed. G. Spadaro. Catania: 63–93.
  (2006) 'Sant'Agata a Bisanzio nel IX secolo: Rileggendo Metodio patriarca di Costantinopoli', in *Euplo e Lucia 304–2004: Agiografia e tradizioni cultuali in Sicilia*, eds. T. Sardella and G. Zito. Florence-Milan: 143–63.
  (2017) 'Note al testo di Metodio, patriarca di Costantinopoli "Encomio di S. Agata" (*BHG* 38)', *Nea Rhome* 14: 37–50.
Criscuolo, U. (1994a) 'Sugli epigrammi iconoclastici di Giovanni (il Grammatico?)', in *Syndesmos: Studi in onore di Rosario Anastasi*, eds. A. Carile et al. Catania. Vol. II: 143–51.
  (1994b) 'Iconoclasmo e letteratura', in *Il Convegno Niceno II (787) e il culto delle immagini*, ed. S. Leanza. Messina: 191–219.
Crostini, B. (2013) 'Book and Image in Byzantine Christianity', in *Aesthetics and Theurgy in Byzantium*, eds. S. Mariev and W. M. Stock. Berlin: 105–26.
Cunningham, I. C. (1982) *Greek Manuscripts in Scotland*. Edinburgh.
Cunningham, M. B. (1991) *The Life of Michael the Synkellos*. Belfast.

(2011) 'Messages in Context: The Reading of Sermons in Byzantine Churches and Monasteries', in *Images of the Byzantine World: Visions, Messages and Meanings: Studies Presented to L. Brubaker*, ed. A. Lymberopoulou. Aldershot: 83–98.

(2015) 'Mary As Intercessor in Constantinople during the Iconoclast Period: The Textual Evidence', in *Presbeia Theotokou: The Intercessory Role of Mary across Times and Places in Byzantium, 4th–9th c.*, eds. L. M. Peltomaa et al. Vienna: 139–52.

(2019) 'The *Life of the Theotokos* by Epiphanios of Kallistratos: A Monastic Approach to an Apocryphal Story', in *The Reception of the Virgin in Byzantium: Marian Narratives in Texts and Images*, eds. T. Arentzen and M. B. Cunningham. Cambridge: 309–23.

Curta, F. (2011) 'Sklaviniai and Ethnic Adjectives: A Clarification', *Byzantion Nea Hellas* 30: 85–98.

Cutler, A. (1977) 'The Byzantine Psalter: Before and after Iconoclasm', in *Iconoclasm: Papers Given at the Ninth Spring Symposium of Byzantine Studies*, eds. A. A. Bryer and J. Herrin. Birmingham: 93–102.

D'Aiuto, F. (1997) 'Note al testo dell'anacreontea di Michele Sincello per la restaurazione del culto delle icone', *RSBN* 34: 37–45.

(2012) 'La questione delle due redazioni del "Menologio Imperiale", con nuove osservazioni sulle sue fonti agiografiche', *RSBN* 49: 275–361.

D'Agostino, M. (1997) *La minuscola 'tipo Anastasio' dalla scrittura alla decorazione*. Bari.

Dagron, G. (1968) 'La Vie ancienne de saint Marcel Acémète', *AnBoll* 86: 271–321.

(1974) *Naissance d'une capitale: Constantinople et ses institutions de 300 à 451*. Paris.

(1981) 'Quand la terre tremble ...', *TM* 8: 87–103 (repr. in *La romanité chrétienne en Orient*. London. 1984).

(1985) 'Rêver de Dieu et parler de soi', in *I sogni nel Medioevo*, ed. T. Gregory. Rome: 37–55.

(1991a) 'Holy Images and Likeness', *DOP* 45: 23–33.

(1991b) 'Le traité de Grégoire de Nicée sur le baptême des Juifs', *TM* 11: 313–57.

(1993) 'Le christianisme byzantin du VIIe au milieu du XIe siècle', in *Histoire du christianisme des origines à nos jours. Tome 4: Évêques, moines et empereurs (610–1054)*, eds. G. Dagron et al. Paris: 9–371.

(1994) 'Théophanô, les Saints-Apôtres et l'église de Tous-les-Saints', *Symmeikta* 9: 201–19.

(1996) *Empereur et prêtre: Étude sur le "césaropapisme" byzantin*. Paris.

Dal Santo, M. (2012) *Debating the Saints' Cult in the Age of Gregory the Great*. Oxford.

Darrouzès, J. (1966) *Documents inédits d'ecclésiologie byzantine*. Paris.

(1970) *Recherches sur les ὀφφίκια de l'Église byzantine*. Paris.

(1984) 'Le traité des transferts: Édition critique et commentaire', *REB* 42: 147–214.

(1987) 'Le patriarche Méthode contre les Iconoclastes et les Stoudites', *REB* 45: 15–57.
Darrouzès, J., and Westerink, L. G. (1978) *Théodore Daphnopatès: Correspondance*. Paris.
Davis, R. (1995) *The Lives of the Ninth-Century Popes (Liber Pontificalis)*. Liverpool.
De Gregorio, G. (2010) 'Epigrammi e documenti: Poesia come fonte per la storia di chiese e monasteri bizantini', in *Sylloge diplomatico-palaeographica I: Studien zur byzantinischen Diplomatik und Paläographie*, eds. C. Gastgeber and O. Kresten. Vienna: 14–28.
De Meester, P. (1949) 'L'archimandritat dans les Eglises de rite byzantin', in *Miscellanea liturgica in honorem L. Cuniberti Mohlberg*. Rome. Vol. II: 115–37.
Der Nersessian, S. (1962) 'The Illustration of the Homilies of Gregory of Nazianzus: Paris. Gr. 510. A Study of the Connections between Text and Images', *DOP* 16: 195–228.
Di Maria, G. (2004) 'Encomio di San Bartolomeo Apostolo', in *Tre laudationes bizantine in onore di San Bartolomeo apostolo*, ed. V. Giustolisi. Palermo: 47–64.
Diehl, C. (1906) 'Une bourgeoise de Byzance au VIIIe siècle', in *Figures Byzantines*. Paris. Vol. I: 111–32.
  (1908) 'Théophano', in *Figures Byzantines*. Paris. Vol. II: 217–44.
  (1931) 'La légende de l'empereur Théophile', *Seminarium Kondakovianum* 4: 33–37.
Declerck, J. (2017) 'Le Parisinus gr. 923: Un manuscrit destiné à l'empereur Basile Ier (867–886)', *Byzantion* 87: 181–206.
Delehaye, H. (1897) 'Les ménologes grecs', *AnBoll* 16: 311–29 (repr. in *Synaxaires byzantines, ménologes, typica*. London. 1977. Ch. III).
  (1906) 'Notes sur un manuscrit grec du Musée Britannique', *AnBoll* 25: 495–99.
  (1910) 'L'invention des reliques de Saint Ménas à Constantinople', *AnBoll* 29: 117–50.
  (1912) 'Saints de Thrace et de Mésie', *AnBoll* 31: 161–300.
  (1926) 'Catalogus codicum hagiographicorum graecorum bibliothecae scholae theologicae in Chalce insula', *AnBoll* 44: 5–63.
  (1927) *Sanctus: Essai sur le culte des saints in l'Antiquité*. Brussels.
  (1934) 'Stoudion – Stoudios', *AnBoll* 52: 64–6.
  (1966) *Les Passions des martyrs et les genres littéraires*, 2nd ed. Brussels.
Deliernaux, N. (2014) 'The Literary Portrait of Byzantine Female Saints', in *Ashgate Research Companion to Byzantine Hagiography. Volume II: Genres and Contexts*, ed. S. Efthymiadis. Farnham: 363–86.
Delouis, O. (2005) 'Saint-Jean-Baptiste de Stoudios à Constantinople: La contribution d'un monastère à l'histoire de l'Empire byzantin (v. 454–1204)'. Unpublished PhD thesis. Universitè Paris I-Sorbonne.
  (2008a) 'Le *Testament* de Théodore Stoudite est-il de Théodore?', *REB* 66: 173–90.

(2008b) 'Église et serment à Byzance: norme et pratique', in *Oralité et lien social au Moyen Âge (Occident, Byzance, Islam): Parole donnée, foi jurée, serment*, eds. M. F. Auzépy and G. Saint-Guillain. Paris: 211–46.

(2011) 'Ecriture et réécriture au monastère de Stoudios à Constantinople (IXe–Xe s.): Quelques remarques', in *Remanier, métaphraser: Fonctions et techniques de la réécriture dans le monde byzantin*, eds. S. Marjanović-Dušanic and B. Flusin. Belgrade: 101–10.

(2014) 'La Vie métrique de Théodore Stoudite par Stéphane Mélès (*BHG* 1755m)', *AnBoll* 132: 21–54.

(2016) 'La profession de foi pour l'ordination des évêques (avec un formulaire inédit du patriarche Photius)', in *Le saint, le moine et le paysan: Mélanges d'histoire byzantine offerts à M. Kaplan*, eds. O. Delouis, S. Métivier and P. Pagès. Paris: 119–38.

Delouis, O., and Peters-Custot, A. (2019) 'Le voyage de Rome dans la fabrique des saints moines byzantins', in *Les mobilités monastiques en Orient et en Occident, de l'Antiquité tardive au Moyen Âge (IVe–XVe siècles)*, eds. O. Delouis, M. Mossakowska-Gaubert and A. Peters-Custot. Rome: 311–36.

Dell'Acqua, F. and Gantner, C. (2019) 'Resenting Iconoclasm: Its Early Reception in Italy through an Inscription from Corteolona', *Medieval Worlds* 9/1: 160–86.

Demoen, K. (1998) 'School Rhetoric in the Byzantine "Dark Ages": The Anti-Iconoclastic Treatises of Theodore the Studite', in *Retórica, política e ideología: Desde la antigüedad hasta nuestros días*, ed. A. López Eire. Salamanca. Vol. I: 123–29.

(2001) 'La poésie de Théodore de Stoudite: Renouveau de l'épigramme grecque profane?', in *La poesia tardoantica e medievale*, ed. M. Salvadore. Alessandria: 149–69.

(2019) 'Monasticism and Iconolatry: Theodore Stoudites', in *A Companion to Byzantine Poetry*, eds. W. Hörandner, A. Rhoby and N. Zagklas. Leiden: 166–90.

Déroche, V. (1993) 'L'autorité des moines à Byzance du VIIIe au Xe siècle', *Revue Bénédictine* 103: 241–54 (= *Le monachisme à Byzance et en Occident du VIIIe au Xe siècle: Aspects internes et relations avec la société*, eds. A. Dierkens et al. Maredsous).

(2011) 'Les réécritures de la *Vie de Jean l'Aumônier* de Léontios de Néapolis (*BHG* 886)', in *Remanier, métaphraser: Fonctions et techniques de la réécriture dans le monde byzantin*, eds. S. Marjanović-Dušanic and B. Flusin. Belgrade: 61–69.

Déroche V., and Lesieur, B. (2010) 'Notes d'hagiographie byzantine: Daniel le Stylite – Marcel l'Acémète – Hypatios de Rufinianes – Auxentios de Bithynie', *AnBoll* 128/2: 283–95.

Detorakes, T. E. (1970) Οι άγιοι της πρώτης βυζαντινής περιόδου της Κρήτης και η σχετική προς αυτούς φιλολογία. Athens.

Detorakes, Th. (1990) 'Η χρονολόγηση του αυτοκρατορικού Μηνολογίου του B. Latysev', *BZ* 83/1: 46–50.

Detoraki, M. (2011) 'Un parent pauvre de la réécriture hagiographique: l'abrégé', in *Remanier, métaphraser: Fonctions et techniques de la réécriture dans le monde byzantin*, eds. S. Marjanović-Dušanic and B. Flusin. Belgrade: 71–83.

(2015) '*Chronicon animae utile*: La Chronique de Georges le Moine et les récits édifiants', in *Myriobiblos: Essays on Byzantine Literature and Culture*, eds. Th. Antonopoulou et al. Berlin: 103–30.

Deubner, L. (1907) *Kosmas und Damian*. Leipzig.

Devreese, R. (1950) 'Une lettre de S. Theodore Studite relative au synode moechien (809)', *AnBoll* 68: 44–57.

Dick, I. (1961) 'La Passion arabe de S. Antoine Ruwah, néo-martyr de Damas (25 déc. 799)', *Le Muséon* 74: 109–33.

Diller-Sellschopp, I. (1982) 'Der Weg des Aschenputtelmärchens vom Orient zu den Brüdern Grimm', *Folia neohellenica* 4: 7–24.

Dobroklonskij, A. P. (1913) *Prepodobnie Feodor', Ispovednik' i Igumen' Studijskij*. Odessa. 2 vols.

Dobrynina, E. N. (2010) 'New Findings on the *Khludov Psalter* Revealed during Restoration', *Nea Rhome* 7: 57–72 (= Ἔξεμπλον. *Studi in onore di I. Hutter*. Vol. II).

Dölger, F. (1953) 'Zur Bedeutung von φιλόσοφος und φιλοσοφία in Byzantinischer Zeit', in *Byzanz und die europäische Staatenwelt*. Munich: 197–208.

Doens I., and Hannick, Ch. (1973) 'Das Periorismos-Dekret des Patriarchen Methodios I gegen die Studiten Naukratios und Athanasios', *JÖB* 22: 93–102.

Donnet, D. (1982) *Le traité de la construction de la phrase de Michel le Syncelle de Jérusalem*. Brussels-Rome.

Dorfmann-Lazarev, I. (2004) *Arméniens et Byzantins à l'époque de Photius: Deux débats théologiques après le triomphe de l'orthodoxie*. Leuven (SCSO 609).

(2016) 'The Armenian-Syrian-Byzantine Council of Širakawan, 862', in *Christ in Armenian Tradition: Doctrine, Apocrypha, Art (Sixth–Tenth Centuries)*. Leuven: 293–313.

Downey, G. (1955) 'Earthquakes at Constantinople and Vicinity', *Speculum* 30: 593–600.

(1955/1956) 'The Church of All Saints (Church of St Theophano) Near the Church of the Holy Apostles at Constantinople', *DOP* 9–10: 301–5.

Dufrenne, S. (1965) 'Une illustration "historique", inconnue, du Psautier du Mont-Athos, *Pantocrator* 61', *CahArch* 15: 83–95.

Dujcev, I. (1957) 'Vuprosut za vizantino-slavjanskite otnosenija i vizantijski opiti za suzdavane na slavjanskata azbuka prez purvata polovina na IX vek', *IzvInstBulgIst* 7: 241–67.

(1966) 'A propos de la vie de saint Pierre d'Atroa', *BSl* 27: 92–97 (repr. in *Medioevo bizantino-slavo*. Rome. 1968. Vol. II: 533–39 and 624f).

Dvornik, F. (1926) *La vie de s. Grégoire le Décapolite et les Slaves macédoniens au IXe siècle*. Paris.

(1933) *Les légendes de Constantin et de Méthode vues de Byzance*. Prague.

(1935) 'Lettre a M. H. Grégoire a propos de Michel III', *Byzantion* 10: 5–9.
(1948) *The Photian Schism: History and Legend*. Cambridge (repr. 1970).
(1953) 'Patriarch Photius and Iconoclasm', *DOP* 7: 67–98.
(1958) 'The Patriarch Photius in the Light of Recent Research', in *Berichte zum XI. Intern. Byzantinistenkongress*. Munich. Vol. III/2: 1–56 (repr. in *Photian and Byzantine Ecclesiastical Studies*. London. 1974. Ch. VI).
(1964) *Byzance et la primauté romaine*. Paris.
(1966) 'Patriarch Ignatius and Caesar Bardas', *BSl* 27: 7–22.
(1973a) 'Photius, Nicholas I and Hadrian II', *BSl* 34: 33–50 (repr. in *Photian and Byzantine Ecclesiastical Studies*. London. 1974. Ch. IX).
(1973b) 'Photius' Career in Teaching and Diplomacy', *BSl* 34: 211–18 (repr. in *Photian and Byzantine Ecclesiastical Studies*. London. 1974. Ch. X).
Ehrhard, A. (1929/1930) 'Ein neues vormetaphrastisches Januarmenologium', *BZ* 30: 305–16.
(1936–1939) *Überlieferung und Bestand der hagiographischen und homiletischen Literatur der griechischen Kirche, von den Anfängen bis zum Ende des 16. Jahrhunderts*. Leipzig. 3 vols. (TU 50–52).
Eleopoulos, N. X. (1967) *Ἡ βιβλιοθήκη καὶ τὸ βιβλιογραφικὸν ἐργαστήριον τῆς μονῆς τῶν Στουδίου*. Athens.
Eleuteri, P., and Rigo, A. (1993) *Eretici, dissidenti, musulmani ed ebrei a Bisanzio: Una raccolta eresiologica del XII secolo*. Venice.
Ephrem Archimandrite. (2006) 'Byzantine Hymns of Hate', in *Byzantine Orthodoxies*, eds. A. Louth and A. Casiday. Aldershot: 151–64.
Efthymiadis, S. (1991a) 'On the Hagiographical Work of Ignatius the Deacon', *JÖB* 41: 73–83.
(1991b) 'John of Sardis and the Metaphrasis of the *Passio* of St Nikephoros the Martyr (*BHG* 1334)', *RSBN* 28: 23–44.
(1993a) 'The Life of St Stephen the Younger (*BHG* 1666): An Additional Debt', *Hell* 43: 206–9.
(1993b) 'Le panégyrique de S. Théophane le Confesseur par S. Théodore Stoudite (*BHG* 1792b): Edition critique du texte intégral', *AnBoll* 111: 259–90.
(1995) 'Notes on the Correspondence of Theodore the Studite', *REB* 53: 141–63.
(1996) 'The Byzantine Hagiographer and His Audience in the Ninth and Tenth Centuries', in *Metaphrasis: Redactions and Audiences in Middle Byzantine Hagiography*, ed. C. Högel. Oslo: 59–80 (repr. in *Hagiography in Byzantium: Literature, Social History and Cult*. Aldershot. 2012. Ch. VIII).
(1998) 'Hagiographica varia', *JÖB* 48: 41–48.
(2002) 'The Biography of Ignatios the Deacon: A Reassessment of the Evidence', *BMGS* 26: 276–83.
(2006) 'Le miracle et les saints durant et après le second iconoclasme', in *Monastères, images, pouvoirs et société à Byzance*, ed. M. Kaplan. Paris: 153–82.
(2006/2007) 'Le monastère de la Source à Constantinople et ses deux recueils de miracles: Entre hagiographie et patriographie', *REB* 64–65: 283–309.

Efthymiadis, S. ed. (2011a) *Ashgate Research Companion to Byzantine Hagiography. Volume I: Periods and Places*. Ashgate Research Companions. Aldershot.
　(2011b) 'Medieval Thessalonike and the Miracles of Its Saints: Big and Small Demands Made on Exclusive Rights (Ninth–Twelfth Centuries)', in *Hagiography in Byzantium: Literature, Social History and Cult*. Aldershot: 1–16. Ch. XI.
Efthymiadis, S. ed. (2014) *Ashgate Research Companion to Byzantine Hagiography. Volume II: Genres and Contexts*. Farnham.
　(2015) 'Une hagiographie classicisante et son auteur: La Vie longue de sainte Thomaïs de Lesbos (*BHG* 2455)', in *Pour une poétique de Byzance: Hommage à Vassilis Katsaros*, eds. S. Efthymiadis et al. Paris: 113–32.
　(2016), 'Ὁ βίος του αγίου Φιλαρέτου του Ελεήμονος και η επιστροφή στη βιβλική απλότητα', *Δελτίο βιβλικών μελετών* 31/B: 16–25.
　(2017) 'De Taraise à Méthode: L'apport des premières grandes figures reconsidéré', *TM* 21/2: 165–86.
Efthymiadis, S., and Featherstone, J. M. (2007) 'Establishing a Holy Lineage: Theodore the Stoudite's Funerary Catechism for His Mother (*BHG* 2422)', in *Theatron: Rhetorische Kultur in Spätantike und Mittelalter*, ed. M. Grünbart. Berlin: 13–51.
Efthymiadis, S., and Kalogeras, N. (2014) 'Audience, Language and Patronage in Byzantine Hagiography', in *Ashgate Research Companion to Byzantine Hagiography. Volume II: Genres and Contexts*, ed. S. Efthymiadis. Farnham: 247–84.
Émereau, C. (1922) 'Hymnographi Byzantini – Quorum nomina in litteras digessit notulisque adornavit (continuatur)', *ÉO* 21/127: 258–79; *ÉO* 22/129 (1923): 11–25; *ÉO* 22/132 (1923): 419–39; *ÉO* 23/134 (1924): 195–200; *ÉO* 23/136 (1924): 407–14; *ÉO* 24/138 (1925): 163–79; *ÉO* 25/142 (1926): 177–84.
Ermerins, F. Z. (1840) *Anecdota Medica Graeca e Codicibus MSS: Exprompsit*. Leiden (repr. Amsterdam. 1963).
Euangelides, T. E. (1895) *Οἱ βίοι τῶν ἁγίων*. Athens.
Eustratiadès, S. (1918) *Κατάλογος τῶν ἐν τῇ μονῇ Βλατέων (Τσάους-μοναστήρι) ἀποκειμένων κωδίκων*. Thessaloniki.
　(1936) 'Θεοφάνης ὁ Γραπτός', *Nea Sion* 31: 339–44, 403–16, 467–78, 525–40, 666–73; 32 (1937): 60–67, 81–96, 187–95, 252–59.
　(1941/1952) 'Ἰωσὴφ ὁ Στουδίτης ἀρχιεπίσκοπος Θεσσαλονίκης', *Makedonika* 2: 25–88.
Evangelatou, M. (2009) 'Liturgy and the Illustration of the Ninth-Century Marginal Psalters', *DOP* 63: 59–116.
Even-Zohar, I. (1978) *Papers in Historical Poetics* (= Papers on Poetics and Semiotics 8). Tel-Aviv.
　(1990) *Polysistem Studies* (= *Poetics Today* 11).
　(2005) *Papers in Culture Research*. Tel-Aviv.
Fanar, E. M. (2006) 'Visiting Hades: A Transformation of the Ancient God in the Ninth-Century Byzantine Psalters', *BZ* 99/1: 93–108.

Featherstone, J. M. (1980) 'The Praise of Theodore Graptos by Theophanes of Caesarea', *AnBoll* 98: 93–150.
  (1981) 'A Note on the Dream of Bardas Caesar in the *Life of Ignatius* and the Archangel in the Mosaic over the Imperial Doors of St Sophia', *BZ* 74: 42–43.
  (2010) 'All Saints and the Holy Apostles: *De ceremoniis, 6–7*', *Nea Rhome* 7: 235–48.
  (2015) 'Icon As Cultural Identity', in *L'aniconisme dans l'art religieux byzantine*, eds. M. Campagnolo et al. Geneva: 105–13.
Fedalto, G. (1988) *Hierarchia Ecclesiastica Orientalis: Series episcoporum ecclesiarum christianarum orientalium*. Vol. 1: *Patriarchatus Constantinopolitanus*. Vol. 2: *Patriarchatus Alexandrinus, Antiochenus, Hierosolymitanus*. Padua.
Feld, K. (2005) *Barbarische Bürger: Die Isaurier und das Römische Reich*. Berlin-New York.
Festugière, A. J. (1962) *Les moines d'Orient*. Paris.
  (1971) *Ste Thècle, Saints Côme et Damien, Saints Cyr et Jean (Extraits), Saint Georges: Collections, grecques de miracles*. Paris.
Flusin, B. (1985) 'Un fragment inédit de la vie d'Euthyme le patriarche?', *TM* 9: 119–31; *TM* 10 (1987): 233–60.
  (1993) 'L'hagiographie monastique à Byzance au IXe et au Xe siècle: Modèles anciens et tendances contemporaines', *Revue Bénédictine* 103: 31–50 (= *Le monachisme à Byzance et en Occident du VIIIe au Xe siècle: Aspects internes et relations avec la société*, eds. A. Dierkens et al. Maredsous).
  (2000) 'Construire une nouvelle Jérusalem: Constantinople et les reliques', in *L'Orient dans l'histoire religieuse de l'Europe: L'invention des origines*, eds. M. Amir Moezzi and J. Scheid. Turnhout: 51–70.
  (2001) 'L'empereur hagiographe', in *L'empereur hagiographe: Culte des saints et monarchie byzantine et post-byzantine*, ed. P. Guran. Bucarest: 29–54.
  (2010) 'Le triomphe des images et la nouvelle définition de l'Orthodoxie: À propos d'un chapitre du *De cerimoniis* (I. 37)', in *Orthodoxy and Heresy in Byzantium: The Definition and the Notion of Orthodoxy and Some Other Studies on the Heresies and the Non-Christian Religions*, eds. A. Rigo and P. Ermilov. Rome: 3–20.
  (2011) 'Vers la Métaphrase', in *Remanier, métaphraser: Fonctions et techniques de la réécriture dans le monde byzantin*, eds. S. Marjanović-Dušanic and B. Flusin. Belgrade: 85–99.
  (2012) 'Récit de sainteté, famille et société: Évelyne Patlagean et l'hagiographie', in *Réseaux familiaux à la fin de l'Antiquité et au Moyen Âge: In memoriam A. Laiou et E. Patlagean*, ed. B. Caseau. Paris: 113–24.
  (2017) 'Aréthas de Césarée et la transmission du savoir', *TM* 21/2: 309–24.
Follieri, E. (1960–1966) *Initia hymnorum ecclesiae graecae*. Vaticano. Vols. I–V, 2 (StT 211–15).
  (1964) 'Problemi di innografia bizantina', in *Actes du XIIe Congrès International d'Études Byzantines 1961*. Belgrade. Vol. II: 311–25.

(1969) *Codices graeci Bibliothecae Vaticanae selecti*. Vaticano.
(1975) 'Santa Agrippina nella innografia en ella agiografia greca', *Byzantino-Sicula* 2: 231–50.
(1977) 'La minuscola libraria dei secoli IX e X', in *La paléographie grecque et byzantine*, eds. J. Glénisson, J. Bompaire and J. Irigoin. Paris: 139–65.
Follieri, E., and Dujcev, I. (1963) 'Un'acolutia inedita per i martiri di Bulgaria dell'anno 813', *Byzantion* 33: 71–106.
Fonkitch, B. L. (1980/1982) 'Scriptoria bizantini: Risultati e prospettive della ricerca', *RSBN* 17–19: 73–118.
(2000) 'Aux origines de la minuscule stoudite (les fragments muscovite et parisien de l'Oeuvre de Paul d'Égine)', in *I manoscritti greci tra riflessione e dibattito, Atti del V Colloquio internazionale di paleografia greca*, ed. G. Prato. Florence. Vol. 1: 169–86.
(2010) 'Sulla datazione dei codici greci del secolo IX', in *The Legacy of Bernard de Montfaucon: Three Hunderd Years of Studies on Greek Handwriting*, eds. A. Bravo et al. Turnhout: 37–43.
Franchi de' Cavalieri, P. (1920) *Note agiografiche 6*. Rome (StT 33).
et al. (1899) *Catalogus codicum hagiographicorum graecorum Bibliothecae Vaticanae*. Brussels.
(1902) 'Ad catalogum codicum hagiographicorum graecorum bibliothecae vaticanae supplementum', *AnBoll* 21: 5–22.
Frazee, C. (1981) 'Saint Theodore of Studios and Ninth-Century Monasticism in Constantinople', *Studia Monastica* 23/1: 27–58.
Fuentes Alonso, J. (1984) *El divorcio del Constantino VI y la doctrina matrimonial de San Teodoro Estudita*. Pamplona.
Galadza, D. (2010) 'Liturgical Byzantinization in Jerusalem: Al-Biruni's Melkite Calendar in Context', *BBGG* III, 7: 69–85.
(2018) *Liturgy and Byzantinization in Jerusalem*. Oxford.
Gallagher, C. (2007) 'Patriarch Photius and Pope Nicholas I and the Council of 879', *The Jurist* 67: 72–88.
Gallavotti, C. (1987) 'Note su testi e scrittori di codici greci. VII: Il codice Barb. Gr. 310; VIII: Il vetus Index Barberinianus e lo stato attuale del codice; IX: Note di commento all'Index Barberinianus; X: Le due parti dell'Antologia Barberiniana; XI: Le nuove anacreontiche sillabiche; XII: Gli alfabetari per la morte di Leone VI', *RSBN* 24: 29–83.
Gallina, M. (2011) 'La descrizione della *Nea Ekklesia* nella *Vita Basilii* tra propaganda dinastica e retorica letteraria', *Studi Medievali Serie 3* 52: 347–73.
Gardner, A. (1905) *Theodore of Studium, His Life and Times*. London.
Garitte, G. (1943) 'Fragments palimpsestes de l'"Agathange" grec', *Le Muséon* 56: 35–53.
Garland, L. (1999) *Byzantine Empresses: Women and Power in Byzantium AD 527–1204*. London-New York.
Garsoïan, N. (1967) *The Paulician Heresy: A Study of the Origin and Development of Paulicianism in Armenia and the Eastern Provinces of the Byzantine Empire*. The Hague-Paris.

Garton, C., and Westerink, L. G. (1979) *Germanos on Predestined Terms of Life*. Buffalo.
Garzya, A. (1981) 'Testi letterari d'uso strumentale', *JÖB* 31/1: 263–71.
Gedeon, M. (1899) 'Στουδικὸν Ἑορτολόγιον', in Βυζαντινόν ἑορτολόγιον. Μνῆμαι τῶν ἀπὸ τοῦ Δ᾽ μέχρι τῶν μέσων τοῦ ΙΕ᾽ αἰῶνος ἑορταζομένων ἁγίων ἐν Κωνσταντινουπόλει, ed. M. Gedeon. Constantinople. Vol. 1: 220–21.
Gemmiti, D. (1993) *Teodoro Studita e la questione moicheiana*. Marigliano.
Genette, G. (1982) *Palimpsestes: La Littérature au second degré*. Paris.
  (1991) *Fiction et diction*. Paris.
Gendle, N. (1981) 'The Role of the Byzantine Saint in the Development of the Icon Cult', in *The Byzantine Saint*, ed. S. Hackel. London: 181–86.
Georgiev, P. (1993) 'Neizpolzuvano svedenie za statuta na slaviniite vuv vizantija v na aloto na IX v.', in *Studia protobulgarica et mediaevalia europensia: V cest na profesor V. Besevliev (In honorem Prof. V. Besevliev)*, ed. V. Gjuzelev. Veliko Tarnovo: 59–62.
Gero, S. (1974/1975) 'John the Grammarian, the Last Iconoclastic Patriarch of Constantinople: The Man and the Legend', *Byzantina* 3/4: 25–35.
  (1975) 'The Eucharistic Doctrine of the Byzantine Iconoclasts and Its Sources', *BZ* 68: 4–22.
  (1977) *Byzantine Iconoclasm during the Reign of Constantine V: With Particular Attention to the Oriental Sources*. Leuven (CSCO 384, Subsidia 52).
  (1978) 'The Legend of Constantine V As Dragon-Slayer', *GRBS* 19: 155–59.
  (1995) 'Jannes and Jambres in the *Vita Stephani Iunioris (BHG* 1666)', *AnBoll* 113: 281–92.
Giakalis, A. (1994) *Images of the Divine: The Theology of Icons at the Seventh Ecumenical Council*. Leiden.
Giannelli, G. (1950) *Codices Vaticani graeci 1485–1683*. Vaticano.
  (1963) 'L'ultimo umanesimo nell'Italia Meridionale', in *SBN* (= *Scripta Minora*) Studi bizantini e neoellenici 10, ed. G. Gianelli. Rome: 307–27.
Giannouli, A. (2014) 'Byzantine Hagiography and Hymnography: An Interrelationship', in *Ashgate Research Companion to Byzantine Hagiography. Volume II: Genres and Contexts*, ed. S. Efthymiadis. Farnham: 285–312.
Gibson, R. (2013) 'Letters into Autobiography: The Generic Mobility of the Ancient Letter Collection', in *Generic Interfaces in Latin Literature: Encounters, Interactions, and Transformations*, eds. Th. D. Papanghelis et al. Berlin: 387–416.
Gill, J. (1968) 'An Unpublished Letter of St Theodore the Studite', *OCP* 34: 62–69.
Gkoutzioukostas, A. (2017) '"Sklavenia" (Σκλαυηνία) Revisited: Previous and Recent Considerations', *Parekbolai* 7: 1–12.
Glynias, J. (2017) 'Prayerful Iconoclasts: Psalm Seals and Elite Formation in the First Iconoclast Era (726–750)', *DOP* 71: 65–94.
Goldfus, H. (2006) 'St Euphemia's Church by the Hippodrome of Constantinople within the Broader Context of Early 7th Century History and Architecture', *Ancient West & East* 5: 178–98.

Gouillard, J. (1960) 'Une oeuvre inédite du patriarche Méthode: La Vie d'Euthyme de Sardes', *BZ* 53: 36–46.
  (1961a) 'Deux figures mal connues du second iconoclasme', *Byzantion* 31: 371–401.
  (1961b) 'Hypatios d'Ephèse ou du Pseudo-Denys à Théodore Studite', *REB* 19: 63–75.
  (1966) 'Fragments inédits d'un antirrétique de Jean le Grammarien', *REB* 24: 171–81 (repr. in *La vie religieuse à Byzance*. London. 1981).
  (1969) 'Un "quartier" d'émigrés palestiniens à Constantinople au IXe siècle?', *RESEE* 7: 73–76.
  (1971) 'Le Photius du Pseudo-Syméon Magistros: Les sous-entendus d'un pamphlet', *RESEE* 9: 397–404.
  (1982) 'La femme de qualité dans les lettres de Théodore Studite', *JÖB* 32/2: 445–52.
  (1987) 'La vie d'Euthyme de Sardes (†831), une oeuvre du patriarche Méthode', *TM* 10: 1–101.
Goullet, M. (2005) *Écriture et réécriture hagiographiques: Essai sur les réécritures de Vies de saints dans l'Occident latin médiéval (VIIIe–XIIIe s.)*. Turnhout.
Gounaridis, P. (2006) 'Constitution d'une généalogie à Byzance', in *Parenté et société dans le monde grec de l'antiquité à l'âge moderne*, eds. A. Bresson et al. Bordeaux: 271–80.
Gounelle, R. (2005) 'Traductions de Textes Hagiographiques et Apocryphes Latins en Grec', *Apocrypha* 16: 35–73.
Grabar, A. (1984) *L'iconoclasme byzantin: Dossier archéologique*, 2nd ed. Paris.
  (1965) 'Quelques notes sur les psautiers illustres byzantin du IXe siècle', *CahArch* 15: 61–82
Gray Birch, W. de (1898) *Catalogue of Seals in the Department of Manuscripts in the British Museum*. London.
Grégoire, H. (1929) 'La vie de saint Blaise d'Amorium', *Byzantion* 5: 391–414.
  (1933) 'Études sur le neuvième siècle', *Byzantion* 8: 515–50.
  (1934) 'Manuel et Théophobe ou la concurrence de deux monastères', *Byzantion* 9: 183–204.
Greenwood, T. (2006a) 'The Discovery of the Relics of St Grigor and the Development of Armenian Tradition in Ninth-Century Byzantium', in *Byzantine Style, Religion and Civilization: In Honour of Sir Steven Runciman*, ed. E. M. Jeffreys. Cambridge: 177–91.
  (2006b) 'Failure of a Mission? Photius and the Armenian Church', *Le Muséon* 119/1–2: 123–68.
Gribomont, A. (2012) 'La question du titre dans la littérature byzantine: Quelques pistes de réflexion autour du terme ὑπόμνημα', *Byzantion* 82: 89–112.
Grierson, P. (1962) 'The Tombs and Obits of the Byzantine Emperors (337–1042)', *DOP* 16: 1–63.
Griffith, S. H. (1982) 'Eutychius of Alexandria on the Emperor Theophilus and Iconoclasm in Byzantium: A Tenth-Century Moment in Christian Apologetics in Arabic', *Byzantion* 52: 154–90.

(1985) 'Theodore Abū Qurrah's Arabic Tract on the Christian Practice of Venerating Images', *JAOS* 105: 50–73.
  (1993) 'Muslims and Church Councils: The Apology of Theodore Abu Qurrah', *Studia Patristica* 25: 270–99.
  (1997) *A Treatise on the Veneration of the Holy Icons by Theodore Abū Qurrah, Bishop of Harrān (c. 755–c. 830 A.D.)*. Leuven.
  (1998) 'What Has Constantinople to Do with Jerusalem? Palestine in the Ninth Century: Byzantine Orthodoxy in the World of Islam', in *Byzantium in the Ninth Century: Dead or Alive?*, ed. L. Brubaker. Aldershot: 181–94.
Grumel, V. (1930) 'Le Filioque au concile photien de 879–880 et le témoignage de Michel d'Anchialos', *EO* 29: 250–64.
  (1934) 'La liquidation de la querelle photienne', *EO* 33: 257–88.
  (1935) 'La politique religieuse du patriarche saint Méthode: Iconoclastes et Stoudites', *EO* 34: 385–401.
  (1938) 'Le décret du synode photien de 879–880 sur le symbole de foi', *EO* 37: 357–72.
  (1939) 'La genèse du schisme photien: La succession d'Ignace', *RSBN* 5: 179–84.
  (1940/1942) 'Le schisme de Grégoire de Syracuse', *EO* 39: 257–67.
  (1945) 'Titulature de métropolites byzantins, I: Les métropolites syncelles', *REB* 3: 92–114.
  (1951) 'Une fable d'Ésope dans Photius: Les trois grappes', *Ann. Inst. de Phil. et d'Hist. Orient. et Slaves* 11: 129–32.
  (1951–1952) 'L'annexion de l'Illyricum oriental, de la Sicile et de la Calabre au Patriarcat de Constantinople', *RechSR* 40: 191–200.
  (1966) 'Quel est l'empereur Constantin le Nouveau commémoré dans le Synaxaire au 3 septembre?', *AnBoll* 84: 254–60.
  (1967) 'La VIe séssion du concile photien de 879–880: À propos de la mémoire liturgique, le 3 septembre, de l'empereur Constantin le nouveau', *AnBoll* 85: 336–37.
Grünbart, M. (2013) 'Das byzantinische Bithynien als Hinterland von Konstantinopel', in *Neue Funde und Forschungen in Bithynien*, eds. P. Winter and K. Zimmermann. Bonn: 111–30.
Grossu, N. (1907) *Prepodobnyĭ Feodor Studit: Ego vremiā, zhizn' i tvoreniia*. Kiev.
Guilland, R. (1926) *Essai sur Nicéphore Grégoras: L'homme et l'oeuvre*. Paris.
  (1970) 'Patrices des règnes de Théophile et de Michel III', *RESEE* 8: 593–610 (repr. in *Titres et fonctions de l'Empire byzantin*. London. 1976. Ch. x).
  (1971) 'Les logothètes: Études sur l'histoire administrative de l'Empire byzantin', *REB* 29: 5–115
Guillou, A. et al., eds. (1983) *Il Mezzogiorno dai Bizantini a Federico II*. Turin.
Gwynn, D. M. (2007) 'From Iconoclasm to Arianism: The Construction of Christian Tradition in the Iconoclast Controversy', *GRBS* 47: 225–51.
Haldon, J. F. (1984) *Byzantine Praetorians: An Administrative, Institutional and Social Survey of the Opsikion and Tagmata, c. 580–900*. Bonn.

(1990) *Byzantium in the Seventh Century: The Transformation of a Culture.* New York.
(1998) 'The Byzantine State in the Ninth Century: An Introduction', in *Byzantium in the Ninth Century: Dead or Alive?*, ed. L. Brubaker. Aldershot: 3–10.
(2001) *The Byzantine Wars: Battles and Campaigns of the Byzantine Era.* Gloucestershire.
(2008) 'The State: Structures and Administration', in *The Oxford Handbook of Byzantine Studies*, eds. E. Jeffreys et al. Oxford: 539–54.
(2014) 'Dark-Age Literature', in *Byzantine Culture*, ed. D. Sakel. Ankara: 71–83.
(2017) 'The Blockade of Constantinople in 813', in *Byzantion'dan Constantinopolis'e İstanbul Kuşatmaları*, eds. M. Arslan and T. Kaçar. Istanbul: 263–79.
Halkin, F. (1944) 'Saint Antoine le Jeune et Pétronas le vainqueur des Arabes en 863 (d'après un text inédit)', *AnBoll* 62: 210–25 (repr. in *Saints moines d'Orient*. London. 1973. Ch. VIII).
(1948) 'Le Synaxaire grec de Christ Church à Oxford', *AnBoll* 66: 59–90.
(1954a) 'Trois dates historiques précisées grâce au Synaxaire', *Byzantion* 24: 7–17.
(1954b) 'Un Ménologe de Patmos (ms. 254) et ses légendes inédites', *AnBoll* 72: 15–34.
(1955) 'La passion de Sainte Théoctiste', *AnBoll* 73: 55–65 (repr. in *Martyrs Grecs IIe–VIIIe s.* London. 1974. Ch. II).
(1956) 'Une passion grecque abrégée de Sainte Lucie', *Classica et Mediaevalia* 17 (= *Mélanges C. Hoeg*): 71–74.
(1957) 'Un nouveau ménologe grec de janvier dans un manuscrit de Glasgow', *AnBoll* 75: 66–71.
(1958) 'Études patristiques et byzantines: Coup d'oeil sur des publications récentes', *AnBoll* 76: 224–44.
(1959) 'Y a-t-il trois Saints Georges évêques de Mytilène et "Confesseurs" sous les Iconoclastes?', *AnBoll* 77: 464–69.
(1960) 'La Vie de Saint Nicéphore, fondateur de Médikion en Bithynie (d. 813)', *AnBoll* 78: 396–430.
(1965) *Euphémie de Chalcédoine: Légendes byzantines.* Brussels.
(1967) 'L'Hagiographie byzantine au service de l'Histoire', in *Proceedings of the XIIIth International Congress of Byzantine Studies*, eds. J. M. Hussey et al. London: 345–54.
(1968) *Manuscrits grecs de Paris: Inventaire hagiographique.* Brussels.
(1969) *Auctarium Bibliothecae Hagiographicae Graecae.* Brussels.
(1970) 'S. Nicéphore de Médikion d'après un synaxaire du mont Sinai', *AnBoll* 88: 13–16.
(1986) *Hagiologie byzantine.* Brussels.
(1988) 'Deux impératrices de Byzance, I: La Vie de l'impératrice sainte Irène et le second concile de Nicée en 787', *AnBoll* 106: 5–27.

Hardt, I. (1810) *Catalogus codicum manuscriptorum Graecorum Bibliothecae Regiae Bavaricae*. Munich. Vol. 4: cod. CCCXLVIII–CCCCLXXII.
Hatlie, P. (1993) 'Abbot Theodore and the Stoudites: A Case Study in Monastic Social Groupings and Religious Conflict in Constantinople (787–826)'. Unpublished PhD thesis. Fordham University.
   (1995) 'Theodore of Stoudios, Pope Leo III and the Ioseph Affair (808–812): New Light on an Obscure Negotiation', *OCP* 61/2: 407–23.
   (1996a) 'Women of Discipline during the Second Iconoclast Age', *BZ* 89/1: 37–44.
   (1996b) 'The Politics of Salvation: Theodore of Stoudios on Martyrdom (*Martyrion*) and Speaking Out (*Parrhesia*)', *DOP* 50: 263–87.
   (1998) 'Some Intertexts of the Vita Stephani Junioris', *BMGS* 22: 199–214.
   (2002) 'A Rough-Guide to Byzantine Monasticism in the Early Seventh Century', in *The Reign of Heraclius (610–641): Crisis and Confrontation*, eds. G. J. Reinink and B. H. Stolte. Leuven: 205–26.
   (2003) '"The Encomium of Ss. Isakos and Dalmatos by Michael the Monk (*BHG* 956d): Text, Translation and Notes', in *EUKOSMIA: Studi miscellanei per il 75° di Vincenzo Poggi S. J.*, eds. V. Ruggieri and L. Pieralli. Catanzaro: 275–311.
   (2007a) *The Monks and Monasteries of Constantinople (ca. 350–850)*. Cambridge.
   (2007b) 'Byzantine Monastic Rules before the Typikon (Sixth through Eighth Centuries)', in *Founders and Refounders of Byzantine Monasteries*, ed. M. Mullett. Belfast: 140–81.
Haugh, R. (1975) *Photius and the Carolingians: The Trinitarian Heresy*. Belmont.
Havlikova, L. (1993) 'A propos de la Christianisation de la Russie au IXe siècle', *BSl* 54: 102–7.
Heldt, J. (1995) 'Die *Vita Nikolaos* des Studiten: Ein Heiligenleben aus mittelbyzantinischer Zeit', *Bysantinska Sällskapet. Bulletin* 13: 29–36.
Helland, T. J. (2007) 'The Slavonic Tradition of Pre-Metaphrastic Reading Menologia for March – Codex Suprasliensis and Its Russian and Ukrainian Parallels', *Scando-Slavica* 53: 59–76.
Henry, P. (1969) 'The Moechian Controversy and the Constantinopolitan Synod of January A.D. 809', *JThSt* 20: 495–522.
Herbers, K. (1993) 'Papst Nikolaus I. und Patriarch Photios: Das Bild des byzantinischen Gegners in lateinischen Quellen', in *Die Begegnung des Westens mit dem Osten*, eds. O. Engels and P. Schreiner. Sigmaringen: 51–74.
   (2008) 'Rom und Byzanz im Konflikt: Die Jahre 869/870 in der Perspektive der Hadriansvita des *Liber pontificalis*', in *Die Faszination der Papstgeschichte: Neue Zugänge zum frühen und hohen Mittelalter*, eds. W. Hartmann and K. Herbers. Cologne-Weimar-Vienna: 55–69.
Hergenröther, J. (1867–1869) *Photius von Konstantinopel: Sein Leben, seine Schriften und das griechische Schisma nach handschriftlichen und gedruckten Quellen*. Regensburg. 3 vols. (repr. Darmstadt. 1966).

Hergès, A. (1898) 'Monastères de Bithynie: Saint Jean le Théologue de Pélécète', *ÉO* 1/9: 274–80.
  (1898/1899) 'Le Monastère des Agaures', *EO* 2: 230–38.
Hermann, B. (1919) *Theoktista aus Byzanz: Die Mutter zweier Heiligen*. Freiburg im Breisgau.
Herrin, J. (2001) *Women in Purple: Rulers of Medieval Byzantium*. London.
  (2006) 'Changing Functions of Monasteries for Women during Byzantine Iconoclasm', in *Byzantine Women: Varieties of Experience ca. 800–1200*, ed. L. Garland. Aldershot: 1–15.
  (2013) *Unrivalled Influence: Women and Empire in Byzantium*. Princeton.
Hild, F., and Hellenkemper, H. (1990) *Kilikien und Isaurien*. Vienna (TIB 5).
Hinterberger, M. (1999) *Autobiographische Traditionen in Byzanz*. Vienna.
  (2000) 'Autobiography and Hagiography in Byzantium', *Symbolae Osloenses* 75: 139–64.
  (2008) 'Wortschöpfung und literarischer Stil bei Methodios I', in *Lexicologica Byzantina: Beiträge zum Kolloquium zur byzantinischen Lexikographie* (= Super alta perennis 4), eds. E. Trapp and S. Schönauer. Gottingen: 119–50.
  (2014a) 'Byzantine Hagiography and Its Literary Genres: Some Critical Observations', in *Ashgate Research Companion to Byzantine Hagiography. Volume II: Genres and Contexts*, ed. S. Efthymiadis. Farnham: 25–60.
  (2014b) 'The Byzantine Hagiographer and His Text', in *Ashgate Research Companion to Byzantine Hagiography. Volume II: Genres and Contexts*, ed. S. Efthymiadis. Farnham: 211–46.
Hirsch, F. (1876) *Byzantinische Studien*. Leipzig (repr. Amsterdam. 1965).
Høgel, C. (2002) *Symeon Metaphrastes: Rewriting and Canonization*. Copenhagen.
  (2003) 'The Two Recensions of the Metaphrastic Menologion', in *Byzantium in the Year 1000*, ed. P. Magdalino. Leiden-Boston: 217–32.
  (2014) 'Symeon Metaphrastes and the Metaphrastic Movement', in *Ashgate Research Companion to Byzantine Hagiography. Volume II: Genres and Contexts*, ed. S. Efthymiadis. Farnham: 181–96.
  (2015) 'The Actual Words of Theodore Graptos: A Byzantine Saint's Letter As Inserted Document', in *Medieval Letters – between Fiction and Document*, eds. Ch. Høgel and E. Bartoli. Turnhout: 307–15.
Hollingsworth, P. A. (1991) 'Moechian Controversy', in *ODB*: 1388–89.
Hoyland, R. G. (1997) *Seeing Islam As Others Saw It: A Survey and Evaluation of Christian, Jewish and Zoroastrian Writings on Early Islam*. Princeton.
Huglo, M. (1951) 'L'ancienne version latine de l'Hymnos Acathiste', *Le Muséon* 64: 27–61.
Hunger, H. (1978) *Die hochsprachliche profane Literatur der Byzantiner*. Munich. 2 vols.
Hurbanic, M. (2005) 'The Byzantine Missionary Concept and Its Revitalisation in the 9th Century: Some Remarks on the Content of Photius' Encyclical Letter *Ad Archiepiscopales Thronos per Orientem Obtinentes*', *BSl* 63: 103–16.
Hutter, I. (1995) 'Scriptoria in Bithynia', in *Constantinople and Its Hinterland*, eds. C. Mango et al. Aldershot: 379–96.

Huxley, G. L. (1975) 'The Emperor Michael III and the Battle of Bishop's Meadow (A.D. 863)', *GRBS* 16: 443–50.
  (1978) 'On the Vita of St John of Gotthia', *GRBS* 19: 161–69.
  (1980) 'The Scholarship of Constantine Porphyrogenitus', *Proceedings of the Royal Irish Academy* Section C 80C: 29–40.
  (1981) 'On the Erudition of George the Synkellos', *Proceedings of the Royal Irish Academy* 81C: 207–17.
Ieraci Bio, A. M. (1989) 'La transmissione della letteratura medica greca nell'Italia meridionale fra X e XV secolo', in *Contributi alla cultura greca nell'Italia meridionale*, ed. A. Garzya. Naples. Vol. I: 133–255.
Irmscher, J. (1980) *Der byzantinische Bilderstreit: Sozialökonomische Voraussetzungen – ideologische Grundlagen – geschichtliche Wirkungen. Eine Sammlung von Forschungsbeiträgen.* Leipzig.
Janin, R. (1954) 'L'église byzantine sur les rives du Bosphore (Côte asiatique)', *REB* 12: 69–99.
  (1969) *La géographie ecclésiastique de l'empire byzantin: Première partie. Le siège de Constantinople et le patriarcat oecuménique.* Vol. III: *Les églises et les monastères*, 2nd ed. Paris.
  (1975) *Les églises et les monastères des grands centres byzantins.* Paris.
Jankowiak, M., and Montinaro, F. (2015) *Studies in Theophanes.* Paris (= *TM* 19).
Jeffreys, E. (2009) 'Why Produce Verse in Twelfth-Century Constantinople?', in *'Doux remède . . .' Poésie et poétique à Byzance*, eds. P. Odorico et al. Paris: 219–28.
Jenkins, R. J. H. (1965) 'A Note on Nicetas David Paphlago and the *Vita Ignatii*', *DOP* 19: 241–47 (repr. in *Studies on Byzantine History of the 9th and 10th Centuries.* London. 1970. Ch. IX).
Jenkins, R. J. H., and Mango, C. (1956) 'The Date and Significance of the Tenth Homily of Photius', *DOP* 9: 123–40.
  (1961) 'A Synodicon of Antioch and Lacedaimonia', *DOP* 15: 225–42.
Jokisch, B. (2007) *Islamic Imperial Law: Harun-Al-Rashid's Codification Project.* Berlin-New York.
Jolivet-Lévy, C. (1991) 'Hagiographie cappadocienne: À propos de quelques images nouvelles de saint Hiéron et de saint Eustathe', in Ευφρόσυνον, Αφιέρωμα στον Μ. Χατζηδάκη, ed. E. Kypraiou. Athens. Vol. I: 205–18 (repr. in *Études cappadociennes.* London. 2002: 471–97).
Jugie, M. (1913) 'La vie et les oeuvres d'Euthyme, patriarche de Constantinople', *EO* 16: 385–95 and 481–92.
  (1918) 'La vie et les oeuvres du moine Théognoste (IXe siècle): Son témoignage sur l'Immaculée Conception', *Bessarione. Rivista di studi orientali* 34: 162–74 and 259–63.
  (1922/1923) 'Le culte de Photius dans l'église byzantine', *ROC* 23: 105–22.
  (1938) 'Les Actes du synode photien de Sainte-Sophie', *EO* 37: 89–99.
Kaegi, W. E. (1966) 'The Byzantine Armies and Iconoclasm', *BSl* 27: 48–70.
Kaldellis, A. (1998) *Genesios: On the Reigns of the Emperors.* Canberra.

(2015) *The Byzantine Republic: People and Power in New Rome*. Cambridge, MA.

Kałżaniacki, E. (1903) 'Die Legende vor der Vision Amphilog's und der λόγος ἱστορικός des Gregorios Dekapolites', *Archiv für Slavische Philologie* 25: 101–8.

Kaplan, M. (1990) 'Les normes de la sainteté à Byzance (VIe-XIe siècle)', *Mentalités* 4: 15–34.

(1992) *Les hommes et la terre à Byzance du VIe au IXe siècle: Proprieté et exploitation du sol*. Paris.

(1993a) 'Les moines et leurs biens fonciers à Byzance du VIIIe au Xe siècle', *Revue Bénédictine* 103: 209–23 (= *Le monachisme à Byzance et en Occident du VIIIe au Xe siècle: Aspects internes et relations avec la société*, eds. A. Dierkens et al. Maredsous).

(1993b) 'Les sanctuaires de Theodore de Sykéòn', in *Les saints et leur sanctuaire à Byzance: Textes, images et monuments*, eds. C. Jolivet-Lévy et al. Paris: 65–79.

(1997) *La chrétienté byzantine du début du VIIe siècle au milieu du XIe siècle*. Paris.

(1999) 'Le saint, l'évêque et l'Empereur: l'image et le pouvoir à l'époque du second iconoclasme d'après les sources hagiographiques', in *Les images dans les sociétés médiévales: pour une histoire comparée*, eds. J. M. Sansterre and J. Cl. Schmitt. Rome (Bulletin de l'Institut Historique belge de Rome 69): 185–201.

(2000) 'Le miracle est-il nécessaire au saint byzantin?', in *Miracle et Karāma*, ed. D. Aigle Turnhout: 167–96.

(2001) 'Quelques remarques sur la vie rurale à Byzance au IXe siècle d'après la correspondance d'Ignace le Diacre', in *The Dark Centuries of Byzantium (7th–9th c.)*, ed. E. Kountura-Galaki. Athens: 365–76.

(2002) 'L'ensevelissement des saints: Rituel de création des reliques et sanctification à Byzance à travers les sources hagiographiques (Vè–XIIè siècles)', *TM* 14 (= *Mélanges G. Dagron*): 319–32.

(2006) 'L'évêque à l'époque du second iconoclasme', in *Monastères, images, pouvoirs et société à Byzance*, ed. M. Kaplan. Paris: 183–205.

(2011) *Pouvoirs, Église et sainteté: Essais sur la société byzantine*. Paris.

(2013) 'La Vie de Théodora de Thessalonique, un écrit familial', in *Approaches to the Byzantine Family*, eds. L. Brubaker and S. Tougher. Aldershot: 285–302.

(2015) 'Le saint byzantin et son hagiographe, Ve–XIIe siècle: Esquisse', in *Myriobiblos: Essays on Byzantine Literature and Culture*, eds. Th. Antonopoulou et al. Berlin: 169–85.

(2017) 'Les moines et les pouvoirs dans le monde byzantin à l'époque iconoclaste', in *Monachesimi d'Oriente e d'Occidente: LXIV settimana di studio della fondazione C.I.S.A.M.* Spoleto: 1021–62.

Karayannopoulos, J. (1986) *L'inscription protobulgare de Direkler*. Athens.

(1989) *Les Slaves en Macédoine: La prétendue interruption des communications entre Constantinople et Thessalonique du 7ème au 9ème siècle*. Athens.

Karlin-Hayter, P. (1966) 'Quel est l'Empereur Constantin le nouveau commémoré in le synaxaire au 3 Septembre?', *Byzantion* 33: 624–26.

(1969) 'La mort de Théophano', *BZ* 62: 13–19.

(1971) 'Études sur les deux histoires du règne de Michel III', *Byzantion* 41: 452–96.

(1977) 'Gregory of Syracuse, Ignatios and Photius', in *Iconoclasm: Papers Given at the Ninth Spring Symposium of Byzantine Studies*, eds. A. A. Bryer and J. Herrin. Birmingham: 141–45.

(1990) 'La mort de Théodora', *JÖB* 40: 205–8.

(1991a) 'L'enjeu d'une rumeur: Opinion et imaginaire à Byzance au IXe s.', *JÖB* 41: 85–111.

(1991b) 'L'adieu à l'empereur', *Byzantion* 61: 112–55.

(1991c) 'Le *De Michaele* du Logothete: Construction e intentions', *Byzantion* 61: 365–95.

(1993) 'Où l'abeille butane: La culture littéraire monastique à Byzance aux VIIIe et IXe siècles', *Revue bénédictine* 103: 90–116 (= *Le monachisme à Byzance et en Occident du VIIIe au Xe siècle: Aspects internes et relations avec la société*, eds. A. Dierkens et al. Maredsous).

(1994) 'A Byzantine Politician-Monk: Saint Theodore Studite', *JÖB* 44: 217–32.

(2001) 'Icon Veneration: Significance of the Restoration of Orthodoxy?', in *Novum Millennium: Studies on Byzantine History and Culture Dedicated to P. Speck*, eds. C. Sode and S. Takács. Aldershot: 171–83.

(2004) 'Notes on the *Acta Davidis, Symeonis et Georgii (BHG* 494)', in *Philomathestatos: Studies in Greek and Byzantine Texts Presented to Jacques Noret for His 65th Birthday*, eds. B. Janssens et al. Leuven-Paris-Dudley: 325–50.

(2006a) 'Restoration of Orthodoxy, the Pardon of Theophilos and the *Acta Davidis, Symeonis et Georgii*', in *Byzantine Style, Religion and Civilization: In Honour of Sir Steven Runciman*, ed. E. Jeffreys. Cambridge: 361–73.

(2006b) 'Methodios and His Synod', in *Byzantine Orthodoxies*, eds. A. Louth and A. Casiday. Aldershot: 55–74.

(2007) 'Being a Potential Saint', in *Eat, Drink, and Be Merry (Luke 12:19) – Food and Wine in Byzantium*, eds. L. Brubaker and K. Linardou. Aldershot: 245–46.

Katsiampoura, G. (2010) 'John VII Grammaticus: Scientist or Magician?', *AIHS* 60: 33–41.

Kavrus, N. F. (1983) 'Студийский скрипторий в IX в. (по материалам рукописей Москвы и Ленинграда)', *VV* 44: 98–110.

Kazhdan, A. (1982) 'Small Social Groupings (Microstructures) in Byzantine Society', *JÖB* 32/2: 3–11.

(1983) 'Hagiographical Notes (Nos. 1–4)', *Byzantion* 53: 538–55 (repr. in *Authors and Texts in Byzantium*. Aldershot. 1993. Ch. III).

(1984) 'Hagiographical Notes (Nos. 5–8)', *Byzantion* 54: 176–92 (repr. in *Authors and Texts in Byzantium*. Aldershot. 1993. Ch. IV).

(1985) 'Hermitic, Cenobitic, and Secular Ideals in Byzantine Hagiography of the Ninth through the Twelfth Centuries', *GOrThR* 30: 473–87.

(1986) 'Hagiographical Notes (Nos. 13–16)', *Byzantion* 56: 148–70 (repr. in *Authors and Texts in Byzantium*. Aldershot. 1993. Ch. VI).

(1988) 'Hagiographical Notes (Nos. 17–20)', *Erytheia* 9/2: 197–209 (repr. in *Authors and Texts in Byzantium*. Aldershot. 1993. Ch. VII).

(1992–1993) 'An Oxymoron: Individual Features of a Byzantine Hymnographer', *RSBN* 29: 19–58.

(1996) 'Joseph the Hymnographer and the First Russian Attack on Constantinople', in *From Byzantium to Iran: In Honour of N. Garsoïan*, eds. J.-P. Mahé and R. W. Thomson. Atlanta: 187–96.

(1997) 'The Formation of Byzantine Family Names in the Ninth and Tenth Centuries', *BSl* 58: 90–109.

(1999) *A History of Byzantine Literature (650–850)*, in collaboration with L. F. Sherry and Ch. Angelidi. Athens.

(2006) *A History of Byzantine Literature (850–1000)*, edited by Ch. Angelidi. Athens.

Kazhdan, A., and Maguire, H. (1991) 'Byzantine Hagiographical Texts As Sources on Art', *DOP* 45: 1–22.

Kazhdan, A., and Sherry, L. F. (1996) 'The Tale of a Happy Fool: The *Vita* of St Philaretos the Merciful (*BHG* 1511z–12b)', *Byzantion* 66: 351–62.

Kazhdan, A., and Sherry, L. F. (1997) 'Some Notes on the Scriptor Incertus de Leone Armenio', *BSl* 58/1: 110–12.

Kazhdan, A., and Talbot, A. M. (1991) 'Women and Iconoclasm', *BZ* 84/85: 391–408 (repr. in A. M. Talbot, *Women and Religious Life in Byzantium*. Aldershot. 2001. Ch. III).

et al. (1991) 'Stoudios Monastery', in *ODB*: 1960–61.

Kekelidze, K. (1965) 'Un monument inconnu de la littérature byzantine en version géorgienne', *BK* 19/20 (nrs. 48/49): 61–68.

Khoury, A. Th. (1969) *Les théologiens byzantins et l'Islam*. Leuven-Paris.

Kiessling, N. (1970) 'Antecedents of the Medieval Dragon in Sacred History', *JBL* 89: 167–75.

Kislinger, E. (1983) 'Eudokia Ingerina, Basileios I. und Michael III.', *JÖB* 33: 119–35.

(2007) 'Nikolaos episkopos Lakedaimonias: Chronologische Präzisierungen zur Bischofsliste im Bodleianus Holkham gr. 6 (Mit einer Tafel)', *JÖB* 57: 27–35

Koder, J. (2013) 'The Authority of the Eparchos in the Markets of Constantinople (according to the *Book of the Eparch*)', in *Authority in Byzantium*, ed. P. Armstrong. Aldershot: 83–108.

Kosinski, R. (2016) *Holiness and Power: Constantinopolitan Holy Men and Authority in the 5th Century*. Berlin.

Kolia-Dermitzaki, A. (2002) 'The Execution of the Forty-two Martyrs of Amorion: Proposing an Interpretation', *Al-Masaq* 14/2: 141–62.
Kolias, G. (1939) *Léon Choerosphactes, magistre, proconsul et patrice*. Athens.
Kolias, G. T. (1953) 'Βιογραφικὰ Στεφάνου Α΄ οἰκουμενικοῦ πατριάρχου', in *Προσφορὰ εἰς Στ. Κυριακίδην* [*Festschrift St. Kyriakides*] (= Ἑλληνικῶν Παράρτ. 4): 358–63.
Komines, A. D. (1966) *To Byzantinon hieron epigramma kai oi epigrammatopoioi*. Athens.
Konidaris, J. (1982) 'Die Novellen des Kaisers Herakleios', in *Fontes Minores V*, ed. D. Simon. Frankfurt am Main: 62–72.
Konstantelos, D. (1989/1991) 'Τὸ ἰδεολογικὸν ὑπόβαθρο στὴν διένεξη μεταξὺ τῶν πατριαρχῶν Ἰγνατίου καὶ Φωτίου', *EkTh* 10: 189–206.
Konstantopoulos, K. M. (1906) 'Βυζαντιακὰ μολυβδόβουλλα ἐν τῷ Ἐθνικῷ Νομισματικῷ Μουσείῳ', *JIAN* 9: 61–146 (repr. in *Byzantiaka Molybdoboulla tou en Athenais Ethnikou Nomismatikou Mouseiou*. Athens. 1917).
Konti, V. (1999) 'Μαρτυρίες για την εικονομαχική έριδα στην Πελοπόννησο. Προβλήματα και προσεγγίσεις', *Symmeikta* 13: 77–95.
Kotzabassi, S. (1992) 'Τὸ μαρτύριο τῶν μβ΄ μαρτύρων τῶν Ἀμορίου ἁγιολογικὰ καὶ ὑμνολογικὰ κείμενα', *EEPhSPTh* 2: 111–53.
  (2007) 'Bemerkungen zu dem Enkomion des Joseph Studites auf den heiligen Demetrios (*BHG* 535)', in *Theatron: Rhetorische Kultur in Spätantike und Mittelalter*, ed. M. Grünbart. Berlin: 157–68.
  (2015) 'Miscellanea Palaeographica', *Parekbolai* 5: 135–43.
Kougeas, S. B. (1913) *Ὁ Καισαρείας Ἀρέθας καὶ τὸ ἔργον αὐτοῦ*. Athens.
Koutava-Delivoria, B. (2002) 'La contribution de Constantin Porphyrogénète à la composition des Geoponica', *Byzantion* 72/2: 365–80.
Kountoura-Galaki, E. (1996) *Byzantine Clergy and Society in the Dark Centuries*. Athens.
  (2004) 'The Cult of the Saints Nicholas of Lycia and the Birth of the Byzantine Maritime Tradition', in *The Heroes of the Orthodox Church: The New Saints (8th–16th c.)*, ed. E. Kountoura-Galaki. Athens: 91–106.
Koutrakou, N. C. (1994) *La propagande impériale byzantine: Persuasion et réaction (VIIIe–Xe siècles)*. Athens.
  (2005) 'Use and Abuse of the 'Image' of the Theotokos in the Political Life of Byzantium (with Special Reference to the Iconoclast Period)', in *Images of the Mother of God: Perceptions of the Theotokos in Byzantium*, ed. M. Vassilaki. Aldershot: 77–89.
Krannich, Th., Schubert, C., and Sode, C. (eds.) (2002) *Die ikonoklastische Synode von Hiereia 754*. Tübingen.
Krausmüller, D. (1998/1999) 'God or Angels As Impersonators of Saints: A Belief and Its Context in the Refutation of Eustratius of Constantinople and in the Writings of Anastasius of Sinai', *Gouden Hoorn* 6/2: 5–16.
  (1999) 'Divine Sex: Patriarch Methodios' Concept of Virginity', in *Desire and Denial in Byzantium*, ed. L. James. Aldershot: 57–65.

(2003) 'Metaphrasis after the Second Iconoclasm: Nicephorus Skeuophylax and His *Encomia* of Theophanes Confessor (*BHG* 1790), Theodore of Sykeon (*BHG* 1749), and George the Martyr (*BHG* 682)', *Symbolae Osloenses* 78/1: 45–70.

(2004) 'Killing at God's Command: Niketas Byzantios' Polemic against Islam and the Christian Tradition of Divinely Sanctioned Murder', *Al-Masaq* 16: 163–76.

(2006) 'Patriarch Methodius, the Author of the Lost First Life of Theodore of Stoudios', *Symbolae Osloenses* 81/1: 144–50.

(2007a) 'The Identity, the Cult and the Hagiographical Dossier of Andrew "in Crisi"', *RSBN* 44: 57–86.

(2007b) 'The Constantinopolitan Abbot Dius: His Life, Cult and Hagiographical Dossier', *BMGS* 31/1: 13–31.

(2007c) 'Lay Founders and First Abbots: The Cases of John II Komnenos and Basil the Macedonian', in *Founders and Refounders of Byzantine Monasteries*, ed. M. Mullett. Belfast: 344–365.

(2009a) 'Exegeting the Passio of St Agatha: Patriarch Methodios (†847) on Sexual Differentiation and the Perfect "Man"', *BMGS* 33/1: 1–16.

(2009b) 'The *Encomium* of Catherine of Alexandria (*BHG* 32b) by the *Protasecretis* Anastasius, a Work of Anastasius *the Stammerer*', *AnBoll* 127/2: 309–12.

(2011) 'Making the Most of Mary: The Cult of the Virgin in the Chalkoprateia from Late Antiquity to the Tenth Century', in *The Cult of the Mother of God in Byzantium: Texts and Images*, eds. L. Brubaker and M. B. Cunningham. Farnham: 219–46.

(2013a) 'The *Vitae* B, C and A of Theodore the Stoudite: Their Interrelation, Dates, Authors and Significance for the History of the Stoudios Monastery in the Tenth Century', *AnBoll* 131/2: 280–98.

(2013b) 'Chastity or Procreation? Models of Sanctity for Byzantine Laymen during the Iconoclastic and Post-Iconoclastic Period', *JLARC* 7: 51–71.

(2013c) 'Byzantine Monastic Communities: Alternative Families', in *Approaches to the Byzantine Family*, eds. L. Brubaker and S. Tougher. Aldershot: 345–58.

(2015) 'Sleeping Souls and Living Corpses: Patriarch Methodius' Defense of the Cult of Saints', *Byzantion* 85: 143–55.

(2016) 'Showing One's True Colours: Patriarch Methodios on the Morally Improving Effect of Sacred Images', *BMGS* 40/2: 298–306.

(2018) 'Affirming Divine Providence and Limiting the Powers of Saints: The Byzantine Debate about the Term of Life (6th–11th Centuries)', *Scrinium* 14: 392–433

(2019) 'Saints As Finders of Relics: Joseph the Hymnographer and John of Galatia', *Erytheia* 40: 53–62.

Kreutz, B. (1991) *Before the Normans: Southern Italy in the Ninth and Tenth Centuries*. Philadelphia.

Krueger, D. (2004) *Writing and Holiness: The Practice of Authorship in the Early Christian East*. Philadelphia.

Krumbacher, K. (1896) 'Ein Dithyrambus auf den Chronisten Theophanes', *SBAW* 4: 583–625.

Kustas, G. L. (1962) 'The Literary Criticism of Photius: A Christian Definition of Style', *Hell* 17: 132–69.

(1964) 'History and Theology in Photius', *GOTR* 10: 37–74.

Kyriakis, E. K. (1993) Βυζάντιο και οι Βούλγαροι (7^{ος}–10^{ος} αι.): Συμβολή στην εξωτερική πολιτική του Βυζαντίου. Athens.

Laiou, A. E. (1989) "Ἡ ἱστορία ἑνὸς γάμου: ὁ βίος τῆς ἁγίας Θωμαΐδος τῆς Λεσβίας', in Ἡ καθημερινή ζωή στό Βυζάντιο, ed. Ch. Maltezou. Athens: 237–51.

(1994) 'Law, Justice and the Byzantine Historians: Ninth to Twelfth Centuries', in *Law and Society in Byzantium: Ninth–Twelfth Centuries*, eds. A. E. Laiou and D. Simon. Washington: 151–85.

(1998) 'The General and the Saint: Michael Maleinos and Nikephoros Phokas', in Εὐψυχία. *Mélanges offerts à H. Ahrweiler*, eds. M. Balard et al. Paris. Vol. 2: 399–412.

Lake, K. (1909) *The Early Days of Monasticism on Mount Athos*. Oxford.

Lamoreaux, J. C. (1992) 'An Unedited Tract against the Armenians by Theodore Abū Qurrah', *Le Muséon* 105: 327–41.

Lampakis, S. (2001) 'Παρατηρήσεις σχετικά μὲ τὶς ὄψεις τῆς ἀρχαιογνωσίας στὸ ἔργο τοὐ Ἰγνατίου Διακόνου', in *The Dark Centuries of Byzantium (7th–9th c.)*, ed. E. Kountura-Galaki. Athens: 109–32.

Lamza, L. (1975) *Patriarch Germanos I von Konstantinopel*. Würzburg.

Laourdas, B. (1950) 'Λανθάνουσα ἐπιστολή τοῦ πατριαρχοῦ Φωτίου πρὸς τὸν αὐτοκράτορα Βασίλειον', Ὀρθοδοξία 25: 472–74.

(1951) 'Παρατηρήσεις ἐπὶ τοῦ χαρακτῆρος τῶν ἐπιστολῶν τοῦ Φωτίου', *EEBS* 21: 74–109.

(1954) "Ὁ Ἀρέθας περὶ εἰκονομαχίας', Θεολογία 25: 614–22.

Latysev, V. (1914) 'Zitie prep: Theodora Studita v miunhenskoj rukopisi n° 467', *VV* 21: 222–54.

Laurent, V. (1964) 'Une homélie inédite de l'archevêque de Thessalonique Léon le Philosophe sur l'Annonciation (25 mars 842)', in *Mélanges Eugène Tisserant*. Vaticano. Vol. II: 281–302.

Lauritzen, F. (2017) 'The Layers of Composition of the *Synodikon* of Alexius Studites', *Studia Ceranea* 7: 121–28.

Lauxtermann, M. (1998) 'Three Biographical Notes', *BZ* 91: 391–405.

(1999) 'Ninth-Century Classicism and the Erotic Muse', in *Desire and Denial in Byzantium*, ed. L. James. Aldershot: 161–70.

(2003) *Byzantine Poetry from Pisides to Geometres: Texts and Contexts*. Vienna. Vol. 1.

(2019) *Byzantine Poetry from Pisides to Geometres: Texts and Contexts*. Vienna. Vol. 2.

Lavagnini, B. (1959–1960) 'Siracusa occupata dagli Arabi e l'epistola di Teodosio Monaco', *Byzantion* 29–30: 267–79.
Lechner, J. (2002) 'Quelques remarques sur le rapport entre texte et image dans le psautier *Athonis Pantocratoris* 61', *Arte medievale* II/1: 25–34.
Lefort, J. (1995) 'Les communications entre Constantinople et la Bithynie', in *Constantinople and Its Hinterland*, eds. C. Mango and G. Dagron. Aldershot: 207–18.
  (1996) 'Constantinople et la Bithynie, ou les fonctions d'un hinterland', *MEFREM* 108: 366–69.
Lemercier, C. (2012) 'Formale Methoden der Netzwerkanalyse in den Geschichtswissenschaften: Warum und Wie?', in *Historische Netzwerkanalysen (Österreichische Zeitschrift für Geschichtswissenschaften 23/1)*, eds. A. Müller and W. Neurath. Innsbruck-Vienna: 16–41.
Lemerle, P. (1965) 'Thomas le Slave', *TM* 1: 255–97.
  (1967) 'Roga et rente d'État', *REB* 25: 78–83.
  (1971) *Le premier humanisme byzantin: Notes et remarques sur enseignement et culture à Byzance des origines au Xe siècle*. Paris.
  (1973) 'L'histoire des Pauliciens d'Asie Mineure d'après les sources grecques', *TM* 5: 1–144.
  (1979) *The Agrarian History of Byzantium from the Origins to the Twelfth Century: The Sources and Problems*. Galway.
Leone, P. L. M. (1989) '*L'Encomium in patriarcham Antonium II Cauleam* del filosofo e retore Niceforo', *Orpheus* 10: 404–29.
Leontaritou, V. A. (1996) Εκκλησιαστικά αξιώματα και υπηρεσίες στην πρώιμη και μέση βυζαντινή περίοδο. Athens.
Leontopoulos, S. P. (1939) 'Ταμεῖον ἐκκλησιαστικῆς ποιήσεως', *Ekklesiastikós Pháros* 38: 305–22.
Leroy, J. (1958a) 'La réforme studite', in *Il monachesimo orientale (OCA 153)*. Rome: 181–214 (repr. in *Études sur le monachisme byzantin: Textes rassemblés et présentés par O. Delouis*, ed. J. Leroy. Bégrolles-en-Mauges. 2007: 155–99).
  (1958b) 'Les *petites Catecheses* de s. Théodore Studite', *Le Muséon* 71: 329–58 (repr. in *Études sur le monachisme byzantin*: Bégrolles-en-Mauges. 2007. Ch. 6).
  (1969) *Studitisches Mönchtum: Spiritualität und Lebensform*, ed. J. Leroy. Graz-Cologne-Vienna.
  (1973) 'Le Patmos St Jean 742 (Gregory 2464), un nouveau manuscrit de Nicolas Studite (†868)', in *Zetesis: Album amicorum door vrienden en collega's aangeboden aan Prof. Dr. E. de Strycker ter gelegenheid van zijn 65e verjaardag*, Antwerp-Utrecht: 488–501.
  (1977) 'Un nouveau manuscrit de Nicolas Stoudite: Le Paris. Gr. 494', in *La paléographie grecque et byzantine*, eds. J. Irigoin et al. Paris: 181–90.
  (2002) 'Le monachisme stoudite', in *Theodore Stoudite, Les Grandes Catecheses (Livre I); Les epigrammes (I–XXIX); precedees d'une etude de J. Leroy sur le*

monachisme stoudite, traduction et notes par F. de Montleau (Spiritualité orientale 79), Abbaye de Bellefontaine: 79–80.
  (2008) *Études sur les grandes catéchèses de S. Théodore studite*, eds. O. Delouis and S. J. Voicu. Vaticano.
Leserri, V. (2004) 'Un'*Epistola* del patriarca Fozio all'imperatore Basilio', *Augustinianum* 44: 461–69.
  (2005) 'L'epistola del patriarca Fozio al papa Niccolò I', *Augustinianum* 45: 259–63.
  (2006) 'Riflessioni su un'esegesi biblica del patriarca Fozio: "Amphilochia"', *Augustinianum* 46: 261–63.
  (2007) 'La morte di Abele e la strage degli innocenti secondo Fozio', *Augustinianum* 47: 227–28.
Letsios, D. (2004) 'Theophilos and His "Khurramite" Policy: Some Reconsiderations', *Graeco-Arabica* 9/10: 249–71.
Lifshitz, F. (1994) 'Beyond Positivism and Genre: "Hagiographical" Texts As Historical Narrative', *Viator* 25: 95–113.
Lilie, R. J. (1996) *Byzanz unter Eirene und Konstantin VI (780–802)*. Frankfurt am Main (Berliner Byzantinische Studien 2).
Lilie, R. J. ed. (1999) *Die Patriarchen der ikonoklastischen Zeit: Germanos I.- Methodios I. (715–847)*. Frankfurt am Main (Berliner Byzantinische Studien 5).
Ljubarskij, J. (1994) 'George the Monk As a Short-Story Writer', *JÖB* 44: 255–64.
Loenertz, R. (1950) 'Le panégyrique de S. Denys l'Aréopagite par S. Michel le syncelle', *AnBoll* 68: 94–107.
Loparev, Ch. (1899) 'Zitie sv. caricy Theofanii i ego pozdnejsie pereskazy', *ZMNP* 325: 343–61.
  (1904) 'De S. Theodoro monacho hegumenoque Chorensi', *Zapiski Klassicheskago otdelniia imperatorskago russkago arkeologischeskago obschestva* 1: 1–16.
  (1910) 'Vizantijskie zitija svjatych VIII-IX vekov', *VizVrem* 17: 1–224.
Lourié, B. (2011) 'The Feast of Pokrov, Its Byzantine Origin, and the Cult of Gregory the Illuminator and Isaac the Parthian (Sahak Partcev) in Byzantium', *Scrinium* 7/1: 231–331.
Louth, A. (2006) 'Photios As Theologian', in *Byzantine Style, Religion and Civilization: In Honour of Sir Steven Runciman*, ed. E. M. Jeffreys. Cambridge: 206–23.
Lowe, V. (1976) 'A Group of Hagiological Studite kontakia pros to toi theoi apo metras: A Critical Edition, with Notes'. Unpublished PhD thesis. University of Oxford.
Löwe, H. (1982) 'Methodius im Reichenauer Verbrüderungsbuch', *DA* 38: 341–62.
Lucà, S. (2016) 'La distribuzione calendariale delle Catechesi di Teodoro di Studio nel Vat. gr. 2112', in *Manuscripta Graeca et Orientalia. Mélanges*

monastiques et patristiques en l'honneur de P. Géhin, eds. A. Binggeli et al. Leuven-Paris-Bristol. 2016: 497–522.
Ludwig, C. (1987) 'Wer hat was in welcher Absicht wie beschrieben? Bemerkungen zur Historia des Petros Sikeliotes', in *Varia II*, eds. A. Berger et al. Bonn (Poikila Byzantina 6): 149–227.
(1997) *Sonderformen byzantinischer Hagiographie und ihr literarisches Vorbild: Untersuchungen zu den Viten des Äsop, des Philaretos, des Symeon Salos und des Andreas Salos*. Frankfurt am Main.
(1998) 'The Paulicians and Ninth-Century Byzantine Thought', in *Byzantium in the Ninth Century: Dead or Alive?*, ed. L. Brubaker. Aldershot: 23–35.
Lukhovitskij, L. (2013) 'Historical Memory of Byzantine Iconoclasm in the 14th c.: The Case of Nikephoros Gregoras and Philotheos Kokkinos', in *Aesthetics and Theurgy in Byzantium*, eds. S. Mariev and W. M. Stock. Berlin: 205–34.
(2014) 'Nikephoros Gregoras' Vita of St Michael the Synkellos: Rewriting Techniques and Reconstruction of the Iconoclast Past in a 14th Cent. Hagiographical Metaphrasis', *JÖB* 64: 177–96.
(2016) 'Recollection, Reevaluation, Distortion: Symeon Metaphrastes' Narrative Techniques in Retelling the History of Iconoclasm', *BZ* 109/2: 785–808.
Luzzi, A. (1996) 'Per l'identificazione degli imperatori bizantini commemorati nel Sinassario di Costantinopoli', *RSBN* 33: 45–66.
(1999) 'Precisazioni sull'epoca di formazione del Sinassario di Costantinopoli', *RSBN* 36: 75–91.
MacDougall, B. (2017) 'Living Images and Authors of Virtue: Theodore of Stoudios on Plato of Sakkoudion and Gregory of Nazianzus on Basil', *BZ* 110/3: 691–712.
Magdalino, P. (1987) 'Observations on the Nea Ekklesia of Basil I', *JÖB* 37: 51–64.
(1988a) 'Basil I, Leo VI, and the Feast of the Prophet Elijah', *JÖB* 38: 193–96.
(1988b) 'The Bath of Leo the Wise and the "Macedonian Renaissance" Revisited: Topography, Iconography, Ceremonial, Ideology', *DOP*. 42: 97–118.
(1993) 'The History of the Future and Its Uses: Prophecy, Policy and Propaganda', in *The Making of Byzantine History: Studies Dedicated to D. M. Nicol on His Seventieth Birthday*, eds. R. Beaton and C. Rouéché. Aldershot: 3–34 (reprinted with postscript in *The Expansion of the Orthodox World: Byzantium, the Balkans and Russia*, ed. J. Shepard. Aldershot. 2007: 29–63).
(1996) *Constantinople médiévale: Études sur l'évolution des structures urbaines*. Paris.
(1998) 'The Road to Baghdad in the Thought-World of Ninth-Century Byzantium', in *Byzantium in the Ninth Century: Dead or Alive?*, ed. L. Brubaker. Aldershot: 195–213.
(2006) *L'Orthodoxie des astrologues: La science entre le dogme et la divination à Byzance (VIIe–XIVe siècle)*. Paris.

(2013) 'Knowledge in Authority and Authorized History: The Imperial Intellectual Programme of Leo VI and Constantine VII', in *Authority in Byzantium*, ed. P. Armstrong. Farnham: 187–211.

(2015a) 'Le patriarche Jean le Grammairien et la théorie de l'aniconisme', in *L'aniconisme dans l'art religieux byzantine*, eds. M. Campagnolo et al. Geneva: 85–94.

(2015b) 'Le culte de saint Nicolas à Constantinople', in *En Orient et en Occident: Le culte de saint Nicolas en Europe*, eds. V. Gazeau et al. Paris: 41–55.

(2017) 'Humanisme et mécénat impérial aux IXe et Xe siècles', *TM* 21/2: 3–21.

Magrì, M. A. (1971) 'Un canone inedito di Teodoro Studita nel Cod: Messanensis GR. 153', in *Umanità e Storia, Scritti in onore di Adelchi Attisani*, ed. R. Franchini. Messina. Vol. II: 85–101.

(1978/1979) 'Il canone In requiem monachi di Teodoro Studita', *Helikon* 18–19: 76–92.

(1979) *Clemente innografo e gli inediti canoni cerimoniali*. Rome.

Maguire, H. (1988) 'The Art of Comparing in Byzantium', *Art Bulletin* 70: 88–93.

Majeska, G. P. (1977) 'The Body of St Theophano the Empress and the Convent of St Constantine', *BSl* 38: 14–21.

Majeska ed. (1984) *Russian Travelers to Constantinople in the Fourteenth and Fifteenth Centuries*. Washington.

(2005) 'Patriarch Photius and the Conversion of the Rus', *Russian History* 32: 413–18.

Makris, G. (2013) 'Zur Dämonisierung des Kaisers Leon V. durch Ignatios Diakonos in der *Vita* des Patriarchen Nikephoros', in *Zwei Sonnen am Goldenen Horn? Kaiserliche und patriarchale Macht im byzantinischen Mittelalter*, eds. M. Grünbart et al. Berlin. Vol. II: 67–74.

Maksimovic, K. (2000) 'Patriarch Methodios I. (843–847) und das studitische Schisma: Quellenkritische Bemerkungen', *Byzantion* 70: 422–46.

Malamut, E. (2004) 'Les itinéraires sacrés de Grégoire le Décapolite', in *Cristianità d'Occidente e Cristianità d'Oriente*. Settimane di Studio della Fondazione Centro Italiano di Studi sull'Alto Medioevo 51. Spoleto: 1191–220.

(2005) 'Thessalonique 830–904', in *Zwischen Polis, Provinz und Peripherie, Beiträge zur byzantinischen Geschichte und Kultur*, ed. L. M Hoffmann. Wiesbaden: 159–90.

Maltese, E. V. (2014) 'Il testo genuino di Teodoro Studita, Epitafio per la madre (BHG 2422), e Giovanni Crisostomo: Unicuique suum', in *ΕΝ ΚΑΛΟΙΣ ΚΟΙΝΟΠΡΑΓΙΑ: hommages à la mémoire de P. L. Malosse et J. Bouffartigue*, ed. E. Amato. Revue des Études Tardo-antiques (RET). Supplément 3. Nanterre: 305–11.

Malyševskij, J. (1887) 'Logofet Feoktist, pokrovitel' Konstantina Filosofa', *Trudy Kievskoj duchovnoj akademii* 28/2: 265–67.

Mamboury, E. (1920) 'Le couvent byzantine de femmes à Prinkipo', *EO* 19: 200–209.
Mango, C. (1959) *The Brazen House: A Study of the Vestibule of the Imperial Palace of Constantinople*. Copenhagen.
  (1960) 'The Legend of Leo the Wise', *ZRVI* 6: 59–93 (repr. in *Byzantium and Its Image*. London. 1984. Ch. XVI).
  (1968a) 'The Monastery of St Abercius at Kurşunlu', *DOP* 22: 169–76.
  (1968b) 'The Byzantine Church at Vize (Bizye) in Thrace and St Mary the Younger', *ZRVI* 11: 9–13.
  (1973) 'Eudocia Ingerina, the Normans and the Macedonian Dynasty', *ZRVI* 14–15: 17–27.
  (1975a) 'The Availability of Books in the Byzantine Empire, A.D. 750–850', in *Byzantine Books and Bookmen*, eds. C. Mango and I. Sevcenko. Washington: 29–45.
  (1975b) 'The Church of Sts Sergius and Bacchus Once again', *BZ* 68: 385–392.
  (1977) 'The Liquidation of Iconoclasm and the Patriarch Photius', in *Iconoclasm: Papers Given at the Ninth Spring Symposium of Byzantine Studies*, eds. A. A. Bryer and J. Herrin. Birmingham: 133–40.
  (1978a) 'The Date of the Studios Basilica at Istanbul', *BMGS* 4: 115–22.
  (1978b) 'Who Wrote the Chronicle of Theophanes?', *ZRVI* 18: 9–17.
  (1982) 'St. Anthusa of Mantineon and the Family of Constantine V', *AnBoll* 100: 401–9.
  (1983) 'The Two Lives of St Ioannikios and the Bulgarians', *HUS* 7 (= *Okeanos: Essays Presented to I. Ševčenko on His Sixtieth Birthday by His Colleagues and Students*): 393–404.
  (1985) 'On Re-Reading the Life of St Gregory the Decapolite', *Byzantina* 13/1: 633–46.
  (1991) 'Greek Culture in Palestine after the Arab Conquest', in *Scritture, libri e testi nelle aree provinciali di bisanzio*, eds. G. Cavallo et al. Spoleto. Vol. I: 149–60.
  (1994) 'Notes d'épigraphie et d'archéologie: Constantinople, Nicée', *TM* 12: 343–58.
  (1999) 'The Relics of St Euphemia and the Synaxarion of Constantinople', *BBGG* 53 (= S. Lucà and L. Perria, *Studi in onore di mgr P. Canart per il LXX compleanno*), vol. III: 79–87.
  (2009) 'The Life of St Theodore of Chora and the Chronicle of Theophanes', in *Captain and Scholar: Papers in Memory of D. I. Polemis*, eds. E. Chrysos and E. A. Zachariadou. Andros: 183–94.
Mango, C., and Efthymiadis, S. (1997) *The Correspondence of Ignatios the Deacon*. Washington (CFHB 29, DOT 11).
Mango, C., and Hawkins, E. J. W. (1965) 'The Apse Mosaics of St Sophia at Istanbul: Report on Work Carried Out in 1964', *DOP* 19: 115–51.
  (1972) 'The Mosaics at St Sophia at Istanbul. The Church Fathers in the North Tympanum', *DOP* 26: 1–41.

Mango, C., and Ševčenko, I. (1973) 'Some Churches and Monasteries on the Southern Shore of the Sea of Marmara', *DOP* 27: 242–48.
Maraval, P. (1989) 'Songes et visions comme mode d'invention des reliques', *Augustinianum* 29: 583–99.
Marin, E. (1897) *Les moines de Constantinople*. Paris.
Marino, S. (1986) 'Considerazioni sulla personalità di Metodio I, patriarca da Costantinopoli', in *Culto delle imagini e crisi iconoclasta*, ed. C. Crimi. Palermo: 117–26.
Markopoulos, A. (1978) 'Ἡ Χρονογραφία του Ψευδο-Συμεών και οι πηγές της'. Unpublished PhD thesis. University of Ioannina.
  (1979) 'La Vie de Saint Georges d'Amastris et Photius', *JÖB* 28: 75–82 (repr. in *History and Literature of Byzantium in the 9th–10th Centuries*. Aldershot. 2004. Ch. II).
  (1983) 'Βίος τῆς αὐτοκράτειρας Θεοδώρας (*BHG* 1731)', *Symmeikta* 5: 249–85.
  (1986) 'Quelques remarques sur la famille des Genesioi aux IXe-Xe siècles', *ZRVI* 24/25: 103–8 (repr. in *History and Literature of Byzantium in the 9th–10th Centuries*. Aldershot. 2004. Ch. XI).
  (1992) 'An Anonymous Laudatory Poem in Honor of Basil I', *DOP* 46 (= *Homo Byzantinus: Papers in Honor of A. Kazhdan*): 225–32.
  (1994) 'Constantine the Great in Macedonian Historiography: Models and Approaches', in *New Constantines: The Rhythm of Imperial Renewal in Byzantium, 4th–13th Centuries*, ed. P. Magdalino. Aldershot: 159–70 (repr. in *History and Literature of Byzantium in the 9th and 10th Centuries*. Aldershot. 2004).
  (1998) 'The Rehabilitation of the Emperor Theophilos', in *Byzantium in the Ninth Century: Dead or Alive?*, ed. L. Brubaker. Aldershot: 37–49.
  (1999) 'La chronique de l'an 811 et le *Scriptor Incertus de Leone Armenio*: problèmes des relations entre l'hagiographie et l'histoire', *REB* 57: 255–62.
  (2013) 'Οι μεταμορφώσεις της μυθολογίας του Βασιλείου Α΄', in *Antecessor: Festschrift für S. N. Troianos zum 80. Geburtstag*, eds. V. A. Leontaritou et al. Athens: 945–70.
  (2015) 'Teachers and Textbooks in Byzantium, Ninth to Eleventh Centuries', in *Networks of Learning: Perspectives on Scholars in Byzantine East and Latin West, c. 1000–1200*, eds. S. Steckel et al. Berlin: 3–16.
  (2016) 'Notes et remarques sur la Vie de saint Pierre d'Atroa', in *Le saint, le moine et le paysan: Mélanges d'histoire byzantine offerts à M. Kaplan*, eds. O. Delouis et al. Paris: 395–405.
  (2017) 'L'éducation à Byzance aux IXe-Xe siècles: Problèmes et questions diverses', *TM* 21/2: 53–73.
Martin, E. J. (1930) *A History of the Iconoclast Controversy*. London (repr. New York. 1978).
Martin-Hisard, B. (1994) 'Le culte de l'archange Michel dans l'empire byzantin (VIIIe-XIe siècles)', in *Culto e insediamenti micaelici nell'Italia meridionale fra tarda antichità e medioevo*, eds. C. Carletti and G. Otranto. Bari: 351–73.

(2014) 'Hagiographie et Liturgie: Pantoléon et *l'Enkômion* pour l'archange Michel (*BHG* 1289)', in Συναξις καθολικη: *Beiträge zu Gottesdienst und Geschichte der fünf altkirchlichen Patriarchate für Heinzgerd Brakmann zum 70. Geburtstag*, eds. D. Atanassova and T. Chronz. Münster-Berlin: 451–76.

Matantseva, T. (1993) 'La Vie d'Hilarion, higoumène de Dalmatos, par Sabas (*BHG* 2177)', *RSBN* 30: 17–29.

(1996a) 'Eloge des archanges Michel et Gabriel par Michel le Moine (*BHG* 1294a)', *JÖB* 46: 97–155.

(1996b) 'Le *Vaticanus graecus* 1669, ménologe prémétaphrastique de novembre', *Scriptorium* 50/1: 106–13.

(1996c) 'Un fragment d'une nouvelle vie de saint Théodore Stoudite, vie D (*BHG* 1755f)', *BF* 23: 151–63.

(1998) 'La conférence sur la vénération des images en décembre 814', *REB* 56: 249–60.

Mathews, Th. (1971) *The Early Churches of Constantinople: Architecture and Liturgy*. University Park.

McCormick, M. (1994) 'Textes, images et iconoclasme in le cadre des relations entre Byzance et l'Occident carolingien', in *Testo e immagine nell'alto medioevo: Spoleto*. Vol. I: 95–162.

McGeer, E. et al. (1996) *Catalogue of Byzantine Seals at Dumbarton Oaks and in the Fogg Museum of Art, Vol. V: The East (Continued), Constantinople and Environs, Unknown Locations, Addenda, Uncertain Readings*. Washington.

Meijer, J. (1975) *A Successful Council of Union: A Theological Analysis of the Photian Synod of 879–880*. Thessaloniki.

Mellas, A. (1984) *Η Χάλκη των Πριγκηπονήσων*. Athens.

Menthon, B. (1935) *L'Olympe de Bithynie: Ses saints, ses couvents, ses sites: Une terre de légendes*. Paris.

Mercati, S. G. (1920) 'Note d'epigrafia bizantina (I.IV)', *Bessarione* 24: 192–205.

(1929/1930) 'Inno anacreontico alla SS. Trinità di Metrofane arcivescovo di Smirne', *BZ* 30: 54–60 (repr. in *Collectanea Byzantina*. Bari. 1970. Vol. I: 443–51).

(1953) 'Epigramma in esametri di Dionisio Studita in lode di san Teodoro e di Anatolio Studiti', *REB* 11: 224–32.

Métivier, S. (2008) 'L'organisation de la frontière arabo-byzantine en Cappadoce (VIIIe–IXe siècle)', in *Puer Apuliae: Mélanges offerts à J. M. Martin*, ed. E. Cuozzo. Paris. Vol. II: 433–54.

(2012) 'Aristocrate et saint: Le cas d'Eudokimos', in *Réseaux familiaux à la fin de l'Antiquité et au Moyen Âge: In memoriam A. Laiou et E. Patlagean*, ed. B. Caseau. Paris: 95–112.

(2017) 'Michel Maléinos, un saint des Phocas?', in *Mélanges J.-C. Cheynet*, eds. B. Caseau et al. Paris (= *TM* 21/1): 451–58.

(2018) 'Peut-on parler d'une hagiographie aristocratique à Byzance (VIIIe–XIe siècle)?', in *Byzantine Hagiography: Texts, Themes and Projects*, ed. A. Rigo. Turnhout: 179–99.

Métivier, S., and Papaconstantinou, A. (2007) 'L'école du monastère de Stoudios: Vie de Nicolas Stoudite', in *Économie et société à Byzance (VIIIe–XIIe siècle)*, ed. S. Métivier. Paris: 219.

Michanian, M., and Prigent, V. (2003) 'Les stratèges de Sicilie: De la naissance du thème au règne de Leon V', *REB* 61: 87–141.

Mioni, E. (1948) 'I Kontakia inediti di Giuseppe Innografo', *BBGG* 2: 87–98 and 177–92.

  (1950) 'L'encomio di S. Agata di Metodio patriarca di Costantinopoli', *AnBoll* 68: 58–93.

  (1967) *Bibliothecae Divi Marci Venetiarum. Codices Graeci manuscripti, vol. 1: Codices in classes a prima usque ad quintam inclusi, Pars prior: classis I– Classis II, codd. 1–120*. Rome.

  (1985) *Bibliothecae Diui Marci Venetiarum codices graeci manuscripti. Volumen II: Thesaurus Antiquus. Codices 300–625*. Rome.

Mitsiou, E. (2012) 'Networks of Nicaea: 13th century Socio-Economic Ties, Structures and Prosopography', in *Liquid and Multiple: Individuals and Identities in the Thirteenth-Century Aegean*, eds. G. Saint-Guillain and D. Stathakopoulos. Paris: 91–104.

Moffatt, A. (1977) 'Schooling in the Iconoclast Centuries', in *Iconoclasm: Papers Given at the Ninth Spring Symposium of Byzantine Studies*, eds. A. A. Bryer and J. Herrin. Birmingham: 85–92.

Mondrian, B. (1993) 'Antoine Éparque et Augsbourg: Le catalogue de vente des manuscrits grecs acquis par la ville d'empire', *BBGG* 47: 227–43.

Moravcsik, G. (1961) 'Sagen und Legenden über Kaiser Basileios I.', *DOP* 15: 59–126 (repr. in *Studia Byzantina*. Amsterdam. 1967).

Morini, E. (1979) 'Ancora sulla Vita di s. Giorgio di Amastride: Note su un recente contributo', *Studi e Ricerche sull' Oriente Cristiano* 2: 127–47.

Morris, R. (1995) *Monks and Laymen in Byzantium 843–1118*. Cambridge.

Müller, C. F. (1891) 'Ignatii Diaconi acrostichon alphabeticum', *Rheinisches Museum, N. F.* 46: 320–23.

Moulet, B. (2011) *Évêques, pouvoir et société à Byzance (VIIIe–XIe siècle): Territoires, communautés et individus dans la société provinciale byzantine*. Paris.

Mullett, M. (1984) 'Aristocracy and Patronage in the Literary Circles of Comnenian Constantinople', in *The Byzantine Aristocracy IX to XIII Centuries*, ed. M. Angold. Oxford: 173–201.

  (1990) 'Writing in Early Medieval Byzantium', in *The Uses of Literacy in Early Medieval Europe*, ed. R. McKitterick. Cambridge: 156–85.

  (1997) *Theophylact of Ochrid: Reading the Letters of a Byzantine Archbishop*. Aldershot.

Naumann, R., and Belting, H. (1966) *Die Euphemia-Kirche am Hippodrom zu Istanbul und ihre Fresken*. Berlin.

Nef, A., and Prigent, V. (2013) 'Guerroyer pour la Sicile (827–902)', in *La Sicilia del IX secolo tra Bizantini e musulmani*, eds. S. Modeo et al. Caltanisseta: 13–40.

Neil, B. (2006) *Seventh-Century Popes and Martyrs: The Political Hagiography of Anastasius Bibliothecarius*. Turnhout.

Neirynck, S., and Van Deun, P. (2018) 'Est-ce qu'on a decouvert la profession de foi de Metrophane de Smyrne?', in *The Literary Legacy of Byzantium: Editions, Translations, and Studies in Honour of J. A. Munitiz*, eds. P. Van Deun et al. Turnhout: 321–32.

Neville, L. (2018) *Guide to Byzantine Historical Writing*. Cambridge.

Niavis, P. (1987) *The Reign of the Byzantine Emperor Nicephorus I (AD 802–811)*. Athens.

(1990) 'Iosêph, Hegoumenos tês monês tôn Katharôn', *Byzantinos Domos* 4: 109–17.

Nicol, D. (1984) 'Prosopography of the Byzantine Aristocracy', in *The Byzantine Aristocracy: IX to XII Centuries*, ed. M. Angold. Oxford: 79–91.

Nikitin, P. (1895) 'O nekotorych grecheskich tekstach zhitij sviatych', *ZapANIst. fil.* Ser. 8, I.1: 1–67.

Nikolaou, K. (1994) 'Οι γυναίκες στο βίο και τα έργα του θεόφιλου', *Symmeikta* 9 (= *Μνήμη Δ.Α. Ζακυθηνοῦ*) Vol. 2: 137–51.

Nissen, Th. (1936/1938) 'Textkritisches zur Vita des Nikolaus Studites', *DChAE* 4: 91–99.

Nogara, A. (1978) 'Sergio il Confessore e il cod. 67 della *Biblioteca* di Fozio patriarca di Costantinopoli', *Aevum* 52: 261–66.

Norden, E. (1898) *Die Antike Kunstprosa vom IV Jahrhundert v. Chr. bis in die Zeit der Renaissance*. Leipzig (repr. 1995).

Noret, J. (1968) 'Ménologes, Synaxaires, Ménées: Essai de clarification d'une terminologie', *AnBoll* 86: 21–24.

Noyé, G. (1998) 'Byzance et Italie méridionale', in *Byzantium in the Ninth Century: Dead or Alive?*, ed. L. Brubaker. Aldershot: 229–43.

Odorico, P. (1983) 'La politica dell'immaginario di Leone VI il Saggio', *Byzantion* 53: 597–631.

(1986) *Il prato e l'ape: Il sapere sentenzioso del monaco Giovanni*. Vienna.

(1990) 'La cultura della syllogé. 1) Il cosiddetto enciclopedismo bizantino. 2) Le tavole dei sapere di Giovanni Damasceno', *BZ* 83: 1–23.

(2001) 'Idéologie politique, production littéraire et patronage au 10° siècle: l'empereur Constantin VII et le Synaxariste Evariste', *MEG* 1: 1–21.

(2002) 'L'auteur byzantin: Un essai de définition', in *Pour une nouvelle histoire de la littérature byzantine: Problèmes, méthodes, approches, propositions*, eds. P. Odorico and A. Agapitos. Paris: 61–80.

(2006) 'Displaying la littérature Byzantine', in *Proceedings of the 21st International Congress of Byzantine Studies (London 21–26 August 2006)*, eds. A. Bryer and E. Jeffreys. Aldershot. Vol. 1: 213–34.

(2011) 'Cadre d'exposition/cadre de pensée – la culture du recueil', in *Encyclopedic Trends in Byzantium?*, eds. P. Van Deun and C. Macé. Leuven: 89–107.

(2014) 'Prolegomènes à la litterature byzantine du IXe et du Xe siècle', in *Byzantine Culture*, ed. D. Sakel. Ankara: 93–108.

Odorico, P., and Agapitos, A. (2004) (eds.) *Les vies des saints à Byzance: Genre littéraire ou biographie historique?* Paris.

Oikonomidès, N. (1972) *Les listes de préséance byzantines des IXe et Xe siècles*. Paris.
  (1985) 'Some Remarks on the Apse Mosaic of St Sophia', *DOP* 39: 111–15.
  (1994) 'Pour une nouvelle lecture des inscriptions de Skripou en Béotie', *TM* 12: 479–93 (repr. in *Social and Economic Life in Byzantium*. Aldershot. 2004. Ch. xxvii).
  (1996) 'St. Andrew, Joseph the Hymnographer, and the Slavs of Patras', in Λειμών: *Studies presented to L. Rydén*, ed. J. O. Rosenqvist. Uppsala: 71–78 (repr. in *Social and Economic Life in Byzantium*. Aldershot. 2004. Ch. ix).
Ostrogorsky, G. (1930) 'Les débuts de la querelle des images', in *Études sur l'histoire et sur l'art de Byzance: Mélanges C. Diehl*. Paris. Vol. 1: 235–55.
  (1952) *Geschichte des byzantinischen Staates*. Munich.
Pankova, M. M. et al. eds. (2007) *Salterio griego Jlúdov (ms. gr. 129, Museo Histórico del Estado, Moscú): Libro de estudios*. Moscow-Madrid.
Papachryssanthou, D. (1973) 'La vie monastique dans les campagnes byzantines du VIIIe au XIe siècles: Ermitages, groupes, communautes', *Byzantion* 43: 158–80.
  (1974) 'La vie de saint Euthyme le Jeune et la métropole de Thessalonique à la fin du IX et au début du Xe siècle', *REB* 32: 225–45.
Papaconstantinou, A. (2012) 'Saints and Saracens: On Some Miracle Accounts of the Early Arab Period', in *Byzantine Religious Culture: Studies in Honor of A. M. Talbot*, eds. D. Sullivan et al. Leiden-Boston: 323–38.
Papadakis, A. (1970) 'The Unpublished Life of Euthymius of Sardis: *Bodleianus Laudianus Graecus 69*', *Traditio* 26: 63–89.
Papadopoulos, G. I. (1890) Συμβολαί εις την ιστορίαν της παρ' ημίν εκκλησιαστικής μουσικής και οι από των αποστολικών χρόνων άχρι των ημερών ημών ακμάσαντες επιφανέστεροι μελωδοί, υμνογράφοι, μουσικοί και μουσικολόγοι. Athens.
Papadopoulos-Kerameus, A. (1899) 'Ὁ Πατριάρχης Φώτιος ὡς πατὴρ ἅγιος τῆς Ὀρθοδόξου Καθολικῆς Ἐκκλησίας', *BZ* 8: 647–71.
  (1900) 'Theophanes Sikelos', *BZ* 9: 370–78.
  (1901) 'Καὶ πάλιν περὶ τῆς δευτέρας ᾠδῆς τῶν ᾀσματικῶν κανόνων', Ἐκκλησιαστικὴ Ἀλήθεια 21: 426–27.
  (1902) "Ὁ ὑμνογράφος Ἰγνάτιος', *Ekklesiastike Aletheia* 26: 37–39, 68–70 and 88–91.
Papaeliopoulou-Photopoulou, E. (1994/1995) 'Προβλήματα βυζαντινῆς ὑμνογραφίας ἢ περί τινων ἀκροστιχίδων τοῦ ὑμνογράφου Γεωργίου', *Diptycha* 6: 431–78.
Papaioannou, S. (2012) 'Rhetoric and the Philosopher in Byzantium', in *Essays in Byzantine Philosophy*, eds. K. Ierodiakonou and B. Bydén. Athens: 171–97.
  (2014) 'Voice, Signature, Mask: The Byzantine Author', in *The Author in Middle Byzantine Literature: Modes, Functions, and Identities*, ed. A. Pizzone. Berlin: 21–40.
Papagianni, E., and Troianos, S. (1984) 'Die Besetzung der Ämter im Grossskeuophylakeion der Grossen Kirche im 12. Jahrhundert', *FM* 6: 87–97.
Papavarnavas, Ch. (2016) 'The Role of the Audience in the Pre-Metaphrastic Passions', *AnBoll* 134/2: 66–82.

Pargoire, J. (1899) 'Une loi monastique de S. Platon', *BZ* 8: 98–101.
  (1900/1901) 'A quelle date l'hégoumène saint Platon est-il mort?', *EO* 4: 164–70.
  (1901a) 'Les monastères de saint Ignace et les cinq plus petit îlots de l'archipel des Princes', *IRAIK* 7: 56–91.
  (1901b) 'Saints Iconophiles', *EO* 4: 347–56.
  (1901/1902) 'Saint Euthyme et Jean de Sardes', *EO* 5: 157–61.
  (1902) 'S. Théophane le Chronographe et ses rapports avec s. Théodore Studite', *VizVrem* 9: 31–102.
  (1903a) 'Saint Méthode de Constantinople avant 821', *EO* 6: 126–31.
  (1903b) 'Saint Méthode et la persécution', *EO* 6: 183–91.
  (1906a) 'Saint Joseph de Thessalonique', *EO* 9: 278–82 and 351–56.
  (1906b) 'Saint Thaddée l'homologète', *EO* 9: 37–41.
  (1907) 'Les oeuvres de Saint Joseph de Thessalonique', *EO* 10: 207–10.
Parry, K. (1989) 'Theodore Studites and the Patriarch Nikephoros on Image-Making As a Christian Imperative', *Byzantion* 59: 164–83.
  (1996) *Depicting the Word: Byzantine Iconophile Thought of the Eighth and Ninth Centuries*. Leiden.
Paschalidis, S. A. (1994a) "Ἕνας ὁμολογητής τῆς δευτέρης Εἰκονομαχίας· ὁ ἀρχιεπίσκοπος Θεσσαλονίκης Ἀντώνιος (†844)', *Βυζαντινά* 17: 189–216.
  (1994b) "Ἡ συνείδηση τῆς Ἐκκλησίας γιὰ τὴν ἁγιότατη τοῦ Μ. Φωτίου καὶ ἡ ἔνταξή του στὸ ἑορτολόγιο. Καταγραφὴ καὶ ἀνάλυση τῶν φιλοφωτιανῶν καὶ ἀντιφωτιανῶν πηγῶν', in *Μνήμη Ἁγίων Γρηγορίου τοῦ Θεολόγου καὶ Μεγάλου Φωτίου, ἀρχιεπισκόπων Κωνσταντινουπόλεως*, eds. Th. Zissis et al. Thessaloniki: 367–97.
  (1999) *Νικήτας Δαβὶδ Παφλαγών: Το πρόσωπο και το έργο του*. Thessaloniki.
  (2004) 'From Hagiography to Historiography: The Case of the *Vita Ignatii* (*BHG* 817) by Nicetas David the Paphlagonian', in *Les Vies de Saints à Byzance. Genre littéraire ou biographie historique?*, eds. P. Odorico and P. A. Agapitos. Paris: 161–73.
Patlagean, E. (1968) 'À Byzance: Ancienne hagiographie et histoire sociale', *Annales. ÉSC* 23/1: 106–26 (repr. in *Structure sociale, famille, Chrétienté à Byzance: IVe–XIe siècle*. London. 1981. Ch. v).
  (1976) 'L'histoire de la femme déguisée en moine et l'évolution de la sainteté feminine à Byzance', *SM*, 3e série, 17, Spoleto: 617–23 (repr. in *Structure sociale, famille, chrétienté à Byzance: IVe-XIe siècle*. London. 1981. Ch. XI).
  (1981) 'Sainteté et pouvoir', in *The Byzantine Saint*, ed. S. Hackel. London: 88–105 (repr. in *Figures du pouvoir à Byzance, IXe–XIIe siècle*. Spoleto. 2001: 173–98).
  (1984a) 'Les debuts d'une aristocratie byzantine et le témoignage de l'historiographie: Système des nombs et liens de parenté aux IXe–Xe siècles', in *The Byzantine Aristocracy: IX to XII Centuries*, ed. M. Angold. Oxford: 23–42 (repr. in *Figures du pouvoir à Byzance: IXe–XIIe siècle*. Spoleto. 2001: 131–57).

(1984b) 'Théodora de Thessalonique. Une sainte moniale et un culte citadin (IXe–XXe siècle)', in *Culto dei santi, istituzioni e classi sociali in età preindustriale*, eds. S. B. Gajano and L. Sebastiani. Rome: 37–67.

(1988) 'Les Stoudites, l'empereur et Rome', in *Bisanzio, Roma e l'Italia nell'alto medioevo*. Spoleto. Vol. 1: 429–60 (repr. in *Figures du pouvoir à Byzance: IXe–XIIe siècle*. Spoleto. 2001: 73–98).

(1989) 'Le Basileus assassiné et la Sainteté Impériale', in *Media in Francia: Recueil de mélanges offert à K. F. Werner*. Maulévrier: 345–61.

Patterson Ševčenko, N. (1998) 'Canon and Calendar: The Role of a Ninth-Century Hymnographer in Shaping the Celebration of the Saints', in *Byzantium in the Ninth Century: Dead or Alive?*, ed. L. Brubaker. Aldershot: 101–14.

(2013) 'The Imperial Menologia and the "Menologion" of Basil II.', in *The Celebration of the Saints in Byzantine Art and Liturgy*, N. Patterson Ševčenko. Farnham: 1–32.

Peeters, P. (1911) 'S. Romain le néomartyr († 1 mai 780) d'après un document géorgien', *AnBoll* 30: 393–427.

(1951) 'Une sainte arménienne oubliée: Sainte Marie la Jeune († 902–903)', *Recherches d'histoire et de philologie orientales* 1: 129–35.

Pelekanides, S. et al. eds. (1979) Οι Θησαυροί του Αγίου Όρους. Εικονογραφημένα χειρόγραφα. Athens.

Pelikan, J. (2011) *Imago Dei: The Byzantine Apologia for Icons*. Oxford.

Pentcheva, B. V. (2006) *Icons and Power: The Mother of God in Byzantium*. University Park.

(2010) *The Sensual Icon: Space, Ritual, and the Senses in Byzantium*. University Park.

Pentkovskij, A. M. (2001) *Tipikon patriarha Aleksija Studita v Bizantii i na Rusi*. Moscow.

Perger, T. (1901) *Scriptores Originum Constantinopolitarum*. Leipzig (repr. New York. 1975).

Peri, V. (1976) 'C'è un concilio ecumenico ottavo?', *AHC* 8: 43–79.

(1988/1989) 'La brama e lo zelo della Fede del popolo chiamato Rhos', *Harvard Ukrainian Studies* 12/13: 39–62.

Perria, L. (1991) 'La minuscola "tipo Anastasio"', in *Scritture, libri e testi nelle aree provinciali di Bisanzio*, eds. G. Cavallo et al. Spoleto. Vol. 1: 271–318.

(1993) 'Scrittura e ornamentazione nei manoscritti di origine studita', *BBGG* 47: 245–80.

Perrone, L. (1990) 'Il Costantinopolitano IV (869–870): Primato romano, pentarchia e comunione ecclesiale alla vigilia della separazione fra oriente e occidente', in *Storia dei concili ecumenici*, ed. G. Alberigo. Brescia: 155–81.

Perry, B. E. (1953) 'An Aesopic Fable in Photius', *BZ* 46: 308–313.

Petit, L. (1900) 'Les évêques de Thessalonique', *EO* 4: 216–17.

(1916) 'Le Synodicon de Thessalonique', *EO* 18: 236–54.

(1926) *Bibliographie des acolouthies grecques*. Brussels.

Pétridès, S. (1903) 'Office inédit de saint Clément', *BZ* 12: 575–81.

Petrov, P. (1966) 'La politique étranger de la Bulgarie au milieu du IXe siècle et la conversion des Bulgares', *BBulg* 2: 41–52.

Phountoules, I. M. (1961) 'Οἱ ὅσοι αὐτάδελφοι Δαβίδ, Συμεών καὶ Γεώργιος, οἱ ὁμολογηταί', in *Λεσβιακὸν ἑορτολόγιον*, ed. I. M. Phoutoules. Athens. Vol. III: 9–10.

Phytrakes, A. (1968) '"Ἅγιος Νικόλαος ὁ Κυδωνιεύς', in *Πεπραγμένα τοῦ Β΄ διεθνοῦς Κρητολογικοῦ συνεδρίου*. Athens, ed. N. M. Panaiotakis. Vol. III: 286–303.

Pignani, A. (2007) *Teodoro Studita: Catechesi-epitafio per la madre*. Naples.

  (2009) 'Ancora sulla Catechesi – epitafio per la madre di Teodoro Studita: In margine a una recente recensione', *Bizantinistica* 11: 183–204.

Pitsakis, K. G. (2009) 'Φώτιος ... ὁ μετονομασθεὶς Ταράσιος· σχετικὰ με μία παράδοξη ταύτιση', in *Realia Byzantina*, eds. S. Kotzabassi and G. Mavromatis. Berlin: 197–206.

Pizzone, A. (2012) 'Theodore and the Black Man: Imagining (through) the Icon in Byzantium', in *Knotenpunkt Byzanz: Wissensformen und kulturelle Wechselbeziehungen*, eds. A. Speer and P. Steinkrüger. Berlin: 47–70.

  (2014) 'Introduction: The Author in Middle Byzantine Literature: A View from Within', in *The Author in Middle Byzantine Literature: Modes, Functions, and Identities*, ed. A. Pizzone. Berlin: 3–18.

Podolak, P. (2015) 'L'agiografia di Dionigi fra Oriente e Occidente: Breve studio del suo sviluppo ed edizione del panegirico di Michele Sinchello (*BHG* 556)', *Byzantion* 85: 179–258.

Polemis, I. D. (1989) 'Φιλολογικὲς παρατηρήσεις σὲ βυζαντινὰ ἁγιολογικὰ καὶ ῥητορικὰ κείμενα', *Hell* 40: 403–8.

Polidori, V. (2014) 'Photius and Metrophanes of Smyrna: The Controversy of the Authorship of the *Mystagogy of the Holy Spirit*', *MEG* 14: 199–208.

Politis, L. (1968) 'Συμπληρωματικοὶ κατάλογοι χειρογράφων Ἁγίου Ὄρους', *Hell* 21: 347–77.

Poljakova, S. V. (1973) 'Fol'klornyj suzet o scastlivom glupce v nekotorych pamjatnikach agiografii VIII v.', *VizVrem* 34: 130–36.

Potache, D. (1981) 'Le theme et la forteresse de Charsianon: Recherches dans la région d'Akdagmadeni', in *Geographica Byzantina*, ed. H. Ahrweiler. Paris: 101–7.

Pott, T. (2000) *La réforme liturgique byzantine: Étude du phénomène de l'évolution non-spontanée de la liturgie byzantine*. Rome.

Prato, G. (1986) 'Attività scrittoria in Calabria tra IX e X secolo', *JÖB* 36: 219–28 (repr. in *Studi di paleografia greca*. Spoleto. 1994: 1–11 + figures).

  (2000) 'Una questione di metodo', in *I manoscritti greci tra riflessione e dibattito: Atti del V Colloquio Internazionale di Paleografia Greca*, ed. G. Prato. Florence. Vol. II: 701–7.

Pratsch, T. (1998) *Theodoros Studites (759–826) - zwischen Dogma und Pragma: Der Abt des Studiosklosters in Konstantinopel im Spannungsfeld von Patriarch, Kaiser und eigenem Anspruch*. Bern.

(2000) 'Ignatios the Deacon – Cleric of the Constantinopolitan Patriarchate, Metropolitan Bishop of Nikaia, Private Scholar, Teacher and Writer (a Life Reconsidered)', *BMGS* 24: 82–101.

(2001) 'Ein Brief Platons in zwei Briefen des Theodoros Studites – eine textkritische Anmerkung', *GBBNPh* 1: 63–74.

(2004) 'Das Todesdatum der Maria (der Jüngeren) von Bizye (*BHG* 1164): † 16. Februar 902', *BZ* 97/2: 567–69.

(2005) *Der hagiographische Topos: Griechische Heiligenviten in mittelbyzantinischer Zeit*. Berlin.

(2007) 'Mönchsorden in Byzanz? – zur Entstehung und Entwicklung monastischer Verbände in Byzanz (8.–10. Jh.)', *Millennium-Jahrbuch* 4: 261–77.

Preiser-Kapeller, J. (2020) 'Letters and Network Analysis', in *Companion to Byzantine Epistolography*, ed. A. Riehle. Leiden: 431–65.

Prell, C. (2012) *Social Network Analysis: History, Theory and Methodology*. Los Angeles-London.

Prieto Domínguez, Ó. (2008) 'Problemas de cronología relativa en dos *corpora* del patriarca Focio: *Epistulae* y *Amphilochia*', *MEG* 8: 255–70.

(2013) 'On the Founder of the Skripou Church: Literary Trends in the Milieu of Photius', *GRBS* 53/1: 166–91.

(2014a) 'The Massive Conversion of Jews Decreed by Emperor Basil I in 873–874: Its Reflection in Contemporary Legal Codes and Its Underlying Reasons', in *Jews in Early Christian Law: Byzantium and the Latin West, 6th–11th c.*, eds. J. Tolan et al. Turnhout: 283–310.

(2014b) 'Recounting Suffering: Patriarchal Tortures in Greek Medieval Literature', in *Agalma: Homenaje a M. García Teijeiro*. Valladolid: 583–88.

(2016a) 'Saint Theokleto: A Female Iconoclast Saint', *AnBoll* 134/2: 293–302.

(2016b) 'Saint Iakobos the Confessor, the Baptiser of Patriarch Photios', *JÖB* 66: 179–86.

(2019a) *Casia de Constantinopla: Poemas*. Madrid.

(2019b) 'The Iconoclast Saint: Emperor Theophilos in Byzantine Hagiography', in *The Emperor in the Byzantine World*, ed. S. Tougher. London: 163–84.

Prigent, V. (2006) 'La carrière du tourmarque Euphèmios, basileus des Romains', in *Histoire et culture in l'Italie byzantine: Acquis et nouvelles recherches*, eds. A. Jacob et al. Rome: 279–317.

(2017) 'À l'ouest rien de nouveau? L'Italie du Sud et le premier humanisme byzantin', *TM* 21/2: 129–64.

Quacquarelli, A. (1975) *Il Leone e il Drago nella Simbolica dell' Età Patristica*. Bari.

Raasted, J. (1981) 'A Byzantine Letter in Sankt Gallen and Lazarus the Painter', *Cahiers de l'Institut du moyen-âge grec et latin* 37: 124–38.

Rapp, C. (1993) 'Epiphanius of Salamis: The Church Father As Saint', in *'The Sweet Land of Cyprus': Papers Given at the Twenty-Fifth Jubilee Spring Symposium of Byzantine Studies*, eds. A. A. Bryer and G. S. Georghallides. Nicosia: 169–87.

(1995) 'Byzantine Hagiographers As Antiquarians, 7th to 10th Century', in *Bosphorus: Essays in Honour of C. Mango*, eds. S. Efthymiadis et al. Amsterdam (= *BF* 21): 31–44.
  (2015) 'Author, Audience, Text and Saint: Two Modes of Early Byzantine Hagiography', *SJBMGS* 1: 111–29.
Rekaya, M. (1974) 'Mise au point sur Théophobe et l'alliance de Bâbek avec Théophile (833/34–839/40)', *Byzantion* 44: 43–67.
Resh, D. (2015) 'Toward a Byzantine Definition of Metaphrasis', *GRBS* 55/3: 754–87.
Reynolds, D. (2017) 'Rethinking Palestinian Iconoclasm', *DOP* 71: 1–64.
Rezác, G. (1958) 'Le diverse forme di unione fra i monasteri orientali', in *Il monachesimo orientale (OCA 153)*. Rome: 99–135.
Ricci, A. (1998) 'The Road from Baghdad to Byzantium and the Case of the Bryas Palace in Istanbul', in *Byzantium in the Ninth Century: Dead or Alive?*, ed. L. Brubaker. Aldershot: 131–49.
  (2012) 'Left Behind: Small Sized Objects from the Middle Byzantine Monastic Complex of Satyros (Küçükyalı, Istanbul)', in *Byzantine Small Finds in Archaeological Contexts*, eds. B. Böhlendorf-Arslan and A. Ricci. Istanbul: 147–62.
Riedel, M. L. D. (2018) *Leo VI and the Transformation of Byzantine Christian Identity: Writings of an Unexpected Emperor*. Cambridge.
Ringrose, K. (1979) 'Monks and Society in Iconoclastic Byzantium', *Byzantine Studies/Études Byzantines* 6 (= *Essays in Honor of P. Charanis Offered by His Students on the Occasion of His Seventieth Birthday*): 130–51.
  (1999) 'Passing the Test of Sanctity: Denial of Sexuality and Involuntary Castration', in *Desire and Denial in Byzantium*, ed. L. James. Aldershot: 123–37.
Rigo, A. (2006) 'Niceta Byzantios, la sua opera e il monaco Evodio', in *'In partibus clius': Scritti in onore di G. P. Carratelli*, ed. G. Fiaccadori. Naples: 147–87.
Rizzo Nervo, F. (1991) 'Teodora Raoulena: Tra agiografia e politica', in *Syndesmos: Studi in onore di R. Anastasi*, ed. A. Carile. Catania. Vol. 1: 147–61.
Robins, R. H. (1993) *The Byzantine Grammarians: Their Place in History*. Berlin.
Rochow, I. (1967) *Studien zu der Person, den Werken und dem Nachleben der Dichterin Kassia*. Berlin.
  (1983) 'Antihäretische Schriften byzantinischer Autoren aus der Zeit zwischen 843 und 1025: Ein Überblick', in *Besonderheiten der byzantinischen Feudalentwicklung*, ed. H. Köpstein. Berlin: 98–102.
  (1991) *Byzanz im 8. Jahrhundert in der Sicht des Theophanes: Quellenkritisch-historischer Kommentar zu den Jahren 715–813*. Berlin.
  (1994) *Kaiser Konstantin V. (741–775): Materialien zu seinem Leben und Nachleben. Mit einem prosopographischen Anhang von C. Ludwig, I. Rochow u. R. J. Lilie*. Frankfurt.
Rognoni, C. (2010) 'Au pied de la lettre? Réflexions à propos du témoignage de Théodose, moine et grammatikos, sur la prise de Syracuse en 878', in

La Sicile de Byzance à l'Islam: De l'archéologie à l'histoire, eds. A. Nef and V. Prigent. Paris: 205–28.
Ronconi, F. (2011) 'Le silence des livres. Manuscrits philosophiques et circulation des idées à l'époque byzantine moyenne', in *Il libro filosofico dall'antichità al XX secolo, Atti del Convegno internazionale, Cassino, 25–26 maggio 2011*, eds. L. Del Corso and P. Pecere. Turnhout (= *Quaestio* 11): 169–207.
  (2012a) 'La main insaisissable: Rôle et fonctions des copistes byzantins entre réalité et imaginaire', in *Scrivere e leggere nell'alto medioevo: LIX settimana di studio della fondazione C.I.S.A.M.* Spoleto: 627–68.
  (2012b) 'La collection brisée: La face cachée de la "Collection philosophique": Les milieux socioculturels', in *La face cachée de la littérature byzantine: Le texte en tant que message immédiat*, ed. P. Odorico. Paris: 137–58.
  (2014) 'Essere copista a Bisanzio: Tra immaginario collettivo, autorappresentazioni e realtà', in *Storia della scrittura e altre storie*, ed. D. Bianconi. Rome: 383–434.
  (2015a) 'La première circulation de la "chronique de Théophane": Notes paléographiques et codicologiques', in *Studies in Theophanes*, eds. M. Jankowiak and F. Montinaro. Paris (= *TM* 19): 121–48.
  (2015b) 'Il Moveable Feast del Patriarca: Note e ipotesi sulla genesi della Bibliotheca di Fozio', in *Nel segno del testo: Edizioni, materiali e studi per Oronzo Pecere*, eds. L. Del Corso et al. Florence: 203–38.
  (2017) 'De Stoudios à la Théotokos Evérgétès: Textes et livres du monachisme méso-byzantin, entre innovations et continuité', in *Monachesimi d'Oriente e d'Occidente: LXIV settimana di studio della fondazione C.I.S.A.M.* Spoleto: 1293–370.
  (2018) 'Le "Schisme photien": La contribution de Francis Dvorník', in *Homage to Francis Dvorník: Francis Dvorník – Scholar and His work*, eds. V. Vavřínek et al. Prague (*Byzantinoslavica* 76/3 Supplementum): 49–64.
Rosenqvist, J. O. (2002) 'A Philological Adventure: Editing the Life of St Niketas of Medikion', *ABzF* 1: 59–72.
Rosser, J. (1974) 'Theophilus' Khurramite Policy and Its Finale: The Revolt of Theophobus' Persian Troops in 838', *Byzantina* 6: 263–71.
  (1983) 'Theophilos (829–842): Popular Sovereign, Hated Persecutor', *Byzantiaká* 3: 37–56.
Rossi Taibbi, G. (1965) *Sulla tradizione manoscritta dell'omiliario di Filagato da Cerami*. Palermo.
Roth, C. (1983) *On the Holy Icons*. Crestwood.
Ruffini, G. R. (2008) *Social Networks in Byzantine Egypt*. Cambridge.
Ruggieri, E. (1985) 'Anthousa di Mantineon ed il canone XX del Concilio di Nicea II (anno 787)', *JÖB* 35: 131–42.
Ruggieri, V. (1991) *Byzantine Religious Architecture (582–867): Its History and Structural Elements*. Rome.
Ruggieri, V., and Nethercott, F. (1986) 'The Metropolitan City of Syllion and Its Churches', *JÖB* 36: 133–56.
Russell, D. A., and Wilson, N. G. eds. (1981) *Menander Rhetor*. Oxford.

Rydén, L. (1985) 'The Bride-Shows at the Byzantine Court: History or Fiction?', *Eranos* 83: 175–91.
  (1986) 'New Forms of Hagiography: Heroes and Saints', in *The 17th International Byzantine Congress: Major Papers*. Washington: 537–54.
  (2002) *The Life of St Philaretos the Merciful Written by His Grandson Niketas*. Uppsala.
Sahas, D. J. (1986) 'What an Infidel Saw That a Faithful Did Not: Gregory Dekapolites (d. 842) and Islam', *GOTR* 31: 47–67.
Salucci, B. (1973) *La scuola calligrafica del monastero bizantino di Studios*. Messina-Florence.
Salvemini, R. (1997) 'Aspetti letterari dell'Epistolario di Fozio', *Annali della Facoltà di Lettere e Filosofia di Bari* 40: 191–208.
  (2000) 'Empietà e follia nella caratterizzazione degli eretici. Alle origini del lessico di Fozio', *Nicolaus* 27: 355–89.
Sansterre, J. M. (1973) 'Les représentants des patriarcats au concile photien d'août-septembre 867', *Byzantion* 43: 195–228.
  (1983) *Les moines grecs et orientaux à Rome aux époques byzantine et carolingienne (milieu du VIe s.–fin du IXe s.)*. Brussels.
  (1994) 'La parole, le texte, et l'imagine selon les auteurs byzantins des époques iconoclaste et posticonoclaste', in *Testo e immagine nell'alto medioevo: Settimane di Studi del Centro Italiano di Studi sull'Alto Medioevo* 41. Spoleto: 197–240.
  (1996) 'Les informations parvenues en Occident sur l'avènement de l'empereur Léon V et le siège de Constantinople par les Bulgares en 813', *Byzantion* 66: 373–80.
Saradi, H. (1995) 'Constantinople and Its Saints (IVth–VIth c.): The Image of the City and Social Considerations', *Studi Medievali* n.s. III/36: 87–110.
Sarris, V. A. (2005) *Η βυζαντινή παραμυθητική επιστολή· από τον Θεόδωρο Στουδίτη εως τον Ευστάθιο Θεσσαλονίκης (9ος–12ος αι.)*. Athens.
Schamp, J. (2008) 'Photios, maître de l'art épistolaire', in *Epistulae antiquae V. Actes du Vᵉ Colloque international 'L'épistolaire antique et ses prolongements européens', Université François-Rabelais*, eds. P. Laurence and F. Guillaumont. Leuven-Paris: 309–25.
  (2011) 'Le projet pédagogique de Photios', in *Encyclopedic Trends in Byzantium?*, eds. P. Van Deun and C. Macé. Leuven: 57–75.
Schiffer, E. (1996) 'Metaphrastic Lives and Earlier *Metaphraseis* of Saint's Lives', in *Metaphrasis: Redactions and Audiences in Middle Byzantine Hagiography*, ed. C. Högel. Oslo: 22–42.
  (2004) '"Hypomnema" als Bezeichnung hagiographischer Texte', in *Wiener Byzantinistik und Neogräzistik: Beiträge zum Symposium vierzig Jahre Institut für Byzantinistik und Neogräzistik der Universität Wien im Gedenken an Herbert Hunger*, eds. W. Hörandner et al. Vienna: 397–407.
Schirò, G., and Gonzato, A. (1960) 'Per un'edizione di "Analecta Hymnica e codicibus eruta Italiae inferioris"', in *Akten des XI: Internationalen Byzantinisten-Kongresses, München 1958*, eds. F. J. Dölger and H. G. Beck. Munich: 539–55.

Schminck, A. (1985) 'Rota tu volubilis: Kaisermacht und Patriarchenmacht in Mosaiken', in *Cupido legum*, eds. L. Burgmann et al. Frankfurt: 211–34.
  (1989) '*In hoc signo vinces* – Aspects du 'césaropapisme' à l'époque de Constantin VII Porphyrogénète', in *Constantine VII Porphyrogenitus and His Age*, ed. A. Markopoulos. Athens: 103–16.
  (2000) 'The Beginnings and Origins of the Macedonian Dynasty', in *Byzantine Macedonia: Identity, Image and History*, eds. J. Burke and R. Scott. Melbourne: 61–68.
  (2005) 'Zur Einzelgesetzgebung der "makedonischen" Kaiser', *FM* 11: 269–324.
Schmit, T. (1906) 'Kachrie-Dzami', *IRAIK* 11: 8–23, 27–29, 260–79 and 295–301.
Schönauer, S. (2010) 'Zu Spielarten der mimesis in der profanen Dichtung der Kassia', in *Imitatio – aemulatio – variatio*, ed. A. Rhoby. Vienna: 243–52.
Schor, A. M. (2011) *Theodoret's People: Social Networks and Religious Conflict in Late Roman Syria*. Berkeley.
Scott, J., and Carrington, P. J. (2011) *The Sage Handbook of Social Network Analysis*. Los Angeles.
Schreiner, P. (1976) 'Legende und Wirklichkeit in der Darstellung des byzantinischen Bilderstreites', *Saeculum* 27: 165–79.
  (1987) 'Das Christentum in Bulgarien vor 864', in *Das Christentum in Bulgarien und auf der übrigen Balkanhalbinsel in der Spätantike und im frühen Mittelalter*, eds. V. Gjuzelev and R. Pillinger. Vienna: 51–61.
  (1988) 'Der byzantinische Bilderstreit: Kritische Analyse der zeitgenössischen Meinungen und das Urteil der Nachwelt bis heute', in *Bisanzio, Roma e l'Italia nell'Alto Medioevo* (Settimane di Studio del centro italiano di studi sull'alto medioevo 34). Spoleto: 319–427.
Schukin, T. (2008) 'Iconoclastic Fragment of the Apologetic Note by John Italos', *Scrinium* 4: 249–59.
Schwartz, E. (1939) *Kyrillos von Skythopolis*. Leipzig.
Seibt, W. (2002) 'Beinamen, "Spitznamen", Herkunftsnamen, Familiennamen bis ins 10. Jahrhundert: Der Beitrag der Sigillographie zu einem prosopographischen Problem', *SBS* 7: p. 119–36.
Senina, T. A. (2008a) 'Notices sur l'atmosphère intellectuelle à l'époque du second iconoclasme', *Scrinium* 4: 318–40.
  (2008b) 'La confession de Théophane et Théodore les Graptoi: remarques et précisions', *Scrinium* 4: 260–98.
  (2009) 'Un saint fouette un autre: Théoktistos le logothète et Euthyme de Sardes', *Scrinium* 5: 391–93.
  (2011/2012) 'Remarques sur les canons en l'honneur des saints patriarches Taraise et Méthode de Constantinople', *Scrinium* 7–8: 69–81.
  (2013) 'Remarques sur l'auteur et la date de *Scriptor Incertus de Leone Armenio*', *Scrinium* 9: 399–409.
  (2014) 'Concerning the Dates of St Makarios of Pelekete's Life and the Dating of His Vita', *Scrinium* 10: 245–50.

(2015) 'Notes hagiographiques sur l'époque du second iconoclasme', *Scrinium* 11: 306–13.
(2016) 'Sur l'origine des sobriquets de Jean le Grammairien *Jannes* et *Sorcier*', *Scrinium* 12: 322–28.
(2019) 'Les motifs hellénistiques dans le poème de Léon le Philosophe *Job*', *Byzantina Symmeikta* 29: 11–24.
Settipani, C. (2006) *Continuité des élites à Byzance durant les siècles obscurs: Les princes Caucasiens et l'empire du VIe au IXe siècle*. Paris.
(2012) 'Les réseaux familiaux dans l'aristocratie byzantine: Quelques exemples du VIe au XIe siècle', in *Réseaux familiaux à la fin de l'Antiquité et au Moyen Âge. In memoriam A. Laiou et E. Patlagean*, ed. B. Caseau. Paris: 287–306.
Ševčenko, I. (1956) 'The Definition of Philosophy in the Life of Saint Constantine', in *For R. Jakobson: Essays on the Occasion of His Sixtieth Birthday*, eds. M. Halle et al. The Hague: 449–57 (repr. in *Byzantium and the Slavs*. Cambridge, MA. 1991).
(1962) 'The Illuminators of the Menologium of Basil II', *DOP* 16: 248–76 (repr. in *Ideology, Letters and Culture in the Byzantine World*. London. 1982. Ch. XI).
(1965) 'The Anti-Iconoclastic Poem in the Pantocrator Psalter', *CahArch* 15: 39–60 (repr. in *Ideology, Letters and Culture in the Byzantine World*. London. 1982. Ch. XIII).
(1977a) 'Hagiography of the Iconoclast Period', in *Iconoclasm: Papers Given at the Ninth Spring Symposium of Byzantine Studies*, eds. A. A. Bryer and J. Herrin. Birmingham: 113–31 (repr. in *Ideology, Letters and Culture in the Byzantine World*. London. 1982. Ch. V).
(1977b) 'L'agiografia bizantina dal IV al IX secolo', in *La civiltà bizantina dal IV al IX secolo: Aspetti e problemi*, ed. A. Guillou. Bari: 87–173.
(1979/1980) 'Constantinople Viewed from the Eastern Provinces in the Middle Byzantine Period', *HUS* 3–4: 712–47 (repr. in *Ideology, Letters and Culture in the Byzantine World*. London. 1982. Ch. VI).
(1981) 'Levels of Style in Byzantine Prose', *JÖB* 31/1: 289–312.
(1982) 'Additional Remarks to the Report on Levels of Style', *JÖB* 32/1: 220–38.
(1987) 'An Early Tenth-Century Inscription from Galakrenai with Echoes from Nonnos and the Palatine Anthology', *DOP* 41: 461–68.
(1992) 'The Search for the Past in Byzantium around the Year 800', *DOP* 46: 280–93.
(1995) 'Was There Totalitarianism in Byzantium? Constantinople's Control over Its Asiatic Hinterland in the Early 9th Century', in *Constantinople and Its Hinterland*, eds. C. Mango and G. Dagron. Aldershot: 91–105.
Shoemaker, S. J. (2008) 'The Cult of Fashion: The Earliest *Life of the Virgin* and Constantinople's Marian Relics', *DOP* 62: 53–74
(2011) 'A Mother's Passion: Mary at the Crucifixion and Resurrection in the Earliest *Life of the Virgin* and Its Influence on George of Nikomedeia's Passion Homilies', in *The Cult of the Mother of God in Byzantium: Texts and Images*, eds. L. Brubaker and M. B. Cunningham. Farnham: 53–67.

Sideras, A. (1994) *Die byzantinischen Grabreden*. Vienna.
Sietis, N. (2018) 'Considerazioni su circolazione e produzione libraria in Bitinia al tempo della controversia iconoclasta: Le fonti agiografiche', in *Un large Moyen Âge? L'œuvre de J. Le Goff et les études byzantines*, eds. B. Campos Rubillar et al. Paris: 207–26.
Signes Codoñer, J. (1995) *El período del segundo iconoclasmo en Theophanes Continuatus*. Amsterdam.
  (2002) 'Helenos y Romanos: La identidad bizantina y el Islam en el siglo IX', *Byzantion* 72: 404–48.
  (2006) 'Lust am Erzählen: Heiligenviten als Grundlage der Geschichtsschreibung im 10. Jahrhundert und der Weg nach Bagdad', in *La litteralité de l'historiographie: Troisième colloque international sur la litterature byzantine*, ed. P. Odorico. Paris: 85–105.
  (2013a) 'Melkites and Icon Worship during the Iconoclastic Period', *DOP* 67: 135–87.
  (2013b) 'Dead or Alive? Manuel the Armenian's (After)life after 838', in *Pour l'amour de Byzance: Hommage à P. Odorico*, eds. Ch. Gastgeber et al. Frankfurt am Main: 231–42.
  (2013c) 'Die melkitischen Patriarchen, Konstantinopel und der Bilderkult in der zweiten Hälfte des 9. Jahrhunderts: Mit besonderer Berücksichtigung vom Brief 2 des Photios und dem sogenannten Brief der drei Patriarchen an Theophilos', in *Zwei Sonnen am Goldenen Horn? Kaiserliche und patriarchale Macht im byzantinischen Mittelalter*, eds. M. Grünbart et al. Münster: 97–134.
  (2014) *The Emperor Theophilos and the East, 829–842: Court and Frontier in Byzantium during the Last Phase of Iconoclasm*. Aldershot.
  (2015) 'Theophanes at the Time of Leo VI', in *Studies in Theophanes*, eds. M. Jankowiak and F. Montinaro. Paris (= *TM* 19): 159–76.
Signes Codoñer, J., and Andrés Santos, F. J. (2007) *La 'Introducción al derecho' (Eisagogé) del patriarca Focio*. Madrid.
Simeonova, L. (1988) *Diplomacy of the Letter and the Cross: Photios, Bulgaria and the Papacy, 860s–880s*, Amsterdam.
Sode, C. (2001) *Jerusalem – Konstantinopel – Rom: Die Viten des Michael Synkellos und der Bruder Theodoros und Theophanes Graptoi*. Stuttgart.
  (2004) 'Creating New Saints: The Case of Michael the Synkellos and Theodore and Theophane the Graptoi', in *The Heroes of the Orthodox Church: The New Saints (8th–16th c.)*, ed. E. Kountoura-Galaki. Athens: 180–89.
Sorlin, I. (1961) 'Les Traités de Byzance avec la Russie au Xe siècle', *Cahiers du monde russe et soviétique* II/3: 313–60.
Sot, M. (1978) 'Historiographie épiscopale et modèle familial en Occident au IXe siècle', *Annales ESC* 33: 433–49.
Spadaro, M. D. (1971) 'Sulle composizioni di Constantino il Filosofo del Vatican 915', *SicGym* 24: 175–205.
Spanos, A. (2010) *Codex Lesbiacus Leimonos 11*. Berlin.
  (2014) 'Political Approaches to Byzantine Liturgical Texts', in *Approaches to the Text. From Pre-Gospel to Post-Baroque*, eds. R. Eriksen and P. Young. Rome: 63–81.

Speck, P. (1963) 'Humanistenhandschriften und frühe Drucke der Epigramme des Theodoros Studites', *Helikon* 3: 41–110.
  (1964) 'Parerga zu den Epigrammen des Theodoros Studites', *Hell* 18: 11–43.
  (1968) *Theodoros Studites: Jamben auf verschiedene Gegenstände*. Berlin.
  (1974a) 'Die ikonoklastischen Jamben an der Chalke', *Hell* 27: 376–80.
  (1974b) 'Petros Sikeliotes, seine Historia und der Erzbischof von Bulgarien', *Hell* 27: 381–87.
  (1974c) *Die kaiserliche Universität von Konstantinopel*. Munich.
  (1978) *Kaiser Konstantin VI. Die Legitimation einer Fremden und der Versuch einer eigenen Herrschaft: Quellenkritische Darstellung von 25 Jahren byzantinischer Geschichte nach dem ersten Ikonoklasmus*. Munich.
  (1984) 'Ikonoklasmus und die Anfänge der Makedonischen Renaissance', *Varia 1* (Poikila Byzantina 4). Bonn: 175–210.
  (1987a) 'Weitere Überlegungen und Untersuchungen über die Ursprünge der byzantinischen Renaissance', in *Varia 2*. Poikila Byzantina 6, eds. A. Berger et al. Bonn: 266–71.
  (1987b) 'Die Ursprünge der byzantinischen Renaissance', in *The 17th International Byzantine Congress: Major Papers*. Washington: 556–76.
  (1994) 'Der 'zweite' Theophanes: Eine These zur Chronographie des Theophanes', *Varia 5* (Poikila Byzantina 13). Bonn: 431–83.
  (1995) 'Ignatios Diakonos, Στίχοι εις τον Αδάμ: Eine Aufführung zur Abschlussfeier', *BSl* 56/2: 353–57.
  (1997) 'Die Vermeintliche Häresie der Athinganoi', *JÖB* 47: 37–51.
  (2000) 'Die griechischen Quellen zur Bekehrung der Bulgaren und die zwei ersten Briefe des Photios', in *Polypleuros nous: Miscellanea für P. Schreiner zu seinem 60. Geburtstag*, eds. C. Scholz and G. Makris. Munich-Leipzig: 342–59.
  (2003) 'The Origins of the Byzantine Renaissance', in *Understanding Byzantium: Studies in Byzantine Historical Sources*, ed. S. Takács. Aldershot: 143–62.
Steckel, S. (2014) 'Networks of Learning in Byzantine East and Latin West: Methodological Considerations and Starting Points for Further Work', in *Networks of Learning: Perspectives on Scholars in Byzantine East and Latin West, c. 1000–1200*, eds. S. Steckel et al. Berlin-Münster: 185–234.
Stein, D. (1980) *Der Beginn des byzantinischen Bilderstreites und seine Entwicklung bis in die 40er Jahre des 8. Jahrhunderts*. Munich.
Stephanou, P. (1952) 'Les débuts de la querelle photienne vus de Rome et de Byzance', *OCP* 18: 270–80.
  (1955) 'La violation du compromis entre Photius et les Ignatiens', *OCP* 21: 291–307.
  (1973) 'Deux conciles, deux ecclésiologies? Les conciles de Constantinople en 869 et en 879', *OCP* 39: 363–407.
Stephenson, P. (2006) '*About the Emperor Nikephoros and How He Leaves His Bones in Bulgaria*: A Context for the Controversial *Chronicle of 811*', *DOP* 60: 87–109.

Stephenson, P., and Shilling, B. (2012) 'Nicholas the Monk and Former Soldier', in *Byzantine Religious Culture: Studies in Honor of A. M. Talbot*, eds. D. Sullivan et al. Leiden-Boston: 421–38.
Sterk, A. (2004) *Renouncing the World Yet Leading the Church: The Monk-Bishop in Late Antiquity*. Cambridge, MA.
Sternbach, L. (1898) 'Methodii patriarchae et Ignatii patriarchae carmina inedita', *Eos* 4: 150–63.
Stiernon, D. (1967) 'Autour de Constantinople IV (869–870)', *REB* 25: 155–88.
  (1970) 'Notice sur s. Jean higoumène de Kathara', *REB* 28: 111–27.
  (1973) 'La vie et l'oeuvre de s. Joseph l'Hymnographe: A propos d'une publication récente', *REB* 31: 243–66.
Storin, B. K. (2017) 'Autohagiobiography: Gregory of Nazianzus among His Biographers', *Studies in Late Antiquity* 1/3: 254–81.
  (2019) *Self-Portrait in Three Colors: Gregory of Nazianzus's Epistolary Autobiography*. Oakland.
Strano, G. (2001) 'La *vita* di Teofano (*BHG* 1794) fra agiografia e propaganda', *Bizantinistica* 3: 47–61.
Stratoudaki White, D. (1974) 'Photios' Letter to the Bishops in Exile', *GOTR* 19: 113–29.
Sullivan, D. (1994) 'Was Constantine VI 'Lassoed' at Markellai?', *GRBS* 35/3: 287–91.
Svoronos, N. (1951) 'Le serment de fidélité à l'empereur byzantin et sa signification constitutionnelle', *REB* 9: 106–42.
Szövérffy, J. (1979) *A Guide to Byzantine Hymnography*. Brookline.
Tafrali, O. (1913) *Topographie de Thessalonique*. Paris.
Taft, R. F. (1994) 'The Synaxarion of Evergetis in the History of Byzantine Liturgy', in *The Theotokos Evergetis and Eleventh-Century Monasticism*, eds. M. Mullett and A. Kirby. Belfast: 274–93.
  (1998) 'Women at Church in Byzantium: Where, When and Why?', *DOP* 52: 27–87.
  (2004) 'The Changing Rhythms of Eucharist Frequency in Byzantine Monasticism', in *Il monachesimo tra eredità e aperture*, eds. M. Bielawski and D. Hombergen. Rome: 425–29.
Talbot, A. M. (1994) 'Byzantine Women, Saints' Lives, and Social Welfare', in *Through the Eye of a Needle: Judaeo-Christian Roots of Social Welfare*, eds. E. A. Hanawalt and C. Lindberg. Kirksville: 105–22.
  (1996a) *Holy Women of Byzantium: Ten Saints' Lives in English Translation*. Washington.
  (1996b) 'Family Cults in Byzantium: The Case of St Theodora of Thessalonike', in Λειμών: *Studies Presented to L. Rydén*, ed. J. O. Rosenqvist. Uppsala: 49–69.
Talbot, A. M. ed. (1998) *Byzantine Defenders of Images*. Washington.
  (2001) 'Les saintes montagnes à Byzance', in *Le sacré et son inscription dans l'espace à Byzance et en Occident*, ed. M. Kaplan. Paris: 263–75.

(2012) 'Anonymous Miracles of the Pege', in *Miracle Tales from Byzantium*, eds. A. M. Talbot and S. F. Johnson. Cambridge, MA: 203–98.

(2015) 'The Relics of New Saints: Deposition, Translation and Veneration in Middle and Late Byzantium', in *Relics and Sacred Matter: The Cult of Relics in Byzantium and Beyond*, eds. H. Klein and C. Hahn. Washington: 215–30.

Talbot, A. M., and McGrath, S. (2006) 'Monastic Onomastics', in *Monastères, images, pouvoirs et société à Byzance*, ed. M. Kaplan. Paris: 89–118.

Tamarkina, I. (2006) 'The Date of the Life of the Patriarch Ignatius Reconsidered', *BZ* 99/2: 615–30.

Tanner, G. (1997) 'The Life of Saint Antony the Younger', *Studia Patristica* 29: 153–57.

Tarquini, S. (1961) 'Teofane Siculo: Canone per s. Marciano di Siracusa', *Archivio italiano per la storia della pietà* 2: 263–77.

Tessari, S. (2014) *Il corpus innografico attribuito a Fozio: Edizione critica e analisi musicale*. Torino.

Théarvič, M. (1904) 'A propos de Théophane le Sicilien', *EO* 7: 31–4, 164–71.

Theodorakopoulos, I. (2004) 'Ὁ Βίος του οσίου Ευδοκίμου και συναφή αγιολογικά κείμενα', in *The Heroes of the Orthodox Church: The New Saints, 8th–16th c.*, ed. E. Kountura-Galaki. Athens: 123–44.

Thomas, J. Ph. (1987) *Private Religious Foundations in the Byzantine Empire*. Washington.

Thomas, J. et al. (2000) *Byzantine Monastic Foundation Documents: A Complete Translation of the Surviving Founders' Typika and Testaments*. Washington.

Thomson, F. J. (1991) 'Les cinq traductions slavonnes du "Libellus de Fide Orthodoxa" de Michel le Syncelle et les mythes de l'arianisme de saint Méthode, apôtre des Slaves, ou d'Hilarion, métropolite de Russie, et de l'existence d'une église arienne à Kiev', *RES* 63: 19–54.

(2007) 'The Name of the Monastery Where Theophanes the Confessor Became a Monk: Πολίχνιον or Πολυχρόνιον?', *AnBoll* 125: 120–38.

Thümmel, H. G. (1981) 'Patriarch Photios und die Bilder', in *Eikon und Logos: Festschrift K. Omash*. Halle: 275–89 (repr. in *Bilderlehre und Bilderstreit: Arbeiten zur Auseinandersetzung über die Ikone und ihre Begründung vornehmlich im 8. und 9. Jahrhundert*. Würzburg. 1991: 115–26).

(1983) 'Eine wenig bekannte Schrift zur Bilderfrage', in *Studien zum 8. und 9. Jahrhundert in Byzanz*, eds. H. Kopstein and F. Winkelmann. Berlin: 153–57.

(1992) *Die Frühgeschichte der ostkirchlichen Bilderlehre: Texte und Untersuchungen zur Zeit vor dem Bilderstreit*. Berlin.

(1993/1994) 'Das Florileg des Niketas von Medikion für die Bilderverehrung', *BZ* 86–87: 40–46.

Timotin, A. (2010) *Visions, prophéties et pouvoir à Byzance: Étude sur l'hagiographie méso-byzantine (IX–XI siècles)*. Paris.

(2012) 'Message traditionnel et message immédiat dans l'hagiographie mésobyzantine (IXe–XIe s.)', in *La face cachée de la littérature byzantine: Le texte en tant que message immédiat*, ed. P. Odorico. Paris: 265–74.

Tihon, A. (1993) 'L'astronomie à Byzance a l'époque iconoclaste (VIIIe–IXe siècles)', in *Science in Western and Eastern Civilization in Carolingian Times*, eds. P. H. Butzer and D. Lohrmann. Basel: 181–203.
Tobias, N. (2007) *Basil I, Founder of the Macedonian Dynasty: A Study of the Political and Military History of the Byzantine Empire in the Ninth Century*. Lewiston.
Tollefsen, T. T. (2018) *St Theodore the Studite's Defence of the Icons: Theology and Philosophy in Ninth-Century Byzantium*. Oxford.
Tomadakes, E. (1971a) Ἰωσήφ ὁ Ὑμνογράφος: Βίος καί Ἔργον. Athens.
 (1971b) "Ἡ ἀκολουθία τῶν ἐν Βουλγαρίᾳ ΙΔ' νεομαρτύρων (814–815 μ.Χ.) καὶ Θεόδωρος ὁ Στουδίτης', *Athena* 72: 333–51.
Tomadakes, N. (1975) 'La lingua di Giuseppe Innografo (poeta greco palermitano)', in *Byzantino-Sicula II: Miscellanea di scritti in memoria di G. Rossi Taibbi*. Palermo: 497–506.
 (1977) 'Σέργιος πατρίκιος ὁμολογητής, πατὴρ τοῦ ἱεροῦ Φωτίου, καὶ ὁ εἰς μνήμην του (13 Μαΐου) κανὼν Ἰωσὴφ τοῦ Ὑμνογράφου', *Εκκλ. Φάρος* 59: 152–61.
Topping, E. C. (1986/88) 'Theodosia: Melodos and Monastria', *Diptycha* 4: 384–405.
Torgerson, J. W. (2015) 'From the Many, One? The Shared Manuscripts of the *Chronicle* of Theophanes and the *Chronography* of Synkellos', in *Studies in Theophanes*, eds. M. Jankowiak and F. Montinaro. Paris (= *TM* 19): 93–117.
Tougher, S. (1994) 'The Wisdom of Leo VI', in *New Constantines: The Rhythm of Imperial Renewal in Byzantium, 4th–13th Centuries*, ed. P. Magdalino. Aldershot: 171–79.
 (1997) *The Reign of Leo VI (886–912): Politics and People*. Leiden.
 (2004) 'Holy Eunuchs! Masculinity and Eunuch Saints in Byzantium', in *Holiness and Masculinity in the Middle Ages*, eds. P. Cullum and K. Lewis. Cardiff: 93–108.
Toynbee, A. (1973) *Constantine Porphyrogenitus and His World*. Oxford.
Travis, J. J. (1984) *In Defence of the Faith: The Theology of Patriarch Nikephoros of Constantinople*. Brookline.
Treadgold, W. T. (1975) 'The Problem of the Marriage of the Emperor Theophilus', *GRBS* 16: 325–41.
 (1979a) 'The Bride-Shows of the Byzantine Emperors', *Byzantion* 49: 402–6.
 (1979b) 'The Chronological Accuracy of the *Chronicle* of Symeon the Logothete for the Years 813–845', *DOP* 33: 159–97.
 (1980) *The Nature of the Bibliotheca of Photius*. Washington.
 (1981) 'Photius and the Reading Public for Classical Philology in Byzantium', in *Byzantium and the Classical Tradition*, eds. M. Mullett and R. Scott. Birmingham: 123–26.
 (1982) 'The Unpublished Saint's Life of the Empress Irene', *BF* 8: 237–51.
 (1988) *The Byzantine Revival 780–842*. Standford.
 (1988/1990) 'Three Byzantine Provinces and the First Byzantine Contacts with the Rus', *HUS* 12–13: 132–44.

(2002) 'Photius before His Patriarchate', *JEH* 53/1: 1–17.
(2004) 'The Prophecies of the Patriarch Methodius', *REB* 62: 229–37.
(2012) 'Opposition to Iconoclasm As Grounds for Civil War', in *Byzantine War Ideology between Roman Imperial Concept and Christian Religion*, eds. J. Koder and I. Stouraitis. Vienna: 33–39.
(2013) *The Middle Byzantine Historians*. Basingstoke.
Troianos, S. (2012) 'Byzantine Canon Law to 1100', in *History of Byzantine and Eastern Canon Law*, eds. W. Hartmann and K. Pennington. Washington: 115–69.
Tsigkos, B. A. (2001) Βίος, Συγγράμματα καί ἀκολουθία τοῦ Ὁσίου Πατρός καί Ὁμολογητοῦ Θεοδώρου τοῦ Στουδίτου. Thessaloniki.
Tsironis, N. (1998) 'Historicity and Poetry in Ninth-Century Homiletics: The Homilies of Patriarch Photios and George of Nicomedia', in *Preacher and Audience: Studies in Early Christian and Byzantine Homiletics*, eds. M. B. Cunningham and P. Allen. Leiden: 295–316.
Turner, D. (1990) 'The Politics of Despair: The Plague of 746–7 and Iconoclasm in the Byzantine Empire', *ABSA* 85: 419–34.
Turner, J. P. (2013) 'The Enigmatic Reign of al-Wāthiq (r. 227/842–232/847)', in *Abbasid Studies IV: Occasional Papers of the School of Abbasid Studies*, ed. M. Bernards. Exeter: 218–31.
Turyn, A. (1964) *Codices Graeci Vaticani saeculis XIII et XIV scripti annorumque notis instructi*. Vaticano.
Yannopoulos, P. (1993) 'Ὁ Βορειοελλαδικός χῶρος σύμφωνα με τον βίο του Ἁγίου Γρηγορίου του Δεκαπολίτου', *Parnassos* 35: 53–75.
(2000) 'Les vicissitudes historiques de la Chronique de Théophane', *Byzantion* 70: 527–53.
(2004) 'Le destinataire anonyme de la *Vita Theophanis* de Méthode le Patriarche', in *Byzance et ses Périphéries: Hommage à A. Ducellier*, eds. B. Doumerc and Ch. Picard. Toulouse: 173–81.
(2005) 'Constantin Porphyrogénète et Théophane le Confesseur', *Byzantion* 75: 362–72.
(2007a) 'Les destinataires de la lettre "Aux moniales" de Théodore Stoudite', *BZ* 100/2: 819–22.
(2007b) 'Une note sur la date de la rédaction de la *Vita Theophanis* par le patriarche Méthode', *Byzantion* 77: 463–65.
(2008) 'Las sources orales de la biographie de Théophane le Confesseur', *JÖB* 58: 217–22.
(2009) 'Les deux versions de la Biographie Abrégée de Théophane le Confesseur (*BHG* 1788 et *BHG* 1788b)', *Parnassos* 51: 239–46.
(2010) 'Le lieu et la date de naissance de Théophane le Confesseur', *REB* 68: 225–30.
(2013) *Théophane de Sigriani le Confesseur (759–818): Un héros orthodoxe du second iconoclasme*. Brussels.
(2014) Μεγαλώ (761–μετά το 818): Η αγνοημένη βυζαντινή οσία. Thessaloniki.
(2016) 'Jean, disciple de Grégoire Décapolite', *Erytheia* 37: 9–18.

Vailhé, S. (1901) 'Saint Michel le Syncelle et les deux frères Grapti, saint Théodore et saint Théophane', *ROC* 6: 311–32, 610–42.
Vaillant, A., and Laskaris, M. (1933) 'La date de la conversion des Bulgares', *RES* 13: 6–15.
Vallejo Girvés, M. (2000) 'Obispos exiliados: Mártires políticos entre el Concilio de Nicea y la eclosión monofisita', in *Tempus Implendi Promissa*, ed. E. Reinhardt. Pamplona: 507–33.
Van de Vorst, Ch. (1912a) 'Un panégyrique de Théophane le Chronographe par S. Théodore Studite', *AnBoll* 31 (1912) 11–23.
  (1912b) 'En quelle année mourut s. Théophane le Chronographe?', *AnBoll* 31: 148–56.
  (1912c) 'Saint Thaddée Studite', *AnBoll* 31: 157–60.
  (1913a) 'La translation de s. Théodore Studite et de s. Joseph de Thessalonique', *AnBoll* 32: 27–62.
  (1913b) 'Note sur s. Macaire de Pélécète', *AnBoll* 32: 270–73.
  (1913c) 'Les relations de S. Théodore Studite avec Rome', *AnBoll* 32: 439–47.
  (1914) 'La Petite catéchèse de s. Théodore Stoudite', *AnBoll* 33: 31–51.
  (1920) 'Note sur S. Joseph l'Hymnographe', *AnBoll* 38: 148–54.
Van de Vorst, Ch., and Delehaye, H. (1913) *Catalogus codicum hagiographicorum Graecorum Germaniae, Belgii, Angliae*. Brussels.
Van den Gheyn, J. (1897) 'S. Macarii Monasterii Pelecetes Hegumeni, Acta Graeca', *AnBoll* 16: 142–63.
Van den Ven, P. (1902) 'La vie grecque de s. Jean le Psichaïte, confesseur sous le règne de Léon l'Arménien (813–820)', *Le Muséon* 21: 103–25.
  (1910) 'Note sur le texte de la Vie de S. Antoine le Jeune', *BZ* 19: 310–13.
  (1955–1957) 'La patristique et l'hagiographie au Concile de Nicée de 787', *Byzantion* 25–27: 325–62.
Van Deun, P. (2006) *Eustratii Presbyteri Constantinopolitani De statu animarum post mortem (CPG 7522)*. Turnhout-Leuven.
  (2008) 'La chasse aux trésors: La découverte de plusieurs oeuvres inconnues de Métrophane de Smyrne (IXe–Xe siècle)', *Byzantion* 78: 346–67.
  (2017) 'Le *Liber de cognitione Dei* de Métrophane de Smyrne (*CPG* 3223): Un bilan des fragments conserves', *Medioevo Greco* 17: 241–81.
Van Deun, P., and De Vos, I. (2010) 'The Panegyric of Polycarp of Smyrna Attributed to Metrophanes of Smyrna (*BHG* 1563)', in *Martyrdom and Persecution in Late Antique Christianity: Festschrift B. Dehandschutter*, ed. J. Leemans. Leuven: 311–31.
Van Dieten, J. L. (1980/1982) 'Synodicon Vetus', *Annuarium Historiae Conciliorum* 12: 62–108.
Van Millingen, A. (1912) *Byzantine Churches in Constantinople, Their History and Architecture*. London.
Varona Codeso, P. (2010) *Miguel III (842–867): Construcción histórica y literaria de un reinado*. Madrid.
Varona, P. (2018) 'Chronographical Polemics in Ninth-Century Constantinople: George Synkellos, Iconoclasm and the Greek Chronicle Tradition', *Eranos* 108, 117–36.

Varona Codeso, P., and Prieto Domínguez, Ó. (2013) 'Deconstructing Photius: Family Relationship and Political Kinship in Middle Byzantium', *REB* 71: 105–48.
Varona, P., and Prieto, O. (2014) 'Three Clergymen against Nikephoros I: Remarks on Theophanes' *Chronicle* (AM 6295–6303)', *Byzantion* 84: 485–510.
Vasilevskij, V. (1893) *Russko-vizantijskie issledovanija*. St Petersburg. 2 vols.
Vasilevskij, V., and Nikitin, P. (1905) *Skažanija o 42 amoriiskikh mučenikhax*, Zapiski Imper. Akademij Nauk VII/2. Saint Petersburg.
Vasiliev, A. A. (1935) *Byzance et les Arabes*, Fr. ed. by H. Grégoire and M. Canard. Vol. 1: *La dynastie d'Amorium (820–867)*. Brussels.
(1946) *The Russian Attack on Constantinople in 860*. Cambridge.
Velkovska, E. (1996) 'Lo studio dei lezionari bizantini', *EO* 13: 253–71.
(2003) 'Libri liturgici bizantini', in *Scientia liturgica: Manuale di Liturgia, Casale Monferrato*, ed. A. J. Chupungco. Vol. 1: Introduzzione alla Liturgia: 243–58.
Vercleyen, F. (1988) 'Tremblements de terre à Constantinople: l'impact sur la population', *Byzantion* 58: 155–73.
Vernadsky, G. (1949) 'The Problem of the Early Russian Campaigns in the Black Sea Area', *ASEER* 8: 3–6.
Vinson, M. (1995) 'The Terms ἐγκόλπιον and τενάντιον and the Conversion of Theophilus in the *Life of Theodora* (BHG 1731)', *GRBS* 36: 89–99.
(1998) 'Gender and Politics in the Post-Iconoclastic Period: The *Lives* of Antony the Younger, the Empress Theodora, and the Patriarch Ignatios', *Byzantion* 68: 469–515.
(1999) 'The *Life of Theodora* and the Rhetoric of the Byzantine Bride Show', *JÖB* 49: 31–60.
(2003) 'Rhetoric and Writing Strategies in the Ninth Century', in *Rhetoric in Byzantium*, ed. E. Jeffreys. Aldershot: 9–22.
(2004) 'Romance and Reality in Byzantine Bride Shows', in *Gender in the Early Medieval World: East and West, 300–900*, eds. L. Brubaker and J. M. H. Smith. Cambridge: 102–20.
Vogt, A. (1932) 'S. Théophylacte de Nicomédie', *AnBoll* 50: 67–82.
Volk, O. (1955) 'Die Byzantinischen Klosterbibliotheken von Konstantinopel, Thessalonike und Kleinasien'. Unpublished PhD thesis. Ludwig-Maximilians-Universität. Munich.
Von Dobschütz, E. (1909a) 'Methodios und die Studiten: Strömungen und Gegenströmungen in der Hagiographie des 9. Jahrhunderts', *BZ* 18: 41–105.
(1909b) 'Die Vita des Johannes Psichaites', *BZ* 18: 714–16.
Von Falkenhausen, V. (1978) *La dominazione bizantina nell'Italia meridionale dal IX all'XI secolo*. Bari.
(1988) 'San Pietro nella religiosità bizantina', in *Bisanzio, Roma e l'Italia nell'Alto Medioevo*. Spoleto. Vol. II: 627–74.
(1989) 'Die Städte im Byzantinischen Italien', *MEFREM* 101/2: 401–64.

Von Glanvell, V. W. (1905) *Die Kanonensammlung des Kardinals Deusdedit*. Paderborn.

Vryonis Jr, S. (1981) 'The Panêgyris of the Byzantine Saint', in *The Byzantine Saint*, ed. S. Hackel. London: 196–227.

Vukašinović, M. (2015) 'Un saint père et une sainte impératrice: Saint Euthyme CP et sainte Théophanô dans une tension du Xe siècle?', *BSl* 73: 90–106.

Walter, C. (1970) 'Heretics in Byzantine Art', *Eastern Churches Review* 3: 40–49.

(1980) 'The Invention of John the Baptist's Head in the Wall-Calendar at Gračanica', *Zbornik za likovne umetnosti* 16: 71–83.

(1987) 'Latter-Day Saints and the Image of Christ in the Ninth Century Byzantine Marginal Psalters', *REB* 45: 205–22.

(1997) 'Iconographical Considerations', in *The Letter of the Three Patriarchs to the Emperor Theophilus and Related Texts*, eds. J. E. Munitiz et al. Camberley: LI–LXXVIII.

(2003) *The Warrior Saints in Byzantine Art and Tradition*. Aldershot.

Wasilewski, T. (1971) 'Macedońska historiografia dynastyczna X wieku jako źródło do dziejów Bizancjum w latach 813–867', *Studia źródłoznawcze. Commentationes* 16: 59–83.

Wellesz, E. (1961) *A History of Byzantine Music and Hymnography*, 2nd ed. Oxford.

Werner, E. (1957) 'Die Krise im Verhältnis von Staat und Kirche in Byzanz: Theodor von Stoudion', in *Aus der byzantinistischen Arbeit der Deutschen Demokratischen Republik 1*, ed. J. Irmscher. Berlin: 113–33.

Westerink, L. G. (1986) 'Leo the Philosopher: *Job* and Other Poems', *Illinois Classical Studies* 11: 193–222.

White, H. C. (2008) *Identity and Control: How Social Formations Emerge*, 2nd ed. Princeton-Oxford.

White, M. (2008) 'The Rise of the Dragon in Middle Byzantine Hagiography', *BMGS* 32/2: 149–67.

(2013) *Military Saints in Byzantium and Rus, 900–1200*. Cambridge.

Wilson, A. (1995) 'Female Sanctity in the Greek Calendar: The Synaxarion of Constantinople', in *Women in Antiquity: New Assessments*, eds. R. Hawleyand and B. Levick. London-New York: 233–47.

Wilson, N. G. (2000) 'Fozio e le due culture: Spunti dall'epistolario', in *Fozio: Tra crisi ecclesiale e magistero letterario*, eds. L. Canfora et al. Brescia: 29–44.

Winkelmann, F. (1985) *Byzantinische Rang- und Ämterstruktur im 8. und 9. Jahrhundert: Faktoren und Tendenzen ihrer Entwicklung*. Berlin.

(1987) *Quellenstudien zur herrschenden Klasse von Byzanz im 8. und 9. Jahrhundert*. Berlin.

Wittig, A. (1989/1991) 'Zu den Briefen des Patriarchen Photios', *EkTh* 10: 163–79.

Wolfram, G. (2003) 'Der Beitrag des Theodoros Studites zur byzantinischen Hymnographie', *JÖB* 53: 117–26.

Wolska-Conus, W. (1970) 'De quibusdam Ignatiis', *TM* 4: 329–60.

(1980) 'Un programme iconographique du patriarche Tarasios?', *REB* 38: 247–54.

Wortley, J. (1969/1970) 'The Date of Photius' Fourth Homily', *Byz* 39: 199–203.
  (1977) 'The Oration of Theodore Syncellus *(BHG* 1058) and the Siege of 860', *Byzantine Studies* 4: 111–26 (repr. in *Studies on the Cult of Relics in Byzantium up to 1204*. Aldershot. 2009. Ch. XIII).
  (1980) 'Legends of the Byzantine Disaster of 811', *Byzantion* 50: 533–62.
  (1982) 'Iconoclasm and Leipsanoclasm: Leo III, Constantine V and the Relics', *BF* 8: 253–79 (repr. in *Studies on the Cult of Relics in Byzantium up to 1204*. Aldershot. 2009. Ch. VII).
  (1999) 'The Byzantine Component of the Relic-Hoard of Constantinople', *GRBS* 40: 353–78.
  (2004) 'Relics of "The Friends of Jesus" at Constantinople', *TM* 17: 143–57 (repr. in *Studies on the Cult of Relics in Byzantium up to 1204*. Aldershot. 2009. Ch. XIV).
  (2005) 'The Marian Relics at Constantinople', *GRBS* 45: 171–87.
Zacos, G., and Nesbitt, J. W. (1984) *Byzantine Lead Seals*. Bern.
Zervoudaki, A. (2002) 'Θεοφάνης ὁ Γραπτός. Βίος καὶ ἔργο'. Unpublished PhD thesis. University of Crete. Rethymnon.
Zlatarski, V. N. (1918) *История на българската държава през средните векове. I. Първо българско царство. 2. От славянизацията на държавата до падането на първото царство* [*Medieval History of the Bulgarian State. 1. History of the First Bulgarian Empire*], 4th ed. Sofia (ed. P. Petrov. 2006).
Zuckerman, C. (2017) 'Emperor Theophilos and Theophobos in Three Tenth-Century Chronicles: Discovering the "Common Source"', *REB* 75: 101–50.

General Index

Abraham, 10, 180, 291
Acathist Hymn, 158
Achillas, hegoumenos of Stoudios, 311, 406
acrostic, 12, 79, 104, 118, 140, 161, 290, 325, 343, 380, 412
Acta of David, Symeon and Georgios, 150, 187, 189, 253, 256, 261, 382–90, 416
Acta of the Ten Martyrs of Constantinople, 319–25
Adrian II, Pope, 288
Aesop, 353, 368
Against Eusebium, 136
Against Iconoclasts, 333
Against the Manicheans, 434
Agapetos, *koubikoularios*, 218
Agapetus, Pope, 156
Agatha of Palermo, 104, 128, 147, 162, 217, 358
Aimilianos, metropolitan of Kyzikos, 83, 147, 163
Ainos, 170, 183
Akakios, hegoumenos of Sakkoudion, 378
Alexandros, Prince (son of Basileios I), 381
Alexios Mouselé, Duke of Sicily, 173–74, 183–84, 264
Al-Ma'mūn, Caliph, 171, 177, 193
Al-Mu'taṣim, Caliph, 177, 240, 245
Al-Wathiq, Caliph, 117, 376
Amastrianon, 263, 278
Amastris, 370
Ambrosios, 291
Amer, emir of Melitene, 245
Amorian dynasty, 210, 223, 229, 260, 268–69, 272, 358
Amorion, 108, 241–42, 245, 376
Amphilochia, 333, 335, 343, 367, 372, 401
Amphilochios, metropolitan of Kyzikos, 335, 356
Anastasios of Perge, 39
Anastasios of St Menas, 186, 193–94, 216
Anastasios Quaestor, 270
Anastasios Traulos, 79, 298
Anastasios, copyist, 101, 376, 414

Anastasios, monk of St Menas, 174–75
Anastasios, patriarch of CP, 320, 322
Anastasius the Librarian, 23, 294, 331, 400
anathema, 185, 282, 321, 330, 332, 348, 355
Anatolios, hegoumenos of Stoudios, 33, 79, 307–8
Andreas *en Krisei*, 26, 30, 199, 248
Andreas of Blachernai, 30, 249
Andreas of Crete, 3
Anthimos, bishop of Constantinople, 156
Anthologia Barberina, 284, 390
Anthologia Graeca, 79, 129
Anthony of Novgorod, 327
Anthos, Stoudite monk, 61
Anthousa, hegoumene of Mantineon, 19, 230
Antichrist, 138, 337, 350, 420, 423
Antigonos, 160
Antioch, 156, 198
Antirrheticus, 119, 340
Antonios II Kauleas, patriarch of CP, 259, 371
Antonios Mauros, 308
Antonios Ruwah, 177
Antonios the Abbot, 59
Antonios the Younger, 139, 193, 245, 256–60, 284, 328
Antonios, bishop of Dyrrhachium, 176, 234
Antonios, bishop of Lakedaimon, 282
Antonios, hegoumenos of Agauroi, 121
Antonios, hegoumenos of Elaiobomoi, 122
Antonios, hegoumenos of Hagios Petros, 43
Antonios, monk of Agauroi, 396
Antonios, patriarch of CP, 138, 145, 176, 190, 286
Apamea, 364–65
Aphousia, 16, 93–94, 159–60, 171, 203, 384, 408
Apollodoros of Carystus, 368
Apologeticus maior, 119
Apostle Bartholomew, 101, 201, 324, 414
Apostle James, 317–18
Apostle Paul, 422

525

Apostle Peter, 216, 422
Apostles, 31, 56, 132, 180, 283, 354
Arabs, 172–73, 176–77, 183, 198, 229, 240–41, 244, 246, 255, 276, 344, 357, 375, 379, 393, 417, 428
  attack, 196, 269
  invasion of Sicily, 226
  occupation of Crete, 220, 375
  raids, 49, 195, 227, 257, 357, 393
Aratus, 10
archimandrites, 288
Arethas, metropolitan of Caesarea, 79, 188, 333, 344, 346–47, 355, 363, 403
Arians, 340, 403, 419
aristocracy, 210, 240, 270, 345, 376, 429
Aristophanes, 129
Aristotle, 289, 333
Arkadios, hegoumenos of Stoudios, 220
Armenians, 153, 379
Arsaber, *protospatharios*, 291
Arsenios, copyist, 298
Arsenios, founding abbot, 59
Arsenios, hegoumenos of Hieron, 434
Arsenios, hermit, 50
Arsenios, hesychast, 421
Arsenios, monk of Medikion, 86
ascetic life, 50, 68, 118, 139, 209
asceticism, 47, 86, 188, 193, 195, 198, 203, 207, 311, 401, 417, 426
Asia Minor, 209, 229, 257, 393
Ašot I, Armenian King, 379
Aspar, cistern of, 246, 341
Athanasios of Alexandria, 39, 318, 340, 419
Athanasios, bishop of Methone, 173
Athanasios, hegoumenos of Paulopetrion, 65–66, 71, 97, 341
Athanasios, hegoumenos of Sakkoudion, 75, 112
Athanasios, hesychast, 351, 400
Athanasios, monk of Medikion, 86
Athos, mount, 314
audience, 3, 8, 27, 55, 78, 80, 134, 148, 265, 308, 389, 403
  male, 260
  monastic, 90, 178, 197
Augusta, title of Empress Theodora, 191, 377, 388

Baanes Angoures, 282
Baghdad, 105
Balkans, 421
Bardanes Tourkos, 42, 106, 149
Bardas, *caesar*, 13, 197, 200, 220, 252–57, 267, 269, 275–78, 280, 293, 312, 317, 319, 322, 387, 431

Bardas, *strategos* of Thrakesion, 63–64, 135, 138, 219
Basileios I, Emperor, 4, 23, 192, 200, 211, 223, 239, 247, 249, 260, 266–69, 277, 283, 288, 295, 305, 312–15, 317, 323, 336, 339, 348, 350, 359–63, 366, 369, 371, 377, 380–82, 390, 401, 421, 424, 432, 434
Basileios the Great, 32, 39, 45, 51, 178
Basileios, copyist, 39
Basileios, father of Eudokimos, 240
Basileios, hegoumenos, 203–4
Basileios, metropolitan, 347
Basileios, *oikonomos*, 122
Battle of Amorion (838), 269
Battle of Anzes (838), 245–46, 251
Battle of Crete (843), 253
Battle of Daras (530), 157
Battle of Markellai (792), 126
Battle of Melitene (837), 157
Battle of Poson (863), 255, 258
Battle of Zapetra (837), 245, 251
Benedict III, Pope, 274, 325
Bible, *see* Scriptures
Bibliotheca, 335, 340, 372
Bizye, 233
Blasios of Amorion, 31, 300, 314
Blasios, monk, 293
Boleron, 174
Boneta, 53, 309
Boris, Bulgarian Khan, 404, 433
Bosphorus, 17, 95, 114, 133, 173, 342
bride-show, 228, 235, 267
Bryennios, nephew of Leon V, 126
Bulgaria, 62, 308
  expedition in (837), 175
Bulgarians, 175, 397, 404, 428

Caliphate
  Abbasid, 154, 198
  Umayyad, 177
Canaan, 145, 148
Canon in terrae motus periculo, 325
canonisation, 6, 47, 63, 98, 117, 340, 358, 368
Cape Akritas, 85, 101, 106, 254
Cappadocia, 229, 240, 363
Carpocrates, gnostic, 336, 353
Catania, 164, 173
Catecheseis, 45, 50, 74, 341
  Magnae, 62, 410
  Parvae, 62, 65, 74, 213, 279
Chalcedon, 17, 283, 286, 310, 364–65
Chalke Gate, 12, 110, 127, 154, 237, 262, 320–21, 327, 361, 386
Chalki, 90, 341

General Index

charity, 67, 132, 179, 181, 211, 227–28, 239, 346
Charlemagne, 66
Charsianon, 229–31, 240, 393
chastity, 46, 55, 102, 214, 217, 242
Chersonesos, 91, 197, 222, 293, 295, 312
Chonai, 305
Chosroes, Sasanian King, 156–57
Christ, 25, 58, 60, 68, 104, 109–10, 236, 239, 261, 311, 333, 336, 350, 352–53, 366
  Christology, 5, 22, 335
  icon of, 102, 110, 127, 154, 178, 185, 320–21, 327, 433
Christodoulos, 12, 160
Christoupolis, 170, 174
Chronicle of 811, 397
Chronicle of Georgios Monachos, 59, 120, 266, 269
Chronography of Georgios Synkellos, 58, 120
Chronography of Theophanes, 57, 59, 101, 120, 124, 156, 321, 328
Chrysocheir, 353
Chrysopolis, 16, 94, 114, 137, 173
church
  All Saints (CP), 233
  Blachernai (CP), 200, 265, 284, 316, 331, 347, 355, 369
  Chalkoprateia (CP), 316, 369
  Georgios of Sykeon (CP), 436
  Hagia Sophia (CP), 36, 42, 66, 95, 99, 109, 114–15, 129, 142, 145, 148, 173, 197, 200, 209, 222, 225, 275, 284, 289, 295, 304, 314, 321–22, 331, 339, 355, 367, 375, 386, 407
    apse of, 327, 334, 336
  Holy Apostles (CP), 114, 143, 145, 149, 163, 263–64, 277–78, 289, 332, 342, 436
  Nea (CP), 284, 363
  Pharos (CP), 263, 335
  Skripou (Boeotia), 422
  St Euphemia (CP), 373
  St John the Baptist (monastery of Stoudios), 33, 51, 77, 313
  St Menas (CP), 363
  St Stephen (Daphne), 210
clairvoyance, 194, 215–16, 221, 223, 269
Claudiopolis, 19
Constitutiones Apostolicae, 85
Contra Iconomachos, 111
convent
  Chrysobalanton (CP), 314, 431
  Kassias (CP), 235
  Kloubiou (CP), 18, 118, 126
  Krisis (CP), 30, 228, 248
  Lydia (Bithynia), 394

Mantineon (Paphlagonia), 19, 229
  Ta Gastria (CP), 256, 267–68, 275
  Theotokos of Prinkipos (Prinkipos), 264
Corinth, 170, 172
Council of Constantinople (869/870), 23, 277, 281, 293, 295, 315, 323, 328, 332, 362, 378, 421–22, 424
Council of Constantinople (879/880), 282, 285, 293, 296, 311, 316, 332, 345, 368, 378, 432
Council of Hagia Sophia (815), 45, 51
Council of Hiereia (754), 25, 51, 58
Council of Nicaea, Second (787), 1, 7, 18, 29, 43–44, 47, 49, 58, 66, 83, 90, 93, 95, 99, 105, 111, 130, 132–33, 144–45, 149, 153, 179, 202, 207, 257, 305, 332–33, 338, 343, 356
Crete, 187, 195–96, 309, 375
Cyclades, 357, 389

Dalmatos, founding abbot, 59
Damascus, 3, 177
Daniel, prophet, 303, 319, 367
'Dark Age', 2–3, 21, 225, 426, 438
David of Thessaloniki, 370
David, presbyteros of Mytilene, 382, 384
Dazimon, 245–46
De administrando imperio, 404
De Ceremoniis, 59, 342
De Theophili imperatoris absolutione, 187, 262, 265, 272, 383, 385
De Theophili imperatoris benefactis, 187, 265, 272
Dekapolis, 177, 201, 206
Dekapolites, father of Eudokia Dekapolitissa, 209
Demetrios, *hypatos*, 56
'devotional symbiosis', 207, 249
Diocletian, Emperor, 58
Diogenes Laërtius, 353
Dionysios, monk of Stoudios, 60–61, 79
Dios, founding abbot, 59, 370
Diospolis, 177
Domitianos, hegoumenos of Sakkoudion, 62, 65
Domnica, hegoumene, 39
Dormition of the Virgin, 32, 94
Dorotheos of Gaza, 213
Dorotheos, copyist, 33
Dorotheos, monk of Stoudios, 236
dreams, 201, 218, 220, 223, 233, 262, 320, 322, 385–86

earthquake, 156, 289, 323, 325, 342, 377, 381
Edessa, 22, 106, 155
edict of 833 (iconoclast), 101, 171, 190, 204
Egypt, 125, 138, 145, 148, 156

Eirene, Empress, 7, 42, 46, 48, 103, 105, 110, 132, 145, 180, 210, 226, 229, 264, 356, 373, 381, 427
  translation of relics, 263
Eirene, hegoumene of Chrysobalanton, 431
Eirene, mother of Photios, 345
Eirene, owner, 311
Eirene, *patrikia*, 60
Eirene, sister of Empress Theodora, 269
Eirenopolis, 169, 202, 207
Eisagogé (Introduction to law), 433
Ekloga, 431
Elias the Younger, 207, 249
Elijah, prophet, 180, 207, 238–39, 249, 363, 366, 369, 380
Elisha, prophet, 380
Elpizon, fortress, 82
Encomium Ignatii, 285, 317
Encomium of St Isaakios and St Dalmatos, 303, 305
Encomium of the Archangel Michael, 304
Encomium of the Archangels Gabriel and Michael, 303–4
Encyclica ad sedes orientales, 357
Encyclica de obitu, 72, 74
enkolpion, 254, 261
Enkomion of Basileios I, 181, 268, 284
Enkomion of Euthymios of Sardis, 105, 298–302
Enkomion of Nicholas of Myra, 368
Enkomion of St Mokios, 314
Enkomion of the Patriarch Antonios II Kauleas, 371, 374
Enkomion of Theodoros Graptos, 359, 361–67
Ephesos, 170, 387
Epicharmos, 368
Epiphanios of Kallistratos, 406, 438
Epiphanios of Stoudios, 220
Epiphanios, monk, 188
Epiphanios, monk of Balaiou, 399
epistolography, 11, 73, 227
Epistula ad Theophilum, 300
Eriste, 351, 400
erotapokriseis, 285, 335, 339
Euchaita, 353, 357
Eucharist, 44, 177–78, 330
Euclid, 10
Eudokia Dekapolitissa, 210–11, 223, 268, 280
Eudokia Ingerina, 210–11, 247, 312
Eudokia, mother of Eudokimos, 229, 325
Eudokia, mother of patriarch Ignatios, 17
Eudokimos, *stratopedarches*, 26, 169, 185, 199, 201, 222, 229–32, 234, 238–41, 245, 249, 271
Eudoxios, metropolitan of Amorion, 83, 106
Eugenios, hegoumenos of Stoudios, 406

Eulalios, ex-monk of Stoudios, 226
Eulampios, archbishop of Apamea, 274, 435
Euodios, hagiographer, 197, 379–82
Euphemia of Chalcedon, 7, 180, 372
  relics, 373
Euphemios, *tourmarches*, 183
Euphrates, bishop, 419
Euphrosyne, Empress, 43, 228, 358
Euphrosyne, hegoumene of Kloubiou, 18
Euphrosyne, *patrikia*, 60
Euphrosynos the Cook, 308
Euschemon, metropolitan of Caesarea, 349, 355, 423
Eusebios of Caesarea, 58, 328
Eusebios, bishop of Nazianzus, 280
Eustathios of Antioch, 340, 419
Eustathios of Kios, 87
Eustolia of Constantinople, 140
Eustratios of Constantinople, 318
Eustratios, hegoumenos of Agauroi, 18, 121–26, 219, 395, 398, 431
Euthymios Zigabenos, 333
Euthymios, brother of Theodoros Stoudites, 47, 52
Euthymios, founding abbot, 59
Euthymios, hegoumenos, 43
Euthymios, metropolitan of Sardis, 20, 83, 101–2, 104–7, 189–90, 212, 215, 254, 298–302, 367, 383, 416
Euthymios, monk, 350
Euthymios, patriarch of CP, 34, 188, 192, 223, 279, 285, 344
Evarestos, hegoumenos of Kokorobion, 293, 300, 313
exarchos, 288
expulsion of demons, 56, 93, 114, 384

family networks, 4, 201, 208, 232, 251
Fathers of the Church, 25, 31, 34, 49, 52, 58, 85, 154, 162, 178, 418
filioque, schism, 292, 359
Flavian of Constantinople, 340
Flavius Iosephus, 37
florilegium, 49, 360
  iconoclast, 9, 99, 357
  iconodule, 58, 85, 162
Formosus, Pope, 297
Franks, 360

Galen, 368
Genesios, 246, 250–53, 256, 273, 419
Georgios Amasianos, *chartoularios*, 289, 350
Georgios Kedrenos, 278, 393
Georgios Monachos, 59, 100, 109, 118–19, 155, 250, 265
Georgios Synkellos, 58–59, 100, 149

General Index

Georgios, bishop of Amastris, 83, 169, 180, 185, 230, 356–58, 373, 390
Georgios, metropolitan of Mytilene, 17, 94, 139, 163, 166, 256, 281, 370, 382–89
    translation of relics, 113, 387
Georgios, metropolitan of Nicomedia, 98, 201, 316, 349, 355, 367–71, 382, 390
Georgios, *protokankelarios*, 174, 180, 194
Germanos I, patriarch of CP, 34, 152, 163, 305, 319–22, 339
    tomb, 157
Glykeria, 85
Golden Gate, 230
Golden Horn, 128, 182, 326
Gotthia, 136
Graptoi brothers (Theodoros and Theophanes), 12, 118, 159–63, 171, 360–67, 383, 388, 417
Gregoria, mother of Ioannes of Kathara, 202, 207
Gregorios Asbestas, archbishop of Syracuse, 185, 273–78, 287, 290, 325, 337, 355, 410–20, 435
Gregorios Dekapolites, 17–18, 20, 168–224, 249, 268, 280, 324–25, 409, 425
    relics, 207, 211
Gregorios of Nazianzus, 10, 51, 134, 154, 178, 336, 348
Gregorios the Illuminator, 336
Gregorios, hegoumenos of Dalmatos, 202, 206–7
Gregorios, monk of Sigriane, 214, 216

Harun al-Rashid, Caliph, 66, 177, 357
healings, 56, 64, 90, 92–93, 107, 122, 149, 155, 214, 229, 231, 243, 247, 250, 257, 283, 288, 312, 327, 394, 402, 404, 419
Hebros, river, 404
Helena, Empress, 110, 157, 162, 381
Helena, sister of Theophilos, 174, 247, 251, 312
Heliodoros, magician, 164
Hellenes, 336, 352
hermit life, 50, 120, 125, 370
Herod, 55, 322
Hesychios, *protonotarios ton Thrakesion*, 385
Hierapolis, 141
Hiereia, 55, 214, 277
Hilaria, sister of David, Symeon and Georgios, 389
Hilarion, founding abbot, 59
Hilarion, hegoumenos of Dalmatos, 20, 37, 65, 83, 139, 171, 182, 189, 206, 209, 215, 221, 305, 345, 407–10
Hilarion, hegoumenos of Pelekete, 97, 163, 199, 370

Hilarion, hegoumenos of Stoudios, 313, 406
Hippocrates, 368
Homer, 10–11
Homilies by Photios, 334, 336, 340, 357
humility, 13, 92, 132, 213, 285, 301, 324, 384, 418

Iakobos of Atroa, 19
Iakobos the Younger, 139
Iakobos, bishop of Anchialos, 69, 139
Iakobos, hegoumenos of St Zacharias, 394, 398
Iakobos, monk of Hagion Panton, 260
Iakobos, monk of Stoudios, 33, 68–69, 97
Iannes and Iambres, 138
Iconoclasm, First (726–787), 2–3, 11, 21, 69, 92, 99, 145, 152, 321, 327–28, 430
Iconoclasm, Second (815–843), 4, 8–11, 22–25, 62, 69, 83, 113–16, 126–27, 133, 159, 166–67, 176, 178, 185, 187, 203, 225, 241, 251–52, 270–71, 320–21, 328, 341, 344–45, 350, 367, 387, 392, 409, 430, 436
iconoclast hagiography, 8, 164, 179, 248
iconography, 6, 25, 115, 132, 165, 179, 336–37, 339
Ignatian party, 253, 259–60, 289–90, 293, 295, 297, 306, 316, 325, 400, 406
Ignatios Diakonos, 11–12, 34, 38, 79, 100, 114, 117, 119, 123, 127–43, 148, 154–55, 169–70, 179–80, 186, 193–94, 206, 209, 212, 216–20, 280–81, 341, 356–57, 366, 396, 407, 409, 414, 425, 427
Ignatios of Antioch, 46, 85
Ignatios, bishop of Lophoi, 351
Ignatios, bishop of Miletus, 60
Ignatios, patriarch of CP, 17, 23, 77, 166, 197–200, 222–23, 247, 252, 254, 256–57, 259, 263, 266, 270, 273–329, 337, 342, 344, 350–51, 354–55, 359, 361, 363, 377–78, 390, 396–97, 399, 404, 406, 411, 420–25, 430, 435
illuminated books, 115, 336–37, 360
Imperial Menologion, 15, 380
incarnation (ἐνσάρκωσις), 25, 58, 104–5, 110, 335
Inger, metropolitan of Nicaea, 122, 219
Ioannes Chalkitos, hegoumenos of Hagia Trias, 341
Ioannes Chrysocheir, *spatharios*, 336, 352
Ioannes Damaskenos, 3, 7, 22, 31, 34, 45, 333
Ioannes Diakonos, 191, 194–95, 198
Ioannes Doxopatres, 198
Ioannes Geometres, 210
Ioannes Grammatikos, monk, 128

Ioannes Hagioelites, 89
Ioannes Kalybites, 39
Ioannes Katasambas/Kakosambas, 383, 418
Ioannes of Galatia, 192, 199, 295, 401
Ioannes of Ruphinianai, 192
Ioannes the Merciful, 248
Ioannes VII Grammatikos, patriarch of CP, 8–9, 11, 56, 71, 93, 99, 103, 111, 115–16, 138, 145, 150, 157, 164–65, 176, 182, 191, 250, 252, 265, 271, 278, 282–83, 298, 332, 334, 359, 384, 386–87, 417, 419, 430
Ioannes, bishop of Amastris, 128
Ioannes, bishop of Gotthia, 180, 356, 370
Ioannes, bishop of Komana, 280, 297
Ioannes, bishop of Leontopolis, 280
Ioannes, bishop of Prousa, 121
Ioannes, copyist, 33, 88
Ioannes, disciple of Gregorios Dekapolites, 146, 186, 194–95, 219, 224
Ioannes, hegoumenos of Elaiobomoi, 123
Ioannes, hegoumenos of Eukairia, 66
Ioannes, hegoumenos of Kathara, 65, 71, 93, 97, 171, 202, 206–8, 224, 305
Ioannes, hegoumenos of Psicha, 19, 83, 91, 97, 163
Ioannes, *logothetes tou dromou*, 296
Ioannes, metropolitan of Chalcedon, 71
Ioannes, metropolitan of Kyzikos, 162
Ioannes, metropolitan of Sardis, 30, 83, 149
Ioannes, monk of Antidion, 219
Ioannes, monk of Latros, 258
Ioannikios, hermit, 16, 18, 20, 26, 43, 57, 75, 87, 113, 118–27, 133, 140, 152, 154, 163, 166, 182, 189, 199, 209, 212–13, 216–22, 248, 283, 317, 342, 370, 383, 392, 395–99, 404, 406, 408–13, 418, 425, 431, 435
Iob, Palestinian monk, 159, 360
Ionas, father of the Graptoi, 161
Ioseph affair, 42–44, 48, 54, 82, 137, 215
Ioseph Hymnographos, 30, 98, 165, 176, 209, 211, 221–24, 230–31, 249, 285, 293, 295, 316, 324–25, 370, 379, 381
Ioseph, archbishop of Thessaloniki, 33, 43, 50, 53–54, 56, 60–61, 76, 81–85, 87, 90, 97, 107, 190, 215
 translation of relics, 75
Ioseph, hegoumenos of Antidion, 126, 395–96, 398
Ioseph, hegoumenos of Herakleion, 257
Ioseph, hegoumenos of Kathara, 42, 124, 136, 216, 396, 415
Ioseph, monk, 229, 231, 239
Irenaeus of Lyons, 25

Isaac, Israelite patriarch, 145
Isaakios, thaumatourgos, 189
Isauria, 189, 193, 201
Isaurian dynasty, 53, 321, 334, 429
Israel, 125, 133, 180
Italy, 165, 176, 184, 323, 437

Jacob, Israelite patriarch, 180
Jerusalem, 112, 151, 159, 177, 302
Jerusalem, Patriarchate of, 21, 60, 161
Jews, 22, 103, 336, 344, 352, 434
Job, 11, 54, 61, 180, 228, 349
Job, or, On Indifference to Grief and on Patience, 10
John Chrysostom, 114, 145, 148, 178, 196, 270, 294, 340
 tomb, 342
 translation of relics, 76, 114
John the Baptist, 279, 305, 322
 head of, 38, 279, 288, 327
 icon of, 327
John the Evangelist, icon of, 258
John VIII, Pope, 296, 421
Joseph of Arimathea, 239
Joseph, Israelite patriarch, 145, 148, 180
justice, 104, 239, 245, 265, 317, 327, 390
Justinian I, Emperor, 152, 156, 158, 191
 mausoleum, 263–64, 278
Justinian II, Emperor, 164

Kallistos, duke of Koloneia, 241–43, 271
Kallonas, *spatharios*, 151
Kalogeros, monk of Stoudios, 73
Kanikleion, 157, 261
Kanon on the Restoration of the holy icons, 153
Karioupolis, 228
Kartalimen, 160
Kassia, 235–38
Khurramite refugees, 251
Kiev, 358
King David, 10, 179–80, 239, 241, 381
King Solomon, 381
Kios, 122
Klemes, hegoumenos of Stoudios, 87, 259–60, 313, 406
Klemes, Stoudite hymnographer, 87
Kletorologion, 331, 432
Komana, 279, 327
Kometas, 79
Konon, 217
Konstantinos Akropolites, 230, 325
Konstantinos Baboutzikos, 255–56
Konstantinos I, Emperor, 110, 207, 239, 250, 380–81

Konstantinos II, patriarch of CP, 120
Konstantinos IV, Emperor, 164
Konstantinos of Tios, 7, 356, 373
Konstantinos Sikelos, 10, 355
Konstantinos the Armenian, 252–53, 271
Konstantinos V, Emperor, 19, 30, 100, 120, 136, 178, 248, 263, 278, 282, 332, 335, 358, 397, 406, 436
   sarcophagus, 252, 263
Konstantinos VI, Emperor, 20, 42–45, 48–56, 101, 110, 124, 132, 164, 210, 213, 228–29, 264, 356, 396, 415
Konstantinos VII Porphyrogennetos, Emperor, 4, 55, 59, 210, 268, 435
Konstantinos, *asekretis*, 427
Konstantinos, brother of Eudokimos, 231
Konstantinos, Prince (son of Basileios I), 207, 239, 249, 433
Konstantinos, *scholarios*, 404
Konstantinos, student, 128
Konstantinos-Kyrillos, evangelist of the Slavs, 371
Kosmas the Melode, 3
Kosmas Vestitor, 270
Krateroi, 375
Kydonia, 309
Kynolykos, 162, 365
Kyrillos of Alexandria, 343

Latros, mount near Ephesos, 258
Laudatio de capitis inventione, 279
Laudatio de decollatione, 279
Laudatio of Platon of Sakkoudion, 31, 34, 48–53, 88, 215, 220
Laudatio of Theoktiste, 31, 34, 45–48, 51, 107
Lazaros the Painter, 325–28
Lazaros, deacon, 155
Lazarus, 128
lectionaries, 33, 69–70
Lemnos, 7, 373
Leo IV, Pope, 274
Leon Choirosphaktes, 298, 346
Leon Diakonos, 232
Leon III, Emperor, 7, 11, 110, 152, 158, 237, 319–22, 328, 373, 414
Leon IV, Emperor, 164, 214
Leon Katakalon/Katakoilas, 342
Leon Laloudios, 282, 332
Leon the Mathematician, 8–9, 176–77, 226, 234, 346, 355, 371
Leon V, Emperor, 9, 12, 16, 36, 54, 56, 60–69, 82–86, 88, 91–95, 99–106, 113, 116, 124, 127, 134–38, 143–44, 151–52, 154, 159, 190, 202–3, 215, 217, 219, 226, 234, 236, 243, 245, 253, 273, 286, 300, 305, 309, 339, 346, 366, 375, 383, 387, 389, 397, 403, 405, 408, 414
Leon VI, Emperor, 4, 181, 192, 211, 223, 232, 239, 249, 267, 269, 272, 277, 284, 314, 319, 342, 346, 363, 372, 430, 435
   new marriage, 259, 285
Leon, *archidiakonos*, 323, 325
Leon, bishop of Catania, 163–65, 169, 185, 230
Leon, *diakonos*, 323
Leon, *hypatos*, 315
Leon, literary patron, 315
Leon, *patrikios*, 60
Leon, Prince (son of Basileios I), 381
Leon, *sakellarios*, 218, 315
Leontios of Damascus, 8
Leontios of Neapolis, 85
Leontios, monk of Stoudios, 23
Lesbos, 385, 388
Libellus of Theognostos, 275, 288, 290, 297, 421
Liber Pontificalis, 331
Libri contra Manichaeos, 297
liturgical calendar, 31–32, 35, 39, 54, 143, 245, 249, 254, 256
Louis II, Frankish Emperor, 337
Lycaonia, 189
Lykos, river, 318

Macedonian dynasty, 23, 109, 223, 239, 249, 268, 331, 336, 380
magic, 103, 138, 157, 164, 381
Magnaura Palace, 13, 111, 210
Makarios, hegoumenos of Pelekete, 16, 20, 28, 65, 83, 92–97, 171, 204–6, 392, 394, 429
Maleinoi, 232, 239
Manichaeans, 112, 336, 352, 434
Manuel Malaxos, 339
Manuel the Armenian, *magistros*, 174, 240, 245–52, 261, 271, 341, 346, 412
Manuel, *logothetes tou dromou*, 275, 296–97, 312, 421
Maria of Amnia, Empress, 42, 55, 210, 228, 264
Maria the Younger in Bizye, 232
Maria, daughter of Theophilos, 173
Maria, mother of Gregorios Dekapolites, 188, 207
Maria, *patrikia*, 237, 320
Marianos, son of Petronas, 257, 260
Markos, hegoumenos of Menas (Thessaloniki), 176, 181
Martiniakoi, 233, 239
Martinos, *artoklines*, 233

General Index

martyrs of Amorion, XLII, 26, 117, 139, 154, 166, 199, 222, 240, 255, 266, 370, 374–82, 390
martyrs of Bulgaria, 33, 70
martyrs of Constantinople, X, 319–25
martyrs of Sinai and Rhaithou, 67
martyrs, Paleo-Christian, 10, 28, 65, 75
Maximos the Confessor, 371
Megalo, nun of Prinkipos, 53, 102, 214, 264
Megas synaxaristês, 254
Melchisedech, 291
Meletios, hegoumenos of Dalmatos, 305
Melissenoi, 242–43
Melissenos, 242
Melkite Church, 22
Menander Rhetor, 88
Menas, bishop of Constantinople, 156
menologion, 6, 28–40, 46, 69, 79, 87–88, 96–97, 101, 135, 139, 143, 163, 234, 307, 322, 361, 367, 376, 399, 420, 426, 439
  Slavonic, 32, 38, 63, 81, 89, 398
Menologion of Basileios II, 230, 271, 345
Merkuras, tax collector, 180
metaphrasis, 11, 15, 28–29, 78, 299, 301, 307, 315
Metaphrastic Menologion, 26, 28, 80
Methodios, patriarch of CP, 8–12, 20, 23, 25, 30, 36, 57, 75–79, 81, 96, 99–167, 176, 182, 185, 187–92, 196, 199, 208, 212–24, 234, 242, 250, 253, 255, 257, 259, 262–63, 266, 273, 276, 278–81, 286, 292, 298–302, 307, 315, 317, 321, 323, 337–39, 342–43, 354, 358, 366–67, 370, 378–79, 383–87, 395, 397, 406, 409–26, 430, 435, 438
metochion, 16–17, 85–86, 121, 193, 257–58, 260
Metopa, 309
Metrophanes, metropolitan of Smyrna, 247, 270, 275, 293, 295–302, 312, 328, 421
  mother, 217, 298, 412
Metrophanes, monk, 350
Michael I, Emperor, 17, 43, 50, 87, 133, 245, 274, 286–87, 294, 301, 304, 397, 404
Michael II, Emperor, 43, 55, 57, 64, 82, 85, 93, 96, 101, 103, 105–6, 123, 127, 134–37, 151, 168, 183, 190, 202, 215, 219, 228, 236, 245, 253, 286, 300, 310, 345, 358, 375, 386, 414, 416
Michael III, Emperor, 23, 75, 108, 110, 114, 145, 157, 162, 210–11, 220, 222–23, 244, 246, 252–55, 260–61, 263, 267–69, 275–80, 288, 290–93, 304–5, 311, 319, 322, 326, 330–31, 358–59, 364, 366, 377, 381, 386, 388, 431–32
Michael IV, Emperor, 15

Michael Maleinos, 232
Michael Monachos, 34, 78, 80, 116, 155, 204, 295, 300–19, 328, 367
Michael Synkellos, 12, 28, 35, 117–18, 151–55, 157–66, 241, 302, 316, 358–65, 390, 417–18
Michael, founder of Michaelitzes, 364
Michael, metropolitan of Synada, 36, 44, 65–66, 83, 95, 97, 141, 163, 166, 345
Michael, patriarch of Alexandria, 346
Miḥna, 171
military saints, 229, 245, 257, 271
miniatures, 115, 165, 336–37
minuscule script, 21, 226, 294, 309
Miracles of Anastasios the Persian, 7
Miracles of St Artemios, 225
Moab, 159
Moechian controversy, 20, 42–44, 48, 50–51, 54–55, 63, 77, 82, 101, 124, 131–32, 213, 341
monastery
  Agapios (Bithynia), 17, 122
  Agathou (CP), 17, 137, 342
  Agauroi (Bithynia), 17, 121–22, 395, 431
  Aninas (CP), 320, 323–25
  Anthemiou (Chrysopolis), 173
  Antidion (Bithynia), 126, 128, 140, 182, 218, 395, 398, 426
  Antipas (CP), 186, 194–95, 325
  Apostles Peter and Paul (Lydia), 16
  Armenianoi (Nicomedia), 340
  Balaiou (Bithynia), 17, 222, 394, 399
  Balentia (Lydia), 17, 394
  Bartholomew (CP?), 196
  Batalas (Bithynia), 340
  Bomoi/Elaiobomoi/Elegmoi (Bithynia), 17, 122–23
  Caesarius (Rome), 314
  Chenolakkos (Bithynia), 101, 122, 212, 414
  Chora (CP), 21, 146, 152, 155–60, 165, 302, 358–61, 365–66
  Christophoros (Bithynia), 16, 41
  Chrysonike (CP), 287
  Dalmatos (CP), 94, 139, 202, 221, 305, 319, 407
  Diomedes (CP), 192
  Elijah (Bithynia), 17, 122
  Eustathiou (Lydia), 16
  Evandros (CP), 244, 326
  Galakrenai (Chalcedon), 303
  Georgios (Bithynia), 16, 41
  Hagias Trias (Chalki), 341
  Hagion Panton (CP), 193, 257–60
  Hagios Petros (Bithynia), 43

General Index

Hagios Porphyrios/of the Eunuchs (Bithynia), 17, 139, 394
Herakleion (Kios), 121, 193, 257, 260, 434
John Chrysostom (CP), 196, 211
Kallistratos (CP), 406–7, 426
Kalonymos/Mikros Agros (Bithynia), 16
Katesia (Nicomedia), 18, 287
Kathara (Bithynia), 16, 19, 41, 94, 202, 206, 407
Kokorobion (CP), 293, 312
Kosmas (Bithynia), 17, 122
Kreskentios (Nicomedia), 404
Latomos (Thessaloniki), 195
Leon Diakonos (CP), 258
Leukades (Bithynia), 17, 122
Manuel (CP), 246, 341
Mar Sabas (Palestine), 22, 151
Medikion (Bithynia), 16, 20, 85–86, 88–89
Megas Agros (Bithynia), 16, 54, 57–59, 102, 206, 214
Menas (CP), 200, 207, 222
Menas (Thessaloniki), 170, 193
Michaelitzes (CP), 364
Mokios (CP), 194, 315, 320, 325
Myele, 61
Niandros (Princes' Islands), 17, 286
Paulopetrion (Cape Akritas), 65, 94, 206
Pelekete (Bithynia), 16, 92, 94, 97, 206, 242
Philippikou (Chrysopolis), 173
Phloros (CP), 262
Phoberou (CP), 327
Photeinoudion (Bithynia), 66
Photnai (Bithynia), 43
Pikridion (CP), 94, 128, 142, 182, 206
Pissadinoi (Bithynia), 294, 400–1, 425–26
Plate (Princes' Islands), 17, 286
Polichniou (Bithynia), 16
Prokopias (CP), 140
Sakkoudion (Bithynia), 16, 19, 41–42, 44, 48–49, 63, 81, 86
Satyros/Anatellon (Chalcedon), 17, 283, 286, 304, 318
Sergios and Bakkhos (CP), 150–51, 190–92, 194, 198–99, 283, 295, 401
St Anna (Kios), 294, 400
Stoudios (CP), 18–19, 28–41, 49–50, 58, 69, 75–81, 84, 87, 89, 93, 112, 115, 141, 166, 168, 196, 209, 220, 223, 235, 247–48, 259, 273, 279, 294, 303–5, 309–14, 378, 398–99, 415, 419, 425
Sykeon (CP), 436
Symboloi (Bithynia), 16, 41, 49, 85–86, 351, 400

Ta Rhomaiou (CP), 158
Tarasios/All Saints (CP), 133, 339–40
Terebinthos (Princes' Islands), 17, 286
Theodoros (Chrysopolis), 17, 114, 137, 145–46, 340
Theophobia (CP), 252
Theotokos (Lydia), 16
Theotokos of Niketiates (Nicomedia), 187, 244
Theotokos of Psicha (CP), 19, 91
Theotokos tes Peges (CP), 288–89, 381
Tripyliana (Bithynia), 16, 41
Tryphon (Cape Akritas), 16, 41, 310
Zacharias (Bithynia), 17, 394, 398, 401, 426
monastic families, 18–19, 193
monasticism, 4, 16, 34, 68, 76, 78, 84, 98, 166, 199, 205, 226, 287, 306, 384
  anchoritic, 178, 203, 213
  Bithynian, 21, 121, 399, 401
  cenobitic, 61, 178, 203, 213
  Constantinopolitan, 59, 221, 370, 407
  monastic culture, 4, 47, 226
  Stoudite, 44, 51, 67, 79
monothelite heresy, 379
mosaics, 284, 331, 334–36
Moses, 125, 132, 138, 142, 180
Mystagogia de spiritu sancto, 297
mysticism, 168, 178, 185, 260
Mytilene, 17, 277, 312, 318, 382, 388

Naples, 170, 172
Narratio de sanctis patriarchis Tarasio et Nicephoro, 77
Narratio historica in festum restitutionis imaginum, 109, 266
Naukratios, hegoumenos of Stoudios, 12, 70–77, 90, 112, 116, 311, 313
Necrologium imperatorum et catalogus eorum sepulchrorum, 263, 278
Nektarios, 291
Neoplatonism, 10, 333
Nestorios, patriarch of CP, 35, 340
Nicholas I, Pope, 277, 288, 291–93, 326, 332, 338, 355, 362, 377, 421, 423
Nicholas of Myra, 104, 192, 222, 300, 438
  chapel of, 222
Nicomedia, 65, 96, 187, 244, 351, 368, 404
Nikephoros Gregoras, 151, 233, 364
Nikephoros I, Emperor, 33, 42, 50–51, 66, 70, 106, 124–25, 133, 136, 144, 196, 202, 226, 308, 356
Nikephoros Phokas, 232
Nikephoros, *chartophylax*, 194
Nikephoros, hegoumenos, 48

General Index

Nikephoros, hegoumenos of Medikion, 20, 84, 89–90, 97, 256–57, 341, 429
Nikephoros, monk and philosopher, 355, 371–74, 390
Nikephoros, patriarch of CP, 6, 17, 37, 42, 44, 56, 58, 82, 87–88, 93, 99, 101, 115, 119, 127, 135, 137, 163–64, 266, 281, 286, 307, 310, 313, 333–34, 337, 339–40, 343–44, 360, 366, 370, 387, 414–15
  translation of relics, 114
Nikephoros, *skeuophylax*, 436
Niketas Byzantios, 355, 371, 379–80
Niketas Choniates, 411–12
Niketas David Paphlagon, 30, 223, 276, 279, 283, 317, 319, 323, 328, 337, 342, 371, 377
Niketas the Patrician, 18
Niketas, hagiographer, 228
Niketas, hegoumenos of Medikion, 20, 54, 66, 81–86, 94, 97, 127, 163, 166, 241, 259, 396, 429
Niketas, *logothetes tou genikou*, 48
Niketas, metropolitan of Heraclea, 189
Niketas, metropolitan of Smyrna, 296
Nikodemos Hagiorites, 254
Nikolaos Joulas, 177
Nikolaos Mystikos, patriarch of CP, 285, 303, 317, 346, 355
Nikolaos, *asekretis*, 333
Nikolaos, hegoumenos of Agauroi, 123
Nikolaos, hegoumenos of Bomoi, 122
Nikolaos, hegoumenos of Nikephoros, 340
Nikolaos, hegoumenos of Pissadinoi, 294, 400
Nikolaos, hegoumenos of Stoudios, 22, 30–31, 78, 81, 87, 220, 247–48, 277, 293–94, 307–14, 378, 406
Nikolaos, hegoumenos of Tarasios, 339
Nikolaos, monk, 192
Nikolaos, soldier, 308
Nomocanon, 339
Noumera, 277, 295

oaths of loyalty, 23, 277
oikonomía, 43, 124, 131, 136, 263, 419
Old Testament, 132, 179–80, 238, 362, 381
Olympos, mount in Bithynia, 42, 49, 86, 120–28, 151, 170, 175, 181, 257, 351, 395, 405–9, 425
  cells, 294, 400–1
omophorion, 317
On Orthography, 226
On the Baptising of Jews, 418
Oration on the Girdle of the Theotokos, 303, 316
Otranto, 170, 172, 174, 176, 183

Pachomios, founding abbot, 59
Palace of Daphne, 210, 280, 389
Palace of the Sources, 380
Palermo, 173
Palestine, 8, 22, 72, 151, 156, 159, 367
Pamphilos Trimalethon, monk of Stoudios, 60
pamphlet, 82, 106–7, 124, 190, 215, 317, 416, 421
Panion, 341
Pankratios of Taormina, 147
Panoplia dogmatica, 333
Pantelleria, 106
Pantoleon, *chartophylax*, 66, 304
Paphlagonia, 210, 227, 267, 317
Paschal I, Pope, 65, 94, 182, 202, 206, 408, 415–16
Passio of the 42 martyrs of Amorion (version B), 243
Passio of the 42 martyrs of Amorion by Euodios (version Z), 379–82
Passio of the 42 martyrs of Amorion by Michael Synkellos (version Γ), 117, 154, 241–43
Passio of the 42 martyrs of Amorion by Sophronios (version Δ), 242, 374–79
Patras, 196, 355
Patria, 237
patronage, 24, 29, 119, 130, 132, 223, 280, 328, 336, 379, 426–27, 436
Paula (Bithynia), 48
Paulicians, 93, 242, 294, 344, 353, 434–35
Paulos III, patriarch of CP, 292, 338
Paulos IV, patriarch of CP, 261
Paulos of Atroa, 19
Paulos of Plousia, 259
Paulos the Confessor, 340
Paulos, anathematised iconoclast, 282, 332
Paulos, archbishop of Thessaloniki, 352
Paulos, hegoumenos of St Zacharias, 394
Paulos, *komes* of Opsikion, 92
Paulos, metropolitan of Caesarea, 423
Paulos, student, 128
Peloponnese, 195, 228, 282, 437
Petronas, *droungarios tes viglas*, 249, 253, 255–61, 269, 271, 328, 387
Petronios, cleric, 368
Petros Monachos, 118, 120–27, 395–98, 431
Petros of Atroa, 17, 19–20, 39, 65, 83, 139, 221, 241, 248, 391–408, 413, 425
Petros of Galatia, 244, 271
Petros Patrikios, 326
Petros Sikeliotes, 434
Petros the Patrician, 244
Petros, bishop of Syllaion, 121, 274, 435
Petros, disciple of Ioannikios, 244, 326
Petros, metropolitan of Nicaea, 54, 71, 83, 163

Petros, metropolitan of Sardis, 274
Petros, monk of Thessaloniki, 184
Phebronia, disciple of Symeon of Lesbos, 384
Phiale, 159
philanthropy, 241, 245
Philaretos the Merciful, 30, 169, 185, 211, 227–32, 248, 358
Philotheos, *protospatharios*, 331, 432
Phirmoupolis, 311
Phlorina-Theoktiste, mother of Empress Theodora, 267
Phokades, 232
Phokas, Emperor, 156
Photeinos, father of Theodoros Stoudites, 45
Photian schism, 257, 259, 308, 369, 372, 406
  reconciliation, 259, 284, 317, 319, 352, 363
Photios, patriarch of CP, 4, 8–10, 12, 23, 110, 161, 167, 197, 200, 222, 250, 252, 257, 263, 270, 275–329, 399–401, 403, 406–7, 411–12, 419, 421–25, 427, 432–35
Phrygia, 95, 424
piety, 49, 85, 92, 141, 188, 193, 201, 210, 239, 286, 327, 337, 345, 354, 359, 386, 390, 424, 435
pilgrimage, 30, 51, 90, 93, 153, 249, 343, 395, 402
pirates, 172, 175, 180
Platanion, 158
Plate, 355
Plateia Petra, 65, 257
Platon of Sakkoudion, 18, 31, 33–34, 42, 46, 48, 78, 84, 86, 88, 94, 97, 191, 213, 314, 418, 429
  exile, 50
  sarcophagus, 82, 90
poetry, 10, 26, 67, 71, 75, 79, 131, 138, 160, 199, 201, 227, 439
  alphabetical, 128, 284
  Anacreontic, 153, 381
  dithyramb, 102
  dodecasyllabic, 116
  epigram, 11, 51, 59–60, 70, 75, 196, 270, 315, 370
  iambic poem, 12, 47, 53, 59, 70, 79–80, 110, 127–28, 154, 159, 313, 339, 346, 364, 427
  idiomelon, 69, 110, 117, 139, 155, 222, 241, 343
  kontakion, 6, 59, 67, 162, 197, 199, 223, 285
Pontius Pilate, 366
posthumous miracles, 56, 107, 133, 184, 214, 229, 243, 260, 262, 271, 391, 402, 409
Praitorion, 160, 358
Prinkipos, 72, 114, 116, 264–65, 311
Priskos, *protopatrikios*, 156

Proklos, patriarch of CP, 197
Prokonnesos, 170–71, 208, 312, 341
Prokopia, Empress, 133, 140, 259, 286
Prokopios Dekapolites, 146, 163, 203–9, 249
  relics, 207
prophecy, 18, 38, 126, 135, 138, 203, 205, 214–17, 220, 222, 228, 256, 258, 269, 313, 317, 345, 387, 431
Propontis, 56, 93, 171, 341
Prote, 16, 86
Prousa, 18
psalter, 73, 84, 97, 300, 337, 417, 426
  Khludov, 115–16, 165
  Pantokrator, 115
  Paris, 115
Pseudo-Athanasios, 318
Pseudo-Leukios Charinos, 335
Pseudo-Symeon, 160, 261, 345, 364
Ptolemy, 10
purge of iconoclasts, 44, 111, 116, 128, 147, 168, 176, 182, 219, 354
Pythagoras, 10

Ravenna, 164
Refutatio et eversio, 119, 136, 266
Refutation of Manichaeism, 434
Refutation of the Iconoclasts, 71
Refutation of the Koran, 379–80
Reggio, 170, 172
repentance after iconoclasm, 85–86, 112, 129, 131, 134, 138, 142, 185, 236, 261, 269, 334, 378, 386, 400, 434
Rhangabe family, 286, 294
Rodoaldus of Porto, 277
Romanos I, Emperor, 420
Romanos II, Emperor, 210, 268
Rome, 30, 60, 72, 101, 116, 122, 151, 170–73, 195–98, 217, 277, 288, 291–94, 314, 326, 360, 414, 416
  Papacy, 156, 290, 295, 330, 332, 337, 360, 421
Ruphinianai, 192
Russians
  attack of Amastris, 357
  attack of CP, 200, 316, 347, 355, 369, 377
  conversion, 357
  raids, 128

Sabaite abbots, 67
Sabas of Pelekete, hagiographer, 92, 94, 392
Sabas, founding abbot, 59
Sabas, hagiographer, 24, 29–30, 37–40, 81, 221, 312, 391–427
Sabas, hegoumenos of Stoudios in 787, 18, 131
Samarra, 154, 255, 376

Samothrace, 54–55, 214
Samuel, patron of Kokorobion monastery, 293
Saphrad, 357
Scriptor incertus, 286, 345, 397
scriptorium, 41, 97, 115, 166, 394
Scriptures, 51, 92, 106, 162, 179, 195, 198, 203, 224, 234, 309, 333
    Old Testament
        Genesis 1: 26, 102
        Genesis 3, 237
        Genesis 4: 8, 353
        Genesis 5: 1, 102
        Genesis 17: 23–27, 353
        Genesis 17: 9–14, 291, 353
        Genesis 50: 1–13, 148
        Exodus 13: 17, 138
        Exodus 4: 24–26, 291
        Numbers 10: 11, 138
        1 Samuel 16: 13, 362
        1 Kings 5: 10–11, 362
        Job, 10
        Psalm 119 (118): 93, 73
        Psalm 119 (118): 94, 73
        Psalm 134: 15, 354
        Psalms, 46, 73, 115, 239, 241, 297, 337, 343
        Ecclesiastes, 297
        Jeremiah 15: 10, 51
    New Testament
        Matthew 5: 28, 424
        Matthew 7: 6, 354
        John 14: 2, 401
        John 14: 28, 401
        Acts 8: 13, 336
        Romans 2: 29, 353
        1 Corinthians 2: 7, 353
        2 Corinthians 11: 28, 401
        Philippians 1: 20, 339
        Philippians 3: 8, 236
        1 Timothy 4: 14, 70
        Hebrews 2: 14, 353
        Hebrews 7: 1-3, 291
        1 Peter 5: 5, 368
Sea of Marmara, 16, 54, 56, 72, 86, 102, 203, 264
Seleucia, 153
Sergios I, patriarch of Jerusalem, 111
Sergios II, patriarch of CP, 342
Sergios Niketiates, *magistros*, 187, 244, 253, 261, 271, 346, 388
Sergios the Confessor, 286, 335, 345–46
Sergios, brother of Photios, 354
Sergios, father of Gregorios Dekapolites, 188
Sergios, hegoumenos of Pelekete, 95
Sergios, poet, 11, 71

Sermo de capitis inventionibus, 279
Sermo historicus, 177
Severos of Antioch, 157
Short History, 340
Sicily, 2, 105, 147, 163, 172, 183, 195, 212, 273
Simeon, Bulgarian King, 420
Simon Magus, 165, 336–37, 353
Sinai, 125
Skepe, 339
skeuophylax, 142
Skylitzes, 250, 253
Slavs, 32, 153, 178, 180, 196, 346
    settlement, 175
Smolyans, 175
Smyrna, 64, 309, 385
social mobility, 63, 391
Socrates, 10
Socrates Scholasticus, 328
Sophia, sister of Empress Theodora, 255
Sophonios, bishop of Adrianoupolis, 378
Sophonios, bishop of Apamea, 378
Sophoronios, hegoumenos of Sakkoudion, 378
Sophronios, deacon, 378
Sophronios, hagiographer, 242–43, 374–79
Sophronios, hegoumenos of Stoudios, 79, 307, 311, 378
Sophronios, monk, 352, 378
Speech about the Holy Icons, 108
spiritual father, 17–18, 21, 43, 55, 57, 79, 89, 182, 192–95, 199, 224, 236, 258, 311, 394, 401, 425
Spiritual Meadow, 217, 272
St Andrew, island of, 101–2, 106, 190, 414, 416
St Menas, 363, 369
St Michael, archangel, 268, 301, 304–5, 324
St Sabas, 152, 156–57, 384
Staurakios, Emperor, 126, 217
Stephanos I, patriarch of CP, 110, 239, 297, 363, 435
Stephanos III, patriarch of CP, 110
Stephanos Kapetolites, 71, 154
Stephanos Meles, 80
Stephanos Molites, 282, 332
Stephanos Sabaites, 367
Stephanos the Protomartyr, 180, 367, 389
Stephanos the Younger, deacon, 7, 26, 69, 99, 173, 199, 360, 369
Stephanos, addressee of Photios, 354
Stephanos, *asekretis*, 103, 141, 151
Stephanos, diakonos of Hagia Sophia, 70, 99
Stephanos, hegoumenos of Megas Agros, 57, 103
Stephanos, hermit, 84
Stephanos, *magistros*, 103
Stephanos, relative of Theodoros Stoudites, 60
Stephen V, Pope, 275, 280, 296

General Index

Stichelegeia, 77
Stichoi on Lazarus, 280
style, 12, 15, 26, 30, 55, 78, 80, 88, 91, 103–4, 117, 136, 144, 148, 165, 182, 235, 240, 315, 384, 402, 414, 438
  Asiatic, 146, 308, 372, 374
  epistolary, 423
  Homeric, 11
  iconoclast, 12
  Methodian, 299, 307
  narrative, 379
  Photian, 357
  Theodoros Stoudites, 11
Stylianos Zaoutzes, *basileopator*, 223
Stylianos, bishop of Neocaesarea, 275, 280, 296–97, 326
Symeon Dekapolites, 16, 18, 105, 150, 170, 175, 181, 186, 188–93, 207, 216, 224
Symeon Logothetes, 183–84, 210, 246, 248, 253–54, 364
Symeon Metaphrastes, 30, 35, 364, 380
Symeon, hegoumenos of Kyzikos, 189
Symeon, stylite of Lesbos, 17, 150, 171, 187, 189, 191, 209, 262, 370, 382–90, 409
Synagogai, 285
synaxarion, 6, 29–30, 33, 40, 54, 75, 81, 83, 87, 89, 91, 96–97, 102, 107, 139, 143, 156, 161, 163, 187, 195, 198, 234, 238–39, 241, 250, 256, 261, 287, 322, 346, 357, 373
Synaxarion Evergetis, 29, 35, 305, 322
Synaxarion of Constantinople, 6, 40, 64–65, 67, 93, 107, 133, 197, 201–2, 204, 230, 245, 248, 254, 256, 271, 282, 284, 289, 304, 313, 326, 345, 347, 368, 370, 387, 408–10, 414
Synesios of Cyrene, 154
synod of 536, 156
synod of 809 (in Constantinople), 43, 50–51, 216
synod of 843 (in Constantinople), 332
synod of 859 (in Constantinople), 295
synod of 860/861 (in Constantinople), 277, 288, 292, 294, 331, 423
Synodicon vetus, 109, 248, 250, 284, 328, 331
Synodikon of Lakedaimon, 283
Synodikon of Orthodoxy, 67, 76, 83–84, 96, 107, 109, 113, 133, 161, 189, 221, 271, 283, 321, 328, 347
Synodikon of Rhodes, 306
Synopsis artis medicae, 8
Syracuse, 100, 147, 170–76, 184, 282
Syria, 266

taktikón Uspenskij, 432
Tarasios, patriarch of CP, 6, 23, 30, 36, 42–44, 50–51, 54, 58–59, 66, 77, 83–84, 90–93, 95, 100, 105, 111, 114, 119, 124, 127–34, 136, 139, 145, 148–49, 153, 166, 180, 202, 209, 291–92, 300, 321, 333, 338–40, 345, 356, 369, 373, 414, 418
Tephrike, 242, 353, 434
Terebinthos, 275
Testament of Theodoros Stoudites, 74
Thaddaios, monk of Stoudios, 62–65, 68, 97
Thales, 10
Thasos, 106
Thekla, saint, 373
Thekla, sister of Michael III, 377
thema, 428
  Anatolikon, 306, 309, 375, 397
  Armeniakoi, 242, 245
  Boukellarioi, 259, 375
  Charsianon, 232, 363
  Kibyrrhaiotai, 95, 245, 376
  Opsikion, 407
  Optimatoi, 18, 234
  Thessaloniki, 174
  Thrakesioi, 17, 64, 255
Theodora I, Empress, 152, 156–57
Theodora of Thessaloniki, 201, 232–33
Theodora Raoulena Paleologina, Empress, 364
Theodora, Empress, 23, 75, 96, 108–14, 117, 123, 142, 145, 148, 150, 157, 160, 162, 168, 181, 187, 210, 224, 235, 238, 244–56, 259–72, 278, 280, 283, 292, 304, 317, 327, 332, 341, 346, 359, 364, 366, 377, 386, 388, 408, 418, 427, 430, 432
Theodore Abū Qurrah, 22, 153
Theodoretos of Cyrrhus, 419
Theodoros Daphnopates, 55, 80
Theodoros Dekapolites, *magistros*, 210, 268
Theodoros Gastes, 282, 332
Theodoros Graptos, 26, 158–63, 166, 361–67, 390, *see* Graptoi brothers
Theodoros Krateros, 243, 375
Theodoros Krithinos, 173, 183–84, 273, 282, 332
Theodoros of Sykeon, 436
Theodoros Santabarenos, hegoumenos of Stoudios, 296, 342, 353, 355, 406, 433
Theodoros Synkellos, 316, 355
Theodoros, archbishop of Syracuse, 274
Theodoros, bishop of Thessaloniki, 176
Theodoros, hegoumenos of Chora, 155–60, 360
Theodoros, hegoumenos of Psicha, 19

Theodoros, hegoumenos of Stoudios, 4–5, 8, 11–12, 16, 18, 23–40, 182, 189, 191, 196, 202–5, 213–15, 220–21, 235–38, 248, 256, 259, 279, 294, 300, 305–10, 314–15, 333–34, 341, 344, 348–49, 351, 356, 370, 375–76, 384–85, 396–97, 404–11, 415, 418, 420, 425–26, 428, 432
 first exile, 48
 translation of relics, 75, 117
Theodoros, metropolitan of Laodicea, 355, 424
Theodoros, monk, 62
Theodoros, *strategos*, 375
Theodosia, Empress, 16, 85
Theodosia, hegoumene of Kloubiou, 118, 140, 163
Theodosia, wife of Caesar Bardas, 431
Theodosios I, Emperor, 120
Theodosios, founding abbot, 59
Theodosios, hegoumenos of Pikridion, 65, 128, 182
Theodosios, hegoumenos of Stoudios, 406
Theodosios, monk, 323
Theodote, *koubikoularea*, 42, 45, 48, 55
Theodotos, patriarch of CP, 85, 116, 145, 243, 301
Theognostos, *grammatikós*, 2, 226
Theognostos, hegoumenos of tes Peges, 275, 277, 288–90, 295, 297, 421
Theognostos, *patrikios*, 92
Theokleto, female saint, 234
Theokletos, bishop of Lakedaimon, 282
Theoktiste, 45–48, 52, 97, 213
Theoktistos, hegoumenos of Cucumo, 147
Theoktistos, hegoumenos of Sakkoudion, 86
Theoktistos, *logothetes tou dromou*, 210, 249, 252–55, 261, 269, 271, 275, 280, 388, 418
Theopaschite heresy, 156–57
Theophanes Continuatus, 2, 108, 160, 246, 250, 252, 254, 256, 258, 261, 326, 345, 364, 419
Theophanes Graptos, 146–47, 153, 158–63, 166, 201, 204, 364–65, 370, *see* Graptoi brothers
Theophanes Presbyteros, 100, 118, 143–49
Theophanes Sikelos, 147, 151, 197
Theophanes, hegoumenos of Bartholomew, 146, 197, 200, 204
Theophanes, hegoumenos of Sigriane, 16, 53–59, 65, 81, 83, 97, 101–3, 138, 163, 191, 265, 283, 317, 373, 398
 death, 85
Theophanes, hymnographer, 147

Theophanes, metropolitan of Caesarea, 352, 359, 361–67, 390
 Theophanes the Confessor, *see* Theophanes, hegoumenos of Sigriane
Theophano, Empress, 232, 239, 256, 259
Theophilos, archbishop of Ephesos, 82, 85
Theophilos, *diakonos*, 60
Theophilos, Doctor, 371
Theophilos, Emperor, 12, 23, 64, 75, 82, 87, 93, 96, 101, 104–9, 117, 124, 126, 128, 139, 145, 151, 154, 157, 159, 162, 164, 170, 173–75, 181, 183, 187–90, 194, 198, 203–4, 208, 215, 226, 229, 231–47, 250–72, 280, 300, 311, 325–26, 343, 345, 359, 364–66, 375–82, 393, 396, 408, 414, 417, 429
 absolution, 187, 327, 398, 434
 rehabilitation, 166, 385, 409
Theophilos, hegoumenos, 43
Theophilos, *praipositos*, 423
Theophilos, *protonotarios*, 141
Theophobos, *patrikios*, 240, 246, 251, 271
Theophylaktos of Ohrid, 14
Theophylaktos, co-Emperor, 404
Theophylaktos, hagiographer, 36, 96
Theophylaktos, metropolitan of Nicomedia, 36, 44, 66, 83, 95–97, 106, 113, 163, 166
Theophylaktos, priest, 63
Theophylaktos, *protospatharios*, 60
Theosteriktos, monk of Medikion, 87–91
Theotokos, 34, 185, 230, 235, 237, 262, 264, 281, 298, 316, 355, 369
 garment of the, 200, 316, 369
 girdle of the, 316, 369
 icon of the, 64, 178, 334, 347
Thesaurus orthodoxae fidei, 411–12
Thessaloniki, 170, 172, 174, 176, 181, 184, 186, 193, 195, 197, 209
Thessaly, 52, 76, 82
Thomaïs of Lesbos, 233
Thomas the Slav, 95, 127, 135, 245, 266, 383, 405
Thomas, patriarch of Jerusalem, 151, 153, 360
Thrace, 311
Tigris, 241, 374
Timotheos, hegoumenos of Stoudios, 33
Timotheos, monk of Symboloi, 86
Titos, monk of Stoudios, 293
Translation of the Patriarch Nikephoros, 11, 114, 143–49
Translation of the Relics of St Euphemia, 7, 356, 373
Translation of Theodoros Stoudites and Ioseph, 76, 82
Trichalix, 122, 219, 395

General Index

Trinity, 298, 335, 403
Triumph of Orthodoxy (11 March 843), 4, 21, 77, 99, 109, 112, 143, 166, 185, 198, 231, 245, 261, 286, 304, 321, 343, 364, 384, 403, 429, 433
typikon, 18, 156, 284
Typikon of Alexios Stoudites, 117
Typikon of the Great Church, 110, 230

uncorrupted body, 7, 145, 149, 231, 234, 321, 373

virginity, 217, 241, 245
Vision of Isaiah of Nicomedia, 272
Vita A of Theodoros Stoudites, 28, 38, 79, 221
Vita A of Theophylaktos of Nicomedia, 36, 96, 113
Vita B of Theodoros Stoudites, 28, 34, 78–79, 116, 155, 204–5, 303, 306, 308, 310, 411
Vita B of Theophylaktos of Nicomedia, 36–37, 96
Vita C of Theodoros Stoudites, 28, 79
Vita D of Theodoros Stoudites, 80
Vita of Andreas en Krisei, 30, 249
Vita of Antonios the Younger, 193, 245, 256–60, 294
Vita of Athanasia of Aegina, 264
Vita of Blasios of Amorion, 31, 34, 38, 79, 308, 314
Vita of Eirene of Chrysobalanton, 21, 261, 263, 285, 385, 431
Vita of Eudokimos, 229–32, 393
Vita of Eustratios of Agauroi, 121, 431
Vita of Euthymios of Sardis, 8, 101, 105–7, 150, 189, 215, 218, 254, 300, 367
Vita of Euthymios the Younger, 347, 400
Vita of Eutychios, patriarch of CP, 31, 34
Vita of Evarestos of Stoudios, 293, 312
Vita of Georgios of Amastris, 34, 36, 38, 128, 130, 170, 180, 356–58
Vita of Georgios of Mytilene, 382–89
Vita of Gregorios Dekapolites, 28, 129–30, 170–86, 193, 204, 206, 216–20
Vita of Hilarion of Dalmatos, 37, 202, 221, 391, 407–10, 413, 425
Vita of Ioannes of Galatia, 192, 295, 324, 401
Vita of Ioannes of Gotthia, 34, 36, 356, 370, 396
Vita of Ioannes Psichaites, 10, 35–36, 91
Vita of Ioannikios by Petros, 189, 216–22, 259, 299, 383, 408–13, 431
Vita of Ioannikios by Sabas, 34, 212, 216–22, 259, 286, 383, 391, 395–99, 407–13, 426
Vita of Ioseph Hymnographos by Ioannes, 191, 194–201
Vita of Ioseph Hymnographos by Theophanes, 146, 169, 194–201

Vita of Konstanti Kaxay, 255
Vita of Leon of Catania, 116, 163–65
Vita of Makarios of Pelekete, 28, 92–97, 204, 206, 391
Vita of Maria the Younger in Bizye, 233
Vita of Michael Maleinos, 232
Vita of Michael of Synada, 36, 66, 96
Vita of Michael the Synkellos, 12, 109, 157–58, 160, 162, 165, 358–61, 364
Vita of Nicholas of Myra by Methodios, 104, 315, 367
Vita of Nicholas of Myra by Michael Monachos, 300, 303, 315, 367
Vita of Nikephoros of Medikion, 35–36, 90–91
Vita of Niketas of Medikion, 34, 36, 89, 91, 120, 126, 248, 409
Vita of Niketas the patrician, 190, 204, 287
Vita of Nikolaos Stoudites, 34, 79, 109, 116, 307–14, 406
Vita of Pankratios of Taormina, 9
Vita of Petros of Atroa, 38, 392–96, 399
Vita of Philaretos the Merciful, 211, 227
Vita of Prokopios Dekapolites, 203–9, 220
Vita of Sabas, 157
Vita of St Andrew the Apostle, 406, 438
Vita of Stephanos the Younger, 7, 47, 70, 99, 159, 179, 225, 321, 360–61
Vita of Symeon the Fool, 217
Vita of Thaddaios Stoudites, 38, 63, 71
Vita of the Empress Eirene, 109, 264–65
Vita of the Empress Theodora, 109, 155, 261–62, 265–72, 383
Vita of the Empress Theophano, 233
Vita of the Patriarch Euthymios, 193
Vita of the Patriarch Germanos, 35, 361
Vita of the Patriarch Ignatios, 263, 274, 279, 289, 316–19, 337
Vita of the Patriarch Methodios, 35, 37, 409–26
Vita of the Patriarch Nikephoros, 11, 34, 134–38, 144, 219, 341, 366
Vita of the Patriarch Tarasios, 34, 38, 127–34, 142, 219
Vita of Theodora of Thessaloniki, 234
Vita of Theodoros of Chora, 28, 59, 155–60, 358, 360
Vita of Theodoros of Edessa, 380
Vita of Theodoros of Sykeon, 436
Vita of Theokletos of Lakedaimon, 282
Vita of Theophanes the Confessor by Methodios, 57, 101–3, 214, 397
Vita of Theophanes the Confessor by Theodoros Stoudites, 53–59, 101–3, 214, 397
Vita retractata of Petros of Atroa, 39, 402–5, 426

Xamelion, 312
Xenophon, 10
Xyraphios, bishop of Dasbentos, 363

Zacharias of Anagni, 277
Zacharias, founder of Menas (Thessaloniki), 176, 181
Zacharias, metropolitan of Chalcedon, 346, 355
Zealots, 113, 274, 432
Zelikians, 112
Zelix, 112, 419
Zoe Tzaoustaina, 239
Zonaras, 274
zygostasia, 44, 49

Index of Manuscripts

Athens

Ethnike Bibliotheke tes Hellados (EBE) 2504 (12th cent.), 89
Ethnike Bibliotheke tes Hellados (EBE) 2534 (12th cent.), 245
Ethnike Bibliotheke tes Hellados (EBE) 991 (16th cent.), 411

Athos

Megistes Lauras Δ 78 (13th–14th cent.), 28, 80
Pantokrator 13 (12th cent.), 28, 156, 361
Pantokrator 61 (9th/13th cent.), 115, 337
Philotheou 8 (11th cent.), 141

Brussels

Brussels Bibliothèque Royale 8163–6931 (17th cent.), 245

Florence

Biblioteca Medicea Laurenziana Plut. 9.21 (14th cent.), 382

Genoa

Biblioteca Franzoniana Urb. 33 (10th–11th cent), 28, 156, 361

Glasgow

Glasgow University Library BE 8.x.5 (10th cent.), 39

Istanbul

Patriarchike Bibliotheke Hagia Trias 88 (late 9th cent.), 367

Patriarchike Bibliotheke Hagia Trias 95 (11th cent.), 141
Patriarchike Bibliotheke Hagia Trias 96 (12th cent.), 306

Jerusalem

Hagios Stavros Gr. 40 (10th–11th cent.), 256

Leiden

Bibliotheek der Rijksuniversiteit Gronovii 12 (Geel nr. 8) (16th cent.), 298

Lesbos

Leimonos 11 (11th cent.), 163, 370

London

British Library Add. 28270 (a. 1111), 271
British Library Add. 36589 (12th cent.), 141
British Library Add. 36636 (11th cent.), 80

Messina

Biblioteca Regionale Universitaria S. Salv. 153 (11th cent.), 68
Biblioteca Regionale Universitaria S. Salv. 30 (1307–8), 305

Meteora

Metamorphoseos 150 (11th cent.), 370
Metamorphoseos 591 (861/2), 294, 400

Moskow

Moskow Gosudarstvennyj Istoričeskij Musej (GIM) Khludov 129D (mid-9th cent.), 115, 165, 337

542   *Index of Manuscripts*

*Moskow Gosudarstvennyj Istoričeskij Musej (GIM)
  Sinod. Gr. 97* (ca. 890), 309
*Moskow Rossijskaja Gosudarstvennaja Biblioteka
  (RGB) Fond. 173, nr. 92.I* (15th cent.), 32, 38
*Moskow Rossijskaja Gosudarstvennaja Biblioteka
  (RGB) Gr. 128* (12th cent.), 28, 80

München

*München Bayerische Staatsbibliothek (BSB)
  Gr. 366* (15th cent.), 35, 91

Oxford

Bodleian Auctarium E.5.12 (Miscellaneus 77)
  (12th cent.), 302
Bodleian Barocci 238 (mid-10th cent.), 140
Bodleian Laud Gr. 69 (10th–11th cent.), 300
Christ Church Wake 5 (9th-10th cent.), 58

Paris

Paris BNF Coislin Gr. 269 (9th–10th cent.), 309
Paris BNF Coislin Gr. 303 (10th–11th cent.),
  120, 360
Paris BNF Gr. 1104 (11th cent.), 77
Paris BNF Gr. 1219 (11th cent.), 324
Paris BNF Gr. 1452 (10th cent.), 33–34, 38, 128,
  140, 358
Paris BNF Gr. 1470 (890), 101, 376, 414
Paris BNF Gr. 1476 (890), 101, 376, 414
Paris BNF Gr. 1491 (9th–10th cent.), 31–32, 34,
  46, 314
Paris BNF Gr. 1582 (14th cent.), 254
Paris BNF Gr. 1710 (960s), 59
Paris BNF Gr. 1711 (1013), 286
Paris BNF Gr. 20 (mid-9th cent.), 115, 337
Paris BNF Gr. 382 (late 10th cent.), 33, 69–70
Paris BNF Gr. 494 (10th cent.), 309
Paris BNF Gr. 510 (ca. 880), 336
Paris BNF Gr. 548 (10th–11th cent.), 28, 206
Paris BNF Gr. 887 (16th cent.), 298
Paris BNF Gr. 910 (9th cent.), 141
Paris BNF Gr. 923 (9th cent.), 360

Patmos

Patmos Gr. 254 (10th cent.), 387
Patmos Gr. 266 (9th cent.), 256
Patmos Gr. 736 (14th cent.), 35
Patmos Gr. 742 (9th cent.), 309

Sinai

Sinai Gr. 515 (12th cent.), 141
Sinai Gr. 562 (11th cent.), 161, 200, 285
Sinai Gr. 581 (11th cent.), 151
Sinai Gr. 583 (early 11th cent.), 151
Sinai Gr. 609 (11th cent.), 96
Sinai Gr. 627 (11th cent.), 370

St Petersburg

*St Petersburg Rossijskaja Nacional'naja biblioteka
  (RNB) Gr. 219* (835), 22, 309
*St Petersburg Rossijskaja Nacional'naja biblioteka
  (RNB) Gr. 265*, 115

Vatican City

Vatican Barberini Gr. 310 (11th cent.), 347, 390
Vatican Gr. 1130 (16th cent.), 177
Vatican Gr. 1259 (13th cent.), 66
Vatican Gr. 1510 (1431), 67
Vatican Gr. 155 (9th-10th cent.), 58
Vatican Gr. 1660 (916), 31–35, 79, 87, 307, 420
Vatican Gr. 1667 (early 10th cent.), 33–34, 37,
  141, 324, 411, 420
Vatican Gr. 1669 (early 10th cent.), 32, 34, 303
Vatican Gr. 1671 (early 10th cent.), 33–34, 322
Vatican Gr. 1753 (15th cent.), 25, 109
Vatican Gr. 1809 (10th cent.), 141
Vatican Gr. 1853 (9th/12th cent.), 32
Vatican Gr. 1882 (10th cent.), 141
Vatican Gr. 1991 (13th cent.), 144
Vatican Gr. 2014 (11th cent.), 265
Vatican Gr. 2079 (9th–10th cent.), 32, 309
Vatican Gr. 415 (10th–15th cent.), 32
Vatican Gr. 511 (11th cent.), 85
Vatican Gr. 655 (16th cent.), 324
Vatican Gr. 825 (12th–13th cent.), 410
Vatican Gr. 984 (9th cent./1354), 37, 141, 324,
  408
Vatican Palatine Gr. 216 (10th cent.), 297

Venezia

Venezia BNM Gr. II 115 (coll. 1058) (11th–12th
  cent.), 33, 69–70
Venezia BNM Gr. Z 359 (coll. 816) (early 11th
  cent.), 143
Venezia BNM Gr. Z 362 (coll. 817) (13th cent.),
  316
Venezia BNM Gr. Z 583 (coll. 595) (early 11th
  cent.), 39

Vienna

*Vienna Österreichische Nationalbibliothek (ÖNB)
  Hist. Gr. 3* (11th cent.), 141
*Vienna Österreichische Nationalbibliothek (ÖNB)
  Hist. Gr. 31* (10th cent.), 245

Lightning Source UK Ltd.
Milton Keynes UK
UKHW022108260121
377741UK00004B/22